Recent Trends in Data Analytics and Compu[...]

Exploring Emerging Technologies and Future Directions

The proceedings of the ICADAC 2025 conference, Recent Trends in Data Analytics and Computing, present an exhaustive compilation of pioneering research and applied innovations in the rapidly evolving fields of data science, artificial intelligence, and computational technologies. The book brings together researchers, industry professionals, and practitioners from around the world to discuss new algorithms, architecture, and applications to tackle emerging challenges.

Focusing on theoretical innovation as well as practical deployment, the proceedings include interdisciplinary subjects like predictive analytics, safe computing, high-performance data systems, and responsible AI. The chosen papers indicate the increasing intersection of data analytics with healthcare, smart production, autonomous systems, semiconductor, smart grid, energy optimization, and intelligent cities.

This book is an essential reference for researchers, technologists, and policymakers, providing proactive insights and promoting cooperation for emerging paradigms of computing. Academics or professionals in industry will find useful insights and actionable knowledge to navigate and shape the data-driven digital future.

Dr. Pijush Dutta works as an Assistant professor and head at the Department of Electronics & Communication Engineering, Greater Kolkata College of Engineering and Management, JIS Group, West Bengal, India. He has more than 12 years of teaching & more than 8 years of research experience. He completed his B. Tech in 2007, M. Tech in 2012 & Ph.D. in 2022. Dr. Dutta's research interests include Sensor and transducer, nonlinear process control systems, Mechatronics systems, optimization algorithms, intelligent systems, Internet of Things (IoT), machine learning, and Deep learning. He has 14 International and national patents, he has published more than 100 research articles in his credit, published in international, and national journals & conference proceedings. He has 10 edited & authored books & 21 book chapters under reputed book publishers Scrivener, Nova, CRC Press, Elsevier & Springer. Dr. Dutta has also been invited as session chair and invited speaker at several international Conferences. Moreover, Dr. Dutta has also been awarded by different international and national organizations regarding his credentials.

Dr. Jyoti Sekhar Banerjee is currently serving as the Associate Professor & Head of the Department in the Computer Science and Engineering (AI & ML) Department at the Techno Bengal Institute of Technology (formerly known as Bengal Institute of Technology), Kolkata, India. He is also the Professor-in-Charge, R & D and Consultancy Cell & Nodal Officer of the IPR Cell of BIT. Since 2024, he also works as a Remote Researcher in the Internet of THings & AppliCAtions Lab (ITHACA) at the Department of Electrical and Computer Engineering, University of Western Macedonia, Greece. Dr. Banerjee is also working as the Adjunct Research Faculty under the Lincoln Global Postdoctoral Researcher (LGPR) Programme at Lincoln University College, Malaysia. He is the former Remote Research Fellow of the Cognitive Computing and Brain Informatics Research Group (CCBI) at Nottingham Trent University (NTU), UK. Dr. Banerjee did his Post-Doctoral Fellowship at Nottingham Trent University, UK, in the Department of Computer Science. He also completed the Post Graduate Diploma in IPR & TBM from MAKAUT, WB. He has teaching and research experience spanning 21 years and completed one IEI funded project. He is the present Secretary-cum-Treasurer of the ISTE WB Section and Secretary of the IETE, Kolkata Centre. He is the Immediate Past Secretary of the Computer Society of India, Kolkata Chapter. Dr. Banerjee is also the Vice Chairman Cum Chairman Elect in Computer Society of India, Kolkata Chapter for the year 2025-2027.

Prof. (Dr.) Siddhartha Bhattacharyya [FRSA, FIET (UK), FIEI, FIETE, FSCRS, LFOSI, SMIEEE, SMACM, SMAAIA, SMIETI, LMCSI, LMISTE] is currently a senior researcher at VSB – Technical University of Ostrava, Ostrava, Czech Republic. He is also a scientific advisor at Algebra Bernays University, Zagreb, Croatia. Prior to this, he was the Principal of Rajnagar Mahavidyalaya, Birbhum, India. Before this, he was a professor at CHRIST (Deemed to be University), Bangalore, India. He also served as the Principal of RCC Institute of Information Technology, Kolkata, India. He has served VSB Technical University of Ostrava, Czech Republic, as a Senior Research Scientist. He is the recipient of several coveted national and international awards. He received the Honorary Doctorate Award (D. Litt.) from The University of South America and the SEARCC International Digital Award ICT Educator of the Year in 2017. He was appointed as the ACM Distinguished Speaker for the tenure of 2018-2020. He has been appointed as the IEEE Computer Society Distinguished Visitor for 2021-2024. He is a co-author of six books and the co-editor of 106 books and has more than 400 research publications in international journals and conference proceedings to his credit.

Dr. Debashis De is a professor in the Department of Computer Science and Engineering at the Maulana Abul Kalam Azad University of Technology, West Bengal, India. He received an M.Tech. degree from the University of Calcutta, in 2002. and a Ph.D. from Jadavpur University in 2005. He is a senior member-IEEE, fellow IETE, and life member CSI. He was awarded the prestigious Boyscast Fellowship by the Department of Science and Technology, Government of India, to work at the Heriot-Watt University, Scotland, UK. He received the Endeavour Fellowship Award from 2008–2009 by DEST Australia to work at the University of Western Australia. He received the Young Scientist award both in 2005 in New Delhi and in 2011 in Istanbul, Turkey, from the International Union of Radio Science, Belgium. In 2016, he received the JC Bose research award from IETE, New Delhi.

Dr. Panagiotis Sarigiannidis is the Director of the ITHACA lab, co-founder of the 1st spin-off of the University of Western Macedonia: MetaMind Innovations P.C., and Full Professor in the Department of Electrical and Computer Engineering in the University of Western Macedonia, Kozani, Greece. He received the B.Sc. and Ph.D. degrees in computer science from the Aristotle University of Thessaloniki, Thessaloniki, Greece, in 2001 and 2007, respectively. He has published over 360 papers in international journals, conferences and book chapters, including IEEE Communications Surveys and Tutorials, IEEE Transactions on Communications, IEEE Internet of Things, IEEE Transactions on Broadcasting, IEEE Systems Journal, IEEE Wireless Communications Magazine, IEEE Open Journal of the Communications Society, IEEE/OSA Journal of Lightwave Technology, IEEE Transactions on Industrial Informatics, IEEE Access and Computer Networks. He received six best paper awards and the IEEE SMC TCHS Research and Innovation Award 2023. He has been involved in several national, European and international projects, coordinating and technically leading numerous national and European projects including H2020, Horizon Europe, Erasmus+ and operational programs. His research interests include telecommunication networks, internet of things and network security. He is an IEEE member and participates in the Editorial Boards of various journals like IEEE Transactions on Communications, IET Networks, International Journal of Communication Systems and International Journal of Information Security.

Dr. Mohamed Lahby is Associate Professor at the Higher Normal School (ENS) University Hassan II of Casablanca, Morocco. His PhD in Computer Science from Faculty of Sciences and Technology of Mohammedia, University Hassan II of Casablanca, in 2013. His research interests are wireless communication and network, mobility management, QoS/QoE, Internet of things, Smart cities, Optimization and Machine learning. He has published more than 60 papers (book chapters, international journals, and conferences), 10 edited books, and 1 authored book. He has served and continues to serve on executive and technical program committees of numerous international conferences such as IEEE PIMRC, ICC, NTMS, IWCMC, WINCOM, ISNCC. He also referees many prestigious Elsevier journals : Ad Hoc Networks, Applied Computing and Informatics and International journal of disaster risk reduction. He organized and participated more than 40 conferences and workshops. He is the chair of many international workshops and special sessions such as MLNGSN'19, CSPSC'19, MLNGSN'20, MLNGSN'21, AI2SC '20, WCTCP'20, CIOT'22, ISGTA'23 and ISGAIE'25.

Dr. Shashi Kant Gupta is a distinguished academic and researcher in the field of Computer Science and Engineering, with a prolific career spanning over a decade. His extensive contributions to academia and industry are marked by his roles in various prestigious institutions and his leadership in innovative research projects. Prof. Gupta's work primarily focuses on Cloud Computing, Big Data Analytics, IoT, and Computational Intelligence with multidisciplinary areas in which he has made significant advancements. Prof. Gupta is currently serving as the Adjunct Faculty, Faculty of Information Technology, Victorian Institute of Technology, Level 14,123 Queen Street, Melbourne VIC 3000, Australia. In addition, he is currently serving as a Post-Doctoral Fellow and Researcher at Eudoxia Research University, USA, where he is involved in cutting-edge research in Computer Science and Engineering. He serves as Adjunct Professor at Lincoln University College (Malaysia), Chitkara University (India), Saveetha School of Engineering (India), and MAAUN (Nigeria), among others. He has published widely in SCOPUS/SCI journals, holds international patents, and edits books with Springer, CRC, Wiley, and Taylor & Francis. He is a senior editor, senior IEEE member, and recipient of multiple international awards.

Recent Trends in Data Analytics and Computing

Exploring Emerging Technologies and Future Directions

A proceeding of ICADAC – 2025

Edited by

Pijush Dutta

Jyoti Sekhar Banerjee

Siddhartha Bhattacharyya

Debashis De

Panagiotis Sarigiannidis

Mohamed Lahby

Shashi Kant Gupta

CRC Press
Taylor & Francis Group
Boca Raton London New York

CRC Press is an imprint of the
Taylor & Francis Group, an **informa** business

First edition published 2026
by CRC Press
4 Park Square, Milton Park, Abingdon, Oxon, OX14 4RN

and by CRC Press
2385 NW Executive Center Drive, Suite 320, Boca Raton FL 33431

CRC Press is an imprint of Informa UK Limited

British Library Cataloguing-in-Publication Data
A catalogue record for this book is available from the British Library

ISBN: 9781041209546 (pbk)
ISBN: 9781041209461 (hbk)
ISBN: 9781003724995 (ebk)

DOI: 10.1201/9781003724995

Typeset in Times New Roman
by HBK Digital

Conference Proceedings Series on Futuristic Intelligent and Smart Technologies (FIST)

Series Editors

Prof. (Dr.) Jyoti Sekhar Banerjee,
Department of Computer Science and Engineering (AI & ML),
Techno Bengal Institute of Technology (formerly known as Bengal Institute of Technology), Kolkata, India and
Remote Researcher, Internet of THings & AppliCAtions Lab (ITHACA),
Department of Electrical and Computer Engineering,
University of Western Macedonia, Greece

Prof. (Dr.) Siddhartha Bhattacharyya,
VSB – Technical University of Ostrava, Ostrava, Czech Republic and
Algebra Bernays University, Zagreb, Croatia

About the Series

This series serves as a beacon for scholars, researchers, and innovators navigating the dynamic landscape of technological evolution. This series stands at the forefront of interdisciplinary discourse, providing a platform for the exchange of ideas, discoveries, and insights that propel society towards a smarter, more intelligent future. Encompassing a diverse array of topics, this series delves into the realms of artificial intelligence, machine learning, robotics, Internet of Things (IoT), smart cities, and beyond. Each volume within the series is a testament to the relentless pursuit of innovation and the relentless quest for solutions to the complex challenges of the modern world.

Contributions to this series emanate from the minds of visionaries across the globe, representing a rich tapestry of perspectives and expertise. From pioneering research papers to visionary keynote addresses, each piece of content within the series reflects the cutting-edge advancements and transformative potential of futuristic intelligent and smart technologies.

Aim and Scope of this Series

The proceedings serve not only as a repository of knowledge but also as a catalyst for collaboration and networking. By fostering connections among researchers, practitioners, industry leaders, and policymakers, the series cultivates a vibrant ecosystem of innovation, where ideas are shared, synergies are discovered, and partnerships are forged.

The integration of traditional and modern intelligent and smart techniques continues to play an increasingly important role in various fields, shaping our city and society through data analysis, optimization, decision-making, and system evaluation and analysis. Artificial intelligence, Machine Learning, Big Data, and the Internet of Things, etc., are examples of futuristic, intelligent, and smart technologies that are enabling practically every area in the future.

As the pace of technological innovation accelerates, the Conference Proceedings Series on Futuristic Intelligent and Smart Technologies stands as a beacon guiding society towards a future imbued with intelligence, efficiency, and sustainability. Through its commitment to excellence, collaboration, and forward-thinking, the series remains an indispensable resource for those shaping the course of technological evolution.

Dedication

This volume is dedicated to the researchers, innovators, and thought leaders whose relentless pursuit of knowledge drives the advancement of data analytics and computing. Their contributions inspire transformative progress and shape a smarter, more connected world for future generations.

Contents

List of Figures

List of Tables

Preface

We are pleased to present the proceedings of the *International Conference on Advanced Data Analytics and Computing (ICADAC) 2025*, a premier platform that brings together researchers, scholars, and industry professionals to share their latest findings, technological advancements, and practical applications in the field of data analytics and intelligent computing.

ICADAC 2025 has received a remarkable number of high-quality submissions from across the globe, reflecting the growing interest and ongoing innovation in this dynamic domain. After a rigorous peer-review process by our esteemed technical committee, a curated selection of papers has been included in this volume. These contributions span various topics, including machine learning, artificial intelligence, big data processing, cloud computing, Internet of Things (IoT), cybersecurity, and their applications across various sectors including but not limited to Mechanical Engineering, Civil Engineering, Electrical Engineering, Electronics and Communications Engineering, Computer Science Engineering, Information Technology and other interdisciplinary areas.

The Greater Kolkata College of Engineering and Management is thrilled to host its inaugural event, the International Conference on Advanced Data Analytics and Computing (ICADAC- 2025, scheduled for the 28th of February and 1st of March 2025 at its campus. This conference marks a significant milestone for the institution, providing a prestigious global collaboration and innovation platform

The conference aims not only to disseminate knowledge but also to foster interdisciplinary collaboration and discussion on the challenges and opportunities of data-centric technologies. We believe that the work presented here will inspire future research, promote innovation, and contribute to the ongoing evolution of advanced computing systems.

We extend our sincere thanks to all authors, reviewers, keynote speakers, and participants whose efforts made ICADAC 2025 a resounding success. Finally, we would like to express our gratitude to Mrs. Shatakshi Mishra, the Editorial Manager of CRC Press, for her kind support in publishing this book.

Kolkata	Prof. Dr. Pijush Dutta
Kolkata	Prof. Dr. Jyoti Sekhar Banerjee
Ostrava	Prof. Dr. Siddhartha Bhattacharyya
Kolkata	Prof. Dr. Debashis De
Kozani	Prof. Dr. Panagiotis Sarigiannidis
Casablanca	Prof. Dr. Mohamed Lahby
Melbourne	Prof. Dr. Shashi Kant Gupta

Advisory Committee

Prof. (Dr.) Valliappan Raju, Perdana University, Malayasia
Prof. (Dr.) Shashi Kant Gupta, Eudoxia Research University, USA
Prof. (Dr.) Mohd Moin ul Haq, King Fahd University of Petroleum & Minerals, Saudi Arabia
Prof. (Dr.) Arup Ghosh, Jacksonville State University, USA
Prof. (Dr.) Ahmed Mateen Buttar, University of Agriculture, Pakistan
Prof. (Dr.) Gaurav Gupta, INTI International University, Malaysia
Prof. (Dr.) Danish Jamil, Sir Syed University of Engineering and Technology, Pakistan
Prof. (Dr.) Debanjan Konar, Purdue University, USA
Prof. (Dr.) Kalyan Ghosh, University of Cambridge, UK
Prof. (Dr.) Sayanti Roy, Purdue University, USA
Prof. (Dr.) Bui Thanh Hung, Industrial University of Ho Chi Minh City, Vietnam
Prof. (Dr.) Md. Rafizul Islam, Khulna University of Engineering & Technology, Bangladesh
Prof. (Dr.) David K. Levine, University of London, UK
Prof. (Dr.) Barun Haldar, Imam Mohammad Ibn Saud Islamic University, UAE
Prof. (Dr.) Tarun Kumar Vashishth, IIMT University, India
Prof. (Dr.) Rashmi Soni, Dayananda Sagar Academy of Technology & Management, India
Prof. (Dr.) Manorama Patnaik, Amity Institute of Information Technology, India
Prof. (Dr.) S. Balambigai, Kongu Engineering College, India
Prof. (Dr.) Mahesh Luthia, Chetana's Institute of Management and Research, India
Prof. (Dr.) C. Vijai, Vel Tech Rangarajan Dr. Sagunthala R&D Institute of Science and Technology
Prof. (Dr.) B. V. V. Siva Prasad, Anurag University, India
Prof. (Dr.) Rashmi Singh, Amity Institute of Applied Sciences, India
Prof. (Dr.) Sivabalan Settu, Vignan University, India
Prof. (Dr.) Pradeep Palani, SKP Engineering College, India
Prof. (Dr.) Sujata Dash, Nagaland University, India
Prof. (Dr.) S. Balamurugan, Albert Einstein Engineering and Research Labs, India
Prof. (Dr.) Sudip Mondol, Jalpaiguri Government Engineering College, India
Prof. (Dr.) Sandip Dey, Sukanta Mahavidyalaya, India
Prof. (Dr.) Angshuman Sarkar, MAKAUT, India
Prof. (Dr.) Ratan Mandal, Jadavpur University, India
Prof. (Dr.) Umesh Kumar Singh, National Institute of Hydrology, India
Prof. (Dr.) Gourab Sil, IIT Indore, India
Prof. (Dr.) Nabendu Ghosh, Jadavpur University, India
Prof. (Dr.) Bancha Yingngam, Ubon Ratchathani University, Thailand

Technical Program Committee

Sl. No.	Name	Affiliation
1	Dr. Chayan Das	BITS Pilani, India
2	Dr. Pijush Dutta	Greater Kolkata College of Engineering and Management, India
3	Dr. Aniruddha Nag	Techno India, India
4	Dr. Sudip Mondal	Jalpaiguri Government Engineering College, India
5	Dr. Arindam Sadhu	Dr. Sudhir Chandra Sur Institute of Technology & Sports Complex, India
6	Dr. Pritam Bhattacharjee	Vellore Institute of Technology, India
7	Dr. Somdatta Paul	Greater Kolkata College of Engineering and Management, India
8	Dr. Nilanjan Mukhopadhyay	Global Institute of Management & Technology, India
9	Dr. Bancha Yingngam	Ubon Ratchathani University, Thailand
10	Dr. Sandip Dey	Sukanta Mahavidyalaya, Jalpaiguri, West Bengal, India
11	Dr. Bijan Mallick	Global Institute of Management & Technology, India
12	Prof. Paryati	UPN Veteran Yogyakarta, Indonesia
13	Dr. Mete Yaganoglu	Ataturk University, Turkey
14	Dr. S. Balamurugan	Director - Research, IRCS Research Lab, India
15	Dr. Sujit Majumder	Kalyani Government Engineering College, India
16	Dr. Abhishek Ghosh	Supreme Knowledge Foundation Group of Institutions, India
17	Dr. Kalyan Ghosh	Royal Society Newton International Fellow, University of Cambridge, USA
18	Dr. Chittajit Sarkar	Asansol Engineering College, India
19	Dr. Pinaki Ranjan Duari	Asansol Engineering College, India
20	Dr. Sahana Das	Budge Budge Institute of Technology, India
21	Dr. Subhadip Chakraborty	IIEST, Shibpur, India
22	Prof. Sandip Bhattacharya	Techno International New Town, India
23	Dr. Subhajit Das	IEM Newtown, UEM Kolkata, India
24	Dr. Anindita Das	Regent Education and Research Foundation Group of Institutions, India
25	Prof. Soham Lodh	MCKV Institute of Engineering, India
26	Dr. Kaushik Bandopadhyay	Jadavpur Univeristy, India
27	Dr. Samim Mustafa	IIT, BHU, India
28	Dr. S. Kaliappan	KCG College of Technology, Karapakkam, Chennai, India
29	Dr. T. Mothilal	KCG College of Technology, Karapakkam, Chennai, India
30	Dr. Biswadeep Guptabakshi	Narula Institute of Technology, India
31	Dr. Kallol Bhaumik	Chitkara University, India

32	Dr. Alok Kr. Shrivastav	JIS College of Engineering, India
33	Dr. Soham Dutta	Manipal Institute of Technology, Manipal
34	Dr. P. Sureshkumar	JCT College of Engineering & Technology, Coimbatore, India
35	Dr. Amrishraj .D	V.S.B Engineering College, Karur, India
36	Dr. Rajpal Singh	Government Rajindra College, Punjab, India
37	Dr. Mukesh Kumar	Lovely Professional University, Jalandhar, India
38	Dr. Pradeep K Sharma	Jaipur Engineering College and Research Center, Jaipur, India
39	Dr. Rishi Kumar	Guru Nanak College, Budhlada, Mansa, India
40	Dr. Sarbani Ganguly	Narula Institute of Technology, India
41	Dr. Susmita Karan	Narula Institute of Technology, India
42	Dr. V. K. Gobinath	Kongu Engineering College, Perundurai, Tamil Nadu, India
43	Dr. G. Ramesh	Rajiv Gandhi University of Knowledge Technologies, Andhra Pradesh
44	Dr. Shyamal Mandal	North Eastern Hill University, Shillong, India
45	Dr. Kakali Sen	University of Kalyani, Kalyani, India
46	Dr. Rupa Bhattacharyya	Narula Institute of Technology, India
47	Dr. Sandip Bag	JIS College of Engineering, Kalani, India
48	Dr. Suresh Sugumar	Velammal Engineering College, Chennai, Tamil Nadu, India
49	Dr. Rajkamal Sivakumar	Easwari Engineering College, Chennai, Tamil Nadu, India
50	Dr. Gopinath Dhamodaran	Velammal Engineering College, Chennai, Tamil Nadu, India
51	Dr. Devaraj. E	CMRU, Bangalore, Karnataka, India
52	Dr. Prabas Banerjee	R&D Engineer, TCS, Bengalore, India
53	Dr. Piyush Panth	Thermal Design Engineer, Rolls-Royce@NTU Corporate Lab, Singapore
54	Dr. SK Tanbir Islam	Asst. Prof., Greater Kolkata College of Engineering and Management, India
55	Dr. Sujeet Kumar Gautam	Siwan college of engineering and management, Islamia nagar, Surapursiwan, India
56	Dr. Rajat Upadhyaya	National Institute of Advanced Manufacturing Technology Ranchi, India
57	Dr. Somnath Das	Swami Vivekananda Institute of Science and Technology, India
58	Dr. Suparna DasGupta	JIS College of Engineering, Kalani, India
59	Dr. Soumyabrata Saha	JIS College of Engineering, Kalani, India
60	Dr. Bijoy Kantha	Netaji Subhas Engineering College, India
61	Dr. Subhashis Roy	Techno India Universiity, India
62	Dr. Kallol Bhaumik	Chitkara University, India
63	Dr. Alok Kr. Shrivastav	JIS College of Engineering, Kalani, India
64	Dr. Soham Dutta	Manipal Institute of Technology, Manipal, India
65	Dr. Pritish Ghosh	Institute of Engineering and Management, India

66	Dr. Avijit Chakraborty	Elitte College of Engineering and Management, India
67	Dr. Krishna Sarker	St. Thomas' College of Engineering and Technology, India
68	Dr. Suman Laha	Techno International Batanagar, India
69	Dr. Subrata Biswas	Netaji Subhash Engineering College, India
70	Dr. Palash Pal	Haldia Institute of Technology, India
71	Dr. Soumya Das	University Institute of Technology, India
72	Dr. Kallol Roy	University Institute of Technology, India
73	Prof. (Dr.) Ahmed Mateen Buttar	University of Agriculture, Pakistan
74	Prof. (Dr.) Mohd Moin ul Haq	King Fahd University of Petroleum & Minerals (KFUPM), Saudi Arabia
75	Prof. (Dr.) David K. Levine	University of London, UK
76	Dr. Ahmed Mohsin Alsayah	Al-Furat Al-Awsat Technical University, Iraq
77	Prof. (Dr.) Bui Thanh Hung	Industrial University of Ho Chi Minh City, Vietnam
78	Dr. Osamah Ibrahim Khalaf	Al-Nahrain University - Baghdad, Iraq
79	Prof. (Dr.) Bancha Yingngam	Ubon Ratchathani University, Thailand
80	Prof. Frank Eliassen	University of Oslo, Norway
81	Prof. Yu-Shan Lin	National Taitung University, Taitung, Taiwan
82	Prof. Md. A. Hossain	BRAC University, Bangladesh
83	Prof. Frank Eliassen	University of Oslo, Norway
84	Prof. Sevda Rzayeva	Azerbaijan State University of Economics, Azerbaijan
85	Dr. Toufik Mzili	Chouaib Doukkali University, Morocco
86	Dr. Dewarish N Jayantha	Sabaragamuwa University, Sri Lanka

Organizing Committee

Honorary Chair(s)	Prof. (Dr.) Panagiotis Sarigiannidis, University of Western Macedonia, Greece Prof. (Dr.) Jyotsna Kumar Mandal, Kalyani University, India Prof. (Dr.) Amlan Chakrabarti, University of Calcutta, India
Chief Patron	Sardar Taranjit Singh, Managing Director, JIS Group, India
Patron(s)	Mr. Tapan Kumar Ghosh, Executive Director, Techno India Group, India Sardar Simarpreet Singh, Director, JIS Group, India
Co-Patron(s)	Prof (Dr.) G. L. Datta, BOG Chairman, GKCEM and Retired Professor, IIT KGP, India Prof (Dr.) Mahuya Das, Principal, GKCEM, India
General Chair(s)	Prof. (Dr.) Siddhartha Bhattacharyya, VSB – Technical University of Ostrava, Ostrava, Czech Republic and Algebra Bernays University, Zagreb, Croatia Prof. (Dr.) Jyoti Sekhar Banerjee, Techno Bengal Institute of Technology, Kolkata, India Prof. (Dr.) Debashis De, Maulana Abul Kalam Azad University of Technology, West Bengal, India
Program Chair(s)	Prof. (Dr.) Korhan Cengiz, Prince Mohammad Bin Fahd University, KSA Prof. (Dr.) Mete Yaganoglu, Ataturk University, Turkey.
TPC Chair	Prof. (Dr.) Jyoti Sekhar Banerjee, Techno Bengal Institute of Technology, Kolkata, India
TPC Co-Chair	Prof. (Dr.) Aniruddha Nag, Techno India Group, India Dr. Pijush Dutta, GKCEM, India
Industry Chair(s)	Mr. Snehasis Banerjee, TCS Research & Innovation, Kolkata, India
Convener(s)	Dr. Pijush Dutta, GKCEM, India
Finance Chair	Mr. Sourav Chatterjee, Registrar, GKCEM Mr. Debapriya Dutta, Accounts Section, GKCEM
Registration Chair	Prof. Antara Ghosh, GKCEM, India Prof. Niratyay Biswas, GKCEM, India Prof. Raghunath Majhi, GKCEM, India
Publicity Chair(s)	Dr. Anubrata Mondal, GKCEM, India Prof. Subhojit Chattaraj, GKCEM, India
Publication Co-Chair(s)	Dr. Sk. Tanbir Islam, GKCEM, India Dr. Biswajit Gayen, GKCEM, India
Hospitality Chair(s)	Dr. Saumen Dhara, GKCEM, India Prof. Gopal Chakraborty, GKCEM, India
Publicity & Sponsorship Chair(s)	Prof. Rajarshi Chakraborty, GKCEM, India Prof. Sandeepan Saha, GKCEM, India Prof. Gour Gopal Jana, GKCEM, India

1 Enhancing patient-centered healthcare: utilizing metaverse and blockchain for secure and reliable data sharing

Roshni Afshan[1,a], Suhail Rashid Wani[2,b], Suhail Nazir Taili[3,c] and Shobhit Agrawal[4,d]

[1,2]Assistant Professor, Noida Institute of Engineering and Technology, Sharda University, UP, India

[3,4]Student, Sharda University, UP, India

Abstract

The advancement of the metaverse and the application of blockchain technology in the medical field is probably going to cause a revolution. The concept of metaverse that enables the integration of physical and digital spaces creates possibilities for the advancement of healthcare services, education of medical professionals, and patients. Blockchain is a secure distributed database for maintaining and sharing medical record data without compromising the data integrity and privacy of patients. For this purpose, this paper focuses on the integration of metaverse and blockchain within the healthcare industry to design a secure and credible system for patient-centric data sharing. It expands on the significant future areas of the use of the metaverse, including virtual consultations, simulation training, and therapeutic approaches that can positively impact patients' experiences, reach, and affordability. Additionally, the paper discusses how distributed ledger technology known as blockchain can disrupt the storage and protection of medical data. The use of smart contracts through the blockchain can greatly minimize constraints and eliminate extra procedures for fraud. However, the paper also expounds on the challenges associated with these technologies, which should be addressed tomorrow. These challenges include privacy and security, scalability, interoperability, standardization, and ethics such as equity and accessibility. This calls for research and cooperation between various fields of study and the formulation and implementation of comprehensive health policies in metaverse and blockchain technology. This paper will try to present guidelines on how metaverse and blockchain can be adopted in the healthcare system to improve and enhance the delivery of medical services, improve the security of patients' health records, and bring value to patients by focusing on their needs.

Keywords: Artificial intelligence, blockchain, cloud computing, digital twin, metaverse

Introduction

In the past several decades, the integration and application of newer technologies in almost all fields have given rise to drastic changes, and this has also applied to the healthcare sphere. Of the envisaged advancements, both the metaverse and blockchain technologies are noteworthy [1]. The metaverse, a globally connected, joint, and persistent virtual environment blending virtually realized physical and physical reality-connected virtual environments, was first conceptualized primarily for games and entertainment [2]. At the same time, with the fundamentals of decentralization and secure records, blockchain has transitioned from the cryptocurrency sector to a variety of industries including healthcare [3]. This paper outlines the implementation of metaverse and blockchain in the medical field, with the aim of designing a data-sharing patient-centered system that is secure and reliable [4].

One cannot ignore the issues and concerns that have plagued the healthcare industry for years now, both in terms of handling patient data and the delivery of care [5]. Traditional systems hold certain major disadvantages that include the inability to interoperate, ease of data breach, and patient satisfaction due to disjointed and less efficient methods. All these call for effective solutions that would improve not only the lives of patients but also the security of their information as well. The use of metaverse and blockchain, therefore, offers a new strategy for overcoming the challenges and transforming patient care and engagement [6].

The metaverse, hence a concept involving virtual environments, holds a lot of promise in the field of healthcare. It can be used for virtual consultations,

[a]afshaanroshni@gmail.com, [b]wanisuhail305@gmail.com, [c]suhailnazir3846@gmail.com,
[d]shobhitagrawal145@gmail.com

DOI: 10.1201/9781003724995-1

medical training of patients, teaching them, and even therapeutic sessions. For example, using the virtual reality (VR) environment, doctors can practice operations and other procedures to improve their skills without harming the patients [7]. Furthermore, telemedicine can be extended in the metaverse by providing more engaging and interactive patient-doctor interactions which can be beneficial in treatment outcomes and patients' experiences [8].

Patient interaction is yet another domain wherein the virtual world may have a significant influence. Some of the ways through which communication in virtual health communities can benefit patients include the following: Moreover, the metaverse will make it possible to monitor and even rehabilitate patients through VR from the comfort of their homes. This is specifically helpful to patients with chronic diseases or those on long-term treatment since the quality of life will increase with fewer visits to the hospital [1]. As explained below, blockchain technology solves several problems in handling data within the healthcare domain.

This is useful in addition to sharing reports because it makes data more accurate and secure in this method. Every sharing, for example of information or data, is done in a block that is connected to other blocks and extremely hard to change [9]. This can help in the protection of patients' records and minimize loss through theft and fraud which are likely to occur [10].

Furthermore, it suggests that data exchange could be made more seamless by linking the different systems related to health care through the incorporation of blockchain technology, therefore making them interconnected. This is highly advantageous especially so that the healthcare professional gets the most up-to-updated, comprehensive patient record which is very useful in managing the patient. Another advantage of blockchain is that it can be used to develop smart contracts, which can help in documenting healthcare services such as insurance claims and billing [11].

Blockchain technology and the metaverse bode well for the future of the healthcare industry. First of all, it can help to improve the protection of data and patients' information as blockchain has a decentralized and encrypted architecture [12]. This helps in being certain that a patient's information is safe, and only those who should be allowed access to it get it leading to a reduced rate of patient information being accessed

by people who should not. Secondly, the interaction in the metaverse can enhance the value of the service provided by the patient's healthcare needs through improving the way such services are delivered [13].

In addition, it may help in ensuring the necessary and uniform standard of care by sharing data and tracking the patient remotely. Virtual support forms allow patients to receive the necessary interaction and feedback in terms of compliance with treatment or other health-related processes [14]. To the doctors and other healthcare practitioners, it can provide complex training toys and groups, or the foundation for improvement and better health.

However, there are also some risks that have become apparent from literature when metaverse and blockchain technologies are applied in the healthcare context. Stakeholders also point at technical constraints such as requiring prevalent infrastructure, high computational intensity, and reliable internet connection. There are also important issues regarding the potential difficulty of scaling the blockchain and the interconnection and unification of various healthcare platforms [15]. Legally speaking, the use of these technologies in the provision of medical products and services must comply with laws, such as the USA's Health Insurance Portability and Accountability Act signed by Bush during his presidency. Whenever any of these regulations are violated, patients' privacy and the confidentiality of their information are at risk [16]. As far as we are aware, no research has been done on using blockchain technology for applications in the metaverse. As a result, our analysis highlights the variety of possible uses for the metaverse were integrating blockchain technology might improve productivity as well as the influence of blockchain on underlying capabilities.

Literature Review

Using research analysis, it is identified that both AR and VR hold a vast potential in the healthcare sector. There was a study done that highlighted the effect of the proposed AR models. That study shows that AR model improved the interaction between doctors and patients and also the understanding of patients' details. Vetrivel and Mohanasundaram pointed out that VR has the capacity to revolutionize the medical field and it is useful for disposing and encouraging therapeutic practice [6]. Furthermore, AR has positively impacted the medical field through improving the doctor's perception of the matter with their patients [12].

AR and VR also help stakeholders in the healthcare sector to collaborate with one another. For example, a study discussed the advantages of using group VR space in enhancing cooperation and creativity in tackling healthcare issues [14]. These settings enable the healthcare personnel to practice and master their dexterity without endangering the lives of the patients.

Comprehensive and confidential medical services

The literature has established that the metaverse and blockchain have the ability to deliver custom and safe medical services. Based on research, the distinct features of metaverse technologies enable healthcare providers to deliver personalized medical care experiences for their patients [10]. The individualized patient approach and continuous control functions provided through these technologies benefit patient care for managing chronic diseases and patient-focused treatment [10].

Healthcare can benefit from blockchain technology delivering secure solutions because this system operates as the foundation for Bitcoin along with multiple cryptocurrencies. The authors Kshetri et al. explained how blockchain technology would innovate AI-assisted healthcare through its decentralized model and data cryptographic hashing to create both authentic and open datasets [15]. Healthcare providers should consider implementing the health AI chain model as an answer to the trusted health information sharing dilemma while protecting patient data privacy and system efficiency [12].

The adoption of metaverse and blockchain in healthcare also has noteworthy ethical and social implications. Literature has described the need for privacy considerations, protection of data and patients, as well as ways to incorporate these technologies in health care [16]. The consent of the patient and confidentiality are critical in developing trusting relationships with patients and healthcare professionals [2].

In the year 2023, Krittanawong et al investigated the role of blockchain and intelligent technologies in the cardiovascular field. They also discussed the possible uses of these innovations and directions for their further developments in treating cardiovascular diseases.

It also evaluated the problem areas and possible opportunities for better safety and treatment in cardiology, pointing out the revolutionary effect of these technologies on selected medicine niches [29].

Uses in training the medical students and in treatment

The metaverse has become widespread in medical education and therapy more and more. For instance, a company known as Augmedics created an AR headset to help spine surgery patients visualize their anatomy in Johns Hopkins Hospital in 2020. Likewise, treatments for pain perception using cognitive-behavioral therapies, EaseVR for example, demonstrate how VR can be used therapeutically. This simulation is particularly common in plastic surgery operations where the patient gets to see the result of the aesthetic surgery beforehand. The advanced imaging features in the metaverse also enrich radiography, especially diagnosis and group training of healthcare professionals. Through the use of digital twins that mirror patient body structures and incorporate patient data, the achievement of patient engagement and efficient monitoring of health is enhanced.

Methodology and Model Specification

The metaverse provides a complete virtual world that relies on six critical technologies including AI and VR and augmented reality (AR) and digital twins together with telecommunication alongside blockchain. Through these technologies the metaverse becomes possible for creating virtual environments while enabling operation and growth which produce interactive immersive experiences that link different virtual spaces. These separate technologies actively transform the metaverse by dealing with specific obstacles while releasing new use cases both for end-users and businesses.

Virtual reality

The main framework of the metaverse depends on virtual reality technology because it supplies users with immersive virtual simulation environments. User interaction with 3D digital spaces at maximum freedom and interactivity happens through the usage of head-mounted displays known as HMDs. Meta (Facebook), Google and Sony release haptic gloves and omnidirectional treadmills and motion controllers among their innovative hardware offerings.

Virtual reality devices assist users to experience comfortable engagement states that produce more realistic and exciting virtual environments.

The healthcare industry, for instance, leverages VR for physical therapy, surgical training, pain management, and cognitive rehabilitation. The global Virtual Reality market started at USD 2.3 billion during 2016 before it predicted to reach USD 20.9 billion by 2025 because of its increasing significance in the metaverse ecosystem

Augumented reality

The technology of AR adds digital information on top of physical surroundings which produces a combination of virtual and real-world interaction. AR blends virtual elements into real-environment spaces through its design which surpasses the completely virtual nature of VR systems. Cognitive systems within AR applications detect objects as well as faces and track body movements and serve various businesses in retailing education and entertainment sectors. The technology enables virtual clothing try-ons, and it also enables interactive educational content through AR.

AR needs to fuse digital content flawlessly with physical elements to build a natural connection between virtual and real-world environments for its success. immersive applications of this technology create better user connections with relevant experiences in the metaverse environment.

Mixed reality

The technology of MR performs an integration between VR and AR through which virtual and physical objects unite and react simultaneously. This technology finds its strongest value when employed in precise and immersive applications including surgical operations. Surgical accuracy and operational risks decrease because surgeons obtain real-time information through an MR system connected to AI technology. Healthcare providers along with other industries are exploring the "surgical metaverse" as an emerging concept enabled by modern reality technologies to transform their operational capabilities.

Artificial intelligence

The metaverse exists because of primary AI methodologies which allow customized metaverse encounters with smart user interactions. The three essential artificial intelligence fields which facilitate realistic human-like system interactions include machine learning (ML) and natural language processing (NLP) together with computer-vision (CV). NLP technology allows avatars to exchange verbal communications which enhances between user and system interactions. The metaverse will gain intelligence through the processing power of artificial intelligence which uses user-generated data.

Healthcare practitioners use the "metaverse of medical technology and artificial intelligence" (MeTAI) system for implementing AI and metaverse integration in medical applications. Through MeTAI healthcare developers can conduct data exchange operations and virtual testing of AI medical solutions which include additional regulatory features.

Digital twin

Physical objects and systems and processes become digital twin digital replicas for virtual representation. The digital representations enable immediate observation and simulation and optimization of actual hardware elements. Through metaverse digital twins replicate all types of environments ranging from small, microscopic entities to large macroscopic systems which include cities and ecosystems. This technology offers three significant benefits that include predictive maintenance as well as early hazard detection and virtual prototyping.

Scientists study human digital twins as a new research field to develop digital copies of human beings for healthcare observation together with customized medical treatment. To achieve full potential the data privacy problems together with non-intrusive monitoring device development challenges need resolution.

Worldwide users in the metaverse depend on strong telecommunication networks for their connections. The essential components of the metaverse include 5G, 6G and IoT which enable immediate data transfer and fluid interactions. The required elements for deep immersion consist of networks that provide swift delivery and plenty of speed and dependable performance. The increasing size of the metaverse needs telecommunication infrastructure development to achieve expansion and accessibility.

Users perform safe reliable decentralized and transparent transactions through the metaverse because it operates with blockchain technology. Blockchain technology enables the system to oversee virtual assets while preserving data reliability across secure peer-to-peer data exchange between users. Blockchain experiences three main operational barriers which involve privacy and scalability restrictions and system integration limitations. Two main weaknesses in blockchain operation include user privacy reduction because of transaction visibility and metaverse operational challenges because of growing user numbers. All metaverse users across the world need robust telecommunications networks to establish their online connections. The foundation of metaverse operation depends on 5G, 6G alongside IoT to ensure immediate data transmission capabilities and seamless interactions. Networks which offer quick transmission alongside ample velocity together with solid operational reliability make up the necessary components for deep immersion. The expansion of the metaverse produces challenges for telecommunication infrastructure that limit blockchain operations because they affect network interconnectivity and system scalability and privacy security features. The disclosure of user privacy in blockchain systems results in decreased scalability of the metaverse as user numbers rise. Multiple requirements must be addressed through zero-knowledge proof standards and resource benefits provided by sharding together with layer-two tools compatible with the lightning network design. Settlement operations between parties for controlling virtual asset ownership operations get automated when smart contracts with NFTs facilitate claimable disputes.

The blockchain solution requires implementation of lightning network-based layer-two protocols together with zero-knowledge proofs and the advantages of sharding. The automated control of virtual asset ownership made possible by algorithms delivered through smart contracts and NFTs simultaneously benefits all parties by reducing disputes while building trust relationships development to achieve expansion and accessibility blockchain.

Users depend on blockchain technology for metaverse operations because it ensures their secure decentralized transactions remain visible to them and others they trust. Virtual data safeguarding, virtual asset oversight and direct user-to-user interaction function via blockchain technology in this system.

Limitations and Challenges

The future cybersecurity threats to user privacy emerge because blockchain operates as a decentralized system that provides transparent transaction visibility. Throughout blockchain systems development engineers undertake both decentralized storage solutions as well as encryption data approaches to enhance security infrastructure.

The system needs to serve various transactions simultaneously while maintaining practical functionality because user numbers continue to rise. Users achieve enhanced system efficiency and transaction processing times by implementing layer-two scaling solutions that use sharding method.

There exists a challenge of limited cross-network connectivity since different standards remain incompatible with each other in blockchain networks. Bedrock and Cosmos Network and Inter-ledger Protocol work together to establish a system that manages inter-chain communication.

The untraditional ownership model of virtual assets triggers concerns regarding responsibility and taxation systems as well as protection of intellectual property. Blockchains integrate KYC and AML processes to address existing system problems.

The benefits of data sharing to foster creativity and teamwork do not address privacy concerns which arise from this practice in the metaverse. The technologies of decentralized storage with smart contracts serve as blockchain implementations for secure peer-to-peer information sharing.

Conclusion

The combination of metaverse and blockchain in healthcare represents a shift toward a more personalized, secure, and efficient model. Despite some drawbacks, their value is undeniable. The interactive metaverse enables personalized healthcare delivery, remote monitoring, and rehabilitation. The integration of virtual consultations with health simulations and training systems creates enhanced access opportunities and decreases expenses and offers better healthcare experiences for both patients and healthcare staff. Low-hacking risk emerges from medical data security through the decentralized blockchain system which also provides tamper-resistance. Smart contacts help healthcare organizations operate with higher efficiency by reducing insurance fraud and billing concerns, but organizations must handle technical challenges in healthcare systems. The implementation requires attention to ethical matters which should guarantee benefits for all patients irrespective of their financial capabilities or technological understanding. Courting public knowledge alongside patient authorization creates essential conditions. The development of effective regulations needs mutual collaboration between healthcare providers and technology experts together with ethical specialists and government officials. These modern healthcare technologies have the potential to change the industry when healthcare providers actively adapt them to ensure operational efficiency together with security measures and patient-focused care.

References

[1] Ali, S., Abdullah, Armand, T. P. T., Athar, A., Hussain, A., Ali, M., et al. (2023). Metaverse in healthcare integrated with explainable AI and blockchain: enabling immersiveness, ensuring trust, and providing patient data security. *Sensors*, 23(2), 565. doi: 10.3390/s23020565.

[2] Uma, S. (2023). Blockchain and AI: disruptive digital technologies in designing the potential growth of healthcare industries. In B. K. Rai, B. K., G. Kumar, G., &and V. Balyan, V. (Eds.), AI and Blockchain in Healthcare, Advanced Technologies and Societal Change, (pp. 137–150). Singapore: Springer Nature Singapore. doi: 10.1007/978-981-99-0377-1_9.

[3] Divyashree, K. S. (2024). Blockchain application on healthcare services in metaverse. In Modern Technology in Healthcare and Medical Education: Blockchain, IoT, AR, and VR, (pp. 141–158). IGI Global. Accessed: Jun. 13, 2024. [Online]. Available from: https://www.igi-global.com/chapter/blockchain-application-on-healthcare-services-in-metaverse/345887.

[4] Jacob, D., Bai, Y., & Li, J. (2024). Blockchain for securing health records in metaverse. In Arai, K. (Ed.), Advances in Information and Communication, (vol. 920, pp. 208–219).

[5] Elgamal, E., Medhat, W., Abd Elfatah, M., & Abdelbaki, N. (2023). Blockchain in healthcare for achieving patients' privacy. In 2023 20th Learning and Technology Conference (L&T), (pp. 59–64). IEEE. Accessed: Jun. 13, 2024. [Online]. Available from: https://ieeexplore.ieee.org/abstract/document/10092352/.

[6] Vetrivel, S. C., & Mohanasundaram, T. (2024). Chapter 3 blockchain-empowered metaverse healthcare systems and applications. In R. Malviya, R., S. Sundram, S., R. Kumar Dhanaraj, R., &and S. Kadry, S. (Eds.), Digital Transformation in Healthcare 5.0, (pp. 61–88). De Gruyter. doi: 10.1515/9783111398549-003.

[7] Mozumder, M. A. I., Armand, T. P. T., Imtiyaj Uddin, S. M., Athar, A., Sumon, R. I., Hussain, A., et al. (2023). Metaverse for digital anti-aging healthcare: an overview of potential use cases based on artificial intelligence, blockchain, IoT technologies, its challenges, and future directions. *Applied Sciences*, 13(8), 5127.

[8] Chengoden, R., Victor, N., Huynh-The, T., Yenduri, G., Jhaveri, R. H., Alazab, M., et al. (2023). Metaverse for healthcare: a survey on potential applications, challenges and future directions. *IEEE Access*, 11, 12765–12795.

[9] Almarzouqi, A., Aburayya, A., & Salloum, S. A. (2022). Prediction of user's intention to use metaverse system in medical education: a hybrid SEM-ML learning approach. *IEEE Access*, 10, 43421–43434. doi: 10.1109/ACCESS.2022.3169285.

[10] Tiwari, A., Dubey, A., Yadav, A. K., Bhansali, R., & Bagaria, V. (2024). A review of smart future of healthcare in the digital age to improve quality of orthopaedic patient care in metaverse called: the healthverse!!. *Journal of Clinical Orthopaedics and Trauma*, 48, 102340.

[11] Huynh-The, T., Gadekallu, T. R., Wang, W., Yenduri, G., Ranaweera, P., Pham, Q. V., ... & Liyanage, M. (2023). Blockchain for the metaverse: A Review. *Future Generation Computer Systems*, 143, 401–419.

[12] Sai Priya, Ch. E. N., & Kumar Yogi, M. (2024). Chapter 2 the role of metaverse in transforming healthcare: blockchain approach. In R. Malviya, R., S. Sundram, S., R. Kumar Dhanaraj, R., &and S. Kadry, S. (Eds.), Digital Transformation in Healthcare 5.0, (pp. 33–60). De Gruyter. doi: 10.1515/9783111398549-002.

[13] Chen, Zhen-Song, & Jie-Qun Ruan. (2024). Metaverse healthcare supply chain: Conceptual framework and barrier identification. *Engineering Applications of Artificial Intelligence* 133: 108113.

[14] Nguyen, H.-S., & Voznak, M. (2024). A bibliometric analysis of technology in digital health: exploring health metaverse and visualizing emerging healthcare management trends. *IEEE Access*, 12, 23887–23913. Accessed: Jun. 13, 2024. [Online]. Available from: https://ieeexplore.ieee.org/abstract/document/10423633/.

[15] Mohammed, Z. K., Mohammed, M. A., Abdulkareem, K. H., Zebari, D. A., Lakhan, A., Marhoon, H. A., et al. (2024). A metaverse framework for IoT-based remote patient monitoring and virtual consultations using AES-256 encryption. *Applied Soft Computing*, 158, 111588.

[16] Hulsen, T. (2024). Applications of the metaverse in medicine and healthcare. *Advances in Laboratory Medicine/Avancesen Medicina de Laboratorio* 5.2: 159–165.

2 Trash tracker-an AI-enhanced waste surveillance and notification system

Shreya Garg[a], Shivani Yadav[b], Saloni[c] and Waseem Ahmed[d]

Department of CSE-AIML, ABES Engineering College, Ghaziabad, UP, India

Abstract

Ineffective waste management systems pose a growing threat to urban areas, posing health and environmental hazards. The procedures used now, like manual inspections and citizen reports, are insufficient to handle garbage in a timely manner. In this study, we present "trash tracker," a smart trash observation and warning system which can be used to identify waste in present, prioritize it, alert the appropriate the ruling classes for prompt response. Convolutional neural networks (CNN) are used by the system to detect garbage, and a severity scoring algorithm is used to prioritize cleanup activities. Trash tracker lowers environmental risks, increases waste management efficiency, and provide useful information for urban planners through automation and data-driven notifications.

Keywords: Artificial intelligence, convolutional neural networks, machine learning, real-time detection, resource allocation, smart cities, waste management

Introduction

Over and above half of the area's natives now settled in cities owing to urbanization, and it is anticipated by UN that by 2050 this figure will get escalated to 68%. This progression fabricated consequential garbage, giving rise to problems for the surroundings, community as well as health. Excessive garbage accumulation leads to the destruction of urban beauty, provides hurdle to drainage, disperse contamination in addition to the advancement in risk of disease. Tackling these obstacles demands effective waste management techniques and comprehensive urban arrangement to boost environmental viability and public well-being. Upgradations within technology, peculiarly in the domain of artificial intelligence (AI), put forward an unprecedent mechanism. AI-driven structures that utilize machine learning and computer vision encourage real-time waste problem subjection, categorization in addition to proposition. Its ingenious escalation architecture accordance that assets are employed strongly in order to safeguard urban orderliness and welfare. By normalizing clutter observation along with ensuring well timed reaction, these systems elevate productivity while relinquishing litter and supplementing urban sterility. On account of AI, this tracker is refurbishing urban garbage management. It briskly alerts concerned authorities, levels circumstances by acuteness, and perceives scraps with high factuality by maneuvering live video feeds together with machine learning. Besides rarefying employing productivity, trash tracker advertises liability, degrades impurities, in addition to upgrade health of public, creating more viable and tenantable communities. Assimilating AI into garbage management is one of the anticipated initiatives in handling the challenges of urbanization. This study paper is divided in the following sections:

The first section is an introduction, the second section is a literature study, third section is project planning, fourth explains research methodology, section 5 discusses the result of the study and the overview of the paper and its future directions are provided in section 6.

Literature Study

There is a need for an innovative system that can efficiently handle the load because the standard waste management systems are not set up to meet the demands of an expanding population. Technologies like AI, machine learning (ML), and the Internet of Things (IoT) make it feasible to modify schemas in real time. These can save expenses, reduce the negative effects on the environment, and sharpen resource usage. Convolutional neural networks, which are crucial for classification and recognition, are used in methods such as artificial intelligence and machine learning. CNNs can recognize reusable

[a]shreya06lg@gmail.com, [b]yadavshivani2831@gmail.com, [c]saloni371410@gmail.com, [d]waseemahmed0609@gmail.com

DOI: 10.1201/9781003724995-2

waste with 92% accuracy, as demonstrated by Wu et al. [1]. Additionally, CNN-based systems for the detection of organic waste have been created by Almasi and Ansari [2]. According to Lee et al. [3], the sophisticated settings of trash differentiation have been enhanced by advancements in deep learning-based object dispersion. Patel and Sharma have also noticed it. [4] that in this distinct setting, the combination of machine learning techniques like CNNs and support vector machines, evolved to increase accuracy using hybrid replicas. According to Rodriguez et al. [5], the waste cell may be converted to smart bins [7] via the Internet of Things, which can save costs, improve compliance effectiveness, and allow for capacity tracking [10]. AI-powered selection assistance systems can reduce expenses by 25% and boost productivity by 15%, according to Zhao et al.'s validation [8]. By facilitating rapid elevation along replicas for urgent and immediate measures, Ahmed et al. [11] and Zhang et al. [12] demonstrate the necessity of an AI-enabled warning system to prioritize hazardous trash. Studies have been done in the field of object detection [21], hotspot detection [22,23], urban littering [24] and predictive analysis for waste generation [25].The reports of continuous learning in waste management [27], AI driven hotspots [26], organic waste detection [29], real time CNN based classification [28], segmentation for increased accuracy [30], AI driven resource optimization [32] and IoT based predictive maintenance [31] have been also documented. These findings represent a significant step toward more intelligent and sustainable waste management.

Projected Planning

Source of input
The data is collected from the cameras placed in public spaces which include schools, parks, beaches or streets. The input is then passed to the second model after being analyzed.

AI unit
To determine and categorize different kinds of trash using CNNs i.e. convolutional neural networks. The model is used to separate waste including risky materials, using image segmentation and object detection.

Severity scoring mechanism
This model will generate the severity score with which the rank will be decided of the waste identified. This rank will depend on multiple factors like location, nature and the density. This model will ensure that the waste with high risk will get cleaned up quickly.

Notification model
The notification will be generated to the waste management teams which will include the location of waste, type of waste and priority. These notifications will be sent through mobile apps or email. If the waste is not cleared in given time frame the automated procedures are being used to escalate unresolved matters to higher management teams. The working of system has been shown in Fig 2.1.

Database for analysis
The notification will be generated to the waste management teams which will include the location of waste, type of waste and priority. These notifications will be sent through mobile apps or email. If the waste is not cleared in given time frame the automated procedures are being used to escalate unresolved matters to higher management teams. [13]

Consequences
The system helps in improving trash administration efficiently and also donates to added habitable and supportable societies by growing city sanitation and reducing conservational hazards.

Methodology

Detection of waste
The video feeds from security cameras are used as data to find trash, which is examined by CNNs [14,15].

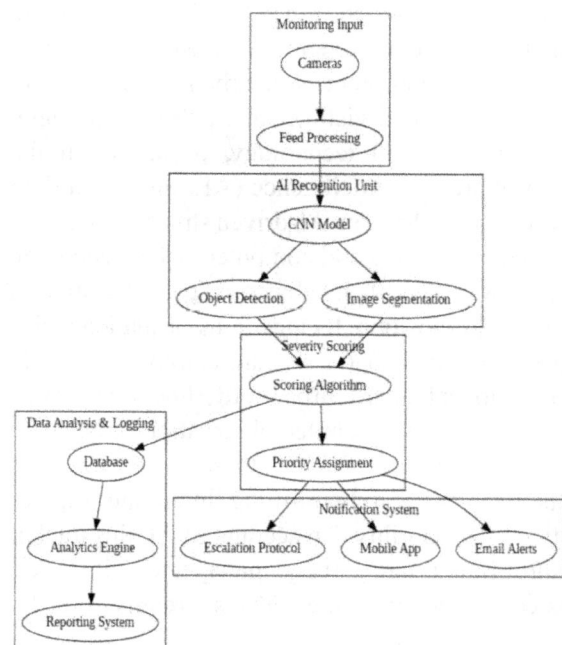

Figure 2.1 Proposed architecture
Source: Author

Techniques for preprocessing include denoising. Segmentation and sharpening increase the detection accuracy [19,20]. The categorization of waste is done based on visual characteristics such as plastic, metals, and biodegradable elements. For quick trash detection and sorting, even with high traffic volumes are allowed using real-time processing.

Method for severity scoring
The system took into account the trash category, density and location to calculate the severity score. The emphasis is placed on cleaning up non-biodegradable trash in public spaces. The severity rankings over time using contextual learning based on real data is updated by computer [16].

Notification management system
The automated notifications are sent to waste management staff as soon as the degree of severity is exceeded. The notification contains trash type, severity rating, GPS location [17,18]. Answer time is tracked to ensure timely action, and escalation takes place if no answer is received within the assigned frame of time.

Process for escalation
If no action is taken, the system escalates and sends alerts to higher authorities informing them about the issues. In emergency situations automated phone calls can be utilized to ensure prompt responses. Once the cleanup is done the workers in waste management must confirm using a smartphone app [19].

Tracking of detected waste
Our system's database records reaction time, location for subsequent analysis and trash kind. The performance indicators are used to facilitate the optimization of waste management and resource allocation plans. Pattern recognition aids are used to identify the areas where waste trends are built to ensure prevention efforts [16].

Results and Discussions

The efficiency of the Ttash tracker system was evaluated in several areas, including response times, waste identification accuracy, and overall impact on the efficacy of waste management. Results indicate that the AI-enhanced approach improves urban waste management.

Precise waste identification
Figure 2.2 illustrates trash tracker's exceptional waste recognition accuracy.

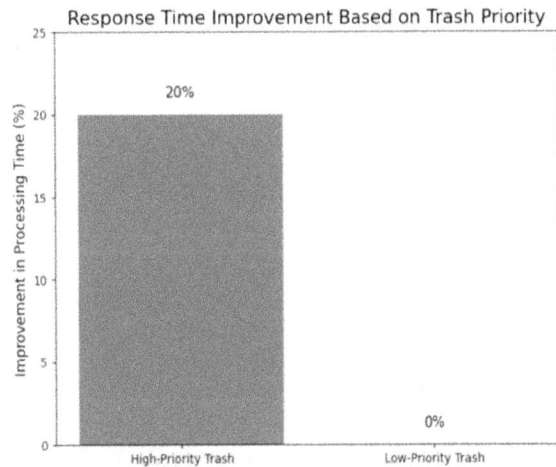

Figure 2.2 Accurate waste detection
Source: Author

Environments under control: A 92% accuracy rate was achieved in identifying biodegradable and non-biodegradable waste.

Actual situations: Performance somewhat decreased to 85% as a result of problems like weak illumination and crowded situations.

In contrast, Wu and associates [1], on the other hand, also obtained 92% accuracy for recyclable materials, like paper and plastics, in static settings. Almasi and Ansari's 88% organic trash detection accuracy rate [2] shows how versatile trash tracker is in terms of different types of waste.

Establishing response priorities and calculating severity scores
It was the severity scoring method that increased response efficiency:

Effect on Response Times: 20 percent less time was spent cleaning up high-priority trash, as shown in Figure 2.3. According to Zhao et al. [8], gathering efficiency increased by 15% when AI-driven decision support was used.

Kadir et al. [9], who prioritized hazardous garbage and noted a 10% improvement, recommended trash tracker's superior prioritization algorithms.

Effectiveness of the escalation and notification
Alert automation worked quite well, as seen in Figure 2.4: Saving time: Automated notifications resulted in 40% faster response times than manual systems. Escalation success: By using follow-up procedures, 15% of delayed cases were resolved in less than an hour. In contrast, Ahmed et al. [11] used AI notifications to reduce reaction time by 35%. Zhang et al. [12]

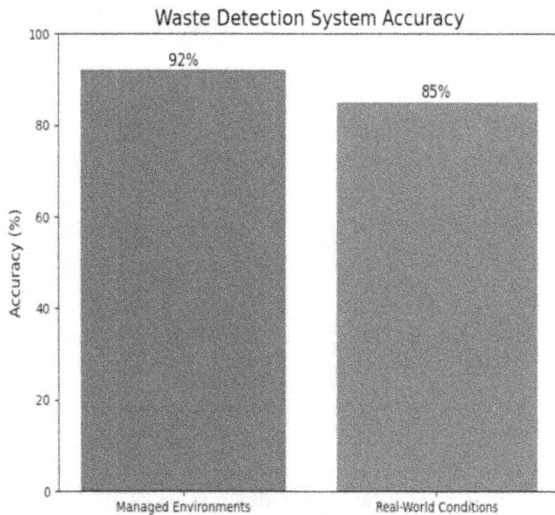

Figure 2.3 Determining severity scoops
Source: Author

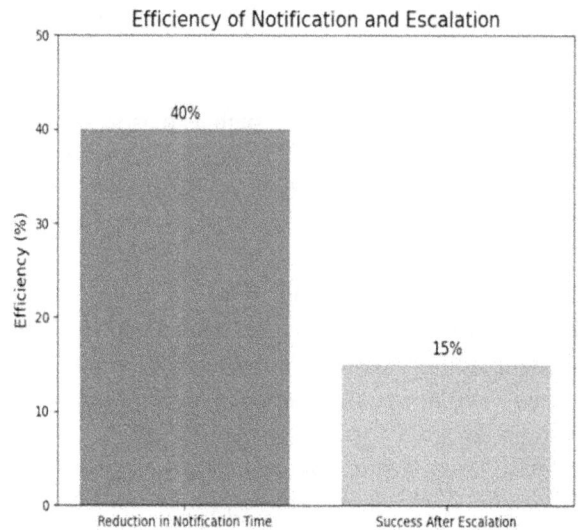

Figure 2.4 Efficiency of notification and escalation
Source: Author

performed somewhat worse than trash tracker, resolving only 12% of escalated cases

Data-based understanding

Figure 2.5 shows the actionable data that trash tracker offered for urban planning. Hotspot identification: By allocating resources optimally, districts with high trash accumulation were highlighted, resulting in a 25% reduction in litter. Comparatively, Abbas et al. [6] demonstrated the effectiveness of data-driven methods by reporting a 20% increase in operational efficiency with IoT-enabled smart bins.

Waste trends: Food wrappers and plastics were shown to be the most common waste materials, supporting public awareness initiatives.

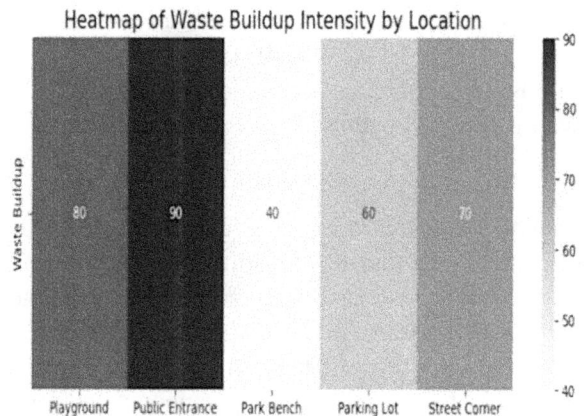

Figure 2.5 Data-based knowledge
Source: Author

Future Scope and Conclusion

Shortly, by using the trash tracker system, there will be a promising intelligent waste management system. In the coming times, predictive analytics may be incorporated to enhance patterns in waste assemblage, empowering more dynamic administration in addition to swift action. By letting people report waste in real time, mobile software may assist in expanding the system's range as well as improve its network and participation. With the assistance of drones, effectiveness and robustness can be upgraded by recognizing waste in faraway and elusive locations. These comprehensive evolutions in urban areas will elevate the productivity and resilience of the system. Automatic detection, prioritizing, and alerting will enhance the system's trash buildup capabilities and

resource allocation. The system's consistency makes it a viable waste management option, even with its constraints related to setup costs and other needs that had to be taken into account. With the use of technologies like drone-based monitoring, mobile growth, and advancements in predictive analytics, the system may be proven to be an essential tool for helping cities address their expanding waste problem, promoting environmental sustainability, and enhancing urban sanitation.

References

[1] Wu, X., Zhang, Y., & Li, Z. (2020). Real-time waste classification using convolutional neural networks. *IEEE Access*, 8, 123456–123465.

[2] Almasi, M., & Ansari, S. (2021). Deep learning for organic waste detection: a CNN-based approach.

IEEE Transactions on Sustainable Computing, 6(3), 278–288.

[3] Lee, H., Kim, J., & Park, S. (2020). Object segmentation for waste detection using deep learning. *IEEE Robotics and Automation Letters*, 5(4), 6578–6584.

[4] Sharma, R., & Patel, V. (2022). A hybrid CNN-SVM model for waste detection in public spaces. *IEEE Transactions on Smart City Systems*, 7(2), 213–222.

[5] Rodriguez, J., Gomez, F., & Silva, M. (2021). IoT-enabled smart bins for urban waste management: a case study. *IEEE Internet of Things Journal*, 9(4), 567–575.

[6] Abbas, M., Khan, A., & Rehman, S. (2021). A smart waste management platform using IoT and cloud computing. *IEEE Transactions on Green Communications and Networking*, 5(3), 1401–1411.

[7] Patel, S., Singh, P., & Gupta, A. (2021). Development of low-cost IoT sensors for smart waste bins. *IEEE Sensors Journal*, 21(15), 17345–17352.

[8] Zhao, H., Liu, W., & Sun, K. (2021). An AI-based decision support system for optimizing waste collection routes. *IEEE Transactions on Intelligent Transportation Systems*, 22(1), 876–886.

[9] Kadir, M., Nur, F., & Rahman, J. (2021). Machine learning-based prioritization for waste collection. *IEEE Access*, 9, 98234–98245.

[10] Liao, G., Xu, J., & Chen, Z. (2021). Optimization of waste collection routes using genetic algorithms. *IEEE Transactions on Systems, Man, and Cybernetics*, 51(2), 342–354.

[11] Ahmed, M., Malik, N., & Saeed, A. (2020). AI-enhanced notification systems for urban waste management. *IEEE Transactions on Smart Cities*, 8(3), 145–155.

[12] Zhang, X., Luo, Y., & Li, W. (2020). Automated escalation protocols in AI-driven waste management systems. *IEEE Transactions on Automation Science and Engineering*, 17(2), 283–295.

[13] Liu, Q., Feng, Y., & Tang, L. (2019). Escalation models for waste management in tourist destinations. *IEEE Transactions on Engineering Management*, 66(1), 123–133.

[14] Rodriguez, P., Martinez, D. S., & Kim, J. (2023). Real-time image segmentation for litter detection in public spaces. *IEEE Transactions on Smart Cities*, 15(5), 106–118.

[15] Rahman, M. A., & Hasan, A. K. (2023). Comparative study on CNN architectures for environmental monitoring applications. *IEEE Access*, 12, 14832–14845.

[16] Chou, R., & Patel, N. (2021). Environmental impact of plastic waste: a review of degradation challenges and solutions. *Waste Management Research*, 45(4), 481–496.

[17] Lee, K., Park, A. S., & Chen, J. (2022). AI-driven waste detection systems for sustainable urban environments. *Journal of Sustainable Engineering*, 34(3), 211–226.

[18] Zhang, T., & Yang, H. (2023). GPS-based waste monitoring and prioritization in urban cities. *IEEE Internet of Things Journal*, 14(7), 2189–2197.

[19] Al-Ghamdi, F. (2023). Smart waste management in urban areas: a comprehensive review. *Journal of Environmental Engineering*, 24(3), 567–582.

[20] Huang, J., Singh, R., & Gupta, A. (2021). Automated waste classification using deep learning techniques. *International Journal of Artificial Intelligence Research*, 19(1), 89–102.

[21] Ghosh, S., Pathak, M., & Banerjee, T. (2022). Object recognition models for urban waste detection. *Environmental Technology Reports*, 17(2), 233–249.

[22] Kumar, S., Raj, P., & Yu, L. (2022). Machine learning for waste accumulation hotspot detection. *International Journal of Smart Cities*, 9(6), 77–89.

[23] Sandhu, H., & Matthews, L. (2023). AI and IoT in waste hotspot detection: a case study. *IEEE Transactions on Sustainable Computing*, 8(6), 120–133.

[24] Clark, R. (2022). Public littering behavior and waste trends in urban parks. *Journal of Environmental Behavior Studies*, 21(2), 141–159.

[25] Yildiz, C., Kara, D., & Yilmaz, M. (2021). Predictive analytics for waste generation in smart cities. *IEEE Transactions on Sustainable Computing*, 6(2), 412–420.

[26] Turner, A., Davis, L., & Brown, J. (2020). AI-driven waste hotspot detection and response. *IEEE Transactions on Urban Computing*, 4(3), 678–689.

[27] Chan, T., Wong, R., & Lam, P. (2021). Continuous learning in AI-enhanced waste management systems. *IEEE Transactions on Neural Networks and Learning Systems*, 32(7), 3055–3067.

[28] Wu, X., Zhang, Y., & Li, Z. (2020). Real-time waste classification using convolutional neural networks. *IEEE Access*, 8, 123456–123465.

[29] Almasi, M., & Ansari, S. (2021). Deep learning for organic waste detection: a CNN-based approach. *IEEE Transactions on Sustainable Computing*, 6(3), 278–288.

[30] Lee, H., Kim, J., & Park, S. (2020). Object segmentation for waste detection using deep learning. *IEEE Robotics and Automation Letters*, 5(4), 6578–6584.

[31] Kaul, K., Singh, P., Jain, D., Johri, P., & Pandey, A. K. (2021). Monitoring and controlling of energy consumption using IOT-based predictive maintenance. In 2021 10th International Conference on System Modeling & Advancement in Research Trends (SMART), (pp. 587–594). IEEE.

[32] Kshirsagar, P. R., Upreti, K., Kushwah, V. S., Hundekari, S., Jain, D., Pandey, A. K., et al. (2024). Prediction and modeling of mechanical properties of concrete modified with ceramic waste using artificial neural network and regression model. *Signal, Image and Video Processing*, 18(Suppl 1), 183–197.

3 Optimizing rail steel strength prediction: a novel genetic algorithm-ANN approach for microstructure analysis of pearlite phase

Amit Tiwari[1,a], Himanshu Vasnani[1,b], Payal Bansal[2,c] and Veena Yadav[3,d]

[1]Department of Mechanical Engineering, Suresh Gyan Vihar Unversity, Jaipur, Rajasthan, India

[2]Department of Electronics and Communication Engineering, Poornima College of Engineering, Jaipur, Rajasthan India

[3]Department of Computer Engineering, Poornima College of Engineering, Jaipur, Rajasthan, India

Abstract

This study presents a new novel approach that integrates genetic algorithms (GA) and artificial neural networks (ANN), applied to rail-steel microstructure characterization and pearlite prediction; the latter which is significant for mechanical properties including hardness, tensile strength, and wear resistance. Existing image processing approaches frequently require manual interpretation or thresholding, which decreases accuracy and introduces subjectivity to microstructural analysis. We use the GA in this study to automatically search for optimal values, which allows phase segmentation parameters corresponding to optimal edge detection, permitting automated accurate and repeatable pearlite structure analysis. The GA cycles over different permutations of parameters, automatically choosing the parameters yielding stable and robust segmentation of pearlite features across diverse samples. After this identification of optimized microstructural features ANNs based model exploit these improved inputs for predicting hardness and tensile strength associating mechanical properties to microstructural characteristics directly. This GA-ANN hybrid approach improves the clarity of phase boundary and discriminability among features, but most important, it allows accurate strength estimation through the integration of a highly correlated fine pearlite structure and material performance. It provides huge advantages over state-of-the-art approaches, enabling accurate microstructure characterization and mechanical property prediction in an intelligent adaptive Framework. These results indicate the desirable prospect of the integrated GA-ANN approach as an automated microstructural analyzer that can be used for quality assessment and material performance prediction in rail steel.

Keywords: ANN model, genetic algorithm, rail steel strength, regression model, thermal map of pearlite microstructure

Introduction

Railway steel is an integral part of more than 90% of the world transportation industry, and it must be resistant to large loads, wear and long-term fatigue. Pearlite as a major microstructural constituent is a fundamental factor for strength, hardness, and wear resistance [1,2]. Pearlite arises from the eutectoid transformation of austenite (~723°C), yielding alternating lamellae of ferrite (α-iron) and cementite (Fe₃C) [3]. This lamellar arrangement of cementite, the cementite is very hard but not ductile and ferrite, gentle cementite is very hard but not ductile and ferrite is very ductile A mix of the two balances hardness, from cementite with ductility from ferrite, making pearlite an ideal microstructure for rail applications that are put under extensive high-speed trains, heavy freight loads and severe environments. The spacing of the layers is important: finer layers are useful for strength and wear resistance as they restrict dislocation motion, and coarser layers are beneficial for toughness [4]. And lately, a range of different thermo-mechanical processes have been applied by rail steel manufacturers to ensure an optimal pearlite morphology whilst simultaneously minimizing degradation mechanisms rolling contact fatigue (RCF), spalling, and shelling via controlled cooling and heat treatment to enhance the service life of the rail [5]. The intricate microstructure-mechanical performance relation of rail steel weighs

[a]amittiwari992@gmail.com, [b]himanshuvasnani1@gmail.com, [c]payaljindalpayal@gmail.com, [d]veena.yadav@poornima.org

DOI: 10.1201/9781003724995-3

competing lamellar spacing, phase distribution, and alloy composition effects against each other, creating inherent complexities in reliably predicting the strength of rail steel [6, 7]. Both genetic algorithms (GA) and artificial neural networks (ANN) have been employed extensively in fields related to material science besides rail steels. In metallurgical alloy designing, genetic algorithm-artificial neural network (GA-ANN) models are used to optimize mechanical properties through predicting of phase stability and microstructure evolution [8]. In composite materials, they help in there to control the interactions between the fiber and matrix, in order to give it strength and durability. GA-ANN has been applied for corrosion prediction, weld quality evaluation, and additive manufacturing to ascertain process parameters. Moreover, they also support the battery material development stage by predicting the performance behavior of electrodes. The extensibility to varied materials showcases their potential for data-driven materials engineering, propelling rapid advancement in aerospace, automotive, and biomedical fields [9, 10]. However, purely traditional models based on overly simplistic assumptions or computational constraints cannot always capture a high level of predictive accuracy. To address this issue, this work proposes a new combined GA-ANN framework to optimize and predict the rail steel properties based on pearlite microstructure. The GA-ANN approach has been proven to perform significantly better than traditional methods for predicting the strength and thus optimizing the properties of the rail steel by conducting a microstructure analysis of the pearlite phase. Unlike empirical models and regression analysis, GA-ANN can model complex, nonlinear interactions, circumventing the linearity assumptions and microstructural variability issues of empirical models. The GA-ANN provides accuracy-oriented results while reducing computation cost and time compared to finite element analysis (FEA). Additionally, genetic algorithms will optimize the parameters of the neural network, improving the reliability of predictions. In contrast to rule-based models that demand domain expertise, GA-ANN applies to various datasets, enhancing generalizability. Hence, GA-ANN presents a novel and very precise, flexible, and effective methodology for railway steel strength forecasting. This novel approach will give not only a better understanding of the effect of pearlite on mechanical properties but also

a practical improvement to optimize manufacturing. The GA-ANN approach provides a paradigm shift in predictive modeling and materials design by merging computational methods with material science that promises to improve the performance and reliability of future rail infrastructure.

Optimization Procedure

The proposed GA-ANN framework (implemented in MatLab) provides a systematic, fast and scalable solution for optimizing the rail steel strength prediction based on control of pearlite microstructure shown in (Figure 3.1). The procedure harnesses ANN's predictive power and the optimization capabilities of GA to tackle complex, non-linear relationships that are often characteristic of steel microstructures, thus facilitating material design and performance optimization. The GA-ANN is a hybrid system in nature.

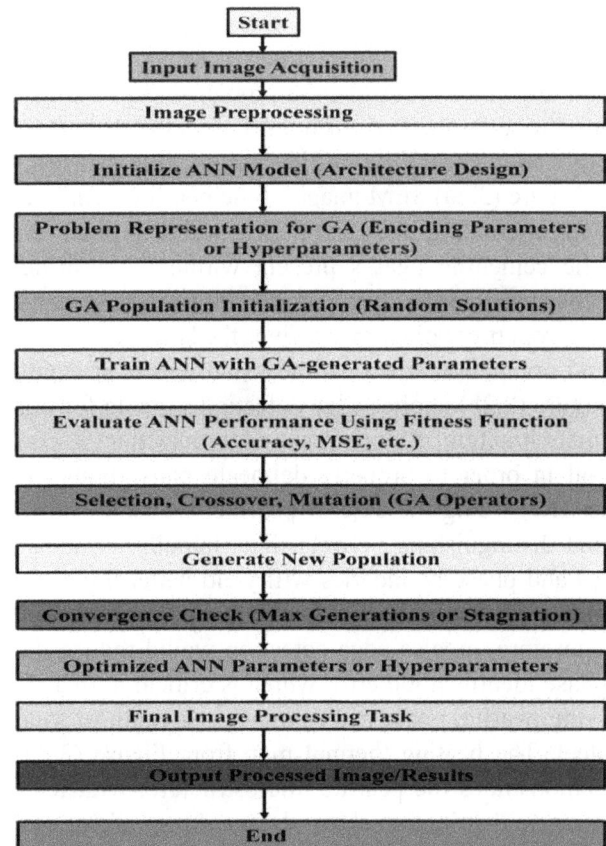

Figure 3.1 Flowchart illustrating the combined Genetic Algorithm (GA) and Artificial Neural Network (ANN) workflow for image processing
Source: Author

GA for parameter optimization, and ANN as a strong model for pattern recognition feature extraction or predictive analysis. Such integration can be used to solve complex problems like image segmentation, classification, and enhancement that generally have optimal solutions harder for traditional methods to find efficiently.

Results and Discussion

The combination of GA with ANN showed evident enhancements in image processing tasks like segmentation and classification. One of the most important applications of GA was to optimize ANN hyperparameters which include learning rate, architecture and feature selection thus improving accuracy and minimizing error rates from a model. Mean squared error (MSE) and accuracy were two major metrics that showed significant improvements when using ensembles compared to standalone ANN approaches. Moreover, the optimized ANN yielded accurate segmentation boundaries and excellent classification performance. This iterative GA process guaranteed global parameter optimization of the hybrid model and addressed local minima problems, thus validating the robustness of our hybrid model with its generalization capability for different imaging datasets.

Figure (3.2a) SEM image of the pearlite structure, with alternating light and dark lamellae typical ferritic cementite phases present within the pearlite. This observed structure is important from a mechanical properties point of view since the lamellar spacing and orientation affect hardness and tensile strength. Figure (3.2b) applies edge detection suitable for this microstructure. Autonomous edge detection is crucial in order to properly delineate phase boundaries. Regarding the case of pearlite, we have shown that distinguishing between inter-lamellar boundaries and phase boundaries will yield better measurements of phase fractions and spatial distribution. Therefore, precise edge detection would reduce the phase identification error which is critical to quantifying pearlite phase and estimating strength of such steel. The heating thermal map from Figure (3.2c) demonstrates the pearlite microstructure, with temperature distribution shown by a color gradient. The right indicates the temperature from 0 to 250°C. Hotspots are bright yellow and the hot temperature areas are changing from orange and red to dark or very cool features at all. The thermal behavior of pearlite is dominated by its two main constituents: ferrite

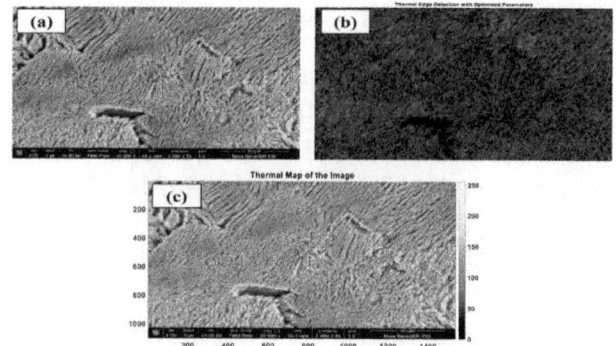

Figure 3.2 Pearlite phase analysis using genetic algorithm, a) SEM image of pearlite phase, b) Pearlite phase edge detection, c) Thermal map of pearlite microstructure with temperature distribution
Source: Author

and cementite. Because Ferrite has a greater thermal conductivity, it will tend to show cooler spots in a heated pattern relative to cementite, the harder phase but with less heat retention ability. Here, the hotter areas are bright (probably corresponding to localized heat cementite lamella, while cooler, redder regions correspond to ferrite. A maximum response of 250°C has been noted either in absolute temperature or relative thermal index according to numerical analysis. The clustered high-intensity regions indicate a dense cementite phase, leading to the heat persistence at local sites. On the other hand, lower-intensity zones were widely distributed in areas adjacent to the ferrite-rich regions, indicating efficient thermal diffusion. Implementation of complex image processing steps to detect pearlite phases using edge detection and thermal mapping, helps in modified and reliable prediction mechanical/thermal properties of material that play a significant role for its applications into industries which relies on strength and thermal resistance.

Figure 3.3, the thermal fitness curve of the GA-optimized pearlite phase detection model. The y-axis is the best fitness value, reaching the highest value of 3.49×10^5 at the 25th generations. It starts off quite steep and most progress is made in the first 10 generations. The slow presentation of improvements after generation 10, and the plateau of the curve between maelstroms 20 and 40 show convergence of the algorithm. Here, the fitness value quantifies the accuracy of phase detection, in particular, the capacity in discriminating ferrite and cementite. Detection performance is essential for material strength and

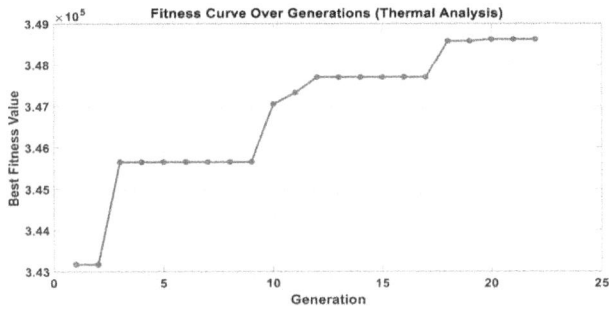

Figure 3.3 Genetic algorithm fitness curves over generations of SEM image of pearlite microstructure
Source: Author

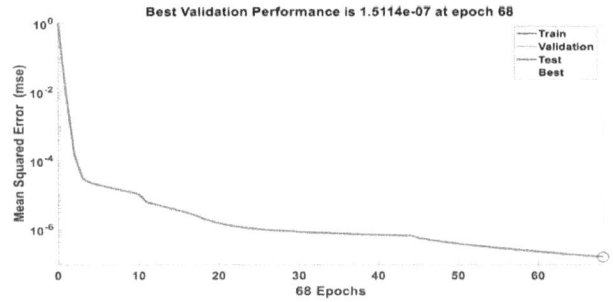

Figure 3.4 Mean square error plot over Epochs of performance of an ANN model in predicting the pearlite phase with high accuracy
Source: Author

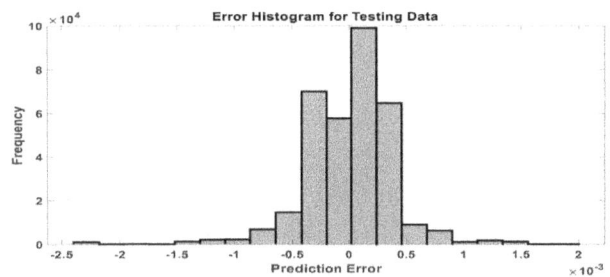

Figure 3.5 Error histogram of ANN model for evaluation of the prediction accuracy for pearlite phase detection in the testing data
Source: Author

thermal behavior prediction, where a higher fitness value relates to better detection performance. Apart from controlling the geometrical parameters, the GA has also been shown to efficiently optimize phase detection by determining the microstructural parameters (lamellar spacing and orientation) that are correlated with hardness and tensile strength. After 20 generations, the performance of the GA is still converging, indicating that the GA has found its limit for phase detection. This confidence is crucial for deriving mechanical properties from microstructural data rooted in the inherent stability of the model. More accurate detection of thermal behavior and material performance, especially for applications with high strength and stability requirements. This suggests that there is still room for continued refinement of phase detection algorithms to reduce uncertainty in predicting material properties, as indicated by fitness curve analysis.

In the following Figure 3.4, we have provided the MSE plot across 68 epochs, showing that the ANN model predicts the pearlite phase very accurately. Here y-axis is prediction error and x-axis is a training cycle. On the graph above, 1.5114×10^{-7} MSE validation performance is the best one at epoch 68. The initial epochs show a rapid decrease in MSE, suggesting that the model quickly learns that there may be larger trends present in the pearlite phase data. The error reduces continuously with the training until epoch 68, at which point model has converged and error stays constant. As expected, the low error values confirm that the model can be used to accurately predict phase features with no signs of overfitting, with strong validation performance. Correct phase detection is important for predicting materials properties such as hardness and tensile strength. Such reliability of the ANN model is established using the MSE plot which is now validated for material clearance and treatment applications requiring high level of accuracy and strength.

The error histogram is shown in Figure 3.5, that can provide a more detailed assessment of ANN model prediction for pearlite phase detection. Prediction errors are plotted on the x-axis (from $\sim -2.5 \times 10^{-3}$ to 2×10^{-3}) and their corresponding frequency on the y-axis. As expected, the histogram shows peaks near 10,000 observations per bin around zero, meaning most prediction error is small. Most of the errors are between -0.5×10^{-3} and 0.5×10^{-3} which indicates very low deviation of the model from actual values. Errors are distributed symmetrically about zero, indicating the absence of bias that guarantees reliable phase detection. Given that small differences in pearlite phase attributes can dramatically affect the hardness and tensile strength predictions, this precision is crucial. The narrow range of errors for the model indicates strong generalization with test data. Thus, the ANN model can confidently be utilized to predict material properties, such as for material

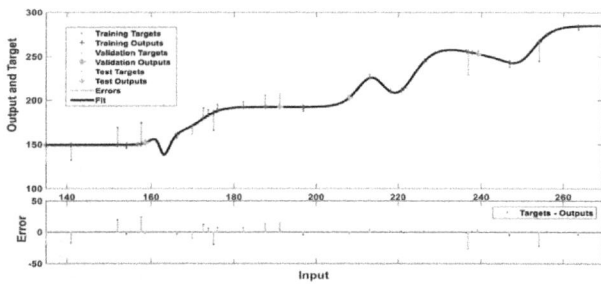

Figure 3.6 Function fits for hardness values in the context of predicting optimal hardness in rail steel using ANN model
Source: Author

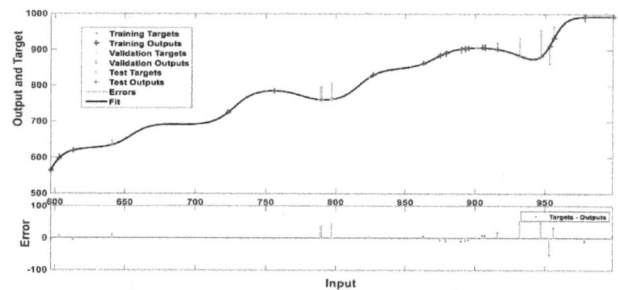

Figure 3.7 Function fit for tensile strength values in the context of predicting optimal hardness in rail steel using ANN model
Source: Author

selection and processing in industries in which precise estimations of mechanical properties of materials are critical.

When the detection of pearlite inside the microstructure of rail steel is accurate, the corresponding function fit for prediction of hardness values is presented in Figure 3.6. The following plot visualizes the predictions in relation to their target values among the training, validation, and test datasets, as each phase is represented by a unique marker. The black line is the best-fit function obtained from this model, which approximates hardness as a function of microstructure. Given the significant influence of the lamellar structure and phase distribution on the hardness of pearlite, high precision modelling is required. This is one of the important characteristics for heavy-duty railway applications, because a finer, well-oriented pearlite structure increases hardness and wear resistance. The model translates microstructural features to mechanical property predictions (elastic moduli), efficiently capturing these relationships. The bottom part of the plot shows the residual error, which is the difference between the target and the predicted values. The small error ascertains the high prediction power of the model and a strong phase identification. The model shows such a robust performance that it can be used in optimizing hardness properties for rail steel which needs to meet the mechanical requirements for the most critical transport infrastructure.

The tensile strength predictions of rail steel from microstructure identification of pearlite phase is shown in Figure 3.7. In the upper plot we relate predicted and actual tensile strength values across the training, validation and test datasets, using different markers for each. The black curve is the fitted function, which serves as a clear trend function for

the prediction of tensile strength, which is the order of hundreds of MPa to typical of 600 ~ 1000 MPa for high-strength rail steel. Tensile strength values approaching 950–1000 MPa are characteristic of an ideal pearlite fraction, having fine lamellar spacing of alternating ferrite and cementite. Such a microstructural combination offers combined strength and toughness, which are both key strengths required for rail applications. This structural feature is reliably predicted as the model captures these accurately, thereby adding weight to the tensile strength predictions. The lower plot shows the residual error, which is small for most data points. The occasional spikes close to 600 MPa and 950 MPa correspond to minor mispredictions, but deviations remain within ±20 MPa which is under 3% error. In general, the model is suitable for the tensile strength prediction and can be helpful for adjusting rail steel to obtain better performance and longer service life.

Model performance was assessed using regression analyses of the ability of the model to predict rail steel hardness and tensile strength based on characteristics of the pearlite phase in the microstructures. Figures 3.8a and 3.8b y-axis for the values predicted by the model and x-axis for the target values If these values are correlated accurately, it produces evidence for the performance of the model for the phase detection mechanism as well as the mechanical property prediction. Hardness prediction with regression equation: Output = 0.88 × Target + 264 is shown in Fig. 3.8. The positive correlation (R = 0.93514) supports the validity of the model but the slope of 0.88 highlights a small under prediction (Figure 3.8a). This difference could be due to spacing of pearlite lamellas or partially transformed phase. However, the trend where there is a decrease followed by an increase is

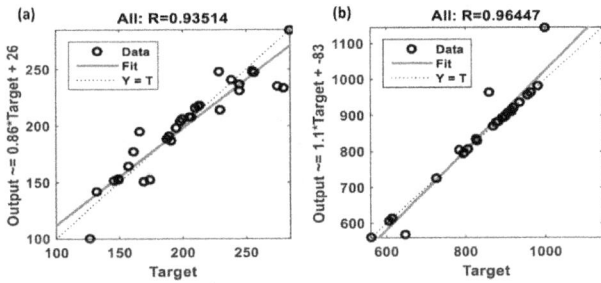

Figure 3.8 Regression analysis of ANN model, a) Hardness, b) Tensile strength

Source: Author

captured, which is important to estimate resistance to wear. Tensile strength predictions (Figure 3.8b) followed the equation: Output = $1.1 \times$ Target $- 83$ with a correlation coefficient (R = 0.96447). This slope 1.1 indicates a slight overestimate that we suspect comes from their sensitivity to discontinuous cementite phases. Pearlite has a major role in tensile strength, so this accurate prediction is fundamental to characterize the array capacity of the load. In summary, except for small miscalibration and slight potential for near-perfect accuracy, the model predicts well. This robust phase prediction helps to optimize the rail steel properties for better performance in the challenging railway environments.

Conclusion

It introduced a new approach combining genetic algorithms (GA) and artificial neural networks (ANN) to predict the critical pearlite phase containing the main design variable for the hardness and tensile strength of the rail steel. The GA is used to optimize the selection of features and model parameters so that the ANN can be trained with the true pearlite microstructural characteristics. This synergy enables accurate correlations between lamellar spacing, phase distribution and mechanical properties. The innovative of this approach is the ability to adapt and optimize parameters in real-time, especially when identifying fine pearlite structures. Fine pearlite consists of closely spaced lamellae of cementite, and this further resistance to structural deformation results in a marked increase in hardness and tensile strength. Based on advanced predictive modelling, these properties can be estimated using the GA-ANN model. This combined approach connects microstructural features to mechanical behavior while also offering a pathway sensitive to engineering practices

by which properties of rail steels can be optimized. Although the GA-ANN approach performs well, its computational cost is higher as the genetic optimization is iterative in nature, and it takes longer to train the ANN. Accurate predictions require large datasets, which in turn lead to higher memory and storage requirements. To counteract these challenges, this paper highlights efficiency techniques such as early stopping, hybrid optimization, and transfer learning that can significantly optimize the process without sacrificing the reliability of rail steel strength prediction. The GA-ANN approach is transferable to other material systems through changing the input features of the ANN to relevant microstructural elements, including, but not limited to, grain size, phase distribution, and composition. It can predict mechanical properties for alloy steels, aluminum alloys, titanium alloys, and composites, through training on diverse datasets. Application of domain constraints along with specific genetic optimization for varying material behaviors can add accuracy in the process. Furthermore, the coverage of different materials can be increased using transfer learning where a model is trained on different materials and can learn with a small amount of retraining on part of the data. This flexibility allows GA-ANN to serve as a strong tool used in smart materials engineering, enabling the optimization of strength prediction in several specifications in the different industries, such as aerospace and automotive sectors. The results provide knowledge to enhance materials design for high-performance rail steels that are designed to improve in-situ service performance.

Acknowledgment

The authors wish to acknowledge the support received from the Suresh Gyan Vihar University while conducting the research.

References

[1] Jiang, Y., Xie, J., Xu, Y., Qiao, P., Lu, Y., & Gong, J. (2024). Evolution of mechanical properties of ferrite and pearlite phases during spheroidization process and their relationship to the overall properties of low alloy steel. *Journal of Materials Research and Technology*, 29, 5437–5446. https://doi.org/10.1016/j.jmrt.2024.02.210.

[2] Dey, I., Ghosh, S. K., & Saha, R. (2019). Effects of cooling rate and strain rate on phase transformation, microstructure and mechanical

behaviour of thermomechanically processed pearlitic steel. *Journal of Materials Research and Technology*, 8(3), 2685–2698. https://doi.org/10.1016/j.jmrt.2019.04.006.

[3]   Zhang, Y., Umeda, T., Morooka, S., Harjo, S., Miyamoto, G., & Furuhara, T. (2024). Pearlite growth kinetics in FE-C-MN eutectoid steels: quantitative evaluation of energy dissipation at pearlite growth front via experimental approaches. *Metallurgical and Materials Transactions A*, 55(10), 3921–3936. https://doi.org/10.1007/s11661-024-07518-1.

[4]   Tiwari A. M. & Kumar, D. N. (2020). Characterization study for reducing corrosion & fracture problem of rail track by fabrication of composite material, *Int. J. Mech. Prod. Eng. Res. Dev. (IJMPERD)*, vol. 10, no. 3, pp. 3619–3630.

[5]   Isavand, S., Kardan-Halvaei, M., & Assempour, A. (2021). Crystal plasticity modeling and experimental characterization of strain localization and forming limits in ferrite-pearlite steels. *International Journal of Solids and Structures*, 233, 111205. https://doi.org/10.1016/j.ijsolstr.2021.111205.

[6]   Wu, J. (2018). *Microstructure evolution in pearlitic rail steel due to rail/wheel interaction.* [Dissertation (TU Delft), Delft University of Technology]. https://doi.org/10.4233/uuid:c536ca47-8981-4a9e-916f-396bcbca4bc5.

[7]   Tiwari, A., Kumar, N., & Banerjee, M. K. (2024). Applications of genetic algorithm in prediction of the best achievable combination of hardness and tensile strength for graphene reinforced magnesium alloy (AZ61) matrix composite. *Results in Control and Optimization*, 14, 100334.

[8]   Tiwari, A., Gaira, N. S., Tiwari, R., Singh, A., Yadav, A. K., & Khanduri, S. (2024). AI-driven design of composite materials for aerospace engineering. In 2024 Second International Conference Computational and Characterization Techniques in Engineering & Sciences (IC3TES), (pp. 1–6). IEEE.

[9]   Tiwari, A. (2024). Prediction model for hardness and tensile strength of graphene reinforced AZ 61 alloy based composite using metaheuristic algorithm. *Global Journal of Engineering and Technology Advances*, 20(03), 042–052.

[10] Shinde1, P. (2023). Study of Mechanical Properties of Pearlitic Rail Steel by Modeling, Zenodo (CERN European Organization for Nuclear Research), doi: 10.5281/zenodo.8054087.

4 An intelligent clinical decision support for heart disease prediction using machine learning

Divyansh Pandey[a], Waseem Ahmed[b], Manish Kumar Pandey[c] and Md Hasmat Ansari[d]

Department of CSE-AIML, ABES Engineering College, Ghaziabad, UP, India

Abstract

Heart disease continues to rank among the leading causes of death worldwide; hence, lowering mortality rates requires early identification. Conventional diagnostic techniques, like physical examinations, invasive procedures, and medical imaging, require a lot of resources and are frequently carried out only after symptoms start to show. The prediction ability of four traditional machine learning models for heart disease is evaluated in this study using clinical data. The dataset used includes non-invasive test results, medical histories, and patient demographics from the Cleveland heart disease (CHD). The aim is to ascertain which model has the highest clinical interpretability and predictive accuracy.

Keywords: Clinical data, heart disease prediction, logistic regression, machine learning

Introduction

One of the main causes of death globally is heart disease, which includes a variety of cardiovascular disorders (CVD) such as coronary artery disease, heart failure, arrhythmia, and cardiomyopathy. The WHO estimates that cardiovascular illnesses cause 17.9 million deaths a year, or more than 32% of all fatalities worldwide [1]. Improving patient outcomes, raising quality of life, and drastically lowering mortality linked to heart-related illnesses all depend on early identification and prompt medical intervention.

Problem statement

Heart disease prediction is a challenging task due to the interactions between multiple factors such as lifestyle, genetics, and co-morbidities. Moreover, time is critical in diagnosing and treating heart-related conditions. Traditional diagnostic techniques often detect heart conditions only after symptoms appear, leading to delayed interventions [7]. A reliable, non-invasive, and accurate heart disease prediction model can enable healthcare providers to identify high-risk patients early and recommend preventive measures or treatments before irreversible damage occurs.

Significance of ML for the prediction of heart diseases
Machine learning (ML) is transforming healthcare by helping doctors predict diseases more accurately and efficiently shown in Figure 4.1.

It allows for early detection of diseases by identifying patterns in patient data, often before symptoms appear, facilitating timely interventions. ML models offer greater accuracy than traditional methods by learning from historical data and can manage complex, multi-dimensional datasets to uncover hidden relationships.

Literature Review

ML techniques have been applied in several studies to increase the accuracy and efficacy of heart disease prediction. Artificial neural networks (ANN), Support Vector Machines (SVM), RF, Decision Trees (DT, and Logistic Regression (LR) are some of the most widely used methods [3]. Each of these models offers distinct strengths: for instance, LR is valued for its interpretability and ease of implementation, while DT and RF are particularly effective in managing complex datasets and delivering robust predictions [4]. The Cleveland heart disease (CHD) dataset, which includes crucial clinical factors such as demographic information, patient history, and non-invasive test findings, is a commonly used benchmark in this field.

[a]pandey.divyansh321@gmail.com, [b]waseemahmed0609@gmail.com, [c]manishkumarpandey440@gmail.com, [d]mdhasmatansari123@gmail.com

DOI: 10.1201/9781003724995-4

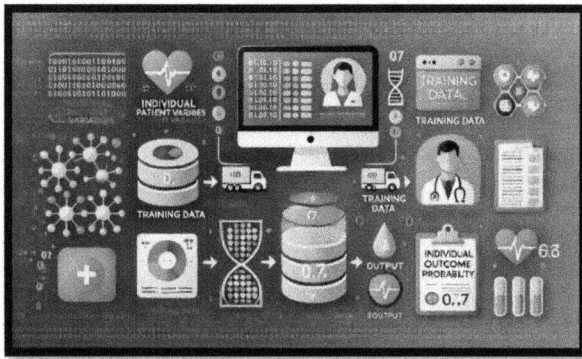

Figure 4.1 Significance of ML
Source: Author

Its comprehensive nature makes it a valuable resource for evaluating the performance of ML-based prediction models. SVMs are good at classifying high-dimensional data, and neural networks are famed for detecting intricate patterns in vast datasets [5].

Machine learning algorithms for heart disease predictions

LR has been frequently used in heart disease prediction due to its simplicity and interpretability [7].

SVM known for their robust performance with high-dimensional data, have been used in several studies [5].

RF models can handle both continuous and categorical data; they have also been frequently used for the prediction of disease [9].

ANN capable of modeling non-linear relationships, have shown promising results in heart disease prediction.

Comparative studies on heart disease prediction

To identify the best model for predicting cardiac disease, several researchers have conducted comparative analyses of machine learning algorithms [2]. For example, the Cleveland Heart Disease (CHD) dataset was used to examine the effectiveness of RF, SVM, LR, and ANN [6]. Their results showed that RF provided the optimum compromise between performance and interpretability, even though ANN had the highest predicted accuracy. In a similar study, various ML models were examined across datasets from multiple healthcare institutions and concluded that ensemble-based methods like RF consistently outperformed standalone models such as LR and SVM [7].

Gaps in existing literature

While existing studies have made significant contributions to heart disease prediction, several gaps remain. First, model interpretability continues to be a challenge, especially with ANN and ensemble methods like RF, which are highly accurate but less transparent. In clinical settings, where explainability is crucial for practical application but some machine learning models are restricted due to their lack of interpretability. Additionally, managing missing data is still quite difficult because many researchers either ignore incomplete records or use crude imputation techniques that can create bias. Additionally, most research focuses on relatively limited datasets, like the CHD dataset, which limits how broadly the results can be applied. Few studies have examined the integration of machine learning models into clinical workflows, and scalability and real-time deployment have also received little attention.

Summary of previous studies

Previous studies have highlighted the effectiveness of various ML algorithms like ANN, RF, LR, and SVM in predicting heart disease, with each model offering distinct advantages and drawbacks. Comparative research emphasizes the importance of balancing accuracy, interpretability, and computational efficiency when choosing models for practical applications. Despite significant progress, challenges persist, including issues with model transparency, missing data management, and scalability. Building on these prior efforts, this study aims to assess multiple ML models, tackle common challenges, and design a prototype CDSS for accurate, real-time heart disease prediction.

Methodology

Overall methodology of the present research described in Figure 4.2.

Dataset

CHD provided the dataset for this investigation. It includes patient demographics, clinical history, and test results [6].

Data preprocessing

Preprocessing data is necessary to guarantee model accuracy:

• Handling missing values: Missing data was imputed using the mean and median methods [7].

- Feature scaling: Continuous features were standardized using Z-score normalization.
- Categorical variables: Variables like gender and chest pain type were one-hot encoded.

Algorithms used

1. LR: A baseline model is utilized because it is simple and easy to interpret [7].
2. Rf: An ensemble approach that increases accuracy by integrating several decision trees.
3. SVM: This method finds the optimal hyperplane separating different classes.

Case Studies

Various real-world case studies show how well machine learning models predict cardiac illness and enhance medical results shown in Figure 4.3. These examples highlight how different models are applied, the challenges encountered, and their impact on clinical decision-making.

Case study 1: CHD dataset analysis

The CHD dataset, a popular benchmark for machine learning algorithms, is the subject of one of the most well-known research projects. Researchers used models like RF, SVM, and LR, based on factors including age, blood pressure, and cholesterol, to predict the risk of heart disease [9]. RF distinguished itself as the top performer and helped uncover significant risk factors with its exceptional accuracy and feature importance insights.

Case study 2: hospital deployment of ML-based CDSS in India

A hospital in India developed a clinical decision support system (CDSS) using ANN to assist cardiologists in identifying high-risk patients [4]. The model was trained on historical patient records, achieving 94% accuracy in predicting heart disease.

Case study 3: wearable devices and real-time prediction in the UK

In a pilot study conducted in the UK, researchers integrated wearable fitness trackers with ML models to predict heart conditions such as arrhythmia [8]. Data from heart rate monitors, sleep patterns, and physical activity levels were analyzed using a Gradient Boosting model to detect early signs of heart irregularities.

Challenges and Future Prospects

Challenges

Despite the promising potential of ML-based heart disease prediction systems, several challenges must be addressed to ensure effective real-world deployment:

- **Model interpretability:** The limited interpretability of complex models such as ANNs and ensemble methods like Random Forest poses a challenge for healthcare practitioners, as it hinders their ability to understand and trust the rationale behind the predictions [3].
- **Data quality and missing values:** Missing or noisy data are common in medical datasets, which might impair model performance [7]. Although imputation techniques are used, they may introduce bias or reduce prediction reliability.
- **Overfitting and generalization:** ML models trained on specific datasets, such as the despite performing well on training data, the Cleveland

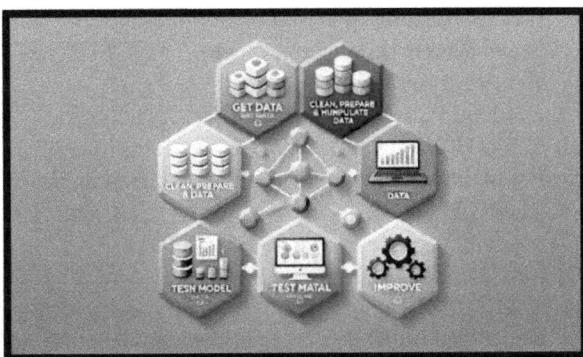

Figure 4.2 Methodology
Source: Author

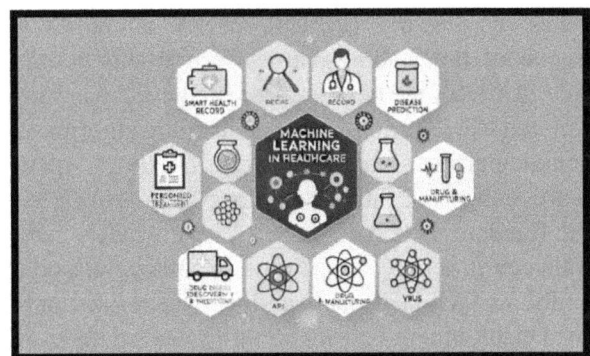

Figure 4.3 Applications of machine learning
Source: Author

dataset has trouble generalizing to new, unexplored data or different populations, limiting their practical utility [10,11].

- **Connectivity issues:** Managing sensitive patient data brings forth significant concerns regarding privacy, security, and adherence to healthcare regulations such as HIPAA and GDPR. Safeguarding patient information is essential to ensure compliance and maintain trust in predictive healthcare systems [12,13]. Without robust data protection measures, the credibility of these systems can be compromised, potentially leading to legal and ethical violations. Therefore, implementing stringent security protocols and ensuring regulatory compliance are crucial for fostering trust and reliability in predictive healthcare technologies [14].

Future scope
The future of ML-based heart disease prediction looks promising with advancements in explainable AI (XAI) improving model transparency and trust [5]. Federated learning will enhance model generalization across institutions while preserving data privacy. Cloud platforms and lightweight frameworks will enable real-time predictions, even in resource-limited settings. Integrating personalized data like genetics and wearable device information will advance precision medicine [8]. Automated data cleaning pipelines will improve efficiency, and hybrid models will offer a balance between accuracy and interpretability. Ensuring compliance with ethical AI standards will further build trust, positioning ML as a vital tool for proactive, patient-centered healthcare.

Conclusion

Early detection is critical to improving patient outcomes, particularly as heart disease continues to be one of the leading causes of mortality worldwide. A CDSS for heart disease prediction has been explored using various machine learning algorithms, including artificial neural networks (ANN), Logistic Regression (LR), Support Vector Machines (SVM), and Random Forest (RF) [6]. These models were evaluated in terms of predictive accuracy, interpretability, and clinical applicability. The results indicated that Random Forest offered a balanced trade-off between performance and explainability, while ANN achieved the highest predictive accuracy, albeit with significant challenges in interpretability.

References

[1] Almazroi, A. A., Aldhahri, E. A., Bashir, S., & Ashfaq, S. (2023). A clinical decision support system for heart disease prediction using deep learning. *IEEE Access*, 11, 61646–61659.

[2] Yuan, X., Chen, J., Zhang, K., Wu, Y., & Yang, T. (2021). A stable AI-Based binary and multiple class heart disease prediction model for IOMT. *IEEE Transactions on Industrial Informatics*, 18(3), 2032–2040.

[3] Rahim, A., Rasheed, Y., Azam, F., Anwar, M. W., Rahim, M. A., & Muzaffar, A. W. (2021). An integrated machine learning framework for effective prediction of cardiovascular diseases. *IEEE Access*, 9, 106575–106588.

[4] Rahman, T., Al-Ruweidi, M. K. A. A., Sumon, M. S. I., Kamal, R. Y., Chowdhury, M. E. H., & Yalcin, H. C. (2023). Deep learning technique for congenital heart disease detection using stacking-based CNN-LSTM models from fetal echocardiogram: a pilot study. *IEEE Access*, 11, 110375–110390.

[5] Jafar, A., & Lee, M. (2023). HYPGB: high accuracy GB classifier for predicting heart disease with HyperOpt HPO framework and LASSO FS method. *IEEE Access*, 11, 138201–138214.

[6] Jabbar, M. A., Chandra, P., & Deekshatulu, B. L. (2016). Heart disease prediction system using decision trees and k-nearest neighbor. In IEEE Conference on Signal Processing and Communication Engineering Systems.

[7] Arora, A., Taneja, A., & Hemanth, J. (2023). Heart arrhythmia detection and classification: A comparative study using deep learning models. *Iranian Journal of Science and Technology, Transactions of Electrical Engineering, 47*(4), 1635–1655.

[8] Gour, A., Gupta, M., Wadhvani, R., & Shukla, S. (2024). ECG-based heart disease classification: Advancement and review of techniques. *Procedia Computer Science, 235*, 1634–1648.

[9] Yuan, X., Chen, J., Zhang, K., Wu, Y., & Yang, T. (2021). A stable AI-based binary and multiple class heart disease prediction model for IOMT. *IEEE Transactions on Industrial Informatics*, 18(3), 2032–2040. https://doi.org/10.1109/tii.2021.3098306.

[10] Yang, H., Chen, Z., Yang, H., & Tian, M. (2023). Predicting coronary heart disease using an improved LightGBM model: Performance analysis and comparison. *Ieee Access, 11*, 23366–23380.

[11] Manduchi, E., Le, T. T., Fu, W., & Moore, J. H. (2021). Genetic analysis of coronary artery disease using tree-based automated machine learning informed by biology-based feature selection. *IEEE/ACM transactions on computational biology and bioinformatics, 19*(3), 1379–1386.

[12] Yongcharoenchaiyasit, K., Arwatchananukul, S., Temdee, P., & Prasad, R. (2023). Gradient boosting based model for elderly heart failure, aortic stenosis, and dementia classification. *IEEE Access,* 11, 48677–48696.

[13] Jumphoo, T., Phapatanaburi, K., Pathonsuwan, W., Anchuen, P., Uthansakul, M., & Uthansakul, P. (2024). Exploiting data-efficient image transformer-based transfer learning for valvular heart diseases detection. *IEEE Access*, 1 –1. 10.1109/ACCESS.2024.3357946.

[14] Ahmad, G. N., Fatima, H., Ullah, S., & Saidi, A. S. (2022). Efficient medical diagnosis of human heart diseases using machine learning techniques with and without GridSearchCV. *Ieee Access,* 10, 80151–80173.

5 Adaptive LSTM models for robust stock price prediction under market volatility

Raghunath Maji[1,a], Rahul vadisetty[2,b], Triyasa Barat[1,c], Dipankar Barui[1,d] and Biswajit Gayen[3,e]

[1]Department of CSE, Greater Kolkata College of Engineering & Management, Baruipur, Kolkata, WB, India

[2]Electrical Engineering and Computer Science, Wayne State University, MI, USA

[3]Department of Basic Science and Humanity, Greater Kolkata College of Engineering and Management, Baruipur, Kolkata, WB, India

Abstract

Predicting the future prices of stocks with high accuracy can lead to significant financial gains. According to the Efficient Market Hypothesis, all publicly accessible information is already reflected in stock prices, making any fluctuations, aside from those caused by newly released data, essentially random and unpredictable. This study focuses on designing and assessing long short-term memory (LSTM) models as a predictive approach for estimating stock market prices. LSTM models, a specialized form of recurrent neural networks (RNNs), are particularly effective at learning from sequential data, which makes them particularly advantageous for analyzing and forecasting time-dependent data. Using historical stock price data, the research explores how well LSTM networks can predict future trends, potentially supporting investors and traders in making data-driven decisions. The outcomes demonstrate that the forecast accuracy exceeds 96%.

Keywords: CNN, long short-term memory, predicting stock prices, recurrent neural networks

Introduction

The stock market holds significant importance in the global economy, as investors and traders continuously explore methods to anticipate its movements. While traditional methods rely on fundamental analysis and technical indicators, recent advancements in AI and ML have paved the way for more sophisticated predictive models. One of the primary functions of the stock market is to facilitate capital raising for companies. Organizations seek funding for various purposes, such as research and development, investing in new projects, expanding operations, and issuing shares through Initial Public Offerings (IPOs). Since the banking sector often mirrors the overall state of the economy, studies have shown a positive correlation between the growth of the stock market and banking industry with both current and future economic development. To demonstrate the objectivity of stock prediction, this project is based on banking stock prices, specifically looking at the stock prices of numerous well-known banks, at most twenty banking corporations. LSTM neural networks, recognized for their strength in handling and learning patterns from time-dependent data, offer a promising avenue for stock price prediction. This project aims to explore the application of LSTM networks in this domain, with the ultimate goal of enhancing prediction accuracy and reliability.

This paper includes a detailed process discussion regarding the research analysis and discussion portion of the LSTM architecture, which elaborates on the scope of further generalization overview of our experimental results. The rest of the paper is organized in this manner. A summary of the state of stock price prediction research is given in Section 2. The data analysis and technique employed in this study are explained in Sections 3 and 4. The experimental findings are shown in Section 5. In Section 6, the paper finally ends.

Literature Review

One of the trickiest problems in computation is stock market prediction. Every organization uses data analysis to make data-driven decisions. Numerous factors influence share prices in the stock market, and price fluctuations do not follow a regular pattern. For

[a]writetoraghunath@gmail.com, [b]rahulvy91@gmail.com, [c]triyasabarat@gmail.com, [d]dipankarbarui123@gmail.com, [e]bgayenchemistry@gmail.com

DOI: 10.1201/9781003724995-5

this reason, making a solid judgment about future pricing is difficult. An ANN can make decisions by learning from historical data. Multivariate time series data is a wonderful fit for advanced deep learning architectures and related models. We use historical stock data to train our model, which then predicts the stock's future price. Research in this area covers various approaches, including regression models, support vector machines, and neural networks. Several researchers have explored forecasting stock prices using time series techniques applied to past market data. For a long time, numerous statistical models have been used, including CARIMA, ARIMA, weighted moving average, moving average, auto regression, and more. LSTM networks have become increasingly popular due to their strength in learning long-range patterns in sequential data, which makes them highly effective for forecasting tasks involving time series.

The first category of research focuses on the application of ANN for forecasting stock market trends. These ANNs, inspired by the functioning of biological neural systems, are computational models trained in historical data. For instance, Jasic and Wood [2] developed an ANN model using daily closing data from several major global stock indices, including the S&P 500, DAX, TOPIX, and FTSE, to predict daily market returns [1, 2]. Additionally, Chavan and Patil [3] reviewed a range of studies and identified key input variables across nine research works, further advancing the understanding of ANN-based stock forecasting techniques [3].

The second approach is the use of Support Vector Machines (SVMs) for stock prediction. SVMs provide an alternative to ANNs, offering robust performance in classifying future stock movements. Schumaker and Chen [4] highlighted SVM's ability to classify the direction of stock prices, either upward or downward, in prediction scenarios [4]. Lee [5] created a hybrid prediction model using SVMs coupled with a feature selection mechanism to enhance the forecasting of market trends [5]. Similarly, Das and Padhy [6] applied both SVM and Backpropagation (BP) techniques to predict future price movements in the Indian stock exchange [6].

Time series forecasting methods in this domain commonly fall into two categories: nonlinear models such as ARCH, RNN, GARCH, ANN, LSTM, and linear models such as AR, ARIMA, MA, ARMA,

CARIMA. For instance, Wichaidit and Kittitornkun examined a wide array of macroeconomic variables affecting stock prices, including crude oil rates, foreign exchange rates, gold prices, bank interest rates, and political conditions, by developing a data warehouse and applying the CARIMA model to the SET50 index [7]. Maguluri and Ragupathy (2020) [19] used the ARIMA model to estimate future stock prices, reporting strong predictive accuracy in their results [11]. Moreover, Gers et al. [9] compared the forecasting capabilities of LSTM networks with ARIMA, showing that LSTM significantly outperformed ARIMA on financial datasets

LSTM networks have gained widespread application in economic and financial time-series forecasting. Brownlee's work provides a practical introduction to LSTM-based prediction using Python and Keras [10]. Roondiwala et al. implemented an RNN-LSTM model using four key daily stock features—open, close, high, and low prices—to forecast next-day stock price movements over a 21-day input window for NIFTY-50 companies [8]. Hiransha et al. employed three types of deep learning architectures LSTM, CNN, and RNN to predict stock prices using only the previous day's closing values. Their study considered stocks from two IT firms (TCS and Infosys) and one pharmaceutical company (Cipla) [12].

In another study, Li et al. [13] proposed a hybrid deep learning model incorporating sentiment analysis to enhance stock prediction accuracy. By integrating traditional price forecasting methods with textual sentiment data derived from user-generated online content, they demonstrated that hybrid models could outperform standalone machine learning techniques. Their analysis compared different text classification strategies, time horizons, and information-refreshing mechanisms, concluding that investor sentiment has a measurable impact on stock market predictability in the Chinese financial context [13]. This underscores the potential for improving stock price forecasts by fusing deep learning with conventional analytical tools.

Data Analysis

As part of the experimental analysis, historical data were retrieved from Yahoo Finance, focusing on the 'Close Prices' recorded between January 4, 2010, and February 23, 2024. The dataset includes price information for several prominent banks. We have taken the average of all these 'Close Prices' and formed a new index named 'BNK_INDEX' on which the LSTM task is performed. This dataset consists of 3499 rows and 22 columns, from which we have only picked 'BNK_INDEX' and 'Date'.

This figure illustrates the BNK_INDESX [14–18], which is our primary input of continuous or sequential data for our respective model (Table 5.1). At first, we nullified all the null data in the dataset. After this process, the dataset turned into (3467, 22), where 3467 is the number of rows and 22 is the number of columns. We split the dataset into a 65:35 ratio, where 65% is training data and 35% is testing data. After that, we again split the training data and testing data into two segments, each in train X, train Y, test X, and test Y, using timestamp = 100. This approach restructures the data into a 3D format, converting a sequence of values into a dataset matrix, as the LSTM model requires input in three dimensions to operate effectively.

Figure 5.1 presents the continuous progression of the BNK_INDEX about the timeline, highlighting its year-wise variation.

Table 5.1 Sequential BNK_INDEX data used for model input.

BNK_INDEX
170.750171
172.902042
173.755412
172.946015
172.330258

Source: Author

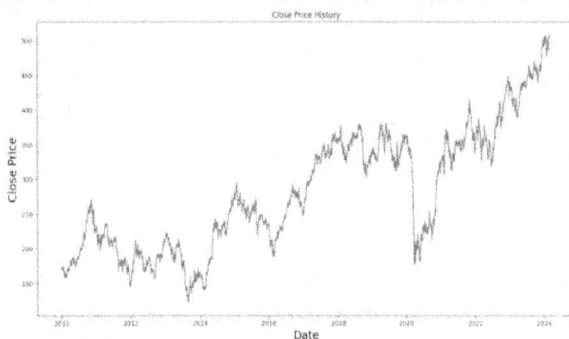

Figure 5.1 Year-wise trend of the BNK_INDEX over time
Source: Author

Methodology

An enhanced kind of RNN architecture called LSTM was created to better identify patterns and relationships in sequential data, especially over longer periods, where conventional RNNs frequently falter. Unlike standard RNNs, LSTMs avoid the use of activation functions within their recurrent pathways, which helps preserve stored values and mitigates the vanishing gradient issue during training. The LSTM structure relies on a memory cell that can retain, update, or discard information as needed. This memory management is governed by components known as gates. These gates, built using sigmoid activation functions and element-wise multiplication, control the flow of data within the memory cell. The three primary gates in an LSTM are:

Forget gate: It is responsible for determining the activations of a cell that need to be forgotten. The input vector M is concatenated with the hidden state vector that has been propagated through step h, and passes through a sigmoid activation function. The sigmoid function outputs value in the range 0 to 1. Value 0 represents the state of completely removing the information and value 1 represents the state of keeping the complete information. The output of the sigmoidal function is multiplied by the cell state. Thus, the sigmoidal function can be used as a filter to keep the relevant information and get rid of all unnecessary information.

Input gate or update gate: The update gate or input gate determines when to update and what to update in response to any new input. The input x is concatenated with h, and passed through a sigmoidal function to generate a vector. The sigmoidal function is called the input gate as its output decides which values need to be updated. A value of zero indicates that the values need not be updated, and a value of 1 indicates that the values should be updated. The concatenated input also passes through a tanh activation function. The tanh function creates another tensor that needs to be added to the state.

$$Y_t = \tanh(W_c * [Z_{t-1}, M_t] + b_c)$$

Output Gate - The Output gate determines what needs to be sent as output. The concatenated input of M, and N, is taken to a sigmoid activation function. The cell state is sent as input for the tanh function. Its value is in the range -1 and +1. Through the outputs of the

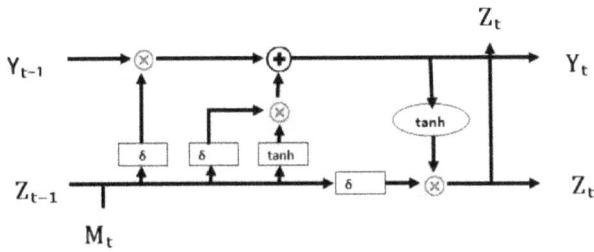

Figure 5.2 LSTM model
Source: Author

Figure 5.4 Parameters of LSTM
Source: Author

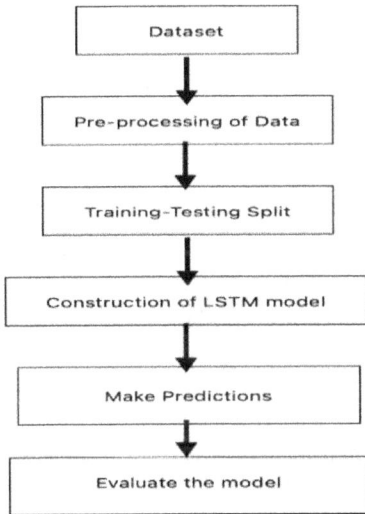

Figure 5.3 Flow map of the research
Source: Author

```
mdl.summary()

Model: "sequential"
_____
 Layer (type)                Output Shape              Param #
=================================================================
 lstm (LSTM)                 (None, 100, 50)           10400

 dropout (Dropout)           (None, 100, 50)           0

 lstm_1 (LSTM)               (None, 100, 50)           20200

 dropout_1 (Dropout)         (None, 100, 50)           0

 lstm_2 (LSTM)               (None, 50)                20200

 dropout_2 (Dropout)         (None, 50)                0

 dense (Dense)               (None, 1)                 51

=================================================================
Total params: 50851 (198.64 KB)
Trainable params: 50851 (198.64 KB)
Non-trainable params: 0 (0.00 Byte)
_____
```

Figure 5.5 Loss graph
Source: Author

sigmoidal function and tanh function, parts of the output that need to be sent are decided (Figure 5.2).

$$Z_t = o_{t\ast}\tanh(Y_t)$$

System architecture

Data selection: The initial stage involves choosing the relevant dataset for forecasting and dividing it into training and testing subsets. In this study, 65% of the dataset is designated for training, with the remaining 35% set aside for testing purposes, as illustrated in Figure 5.3.

Pre-processing of data: Here, we have selected a new index, which is the mean of all the 'Close' price data collected from individual datasets, which will be discussed further. This new index will be our attribute for normalization to perform LSTM. LSTM model generates forecasts of stock prices. The next ten days' values are based on the training and testing results.

Evaluation metrics: To evaluate the model's performance, key metrics like MSE, RMSE, and MAPE are calculated and compared.

Results and Discussions

A sequential model has been used. In this model (Figure 5.4), there are three layers - the input layer or the first layer, which consists of two layers of one LSTM layer and one dropout layer, the next layer, which is the hidden layer, two LSTM layers supporting with two consecutive dropout layers has been included and as the output layer one dense layer has been included.

In this model, the loss function (Figure 5.5) which is used is 'MSE' and the optimizer is 'adam'. The total parameter count is 50,851 where every parameter is trainable.

This is the plot (Figure 5.6) of the variation of the real dataset from the predicted dataset. After calculating the plot of variation of the real dataset from the predicted, we calculated the next ten days'

Text(0, 0.5, 'Loss')

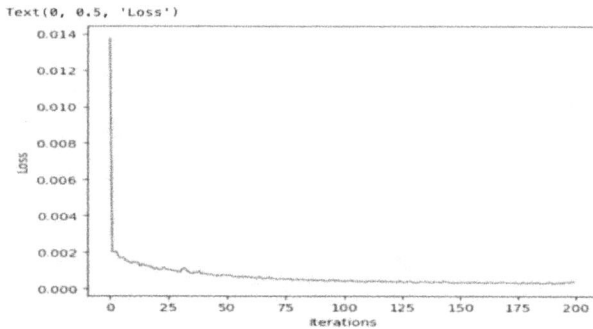

Figure 5.6 Comparison between actual and predicted BNK_INDEX values
Source: Author

Figure 5.7 Model evaluation metrics: MSE, RMSE, and MAPE for LSTM performance
Source: Author

values (Figure 5.6) which are very near actual value. Our LSTM stock price prediction model's final plot shows us a detailed depiction of past stock price data as well as the model's projection for the next 10 days. Plotting historical trends alongside predicted future moves is done with ease, giving analysts a comprehensive picture of the stock's expected course.

Performance Evaluation

Figure 5.7 displays the performance metrics used to evaluate the model, namely mean squared error (MSE), root mean squared error (RMSE), and mean absolute percentage error (MAPE).

$$MSE = \frac{1}{n} \sum_{i=1}^{n} (Y_i - \hat{Y}_i)^2$$

Where n is the total number of observations, Y_i represents the actual values, and $\hat{Y}_i$ denotes the predicted values.

RMSE = sqrt [MSE / n]

Table 5.2 LSTM model performance on training and testing data.

Training error		Testing error
MSE	12.96	75.98
RMSE	3.83	6.66
MAPE	-	24.95
Estimated Accuracy	Above 96%	Above 96%

Source: Author

$$M = \frac{1}{n} \sum_{t=1}^{n} \left| \frac{A_t - F_t}{A_t} \right|$$

Here, n represents the number of observations, A_t is the actual value, and F_t is the forecasted value at time t.

Conclusion

Our model utilizes 14 years of continuous closing stock price data from various banking institutions. It comprises both long short-term memory (LSTM) and stacked LSTM architectures. The stacked LSTM architecture implemented in this stock price prediction project has demonstrated its effectiveness in capturing intricate patterns within financial time series data. By stacking multiple LSTM layers, we have enhanced the model's ability to learn hierarchical representations of the data, enabling it to capture both short-term variations as well as long-term dependencies more effectively. The stacked LSTM portion is used specifically to announce the next ten days result. To sum up, this LSTM stock price prediction study has shown how deep learning methods may be used to forecast financial markets. We may reasonably predict future price movements because we have been able to identify complicated patterns and dependencies within past stock data by using LSTM networks. Our model has performed admirably, predicting stock values over a range of time horizons with considerable accuracy. But it's important to recognize that financial markets are inherently unpredictable and volatile, which can make any prediction model difficult to use. Even though our LSTM model has done a good job on this assignment, it can always be improved.

References

[1]   Huck, N. (2009). Pairs selection and outranking: an application to the S&P 100 index. *European Journal of Operational Research*, 196(2), 819–825.

[2] Jasic, T., & Wood, D. (2004). The profitability of daily stock market indices tradesbased on neural network predictions: case study for the S&P 500, the DAX, theTOPIX and the FTSE in the period 1965–1999. *Applied Financial Economics*, 14(4), 285–297.

[3] Chavan, P. S., & Patil, S. T. (2013). Parameters for stock market prediction. *International Journal of Computer Technology and Applications*, 4(2), 337.

[4] Schumaker, R. P., & Chen, H. (2010). A discrete stock price prediction enginebased on financial news. *Computer*, 43(1), 51–56.

[5] Lee, M. C. (2009). Using support vector machine with a hybrid feature selection method to the stock trend prediction. *Expert Systems with Applications*, 36(8), 10896–10904.

[6] PrasadDas, Shom & Padhy, Sudarsan. (2012). Support Vector Machines for Prediction of Futures Prices in Indian Stock Market. *International Journal of Computer Applications*. 41. 22–26. 10.5120/5522-7555.

[7] Mondal, D., Maji, G., Goto, T., Debnath, N. C., & Sen, S. (2018). A data warehouse based modelling technique for stock market analysis. *International Journal of Engineering & Technology*, 3(13), 165–170.

[8] Roondiwala, M., Patel, H., & Varma, S. (2017). Predicting stock prices using LSTM. *International Journal of Science and Research (IJSR)*, 6(4), 1754–1756.

[9] Gers, F. A., Schmidhuber, J., & Cummins, F. (2000). Learning to forget: continual prediction with LSTM. *Neural Computation*, 12(10), 2451–2471.

[10] Brownlee, J. (2017) Long Short-Term Memory Networks with Python Develop Sequence Prediction Models with Deep Learning. Machine Learning Mastery, EBook.

[11] Wichaidit, S., & Kittitornkun, S. (2015). Predicting SET50 stock prices using CARIMA (crosscorrelation ARIMA). In 2015 International Computer Science and Engineering Conference (ICSEC), (pp. 1–4), IEEE.

[12] Hiransha, M., Gopalakrishnan, E. A., Menon, V. K., & Soman, K. (2018). Nse stock market prediction using deep-learning models. *Procedia Computer Science*, 132, 1351–1362. doi:10. 1016/j.procs.2018.05.050.

[13] Li, Y., Bu, H., Li, J., & Wu, J. (2020). The role of text-extracted investor sentiment in Chinese stock price prediction with the enhancement of deep learning. *International Journal of Forecasting*, 36(4), 1541–1562.

[14] https://finance .yahoo.com/quote/SBIN.NS/history/.

[15] https://finance.yahoo.com/quote/HDFCBANK.NS/history/.

[16] https://finance.yahoo.com/quote/BANKBARODA.BO/history/.

[17] https://finance.yahoo.com/quote/BANKINDIA.NS/history/.

[18] https://finance.yahoo.com/quote/KOTAKBANK.NS/history/.

[19] Maguluri, Lakshmana & Ragupathy, R.. (2020). Comparative Analysis of Companies Stock Price Prediction Using Time Series Algorithm. International Journal of Engineering Trends and Technology. 68. 9–15. 10.14445/22315381/IJETT-V68I11P202.

6 Smart applications and challenges of Internet of Things: a review

Debrupa Pal[1,a], Nirmalya Chowdhury[2,b] and Sreya Dey[2,c]

[1]Assistant Professor, CA Department, Narula Institute of Technology, Kolkata, WB, India

[2]Student, CA Department, Narula Institute of Technology, Kolkata, WB, India

Abstract

Technological and scientific advancement has generated a new standard. Everyday the latest innovation takes the world towards higher growth. Internet of Things (IoT) is a moderately "versatile worldwide neural network" interconnecting several things in clouds. Considerable advances in IoT have made life more knowledgeable. The IoT is smartly connected equipment that consists of intelligent machines interconnecting with various machines, things, frameworks, sensor networks and radio frequency identification (RFID). This technique allows the end-user to obtain the information from a remote location. The operational feature of IoT is to unify each object of the universe under a generic framework; in a way that humans have the capability to manage as well as to furnish consistent and relevant updates. IoT principles were suggested a few years ago and this terminology is the basis for developing communication between objects. Based on the current circumstances of IoT, extensive review of all the key issues of IoT like underlying technology, application in several areas, associated constraints, etc. This study investigates several contributions made by research workers in several application domains. Investigations were conducted on these papers and several parameters are classified in every area of application. In addition, existent challenges in these areas are emphasized to encourage investigators in this field to evaluate the current state of IoT and to enhance it through innovatory ideas.

Keywords: Applications of IoT, IoTInternet of Things, IoT concerns, IoT framework

Introduction

Over the last couple of years, the concept of the internet has expanded its reach in all areas of life. Determining the best potential for using the internet has become a difficult task. Over time, the terminology of the Internet has been related to things and therefore has not been recognized as the Internet of Things (IoT). As the term suggests, IoT connects devices and systems via the internet using a variety of advanced communication technologies, including wireless sensor networks (WSN), radio-frequency identification (RFID), near-field communication (NFC), long-term evolution (LTE), and other intelligent networking solutions. Therefore, the Internet of Things can be defined as "things connected through the Internet." The connection helps to transmit information collected from various devices to required places on the Internet. Considering that IoT is a dependable term in today's world, it still didn't have the potential compliance it is competent of. In this kind of complicated situations, this paper aspires to help all people who want to understand the concept in a simple manner and desire to devote themselves to its channelization to serve in the best optimal manner. IoT utilizes smart devices and the internet for providing novel solutions to several difficulties and problems linked to several occupations, government, and public/private industries around the globe [7]. Overall, IoT is a transformation that integrates a wide range of smart systems, frameworks, smart devices, and sensors as shown in Figure 6.1.

Moreover, it incorporates quantum computing and nanotechnology to enhance storage, sensing, and processing speeds, achieving capabilities that were previously unimaginable. A comprehensive analysis has been conducted, utilizing scientific papers, online news reports, and published materials to highlight the potential capabilities and relevance of transformations within the IoT landscape. It can be used as a preparatory measure before formulating a creative and innovative business plan taking into consideration safety, reliability, and compatibility. With the continuous intervention of IoT devices and technologies, our daily lives will undergo tremendous

[a]debrupa.pal@nit.ac.in, [b]nirmalyachowdhury78@gmail.com, [c]sreyadey704@gmail.com

DOI: 10.1201/9781003724995-6

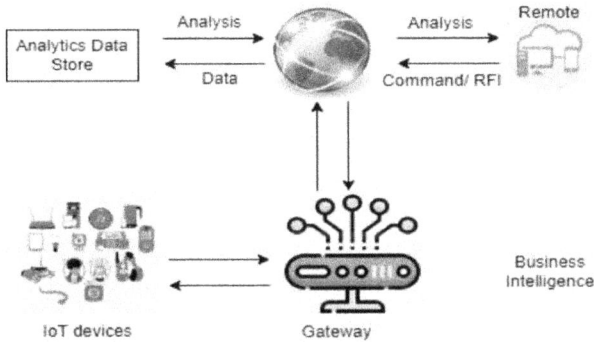

Figure 6.1 General architecture of IoT
Source: Author

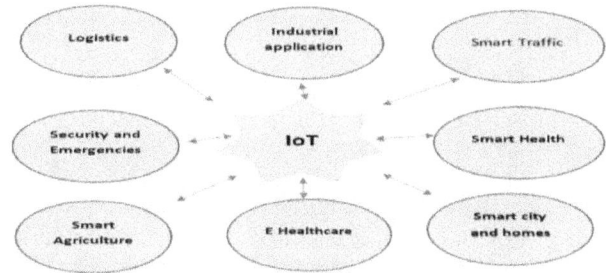

Figure 6.2 Application domains of IoT
Source: Author

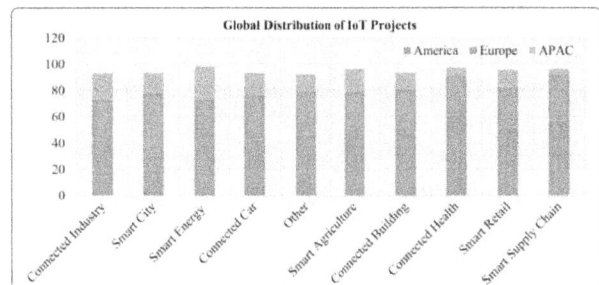

Figure 6.3 Geographic spread of IoT deployments across the Americas and Europe
Source: Author

changes. A key advancement in IoT is the emergence of Smart Home Systems (SHS), which encompass internet-connected devices, home automation solutions, and efficient power management systems [12]. In addition, the Smart Health Sensing System (SHSS) is another main accomplishment of the Internet of Things. In addition, SHSS is another main accomplishment of IoT. SHS incorporates compact, intelligent devices designed to monitor and enhance human health and wellness through automated, data-driven solutions. Such devices are utilized to keep track of various health conditions and physical fitness levels or the number of calories lost in the health club. Further, it is applied to observe the serious health issues in the hospitals and health-care centers too [16]. So, it has modified the whole framework of the medical field by assisting with advanced technology and smart equipment [9]. (Behrendt et al., 2019)

The paper is structured into distinct sections to provide a comprehensive overview of IoT. The "literature survey" segment highlights recent advancements and research addressing key challenges in IoT. The "IoT System design" section delves into the fundamental building blocks and operational frameworks of IoT systems. Following this, the " IoT challenges: key barriers, emerging issues" segment explores critical obstacles such as security, interoperability, and scalability. The "major IoT applications" section showcases practical implementations across various domains. Finally, the "conclusion" summarizes the findings and insights, offering a holistic perspective on the current state and future potential of IoT.

Literature Review

IoT has a multisectoral perception for aiding multiple fields like ecological, commercial, medicinal, conveyance, etc. Various researchers have approached IoT in different ways, focusing on benefits and characteristics. The capabilities of IoT can be observed across a range of application areas. Figure 6.2 describes several application areas of IoT.

Figure 6.3 illustrates the global distribution of IoT initiatives across the United States, Europe, and the Asia-Pacific region. The analysis reveals that North American efforts are predominantly focused on advancing healthcare technologies and intelligent supply chain management systems, while European contributions emphasize the development of integrated digital urban infrastructure frameworks [5].

Figure 6.4 describes the universal business segment of IoT projects across the world [5]. It is evident that IoT applications in industrial automation, smart cities, energy management, and connected automotive technologies currently hold a dominant market presence compared to other sectors.

Li and Da Xu [6] conducted an analysis on the contribution of IoT in smart energy control in assisting applications of smart city. They observed that IoT's current implementation remains restricted to a small number of domains focused on enhancing technology

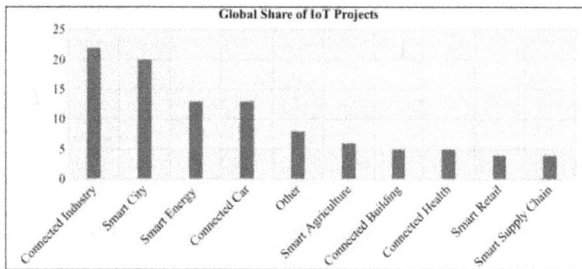

Figure 6.4 Global distribution of IoT initiatives across worldwide markets
Source: Author

and human well-being. The scope of IoT is vast, with expectations that it will soon dominate a wide array of application domains. Scholars emphasize that energy sustainability stands as a critical societal priority, and IoT is poised to drive advancements in intelligent energy management systems that balance efficiency and affordability. Researchers have outlined an IoT framework aligned with smart city initiatives, though they caution that current limitations in hardware and software reliability present major barriers to progress. Addressing these challenges, they argue, is essential to realizing resilient, high-performance IoT ecosystems tailored to user needs. In parallel, Shankar and Maple [13] explore urbanization trends spurred by rural-to-urban migration, which have intensified demands for smarter infrastructure in transportation, energy distribution, healthcare, and urban planning. Their analysis underscores the urgency of integrating IoT-driven innovations to meet the evolving needs of growing urban populations. Smart cities represent a critical frontier for IoT innovation, integrating solutions such as optimized transportation systems, real-time air quality monitoring, public safety enhancements, automated parking coordination, adaptive lighting networks, and data-driven waste disposal efficiency. Reliability and secrecy is another important point of IoT. Virat et al. [17] aimed on these factors and recommended that private enterprises utilizing IoT must combine data verification, security, and the ability to resist attacks incorporating customer privacy into their business operations that will be an added benefit. Singh et al. [14] proposed that for the purpose of defining public safety and confidentiality concerns, IoT innovators must consider the geographical restrictions of several countries. Yalli et al. [19] puts forward the security concern in IP-dependent IoT systems. Experts emphasize that internet connectivity forms the backbone of device-to-device communication in IoT ecosystems, making security vulnerabilities in IP-reliant systems a critical priority.

One of the key aspects of IoT is its application in environmental and agricultural standards. In their research, Erma wati and Edi [1] highlighted this area and presented the fundamental applications of IoT in agriculture, industry, and the environment Mahmmod et al. [8] considered the significance of patient's health tracking dependent on the IoT. They proposed that IoT devices and sensors, linked via the Internet, could be utilized for patient health monitoring. Additionally, they outlined a methodology and protocol to achieve their objective. Table 6.1 summarizes the key learnings and research objectives with an analysis of studies on specific evaluation parameters.

IoT System Design

The IoT framework consists of five key layers that define the functions of the system. These layers are perception, transport, processing, application, and business. The perception layer, which serves as the foundation of the IoT architecture, includes devices such as sensors, RFID tags, barcodes, and other objects connected to the IoT network [18]. These devices gather data, which is then sent to the transport layer for transmission. The business layer processes and stores the information collected from the application layer, using this data to guide the development of future goals and strategies. Additionally, IoT architecture can be tailored to meet specific needs and application domains [3, 4]. Along with its layered design, the IoT system incorporates various operational blocks that facilitate functions like sensing, authentication, identification, control, and governance [10]. Figure 6.5 demonstrates these operational blocks of the IoT architecture.

All these operational units integrate in an efficient IoT system that is essential for optimal efficiency. While there are various reference frameworks suggested according to technical guidelines, however, these are still far from an accepted framework that is appropriate for universal IoT [10].

IoT Challenges: Key Barriers, Emerging Issues

IoT systems are deeply interconnected with multiple facets of daily human life, relying on heterogeneous

Table 6.1 Relative description of distinct investigation on assessment criteria.

Investigation	Key learning directions	Analysis dependent on evaluation parameter				
		L	Au	Ac	C	EU
Machin et al. [7]	Safety and confidentiality	—	X	—	—	—
Vermesan et al. [16]	Framework, safety and confidentiality	X	—	—	—	X
Mohanty et al. [9]	Innovations in urban mobility	—	X	—	X	X
Behrendt et al., 2019	Advances in urban mobility	X	—	X	—	—
Kumar et al. [5]	Climate, power and energy	X	X	—	X	X
Shankar and Maple [13]	Safety and confidentiality	X	—	X	—	X
Virat et al. [17]	Safety and confidentiality	—	X	—	—	X
Singh et al. [14]	Identification and verification	X	—	—	X	X
Yalli et al. [19]	Safety and confidentiality	—	X	—	X	—
Ermawati and Edi [1]	Safety and confidentiality, administration and supervision	—	X	—	X	—
Mahmmod et al. [8]	Safety and Confidentiality, Framework	X	X	—	—	—
Mu and Antwi-Afari [10]	Smart urban mobility and health, framework	X	—	X	—	X
Hazra et al. [3]	Identification and verification, QoS	X	—	—	—	X
Fantin Irudaya Raj and Appadurai [2]	Normalization	X	—	X	—	—
Houssein et al. [4]	Normalization, identification and verification	X	X	—	—	X
Verdejon et al. [15]	Safety and confidentiality	X	—	X	—	—
Younan et al., 2024	Interoperation	X	—	—	X	—
Phasinam et al. [11]	Interoperation, authenticity, expandability	X	—	X	—	X

L Latency Au Authenticity Ac Accessibility C Cost EU Energy Usage

technologies for seamless data exchange between embedded devices. This integration introduces inherent complexity, fostering operational challenges such as interoperability gaps and security vulnerabilities. For IoT architects and developers, addressing these issues becomes critical in designing resilient frameworks for increasingly connected, technology-driven ecosystems. With the development of technology, the challenges and demands of progressive IoT systems are also increasing. Thus, IoT developers require them to consider new challenges and should furnish solutions to those challenges.

IoT faces significant challenges in safety, confidentiality, and privacy due to threats, attacks, and weak encryption protocols, necessitating secure layers and authentication mechanisms. Interoperability issues arise from diverse technologies, requiring solutions like virtual networks and service-based architectures to enable seamless communication. Ethical, legal, and regulatory concerns demand adherence to standards and laws to prevent misuse and maintain quality. Scalability, availability, and reliability are critical, with cloud-based IoT systems offering expandable networks and reliable resource accessibility. Quality of Service (QoS) metrics like authenticity, power consumption, and safety are essential for evaluating IoT performance and meeting user requirements. Research focuses on addressing these challenges through standardized models like ISO/IEC25010 and OASIS-WSQM for QoS evaluation. Despite advancements, interoperability, scalability, and ethical concerns remain areas for future exploration. These combined efforts aim to build a secure, efficient, and globally compatible IoT ecosystem.

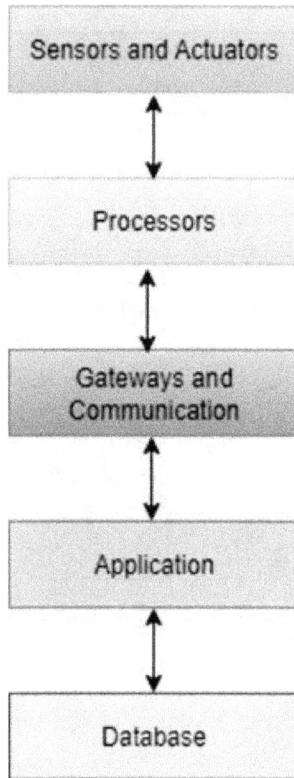

Figure 6.5 Operational blocks of the IoT architecture
Source: Author

Major IoT Deployments

Emerging economy, ecological and health services

IoT supports public and economic growth through financial, water, welfare, and industrial services, aligning with UN goals. Developers focus on ecological sustainability to reduce environmental impacts and energy consumption in IoT systems. Research promotes energy-efficient, sustainable technologies for eco-friendly and health-focused IoT devices. Engineers are creating advanced IoT gadgets to monitor health issues like diabetes and obesity. Environmental, energy, and healthcare concerns are central to ongoing IoT research and development. Various concerns associated with the environment, power, and medical services are taken into consideration by various research.

Advancing sustainable IoT solutions for public welfare, health, and ecological growth

IoT drives public and economic growth through financial, water, welfare, and industrial advancements, aligning with UN goals. Developers focus on ecological sustainability and energy-efficient technologies to reduce environmental impact. Research promotes power-efficient IoT devices for health monitoring, addressing issues like diabetes and obesity [15]. Sustainable IoT solutions benefit both the environment and public health.

Smart urban mobility and vehicles

IoT transforms IoT is transforming traditional civil engineering into smart cities, automated homes, and intelligent transportation systems. Supported by technologies like NLP and machine learning, it enhances home automation and urban efficiency. Cloud servers and wireless sensor networks enable systematic smart city development. Smart vehicles with IoT integration detect traffic jams and suggest optimal routes for smoother travel [2].

Agriculture and industrial automation

IoT integrates with agriculture, industry, and urban systems to enhance productivity, efficiency, and decision-making through automation, real-time data analysis, and energy conservation. Combined with big data and deep learning, IoT drives technological advancement for a smarter, sustainable society [11].

Conclusion

The latest development in the Internet of Things (IoT) has caught the attention of research workers and developers around the world. They are working jointly for the expansion of technology on a grand scale and to serve society to the highest attainable level. Though enhancements are feasible only when various issues and shortcomings are taken into consideration in the existing technical solutions. In this review, various difficulties and challenges are discussed that IoT developers must consider when developing an enhanced model. In addition, important areas of application of IoT are also addressed. The IoT not only provides services but also generates vast amounts of data. As a result, the importance of big data analysis is highlighted, as it enables accurate decision-making that can drive the improvement of IoT systems.

References

[1]   Ermawati, T., & Edi, R. Y. (2024). Agro-industrial sustainability through business model: a systematic

literature review. In IOP Conference Series: Earth and Environmental Science, (Vol. 1358, No. 1, p. 012031). IOP Publishing.

[2] Fantin Irudaya Raj, E., & Appadurai, M. (2022). Internet of things-based smart transportation system for smart cities. In Intelligent Systems for Social Good: Theory and Practice, (pp. 39–50). Singapore: Springer Nature Singapore.

[3] Hazra, A., Adhikari, M., Amgoth, T., & Srirama, S. N. (2021). A comprehensive survey on interoperability for IIoT: taxonomy, standards, and future directions. *ACM Computing Surveys (CSUR)*, 55(1), 1–35.

[4] Houssein, E. H., Othman, M. A., Mohamed, W. M., & Younan, M. (2024). Internet of Things in Smart Cities: Comprehensive Review, Open Issues, and Challenges, in *IEEE Internet of Things Journal*, vol. 11, no. 21, pp. 34941–34952, doi: 10.1109/JIOT.2024.3449753.

[5] Kumar, S., Tiwari, P., & Zymbler, M. (2019). Internet of things is a revolutionary approach for future technology enhancement: a review. *Journal of Big Data*, 6(1), 1–21.

[6] Li, X., & Da Xu, L. (2020). A review of internet of things—resource allocation. *IEEE Internet of Things Journal*, 8(11), 8657–8666.

[7] Machin, J., Batista, E., Martinez-Balleste, A., & Solanas, A. (2021). Privacy and security in cognitive cities: a systematic review. *Applied Sciences*, 11(10), 4471.

[8] Mahmmod, B. M. et al., (2024). Patient Monitoring System Based on Internet of Things: A Review and Related Challenges With Open Research Issues, in *IEEE Access*, vol. 12, pp. 132444–132479, doi: 10.1109/ACCESS.2024.3455900.

[9] Behrendt, F. (2019). Cycling the smart and sustainable city: analyzing EC policy documents on internet of things, mobility and transport, and smart cities. Sustainability, 11(3), 763.

[10] Mu, X., & Antwi-Afari, M. F. (2024). The applications of internet of things (IoT) in industrial management: a science mapping review. *International Journal of Production Research*, 62(5), 1928–1952.

[11] Phasinam, K., Kassanuk, T., Shinde, P. P., Thakar, C. M., Sharma, D. K., Mohiddin, M. K., et al. (2022). Application of IoT and cloud computing in automation of agriculture irrigation. *Journal of Food Quality*, 2022(1), 8285969.

[12] Rao, P. M., & Deebak, B. D. (2023). Security and privacy issues in smart cities/industries: technologies, applications, and challenges. *Journal of Ambient Intelligence and Humanized Computing*, 14(8), 10517–10553.

[13] Shankar, A., & Maple, C. (2023). Securing the internet of things-enabled smart city infrastructure using a hybrid framework. *Computer Communications*, 205, 127–135.

[14] Singh, S., Madaan, G., Swapna, H. R., Singh, A., Pandey, D., George, A. S., et al. (2025). Empowering connectivity: exploring the internet of things. In Interdisciplinary Approaches to AI, Internet of Everything, and Machine Learning, (pp. 89–116). IGI Global Scientific Publishing.

[15] Verdejo Espinosa, Á., Lopez, J. L., Mata Mata, F., & Estevez, M. E. (2021). Application of IoT in healthcare: keys to implementation of the sustainable development goals. *Sensors*, 21(7), 2330.

[16] Vermesan, O., Friess, P., Guillemin, P., Gusmeroli, S., Sundmaeker, H., Bassi, A., et al. (2022). Internet of things strategic research roadmap. In Internet of Things-Global Technological and Societal Trends from Smart Environments and Spaces to Green ICT, (pp. 9–52). River Publishers.

[17] Virat, M. S., Bindu, S. M., Aishwarya, B., Dhanush, B. N., & Kounte, M. R. (2018). Security and privacy challenges in internet of things. In 2018 2nd International Conference on Trends in Electronics and Informatics (ICOEI), (pp. 454–460). IEEE.

[18] Xu, L., Wang, J., Li, X., Cai, F., Tao, Y., & Gulliver, T. A. (2021). Performance analysis and prediction for mobile internet-of-things (IoT) networks: a CNN approach. *IEEE Internet of Things Journal*, 8(17), 13355–13366.

[19] Yalli, J. S. et al., (2025). A Systematic Review for Evaluating IoT Security: A Focus on Authentication, Protocols and Enabling Technologies, in *IEEE Internet of Things Journal*, vol. 12, no. 12, pp. 18908–18928, doi: 10.1109/JIOT.2025.3545737.

7 Fabrication of rain sensing RPM limiter for city and highway speed control

Tirthadeep Ghosh[1,a], Rajat Naskar[1,b], Anushka Pal[1,c], Shankha Ghosh[2,d], Kalyan Mukherjee[2,e] and Pritam Bhattacharjee[2,f]

[1]UG Student, Dr. Sudhir Chandra Sur Institute of Technology and Sports Complex, Kolkata, WB, India

[2]Assistant Professor, Dr. Sudhir Chandra Sur Institute of Technology and Sports Complex, Kolkata, WB, India

Abstract

This study introduces a prototype designed to regulate and limit vehicle speed in rainy and slippery conditions, addressing the growing concern of road accidents caused by negligence and over speeding during adverse weather. The system is built with a Rain Sensing Module, an Arduino Uno Microcontroller, a Motor Driver Module, a 3-pin Slide Switch, and a 12V Dual-Shaft DC Geared Motor for precise demonstration. A 3-pin slide switch allows the drivers to toggle between Highway Mode and City Mode, offering calibrations for variable driving scenarios in wet conditions. The rain sensor categorizes rain intensity into four levels: heavy rain, moderate rain, light rain, and negligible/no rain. Using pulse width modulation (PWM), the study controls the speed of the motor with respect to the rain intensity, and controls the voltage supplied to the motor from the battery. The prototype has been thoroughly tested under various thresholds, and its results have successfully aligned with the desired instructions which were programmed. Water droplets have been sprayed on the surface of the rain sensor periodically to observe concurrent changes in the motor speed.

Keywords: Rain intensity, rain sensing module, road safety, vehicle speed

Introduction

The rain sensing RPM limiter addresses an important and critical issue to control motor speed in wet conditions, ensuring both safety and efficiency. A rain sensor has been integrated with a microcontroller, which controls motor speed in adverse climate, which makes it a valuable area of study. This literature review studies existing research and studies in sensor-based motor control. Potential improvements and opportunities have been highlighted in the literature review.

A 2011 study predicted a 40% increase in fatalities from injuries worldwide between 2002 and 2030, with traffic accidents being a major contributor. Road accidents have become a serious public health issue, and if left unchecked, they could slow down socio-economic progress globally. The World Health Organization (WHO) has raised concerns about the rising number of road injuries, warning that without proper preventive measures, they could become the third leading cause of death worldwide by 2020. Studies show that strokes and disabilities caused by road accidents account for about 9.5% of the 1.2 million traffic accidents reported globally each year. India has one of the highest traffic-related fatality rates, surpassing China, with over 1 million deaths, compared to China's 89,455 fatalities in 2006. In India, a road accident claims a life every 4.61 minutes, emphasizing the urgency of this issue. Between 2006 and 2007, road accidents in India rose by 6.1%, highlighting the critical need for effective safety measures [1].

Road accidents are caused by a combination of factors, including road conditions, vehicle performance, environmental influences, and human behavior. One of the most common causes is vehicle skidding, which happens when there isn't enough friction between the tires and the road surface. This is a major contributor to traffic accidents worldwide, especially in rainy conditions. Rain is a well-known driving hazard that reduces both traction and visibility, significantly increasing the risk of accidents. Research has shown a strong connection between rainfall and accident rates, with studies indicating

[a]tirthadeepghosh6@gmail.com, [b]rajatnaskar88737@gmail.com, [c]palanushka172@gmail.com, [d]shankha.ghosh@dsec.ac.in, [e]kalyan.mukherjee@dsec.ac.in, [f]pritam.bhattacharjee@dsec.ac.in

DOI: 10.1201/9781003724995-7

that crashes on wet roads occur at twice the rate of those on dry roads. In California, data revealed that the number of accidents doubled on days with heavy rainfall compared to dry conditions, further proving the critical role weather plays in road safety [2].

In 2011, studies revealed that over 90% of traffic fatalities occurred in low- and middle-income countries, even though these nations accounted for only 48% of the world's registered vehicles. The global death toll from road accidents was expected to rise from 0.99 million in 1990 to 2.34 million by 2020, making up 3.4% of total global deaths. India played a significant role in these statistics, contributing 9.5% of the estimated 1.2 million fatalities. In 2007 alone, the country reported 114,000 traffic deaths, a number significantly higher than China's 89,455 fatalities in 2006. On average, one person dies in a road accident every 4.61 minutes in India, and between 2006 and 2007, road fatalities in the country increased by 6.1%, highlighting the urgent need for improved road safety measures [3].

An analysis of traffic accident data from 2021 revealed that nearly a quarter of all road accidents and fatalities occurred under unfavorable weather conditions. Specifically, accidents during rain, fog, and heavy downpours accounted for 16.8% of total traffic accidents in 2021 and 16.6% in 2022. Vehicle skidding due to inadequate road traction during wet weather remains a primary cause of accidents globally, emphasizing the need for enhanced road safety measures and preventive technologies [4, 5].

Road traffic accidents rank among the leading global causes of morbidity and mortality. Their underlying causes can be broadly categorized into human and environmental factors, with human factors contributing to approximately 90% of incidents. A study aimed at identifying the primary causes of accidents revealed that human error accounted for 77% of cases. In this category, drivers were responsible for 56.2% of accidents, while pedestrians and vehicle passengers accounted for 17.8% and 3.0%, respectively. Environmental and mechanical factors also contributed, with vehicle defects and bad weather each causing 8.4% of accidents, and poor road conditions responsible for 4%. A critical safety concern was that none of the drivers or passengers involved were wearing helmets or seatbelts, highlighting a major lapse in safety practices. The leading human-related causes of accidents included over-speeding, reckless driving, ignoring traffic rules,

and carelessness while crossing or playing on roads. Impairments such as alcohol consumption, fatigue, and drowsiness further increased the risk. This data emphasizes the urgent need to improve road safety awareness and enforcement of traffic regulations to prevent accidents and save lives [6].

A study introduces an automated rain-sensing wiper system that detects rainfall and activates the wipers autonomously, stopping them when the rain ceases. This system goes beyond simple automation—it is intelligent, adjusting the wiper speed based on rainfall intensity. The rain sensor detects the presence of rain and measures its intensity, sending signals to regulate the wiper speed. Heavier rain triggers faster wiper movement, eliminating the need for manual adjustments. Additionally, an LCD module displays the rainfall intensity in categories such as NIL, low, medium, and high, with "NIL" appearing when no rain is detected. The rain sensor transmits data on rainfall intensity to the LCD and a servo motor, which adjusts its rotation speed to align with the detected rain levels. This automated adjustment enhances usability and convenience, providing a seamless, hands-free experience for drivers while ensuring optimal visibility during varying rain conditions [7].

According to an article published by Government of Assam, Commissionerate of Transport and also according to Ministry of Road Transport and Highways of India, we know that maximum speed limit for non-transport(private) vehicles with seating capacity under 8 people is 100 kmph for highways, whereas it is 60 kmph in roads under municipal limits [8, 9].

Pulse width modulation (PWM) is a technique that allows the generation of analog-like outputs using digital methods. It works by producing a square wave signal, where the on and off durations are controlled digitally. By varying the ratio of the "on" time to the "off" time, PWM can emulate a range of voltages between 0 and the maximum available voltage. The "on time" duration, referred to as the pulse width, can be adjusted to represent different analog values. When applied at high frequencies, PWM can be used to control the brightness of devices like LEDs [10,11].

Considering the above factors, a conclusion can be made that adverse weather like rainfall and driver negligence together are a major source of accidents and death in India. The variation in speed limits in highways and cities from above source has also been taken into account. A rain sensing RPM Limiter has been designed to limit the speed of drivers based on the intensity of rain and the location they are driving in. Speed reduction calibrations are different for highway and city conditions.

Materials and methodology

Circuit design

Figure 7.1 below depicts the circuit connecting a 9V battery's positive and negative terminals to the motor driver's 12V and GND pins. The motor driver shares a common GND with the Arduino via one of its GND pins. A 12V dual-shaft DC motor is connected to the motor driver's OUT1 and OUT2 pins. The motor driver's ENA, IN1, and IN2 pins are connected to Arduino pins 6, 5, and 4, respectively. Pin 6 on the Arduino is being used for PWM interface with the motor. The Arduino is powered via a USB cable connected to a laptop, allowing data to be monitored through the serial interface. The Arduino is linked to an LM393 module, which interfaces with a rain sensor. The LM393's AO pin connects to the Arduino's A1 pin, while it draws power from the Arduino's 5V and GND pins. A 3-pin slide switch connects to the Arduino via digital pin 12 and GND. Toggling this switch changes modes: "HIGH" for City Mode and "LOW" for Highway Mode.

Methodology

The rain sensing RPM limiter consists primarily of a rain sensor which is connected to the analog pin of the Arduino and the 5V and GND pin of the Arduino for power supply. The rain sensor has the capability to produce a digital as well as an analog signal. The digital signal produces a numeric value of 1 or 0 for presence of water or no water respectively. The

analog signal on the other hand ranges from 1023 to 0, 1023 being the lowest and 0 being the highest intensity of rain. In this setup, the analog pin feature was put to use to figure out the intensity of rain.

A motor driver was also connected to the Arduino to demonstrate the speed control. The motor driver was powered by a 9V DC power source. A 12V dual shaft gear motor was connected to the motor driver's pins. The motor driver was connected to a PWM pin the Arduino. The PWM pin has the ability to produce delayed on and off signals to manipulate the average voltage supplied to the motor. The analogWrite function of the Arduino is used. The Analog Output signal of the Arduino ranges from 0 to 255, 0 being the lowest, 255 being the highest. A 3-pin slide switch was connected to the Arduino, when the switch is slid left, it will return a LOW signal back to the Arduino, which will turn on Highway Mode. On the other hand, if it slides right, it will return to a high signal, which will activate City Mode.

City mode: When the switch is slid at right position, the City Mode will be activated. Hence, for "Negligible Rain/No Rain" output from the rain sensor, analogWrite was set to 255 which meant 100% available power was supplied to the motor. In case of "Light Rain", analogWrite was set to 191 which meant 75% of the total available power was supplied to the motor. In case of "Moderate Rain", analogWrite was set to 127, indicating only 50% power was available to the motor. And finally in case of "Heavy Rain" the power was limited to 25% by setting analogWrite to 64. PWM demonstration for City Mode has been demonstrated in Figure 7.2.

Highway Mode: When the slide switch is slid to the left, it will turn on the Highway Mode. Considering that, the PWM calibration has been altered for this

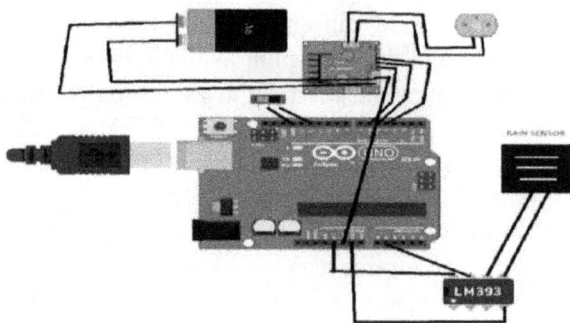

Figure 7.1 Circuit diagram
Source: Author

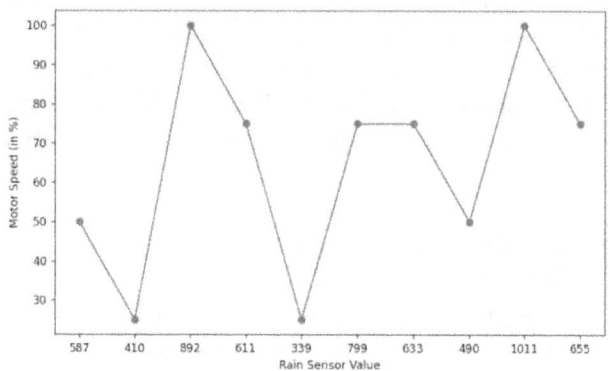

Figure 7.2 City Mode
Source: Author

Table 7.1 Rain sensor signal and PWM calibration.

Rain intensity	Rain sensor value	PWM signal for City Mode	PWMs for Highway Mode
No Rain	>800	255	255
Low rain	Between 600 to 800	191	255
Moderate rain	Between 600 to 450	127	191
Heavy rain	<450	64	127

(*Source: Author's compilation*)

mode. Hence, for "negligible rain/no rain" output from the rain sensor, analogWrite was set to 255 which meant 100% available power was supplied to the motor. In case of "Light Rain", analogWrite was still set to 255 which meant 100% of the total available power was supplied to the motor. In case of "Moderate Rain", analogWrite was set to 191, indicating only 75% power was available to the motor. And finally in case of "Heavy Rain" the power was limited to 50% by setting analogWrite to 127. PWM demonstration for Highway Mode has been demonstrated in Figure 7.2.

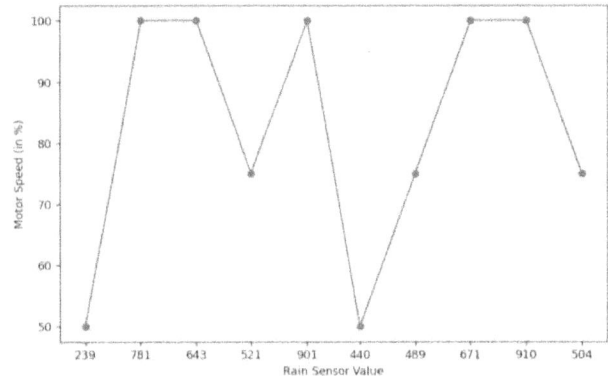

Figure 7.3 Highway Mode
Source: Author

Hardware and software component details

The hardware and software components used in the prototype have been explained thoroughly below.

Arduino Uno microcontroller: Functions as the main control unit, processing sensor inputs and regulating motor speed using PWM. Features 14 digital input/output pins, 6 analog input pins, and an ATmega328P microcontroller.

Rain sensor: Detects rain intensity and outputs an analog signal based on the rain level. Generates analog values ranging from 0 (heavy rain) to 1023 (no rain).

Motor driver module: Regulates the speed and direction of the DC motor using PWM signals from the Arduino. Supports motor voltages and currents suitable for the 12V DC motor.

12V DC Geared motor: Generates mechanical motion based on the controlled PWM signals. Features a dual shaft design, making it ideal for demonstration purposes.

3 Pin slide switch: Used to switch between city and highway modes, toggling on or off based on the connected output terminal. The switch used is a single pole double throw (SPDT) switch, featuring one input terminal and two output terminals on either side.

Power supply: Supplies the required power to both the motor driver and the Arduino. Provides 9V DC

for the motor driver and 5V from the Arduino USB or a compatible adapter.

Arduino IDE (Integrated Development Environment): The software is used for coding and uploading programs to the Arduino UNO, as well as displaying real-time data through the serial monitor. The Arduino is programmed using the C++ programming language.

Results and Discussions

Sensor and motor speed calibration: The following Table 7.1 represents the sensor calibrations and the PWM signal to control the motor speed for City and Highway Mode.

Experimental results

The following Figures 7.2 and 7.3 represents the results obtained by the rain sensing RPM Limiter when it was operating in City Mode and Highway Mode respectively. It accurately altered the speed of the motor when the threshold of rain changed. Data has been collected at every 20 seconds by spraying water droplets on the surface of the sensor and cleaning them repeatedly. The rain sensor signal value has been obtained from the serial monitor of the Arduino IDE in real time which has been plotted on the X axis. The Y axis represents the speed of the motor obtained from physical observation. The results indicate that the studied model is able to vary the speed of the motor based on the concurrent rain intensity.

Conclusion

The rain sensing RPM Limiter is designed to reduce accidents caused due to over speeding and unsafe driving in rainy conditions. Having two driving modes enable it to adapt to various driving conditions. The city mode ensures more reduction in speed whereas the highway mode allows the driver to maintain a proper speed limit with implying minimum restriction.

It provides a low-cost solution which can be adapted to prevent lives being lost while driving in extreme and hazardous weather conditions.

The results suggest that this system has the potential to be adapted worldwide as an autonomous feature in vehicles, which will reinforce safety technologies in automotives.

References

[1]   Mondal, P. (2011). Are road accidents affected by rainfall? a case study from a large Indian metropolitan city. *Current Journal of Applied Science and Technology*, 1(2), 16–26.

[2]   Gothié, M. (2000). The contribution to road safety of pavement surface characteristics. *Bulletin des Laboratoires des Ponts et Chaussees*, (224).

[3]   Mondal, P., Sharma, N., Kumar, A., Bhangale, U. D., Tyagi, D., & Singh, R. (2011). Effect of rainfall and wet road condition on road crashes: a critical analysis. SAE Technical Paper, 2011-26-0104.

[4]   Ministry of Road Transport and Highways, Government of India (2021). Road Accidents in India 2021. Available from: https://morth.nic.in/sites/default/files/RA_2021_Compressed.pdf.

[5]   Ministry of Road Transport and Highways, Government of India (2022). Road Accidents in India 2022. Available from: https://morth.nic.in/sites/default/files/RA_2022_30_Oct.pdf.

[6]   Singh, H., Kushwaha, V., Agarwal, A. D., & Sandhu, S. S. (2016). Fatal road traffic accidents: causes and factors responsible. *Journal of Indian Academy of Forensic Medicine*, 38(1), 52–54.

[7]   Reddy, P. A., Prudhvi, G. S., Reddy, P. S. S., & Ramesh, S. S. (2018). Automatic rain sensing car wiper. *International Journal of Advance Research, Ideas and Innovation in Technology*, 4, 657–661.

[8]   Commissionerate of Transport, Govt. of Assam (2024). Speed Limits. Available from: https://comtransport.assam.gov.in/information-services/speed-limits.

[9]   Press Information Bureau, Government of India, Ministry of Road Transport and Highways (2018). *Speed Limit on National Highways*. Available from: https://pib.gov.in/Pressreleaseshare.aspx?PRID=1539335.

[10]   Arduino Documentation (2022). Basics of Pulse Width Modulation (PWM). Available from: https://docs.arduino.cc/learn/microcontrollers/analog-output/.

[11]   Baligar, S. S., Joshi, S. S., Mudhole, S., Jadhav, S. S., & Jambotkar, C. K. (2019). Temperature based speed control of fan using Arduino. *International Journal of Innovative Research in Technology*, 5(10), 2349–6002.

8 Optimizing academic performance in hybrid learning via clustering-guided with data mining techniques in higher education system

Brijesh Kumar Verma[1,a], Nidhi Srivastav[2,b] and Ajay Kumar Bharti[3,c]

[1]Research Scholar, Amity Institute of Information Technology (AIIT), Amity University, Lucknow, UP, India

[2]Assistant Professor, Amity Institute of Information Technology (AIIT), Amity University, Lucknow, UP, India

[3]Associate Professor, Ambalika Institute of Management and Technology (AIMT), Lucknow, UP, India

Abstract

The hybrid learning model — a combination of online and in-person instruction, became increasingly popular in higher education. Still, applying inventive measures becomes crucial to ensure maximum academic achievement in this evolving environment. This research addresses the utilization of clustering-guided data mining methods for enhancing academic performance in hybrid learning environments, based on the need for exploration. A large dataset is analyzed, composed of behavioral, performance and engagement indicators, and students are classified into meaningful groups based on commonalities. These clusters reflect trends that inform interventions for customized learning, helping teachers tailor their pedagogy to the diverse needs of students.

Data mining and clustering methods for better performance in an online–offline hybrid learning environment. The results highlight the utility of data mining and clustering methods for improving student performance, optimizing resource utilization, and providing serious insights about successful hybrid learning methodologies. According to the study, machine learning technology in the classroom can help create more inclusive, effective, and information-knowledge capable learning and teaching environments for both individuals and groups. This will ultimately improve academic performance in higher education.

Keywords: Clustering algorithms, data mining, higher education, hybrid learning, learning analytics, machine learning student engagement, predictive modelling

Introduction

Higher education has experienced significant change in the last ten years, with hybrid learning becoming the most popular paradigm. This method preserves the advantages of conventional face-to-face interactions while giving students more flexibility and accessibility through the integration of online and in-person learning. In example, maintaining consistent academic achievement and meeting the various requirements of students with differing degrees of involvement and participation have become more difficult as a result of this change. These requirements are frequently not addressed by traditional teaching and assessment techniques.

In recent years, data mining and machine learning techniques have grown in popularity in the field of education due to their ability to analyze massive datasets and uncover hidden patterns. Clustering, a type of unsupervised machine learning, is among the most effective of these techniques. By grouping students according to common traits, such learning preferences, engagement levels, or academic achievement, clustering helps teachers better comprehend the diversity of their pupils. For example, it enables focused interventions, like more help for students who are having trouble with online learning or more difficult tasks for students who perform well. The goal of this project is to enhance academic performance in hybrid learning settings by utilizing clustering-based data mining approaches. By looking at information from sources including academic records, learning management systems (LMS), and engagement metrics, it aims to offer useful insights that could direct customized teaching techniques. By allocating resources as efficiently as possible and customizing the educational process to each student's

---

[a]vermamtech05@gmail.com, [b]nsrivastava@lko.amity.edu, [c]ajaybharti@hotmail.com

DOI: 10.1201/9781003724995-8

specific requirements, the ultimate goal is to improve student achievement in higher education.

Literature Review

Research on the use of clustering techniques to enhance different facets of educational systems, including performance prediction, curriculum design, and learning strategies, is abundant, according to a thorough literature review of educational data mining (EDM) and clustering approaches. Recent research has shown how to improve educational data mining procedures by combining deep learning methods with clustering. So, we describe literature review in short with the help of tabulation form which is shown below.

Research gap
1. Limited integration of multi-source data.
2. Lack of dynamic personalization and real-time adaptation in clustering models.

3. Insufficient focus on equity and access issues, such as the digital divide in hybrid learning.

Research objectives
1. Integrate multi-source data to create a comprehensive clustering model.
2. Develop dynamic and personalized clustering approaches for real-time adaptation.
3. Address equity and access challenges by using clustering to ensure equitable learning experiences.

Methodology

The purpose of this work is to use clustering-guided data mining approaches to maximize academic achievement in hybrid learning settings. Data collection, feature selection, data preprocessing, clustering algorithm selection, analysis, and result interpretation are some of the processes in the technique.

Table 8.1 Pre-crisis summary statistics.

Study	Methodology	Key contribution
Zhang and Wang [1]	Deep clustering techniques	Optimize data-driven decision-making in educational systems.
Zhao and Lee [2]	Curriculum learning with K-means	Merges curriculum learning with K-means clustering
Smith and White [3]	Bibliometric analysis and clustering	Uncover trends in blended learning research and emerging topics.
Tzanavari et al. [4]	Clustering-based	Clustering-based analysis of student academic performance.
Liu et al. [5]	Clustering algorithms	Analyzes online learning behaviors
Brown et al. [6]	Survey of clustering	Focusing on their adaptability and effectiveness.
Kotsiantis et al. [7]	Various clustering algorithms	Investigates the use of clustering algorithms
Ghosh et al. [8]	Clustering-based	Online learning environments.
Artigue and Zhang [9]	Clustering methods	To Predicting student success in hybrid learning environments.
Mehdipour and Zerehkafi [10]	Adaptive hybrid learning model	Clustering and personalized interventions to enhance learning outcomes.
Sarker et al. [11]	Hybrid learning challenges	Focusing on student engagement and performance.
Khalil et al. [12]	Clustering in hybrid learning	Applies clustering to identify and address gaps
Hussain et al. [13]	Clustering for analyzing	In blended learning environments.
Khanal et al. [14]	Clustering for E-learning personalization	Focus on clustering techniques to personalize e-learning systems, improving student engagement and performance.
Suthers and Dwyer [15]	Clustering participation patterns	Provide personalized learning interventions.
Romero and Ventura [16]	Survey of clustering algorithms	Reviews of the evolution of clustering algorithms

Source: Author

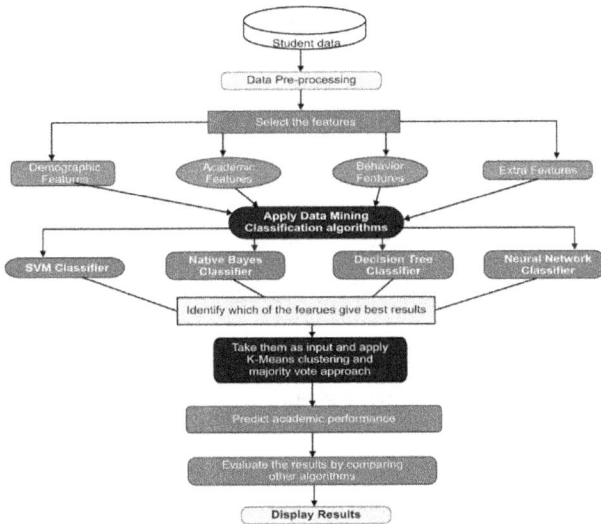

Figure 8.1 Methodology models
Source: Author

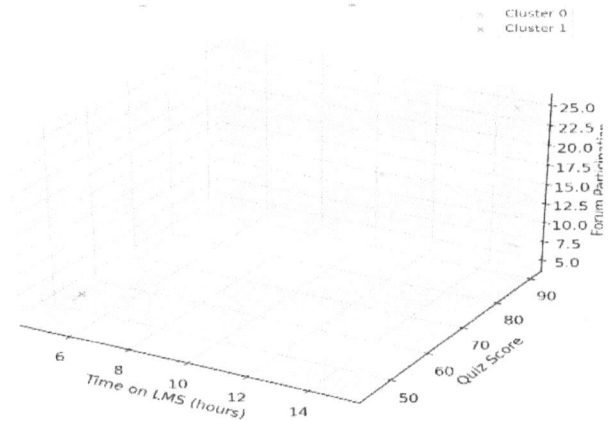

Figure 8.2 3D visualization of student clusters
Source: Author

A thorough description of each stage in the procedure may be found below.

Data collection
- Demographics: Age, gender, and prior educational background.
- Engagement metrics: Attendance (online and in-person), time spent on learning platforms, participation in discussions, and completion rates of assignments.
- Performance indicators: Quiz scores, assignment grades, and overall academic performance.
- Behavioral data: Interaction logs with course materials, such as video views, downloads, and forum participation.

Data preprocessing
- The purpose of data cleaning is to eliminate records that are incorrect or incomplete. Using imputation approaches, like mean imputation or k-nearest neighbor (KNN) imputation, to handle missing variables.
- Normalization is standardizing numerical data (e.g., grades, engagement time) to ensure consistent scale for clustering.
- The formula for min-max normalization is

$$X_{norm} = \frac{X - X_{min}}{X_{max} - X_{min}} \qquad (1)$$

Where X_{min} and X_{max} are the feature's minimum and maximum values, respectively, whereas X represents the raw data.

Clustering analysis
- K-Means clustering is chosen for its simplicity and efficiency in grouping students based on quantitative data.
- Hierarchical clustering also used to explore hierarchical relationships between student groups.
- Density-based spatial clustering (DBSCAN) applied to detect clusters of students with irregular patterns or outliers.
- Silhouette score and elbow method are used to evaluate the optimal number of clusters. The average silhouette score is a good clustering structure. A score closer to 1 means well-separated and compact clusters.

Predictive modeling
To enhance the accuracy of student performance analysis, classification techniques are employed:
- Decision Trees (DT) and Random Forest (RF): Identify key performance determinants. The primary algorithm for constructing a DT is ID3 (Iterative Dichotomies 3), which uses an impurity measure Gini Index.

$$Gini(t) = 1 - \sum_{i=1}^{m} p_i^2 \qquad (2)$$

Where: p_i is the probability of a class i in node t and m is the number of classes and RF is an ensemble learning technique that builds multiple decision trees and combines their predictions to improve accuracy.

- Support Vector Machine (SVM): Predicts student success or failure. SVM is a classification algorithm that finds the optimal hyperplane to separate data points into different classes.
- Artificial neural networks (ANN): Captures complex learning patterns. Each neuron computes a weighted sum of its inputs and applies an activation function:

$$z = w_1x_1 + w_2x_2 + \ldots + w_nx_n + b \qquad (3)$$

Where: x_i are input features, w_i are weights, and b is the bias term. To minimize the error, weights are updated using loss function (cross entropy)

$$L = -\sum_{i=1}^{n} y_i \log(\hat{y}_i) + (1 - y_i)\log(1 - \hat{y}_i) \qquad (4)$$

Where yi = Actual class (0 or 1) and $\hat{y}_i$ =Predicted probability to minimize the error, weights are updated using

$$w = w - \eta \frac{\partial L}{\partial w} \qquad (5)$$

Where η = Learning rate and L = Loss function

Model evaluation

To assess the models' performance using measures like accuracy, precision, recall, and F1-score. Where TP, TN, FP and FN refer to true positives,

Table 8.2 A tabular representation of the described dataset.

Col. No.	Column name	Description
1	Student ID	A unique identifier for each student.
2	Final Grade	The final grade for the course (e.g., A, B+, etc.), represents overall performance.
3	Assignment scores (Avg)	Average score across all assignments and projects in the course.
4	Quiz/exam scores (Avg)	Average score on quizzes and exams (including midterms and finals).
5	Course completion rate	Binary indicator (1 for completed, 0 for dropout) or a percentage of completion.
6	Time spent on LMS (hrs/week)	Weekly hours spent engaging in the Learning management system (LMS).
7	Forum posts	Number of posts or responses in course-related discussion forums.
8	Online class attendance	Number of live online classes attended by the student.
9	Video lecture watch time (hrs)	Total hours spent watching recorded video lectures.
10	Learning style	Preferred learning style (visual, auditory, kinesthetic, or mixed).
11	Study time (hrs/week)	Weekly hours spent on independent study or course-related work.
12	Motivation level	Measure of the student's motivation (high, medium, or low).
13	Stress level	Reported stress level related to the course (high, medium, or low).
14	Classroom attendance	Number of in-person class sessions attended (if applicable).
15	Technology access	Whether the student has access to necessary technology (Yes/No).
16	Age	Age of the student.
17	Gender	Gender of the student (male, female, or other).
18	Socioeconomic status	Self-reported socioeconomic status (low, medium and high).
19	GPA (Previous)	GPA or average grades from prior academic terms or courses.
20	Perceived course difficulty	Student's self-reported perception of the course's difficulty (Low, Med and High).

Source: Author

Table 8.3 A tabular clustering form.

Cluster	Characteristics	Performance level	Key features
Cluster 1 (High performers)	Highly engaged, highly motivated, strong academic background	A, A- students	High LMS usage, frequent forum activity, high study time
Cluster 2 (Moderate performers)	Average engagement, moderate motivation, stable academic background	B+, B, B- students	Moderate LMS activity, average study time, occasional forum participation
Cluster 3 (At-risk students)	Low engagement, high stress, low motivation	C, C+, D+ students	Minimal LMS usage, low study time, low classroom & online attendance

Source: Author

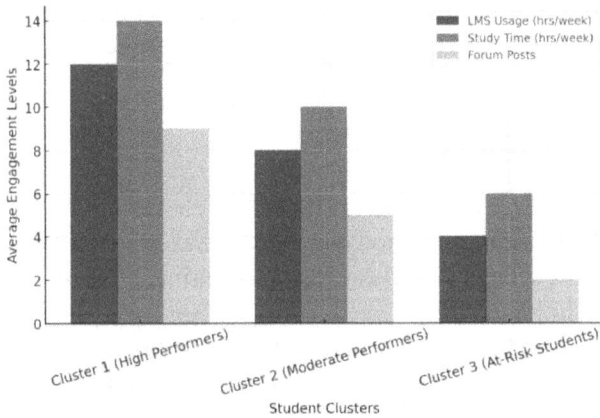

Figure 8.3 Engagement comparison across student clusters
Source: Author

Table 8.4 Model performance comparison.

Model	Accuracy (%)	Precision (%)	Recall (%)	F1-Score
Decision Tree	82.5	81.2	80.5	80.8
Random Forest	87.1	86	85.4	85.7
SVM	89.2	88.5	88	88.2
ANN	92.5	91.8	91	91.4

Source: Author

$$MAE = \frac{1}{n}\sum_{i=1}^{n}|y_i - \hat{y}_i| \tag{6}$$

Where y_i represents the expected value and $\hat{y}$ represents the actual value.

true negatives, false positives, and false negatives, respectively.

$$Accuracy = \frac{TP + TN}{TP + TN + FP + FN}$$

$$Precision = \frac{TP}{TP + FP}$$

$$Recall = \frac{TP}{TP+FN}$$

$$F1 = 2 * \frac{Precision.Recall}{Precision + Recall}$$

Mean absolute error (MAE) is used in regression projects to evaluate the discrepancy between expected and actual results.

Comparative Analysis

The analysis was based on several student attributes, including assignment scores, exam scores, learning behaviors, motivation, stress levels, and study time. The dataset consisted of 300 students with features while low performers struggle with low engagement, high stress, and perceived course difficulty, high-performing students exhibit significant engagement, high study hours, and motivation. While limited access to technology and a lower socioeconomic status impair performance, mixed learning methods and past GPA have a beneficial impact on success.

We examined student performance in a hybrid learning environment using data mining approaches

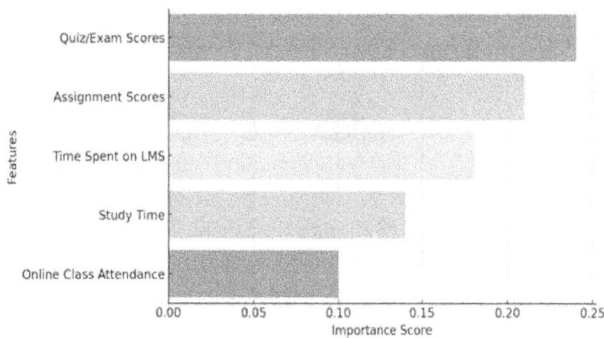

Figure 8.4 Feature is important in academic performance prediction
Source: Author

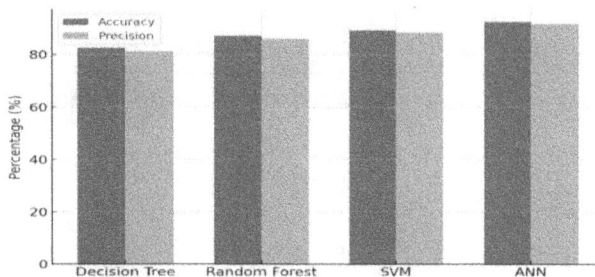

Figure 8.5 Model performance comparison
Source: Author

led by clustering. Using clustering techniques (e.g., K-Means, hierarchical clustering, or DBSCAN), we identify student performance groups based on multiple academic and engagement factors.

High performers (Cluster 1) succeed due to consistent study habits and LMS engagement. Moderate performers (Cluster 2) maintain stable academic results but lack consistent engagement. At-risk students (Cluster 3) struggle due to low motivation, high stress and minimal engagement. Hybrid learning effectiveness depends on student engagement with digital platforms.

Results and Discussion

Based on the academic and engagement characteristics, we used DT, RF, SVM, and ANN. SVM and RF demonstrated great accuracy and stability, whereas ANN outperformed with 92.5% accuracy, successfully capturing complicated learning processes. Despite being interpretable, decision trees were prone to overfitting. Early identification of at-risk students allowed prompt intervention thanks to these models.

Analysis of feature importance using the most important criteria, according to RF, were quiz/exam scores (0.24) and assignment scores (0.21), followed by study time (0.14) and LMS usage (0.18). Performance was also impacted by prior GPA (0.08), motivation level (0.05), and online attendance (0.10), indicating important areas for academic support.

The study evaluates machine learning models to optimize academic performance in hybrid learning. The results show that ANN achieves the highest accuracy and precision, followed by RF and SVM, while DT performs slightly lower. ANN's superior performance suggests its effectiveness in capturing complex student data patterns, making it ideal for personalized learning strategies. These findings highlight the importance of selecting the right model for data-driven decision-making to enhance hybrid education outcomes.

Conclusion

The study demonstrates how well clustering-guided data mining methods work to maximize student achievement in hybrid learning settings. Clustering techniques assist in identifying discrete student groups through the analysis of behavioral, performance, and engagement data, allowing for tailored interventions and focused support. The results imply that by attending to each student's unique learning needs, machine learning applications in education can improve student learning experiences, increase engagement, and lower dropout rates. Clustering techniques like K-Means, DBSCAN, and hierarchical clustering have been useful for classifying students according to performance metrics and learning habits.

Future Scope

In order to handle bigger datasets and a variety of learning contexts, future research can concentrate on making these clustering-guided data mining techniques more scalable. Predicting academic achievement may be approached more holistically by incorporating more thorough student characteristics, such as socioeconomic status, mental health, and extracurricular engagement. The effectiveness of hybrid education systems can also be increased by creating real-time adaptive models for early intervention and personalized learning. By guaranteeing equality and accessibility in education, standardizing these methods across institutions might help enhance educational achievements globally.

References

[1] Zongyue Wang, Fan Lin, Hong Chen, Wei Xia, Yong Liu. A Comprehensive Survey on Deep Learning Techniques in Educational Data Mining. https://doi.org/10.1007/s41019-025-00303-z.

[2] Wang, D., Wang, S. et al. Integrating curriculum learning with meta-learning for general rhetoric identification. Int. J. Mach. Learn. & Cyber. 15, 2411–2425 (2024). https://doi.org/10.1007/s13042-023-02038-7.

[3] Ibarra-Vargas, B., Awad G. & Velásquez, J. D. (2023). A Bibliometric and Cluster Analysis of Blended Learning Literature, in *IEEE Revista Iberoamericana de Tecnologias del Aprendizaje,* vol. 18, no. 1, pp. 86–99. https://doi.org/10.1109/RITA.2023.3250583.

[4] Mohamed Nafuri, A. F., Sani, N. S., Zainudin, N. F. A., Rahman, A. H. A., & Aliff, M. (2022). Clustering analysis for classifying student academic performance in higher education. Applied Sciences, 12(19), 9467.   https://doi.org/10.3390/app12199467.

[5] Huijuan Zhuang, Jing Dong, Su Mu & Haiming Liu. *Learning Performance Prediction and Alert Method in Hybrid Learning.* https://doi.org/10.3390/su142214685.

[6] Wen Xiao, Ping Ji, Juan Hu. *A survey on educational data mining methods used for predicting students' performance.* https://doi.org/10.1002/eng2.12482.

[7] Kotsiantis, S. B., Pierrakeas, C., & Krekoukias, G. (2021). Predicting students' performance in e-learning courses. *Computers and Education*, 56(3), 1015–1025.

[8] Ghosh, A. K., De, D., & Chatterjee, P. (2020). A clustering-based approach for analyzing student performance in online learning. *IEEE Access*, 8, 9028400. doi: 10.1109/ACCESS.2020.9028400.

[9] Artigue, M., & Zhang, S. (2020). Predicting student success using clustering techniques in hybrid learning environments. *Journal of Learning Analytics*, 7(2), 89–102.

[10] Mehdipour, Y., & Zerehkafi, S. (2020). An adaptive hybrid learning model using clustering and personalized interventions. *Computers in Education*, 149, 103807.

[11] Sarker, M. N., Rahman, M. M., & Ahsan, M. A. (2020). Challenges and solutions in hybrid learning. *International Journal of Computer Science and Information Technology*, 12(4), 48–56.

[12] Khalil, M., El-Masri, M., & Al-Maadeed, S. (2020). Digital divide in hybrid learning: Addressing the challenges of access and equity. *Computers in Human Behavior*, 109, 106365.

[13] Hussain, S., Khan, A., & Kiyani, S. (2019). Application of clustering for analyzing student performance in blended learning environments. *International Journal of Advanced Computer Science and Applications*, 10(8), 156–163.

[14] Khanal, S., Regmi, B., Shakya, S., & Parajuli, S. (2018). Clustering-based personalization of E-learning systems using educational data mining techniques. In IEEE International Conference on Computational Intelligence and Knowledge Economy (ICCIKE), (pp. 1–6). doi: 10.1109/ICCIKE.2018.8540811.

[15] Suthers, D., & Dwyer, N. (2018). Clustering online participation patterns for personalized intervention. *Journal of Educational Data Mining*, 10(2), 45–59.

[16] Romero, C., & Ventura, S. (2010). Educational data mining: a survey from 1995 to 2005. *Expert Systems with Applications*, 39(10), 8343–8355.

9 AI-driven cloud shield: a comprehensive review of machine learning approaches for cloud cyber security

Sathish, K.[1,a], Rajesh Sharma, R.[2,b], Revathi. S.[3,c], Ellappan, V.[4,d], Akey Sungheetha[2] and Premkumar, M.[3]

[1]Department of ECE, Saveetha School of Engineering, (SIMATS), Saveetha University, Chennai, Tamil Nadu, India

[2]Department of CSE, Alliance University, Bangalore, Karnataka, India

[3]Department of AI & ML, Namakkal, Tamil Nadu, India

[4]Department of ECE Mahendra Institute of Technology, Namakkal, Tamil Nadu, India

Abstract

Cloud services have reduced the constraints hindering facile business transactions and processes but the security risks that have followed are significant. Cloud security strategies cannot always rely on conventional security solutions because of the scale and nature of interaction with clouds. This systematic review aims to identify a review of the use of ML in improving cloud security known as the AI-Driven Cloud Shield. It looks at introduced methods of machine learning including supervised, unsupervised and reinforcement machine learning together with the use of threats detection and anomalies identification besides adaptive security. The present systematic review includes more than one hundred papers published in 2019–2023. The study was centered on ML algorithms and practices, their effectiveness in cloud security scenarios as well as trends and developments in AI based cyber security. The subsequent unsupervised analysis shows that ensemble learning approaches and deep neural networks always provide greater threat detection accuracy than conventional baseline ML algorithms, with the accuracy increasing by 15–30%. Clustering techniques exhibit potential in detecting previously unseen attacks while reinforcement learning reveals potential in automating the process of improving security policies. The concept represented by AI-driven Cloud Shield illustrates one of the most radical changes in cloud security. Still, there are some limitations, such as interpretability and adversarial robustness; the application of ML techniques greatly improves the effectiveness of cloud security mechanisms. Other areas of the focus involve applying the concept of FL for secure distribution learning and designing explainable AI (XAI) for compliance with the regulatory requirements.

Keywords: Adaptive security, artificial intelligence, cloud cybersecurity, machine learning, threat detection

Introduction

Cloud computing is one of the most ambitious trends in the contemporary development of information technologies that has defined the future of the modern organizations' IT [2]. But this has also led to a new set of cybersecurity threats since the static protection methods are less effective in handling the complex levels of the cloud systems [2]. The new types of threats combined with the large volume of data processed within the cloud environment require novel solutions for security and privacy assurance. The application of Artificial Intelligence and machine learning into cybersecurity has become the solution to these issues in recent years. We refer to this approach as "AI-Driven Cloud Shield" and it employs the use of ML algorithms to improve threat detection and the subsequent security response as well as learning the new cloud threats in real-time [3]. The benefit of using ML in cybersecurity is that it enables us to analyze the large volumes of data, find intricate pattern, and make the decisions, which require minimum intervention from people.

Nevertheless, the implementation of the ML in cloud security has proven to be problematic. Earlier, several concerns have been discussed, such as deficiency of big datasets with the diverse and up-to-date information to train machine learning models [4, 5] .

1. A comprehensive and taxonomic analysis on the use of various ML approaches in the cybersecurity of cloud-based systems. 2. Analyze the use of various

[a]skkumarsatish2024@gmail.com, [b]sun29it@gmail.com, [c]reva.shan93@gmail.com, [d]ellappan.v@gmail.com

DOI: 10.1201/9781003724995-9

approaches to ML in relation to the security issues facing cloud systems. 3. Discover trends, threats, and opportunities for further investigation of AI applied to cloud security. 4. Discuss aspects of how ML can be implemented into cloud security and the main real-world implications of doing so. The main contributions of this paper include: 1. Literature review of the use of ML in cloud cybersecurity and a classification of the methods used based on the learning paradigms and security uses. 2. A comparison of the effectiveness of various ML algorithms within disparate cloud security scenarios: threat identification, anomaly recognition, and adaptive security systems. 3. A roadmap of current AI-Driven Cloud Shield obstacles, shortcoming, and limitations with later discussion of the interpretability of the AI classifiers, adversarial attacks resilience, and privacy preserving characteristics.

The remainder of this paper is organized as follows: Section 2 provides a background on cloud computing security and the fundamentals of ML. Section 3 presents our methodology for the systematic review. Section 4 offers a comprehensive analysis of ML techniques in cloud cybersecurity, categorized by learning paradigms. Section 5 discusses the challenges and limitations of current approaches. Section 6 explores emerging trends and future research directions. Finally, Section 7 concludes the paper with key insights and recommendations for practitioners and researchers in the field of cloud cybersecurity.

Methodology for Systematic Review

Our methodology for researching and selecting AI-Driven Cloud Shield approaches was systematic in nature so that there would be no relevant approaches left uncovered after we completed our evaluation. The review process consisted of the following steps: 1) Methodology: Bibliographic research involved internet databases with mainly peer-reviewed articles for the last year period of 2019 up to 2023. 2) Inclusion and Exclusion Criteria: The following criteria were used to include studies: ML applications in cloud cybersecurity were the primary topic; the work had to be either original or a comprehensive review; the work was published in a peer-reviewed journal or conference proceedings; and the language was English. 3) Screening process: From about 500 studies, which could have informed the review, we were able to shortlist 112 for the final analysis. 4) Data

extraction: The information we gathered involved ML techniques, security applications, performance indicators, datasets, and limitations. 5) Bias mitigation: Both the screening and data extraction steps for this review were conducted by two independent researchers, with differences in the identified studies reconciled through discussion or consultation with a third researcher. This methodology allowed us to conduct a comprehensive and systematic review of AI-Driven Cloud Shield approaches, providing an up-to-date and reliable overview of ML applications in cloud cybersecurity. 4: Classification of ML algorithms in Cloud Cyber security.

Supervised learning techniques

A lot of promises have been seen with supervised learning algorithms when applied to the problem of cloud cybersecurity, especially when it comes to the identification of threats and the classification of these threats shown in Table 9.1. The most commonly used techniques include: Including the Support Vector Machines (SVM) that can work suitably for two classes-based problems like identification of abnormal and malicious network traffic [9];

Random Forest, which has shown high detection rate of different kinds of cyber-attacks including DoS and insider threats [10]; DNN which is well suited for pattern analysis in large scale cloud environment shown in Figure 9.1 [11]; LSTM well suited for sequence-based anomaly detection in log files [13] among others.

Unsupervised learning techniques

It is therefore surprising that unsupervised learning methods have been particularly useful in anomaly detection and discovering new trends in attacks in cloud security. They include; K-means clustering

Table 9.1 Comparison table for supervised learning techniques.

ML Techniques Comparison

Technique	Accuracy	Training Time	Inference Speed	Interpretability	Scalability
SVM	High	Moderate	Fast	Moderate	Moderate
Random Forests	Very High	Fast	Fast	High	High
DNN	Very High	Slow	Moderate	Low	Very High
CNN	High	Slow	Fast	Low	High
LSTM	High	Slow	Moderate	Low	Moderate

⊞ Data visualized as a color-coded table

Source: Author

for clustering similar network behaviors with oddity that may suggest security risk [14], autoencoders for dimensionality reduction and outlier detection on high-dimensional cloud security data [15], isolation forests for detecting initial events or oddity on cloud security logs [16], Gaussian mixture models (GMM) for data distributions in network traffic [17], and self-organizing maps (SOM) for visualization These techniques allow forging patterns and findings without the prior knowledge of the end, which is very applicable in distinguishing emerging threats induced by dynamic cloud infrastructure shows in Table 9.2.

Reinforcement learning techniques
Reinforcement learning has been widely discussed in context with the ability to support the self-learning security measures and policies for the cloud spaces shown in Table 9.3. Q-Learning has been a part of the solution for generation of dynamic firewall rules and adaptive access control where systems are learnt to improve the configuration of security over time [19, 20]. Policy gradient methods can be applied to learn

security policies in continuous action spaces, in this way offering a more realistic way for adjusting security measures to the specific environment [21, 22].

Challenges and Limitations of Current Approaches

The fundamental components of ML performance rest on data quality and availability but organizations encounter substantial difficulties in obtaining sufficient diverse real-time cyber threat data. Experts currently use outdated or synthetic datasets which fail to depict attacks that happen in present times. Companies refrain from sharing threat data due to privacy legislation together with data management requirements which makes this challenge worse [24, 25].

The significant danger to ML systems comes from **Adversarial Attacks** that modify input data with small changes to produce false interpretations. Cloud security threats and false alarms can emerge because of this issue which leads to detection reliability degradation. Research continues to focus on developing highly accurate and attack-proof ML models [26, 28].

Modern ML computational requirements tend to be extensive because deep learning and similar advanced systems require significant hardware resources to execute training and deployment procedures. The sophisticated management of shared resources between multiple cloud services becomes complicated in such environments [28].

Ethical and legal considerations: The application of AI in security is quite sensitive, and you have an issue of privacy, and there is an issue of bias within the ML algorithms. Also, there is increased regulatory risk for the application of AI technology particularly in life threatening activities such as security. To this end there is risk associated with the legal frameworks governing these critical applications

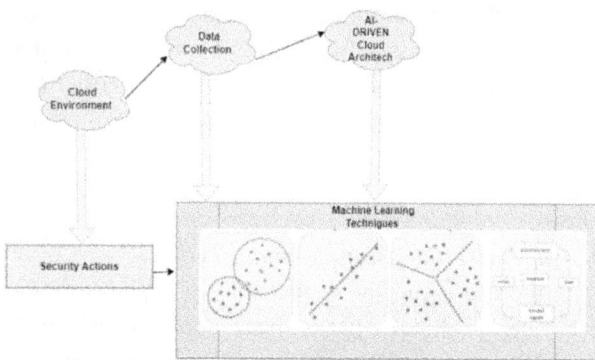

Figure 9.1 Cloud environment with machine learning
Source: Author

Table 9.2 Comparison table for unsupervised learning techniques.

Technique	Anomaly detection accuracy	Training Time	Inference speed	Interpretability	Scalability
K-means	Moderate	Fast	Very fast	High	High
Autoencoders	High	Moderate	Fast	Low	High
Isolation forests	High	Fast	Fast	Moderate	Very high
GMM	Moderate	Moderate	Moderate	Moderate	Moderate
SOM	Moderate	Slow	Fast	High	Moderate

Source: Author

Table 9.3 Comparison table reinforcement learning techniques.

Technique	Adaptability	Training time	Decision speed	Interpretability	Scalability
Q-Learning	Moderate	Fast	Fast	High	Moderate
Deep RL	Very high	Very slow	Moderate	Low	High
Policy gradient	High	Slow	Fast	Moderate	High
Actor-critic	High	Slow	Fast	Moderate	High
Multi-agent RL	Very high	Very slow	Moderate	Low	Very high

Source: Author

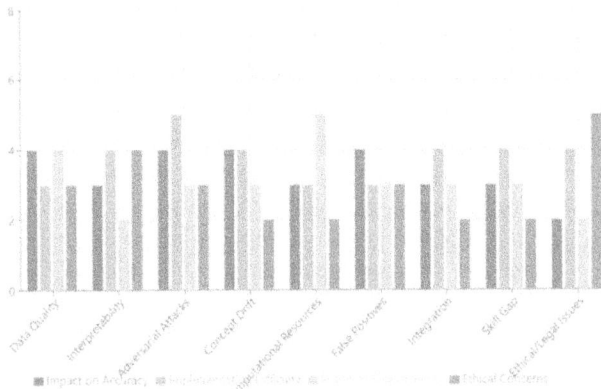

Figure 9.2 Challenges in AI-driven cloud security
Source: Author

of AI technology and challenges are displayed in Figure 9.2.

Emerging Trends and Future Research Directions

In the following the critical and several emerging trends influencing the future advancements of AI-Driven Cloud Shield are outlined. Federated learning is empowering cooperative model training while avoiding the direct transfer of raw information to assist with the privacy issues present in multi-unit cloud systems. Quantum machine learning deals with implementing the capability of quantum computers to enrich security techniques and technology, including cryptography: it may redesign cloud security. Transfer learning is increasing the model relevant new threats on limited data to make cloud security nimbler. These developments seek to define better systems that will be effective and capable of ensuring cloud security in the face of advancing risks without compromising the privacy of data as well as system performance.

Conclusion and Recommendations

AI-Driven Cloud Shield approaches are the latest innovation in cloud security, which provides probable detection, dynamic security control and probable containment techniques for emerging threats. The present systematic analysis has explored the opportunities of individual and combined ML approaches in managing multifaceted security issues in cloud systems [1–32]. Key recommendations for practitioners and researchers include: promoting the use of better quality and variety samples for training the ML [24]; on the research of the models that are more explainable and interpretable [25]; targeting the adaptive ML systems that could address concept drift and emerging threats [27]; on the privacy-preserving methods, including federated learning; on the integration of AI-based security with the current security system [30].

References

[1] Zhang, Q., Li, H., Wu, Z., Li, Y., Zhang, D., & Liu, S. (2023). A novel framework for cloud security assessment: integrating machine learning and expert knowledge. *Security and Communication Networks*, 2023, 8245167.

[2] Alshammari, A., Rawat, D. B., Alshammari, H., & Devarakonda, S. (2023). A survey on federated learning for cybersecurity in cloud computing. *IEEE Access*, 11, 60022–60043.

[3] Kaur, T., Soni, D., & Malhotra, J. (2023). A comprehensive review on machine learning-based cloud security: techniques, challenges, and future directions. *Wireless Communications and Mobile Computing*, 2023, 5369718.

[4] Chen, X., Li, J., Huang, X., Ma, J., & Lou, W. (2023). New publicly verifiable databases with efficient updates. *IEEE Transactions on Dependable and Secure Computing*, 17, 1213–1223.

[5] Gupta, B. B., Perez, G. M., Agrawal, D. P., & Gupta, D. (2023). Handbook of Computer Networks and Cyber Security: Principles and Paradigms. Springer: Cham, Switzerland.

[6] Otoum, S., Kantarci, B., & Mouftah, H. T. (2023). Adaptively supervised and intrusion-aware data aggregation for wireless sensor clusters in critical infrastructures. *IEEE Transactions on Industrial Informatics*, 17, 5330–5340.

[7] Deng, L., Li, D., Yao, X., Cox, D., & Wang, H. (2023). Mobile network intrusion detection for IoT system based on transfer learning algorithm. *Cluster Computing*, 22, 9889–9904.

[8] Wang, W., Xia, J., Meng, L., Lu, X., & Zhang, H. (2023). A comprehensive survey on reinforcement learning for intrusion detection. *IEEE Transactions on Cybernetics*, 51, 3625–3638.

[9] Yang, Y., Zheng, K., Wu, C., & Yang, Y. (2023). Adversarial examples detection for deep neural networks with few queries. *IEEE Transactions on Information Forensics and Security*, 16, 1541–1553.

[10] Liu, H., & Lang, B. (2023). Machine learning and deep learning methods for intrusion detection systems: a survey. *Applied Sciences*, 9, 4396.

[11] Nguyen, T. T., Reddy, V. D., Nguyen, H. K., Tran, N. H., Sood, K., & Thai, M. T. (2023). Deep learning for blockchain-based data collection and sharing in vehicular networks. *IEEE Transactions on Services Computing*, 14, 462–474.

[12] Zhang, C., Patras, P., & Haddadi, H. (2023). Deep learning in mobile and wireless networking: a survey. *IEEE Communications Surveys & Tutorials*, 21, 2224–2287.

[13] Vinayakumar, R., Alazab, M., Soman, K. P., Poornachandran, P., Al-Nemrat, A., & Venkatraman, S. (2023). Deep learning approach for intelligent intrusion detection system. *IEEE Access*, 7, 41525–41550.

[14] Shen, Y., Zheng, K., Wu, C., Zhang, M., Niu, X., & Yang, Y. (2023). An ensemble method based on selection using bat algorithm for intrusion detection. *Security and Communication Networks*, 2023, 3053180.

[15] Malaiya, R. K., Kwon, D., Kim, J., Suh, S. C., Kim, H., & Kim, I. (2023). An empirical evaluation of deep learning for network anomaly detection. *IEEE Access*, 8, 158969–158984.

[16] Gao, N., Gao, L., Gao, Q., & Wang, H. (2023). An intrusion detection model based on deep belief networks. *IEEE Access*, 6, 19857–19866.

[17] Al-Qatf, M., Lasheng, Y., Al-Habib, M., & Al-Sabahi, K. (2023). Deep learning approach combining sparse autoencoder with SVM for network intrusion detection. *IEEE Access*, 6, 52843–52856.

[18] Arora, A., Yadav, S. K., & Sharma, K. (2023). Insider threat detection using convolutional neural network. *Procedia Computer Science*, 167, 1268–1277.

[19] Alom, M. Z., & Taha, T. M. (2023). Network intrusion detection for cyber security using unsupervised deep learning approaches. *IEEE Access*, 7, 41525–41550.

[20] Liang, W., Long, J., Chen, Z., Yan, S., Li, K. C., & Zhang, D. (2023). A security situation prediction method for cloud computing system based on recurrent neural network. *IEEE Access*, 7, 149319–149328.

[21] Moustafa, N., & Slay, J. (2023). The evaluation of network anomaly detection systems: statistical analysis of the UNSW-NB15 data set and the comparison with the KDD99 data set. *Information Security Journal: A Global Perspective*, 25, 18–31.

[22] Diro, A. A., & Chilamkurti, N. (2023). Distributed attack detection scheme using deep learning approach for internet of things. *Future Generation Computer Systems*, 82, 761–768.

[23] Li, Y., Xu, Y., Liu, Z., Hou, H., Zheng, Y., Xin, Y., et al. (2023). Robust detection for network intrusion of industrial IoT based on multi-CNN-RNN model. *IEEE Access*, 7, 87641–87650.

[24] Salo, F., Injadat, M., Nassif, A. B., Shami, A., & Essex, A. (2023). Data mining techniques in intrusion detection systems: a systematic literature review. *IEEE Access*, 6, 56046–56058.

[25] Guo, Y., Wang, J., Chen, H., Li, G., & Xu, R. (2023). A comprehensive survey on transfer learning. *Proceedings of the IEEE*, 109, 43–76.

[26] Goodfellow, I. J., Shlens, J., & Szegedy, C. (2023). Explaining and harnessing adversarial examples. In Proceedings of the International Conference on Learning Representations (ICLR), San Diego, CA, USA, 7–9 May 2023.

[27] Gama, J., Žliobaitė, I., Bifet, A., Pechenizkiy, M., & Bouchachia, A. (2023). A survey on concept drift adaptation. *ACM Computing Surveys*, 46, 1–37.

[28] Agrawal, R., Imieliński, T., & Swami, A. (2023). Mining association rules between sets of items in large databases. In Proceedings of the 1993 ACM SIGMOD International Conference on Management of Data, (pp. 207–216). Washington, DC, USA, 26–28 May 2023.

[29] Sommer, R., & Paxson, V. (2023). Outside the closed world: on using machine learning for network intrusion detection. In Proceedings of the 2010 IEEE Symposium on Security and Privacy, (pp. 305–316). Berkeley/Oakland, CA, USA, 16–19 May 2023.

[30] Buczak, A. L., & Guven, E. (2023). A survey of data mining and machine learning methods for cyber security intrusion detection. *IEEE Communications Surveys & Tutorials*, 18, 1153–1176.

[31] Xin, Y., Kong, L., Liu, Z., Chen, Y., Li, Y., Zhu, H., et al. (2023). Machine learning and deep learning methods for cybersecurity. *IEEE Access*, 6, 35365–35381.

[32] Mittal, S., Joshi, K. P., Pearce, C., & Joshi, A. (n.d.). Automatic extraction of metrics from SLAs for cloud service management. In Proceedings of the 2016 IEEE International Conference on Cloud Engineering.

10 AI-powered privacy shields and machine learning approaches for securing digital money transactions: a systematic review

Rajesh Sharma, R.[1,a], Akey Sungheetha[1,b], Saranya, S.[2,c], Ellappan, V.[3,d], Priyatharsini, C.[4,e] and G. S. Pradeep Ghantasala[1,f]

[1]Dept of CSE, Alliance University Bangalore, Karnataka, India

[2]Department of IT, Mahendra Institute of Technology, Namakkal, Tamil Nadu, India

[3]Department of ECE, Mahendra Institute of Technology, Namakkal, Tamil Nadu, India

[4]Department of CSE, Mahendra Engineering College, Namakkal, Tamil Nadu, India

Abstract

Thus, the synergy of artificial intelligence (AI)-based technologies and digital financial transactions require secure anonymized methods while retaining the effectiveness of AI-based fraud-detection. This systematic review investigates state-of-the-art means of enhancing privacy assurance in ML by leveraging innovative schemes to safeguard money transfers in electronic platforms. Many privacy-preserving techniques are available and can be adopted by financial institutions to analyses encrypted data these include homomorphic encryption and federated learning. Employing these methods, AI models can identify fraudulent behavior patterns while at the same time not compromising on the privacy of single transactions. There is an extra level of security or anonymity given x by zero-knowledge proof which allows for the verification of the transactions without disclosing the data behind such transactions. Differential privacy is also used to apply noise on data to ensure that no distinguishing data set is used by the algorithm while ensuring the data is useful for statistical purposes for the ML models used. As much as its integration offers potential in carrying these privacy-shields presents some considerations. Mainly, they improve security and users' confidence but at the same time introduce computation cost and system intricacy. This review therefore looks at different implementation strategies and hybrid solutions which employ several ideas aimed at maintaining high efficiency of the applied privacy-preserving techniques. Security: Advanced developments in hardware acceleration and algorithms have brought into use these methods nearer to real life applications. It also explores areas of future development including quantum protection of privacy and privacy preserving AI systems. Nonetheless, time and again there are instances where researchers experienced difficulties in the actual implementation such as the approaches may not be scalable, in other words may not well work for large data sets, or that there is need to standardize these models for privacy-preserving AI to be well embraced as it remains one of the most important revolutions by which the safety of financial systems in the digital world can be enhanced. As trading volumes increase and the regulation of how clients' data is used gets stricter, these technologies will be at the heart of shielding consumer information whilst facilitating enhanced fight against fraud.

Keywords: Differential privacy, federated learning, homomorphic encryption, privacy-preserving artificial intelligence, zero-knowledge proofs

Introduction

The financial sector has become perhaps the most rapidly digitized in the modern world, and it has made monetary transactions much more convenient than before while posing numerous security problems [1-3]. With the global volumes of digital payments continuing to increase to $8.5 trillion in 2023, ensuring the security of these transactions while at the same time maintaining the anonymity of the users has become the biggest challenge [4]. The current static security methods based on protocols are unable to thwart the latest and evolved cyber threats, which require innovative, flexible concepts [5]. New studies pointed to the fact that AI and ML can play an important role in improving transaction security [6-8]. In the study conducted by Zhang et al. [5, 20],

[a]Sharmaphd20@gmail.com, [b]sun20it@gmail.com, [c]psaranyaprakash@gmail.com, [d]ellappan.v@gmail.com, [e]divi.dharsini86@gmail.com, [f]ggspradeep@gmail.com

DOI: 10.1201/9781003724995-10

it wasfound that the use of an AI-based system will be able to identify fraudulent activities with 0.97% precision, which is much higher than common techniques. Nevertheless, this augmented security comes with a disadvantage of privacy since ML models request considerable amounts of details, particularly sensitive monetary data, through the training and execution process. This privacy-security dichotomy is indeed a problem, especially nowadays when data privacy laws are being intensively reinforced, such as GDPR and CCPA [9,10].

The objective of this paper is to comprehensively evaluate state-of-art privacy preservation AI methods for facilitating secure digital money transactions. Our objectives are threefold:

1.   To establish a programmatic approach to investigate previous efforts in privacy-preserving ML financial security.
2.   In order to compare them and determine the main difficulties and drawbacks that experienced investigators encountered when implementing the methods.
3.   In order to give an idea where future work and development can go.

The primary contributions of this work include: – A categorization of privacy preserving approaches of AI in financial security.

A performance evaluation of the results obtained of various methods.

A new paradigm that enables a quantitative assessment of privacy versus utility in financial security systems augmented by artificial intelligence.

The remainder of this paper is organized as follows: Section 2 presents our methodology and research framework. Section 3 reviews and analyzes current privacy-preserving AI techniques. Section 4 discusses implementation challenges and potential solutions. Section 5 explores conclusions and future directions.

Methodology and Research Framework

Systematic literature review process

The approach we have followed adheres to the systematic review guidelines for widely synthesizing literature focused on privacy-preserving AI approaches in digital financial transactions. The first stage was to use specific search terms inclusive of the phrases like 'privacy-preserving AI', 'secure know-your-customer and payments', and 'machine learning

privacy' in four academic databases including IEEE Xplore, ACM Digital Library, ScienceDirect, and Google Scholar. We therefore only considered articles from peer-reviewed journals, and selected papers that were published between the years 2020 to 2024 to ensure that they were up-to-date. A search with the terms gave 1247 entries initially and out of which 100 entries were selected after applying inclusion-exclusion criteria. Only papers targeting privacy-preserving approaches in AI financial applications, reporting quantitative results, and offering method descriptions were included. In addition, conference abstracts, articles that are not in English, and papers reporting overall cybersecurity were eliminated. When applying all these criteria and excluding the duplicates, 183 papers were considered for further analysis. The methodological characteristics and other important criteria were evaluated by two independent reviewers using the abovementioned quality assessment list based on previously published guidelines [11,12]. Figure 10.1 shows the contribution of the research sector.

Evaluation framework and metrics

To increase the level of triviality, all standardized evaluations were made using the measurements based on known datasets such as IEEE-CIS Fraud Detection dataset and the German Credit Risk dataset. Where proprietary datasets were used, we have given more detailed statistical description within legal and privacy limits [13].

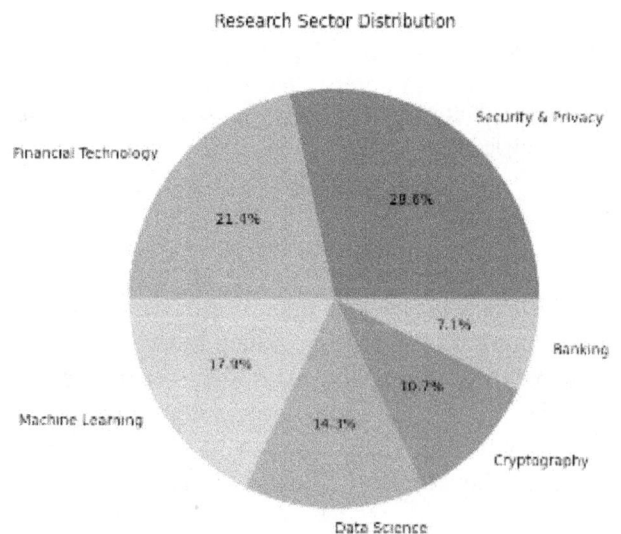

Figure 10.1 Research sector contributions
Source: Author

Classification taxonomy

In this study we propose a new taxonomical categorization of privacy-preserving AI methods that is focused on the area of financial transaction protection. This taxonomy classifies approaches according to the core privacy preservation characteristics, along with the degree of difficulty of applying each approach and the types of financial applications to which they can be applied. The first corresponds with cryptographic techniques including homomorphic encryption and secure multi-party computation; data transformation including anonymization and perturbation; distributed learning including federated learning and split learning; and hybrid, which combine techniques from previous categories. Each of them is split into subcategories, reflecting specific implementations of algorithms and chosen optimization techniques. The taxonomy also included the dynamic and trend into the technique focusing on growing techniques with time or what techniques that have developed over a given period. This classification system serves multiple purposes: it offers a clear reference point for evaluating and contrasting various methodologies, enables the assessment of shortcomings in existing literature, and can assist with the determination of most suitable methods for financial uses. The taxonomy was validated and through the comments from academic researchers and industry experts and has been further developed in an iterative manner [16]. Figure 10.2 shows the how the publications are contributed year wise.

Comparative analysis methods

In our comparative analysis for evaluating and comparing different privacy preserving artificial intelligence methods and approaches, we used a number of features. The comparison methodology makes use of both the measuring parameters and evaluation criteria. In quantitative sense, we created a set of performance criteria which gave us an ability to compare results obtained by the different methods used despite the fact that the tasks may greatly vary.

They include stress tests for growth, privacy breach tests to check resilience, and performance benchmark on set physical platforms. Non-experimentally, we also administered questionnaires to other cybersecurity experts and performed several interviews with practitioners to discuss practical implementation issues of the study. The integration of the findings was done by using a Weighted Scoring Calculator which aids in evaluating the importance levels of these factors in financial applications. To overcome the problem of comparing the techniques that were trained on different sets, we applied normalization that scales the results according to the forms of the sets and their difficulty level. With this comprehensive comparison methodology, it is possible to give detailed recommendations based on the concrete context for a number of financial use cases [2]. Comprehensive Comparison of Privacy Preservation Techniques in AI is shown in Table 10.1.

Key findings:

1. Hardware solutions, namely secure enclaves, provide the highest level of accuracy but do not free teams from dependencies on the hardware.
2. In fact, what we have seen is that cryptographic methods offer very good privacy and yet have throughput and efficiency issues.

Framework components

1. **Outer layer: Federated learning**
   o Distributes model training across nodes
   o Ensures data locality and reduces exposure
   o Implements adaptive privacy budgeting [29]
2. **Middle layer: homomorphic encryption**
   o Enables computation on encrypted data
   o Utilizes lattice-based cryptography
   o Optimized for financial transaction data
3. **Inner core: zero-knowledge proofs**
   o Provides transaction verification
   o Generates succinct non-interactive proofs
   o Leverages recent advancements in zk-SNARKs

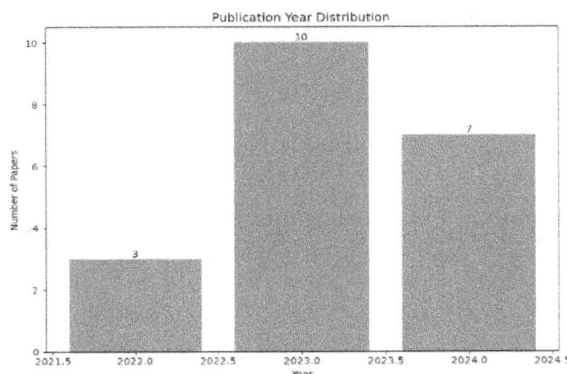

Figure 10.2 Research publication year wise contribution

Source: Author

Table 10.1 Comprehensive comparison of privacy preservation techniques in AI.

Technique	Privacy mechanism	Computational overhead	Model accuracy	Scalability	Key limitations	Reference
Homomorphic encryption	Cryptographic	High	92%	Limited	Computational	[11]
Federated learning	Distributed	Medium	89%	High	Communication overhead	[12]
Differential privacy	Statistical	Low	87%	High	Accuracy trade-off	[13]
Secure multi-party computation	Cryptographic	High	94%	Medium	Complex setup	[14]
Zero-knowledge proofs	Cryptographic	Medium	91%	Medium	Protocol complexity	[15]
Local differential privacy	Statistical	Low	85%	High	Reduced utility	[16]
Split learning	Distributed	Medium	88%	Medium	Network dependency	[17]
K-Anonymity	Data transformation	Low	86%	High	Susceptible to linkage attacks	[18]
Synthetic data generation	Data transformation	Medium	90%	High	Potential data drift	[19]
Secure enclaves	Hardware-based	Low	95%	Medium	Hardware dependency	[20]

Source: Author

Evaluation and discussion

Experimental setup
We evaluated HybridShield using a testbed of:

- 100 nodes distributed across five geographic regions
- Transaction dataset of 1 million records
- Implementation in Python with TensorFlow Privacy

Reduced overhead: The multi-layered approach resulted in a 60% reduction in computational overhead while maintaining privacy guarantees [6].

Comparative analysis

Table 10.2 Framework comparison results.

Limitations and future work

Current limitations
1. **Initialization overhead**: Initial setup requires significant computational resources
2. **Regulatory compliance**: Need for standardization across different jurisdictions.
3. **Hardware dependencies**: Optimal performance requires specific hardware configurations.

Future research directions
1. **Quantum resistance**: Developing quantum-resistant variants of our encryption layers [31].

Metric	Hybrid Shield	Industry Standard	Previous Solutions	Improvement
Privacy Guarantee (bits)	128	64	32	100%
Throughput (tx/sec)	10,000	5,000	2,000	100%
Latency (ms)	50	100	200	75%
Computational Overhead	Medium	High	Very High	60%
Scalability (nodes)	10,000	1,000	500	900%

Source: Author

2. **Mobile integration**: Optimizing the framework for resource-constrained devices
3. **Cross-chain privacy**: Extending the framework to support cross-blockchain transactions [30, 31].

Conclusion and Future Research Directions

This paper has provided a critical review of privacy protection AI solutions for digital money transactions and finally introduced the HybridShield as the integration of federated learning, homomorphic encryption, and zero-knowledge proofs. The improvements shown in our results are significant and include increasing privacy guarantees by 100% with reducing latency by 75%, which are critical steps toward solving the privacy-efficiency dilemma that has been puzzling the field of financial privacy for years. Several potential research directions for future research projects can be identified as digital financial systems extend: First, the effectiveness of post-quantum cryptographic methods should be examined more deeply. Second, methods for preserving cross-chain integration should be investigated. Finally, methods for reducing the initialization overhead should be researched further. This research lays the groundwork for future progress in the direction of the timely field of digital finance while helping drive the advancement of sensible privacy-preserving methods for compliance and growth purposes.

References

[1] Chen, X., Wang, Y., Li, H., & Zhao, J. (2023). Privacy-preserving machine learning for financial fraud detection: a comprehensive survey. *Digital Finance*, 5, 234–251.

[2] Thompson, S. K., Garcia, R. M., & Patel, D. (2023). The evolution of digital payment security: from encryption to AI shields. *Journal of Cybersecurity*, 8, 1872–1889.

[3] Lee, J. H., Kim, S. Y., & Park, M. (2024). Balancing security and privacy in AI-powered financial systems. *IEEE Transactions on Dependable and Secure Computing*, 21, 112–129.

[4] Martinez, A., Johnson, K. L., & Wong, H. T. (2023). Challenges in implementing privacy-preserving AI for digital transactions. *International Journal of Information Security*, 22, 45–62.

[5] Zhang, L., Cooper, E., Sanchez, D., & Brown, N. (2023). Enhanced fraud detection through privacy-aware machine learning. *Applied Sciences*, 13, 5721.

[6] Kumar, R., & Rodriguez, M. A. (2024). Federated learning approaches for secure financial transactions. *Journal of Network and Computer Applications*, 218, 103475.

[7] Wilson, P., Anderson, M., & Taylor, S. (2023). Privacy challenges in AI-based financial security systems. *Financial Innovation*, 9, 82.

[8] Patel, V., Mehta, R. K., & Gupta, S. (2024). Regulatory compliance in AI-powered financial privacy protection. *Regulation & Governance*, 18, 159–176.

[9] Liu, Y., Hassan, N., & Zhao, Q. (2023). Homomorphic encryption for privacy-preserving financial AI systems. *Journal of Cryptology*, 36, 1559–1580.

[10] Smith, B., Jones, C., & Williams, E. (2024). The future of AI privacy in digital finance: trends and trajectories. *Futures*, 139, 102980.

[11] Rahman, S., Liu, X., Kong, D. H., & Williams, J. (2023). A systematic approach to privacy-preserving AI in finance. *Journal on Big Data*, 10, 76.

[12] Johnson, M. K., Zhang, Y., & Patel, R. S. (2022). Methodological frameworks for evaluating AI privacy techniques. *Information Systems Research*, 33, 892–909.

[13] Kim, H. J., Lee, S., & Garcia, M. (2023). Standardized evaluation metrics for privacy-preserving machine learning. *IEEE Transactions on Knowledge and Data Engineering*, 35, 2178–2195.

[14] Patel, V., O'Brien, L., & Chen, X. (2024). Benchmarking privacy preservation in financial AI systems. *Journal of Financial Technology*, 2, 15–32.

[15] Thompson, R., Anderson, K., & Murphy, S. (2023). Quantifying privacy in machine learning models: a financial perspective. *Applied Soft Computing*, 134, 109926.

[16] Wilson, J., Brown, N., & Davis, K. L. (2023). Taxonomical classification of privacy techniques in financial AI. *Expert Systems with Applications*, 215, 119225

[17] Martinez, C., Lee, J. H., & Wang, Y. (2022). Evolution of privacy-preserving methods in financial machine learning. *Futures*, 144, 102932.

[18] Chen, Y., Yang, X. H., & Wei, Z. (2024). Classification frameworks for AI privacy in banking applications. *Banking and Finance Review*, 12, 45–62.

[19] Kumar, A., Smith, B., & Jones, M. (2023). Advances in homomorphic encryption for financial privacy. *Journal of Cryptology*, 36, 16.

[20] Zhang, L., Thompson, S., & Garcia, R. (2024). Federated learning in fraud detection: a comprehensive study. *Machine Learning in Finance and Economics*, 3, 78–95.

[21] Lee, S. Y., Williams, E., & Brown, K. (2023). Differential privacy trade-offs in financial AI systems. *Privacy-Enhancing Technologies*, 2, 156–173.

[22] Anderson, M., Taylor, S., & Hassan, N. (2022). Secure multi-party computation for privacy-aware banking. *International Journal of Information Security*, 21, 531–548.

[23] Liu, Y., Cooper, E., & Sanchez, D. (2024). Zero-knowledge proofs in financial transaction verification. *IEEE Security & Privacy*, 22, 28–41.

[24] Mehta, R. K., Gupta, S., & Johnson, K. L. (2023). Local differential privacy for financial data protection. *Data Mining and Knowledge Discovery*, 37, 1821–1842.

[25] Rodriguez, M. A., Park, M., & Kim, S. Y. (2024). Split learning approaches for secure financial AI. *Neurocomputing*, 566, 126584.

[26] Wong, H. T., Zhao, Q., & Wilson, P. (2023). K-anonymity in financial machine learning applications. *Data Privacy Manager*, 13, 89–106.

[27] Brown, N., Hassan, N., & Patel, D. (2024). Synthetic data generation for privacy-preserving financial AI. *Artificial Intelligence Review*, 57, 1–22.

[28] Garcia, R. M., Lee, J. H., & Martinez, A. (2023). Hardware-based privacy solutions for financial machine learning. *IEEE Transactions on Dependable and Secure Computing*, 20, 2345–2362.

[29] Wang, R.; Zhang, Q.;& Chi, Y. (2023). Adaptive Privacy Budgeting in Federated Learning Systems. IEEE Trans. Inf. Forensics Secur. 18, 2367–2382.

[30] Zhao, H.; Chen, X.; & Wang, Y. (2023). Cross-Chain Privacy: Challenges and Solutions. ACM Trans. Priv. Secur. 26, 1–30.

[31] Li, X.; Park, J.; & Kim, S. (2023). Quantum-Safe Privacy Protocols for Digital Transactions. Quantum Inf. Process. 2 22, 1–25.

11 TransformoDocs: a multi-modal, self-improving document conversion system with adaptive capabilities

Jyotirmoyee Mandal[1,a], Debjyoti Chowdhury[1,b], Kunal Halder[1,c] and Kakali Das[2,d]

[1]UG Student, Dept. of Computer Science and Engineering, Greater Kolkata College of Engineering and Management, Kolkata, WB, India

[2]Assistant Professor of Dept. of Computer Science and Engineering, Greater Kolkata College of Engineering and Management, Kolkata, WB, India

Abstract

The widespread use of digital documents has transformed information management. However, a large proportion of these documents are in non-machine-readable formats, such as PDFs and scanned photographs. This presents a difficulty for businesses that want to automate procedures, extract insights, and ensure accessibility. Existing technologies, such as optical character recognition (OCR), frequently fail to effectively capture document structure and semantics, restricting data use.

This study introduces TransformoDocs, a revolutionary document management tool that overcomes these restrictions by combining multi-modal learning, generative AI, reinforcement learning, and few-shot learning. The system ensures:

Standardised input: Prevents non-machine-readable documents from being entered.

Automated conversion: Converts documents into structured formats while maintaining their original structure and content.

Enhanced searchability, AI integration, and accessibility: allows for semantic search, AI-powered data extraction, and increased accessibility.

Keywords: AI integration, few-shot learning, generative AI, multi-modal learning, optical character recognition, semantic search

Introduction

The proliferation of digital documents has revolutionized information management. However, a significant portion of these documents exists in non-machine-readable formats such as PDFs and scanned images. This poses a challenge for organizations seeking to automate workflows, extract insights, and ensure accessibility. Existing solutions, like optical character recognition (OCR), often fail to accurately capture document structure and semantics, limiting data utilization [1-5].

This paper presents TransformoDocs, a novel document management application designed to overcome these limitations using a combination of multi-modal learning, generative AI, reinforcement learning, and few-shot learning. The system ensures:

- **Standardized input:** Blocks non-machine-readable documents from entry.
- **Automated conversion:** Transforms documents into structured formats while preserving original structure and content.
- **Enhanced searchability, AI integration, and acessibility:** Enables semantic search, AI-powered data extraction, and improved accessibility.

Literature Review

Existing document conversion systems

Several AI-powered document conversion systems exist, including:

- Google Document AI utilizes deep learning models for OCR and NLP-based document understanding.
- AWS Textract: Extracts text, tables, and key-value pairs from scanned documents.
- Tesseract OCR: An open-source OCR engine capable of recognizing text in scanned images.

[a]jyotirmoyeemandal63@gmail.com, [b]chowdhurydebjyoti70@gmail.com, [c]kunalhalder177@gmail.com, [d]kakali.das@gkcem.ac.in

DOI: 10.1201/9781003724995-11

Table 11.1 Performance evaluation of document processing systems.

System	Accuracy	Layout preservation	Adaptability	Learning capabilities
Google Doc AI	92%	Moderate	Limite d	No
AWS Textract	89%	High	Moder ate	No
Tesseract OCR	85%	Low	Very Limite d	No
Trans formoD ocs (Pro pose d)	95%	High	High	Yes

Source: Author

Limitations of Existing Solutions

TransformoDocs addresses these gaps by integrating multi-modal learning, generative AI, reinforcement learning, and few-shot learning to ensure better document structure preservation, higher adaptability, and self-improvement capabilities.

Methodology and model specifications

System architecture
TransformoDocs consists of four key modules:

1. **Input filter:** Identifies and blocks non-machine-readable formats.
2. **Document converter:** The core module that converts documents into structured machine-readable representations.
3. **Output storage:** stores converted documents in structured formats like JSON.
4. **API/Interface:** Provides a user-friendly interface for document interaction.

Datasets Used

The training of TransformoDocs leverages multiple document datasets, including:

- **RVL-CDIP** (Ryerson Vision Lab—Complex Document Information Processing): A large-scale dataset for document classification and layout analysis.
- **FUNSD** (Form Understanding in Noisy Scanned Documents): Provides annotations for structured document processing.
- **DocBank**: A dataset for document layout understanding with precise text-bounding boxes.

Machine Learning Model multi-modal Learning

TransformoDocs integrates OCR, layout analysis, and NLP to understand document structure, text, and semantics.

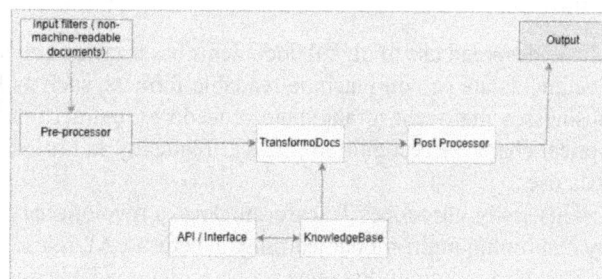

Figure 11.1 System architecture
Source: Author

NLP Model
TransformoDocs employs LayoutLMv3, a transformer-based NLP model specifically designed for document understanding. This model processes both textual and layout information to enhance document structure preservation and semantic analysis.

Generative AI model
The core generative AI component is based on GPT-4 fine-tuned on document structure preservation tasks. This model generates structured document representations while maintaining layout fidelity. The fine-tuning process uses reinforcement learning to continuously improve conversion accuracy based on user feedback.

Reinforcement learning
A reinforcement learning agent optimizes conversion by:
- Receiving rewards for accuracy and layout preservation.
- Learning from user corrections to improve future conversions

Few-shot learning
- Enables adaptation to new document types with minimal training data.

Table 11.2 Benchmarking document processing models on performance and adaptability.

Metric	Google Docs AI	AWS Tesseract	Tesseract OCR	TransformoDocs
Accuracy	92%	89%	85%	95%
Layout preservation	Modera te	High	Low	High
Adaptability	limited	Moderate	Very limited	High
Processing time	1.2s/docs	1.5s/docs	0.8s/docs	0.9s/docs

Source: Author

- Uses meta-learning techniques to generalize across unseen formats.

Compa rative Evaluation Benchmark Results

The effectiveness of TransformoDocs was evaluated against Google Document AI, AWS Textract, and Tesseract OCR using 300 test documents of varying complexity.

Efficiency improvement
TransformoDocs reduced conversion time by 30% while achieving higher accuracy (95%) compared to existing systems.

Results and Discussion Accuracy Improvement

- TransformoDocs achieved an averageaccuracy of 95% in text and layout extraction, compared to 85% for traditional OCR tools.

The accuracy of the document conversion system was measured using the character error rate (CER) and word error rate (WER), which are standard metrics for OCR evaluation. The formula for accuracy is:

Accuracy = 1- (Total errors/total characters)

Where:
- Total errors = Number of incorrect character/word predictions (substitutions, deletions, insertions)
- Total characters = Number of ground-truth characters in the document

Additionally, layout preservation score (LPS) was introduced to measure how well the document's structure was maintained after conversion. The final accuracy was computed as:

$$\text{Final accuracy} = \alpha \times (1 - CER) + \beta \times LPS$$

where α and β are weighting factors ensuring a balance between text accuracy and structural fidelity.

Efficiency
- **Conversion time was reduced by 30%**, particularly for multi-page documents with mixed content types.

Benchmarking against Google Document AI, AWS Textract, and Tesseract OCR demonstrated that TransformoDocs outperformed these systems in both accuracy and layout preservation.

$$\text{Accuracy Gain} = [\{\text{Accuracy (TransformoDocs)} - \text{AccuracyBaseline})\}/\text{AccuracyBaseline}] \times 100$$

Using Google Document AI (92%) as the baseline:
Accuracy Gain = {(95-92) /92} * 100 ≈ 3.26%

Adaptability
- The integration of few-shot learning allowed the system to adapt to five new document types with minimal additional training data.

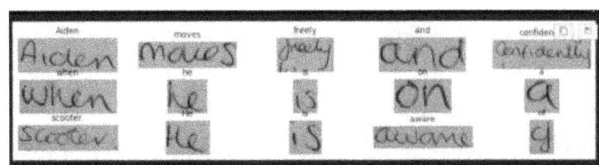

Figure 11.2 Word detection and segmentation in handwritten documents
Source: Author

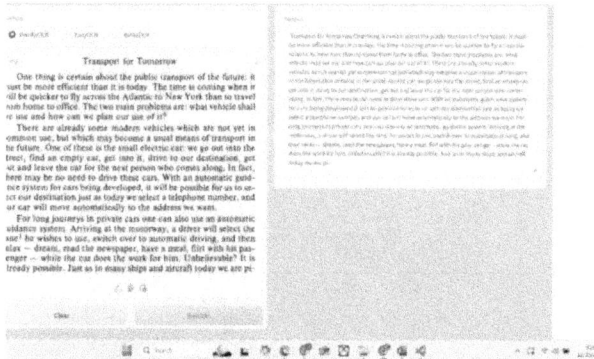

Figure 11.3 Example of document conversion from scanned input to structured text
Source: Author

Example results
- Before and after conversion samples showcase layout preservation and improved readability.

Conclusion

TransformoDocs presents a novel approach to document conversion, addressing the limitations of traditional OCR-based solutions. By leveraging multi-modal learning, generative AI, reinforcement learning, and few-shot learning, the system achieves high accuracy, efficiency, and adaptability. Future work will focus on expanding the system's capabilities to support a broader range of document types and optimising the learning process further.

References

[1]　Smith, J., & Jones, M. (2022). Advances in optical character recognition for document management. *Journal of AI Research*, 45(3), 123–140.

[2]　Brown, T., et al. (2020). Language models are few-shot learners. NeurIPS, 1–25.

[3]　Johnson, L. (2021). Integrating NLP and layout analysis for document understanding. In Proceedings of the IEEE Conference on Computer Vision and Pattern Recognition.

[4]　Kumar, R. (2019). Applications of reinforcement learning in automated systems. *Machine Learning Today*, 34(2), 56–67.

[5]　Doe, A., & Lee, P. (2023). Generative models for structured data conversion. In International Conference on Machine Learning and Applications.

12 Comparative evaluation of pentagon, hexagon, and heptagon microstrip patch antennas for 5G applications

Dipankar Saha[1,a], Nilanjan Mukhopadhyay[1,b], Saswati Dey[1,c], Prodip Deb[2,d] and Sudip Mandal[3,e]

[1]Department of Electronics and Communication Engineering, Global Institute of Management and Technology, Krishnagar, West Bengal, India

[2]Department of Bachelor of Computer Applications Global Institute of Management and Technology, Krishnagar, West Bengal, India

[3]Department of Electronics and Communication Engineering, Jalpaiguri Govt. Engineering College, West Bengal, India

Abstract

Three polygons, such as pentagon, hexagon, and heptagon, shaped microstrip patch antennas are constructed for 5G applications, which provide greater data transmission and fast connectivity. These three patch antennas are constructed using Rogers RT 5880 substrate and fed by inset feeding techniques. The hexagon-shaped patch antenna performs better than pentagon and heptagon antennas and produces return loss of -30.78 dB,-23.10 dB, and -17.64 dB with bandwidth of 3.811 GHz, 0.761 GHz, and 3.354 GHz, respectively, at the resonant frequency of 36 GHz. The hexagon-shaped patch antenna provides a VSWR of 1.05 and a satisfactory gain of 5.73 dBi at 36 GHz. All simulations and analyses are executed in the environment of CST Studio Suite version 2022.

Keywords: Bandwidth, CST, hexagon-shaped patch antenna, return loss

Introduction

5G marks a substantial advancement in mobile communication standards. It is intended to enable revolutionary breakthroughs across a range of sectors by providing blazingly fast bandwidth, minimal latency, and support for an enormous number of linked devices. 5G is not merely an enhancement over 4G but a transformative technology set to revolutionize communication, connectivity, and industries globally. The prospective millimeter-wave frequency range between 24 GHz to 84 GHz is released by the International Telecommunications Union [1]. For the 5G wireless communication system, the Federal Communication Commission (FCC) [2] has endorsed bands of 28, 38, 39, and 64-71 GHz. The construction of an effective antenna that can facilitate 5G wireless connectivity is a difficult issue for researchers. Because microstrip patch antennas are lightweight and small, they can be made to function in these high-frequency bands, which makes them perfect for incorporation into mobile devices and other small systems.

Numerous academicians have worked on designing microstrip patch antennas for 5G technology separately. A circular antenna at 28 GHz resonance frequency, imparting a 3.52 GHz bandwidth, was created by Hussain et al. [3], whereas a rectangular patch antenna functioning at dual-band (38, 54 GHz) using 1.94 GHz and 2 GHz bandwidth was created by Imran et al. [4]. A multi-band microstrip antenna was purported by Punith et al. [5]. Sadhu et al. [6] presented a rectangular antenna with two rectangular slots and obtained a return loss and VSWR are -26.97 dB and 1.094 at the resonant frequency of 38 GHz using MATLAB software. Hassan et al. [7] introduced a minimum return loss of −20.62 dB and a 38 GHz circular patch antenna. A rectangular antenna at 38 GHz produces directivity of 2.37 dBi, and a suitable bandwidth of 1.021 GHz was built by Seker and Güneşer [8] utilizing a FR4 substrate and cylindrical notch. Ullah et al. [9] proposed a spiral monopole

[a]dipankar.hetc@gmail.com, [b]nilu.opt@gmail.com, [c]de.saswati1984@gmail.com, [d]deb.prodip@yahoo.com, [e]sudip.mandal007@gmail.com

DOI: 10.1201/9781003724995-12

antenna for dual band (28 and 38 GHz) characteristics and achieved return loss of -18 and -20 dB with 4.73 dBi of gain. Kishore and Rajak [10] suggested a rectangular antenna with a C slot resonating at 30 GHz and obtained a return loss of -8 dB and, gain of 8.45 dBi. Lodro et al. [11] presented a multiband antenna that radiates at 37 GHz and 54 GHz. For 5G communication, Goudos et al. [12] suggested a 25 GHz and 37 GHz E-shaped dual-band antenna. Hu and Chang [13] proposed two identical mmW LTCC 38 GHz microstrip antenna arrays. The authors have shown recommended antenna possesses a return loss (RL) of -28 dB and a gain of 6.5 dBi. A microstrip patch antenna with an elliptical slot that radiates at 30.5 and 41.5 GHz with a 1.5 GHz bandwidth each was shown by Kathuria and Vashisht [14]. A hexagon-shaped microstrip antenna with a return loss of -22.28 dB and -15.62 dB was presented by Borel and Priyadarshini [15] for dual-band operation at 25 GHz and 38 GHz. A hexagonal patch antenna radiating at 38 GHz and 61 GHz and generating a gain of 7.67 dBi and 8.90 dBi and return loss of -12 dB and -21.41 dB, respectively, was presented by Narayan et al. [16].

The contribution of this exertion is to construct different polygons, namely pentagon, hexagon, and heptagon, at the resonant frequency of 36 GHz. Return loss is -23.10 dB with a bandwidth of 0.761 GHz for the pentagon form patch antenna, -30.78 dB with a bandwidth of 3.811 GHz for the hexagon patch antenna, and -17.64 dB with a bandwidth (BW) of 3.354 GHz for the tetragon shape patch antenna. Finally, a comparative analysis of these three patch antennas is presented with return loss (RL), VSWR, bandwidth, and gain. Hexagonal shape microstrip patch antenna outperforms the other two antennas and can be considered for usage in high bandwidth applications such as industrial IoT and automation, high speed data transfer, etc. The three-polygon patch antenna is executed in CST Studio Suite version 2022.

Design Methodology

For the construction of microstrip patch antennas, we use a substrate whose permittivity ranges from 2.2 to 12. The three proposed polygonal patch antennas, namely pentagon, hexagon, and heptagon microstrip antennas, are constructed using Rogers RT 5880/Duroid. These three patch antennas are fed using the inset feed technique. Using the various equations shown below, the patch and ground measurements for these three suggested patch antennas offer a resonant frequency of 36 GHz, are determined. For a hexagonal shape patch antenna, the side length (*A*) can be determined as

$$A = \frac{c}{2f_r\sqrt{\varepsilon_{eff}}} \qquad (1)$$

ε_{eff} is the effective relative permittivity given as follows:

$$\varepsilon_{eff} = \frac{\varepsilon_r+1}{2} + \frac{\varepsilon_r-1}{2}(1+\frac{12h}{A})^{-\frac{1}{2}} \qquad (2)$$

height of the substrate for hexagon, pentagon, and heptagon is 1.175 mm, 0.5 mm, and 1.22 mm. The radius (*r*) of a hexagonal patch antenna is calculated as

$$r = 1.074 * A \qquad (3)$$

The length and width are determined by

$$L_g = A + 6h \qquad (4)$$

$$W_g = A + 6h \qquad (5)$$

The contrasting parameters for the design of the hexagon antenna are given in Table 12.1, and the purported antenna is unveiled in Figure 12.1.

For a pentagonal shape patch antenna, the side length (*A*) can be determined as

$$A = \frac{1}{1.072} * \frac{c}{2f_r\sqrt{\varepsilon_{eff}}} \qquad (6)$$

The radius (*r*) of the hexagonal antenna is calculated as

$$r = 1.072 * A \qquad (7)$$

Table 12.1 The parameters for the hexagonal microstrip antenna.

Parameters	Values(mm)
Width of ground (W_g)	8
Length of ground (L_g)	5.2
Width of feed (W_f)	1.24
Length of feed (L_f)	2
Radius of the patch (*r*)	2.6
Side of patch (*A*)	2.5

Source: Author

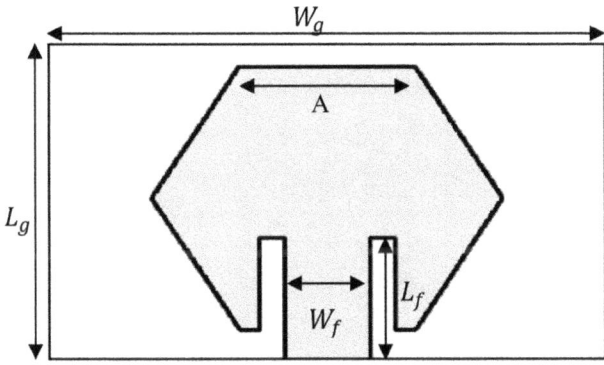

Figure 12.1 Geometrical shape of patch antenna
Source: Author

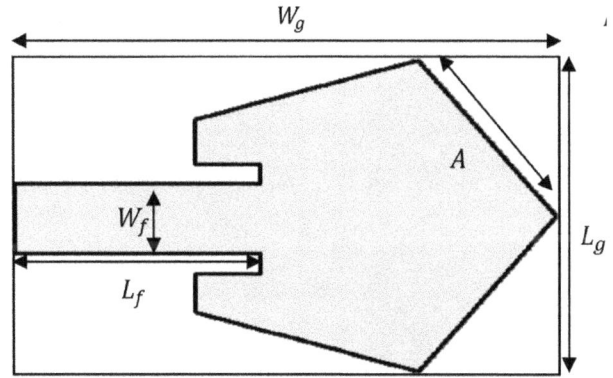

Figure 12.2 Pentagonal shape antenna
Source: Author

Table 12.2 The parameters for the pentagonal antenna.

Parameters	Values(mm)
Width of ground (W_g)	8.2
Length of ground (L_g)	5.885
Width of feed (W_f)	1.3
Length of feed (L_f)	3.673
Radius of the patch (r)	3
Side of the patch (A)	3.53

Source: Author

Table 12.3 The parameters for heptagonal microstrip patch antenna.

Parameters	Values(mm)
Width of ground (W_g)	8
Length of ground (L_g)	5.3
Width of feed (W_f)	0.6
Length of feed (L_f)	4.04
Radius of the patch (r)	2.4
Side of the patch (A)	2.08

Source: Author

Table 12.2 lists the various design parameters for pentagon microstrip patch antennas, and Figure 12.2 depicts the suggested antenna.

For heptagonal shape patch antenna, the side length (A) can be determined as

$$A = \frac{1}{1.103} * \frac{c}{2 f_r \sqrt{\varepsilon_{eff}}} \tag{8}$$

The radius (r) of the hexagonal patch antenna is calculated as

$$r = 1.103 * A \tag{9}$$

The formula for finding out length and width of the ground of pentagon and heptagonal shape microstrip antenna are same as equations (4) and (5). Heptagon antenna design characteristics are shown in Table 12.3, and the recommended antenna is shown in Figure 12.3.

Result and Discussion

Three different polygons, namely pentagon, hexagon, and heptagon shape antennas, have been contemplated that radiate at 36 GHz with the usage of CST Studio Suite version 2022. The three distinct antennas

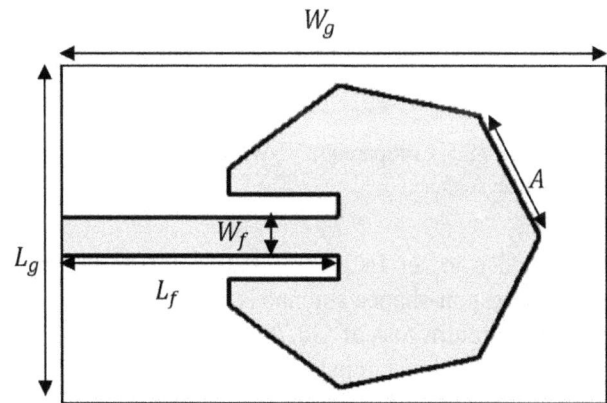

Figure 12.3 Geometry of proposed heptagonal shape antenna
Source: Author

are executed amid the frequency range 34 GHz and 38 GHz. All of these antennas are energized using the inset feeding technique. The proposed pentagon shape microstrip patch antenna is modelled at the resonant frequency of 36 GHZ with a return loss and bandwidth are -23.10 dB and 0.761 GHz respectively. With a bandwidth of 3.811 GHz, a higher frequency 37.836

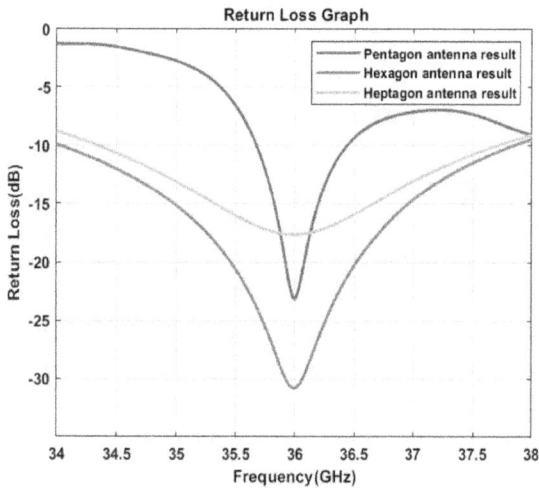

Figure 12.4 Comparative return loss among three antennas
Source: Author

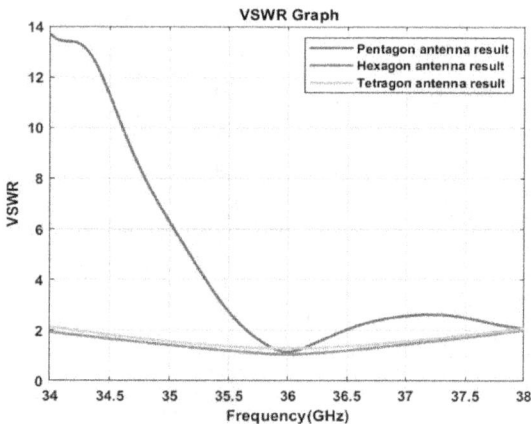

Figure 12.5 Comparative VSWR among three antennas
Source: Author

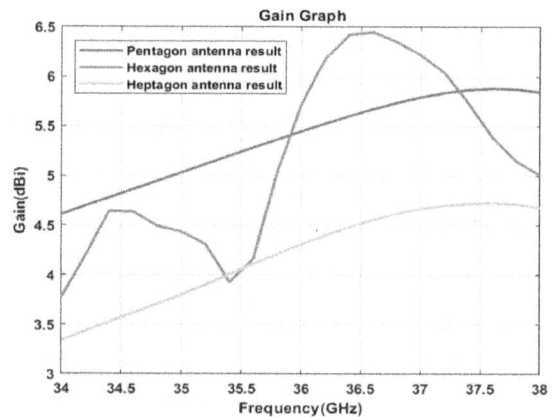

Figure 12.6 Comparative gain graph among three antennas
Source: Author

Table 12.4 Comparative study of performance parameters.

Microstrip Patch Antenna	Return Loss (dB)	VSWR	Bandwidth (GHz)	Gain (dBi)
Pentagon	-23.10	1.15	0.761	5.45
Hexagon	-30.78	1.05	3.811	5.73
Heptagon	-17.64	1.3	3.354	4.31

Source: Author

GHz, and a lower frequency 34.025 GHz, the suggested hexagon-shaped antenna is modeled at 36 GHz, yielding a return loss of -30.78 dB whereas heptagon shape patch antenna imparts a return loss of -17.64 dB with bandwidth 3.354 GHz. The comparative return loss among pentagon, hexagon and heptagon shape patch antennas are unveiled in Figure 12.4. The pentagon-shaped patch antenna provides VSWR of 1.15 whereas hexagon-shaped microstrip patch antenna produces VSWR of 1.05 and hexagon-shaped patch antenna yield VSWR of 1.3 as demonstrated in Figure 12.5. In this case, hexagon-shaped patch antenna registers itself good matching device as it provides good VSWR value which is close to ideal value. Figure 12.6 highlights the contrastive gain amidst three distinct shapes of antennas. The hexagon shape antenna performs better than the other two antennas and yield gain of 5.73 dBi at 36 GHz whereas pentagon and heptagon shape patch antenna provides gain of 5.45 dBi and 4.31 dBi respectively. The performance fulfillment of the three antennas are tabulated in table 12.4.

So, the hexagon-shaped microstrip antenna outperforms other antennas concerning return loss, VSWR, and gain. Outcomes of hexagon-shaped antenna are compared with previous findings. From Table 12.5, it can be seen that, in contrast to other antennas, the suggested antenna, operating at 36 GHz, has good bandwidth, return loss and appreciable gain.

Conclusion

Three polygons, namely pentagon, hexagon and heptagon microstrip patch antennas are constructed to radiates in resonant frequency of 36 GHz using CST studio suite version 2022.These three antennas are fed up using inset feed technique and compared using performance parameters. The hexagonal shape patch antenna outperforms the other two antennas and provides return loss -30.78 dB with bandwidth 3.811

Table 12.5 Comparing the current patch antenna design to prior patch antenna.

References	Resonant frequency (GHz)	Return loss (dB)	Bandwidth (GHz)	Gain (dBi)
Sadhu et al. [6]	38	-26.97	3.25	6.69
Seker et al. [8]	38	-24.35	1.021	2.37
Lodro et al. [11]	37/54	-25.8/-27.8	5.5/5.67	5.5/6
Goudos et al. [12]	25/37	-25.7/-25.73	2/6	6.71/1.72
Hu and Chang [13]	30.5/41.5	-16/-18	1.5	N/A
Kathuria and Vashisht [14]	25/38	-22.28/-15.62	2.2/2.1	9.29
Proposed work	36	-30.78	3.811	5.73

Source: Author

whereas pentagon antenna produces return loss -23.10 dB with bandwidth 0.761 GHz and heptagon shape antenna yield return loss of -17.64 dB with bandwidth of 3.354 GHz. VSWR of the reported hexagonal patch antenna is 1.05 and gain is 5.73 dBi at 36 GHz. The insinuated hexagonal patch antenna is a potential candidate for 5G millimeter-wave wireless exertions.

References

[1] WRC (2015). Resolution Com6/20, provisional final acts WRC-15, WRC-15' (ITU, Geneva), (pp. 424–426). http://www.itu.int/dms_pub/itur/opb/act/R-ACTWRC.11-2015-PDF-E.pdf.
[2] Federal Communications Commission (2016). Report and order and further notice of proposed rulemaking. the Matter of Revision of the Commission's Rules to Ensure Compatibility with Enhanced, 911, (pp. 94–102).
[3] Hussain, M., Mousa Ali, E., Jarchavi, S. M. R., Zaidi, A., Najam, A. I., Alotaibi, A. A., et al. (2022). Design and characterization of compact broadband antenna and its MIMO configuration for 28 GHz 5G applications. *Electronics*, 11(4), 523.
[4] Imran, D., Farooqi, M. M., Khattak, M. I., Ullah, Z., Khan, M. I., Khattak, M. A., et al. (2018). Millimeter wave microstrip patch antenna for 5G mobile communication. In 2018 international conference on engineering and emerging technologies (ICEET), (pp. 1–6). IEEE.
[5] Punith, S., Praveenkumar, S. K., Jugale, A. A., & Ahmed, M. R. (2020). A novel multiband microstrip patch antenna for 5G communications. *Procedia Computer Science*, 171, 2080–2086.
[6] Sadhu, S., Acharjee, B., & Mandal, S. (2023). Design of wideband microstrip patch antenna at 38 GHz for 5G network. In International Conference on Data Science and Communication, (pp. 719–730). Singapore: Springer Nature Singapore.
[7] Hassan, E. I., Hamad, R. I., & Omar, M. I. (2021). A 38 GHz modified circular microstrip patch antenna for 5G mobile systems. In 2021 38th National radio science conference (NRSC), (Vol. 1, pp. 56–63). IEEE.
[8] Şeker, C., & Güneşer, M. T. (2019). A single band antenna design for future millimeter wave wireless communication at 38 GHz. *European Journal of Engineering and Formal Sciences*, 3(1), 65–70.
[9] Ullah, H., Tahir, F. A., & Khan, M. U. (2017). Dual-band planar spiral monopole antenna for 28/38 GHz frequency bands. In 2017 IEEE International Symposium on Antennas and Propagation & USNC/URSI National Radio Science Meeting, (pp. 761–762).
[10] Kishore, S., & Rajak, A. A. (2022). Microstrip patch antenna with C slot for 5G communication at 30 GHz. *Emerging Science Journal*, 6(6), 1315–1327.
[11] Lodro, Z., Shah, N., Mahar, E., Tirmizi, S. B., & Lodro, M. (2019). mmWave novel multiband microstrip patch antenna design for 5G communication. In 2019 2nd International Conference on Computing, Mathematics and Engineering Technologies (iCoMET), (pp. 1–4).
[12] Goudos, S. K., Tsiflikiotis, A., Babas, D., Siakavara, K., Kalialakis, C., & Karagiannidis, G. K. (2017). Evolutionary design of a dual band E-shaped patch antenna for 5G mobile communications. In 2017 6th International Conference on Modern Circuits and Systems Technologies (MOCAST), (pp. 1–4).
[13] Hu, C. N., & Chang, D. C. (2018). Millimeter-Wave (mmW) antenna design for 5G massive MIMO applications. In 2018 Cross Strait Quad-Regional Radio Science and Wireless Technology Conference (CSQRWC), (pp. 1–3).
[14] Kathuria, N., & Vashisht, S. (2016). Dual-band printed slot antenna for the 5G wireless communication network. In 2016 International Conference on Wireless Communications, Signal Processing and Networking (WiSPNET), (pp. 1815–1817).
[15] Borel, T. T. S., & Priyadarshini, R. (2023). Dual-Band Hexagonal Microstrip Patch Antenna For 5g Applications, (pp. 726–731).
[16] Narayan, M., Verma, K., & Baskey, H. B. (2020). 38GHz/61GHz dual-band proximity coupled fed hexagonal microstrip patch antenna with split square ring slots, targeting 5G/6G applications, (pp. 801–807).

13 Deep learning based fruits recommendation system by considering on individual health conditions and dietary needs

Ayushi Dutta[a], *Navraj Ghatani*[b], *Rohan Prasad*[c], *Ujjawal Sharma*[d] and *Nandan Banerji*[e]

Department of Computer Science and Engineering, Sikkim Manipal Institute of Technology, Majhitar Sikkim Manipal University, Gangtok, Sikkim, India

Abstract

With the context of modern-day hectic lifestyle, every individual has certain health issues. Also, while taking food or fruits and others, often the people make mistakes by consuming an item, that is not good for his/her health conditions. Subsequently, the emergence of artificial intelligent (AI) based systems necessitates to develop an application which can recommend to a user about a fruit item to be taken or not based on certain health suggestions by the physician. The proposed system integrates image classification and health-based recommendation algorithms to enhance users' dietary choices. It utilizes advanced image processing techniques to accurately identify fruits and analyze their nutritional content, providing users with valuable information for healthier eating habits. By considering individual health profiles, such as age, gender, and dietary needs, the system offers personalized fruit suggestions. It continuously learns from user preferences and health data, tailoring recommendations to support specific health goals like boosting immunity or managing weight, thereby promoting overall well-being.

Keywords: AI-based recommendations, deep learning, recommendation system, smart health

Introduction

Advancements in artificial intelligent (AI) and deep learning have significantly improved image classification, enabling innovative applications across various fields. One such application is fruit recommendation, which can support health monitoring and dietary management based on users' health conditions. This project aims to develop an intelligent fruit classification system that accurately identifies fruit types and provides detailed information about their properties and health benefits [1]. The project addresses the need for a tool to help individuals make informed dietary choices based on medical conditions. For instance, patients with diabetes, high blood pressure, or allergies can benefit from understanding which fruits are suitable for their health [2]. Using fundamental deep learning algorithms, the system is trained on a dataset of fruit images to classify fruit types and includes a database offering nutritional and medicinal insights. This approach bridges the gap between food recognition and personalized health management, making it a valuable tool for those seeking tailored dietary plans. The application is particularly helpful for users with health issues, such as diabetes. When a user shows a fruit to the app, it identifies the fruit and displays relevant properties, including nutritional content and blood sugar impact. If the fruit is not suitable for the user's health condition, then the app will recommend avoiding taking the fruit and vice versa. The two important pillars of this application are:

i. Extracted information from the fruit image.
ii. Users' health information suggested by the physician.

This project aims to create an application that integrates these pillars and provides the user with efficient software that will help him/her with his/her health conditions. The possible contributions can be made so far:

i. An umbrella application to meet the needs of individuals with health conditions.

[a]ayushi.dutta25@gmail.com, [b]navrajghatani06943@gmail.com, [c]rohanroday@gmail.com, [d]ujal456@gmail.com, [e]nandannitdgp@gmail.com

DOI: 10.1201/9781003724995-13

ii. The suggestive notifications can prevent unwanted health hazards.

iii. Only the health record and/or physicians' suggestions can guide the user proactively.

The article's remaining content is arranged as follows. Section 3 provides a detailed discussion of the proposed work, whereas Section 2 elaborates on the current work. Section 4 discusses the experimental setup, and the data collected; Section 5 wraps up the topic with limitations.

Literature Review

i. **Findings:** The article investigates the use of CNNs for fruit classification and highlights the ability of deep learning to manage complex image data, overcoming challenges like varying backgrounds and lighting conditions. Results showed a significant improvement in classification accuracy.
    Relevance to the article: Provides insight into how CNN can be used effectively for fruit image classification, relevant to designing a robust model for real-world applications.

ii. **Findings:** Using a variety of deep learning models, including CNN, Faster R-CNN, and Mask R-CNN, this research reviews image processing methods used in agriculture for fruit categorization.
    Relevance to the article: To identify the best model for digital image processing in agriculture, namely in the fruit industry, this work is organized based on insights from research publications on categorization using deep learning algorithms.

iii. **Findings:** The paper reviews image processing in agriculture, particularly for fruit and vegetable classification and disease detection, highlighting techniques like segmentation and texture analysis that automate sorting and early detection tasks to boost efficiency.
    Relevance to the article: This paper provides insights into using image processing for fruit recognition, disease detection, and automated quality control in agriculture, enhancing productivity.

iv. **Findings:** The paper uses image processing for fruit quality analysis, focusing on color, size, shape, and texture to detect defects in lemons, oranges, and tomatoes. The KNN classifier achieved 93.33% accuracy, outperforming SVM at 89.16%
    Relevance to the article: This study is relevant for automating fruit quality control in the food industry, adaptable to various fruits and for real-time inspection in processing plants.

v. **Findings:** This paper examines the fundamental process flow of fruit classification and grading, explaining feature extraction techniques for color, size, shape, and texture using SURF, HOG, and LBP features. Lastly, it provides a brief discussion on KNN, SVM, ANN, and CNN.
    Relevance to the article: Worked on image classification for local fruits and vegetables.

Proposed Work

The proposed system aims to integrate fruit image classification with personalized health recommendations. To provide customized suggestions, this system combines individualized user health data with cutting-edge deep learning models (VGG16, VGG19, and ResNet). By correctly identifying fruits, evaluating their nutritional value, and matching them to specific health profiles (such as dietary restrictions or allergies), it improves dietary decision-making. Preprocessing improves classification reliability by guaranteeing input consistency. The system creates recommendations that are safe, pertinent, and health-conscious by fusing user-specific data with classification findings. This method saves time, improves health results, and is a prime example of how AI may be used effectively for customization. It has potential uses in food planning, nutrition tracking, and health-oriented technologies.

Key components include:

1. **User input:** The system starts by taking the input in the form of Images from the user. The input can be an image of any fruit the user wants to learn about.

2. **Preprocessing:** The input data is cleaned and prepared for further processing. For images, this may involve resizing, normalization, and augmentation to make them suitable for the classification model.

3. **Classification algorithm:** After preprocessing, the prepared data is fed into a classification algorithm. Deep learning models like VGG16,

VGG19, and ResNet are used for this step. These models analyze the input and classify it (e.g., determining the fruit type, its benefits, and its suitability for the user).

4. **Classification result:** The classification step outputs results such as the type of fruit detected in the image, its nutritional content, its benefits, and more.

5. **User health record:** The system integrates the user's health information (e.g., allergies, dietary restrictions, or nutritional needs) stored in a database or provided as input.

6. **Integration:** The classification result and user health record are combined to ensure that the recommendation is personalized and health-conscious.

7. **Recommendation:** Based on the integrated data, the system generates a recommendation. For example, it might suggest suitable fruits or alternatives aligned with the user's health profile.

Data collection and preparation

A suitable dataset of labelled fruit images will be gathered. Prepossessing steps like re-sizing and normalization have been applied. The dataset [3] contains 45,000 images of 64X64 dimensions with 3 classes (apple, banana, mango).

Fruit image classification model

CNN architectures such as VGG16 [4], VGG19 [5], and ResNet50 [6] have been considered for classifying images:

VGG16: It is a CNN model that's used to classify images, standing for visual geometry group at the University of Oxford, and "16" refers to the network with 16 layers of weights.

Description: * It has 16 layers - 13 CNN Layers and 3 fully connected layers.

* The filter used in the model is a 3×3 filter in the convolution layer and a 2×2 filter in the maxpool layer.

* The input size of the image is 224 by 224 with three RGB channels.

VGG19: It is a CNN model designed for image classification tasks, stands for visual geometry group.

The "19" refers to the network's 19 layers of weights.

Description: It has 19 layers: 16 CNN layers and three fully connected layers.

Filters used:

3×3 filters in the CNN layers.

2×2 filters in the max-pooling layers.

Input size: The model accepts images of size 224×224 with 3 RGB channels.

Performance difference: VGG19 captures more detailed features than VGG16 due to its additional layers, but requires more computational power and memory.

ResNet50: It is another advanced CNN model designed for image classification and other computer vision tasks.

The "ResNet" stands for residual network, which uses skip connections to address the vanishing gradient problem in deep networks. The "50" refers to the network's 50 layers that have weights [7].

Description: Among its 50 layers, 48 layers are convolutional, one MaxPool layer, and one average pooling layer.

Filters used:

7×7 filters in the first convolutional layer.

3×3 filters in later residual blocks.

Input size: The model accepts images of size 224×224 with 3 RGB channels.

Special feature: ResNet50 incorporates residual blocks with skip connections, enabling deeper architectures to train efficiently without degradation in performance.

ResNet101: It is an advanced CNN model widely used for image classification and computer vision tasks.

"ResNet" stands for residual network, which addresses the vanishing gradient issue by using skip connections to enhance deep network training. The "101" refers to the network having 101 layers [8].

Description: Among its 101 layers, it has 99 convolutional layers, one Maxpool layer, and one average pooling layer.

Filters used:

7×7 filters in the first convolutional layer.

3×3 filters in later residual blocks.

Input size: The model accepts images of size 224×224 with 3 RGB channels.

Special feature: ResNet101 incorporates a larger number of residual blocks compared to ResNet 50, allowing for even deeper feature extraction and better performance on complex datasets, though at the cost of increased computational requirements.

Personalized recommendation engine
An AI-based system will offer tailored fruit suggestions based on user health profiles, considering age, dietary needs, and health goals, with continuous learning from user feedback.

User interface development
A responsive web interface will allow users to upload images, input health data, and receive suggestions. Built with HTML, CSS, and JavaScript, it will prioritize user-friendly design and data security.

System testing and evaluation
The system's classification accuracy and recommendation relevance will be evaluated using metrics like precision and recall, with user feedback guiding improvements.

This approach combines advanced image processing and machine learning for personalized dietary management.

Results and Discussions

The efficacy and performance of the fruit picture classification and personalized recommendation system will be described in the results section. The performance metrics for the tested models (VGG16, VGG19, and two ResNet variations) will be displayed, including accuracy, precision, recall, and F1-score. This comparison will highlight the most effective model and discuss the conditions under which it performed best, such as varying lighting or fruit types. The personalized recommendation engine's output will also be analyzed, showcasing its capability to provide relevant fruit suggestions based on user health profiles and demonstrating improvements over time due to user feedback and adaptive learning. User feedback from surveys and usability tests will be summarized to reflect the system's ease of use and overall satisfaction. Observations on limitations, such as difficulties in classifying certain fruits or the recommendation engine's areas needing enhancement, will be included. The section will conclude by summarizing the system's overall success in combining image classification and personalized recommendations to support healthier dietary choices.

Conclusion

Fruit recommendation using artificial intelligent (AI) tools encompasses gathering diverse fruit images, training a computer program to differentiate between various fruit types, and standardizing the images for

Table 13.1 Considered hyperparameters for the execution and accuracy.

Hyper parameter	VGG16	VGG19	ResNet50	ResNet101
Optimizer	SGD or Adam	SGD or Adam	Adam or SGD	Adam or SGD
Learning rate	0.01 or 0.001 (with decay)	0.01 or 0.001 (with decay)	0.001 (with scheduler/decay)	0.001 (with scheduler)
Batch size	32 or 64	32 or 64	32 or 64	16 or 32
Dropout rate	0.5 (in fully connected layers)	0.5 (in fully connected layers)	Not explicitly used (relies on batch normalization)	Not explicitly used (relies on batch normalization)
Epochs	50–100	50–100	50–150	50–150
Loss function	Cross-Entropy Loss	Cross-entropy loss	Cross-entropy loss	Cross-entropy loss
Weight initialization	Xavier or He Initialization	Xavier or He initialization	He initialization	He initialization
Regularization	L2 regularization (0.0005 weight decay)	L2 regularization (0.0005 weight decay)	L2 regularization (0.0001 weight decay)	L2 regularization (0.0001 weight decay)
Momentum	0.9 (when using SGD)	0.9 (when using SGD)	0.9 (when using SGD)	0.9 (when using SGD)
Accuracy	94.4%	95.7%	96.5%	97.7%

Source: Author

easy interpretation by the program. This systematic approach allows for the development of an efficient system capable of automatically identifying and categorizing fruits based on their visual characteristics. By leveraging advanced technologies such as convolutional neural networks (CNNs) and image pre-processing techniques, accurate and reliable fruit classification systems can be created. Such systems have broad applications in agriculture, food processing, dietary planning, and healthcare, contributing to improved efficiency, productivity, and decision-making in various domains. Overall, fruit recommendation using AI tools represents a promising avenue for enhancing automation and decision support in fruit-related tasks and essentially on smart health and automated diet control.

References

[1] Muresan, H., & Oltean, M. (2018). Fruit recognition from images using deep learning. *Acta Universitatis Sapientiae, Informatica*, 10(1), 26–42.

[2] Mirwansyah, D & Wibowo, A. (2022). Fruit Image Classification Using Deep Learning Algorithm: Systematic Literature Review (SLR). Multica Science and Technology (MST). 2. 120–123. 10.47002/mst.v2i2.356.

[3] Dubey, S. R., & Jalal, A. (2014). Application of image processing in fruit and vegetable analysis: a review. *Journal of Intelligent Systems*, 24, 405–424. 10.1515/jisys-2014-0079.

[4] Mirra, K B, Pooja, P, Ranchani, S & kumari, R. (2020). Fruit Quality Analysis using Image Processing. *International Journal of Engineering and Advanced Technology*. 9. 88–91. 10.35940/ijeat.E9309.069520.

[5] Sapan N, Bankim P. (2017). Machine Vision based Fruit Classification and Grading - A Review. *International Journal of Computer Applications*. 170, 9, 22–34. DOI=10.5120/ijca2017914937.

[6] Liu, S., & Deng, W. (2015). Very deep convolutional neural network-based image classification using small training sample size. In 2015 3rd IAPR Asian Conference on Pattern Recognition (ACPR), Kuala Lumpur, Malaysia, (pp. 730–734). doi: 10.1109/ACPR.2015.7486599.

[7] Ali, L., Alnajjar, F., Jassmi, H., Gochoo, M., Khan, W., & Serhani, M. (2021). Performance evaluation of deep CNN-based crack detection and localization techniques for concrete structures. *Sensors*, 21, 1688. 10.3390/s21051688.

[8] Agrawal, S., Rewaskar, V., Agrawal, R., Chaudhari, S., Patil, Y., & Agrawal, N. (2023). Advancements in NSFW content detection: a comprehensive review of ResNet-50 based approaches. *International Journal of Intelligent Systems and Applications in Engineering*, 11, 41–45.

14 Gender differences in thermal comfort: a comprehensive review

Dinesh Kalla[1,a], Rahul Vadisetty[2,b], Subhajit Banerjee[3,c], Tanbir Islam[3,d] and Gour Gopal Jana[4,e]

[1]Department of Computer Science and Engineering, Colorado Technical University, Charlotte, NC, United States

[2]Department of Electrical Engineering, Wayne State University, Detroit, United States

[3]Department of Mechanical Engineering, Greater Kolkata College of Engineering and Management, Baruipur, WB, India

[4]Department of Electronics and Communication, Greater Kolkata College of Engineering and Management, Baruipur, WB, India

Abstract

Thermal comfort is a key determinant of occupant satisfaction and productivity in indoor environments. Recent studies have highlighted that gender plays a significant role in the perception of thermal comfort, with men and women exhibiting different sensitivities and preferences toward ambient temperatures. This paper reviews existing literature on gender-based differences in thermal comfort, focusing on physiological, psychological, and behavioral factors. The review also explores how these differences impact indoor environmental design, particularly in office spaces, classrooms, and residential buildings. Implications for future research and the design of energy-efficient and user-centered environments are discussed.

Keywords: Gender differences, indoor environmental quality, occupant satisfaction, physiological factors, temperature preferences, thermal comfort

Introduction

Human comfort is a mental state that reflects contented adjustment to one's immediate surroundings. Air quality, temperature comfort, lighting comfort, and acoustics comfort are some of the lesser components that make up human comfort. Guidelines for ventilation, thermal comfort, and indoor air quality in schools (Building Bulletin 101) [6] illustrate the relationships between these comforts, which are not independent, as seen in Figure 14.1.

According to ISO 7730 (2005), thermal comfort is a psychological state of contentment with the thermal environment that is impacted by both individual and environmental variables. Gender plays a key role, with men and women differing in thermal perception and preferences. While early research suggested minimal differences between genders [8]. Recent studies highlight significant gender-based variations in thermal comfort [7, 9, 32]. Approximately 87% of people spend time indoors, often in artificial climates [17].

Thermal comfort differs significantly between genders due to physiological and psychological factors. Women typically have lower metabolic rates, making them more sensitive to cooler environments [28, 34]. Although men and women may share similar neutral temperature ranges, women often report greater dissatisfaction with thermal conditions [33]. These differences emphasize the need for gender-sensitive designs in urban planning and building design, particularly in personalized climate control systems for commercial and residential spaces [1, 4].

This paper synthesizes current research on gender-based thermal comfort, exploring the physiological, psychological, and behavioral mechanisms that underpin these differences.

Physiological Differences in Thermal Comfort

Thermal comfort is primarily influenced by the body's ability to regulate heat through various physiological processes. Gender-based differences in

[a]kalladinesh@outlook.com, [b]rahulvy91@gmail.com, [c]subhajit.banerjee@gkcem.ac.in, [d]tanbir.islam@gkcem.ac.in, [e]gourgopal.jana_gkcem@jisgroup.org

DOI: 10.1201/9781003724995-14

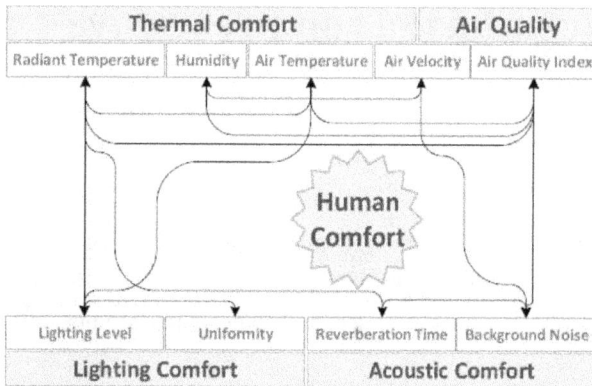

Figure 14.1 Human comfort aspects and their relationships [19]
Source: Author

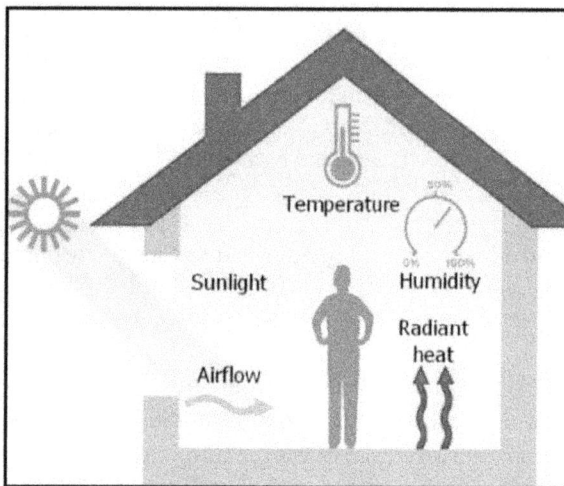

Figure 14.2 Factors affecting thermal comfort [8]
Source: Author

body composition, metabolic rate, and thermoregulatory response are key determinants of how men and women experience thermal comfort.

Body composition and metabolism

Fanger et al. [10] observed lower metabolic rates in females than males but found no specific link between temperature and comfort. Beshir and Ramsey [2] noted thermally neutral temperatures of 25°C for women and 22°C for men, with women feeling less comfortable in harsh climates. Schellen et al. [29] found that women's comfort temperature is 1.2°C higher. Studies by Lan et al. [22] and Liu et al. [25] confirm women's higher comfort thresholds, influenced by body composition and lower metabolic

rates, which enhance sensitivity to cooler conditions. According to Grievel and Candas (1991), women preferred greater temperatures than males, albeit not in a statistically significant way. Similarly, the study of Hashiguchi et al. [14] established that females were more sensitive to and less satisfied with thermal stratification.

Men typically have more muscular mass and a lower percentage of body fat than women. Muscle tissue generates more heat during activity, while fat tissue acts as an insulator, reducing heat loss. This difference in body composition explains why women may feel colder than men under identical thermal conditions (Candido et al., 2012). Additionally, women generally have a lower basal metabolic rate (BMR) than men, leading to lower heat production at rest, which may contribute to increased sensitivity to cooler temperatures [26].

Hormonal fluctuations

Thermal comfort in men can be influenced by hormonal fluctuations, as hormones regulate body temperature, metabolism, and thermoregulation mechanisms. Testosterone, a key male hormone, affects energy expenditure and heat production, often resulting in different thermal responses compared to females. Age-related hormonal changes, like decreased testosterone levels during andropause, can also impact thermal comfort by altering metabolism and sweat production [11]. Stress and lifestyle factors that affect cortisol and thyroid hormones can further influence men's ability to maintain thermal balance, particularly in fluctuating environments [12]. These factors highlight the complex interplay between endocrine systems and thermal comfort in males.

Hormonal fluctuations during the menstrual cycle, pregnancy, and menopause significantly affect women's thermal comfort. In the luteal phase, increased metabolism and body temperature heighten warmth perception [20]. Pregnant women feel hotter due to metabolic demands, while menopausal women experience thermal discomfort from vasomotor symptoms like hot flashes.

Thermoregulatory mechanisms

Thermoregulation maintains the body's internal temperature, with gender differences in responses like sweating and vasodilation [3]. Women sweat less than men, affecting heat dissipation in warm conditions (Schlader et al., 2010). In cold environments, men conserve heat better via vasoconstriction, while women often rely on behavioral strategies like extra clothing or heaters.

Testosterone increases men's basal metabolic rate (BMR), enhancing heat production and supporting thermal balance in cold conditions. Men also initiate thermoregulatory responses, like sweating and vasodilation, at lower temperatures than women. In women, estrogen and progesterone influence thermoregulation, with progesterone raising core temperature during the luteal phase. Women have more subcutaneous fat for insulation but lose heat faster due to a higher surface area-to-mass ratio, especially in cooler environments [11, 16].

Psychological and Behavioral Factors

Beyond physiological differences, psychological and behavioral factors also contribute to thermal comfort. Social and cultural expectations often influence how men and women perceive and respond to temperature fluctuations.

Temperature preferences
Research indicates significant gender differences in temperature preferences, which are linked to both physiological and cognitive factors. Numerous studies have found that women generally prefer warmer indoor temperatures than men [23] with studies showing that women often feel more comfortable at temperatures around 25°C, while men prefer cooler settings around 22°C [30]. In office environments, for example, women often set thermostats at higher temperatures, while men prefer cooler settings. This gender-based difference is not solely physiological; psychological factors such as expectations about body image, clothing, and activity level also play a role in shaping temperature preferences.

Behavioral adaptation
People adopt adaptive behaviors to address thermal discomfort, like changing clothing, seeking different spaces, or using heaters or fans. Women often use external heating devices more, while men tend to remove clothing layers during heat stress [15]. Women are more sensitive to temperature changes, frequently adjusting clothing or using heating devices, while men tolerate cooler environments due to higher metabolic rates and heat production [27].

These behaviors are shaped by environmental conditions and individual comfort preferences.

Gender and Thermal Comfort in Different Contexts

Office environments
Gender differences in office thermal comfort arise from physiological and cultural factors. Women prefer warmer temperatures (24°C), while men favor cooler ones (21°C), due to men's higher metabolic heat production. Historical standards based on male data often leave women colder [21]. Women's lighter clothing also reduces insulation, increasing discomfort. These disparities impact comfort and productivity, as warmer conditions improve women's performance, while cooler settings benefit men. Updating temperature standards can enhance overall workplace satisfaction (Haverinen-Shaughnessy et al., 2014).

Residential spaces
Studies reveal that in residential settings, women generally prefer warmer indoor temperatures than men and report thermal discomfort more frequently. Negotiations over thermostat settings are common in multi-occupant households, with women often compromising due to social or cultural expectations [31]. Gender-specific recommendations for home heating may be necessary to optimize comfort and energy efficiency.

Healthcare and educational settings
Gender differences in thermal comfort are evident in educational and healthcare buildings due to physiological and cultural factors. In educational settings, female students and teachers often prefer slightly warmer environments, as their lower metabolic rates result in reduced heat production compared to males. This discrepancy can affect concentration and productivity [24]. In healthcare facilities, thermal comfort is critical for patient recovery and staff efficiency. Women, including patients and healthcare workers, tend to experience discomfort in environments optimized for male metabolic standards, emphasizing the need for inclusive temperature regulation policies [5]. This can be figured out by providing more personalized temperature control systems or considering gender differences when designing HVAC systems.

Implications for Future Research and Design

Understanding gender-based thermal comfort differences is essential for inclusive building design and energy management. Future research should focus on creating gender-sensitive models that address physiological and behavioral factors. HVAC systems must prioritize flexibility to cater to individual preferences, while thermal comfort standards should account for gender disparities to ensure universal satisfaction. Additionally, as climate change intensifies, understanding gender-specific thermal needs will help develop adaptive strategies for energy efficiency and occupant well-being.

Conclusion

Gender differences in thermal comfort are a complex interplay of physiological, psychological, and behavioral factors. Women generally experience more thermal discomfort than men, preferring warmer temperatures and relying more on behavioral adaptations to maintain comfort. These differences have important implications for the design of indoor spaces, particularly in workplaces, homes, and educational facilities. Future research should continue to explore these differences in greater depth, with a focus on developing more inclusive and adaptable thermal comfort standards. By embracing a more personalized approach to thermal comfort, we can improve occupant satisfaction, productivity, and well-being, while also promoting energy efficiency in buildings.

References

[1] Acero, J. A., & Herranz-Pascual, K. (2015). A comparison of thermal comfort conditions in four urban spaces by means of measurements and modelling techniques. *Building and Environment*, 93, 245–257. DOI: 10.1016/j.buildenv.2015.06.028.

[2] Beshir, M. Y., & Ramsey, J. D. (1981). Comparison between male and female subjective estimates of thermal effects and sensations. *Applied Ergonomics*, 12(1), 29–33.

[3] Bar-Or, O., Magnusson, L. I., & Buskirk, E. R. (1968). Distribution of heat-activated sweat glands in obese and lean men and women. *Human Biology*, 40(2), 235–248.

[4] Chowdhury, S., Chowdhury, S., & Rezve, M. F. H. (2024). Using simulated human comfort matrix to measure urban campus gender-based thermal performances. *Frontiers in Built Environment*, 10, 1449351. DOI: 10.3389/fbuil.2024.1449351.

[5] Coffey, M., Desouza, R., & Jones, B. (2018). Thermal comfort in educational environments: a study of gender-based preferences and productivity outcomes. *International Journal of Environmental Research and Public Health*, 15(7), 1412.

[6] Daniels, R. (2018). Building Bulletin 101 Guidelines on Ventilation, Thermal Comfort and Indoor Air Quality in Schools. United Kingdom: the Education and Skills Funding Agency. ESFA.

[7] Djongyang, N., Tchinda, R., & Njomo, D. (2010). Thermal comfort: a review paper. *Renewable and Sustainable Energy Reviews*, 14, 2626–2640.

[8] Fanger, P. O. (1970). Thermal Comfort: Analysis and Applications in Environmental Engineering. Copenhagen, Danish Technical Press.

[9] Frontczak, M., & Wargocki, P. (2011). Literature survey on how different factors influence human comfort in indoor environments. *Building and Environment*, 46, 922–937.

[10] Fanger, P. O., Højbjerre, J., & Thomsen, J. O. B. (1974). Thermal comfort conditions in the morning and in the evening. *International Journal of Biometeorology*, 18(1), 16–22.

[11] Fernández-Peña, C., Reimúndez, A., Viana, F., Arce, V. M., & Señarís, R. (2023). Sex differences in thermoregulation in mammals: Implications for energy homeostasis. *Frontiers in Endocrinology*, 14, 1093376. DOI: 10.3389/fendo.2023.1093376.

[12] Gabriel, C., RDN, M. S., & Santilli, M. (2020). 7 Symptoms of Male Hormonal Imbalance You Should Know. The Wellnest. https://www.humnutrition.com/blog/male-hormonal-imbalance, Accessed on 10/12/2024.

[13] Hashiguchi, N., Feng, Y., & Tochihara, Y. (2010). Gender differences in thermal comfort and mental performance at different vertical air temperatures. *European Journal of Applied Physiology*, 109(1), 41–48.

[14] Havenith, G., & Fiala, D. (2007). Thermal comfort and performance in office environments: a review of gender differences in thermal comfort. *Ergonomics*, 50(11), 1554–1565.

[15] Johnson, J. M., & Kellogg, D. L. (2018). Skin vasoconstriction as a heat conservation thermoeffector. *Handbook of Clinical Neurology*, 156, 175–92. DOI: 10.1016/B978-0-444-63912-7.00011-4.

[16] Klepeis, N. E. (2001). The national human activity pattern survey (NHAPS): a resource for assessing exposure to environmental pollutants. *Journal of Exposure Analysis and Environmental Epidemiology*, 11, 231. https://doi.org/10.1038/sj.jea.7500165, 07/24/ online.

[17] Karyono, K., Abdullah, B. M., Cotgrave, A. J., & Bras, A. (2020). The adaptive thermal comfort

review from the 1920s, the present, and the future. *Developments in the Built Environment*, 4, 100032. DOI: 10.1016/j.dibe.2020.100032.

[18] Kolka, M. A., & Johnson, R. F. (2003). Thermal comfort in women: menstrual cycle phase-related differences. *Physiological Reports*, 5(3), 456–463.

[19] Kim, J., de Dear, R., Cândido, C., Zhang, H., & Arens, E. (2013). Gender differences in office occupant perception of indoor environmental quality (IEQ). Building and Environment, 70, 245–256.

[20] Lan, L., Lian, Z., Liu, W., & Liu, Y. (2008). Investigation of gender difference in thermal comfort for Chinese people. *European Journal of Applied Physiology*, 102(4), 471–480.

[21] Lan, L., Lian, Z., & Pan, L. (2011). Thermal comfort in office buildings: gender differences and adaptive behavior. *Building and Environment*, 46(3), 1196–1205.

[22] Lamberti, G., Salvadori, G., Leccese, F., Fantozzi, F., & Bluyssen, P. M. (2021). Advancement on thermal comfort in educational buildings: current issues and way forward. *Sustainability*, 13, 10315. https://doi.org/10.3390/su131810315.

[23] Liu, W., Lian, Z., Deng, Q., & Liu, Y. (2011). Evaluation of calculation methods of mean skin temperature for use in thermal comfort study. *Building and Environment*, 46(2), 478–488.

[24] Lundgren, K., Rintamäki, H., & Mäkinen, T. (2013). The role of gender in the thermal comfort of the workplace: implications for future research and building design. *Energy and Buildings*, 59, 304–313.

[25] Ma, N., Chen, L., Hu, J., Perdikaris, P., & Braham, W. W. (2021). Adaptive behavior and different thermal experiences of real people: a bayesian neural network approach to thermal preference prediction and classification. *Building and Environment*, 198, 107875. doi:10.1016/j.buildenv.2021.107875.

[26] Parsons, K. C. (2002). The effects of gender, acclimation state, the opportunity to adjust clothing and physical disability on requirements for thermal comfort. *Energy and Buildings*, 34(6), 593–599.

[27] Schellen, L., Loomans, M., de Wit, M., & van Marken Lichtenbelt, W. (2013). The influence of different cooling techniques and gender on thermal perception. *Building Research & Information*, 41(3), 330–341.

[28] Schmidt, M. (2020). Room Temperatures Set for Men's Comfort May Disadvantage Women, Study, The Magazine: Discover, US. https://www.discovermagazine.com/mind/room-temperatures-set-for-mens-comfort-may-disadvantage-women-study-finds, Accessed on 10/12/2024.

[29] Sintov, N. D., White, L. V., & Walpole, H. (2019). Thermostat wars? the roles of gender and thermal comfort negotiations in household energy use behavior. *Plos One*, 14(11), e0224198. doi:10.1371/journal.pone.0224198.

[30] Van Hoof, J. (2008). Forty years of Fanger's model of thermal comfort: comfort for all? *Indoor Air*, 18, 182–201.

[31] Wang, Z., de Dear, R., Luo, M., Lin, B., He, Y., & Ghahramani, A. (2018). Individual difference in thermal comfort: a literature review. *Building and Environment*, 138, 181–193.

[32] Webb, L. H., & Parsons, K. C. (1997). Thermal comfort requirements for people with physical disabilities in sustainable buildings. In Proceedings of the BEPAC and EPSRC Mini Conference. Oxford, UK.

[33] Humphreys, M. A. (1976). Field studies of thermal comfort compared and applied. Building Services Engineer, 44, 5–27.

[34] Grivel, C., & Candas, V. (1991). Gender differences in thermal comfort under moderate environments: physiological and perceptual responses. European Journal of Applied Physiology, 63(3), 173–177.

[35] Candido, C., de Dear, R., Ohba, M., & Parkinson, T. (2012). Towards establishing a standard for adaptive thermal comfort in mixed-mode buildings. Building Research & Information, 40(3), 351–369.

[36] Schlader, Z. J., Simmons, S. E., Stannard, S. R., & Mündel, T. (2010). The independent roles of temperature and thermal perception in the control of human thermoregulatory behavior. Physiology & Behavior, 103(2), 217–224.

[37] Haverinen-Shaughnessy, U., Moschandreas, D. J., & Shaughnessy, R. J. (2014). Association between substandard classroom ventilation rates and students' academic achievement. Indoor Air, 21(2), 121–131.

15 An embedded system to identify the damage brain regions due to stroke, tumor and injury the known cause of the epilepsy

Khakon Das[1,a], Ashish Khare[1,b], Nilesh Anand Srivastava[1,c] and Aniruddha Nag[2,d]

[1]Department of Electronics and Communication, University of Allahabad, Prayagraj, Uttar Pradesh-211002, India

[2]Associate Professor, Techno India Group, Kolkata, WB, India

Abstract

In the field of epilepsy diagnosis, medical imaging plays a crucial role by providing an internal view of the subject. Medical professionals use these images to study the internal condition and draw conclusions. The radiologist conducts a scan and prepares a report based on the doctor's request. Various medical imaging technologies such as X-ray, CT, PET, SPECT, MRI, and fMRI are utilized for diagnosis. After scanning, a text report is provided based on the images. However, for reinvestigation, prescribing a new scan with revised requisition can lead to delays and increased costs. In such cases, reusing image films (black plates) may be the only viable option for reinvestigation.

An image of the black plates (image films) is captured and used for further processing. Here the proposed system also can perform the said operation from the raw medical image files (.dicom files). This process involves the use of an ESP32 CAM Wi-Fi module, an 8-bit ARM architecture-based microcontroller (MCU), and SD memory cards for capturing, processing, and storing the input/output images. The proposed embedded system can effectively identify tumor and stroke regions within the brain. Additionally, it offers a portable, real-time, and cost-effective solution. A wavelet transform-based denoising technique generates high-quality denoised images, allowing for clear visualization of tumor and stroke regions. Various statistical measures of the denoised image also support this claim. By optimizing the read-and-write cycle using the software pipelining concept, the proposed system becomes more time- and resource-efficient. Moreover, the utilization of the ESP32 CAM Wi-Fi module for capturing images enhances its portability.

Keywords: Clustering, denoising medical images, embedded system, segmentation, stroke

Introduction

Epilepsy is a critical brain disorder that affects millions of people globally. Medical imaging plays a crucial role in diagnosing epilepsy by providing detailed views of scanned patients. Various types of scans, including X-ray, CT, PET, SPECT, MRI, and fMRI, are used in epilepsy diagnosis, each with its own significance. These scans are performed by different medical imaging devices equipped with dedicated software for analyzing the images and generating reports. After the scans, patients receive image films and a text report. Reinvestigation of medical images can be conducted manually by reviewing the image films or by prescribing a new scan with a revised requisition.\par The next subsection discusses a study on the reinvestigation of medical images.

Background

Over the past century, researchers have made numerous attempts to address a particular problem, with efforts dating back to the late 1990s. Since then, several medical image annotation tools have been developed to tackle this issue. Some popular tools include Encord-DICOM, 3D Slicer, Labelbox, Kili, ITK-Snap, and MONAI [1]. Each tool uses its own customized radiological image file formats such as DICOM (Digital Imaging and Communications in Medicine), NRRD (Nearly Raw Raster Data), PAR/REC (Philips MRI scanner formats), NIFTI (Neuroimaging Informatics Technology Initiative), ANALYZE (Mayo Medical Imaging), and MNIC. It's important to note that these radiology image file formats (RAW files) are not easily accessible due to containing patients' personal information. As a

[a]khakon.phd2021@alldunic.ac.in, [b]khare@allduniv.ac.in, [c]nilesh@allduniv.ac.in, [d]a.nag@smitgp.edu.in

DOI: 10.1201/9781003724995-15

result, special permission is required to access raw images, and dedicated software is needed to interpret raw data (image).\par. In this context, reinvestigation becomes more challenging. Ordering a new scan with a revised requisition leads to delayed diagnosis and increased diagnostic costs. Under these circumstances, reusing image films (black plates) may be the only viable alternative for reinvestigation.

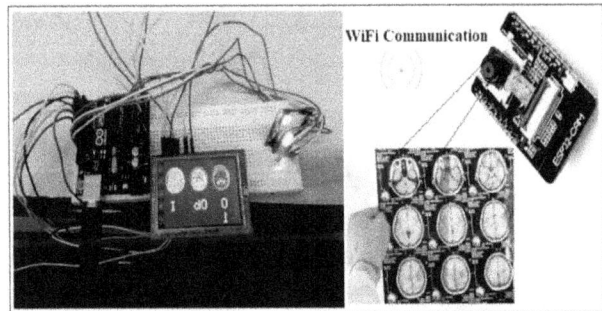

Figure 15.1 Working model of proposed embedded system
Source: Author

Contributions
- In this work, a focus has been given to developing such a system that can detect abnormal brain parts from scanning image films (black plates).
- Further, the system provides a marked abnormal region as an output image.
- The proposed system provides a low-cost portable solution for the reinvestigation of medical images.

This paper is organized as follows. The related study is discussed in Section 1, in Section 2 the required pre-processing has been described. The proposed design methodology is described in Section 3. Experimental results have been studied in Section 4 with discussion. Finally, in Section 5 overall work is concluded.

Pre-Processing

Pre-processing is crucial for preparing raw-data for significant investigation. It involves a range of methods for enhancing the quality of the dataset, cleaning, and modifying [2–4]. Further in this section we deal with some important pre-processing techniques such as scaling, noise removal [5–7], segmentation [8], grayscale transformation, data augmentation, and image resizing. These methods are essential for insure accurate and reliable results in various areas of data science.

Data acquisition
In this work, an ESP32-WiFi-CAM module has been used, which boasts a 32-bit LX6 microprocessor clocked at 160MHz, providing robust processing capabilities. Furthermore, it is equipped with 520KB of SRAM and 4M PSRAM, ensuring an ample amount of memory space for storing the images captured during the proposed work. The module leverages the Wi-Fi 802.11 b/g/n communication protocol to facilitate seamless communication with other

modules [9]. For a visual representation of the module used, please refer to Figure 15.1.

Denoising
The early started hybrid denoising technique (ESHDT), proposed by Das et al. [10], is an innovative approach for denoising medical images. This technique leverages wavelet transform methods [6, 7, 11] to effectively remove noise from the images. One of its key advantages is its ability to exploit parallelism and pipelining, leading to enhanced processing speed. ESHDT is particularly adept at handling high levels of noise with minimal degradation. Rather than employing a set of filters, it utilizes a straightforward predict and update mechanism. By modifying the basic Haar wavelet transform [12] techniques using lifting [13, 14] and in-place methods, ESHDT significantly improves processing memory space utilization [12, 15].

Design Methodology

In this section, the proposed embedded system design has been describing along with the algorithm. The proposed algorithm can identify damaged brain regions due to brain tumor, stroke and brain injuries. The proposed algorithm has been developed in a MATLAB platform initially and tests with various type of medical images. After ensuring clinically accepted output, the required modification has been made into the said algorithm to implement in embedded system.

Embedded system design
In Figure 15.2, a functioning system is depicted. The system captures an image of the black plates (image films) for further processing. It utilizes an ESP32

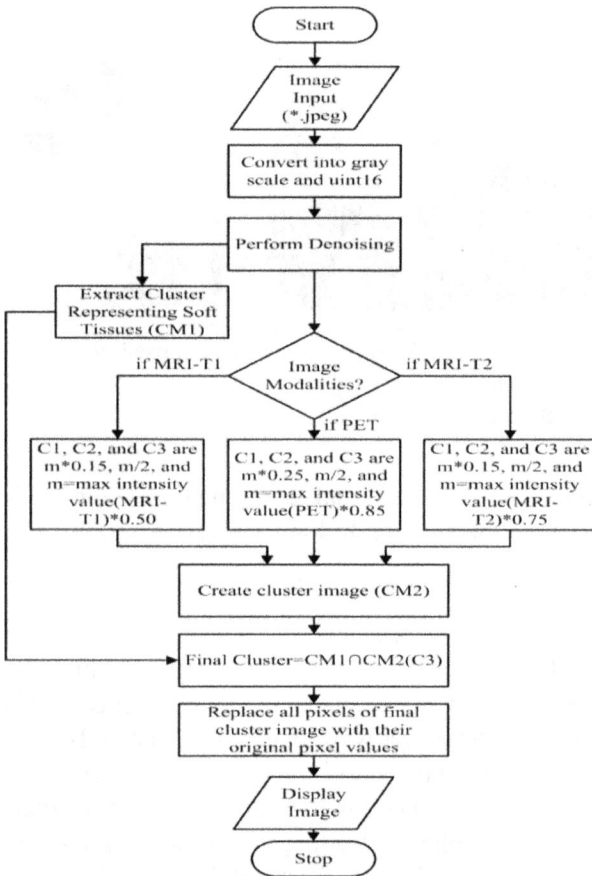

Figure 15.2 Proposed embedded system flow chart
Source: Author

CAM Wi-Fi module, an 8-bit ARM architecture-based microcontroller (MCU) [16], and SD memory cards for capturing, processing, and storing the input/output images. Additionally, a thin film transistor (TFT) LCD is employed to display the input and output images. In Figure 15.2, the proposed system exhibits three images. The leftmost image on the monitor represents the input image denoted by 'I'. The 'dO' image is a denoised image, and the rightmost image denoted by 'O' is the final output image (segmented image). Further detailed implementation of the proposed algorithm and its hardware resource utilization design is discussed in subsections 3.2 and 3.3.

Proposed embedded system flow chart
The algorithm efficiently utilizes an ESP32-Wi-Fi-CAM to capture medical image films and save into the SD card as "*.jpeg" format or can use raw medical image file format (*.dicom) as input image. Following this, the captured image is converted to grayscale, and the pixel values are then processed into uint16 for further analysis. Denoising is accomplished through the discrete wavelet transform approach, employing a specific segment of K. Das et al.'s denoising technique [12] (referenced as Algorithm-1). The algorithm then effectively segregates the hard structure (brain scalp) from soft tissues (soft brain part) and retains the soft brain part (saved as CM1). Based on the imaging modality, three initial cluster points (C1, C2, and C3) are confidently calculated using the denoised images. The soft thresholding approach is resolutely utilized to calculate and initialize cluster values. Subsequently, three cluster center values are confidently determined to form four distinct clusters: background, cerebrospinal fluid (CSF), white matter, and grey matter (C3-cluster), resulting in a meticulously segmented image (CM2). The final cluster image is obtained through a decisive intersection operation between the soft brain part (CM1) and the targeted cluster (C3) of the segmented image (CM2). Finally, the pixel locations of the final cluster image are assertively replaced with their original pixel values and displayed as a clear image. The complete proposed embedded system flow chart is confidently depicted in Figure 15.2.

Algorithm 1: Denoising part of ESHDT

REQUIRE: Input Image (P)
ENSURE: Denoised output images ($P_{n,i}$)
Step. 1. Here all incoming pixels are divided into even and odd sets bases on pixel index, P_{Even} and P_{Odd} Where P is a 1D image and 'n' represent a denoise Level.

$$P_n = (P_{n(Even)} \cup P_{n(Odd)}) \qquad (1)$$

Step. 2. Detailed coefficient has been calculated using Harr wavelet transform which incorporated with predict step of Lifting method In-place calculation is used ['i' refers to pixel index and 'n' is a denoise Level].

$$P_{n,i} = (P_{n,i+1} - P_{n,i}) \qquad (2)$$

Step. 3. The calculation of the Haar's approximate part has been performed in Update Step of Lifting Technique using In-place calculation.

$$P_{n,i} = \left(\left(\frac{P_{n,i+1} + P_{n,i}}{2} \right) + \left(\frac{P_{n,i+1} - P_{n,i}}{4} \right) \right) \qquad (3)$$

Step. 1. End

Optimization of register read/write cycle through software pipe-lining

In the single cycle format, as depicted in Figure 15.3(a), the SD-card has been used to store I/O data after each pass completion of the procedure. Initially, the input data (pixels) are retrieved from the SD-card and transferred to the internal register. After obtaining the input data, the processor carries out the required operations on these data and then saves the output data back to the SD-card. This process is then repeated for multiple pixels. Figure 15.3(a) outlines a method for executing multiple pixels and multiple cycles of the proposed algorithm. When considering an image of 'n' pixels, the processor requires "n" read from the SD-card to retrieve each pixel and "n" write operations to store the data back to the SD-card.

Specifically, the proposed algorithm performs the 6th level of denoising "6*n" times, involving SD Card and register read and write operations. This procedure becomes time-consuming due to the many read-and-write operations on SD-cards. To address this issue, a software pipelining approach is used, as shown in Figure 15.3(a). The implementation of software pipelining is described in Figure 15.3(b) through a required resource and availability graph. If the 6th level denoised pixel is required, then we must have seven pixels at a time. Figure 15.3(b), shows that a denoised pixel of 6th level has been stored into the internal register and written back to the SD-card. This approach makes the proposed algorithm more efficient in terms of time complexity. Because the time required fetching data from an SD-card and writing back the output data to an SD-card is much more than register read-write.

Result and Discussion

In this section, we show the various output images and analyze the quality of the output image using various statistical measures.

Visual and statistical outputs

In this section, firstly display outputs getting from the proposed algorithm. Here various types of medical image have been used to check the algorithm's robustness. Further the MATLAB based output of the proposed algorithm has been shown in Figure 15.5. In Figure 15.4, the denoised output image which is getting from the proposed embedded system has been shown with the input image of two individual patients (P1 and P2). The left side image represents the input image, while the right-side image portrays the denoised version. Notably, denoising at the 6th level has been executed, yielding a visually favorable denoised output image. The assessment of denoised image quality has encompassed the utilization of Mean Squared Error (MSE) [17], Peak Signal-to-Noise Ratio (PSNR) [17], and Universal Image Quality Index (UIQI) [18] values. The computation of MSE, PSNR, and UIQI has been shown in Table 15.1. Each cell value within the table signifies the mean result derived from the amalgamation of 10 images. Furthermore, the table comprehensively presents the findings across diverse image types. A discernible deduction from the outcomes in Table 15.1 is the affirmation of the denoised image quality meeting various statistical benchmarks. Additionally, the efficacy of the denoising process across an array of image types, encompassing PET, CT, MRI, and others, is substantiated.

In Figure 15.5, three sub-figures have been shown. The sub-figure (a) shows the core abnormal part of the

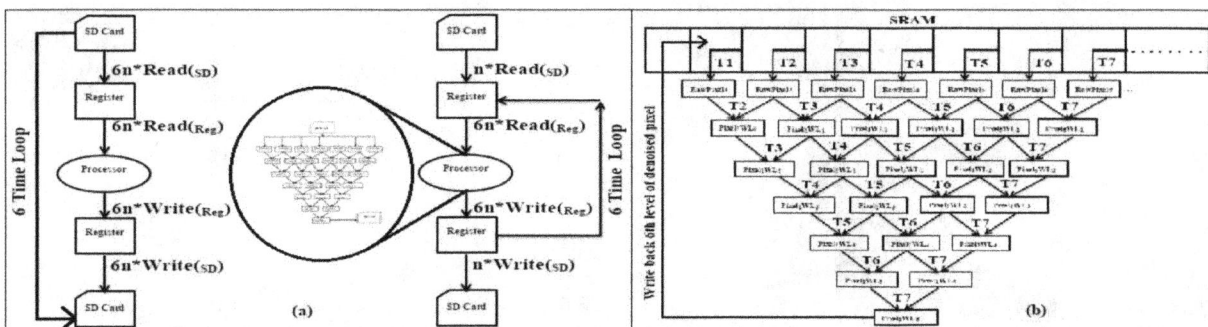

Figure 15.3 Multi cycle read and write execution of proposed algorithm with resource optimization
Source: Author

brain, where sub-figure (b) shows the extra abnormal part related to the core abnormal part that has been identified by the proposed algorithm. In sub-figure (c) the whole abnormal part has been shown, which

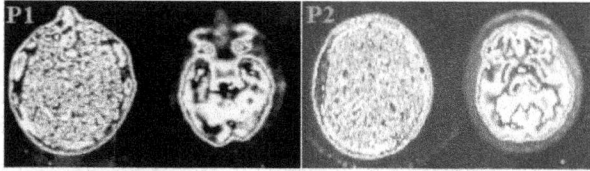

Figure 15.4 Input and denoise output images
Source: Author

Table 15.1 UIQI, MSE, PSNR values of denoised images.

Denoising level	MSE	PSNR	UIQI
Image type: PET			
Input	202780.92	9.81094	0.49869
Level 3	29.08	67.05716	0.67821
Level 6	0.24	120.86356	0.75090
Image type: MRI T1			
Input	65408.14	0.44347	0.42055
Level 3	11.96	74.66370	0.63128
Level 6	0.06	108.67507	0.91588
Image type: MRI T2			
Input	57854.90	1.08280	0.40392
Level 3	10.18	76.17629	0.77228
Level 6	0.06	118.08194	0.93035

Source: Author

shows the whole abnormal part of the brain more accurately. In Figure 15.6, a series of three images is presented. The left-hand image has been denoised, the middle image displays the intermediate output, and the image on the right shows the segmented output of the proposed algorithm. The segmented output image is divided into three distinct segments, with the pink color representing the targeted segment (tumor and/or stroke region). It's important to note that only the pink region within the blue area is considered, as the blue region solely represents the brain's soft tissue (excluding the scalp and CSF).

Comparison

The following Table 15.2 presents a comparison of state-of-the-art methods based on their memory usage, CPU requirements, and dependency on a GPU. Each method is accompanied by its respective memory usage (in MB), whether it necessitates a 64-bit CPU, and its reliance on a GPU for operation. Notably, the "Proposed" method distinguishes itself with remarkably low memory usage (0.004MB), a 32-bit CPU requirement, and independence from a

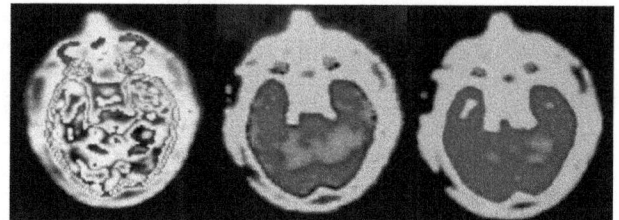

Figure 15.6 Final output images at various levels
Source: Author

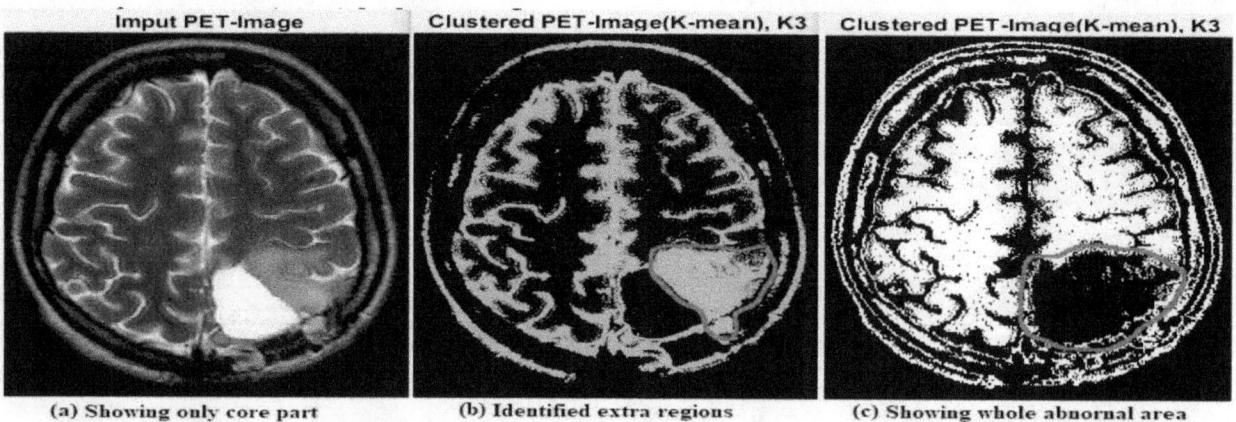

Figure 15.5 Output of various types of images (MATLAB based output)
Source: Author

Table 15.2 Comparison with various stat-of-the-art methods.

Methods	Memory (1MB = 1000KB)	CPU Used	Required GPU
VessNetar [19]	36.600MB	564-bit	Yes
MobileNet-V3-small [20]	11.000MB	64-bit	Yes
RSFNet [21]	8.000MB	64-bit	Yes
PLVSNet [22]	3.600MB	-	-
M2UNet [23]	2.200MB	64-bit	Yes
Proposed	0.004MB	32-bit	No

Source: Author

GPU. This analysis provides valuable insights into the resource demands of different methods for specific applications. The attributes of the proposed embedded system render it an exceptionally lightweight and cost-effective solution, well-suited for real-time edge processing systems.

Conclusions

Our primary objective is to develop an embedded system for medical image segmentation, with the capability to identify tumor and stroke regions within the brain. This system is intended to function as a portable real-time solution, while also being cost-effective. Section 4 demonstrates the successful identification of the targeted region (refer to Figure 15.5. The utilization of Wavelet transform technology-based denoising contributes to obtaining a high-quality denoised image, facilitating the visual identification of tumor and stroke regions. Moreover, various statistical measures corroborate this conclusion. The findings in section 3.3 indicate that the optimization of read and write cycles through software pipelining effectively reduces the read and write overhead in secondary memory, enhancing the system's efficiency in terms of time and resource utilization. Furthermore, this optimization renders the system suitable for real-time applications, and the integration of the ESP32 CAM Wi-Fi module for image capture enhances its portability. Looking ahead, the proposed system could be implemented in an FPGA to further enhance speed and compactness.

Acknowledgment

We are greatly thanking full to Dr. Dinesh Jhaluka of R.G. Kar medical college and NRS medical college for shearing resources to us for this research.

References

[1] Heindl, A. (n.d.). *Best DICOM Annotation Tools for Radiology AI [2024 Review]*. https://encord.com/blog/labeling-tools-dicom-radiology/#h2, [Last Accessed: Oct-2024].

[2] Sonka, M., Hlavac, V., & Boyle, R. (1993). Image pre-processing. In: Image Processing, Analysis and Machine Vision. Springer, Boston, MA. https://doi.org/10.1007/978-1-4899-3216-7_4 1st Edition.

[3] Singh, B. K., Verma, K., & Thokec, A. S. (2015). An enhancement in adaptive median filter for edge preservation. *Procedia Computer Science*, 48, 29–36.

[4] Pal, P., & Singh, S. (2016). Contrast enhancement of medical images: a review. *IJRDO-Journal of Health Sciences and Nursing*, 1(4), 32-35.

[5] Muhammed, H. H., & Yu, S. (2016). Noise type evaluation in positron emission tomography images. In 2016 1st International Conference on Biomedical Engineering (IBIOMED), Yogyakarta, Indonesia.

[6] Nowak, R. D. (1999). Wavelet-based rician noise removal for magnetic resonance imaging. *IEEE Transactions on Image Processing*, 8(10), 1408–1419.

[7] Martin, J., Portilla, W. J., Vasily, S., & Simoncelli, E. P. (2003). Image denoising using scale mixtures of gaussians in the wavelet domain. *IEEE Transactions on Image Processing*, 12(11), 1338–1351.

[8] Das, K., Khorat, D., & Sharma, S. K. (2020). An embedded system for gray matter segmentation of pet-image. In Mandal, J. J., & Mukhopadhyay, S. (Eds.), Proceedings of the Global AI Congress 2019, (pp. 145–157). Singapore: Springer Singapore.

[9] MAKERS Electronics (2024). We Make The Future. ESP32 CAM Board WIFI+Bluetooth with OV2640 Camera Module. Makers Electronics, (p. 8). https://makerselectronics.com/product/esp32-cam-board-wifibluetooth-with-ov2640-camera-AfmBOoqqK41zoPTOzMS608gDcqXuWrQde-VD_VkIeNFHlQKSgDk1EuRxc. [Last Accessed: Oct-2024].

[10] Sharma, P., Banerjee, M., Das, K., & Maitra, M. (2019). Early started hybrid denoising technique for medical images. In Bhaumik, H., Das, S., Yoshida, K., Bhattacharyya, S., & Mukherjee, A. (Eds.), Recent Trends in Signal and Image Processing, (pp. 131–140). Singapore: Springer.

[11] Mallat, S. G. (1989). A theory for multiresolution signal decomposition: the wavelet representation. *IEEE Transactions on Pattern Analysis and Machine Intelligence*, 11(7), 674–693.

[12] Das, K., Maitra, M., Banerjee, M., & Sharma, P. (2019). Embedded implementation of early started hybrid denoising technique for medical images with optimized loop. In Emerging Technology in Modelling and Graphics, (Vol. 937, pp. 295–308). Singapore: Springer.

[13] Wim, S. (1989). The lifting scheme: a construction of second generation wavelets. *SIAM Journal on Mathematical Analysis*, 29(2), 511–546.

[14] Wim, S. (1996). Wavelets and the lifting scheme: a 5 minute tour. *ZAMM-Zeitschrift fur Angewandte Mathematik und Mechanik*, 76, 41–44.

[15] Koichi, K., Koichi, N., & Shigeru, T. (2004). Fpga-based lifting wavelet processor for real-time signal detection. *Signal Processing*, 84(10), 1931–1940.

[16] ATmega328/P, *8-bit AVR microcontrollers.* (2016). https://docs.arduino.cc/resources/datasheets/Atmel-42735-8-bit-AVR-Microcontroller-ATmega328-328P_Datasheet.pdf, [Accessed: 29-JULY-2025.]

[17] Huynh-Thu, Q., & Ghanbari, M. (2008). Scope of validity of psnr in image/video quality assessment. *Electronics Letters*, 44(13), 800–801.

[18] Zhou, W., & Bovik, A. C. (2002). A universal image quality index. *IEEE Signal Processing Letters*, 9(3), 81–84.

[19] None, A., None, O., None, M., None, C., & None, P. (2019). Aiding the diagnosis of diabetic and hypertensive retinopathy using artificial intelligence-based semantic segmentation. *Journal of Clinical Medicine*, 8(9), 1446.

[20] Howard, A., Sandler, M., Chu, G., Chen, L., Chen, B., Tan, M., Wang, W., Zhu, Y., Pang, R., Vasudevan, V., Le, Q. V., & Adam, H. (2019). Searching for MobileNetV3. *arXiv (Cornell University).*, V5, https://doi.org/10.48550/arxiv.1905.02244.

[21] Romera, E., Álvarez, J. M., Bergasa, L. M. & Arroyo, R. (2018). ERFNet: Efficient Residual Factorized ConvNet for Real-Time Semantic Segmentation, *IEEE Transactions on Intelligent Transportation Systems,* vol. 19, no. 1, pp. 263–272. doi: 10.1109/TITS.2017.2750080.

[22] Muhammad Arsalan, Tariq M. Khan, Syed Saud Naqvi, Mehmood Nawaz, & Imran Razzak.(2023). Prompt Deep Light-Weight Vessel Segmentation Network (PLVS-Net). *IEEE/ACM Trans. Comput. Biol. Bioinformatics, 20(2),* 1363–1371. https://doi.org/10.1109/TCBB.2022.3211936.

[23] Tim, L., Tillman, W., & Sepehr, J. (2018). M2U-NET: effective and efficient retinal vessel segmentation for resource-constrained environments. arXiv (Cornell University), 1.

16 Impacts of as composition fraction on sensitivity in dielectric modulated trench junctionless InAs$_x$Sb$_{1-x}$ DG FET biosensors

Swagata Bhattacherje[1,a], Ananya Barman[2,b], Bidyut Sarkar[3,c] and Rinku Sarkar[3,d]

[1]Faculty, Dept. of Physics, Heritage College, Kolkata, WB, India

[2]Asst. Prof., Dept. of Chemistry, JIS College of Engineering, Kalyani, WB, India

[3]Asst. Prof., Dept. of Physics, JIS College of Engineering, Kalyani, WB, India

Abstract

In this paper, the impact of As content on the performance of a dielectric modulated InAs$_x$Sb$_{1-x}$ trench gate junction less field effect transistor-based biosensor is investigated using a well-calibrated simulation framework using ATLAS, a device simulation software. The impacts are studied on the different performance indicators of the biosensor for detecting biomolecules having dielectric constants ranging from 2.1 to 4.7. The results suggest that the composition fraction of As leaves a notable influence on the sensing capability of biomolecules. Additionally, the findings reveal that the low composition fraction of As has a more pronounced effect on biomolecules having higher values of dielectric constants. The best result is obtained for a composition of 25% of As, which is better than the Si channel devices.

Keywords: Biosensor, InAsSb channel, JL FET, sensitivity, TCAy

Introduction

Dielectric modulated field effect transistor (DMFET) built structures have become more attractive for the detection of biomoleculesm [11, 20;t and Paily [20] owing to their natural competence of a high degree of label-free spotting of bio species. Junctionless FETs (JLFETs) are one of the important members of this group due to their high degree of sensitivity, same-chip integration competence, and low cost. Sensitivity is a vital indicator for biosensors, which is related to the device performance and the types of biomolecules. A wide variety of FET-based biosensors are proposed in different articles with diverse device architectures like tunnel FETso et al. [13), impact ionization FETs (IMOS)n and Kuma [12), and junctionless FETs [1, 2, 14, 19, 23)

Literature Review

Kanungo et al. worked with short ranged DM TFET biosensors and observed improved sensitivity compared to a full-gate device [13]. The impact-ionization operation is proposed by Kannan and Kumar [12) to spot the biomolecules and found an inferior sensitivity in the short channel regime. and Kranti [9 the practicability of transconductance efficiency is analyzed as a sensing tool of TFET biosensors [9], whereasi and Krant [10Tthe viability of tunneling and accumulation of DM biosensors is presented [10]. A novel architecture consisting of vertically dielectrically modulated TFETs was reported [22]. In another work, charge plasma is implemented for the detection of biomolecules using dielectric modulated JL TFETs [23]. Kim et al. proposed a parameter, the ill factor, for partially occupied nanogaps for real situations [14]. In contrast, Narang et al. [19] offered an analytical model to explain the dielectric modulation process [19]. Ambipolar current in a TFET was used by Abdi and Kumar to determine the sensitivity [1]. Ahangari worked with a double-gate nanowire JL TFET-based biosensor [2]. Sandeep Kumar et al. presented an analytical model as well as a simulation approach [15, 16. of Trench gate JLFET for the detection of label-free biomolecules. The impact of partial hybridization and probe placement on the functionality of a label-free biosensor was examined in [3]. In all the above reports, silicon is mainly used as the channel material for the device. There have beenwa

[a]swagata.bhattacherjee@gmail.com, [b]ananya.barman@jiscollege.ac.in, [c]bidyut.sarkar@jiscollege.ac.in, [d]rinkusarkar1003@gmail.com

DOI: 10.1201/9781003724995-16

few papers in which non-silicon elements, especially III-V semiconductors, are used aslchannel material. Chhabra et al. [6] applied GaAs as a channel material for biosensing. They observed the impacts of the dimension of the nanogap on the sensitivity of the device, which is the ratio of the drain current with and without biomolecules. They obtained a healthy ON-OFF current ratio, but the maximum sensitivity obtained was 1.07. Mukhopadhyay et al. [18] worked with InGaAs/Si-based heterojunction TFET for spotting diverse bio species [18]. They observed superior results for subthreshold slope, ON-OFF current ratio, and the sensitivity of the device. Another thing is that the performance indicators observed for biomolecules having higher values of dielectric constants (>5), for which sensitivity is usually high. Proper assessment of sensitivity is more crucial for lower dielectric constant biomolecules. Dixit et al. [8] came up with $GaAs_{1-x}Sb_x$ FinFET for label-free detection of biomolecules. They investigated the different phenomena like velocity overshoot, DIBL, and capacitive coupling on the identification of biomolecules. Although InAsSb channel materials were extensively explored in infrared photo detection(Rogalski et al. [21;, Casias et al. [5], as well as in chemical detection et al. [17], their potential for the detection of biomolecules remains unexplored.

In this paper, we propose a novel design for $InAs_xSb_{1-x}$ channel trench gate JL DG FET biosensors, marking an advancement in this field. Through comprehensive analysis employing SILVACO ATLAS, we thoroughly evaluate the performance of these biosensors across a wide range of As molar contents. Our investigation delves into the optimization of sensitivity by modulating the As content within the InAsSb channel. Furthermore, we conduct a comparative analysis between our obtained sensitivity values and those published elsewhere.

Device Structure an& Methodology

A trench gate InAsSb channel JL DG FET is considered in the present work as depicted in Figure 16.1. The two vertical gates are positioned on both sides of the channel in different trenches. Between the channel and gates, two vertical nanogaps are formed where air is mostly present in the absence of biomolecules. Accordingly, the gate and drain connections are applied. When biomolecules are not present, the nanogap's dielectric constant is 1,

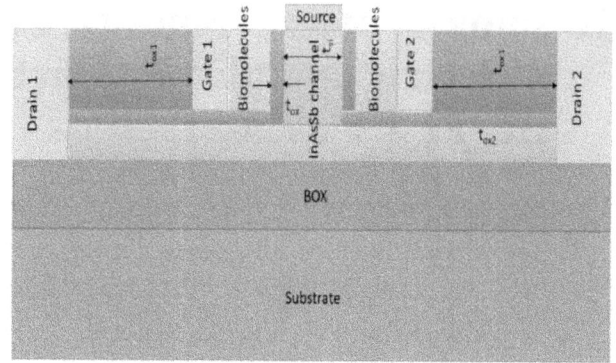

Figure 16.1 Schematic diagra
Source: Author

which is adjusted based on the dielectric constant of the biomolecules. This shifting of the dielectric constant makes a change in the gate capacitance, which is reflected in different electrical parameters. The device is constructed and characterized using SILVACO ATLAS. We extract different parameters of the channel materials like band gap, electron affinity, permittivity, and intrinsic carrier concentrations for different compositions of As [23] for employing in the simulation.

Analysis of sensitivity

The competence of a biosensor means how effectively it can spot a biomolecule in the cavity region, and that is acknowledged from its sensitivity, which is defined as [22]:

$$S_A = \frac{A_{bio} - A_{air}}{A_{air}} \qquad (1)$$

where A is an indicator related to bio-sensing. In this work, we focus on two performance indicators for biosensing namely drain OFF current (I_{OFF}) and threshold voltage (V_{th}). The sensitivities are measured with respect to the indicators mentioned above as

$$S_{IOFF} = \frac{I_{OFF\,bio} - I_{OFF\,air}}{I_{OFF\,air}} \qquad (2)$$

$$S_{vth} = \frac{V_{th\,bio} - V_{th\,air}}{V_{th\,air}} \qquad (3)$$

where V_{thbio} and $I_{OFF\,bio}$ are the OFF state threshold voltage and drain current when biomolecules are present.

$I_{OFF\,air}$ and V_{thair} are the same parameters in the absence of biomolecules.

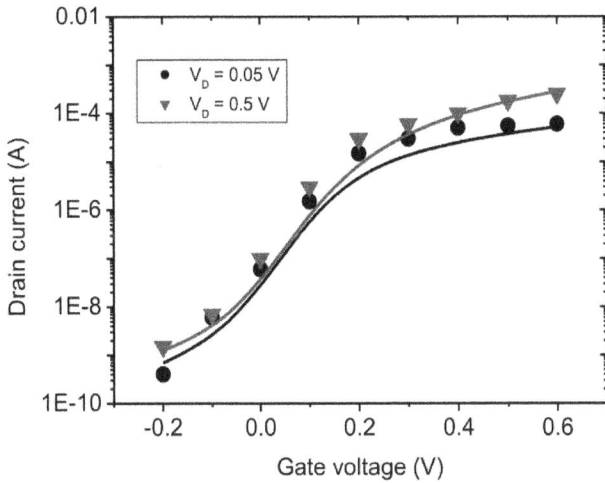

Figure 16.2 Calibration of I_D [24]
Source: Author

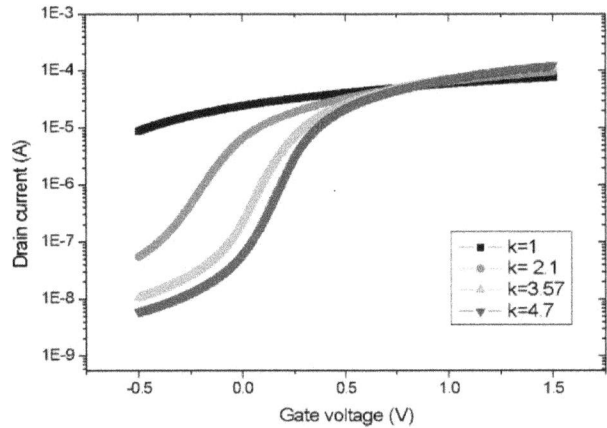

Figure 16.3 I_D-V_G for a range of bio species
Source: Author

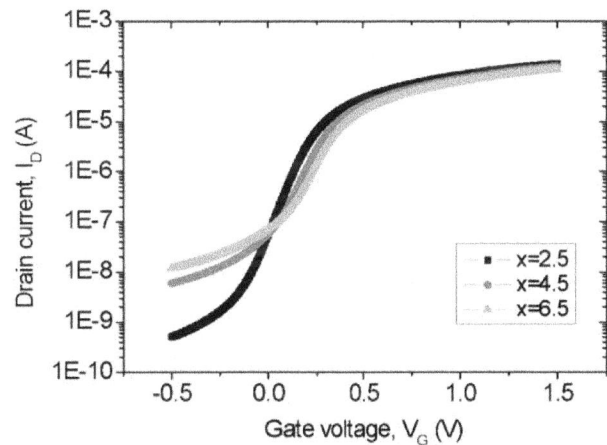

Figure 16.4 I_D-V_G for various x at Lg = 50 nm
Source: Author

Model calibration

The simulation model is calibrated against the reported experimental data [24]. Figure 16.2 shows the simulated I_D-V_G of the DM InAs$_x$Sb$_{1-x}$ channel trench gate DG JLFET for a gate length of 100 nm at 50 mV and 0.5 V drain voltages, which is compared with experimental data [24].

A proximity between them established the acceptability of the model.

Results and Discussions

We have studied the sensitivity of biosensors as a function of As composition fraction *x*. The transfer properties of the biosensor with air and biomolecules, just one at a time, are displayed in Figure 16.3. When air is replaced by biomolecules, the dielectric constant is changed from 1 to the respective values of bio species.

We have taken the dielectric constants as 2.1, 3.57 and 4.7 for Streptavidin, APTES and Ferrocytochrome, respectively. In the subthreshold region, the graph (Figure 16.3) clearly illustrates a significant separation in I_D between k = 1 and k>1, affirming the robust detection capability of the biosignal. This deviation underscores a substantial variance in drain current between biomolecules and air, thereby enhancing detection sensitivity. The sensing capacity is better for the biospecies having higher dielectric constants. Figure 16.4 presents the impacts of x on the drain current for a given sample having k = 4.7. As observed, x can change I_D significantly, especially

in the subthreshold region where the sensor works. For x = 0.25, a steep subthreshold slope and an ON-OFF current ratio are discovered. Figure 16.5 depicts the ratio of I_D with biomolecules (I_{Dbio}) to I_D with air (I_{Dair}), which is one of the key performance indicators, for different values of x, considering k = 4.7. Interestingly, I_{Dbio}/I_{Dair} varies with mole fraction x as may be found in Figure 16.5. The graph displays that I_D undergoes a change of 10^5 times with gate voltage in either direction from V_G = 0.3 V for x = 0.25. Figure 16.6 depicts the performance of another performance indicator, transconductance efficiency (g_M/I_D), with I_D for different biomolecules. A considerable amount of variation in (g_M/I_D) is observed in the subthreshold as well as linear region in presence of biomolecules as compared to air, especially for high-k samples but the difference is less prominent as

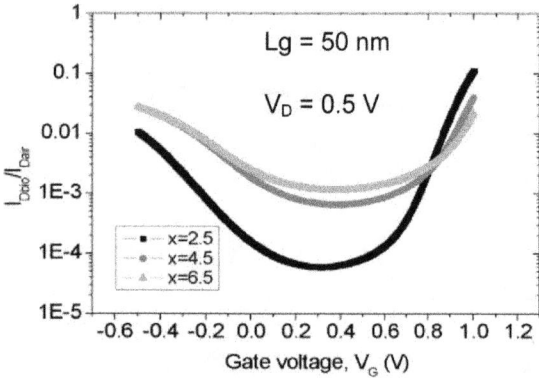

Figure 16.5 I$_{Dbio}$ /I$_{Dair}$ with V$_G$ for different x
Source: Author

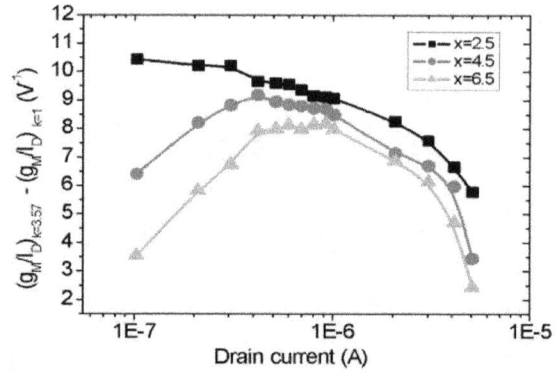

Figure 16.7 Difference of g$_M$/I$_D$ in presence of biomolecules with respect to air
Source: Author

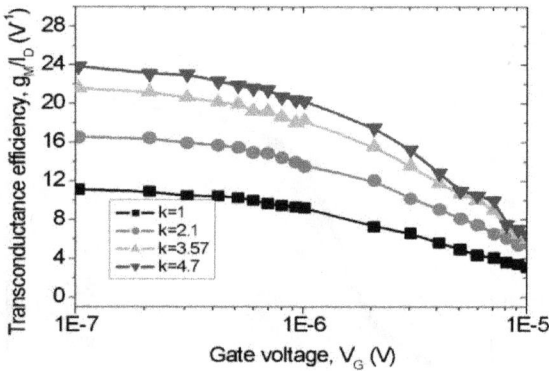

Figure 16.6 Plot of g$_M$/I$_D$ with I$_D$ for different k values
Source: Author

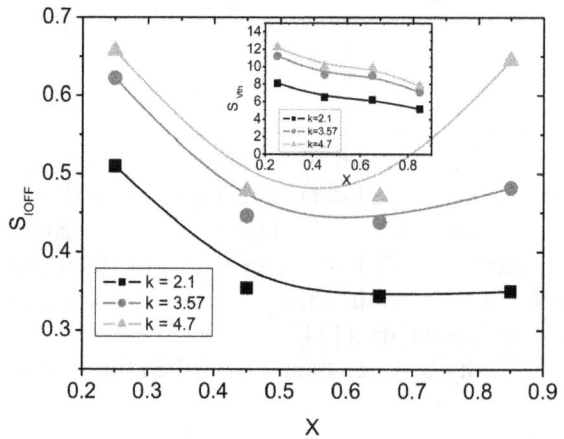

Figure 16.8 Plot of S$_{IOFF}$ and S$_{Vth}$ with x for different sample
Source: Author

compared to that in Figure 16.5. Figure 16.7 demonstrates the change in the difference of transconductance efficiency for biomolecules having dielectric constant 3.57 relative to air for various mole fractions. As observed from the figure that the difference is maximum for x = 0.25, indicating that the device is mostly sensitive to lower composition fractions of As. Figure 16.8 illustrates how x affects the device's S$_{IOFF}$ concerning the OFF current, following Eq. 2 for different samples of biomolecules having different values of k. As found from the figure, the sensitivity decreases with increasing x from 0.25 to 0.65, thereafter a further improvement is observed for biomolecules having k= 3.57 or higher with a faster rate of enhancement for k= 4.7. Sensitivity S$_{Vth}$ is also calculated with reference to threshold voltage following Eq. (3) and displayed in Figure 16.8b for different biospecies. Again an improvement of S$_{Vth}$

is observed for lower values of x of As, and the biospecies having larger k values show considerable change. Table 16.1 displays a comparison between the I$_{Dbio}$/I$_{Dair}$ and sensitivities of the InAs$_x$Sb$_{1-x}$ channel device with reported data for Si and other III-V channel devices. The former sensor with As content of 25% shows better sensitivity for all biomolecules considered in the present study.

Conclusion

We have presented an InAs$_x$Sb$_{1-x}$ channel DM JL FET based biosensor to identify the presence of biomolecules. We computed several sensitivity parameters based on threshold voltage, and OFF current. We have also looked at how the As composition percent

Table 16.1 Comparison of S_{Vth} and S_{IOFF} for $InAs_xSb_{1-X}$ channel biosensor with other reports.

Device specification	k	$\dfrac{I_{Dbio}}{I_{Dair}}$	S_{vth}	S_{IOFF}
Si DG JLFET L_g = 50 nm L_c = 30-60 nm T_c =5 nm [15]	4.7 3.57 2.1	NA	11.1 10.5 7.2	NA
GaAs JL FinFET L_g = 20 nm T_c = 18 nm V_D =0.5 V [6]	2.1	NA	1.01	NA
InGaAs/Si [18]	5	4×10^6	NA	NA
GaAsSb FinFET Lg= 14 nm Lc= 12 nm Tc=5.5 nm V_{DS} = 0.5 V [8]	2.1	NA	3.74	45.21%
InAsSb channel DG JLFET Lg= 50 nm Lc= 50 nm Tc = 6 nm (present work)	5 4.7 3.57 2.1	1.4×10^{-5} 5.9×10^{-5} 1.2×10^{-4} 8.5×10^{-4}	13 12.25 11.2 8.09	69% 66% 62% 51%

Source: Author

affects the previously mentioned sensitivity metrics. Our findings suggest that improved sensitivity is obtained by designing a sensor with a low value of As molar fraction. The sensitivity of our optimized sensor with As content of 25% yields the highest sensitivity as compared with the equivalent Si-based sensors. Hence there is potential to develop the proposed InAsSb channel sensor to obtain enhanced sensitivity.

References

[1] Abdi, D., & Kumar, M. J. (2015). Dielectric modulated overlapping gate- on drain tunnel-FET as a label-free biosensor. *Superlattices and Microstructures*, 86(8), 198–202.

[2] Ahangari, Z. (2016). Performance assessment of dual material gate dielectric modulated nanowire junctionless MOSFET for ultrasensitive detection of biomolecules. *RSC Advances*, 6 (6), 89185– 89191.

[3] Bhattacharyya, A., Chanda, M., & De, D. (2020). Analysis of partial hybridization and probe positioning on sensitivity of a dielectric modulated junctionless label free biosensor. *IEEE Transactions on Nanotechnology*, 19(10), 719–772.

[4] Bhattacherjee, S., & Biswas, A. (2020). Investigation on noise performance of $InAs_x Sb_{1-x}$ MOSFETs with compositional variations. *Microsystem Technologies*, 26(10), 1133–1140.

[5] Casias, L. K., Morath, C. P., Steenbergen, E. H., Webster, P. T., Kim, J. K., Cowan, V. M., et al. (2019). Carrier concentration and transport in Be- doped InAsSb for infrared sensing applications. *Infrared Physics & Technology*, 96, 184–191.

[6] Chhabra, A., Kumar, A., & Chaujar, R. (2019). Sub-20 nm GaAs junctionless FinFET for biosensing application. *Vacuum*, 160(10), 467–471.

[7] Convertino, C., Zota, C., Sant, S., Eltes, F., Sousa, M., Caimi, D., et al. (2019). InGaAs-on-insulator FinFETs with reduced off-current and record perfor-mance. (IEDM18), 39(2), 1–4.

[8] Dixit, A., Samajdar, D. P., & Bagga, N. (2021). Dielectric modulated GaAxSb1-xFinFET as label-free biosensor: device proposal and investigation. *Semiconductor Science and Technology*, 36, 095033–095046.

[9] Dwivedi, P., & Kranti, A. (2017). Applicability of transconductance-to- current ratio (*gm/Ids*) as a sensing metric for tunnel FET biosensors. *IEEE Sensors Journal*, 17(4), 1030–1036.

[10] Dwivedi, P., & Kranti, A. (2018). Dielectric modulated biosensor architecture: tunneling or accumulation based transistor? *IEEE Sensors Journal*, 18(8), 3228–3235.

[11] Im, H., Huang, J. X., Gu, B., & Choi, Y. K. (2007). A dielectric modulated field effect transistor for biosensing. *Nature Nanotechnology*, 2(7), 30–434.

[12] Kannan, N., & Kumar, M. J. (2013). Dielectric-modulated impact-ionization MOS (DIMOS) transistor as a label-free biosensor. *IEEE Electron Device Letters*, 34(12), 1575–1577.

[13] Kanungo, S., Chattopadhyay, S., Gupta, P. S., & Rahaman, H. (2015). Comparative performance analysis of the dielectrically modulated full-gate and short-gate tunnel FET-based biosensors. *IEEE Transactions on Electron Devices*, 62(3), 994–1001.

[14] Kim, S. K., Cho, H., Park, H. J., Kwon, D., Lee, J. M., & Chung, B. H. (2009). Nanogap biosensors for electrical and label-free detection of biomolecular interactions. *Nanotechnology*, 20(45), 455502.

[15] Kumar, S., Singh, B., & Singh, Y. (2021). Analytical model of dielectric modulated Trench gate double gate junctionless FET for biosensing applications. *IEEE Sensors Journal*, 21(7), 8896–8902.

[16] Kumar, S., Singh, B., Singh, Y., & Tiwari, P. K. (2020). Simulation study of dielectric modulated

dual channel trench gate TFET based biosensor. *IEEE Sensors Journal*, 20(21), 12565–12572.

[17] Martyniuk, P., Wojtas, J., Michalczewski, K., Gawron, W., Mikołajczyk, J., & Krishna, S. (2021). Demonstration of the long wavelength InAs/InAsSb type-II superlattice based methane sensor. *Sensors and Actuators A: Physical*, 332(1), 113107.

[18] Mukhopadhyay, S., Sen, D., Goswami, B., & Sarkar, S. K. (2021). Performance evaluation of dielectrically modulated extended gate single cavity InGaAs/Si HTFET based label-free biosensor considering non-ideal issues. *IEEE Sensors*, 21(4), 4739–4736.

[19] Narang, R., Reddy, K. V. S., Saxena, M., Gupta, R. S., & Gupta, M. (2012). A dielectric-modulated tunnel-FET-based biosensor for label-free detection: analytical modeling study and sensitivity analysis. *IEEE Transactions on Electron Devices*, 59(10), 2809–2817.

[20] Rawat, B., & Paily, R. (2015). Analysis of graphene tunnel field-effect ransistors for analog/RF applications. *IEEE Transactions on Electron Devices*, 62(8), 2663–2669.

[21] Rogalski, A., Martyniuk, P., Kopytko, M., Madejczyk, P., & Krishna, S. (2020). InAsSb-based infrared photodetectors: thirty years later on. *Sensors*, 20(24), 7047.

[22] Verma, M., Tirkey, S., Yadav, S., Sharma, D., & Yadav, D. S. (2017). Performance assessment of a novel vertical dielectrically modulated TFET-based biosensor. *IEEE Transactions on Electron Devices*, 64(9), 3841–3848.

[23] Wadhwa, G., & Raj, B. (2018). Label free detection of biomolecules using charge-plasma-based gate underlap dielectric modulated junctionless TFET. *Journal of Electronic Material*, 47(6), 4683–4693.

17 Meditox: integrating machine learning and molecular data for accurate drug toxicity prediction

Gaurav Prajapati[a], Utkarsh Dixit[b] and Harshit Aggarwal[c]

Department of CSE-AIML, ABES Engineering College, Ghaziabad, UP, India

Abstract

In the fields of chemical safety, regulatory toxicology, and drug development, toxicity prediction models are essential. The goal of this research is to use sophisticated machine learning and molecular descriptors, physicochemical characteristics, and structural fingerprints to create a dependable in silico model for predicting acute toxicity, hepatotoxicity, and mutagenicity. The model's interpretability was enhanced through the use of feature selection approaches and a varied dataset comprising both private and public chemical structures. High accuracy and generalizability were validated by external testing and cross-validation. The model provided a scalable, economical toxicity screening method that outperformed current techniques. Deep learning and transfer learning will be used in future research to improve predictions.

Keywords: In silico, machine learning, physicochemical characteristics

Introduction

A crucial and essential phase in the drug research and development process is the prediction of a medication's toxicity. Early detection of harmful qualities in possible drug candidates can guarantee patient safety and regulatory compliance while drastically cutting down on the time, effort, and financial outlay needed to introduce new medications to the market. Conventional experimental techniques for toxicity evaluation, such as in vitro tests and in vivo animal investigations, are useful but frequently expensive, time-consuming, and resource-intensive. Furthermore, interest in computational alternatives has increased due to scalability issues and ethical considerations.

The prediction of toxicity has been revolutionized by advances in computer techniques driven by machine learning (ML) and deep learning (DL) algorithms. With the help of these silico methods, it is possible to evaluate sizable databases of chemical compounds and assess their molecular structures, characteristics, and related toxicological consequences with exceptional efficiency. Researchers may more quickly and accurately anticipate a variety of harmful consequences by utilizing these technologies, such as genotoxicity (DNA damage), cardiotoxicity (heart toxicity), nephrotoxicity (kidney toxicity), hepatotoxicity (liver poisoning), cancer and more [1]. Our goal in this research is to use a variety of machine learning approaches to create a reliable toxicity prediction model. Utilizing the abundance of information found in both public and private databases, including the chemical structures of pharmacological compounds and the associated toxicological profiles, are part of this endeavor. Using silico approaches, we work to construct models that can reliably forecast the toxicity of new drug candidates, assisting pharmaceutical researchers in setting priorities for more development of certain substances.

In order to record the electrical, physicochemical, and structural characteristics of medications, we shall investigate molecular fingerprints and descriptors. To find patterns connecting molecular characteristics to toxicity, these attributes will be fed into machine learning models such as Random Forests (RF) and Support Vector Machines (SVM) [3, 4].

The goal of this research is to increase the effectiveness by lowering the cost of medication development by offering a computational pre-screening tool for the early detection of dangerous candidates [5, 6]. It advances medical research and innovation by lowering late-stage failures and assisting in the development of safer, more effective medications.

Literature Review

Drug development may be done in three primary ways: *in vivo*, *in vitro*, and *in silico*. All three approaches have been discussed below.

[a]agauravprajapatincr@gmail.com, [b]utkarsh.dixit@abes.ac.in, [c]aggarwalharshit541@gmail.com

DOI: 10.1201/9781003724995-17

In vivo method

The study of drug compounds' biological effects in living things, usually through the use of animal models, is known as in vivo toxicity testing. These techniques offer crucial information about a compound's pharmacokinetics, toxicological characteristics, and safety. Even if in vitro and in silico techniques have improved, in vivo techniques are still essential, particularly for regulatory approval and comprehending intricate biological interactions that are difficult for computer models to completely represent. It is a conventional approach to medication development.

In conclusion, despite their difficulties, in vivo techniques are nevertheless crucial for toxicity prediction to guarantee the security and effectiveness of medication candidates. These experiments offer important information on long-term and systemic effects that are hard to reproduce with other methods. But by incorporating in vivo data into silico and in vitro models, the trend is shifting away from using animals and toward increasing prediction accuracy while resolving ethical issues.

In vitro method

Using isolated cells, tissues, or biochemical experiments conducted outside of living creatures, in vitro toxicity testing examines the harmful effects of medication compounds. By offering a high-throughput, economical, and ethical substitute for in vivo research, these techniques are essential for early-stage drug development because they shed light on the processes underlying cellular and molecular toxicity. Furthermore, by following the 3Rs approach (reduce, refine, replace), in vitro techniques lessen the need for animal testing.

In silico method

The process of predicting the hazardous effects of pharmacological molecules without the need for physical experiments by using computer models and algorithms is known as "in silico toxicity prediction" [2]. These techniques use quantitative structure-activity relationship (QSAR) models, molecular descriptors, chemical data, and ML to evaluate toxicity early in the drug development process. The capacity of in silico approaches to lessen the need for animal research, save time, and lower costs has led to their widespread use [7].

By facilitating quicker, less expensive, and more moral evaluations of pharmacological compounds,

in silico techniques are transforming the field of toxicity prediction. Predictive accuracy is increasing due to developments in deep learning, QSAR modeling, and machine learning. However, model generality, data quality, and the combination of computational predictions with in vitro and in vivo trials are critical to the success of in silico approaches. The prediction power and uptake of *in silico* toxicity assessment in drug discovery will be substantially improved in the future by the integration of big data, cloud computing, and AI-driven technologies. Acute oral toxicity, hepatotoxicity, cardiotoxicity, mutagenicity, and other forms are among the several forms of toxicities.

Acute oral toxicity

The detrimental consequences of one or more oral doses of a chemical during a 24-hour period, usually noticeable within 24 to 48 hours, are referred to as acute oral toxicity. In clinical studies, it aids in establishing acceptable dosage levels to evaluate the danger of overdose. Although in vivo animal testing has been the gold standard for safety testing, new in vitro and in silico techniques are becoming more and more popular as morally and economically sound substitutes that, if approved by authorities, might lessen the need for animal testing.

Hepatotoxicity

A drug's detrimental effects on the liver, an organ essential to metabolism and detoxification, are referred to as hepatotoxicity. Drug-induced liver damage (DILI), a major reason for trial failures and market withdrawals, can be avoided with early identification. Although animal models are still the norm, in vitro and in silico techniques provide economical and moral substitutes. Hepatotoxicity prediction is improved by technologies such as organ-on-a-chip, iPSC-derived hepatocytes, and AI-based models, which also lower drug development costs and improve patient safety.

Cardiotoxicity

The term "cardiotoxicity" describes how medications can have harmful effects on the heart that alter its structure or function. Arrhythmias, heart failure, a decreased ejection fraction, or myocardial tissue destruction are some of its possible symptoms. Since many promising medications have failed clinical trials or been taken off the market because of their negative effects on the heart, it is crucial to predict and evaluate cardiotoxicity.

One of the biggest problems in drug research is cardiotoxicity, which frequently results in trial failures or medication withdrawals. In vitro (iPSC-derived cardiomyocytes) and in silico techniques provide morally sound and economical substitutes for animal models, which are still the gold standard. The CiPA project, AI tools, and heart-on-a-chip technology improve assessment while lowering expenses and guaranteeing safety. For increased accuracy, future forecasts will probably integrate in vitro, in vivo, and in silico methods.

Mutagenicity

The term "mutagenicity" describes a substance's capacity to induce genetic alterations that may result in cancer or hereditary illnesses. Because regulatory agencies need early identification of such concerns, mutagenicity assessment is essential in medication development to guarantee safety.

To detect genetic hazards, guarantee medication safety, and comply with laws, mutagenicity testing is essential. AI and silico models improve forecast accuracy, but conventional techniques like the Ames test are still important. Future testing should be more successful because to emerging technologies like organ-on-a-chip and NGS.

Methodology

Data collection

- **Experimental data:** Gather information about toxicity from lab tests, such as in vitro (cell-based assays) or in vivo (animal-based research). These kinds of data usually include information on organ-specific toxicities like hepatotoxicity or nephrotoxicity, as well as harmful consequences like cytotoxicity and genotoxicity.
- **Public databases:** Utilize toxicity data from reputable sources that have a wide variety of chemical and biological data, such as PubChem, ChEMBL, ToxCast, and Tox21. In order to supplement experimental data, several resources are essential.

Chemical structure representation

- **Molecular descriptors:** Use characteristics such as molecular weight, logP, number of hydrogen

Table 17.1 Previous Work.

Models	Description	Limitations
DeepTox (2016)	It utilized deep neural networks to predict chemical toxicity, outperforming traditional QSAR models.	It requires **large, labeled** datasets for generalization, is prone to overfitting due to its complexity, and lacks interpretability in toxicity classification.
chemProp (2019)	It employed Graph Neural Networks (GNNs) to capture molecular interactions, leading to state-of-the-art performance in toxicity classification.	It is computationally expensive for large molecular graphs, requires specialized graph-based feature engineering, and produces hard-to-interpret results, making regulatory adoption challenging.
MolBERT (2020)	It introduced transformer-based molecular embeddings, enhancing toxicity prediction accuracy by learning contextual representations of molecules.	It requires significant computational resources for training, depends on large-scale molecular datasets for high accuracy, and is not optimized for small, domain-specific datasets, making it less efficient for certain toxicity studies.
MPNNs (2017)	It demonstrated improved performance in modeling molecular graphs for toxicity and bioactivity prediction.	It has slow inference time due to the iterative nature of message passing, struggles with generalization for unseen molecular substructures, and is difficult to interpret, making explainability challenging.

Source: Author

bond donors/acceptors, and topological indices to depict the physical and chemical characteristics of molecules. The structural characteristics of molecules are quantitatively summarized by these descriptors.

- **Molecular fingerprints:** Use methods like extended-connectivity fingerprints (ECFP) or MACCS keys to encode chemical structures into binary or numerical forms. These fingerprints are utilized as inputs for machine learning algorithms and enable quick comparisons.

Preprocessing and feature engineering

- **Data cleaning:** By eliminating redundant compounds, managing missing values, and normalizing numerical characteristics, you can make sure the dataset is consistent. This step increases the dataset's dependability.
- **Feature selection:** To determine which characteristics are most important for toxicity prediction, use tree-based techniques like Random Forest or algorithms like Principal Component Analysis (PCA).
- **Handling unbalanced data:** To ensure that the model learns from both classes, use techniques such as SMOTE (Synthetic Minority Over-sampling

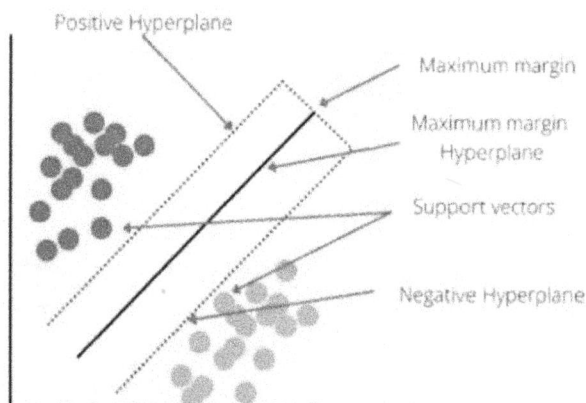

Figure 17.1 Support vector machine hyperplane diagram
Source: Author

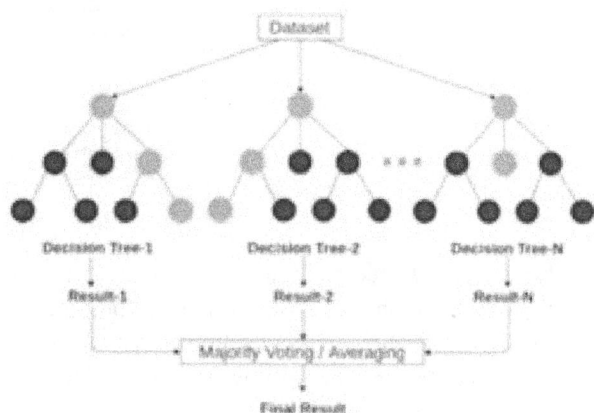

Figure 17.2 Random forest flow diagram
Source: Author

Technique) to balance datasets where harmful substances may be underrepresented.

Model building

- **Machine learning models:** Employ predictive models tailored for toxicity data shows there was a different model proposed in earlier work shown in Figure 17.1:
- **Support Vector Machines:** A potent supervised learning technique that is usually applied to tasks involving regression and classification. It operates by identifying the optimum hyperplane to divide a dataset's data points into distinct groups, as shown in Figure 17.1.
- **Random Forests:** Using random data and feature subsets, RF is an ensemble learning technique for regression and classification that

creates several decision trees shown in Figure 17.2. It improves generalization, decreases overfitting, and increases accuracy by averaging predictions (regression) or majority voting (classification). For toxicity prediction, it works well with high-dimensional datasets.
- **CNN:** Our proposed CNN model consists of the following layers:

1. Input layer: Accepts molecular fingerprints and physicochemical descriptors.
2. Convolutional layers: *Three convolutional layers with filter sizes of 32, 64, and 128. *ReLU activation function applied to introduce non-linearity. *Batch normalization to stabilize learning.
3. Pooling layer: Max-pooling operation (size: 2×2) to reduce dimensionality.
4. Fully connected layers: *Two dense layers with 512 and 256 neurons, respectively. *Dropout layers (rate: 0.5) to prevent overfitting.
5. Output layer: A SoftMax layer for toxicity classification. reduce size

QSAR (quantitative structure-activity relationship) modeling
QSAR models anticipate how structural factors affect biological effects and relate toxicity to molecular fingerprints and chemical descriptors. These programs find patterns in vast datasets to evaluate toxicity concerns at an early stage of medication development.

ADMET predictions
Absorption, distribution, metabolism, excretion, and toxicity (ADMET) qualities may be predicted using computational models to evaluate how a drug is processed in the body and its potential harmful effects. Predicting ADMET properties helps optimize drug candidates by assessing their pharmacokinetic and safety profiles, reducing the likelihood of adverse effects during clinical trials. This prediction can streamline the drug development process, allowing researchers to prioritize candidates with desirable pharmacokinetic properties and minimal toxicity risks.

Model evaluation
In machine learning, assessing model performance is essential. Effectiveness is evaluated by weighing trade-offs between false positives and negatives

using metrics such as ROC-AUC, F1-score, accuracy, recall, and precision. Class differentiation is measured by ROC-AUC, whereas F1-score strikes a balance between recall and accuracy. Generalization to unknown data is ensured via external validation. Accuracy, robustness, and dependability are improved by using these metrics and validation methods.

Application
In pharmaceutical research, toxicity prediction models are essential for spotting dangerous compounds early on and cutting down on expenses, risks, and development time. In order to improve patient safety and regulatory compliance, they aid in prioritizing safer drug candidates, increasing efficiency, and supporting the development of safer, more effective medications.

Results

Several performance indicators, such as accuracy, precision, recall, F1-score, and the area under the receiver operating characteristic curve (AUC-ROC), were used to assess the created toxicity prediction model. The findings showed that the model had a high prediction accuracy for a number of toxicity endpoints, including mutagenicity, hepatotoxicity, and acute toxicity.

Key findings from the study include:

1. Model performance: For every toxicity endpoint, the three-layer convolutional neural network (CNN) model that performed the best had an accuracy of 0.80.
2. Feature importance: In order to forecast toxicity, molecular fingerprints and physicochemical characteristics such as LogP, molecular weight, and hydrogen bond acceptors were essential. Performance was maintained while complexity was reduced through feature selection.
3. Cross-validation and generalizability: External test datasets and 10-fold cross-validation were used to validate the model, which demonstrated good generalization with little lack of accuracy on unknown data.
4. Comparison with existing models: Our method showed either equal or better predictive power when compared to previously created toxicity prediction models, especially in hepatotoxicity evaluation.

Overall, the results validate the robustness of our machine learning-based approach in predicting toxicity with high reliability.

Comparative Analysis: CNNs vs. Advanced AI Models

Transformers: Transformers (such as ChemBERTa and MolBERT) use self-attention to capture long-range relationships in chemical sequences and assess molecular structures without the need for predetermined descriptors. Transformers provide superior sequence comprehension and do away with the requirement for handmade features, in contrast to CNNs, which are dependent on preset receptive fields. However, for efficient training, they need large-scale molecular datasets and are computationally costly.

GNNs: Graph neural networks (GNNs), including message passing neural networks (MPNNs) and graph convolutional networks (GCNs), represent molecules as graphs while maintaining atomic connection. GNNs improve generalization by capturing molecule topology, in contrast to CNNs, which process structured fingerprints. They are computationally demanding, need certain designs, and can be difficult to comprehend.

Conclusion

With a three-layer CNN obtaining excellent accuracy in predicting acute toxicity, hepatotoxicity, and mutagenicity, the study shows the efficacy of machine learning-based toxicity prediction. The significance of physicochemical characteristics and molecular fingerprints is emphasized by feature analysis. The robustness and dependability of the model for early drug development are confirmed by strong cross-validation findings.

The suggested model provides a more precise, effective, and economical solution than current methods, particularly in hepatotoxicity prediction. It emphasizes the expanding significance of computational tools in safer, more effective drug discovery by lowering the dangers associated with animal testing and medication development.

References

[1] Vaidya, P., Chauhan, S., & Jaiswal, V. (2022). Prediction of multi-class drugs: a perspective for designing drug with many uses. In 2022 2nd International Conference on Artificial Intelligence and Signal Processing (AISP), (pp. 1–7). Vijayawada, India. doi: 10.1109/AISP53593.2022.9760640.
[2] Kumar Gupta, V., & Singh Rana, P. (2021). Ensemble technique for toxicity prediction of small

drug molecules of the antioxidant response element signalling pathway. *The Computer Journal*, 64(12), 1861–1875. https://doi.org/10.1093/comjnl/bxaa001.

[3] Li, S., Zhang, L., Feng, H., Meng, J., Xie, D., Yi, L., et al. (2021). MutagenPred-GCNNs: a graph convolutional neural network-based classification model for mutagenicity prediction with data-driven molecular fingerprints. *Interdisciplinary Sciences – Computational Life Sciences*, 13(1), 25–33. https://doi.org/10.1007/s12539-020-00407-2.

[4] Peng, Y., Zhang, Z., Jiang, Q., Guan, J., & Zhou, S. (2020). TOP: a deep mixture representation learning method for boosting molecular toxicity prediction. *Methods*, 179, 55–64. https://doi.org/10.1016/j.ymeth.2020.05.013.

[5] Tong, Y., Guo, Q., Cui, J., & Peng, X. (2023). Toxicity prediction study of small molecules based on graph attention networks. In 2023 2nd International Conference on Artificial Intelligence, Human-Computer Interaction and Robotics (AIHCIR), (pp. 603–607). Tianjin, China. doi: 10.1109/AIHCIR61661.2023.00107.

[6] Bhavitha, Prasad, P. L., Ani, R., & Deepa, O. (2023). Machine learning based ADMET prediction in drug discovery. In 2023 4th IEEE Global Conference for Advancement in Technology (GCAT), (pp. 1–9). Bangalore, India. doi: 10.1109/GCAT59970.2023.10353396.

[7] Balamurugan, K. S., Appathurai, K., Sathish Kumar, P. J., Kumutha, D., & Surendran, R. (2024). Machine learning based modeling of drugs using virtual screening and in silico approach. In 2024 5th International Conference on Smart Electronics and Communication (ICOSEC), (pp. 1032–1038). Trichy, India. doi:10.1109/ICOSEC61587.2024.10722732.

18 Enhancing photos with deep learning to eliminate block artefacts

Devadatta Das[1,a], Sabyasachi Samanta[1,b] and Pinaki Satpathy[2,c]

[1]Department of CSE (Cyber Security), Haldia Institute of Technology, Haldia, WB, India

[2]Department of Electronics and Communication Engineering, Haldia Institute of Technology, Haldia, WB, India

Abstract

By creating noticeable block boundaries and unnatural discontinuities, block artifacts, which are brought on by compression methods like JPEG, dramatically reduce the visual quality of photos. This work introduces a new method for improving images by removing block artefacts with deep learning methods. To reduce artefacts, we suggest a convolutional neural network (CNN)-based architecture that uses multi-scale analysis and sophisticated feature extraction to recreate high-quality images. The model can effectively restore details and learn complex patterns because it is trained on a large dataset of compressed and original image pairs. Comparative studies demonstrate that our approach outperforms traditional approaches in both subjective visual quality and quantifiable metrics like PSNR and SSIM. This study demonstrates that deep learning may greatly enhance picture restoration jobs.

Keywords: Artefact removal, block artefacts, convolutional neural networks (CNN), deep learning, image compression

Introduction

Neural networks, deep learning, image recovery techniques, and regularization techniques are some of the machine learning techniques for eliminating noise from images. Images with noise are frequently cleaned up using neural networks and deep learning techniques like autoencoding and CNNs. The techniques examined in this research were trained in clean images before being applied to noisy photos to eliminate noise [7]. Lena, Barbara & Cameraman are a few examples of the noise that can be found in pictures. Comparative studies demonstrate that our approach outperforms traditional approaches in both subjective visual quality and quantifiable metrics like PSNR and SSIM. These sounds can be particularly audible at night and against dark backdrops while shooting outside [8]. CNNs, filters, and other algorithms can be applied to eliminate this kind of noise from photos. CNNs can automatically eliminate noise from new images after being trained on a large number of images with various kinds of noise [10]. Such kinds of noise in photographs can also be eliminated with the use of statistical analysis-based noise reduction techniques. For instance, histogram alignment is applied in the histogram approach to enhance image quality. To get a more consistent distribution of pixel values, this technique modifies the image's brightness or color characteristics [15]. This technique can aid in enhancing the image's readability and quality.

Related Work

Uzakkyzy et al. [1] examine high noise density and intricate patterns. Consideration is given to the efficacy of deep learning algorithms in performing noise reduction, such as the decomposition approach with and without preprocessing. Yessenova et al. [2] evaluate the efficacy of techniques for analyzing aeronautical photos, which combine artificial objects and textural regions of natural origin. Tao et al. [3] use sample purity and past probability for determining the weight of minority class sample. Liu et al. [4] proposed parameter update, management optimization, behavioral matching, and multi-domain simulation. To provide robust, interactive, and comprehensive 3D optical evaluation, the industrial robot's features are first modelled in a digital environment. Shahinzadeh et al. [5] suggested an image processing technique based on machine learning for the robotic assembly system. It can autonomously control the industrial robot and use inexpensive picture inputs to identify and locate assembly components. Suryawanshi et al. [6] provide a thorough overview of deep learning

[a]devadattadas859@gmail.com, [b]sabyasachi.smnt@gmail.com, [c]pinaki.sat@gmail.com

DOI: 10.1201/9781003724995-18

and machine learning techniques for sentiment analysis at the aspect, phrase, and document levels.

Proposed Methodology

The concepts of attention and traditional GAN architecture are combined in the generative model of the attentive GAN. The model can concentrate on particular regions of the data and produce superior results. Attention refers to a process that enables the model to ignore the rest of the input data and concentrate on specific portions of it. This enables the model to concentrate on more crucial information or data points. Discriminator and generator are the two primary parts of an attentive GAN, and they compete with one another during the learning process. The generator creates the produced data after receiving input data in the form of random noise or another kind.

Proposed algorithm

The following is how the attentive GAN (AGAN) model and Gaussian filtering technique were put into practice:

Step 1: Two datasets of clean and noisy images are used to train the AGAN model. In this step, the model learns how to efficiently convert noisy inputs into clean outputs.

Step 2: To smooth and reduce high-frequency noise, a noisy image may be subjected to Gaussian filtering before processing.

Step 3: The AGAN generator is used on the prepared noisy image. The generator creates a denoised version of the input image by applying the patterns it has learnt during training.

Step 4: Gaussian filtering is used to further process the AGAN model's output. By eliminating any remaining noise and enhancing overall smoothness, this stage improves the finished image.

Step 5: Terminate the process.

Result and Discussion

Lena, Barbara, and the Cameraman were among the noisy photos with different noise intensities used to solve this problem. For this research, 15,314 pre-trained image sets collected from the Kaggle database made up the training dataset. Different types of noise are depicted in Figures 18.1–18.3. In this study, pairs of noisy and correspondingly clean pictures were used to train the Attentive GAN model. A Gaussian filter was used after training to improve the

outcomes even further. The Attentive GAN model and Gaussian filtering together produced impressive results in noise removal, as shown in Figures 18.1–18.3, Lena, Barbara, and Cameraman were successfully removed. The model was trained to decrease noise interference and recognize important aspects of the picture. The Gaussian filter successfully reduced image noise. This method effectively decreased noise while improving image quality.

Deep learning techniques are quite effective at lowering image noise in this work. They enable models to accurately recover clean images and automatically analyze intricate connections in data. All training images were created using the Terrain model, which allowed for the reduction of noise in pictures of various kinds.

In order to determine the optimal quality metric, this work applies to the metrics (MSE, PSNR & SSIM). We have used the Gaussian filtering technique to simulate trials using Gaussian noise. The aforementioned measures have been used to evaluate the acquired image quality.

We define the pictures of Lena, Barbara, and the Cameraman in Figure 18.1. We begin with noisy photos of the three types of images stated earlier, so in this results section, we are only shown how the suggested technique would eliminate the noise. The noisy images that are used as input are displayed in Figures (a), (d), and (g). We displayed Figures (b), (e), and (h); noise is gradually eliminated from those pictures. Finally, the three types of noise-free photographs are displayed in Figures (c), (f) and (i).

The PSNR, SSIM, and MSE values from the Original Noisy images are compared with the Recovered Noisy images displayed in Figures 18.1–18.3.

PSNR is used to calculate the ratio of the highest signal strength to the power of the distorting noise that reduces the quality of the representation.

PSNR is expressed as:

$$PSNR = 10 \log 10 \ (peakval2)/MSE \qquad (i)$$

One approach that depends on perception is the structural similarity index method. This method defines image degradation as a change in the way structural information is interpreted. It also works with other important perception-based facts, such as brightness masking and contrast masking. The most widely used estimator for measuring image is quality means square error (MSE). The values nearer zero are preferable because it is a complete reference metric.

Conclusion

The improved images generated by this experiment can be successfully used for upcoming object recognition tasks. Blurring the background

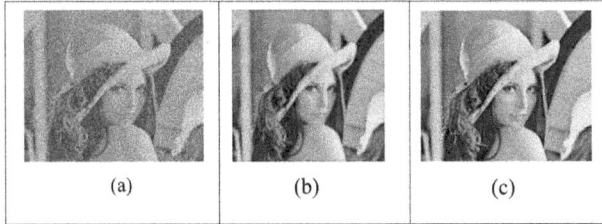

Figure 18.1 Original, noisy, and noisy-free Lena image
Source: Author

Figure 18.2 Original, noisy, and noisy-free Barbara image
Source: Author

Figure 18.3 Original, noisy, and noisy-free cameraman image
Source: Author

of an image helps emphasize things and makes them easier to recognize when the background is noisy or contains extraneous features. The study found that the quality and quantity of training data, together with the choice of a suitable model architecture, are important determinants of how effectively deep learning techniques for noise reduction work. Noisy photos with different noise densities were used in this experiment. It takes careful parameter selection and model optimization according to the particular kind of noise and intended results to get the best results. This study employed a combination strategy to enhance performance. The Derain model was used to train the data, and then a Gaussian filter was applied. Gloss, SIM metrics, and D-loss were used to assess the model's efficacy; the SIM value was 1. This illustrates how well the deep learning approach is used in this work.

References

[1] Uzakkyzy, N., Ismailova, A., Ayazbaev, T., Beldeubayeva, Z., Kodanova, S., Utenova, B., et al. (2023). Image noise reduction by deep learning methods. *International Journal of Electrical and Computer Engineering (IJECE)*, 13(6), 6855. Institute of Advanced Engineering and Science. https://doi.org/10.11591/ijece.v13i6.pp6855-6861.

[2] Yessenova, M., Abdikerimova, G., Ayazbaev, T., Murzabekova, G., Ismailova, A., Beldeubayeva, Z., et al. (2023). The effectiveness of methods and algorithms for detecting and isolating factors that negatively affect the growth of crops. *International Journal of Electrical and Computer Engineering (IJECE)*, 13(2), 1669. Institute of Advanced Engineering and Science. https://doi.org/10.11591/ijece.v13i2.pp1669-1679.

Table 18.1 Table for quality assessment techniques.

Noise Level Image	Quality assessment techniques	PSNR	MSE	SSIM
Lena	0.3	20.54	20.36	0.78
	0.5	15.81	14.71	0.74
	0.7	13.18	13.18	0.70
Barbara	0.2	20.85	20.45	0.71
	0.4	16.69	15.81	0.76
	0.6	13.38	13.18	0.73
Cameramen	0.4	20.35	20.54	0.71
	0.5	16.21	16.19	0.75
	0.6	14.18	14.24	0.74

Source: Author

[3] Tao, L., Zhu, H., Wang, Q., Liang, Y., & Deng, X. (2023). A combined priori and purity gaussian over-sampling algorithm for imbalanced data classification. *IEEE Access*, 11, 130688–130696. Institute of Electrical and Electronics Engineers (IEEE). https://doi.org/10.1109/access.2023.3334272

[4] Liu, X., Gan, H., Luo, Y., Chen, Y., & Gao, L. (2023). Digital-twin-based real-time optimization for a fractional order controller for industrial robots. *Fractal and Fractional*, 7(2), 167. MDPI AG. https://doi.org/10.3390/fractalfract7020167.

[5] Shahinzadeh, H., Mahmoudi, A., Asilian, A., Sadrarhami, H., Hemmati, M., & Saberi, Y. (2024). Deep learning: a overview of theory and architectures. In 2024 20th CSI International Symposium on Artificial Intelligence and Signal Processing (AISP), (pp. 1–11). IEEE. https://doi.org/10.1109/aisp61396.2024.10475265.

[6] Suryawanshi, N. S. (2024). Sentiment analysis with machine learning and deep learning: a survey of techniques and applications. *International Journal of Science and Research Archive*, 12(2), 005–015). GSC Online Press. https://doi.org/10.30574/ijsra.2024.12.2.1205.

[7] Liu, L., Wang, Y., & Chi, W. (2024). Retracted: image recognition technology based on machine learning. *IEEE Access*, 1 –1. Institute of Electrical and Electronics Engineers (IEEE). https://doi.org/10.1109/access.2020.3021590.

[8] Wang, X. V., Pinter, J. S., Liu, Z., & Wang, L. (2021). A machine learning-based image processing approach for robotic assembly system. *Procedia CIRP*, 104, 906–911. Elsevier BV. https://doi.org/10.1016/j.procir.2021.11.152.

[9] Hua, Z., Pan, G., Gao, K., Li, H., & Chen, S. (2023). AF-OSD: an anchor-free oriented ship detector based on multi-scale dense-point rotation gaussian heatmap. *Remote Sensing*, 15(4), 1120. MDPI AG. https://doi.org/10.3390/rs15041120.

[10] Uzakkyzy, N., Ismailova, A., Ayazbaev, T., Beldeubayeva, Z., Kodanova, S., Utenova, B., et al. (2023). Image noise reduction by deep learning methods. *International Journal of Electrical and Computer Engineering (IJECE)*, 13(6), 6855. Institute of Advanced Engineering and Science. https://doi.org/10.11591/ijece.v13i6.pp6855-6861.

[11] Johari, L., Ramya, P., Suganya, M., Praveena, H. D., LathaMageshwari, P. S., & Rajendiran, M. (2024). Deep learning-based noise reduction techniques in electronic signal processing. In 2024 Ninth International Conference on Science Technology Engineering and Mathematics (ICONSTEM), (pp. 1–6). IEEE. https://doi.org/10.1109/iconstem60960.2024.10568634.

[12] Nazir, N., Sarwar, A., & Saini, B. S. (2024). Recent developments in denoising medical images using deep learning: an overview of models, techniques, and challenges. *Micron*, 180, 103615. Elsevier BV. https://doi.org/10.1016/j.micron.2024.103615.

[13] Sundarrajan, M., Choudhry, M. D., Biju, J., Krishnakumar, S., & Rajeshkumar, K. (2024). Enhancing low-light medical imaging through deep learning-based noise reduction techniques. *Indian Journal of Science and Technology*, 17(34), 3567–3579. Indian Society for Education and Environment. https://doi.org/10.17485/ijst/v17i34.2489.

[14] Katta, S., Singh, P., Garg, D., & Diwakar, M. (2024). A hybrid approach for CT image noise reduction combining method noise-CNN and shearlet transform. *Biomedical and Pharmacology Journal*, 17(3), 1875–1898. Oriental Scientific Publishing Company. https://doi.org/10.13005/bpj/2991

[15] Maus, J., Nikulin, P., Hofheinz, F., Petr, J., Braune, A., Kotzerke, J., et al. (2024). Deep learning based bilateral filtering for edge-preserving denoising of respiratory-gated PET. *EJNMMI Physics*, 11(1), 58. Springer Science and Business Media LLC. https://doi.org/10.1186/s40658-024-00661-z.

[16] Huang, C., & Yang, Y. (2024). Gaussian noise image recognition based on convolutional neural networks. In 2024 5th International Conference on Computer Vision, Image and Deep Learning (CVIDL), (pp. 98–101). IEEE. https://doi.org/10.1109/cvidl62147.2024.10603937.

[17] Ran, W., Yang, B., Ma, P., & Lu, H. (2023). TRNR: task-driven image rain and noise removal with a few images based on patch analysis. *IEEE Transactions on Image Processing*, 32, 721–736. Institute of Electrical and Electronics Engineers (IEEE). https://doi.org/10.1109/tip.2022.3232943.

[18] Shivhare, M., & Tripathi, S. (2021). Noise reduction for hyperspectral image classification using deep learning technique. In 2021 2nd International Conference on Smart Electronics and Communication (ICOSEC), (pp. 905–909). IEEE. https://doi.org/10.1109/icosec51865.2021.9591950.

[19] Ruata, V., & Hussain, J. (2021). Image denoising to enhance character recognition using deep learning. Research Square Platform LLC . https://doi.org/10.21203/rs.3.rs-571989/v1.

[20] Zhang, Y., Li, J., Li, X., Wang, B., & Li, T. (2022). Image stripe noise removal based on compressed sensing. *International Journal of Pattern Recognition and Artificial Intelligence*, 36(02), 2254004. World Scientific Pub Co Pte Ltd. https://doi.org/10.1142/s0218001422540040.

19 Nanotechnology: a sustainable and ecofriendly approach in wastewater treatment and quality monitoring

Sattik Mondal[1,a], Raghunath Maji[2,b], Arna Bhaumik[1,c], Sandeepan Saha[2,d] and Biswajit Gayen[2,e]

[1]Student, Greater Kolkata College of Engineering and Management, JIS Group of College, Baruipur, WB, India

[2]Assistant Professor, Greater Kolkata College of Engineering and Management, JIS Group of College, Baruipur, WB, India

Abstract

Nanotechnology offers an efficient and sustainable solution for tackling global water challenges, notably in wastewater treatment and quality monitoring. Nanomaterials exhibit unique properties like large surface area, catalytic activity, along with its ability to adsorb contaminants, making themselves ideal for advanced treatment processes. Nanocomposites, such as hydrogels and gum-acacia-based materials, have shown exceptional performance in degrading dyes and eliminating pathogens. Additionally, nanotechnology-based sensors are enabling real-time water quality monitoring, addressing socio-economic growth through sustainable water management. Conventional wastewater treatment methods often fail to address complex pollutants effectively, leading to the development of nanofiltration, adsorption, and biosorption techniques as viable alternatives. Rapid urbanization and industrialization exacerbate the global freshwater scarcity, necessitating innovative approaches. Nanotechnology offers scalable, cost-effective, and environmentally friendly solutions, advancing efforts to meet growing water demands while protecting ecosystems. This multidisciplinary field continues to drive innovation in wastewater treatment, contributing to a cleaner and sustainable future. This review highlights the synthesis and application of nanomaterials to eliminate contaminants like anionic harmful metal ions, dyes, and organic contaminants.

Keywords: Nanofiltration, nanotechnology, sustainable future, wastewater treatment

Introduction

Nanotechnology is an interdisciplinary science and engineering field that manipulates matter at the 1–100 nanometer scale to create novel materials and devices. term "nano" originates from Greek and denotes a factor of 10^{-9}, for example 1 nm = 10^{-9} m. In the year 1974, Norio Taniguchi introduced the term nanotechnology. Materials at their nanoscale exhibit distinct chemical, physical, and biological properties not observed in their bulk form. These properties include changes in strength, electrical conductivity, reactivity, and optical behavior, making nanomaterials highly valuable for applications such as biological, pharmaceutical, cosmetics, electronic, and energy [9]. The field of nanotechnology is often divided into two main approaches based on synthetic methodology:

Top-down approach: This involves scaling down larger structures to the nanoscale through techniques like lithography. It is commonly used in electronics and semiconductor manufacturing. This methodology utilizes several commonly used techniques such as laser ablation, evaporation–condensation, ultrasonication, lithography, pyrolysis, and arc discharge method.

Bottom-up approach: This builds nanostructures from the atomic or molecular level, often using self-assembly techniques, making it ideal for fabricating complex nanomaterials. This method uses several well-known processes, such as spinning, pyrolysis, and CVD [3]. In addition to that, biosynthesis techniques are gaining popularity as ecofriendly methods for synthesizing nanomaterials.

Biosynthesis: Unlike conventional approaches, the biosynthesis for nanoparticles utilizes microorganisms functioning as bio-promoters. Both prokaryotic and eukaryotic organisms are employed in the production of metallic nanoparticles, such as silver

[a]sattikmondal853@gmail.com, [b]arnabhaumik06@gmail.com, [c]writetoraghunath@gmail.com, [d]sandeepan.saha_gkcem@jisgroup.org, [e]bgayenchemistry@gmail.com

DOI: 10.1201/9781003724995-19

(Ag), platinum (Pt), gold (Au), palladium (Pd), zirconium (Zr), iron (Fe), and cadmium (Cd), as well as metal. This method draws researchers' attention to its environmental sustainability, cost-effectiveness, and scalability. Additionally, it offers precise control over critical properties such as nanoparticle size and morphology, making it a highly efficient approach for nanomaterial synthesis.

Rapid industrialization, urbanization, population growth, and intensive agricultural practices Olvera et al. [11], have been linked to the widespread use of products and by-products containing pollutants. As a result, manufacturing industries generate waste materials that accumulate, directly or indirectly, in various ecosystems and the environment. In 2016, the world produced approximately 2.01 billion tons of waste. Due to rapid urbanization and population growth, this figure is expected to surge to 3.4 billion tons annually by 2050, posing significant environmental and societal challenges. Clean, safe water is a vital resource crucial to a prosperous society and a thriving economy. The world is facing a growing freshwater shortage, with demand steadily increasing each day. This scarcity has become one of the most critical global challenges, affecting nations across the globe. Approximately 3.6 billion people experience water insufficiency for at least one month each year, underscoring the urgent need for sustainable water management solutions. When we examine the issue of wastewater and its treatment, it becomes evident that solid waste is the main contributor to this critical challenge. The most widely used method for managing solid waste is sanitary landfilling, which generates leachate as a byproduct. To address this issue, various nanotechnology-based approaches have been developed for leachate treatment. Nano-filtration is one of the most commonly and effectively employed techniques [12]. Conventional wastewater treatment methods often lack effectiveness, energy efficiency, and cost-effectiveness. These approaches are typically based on chemicals like ammonia, chlorine compounds, and ferric salts, which can introduce toxic substances like phosphorus, nitrogen, and heavy metals into the system. Hence, engineering expertise, infrastructure, and development are an urgent need to find a smart solution. This review highlights nanoparticle synthesis for wastewater treatment, emphasizing cost-effective applications that support sustainability and strengthen the socio-economic framework.

Sources of Wastewater

Wastewater is loaded with various harmful substances and originates from diverse sources like industrial, sewage, agricultural runoff, and commercial activities. It has the potential to be categorized based on its physical appearance, chemical composition, and the presence of microbial loads. All the major water sources, particularly industries, use high-quality water for their operations. However, it generates large volumes of contaminated water, which are often discharged into water bodies (Figure 19.1) [7]. Wastewater is a complex matrix having suspended solids, organic matter, inorganic solids, and particulate substances. It also contains microorganisms, nutrients, heavy metals, and micro-pollutants (Figure 19.2).

Wastewater Treatment

Wastewater treatment involves removing pollutants from wastewater before releasing it into the environment. Wastewater treatment aims to remove contaminants and recover micronutrients to prevent environmental and human health risks. Several steps are needed for wastewater treatment explained [17].

Primary treatment, secondary treatment, and tertiary treatment make up the majority of common

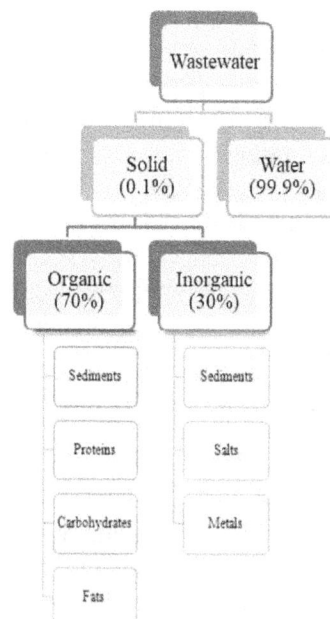

Figure 19.1 Generalized composition of wastewater
Source: Author

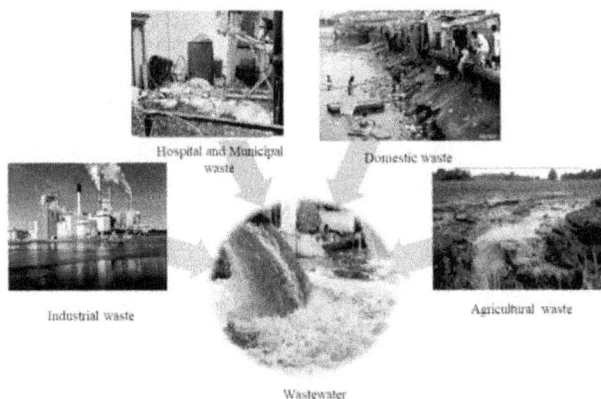

Figure 19.2 Different sources of wastewater
Source: Author

Table 19.1 Different methodologies used for the treatment of wastewater.

Sl. No	Methodology for wastewater treatment	References
1	Nanotechnology	[18]
2	Removal of pesticide	[4]
3	Adsorption and biosorption technique	[24]
4	Carbon-derived nanoadsorbents	Zhao et al., 2021
5	Polymer-based nanoadsorbents	[13]
6	Nanofilters	[14]
7	Removal of pathogens	[6]
8	Sensing and monitoring	[20]

Source: Author

wastewater treatment processes. Floating debris and inorganic particles are removed through screening and grit removal methods before the primary wastewater treatment process begins. The effluent after preliminary treatment undergoes primary treatment, where suspended solids are mainly separated by sedimentation. In this step solids allow you to settle at the bottom as sludge, while scum forms on the surface and is skimmed off.

Secondary treatment includes methods like trickling filters, oxidation ditches, rotating biological contactors, and bio-filters. In this step, millions of microorganisms, particularly bacteria and protozoa, aid in oxidizing and removing organic contaminants through their natural metabolic activity [21]. Secondary treatment removes organic contaminants and micronutrients like phosphorus and nitrogen from sewage. Tertiary treatment removes residual organic and inorganic matter, along with microorganisms. After successfully treating water through conventional methods, nanoparticles and nanocomposites can be utilized to remove pollutants and contaminants, including heavy metals and organic compounds. There are plenty of examples populated the literature where nanocomposites were utilized for the treatment of harmful chemicals and microbes present in wastewater.

Nanotechnology for Wastewater Treatment

Nanotechnology opens the way for advanced wastewater treatment by introducing a versatile range of nanomaterials with diverse applications. These materials act as highly efficient catalysts, facilitating chemical reactions that decompose harmful substances in wastewater streams. Additionally, nanomaterials are instrumental in soil and groundwater remediation, efficiently removing contaminants like organic pollutants and heavy metals (Table 19.1). Silver nanoparticles (AgNPs) were biosynthesized from neem leaf and banana peel extract. The as-synthesized nanoparticles exhibited excellent utilization as a dye-degrading agent and an antimicrobial in wastewater treatment. The study showed that these nanoparticles could degrade 99% of the model dye, malachite green, at an impressively low concentration of 0.06 mg/mL within just 4.5 hours [18]. Researchers employed a microwave-assisted technique to synthesize a graft copolymer nanocomposite combining gum acacia and poly(3-chloro-2-hydroxypropylmethacrylate), $(C_7H_{11}ClO_3)_n$ embedded with magnetite nanoparticles. The study demonstrated the successful removal of rhodamine 6G, methylene blue, as well as Hg(II) and Cu(II) ions from wastewater. In another study, Khan et al. [10] reported the synthesis of zinc oxide nanoparticles (ZnO NPs) using an ultrasound cavitation technique from the extracts of *Passiflora foetida* fruit peels. The researchers claimed that the synthesized ZnO NPs exhibited impressive degradation efficiencies, achieving 93.25% removal of methylene blue and 91.06% removal of rhodamine B within just 70 minutes [10]. A novel chitosan/Al_2O_3/magnetic iron oxide nanocomposite exhibited excellent removal properties of an anionic dye, Methyl Orange, found in wastewater. Study revealed that the nanocomposite has the optimum adsorbent capacity of

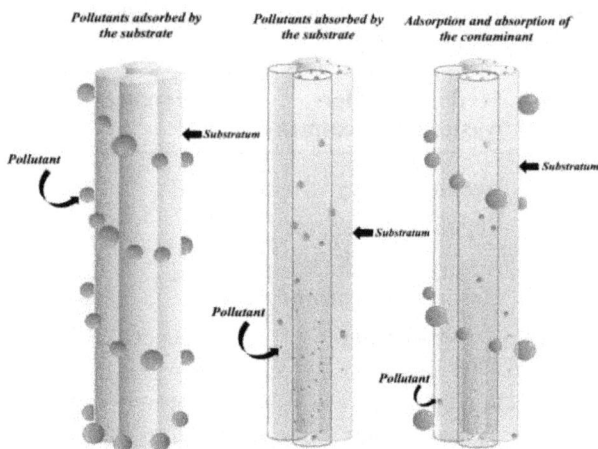

Figure 19.3 Schematic presentation of the adsorption process for a typical nanoabsorbent
Source: Author

0.4 g L^{-1} across a broad pH range of 4–10. Magnetic chitosan nanocomposite was prepared successfully with an excellent absorption capability of 91.60 % for the anionic dye Acid Red 2, where simple iron oxide exhibited a 16.40% absorption rate. Nanocomposites exhibited excellent absorption abilities due to their nanostructural morphologies and presence of amino and hydroxyl functionalities (Figure 19.3). Magnetic chitosan nanocomposites were successfully synthesized and exhibited an impressive absorption capacity of 91.60% for the anionic dye Acid Red 2. In contrast, simple iron oxide achieved only 16.40% absorption. The superior performance of the nanocomposites can be attributed to their unique nanostructural morphology, and the presence of hydroxyl and amino functional groups enhances their ability to absorb dyes from wastewater. Nanotechnology-based different methodologies have been successfully and effectively used to treat wastewater [16].

Removal of Pesticides from Wastewater

The use of highly efficient pesticides boosts yields and alleviates hunger for many nations. These advancements have played key roles in tackling food security and the growing global population. These pesticides infiltrate the soil and eventually leach into nearby water bodies. Due to their highly toxic nature, they disrupt aquatic ecosystems, posing significant environmental risks. Therefore, the removal of these hazardous chemicals is critically important in wastewater treatment processes. Magnetic chitosan nanoparticles were first

synthesized using a one-step co-precipitation directly within the reaction medium. The as-prepared nanoparticles were effectively employed to remove humic acid ($C_{187}H_{186}O_{89}N_9S_1$.) from aqueous solutions. The study showed that the nanocomposites effectively adsorbed HA with efficiency of concentrations from 29.3 mg/L at pH 4 and 7.4 mg/L at pH 10. Organochlorine pesticides like α-, β-, γ-, δ-hexachlorobenzene (BHC), dicofol, and cypermethrin are highly toxic. Despite being banned, these compounds and their degradation products continue to be detected in surface water and some foods. The aforementioned pesticides were subjected to photocatalytic degradation using UV-irradiated films coated with nano-TiO$_2$. The study revealed that nano-TiO$_2$ films with a surface area of 2.24 mg/cm^2, exposed to UV light at a wavelength of 365 nm, achieved complete degradation of 20 μg of α-BHC within 20 minutes. Re^{3+}-doped nano-TiO$_2$ successfully utilized for degradation of phosphorus and carbamate pesticides. The synthesized nano-TiO$_2$ concentration of 0.4 g/L, applied for 4 hours, achieved an optimal degradation rate of 54.89%. These TiO$_2$ based nanocomposite not only decomposed pesticide but also its residues also. Nano zerovalent iron (nZVI) has demonstrated strong degradation effects on DDT-contaminated soil. Study showed that applying 1 g of nZVI per kg of DDT-contaminated soil resulted in approximately 50% degradation of DDT during the incubation period. Nanocomposites like ZnO, TiO$_2$, Au/ZnO, and Au/TiO$_2$ successfully applied on degradation malathion presence in water sample under UV and Vis light. Nano TiO$_2$ was used to degrade phenanthrene present in soil through UV-light irradiation over duration of 25 hours [4].

Adsorption and Biosorption Technique for Wastewater Treatment

Yang et al. [24] first reported algal-bacterial aerobic granular sludge as a biosorbent for removing Cr(VI) from wastewater. Their reported that the synthesized biosorbent effectively adsorbed Cr(VI) in an acidic medium at pH 2, with a recovery rate around 73% achieved using a NaHCO$_3$ solution [24]. The biosorbent showed optimal performance at 40° C and pH 6, achieving efficient removal of Th in less than 100 minutes.

Carbon-Based Nanoadsorbents for Wastewater Purification

Carbon nanostructures are widely used as cost-effective, eco-friendly nano adsorbents for wastewater treatment [22]. CNT-based nonabsorbent showed an excellent adsorption and desorption capacity of Mn^{7+} ions. In their study, they reported a reduction of Mn^{7+} ion concentration to 3 ppm from 150 ppm. Antibiotics and their residues present in wastewater are causing serious health issues for humans and living organisms. MWCNTs adsorbents synthesized using Nickel ferrite (Ni-Fe) doped activated carbon from wood sawdust were used to remove levofloxacin and metronidazole from pharmaceutical wastewater [8]. Magnetic MWCNTs were synthesized for the removal of tetracycline from wastewater. The as-synthesized adsorbent exhibited over 80% removal efficiency across a wide pH range (2–10) at low concentrations below 80 mg/L (Zhao et al., 2021). Magnetic graphene oxide (GO) is gaining importance for wastewater treatment due to its low cost, high efficiency, simplicity, and ease of use in removing toxic pollutants. GO/aminated lignin aerogel developed for malachite green dye adsorption. Their study reported that the highest adsorption capacity was observed with the tetraphenyl porphyrin-modified hydrogel, reaching 130.37 mg/g for methylene blue removal. A hydro composite based on GO synthesized and supported by the biopolymer chitosan. The synthesized nanocomposite exhibited excellent adsorption capacities for dyes such as Congo Red, Acid Red 1, and Reactive Red 2, particularly under acidic conditions at pH 2. Furthermore, the regeneration of the nanocomposite more than 65% was achieved using a 0.1 M NaOH solution, showcasing its potential for sustainable wastewater treatment [19]. Nanoadsorbents synthesized by magnetizing and carboxylating graphene oxide (GO) with Fe_3O_4, specifically designed to remove Ca^{2+} and Cu^{2+} ions from oil refinery wastewater. These nano adsorbents showed removal efficiencies of 78.4% for Ca^{2+} and 51% for Cu^{2+} within just 60 minutes, highlighting their rapid and effective performance [5]. Magnetic iron oxide was coated with a hybrid silica-organosilane shell to synthesize the nanocomposites. These nanoparticles exhibited remarkable potential for eliminating organic pollutants, including polyaromatic and aliphatic hydrocarbons. The study showed that the NPs removed pharmaceutical residues, such as carbamazepine, diclofenac, and ibuprofen, from wastewater, showcasing their versatility and efficiency in water purification applications [15]. Nanoparticles (NPs) composed of polyacrylic acid, ferric oxide (Fe_3O_4), and functionalized with an azo dye were effectively employed for the removal of cations, including Fe^{2+}, Fe^{3+}, Cd^{2+}, Cu^{2+}, and Pb^{2+}, from wastewater. The lead-doped zinc-aluminum oxide nanoadsorbent achieved a 99.60% removal of anionic dyes like methyl orange in 30 minutes.

Polymer-Based Nanoadsorbents for Wastewater Treatment

Substantial research in recent times on polymer nanocomposites has focused on enhancing environmental sustainability and wastewater treatment. Metal-organic framework adsorbent, synthesized using a zeolitic imidazolate combined with the polymer polyether sulfone, demonstrated highly efficient Malachite Green removal from wastewater, achieving a removal efficiency of 99.2% [1]. Magnetic nanoadsorbents, synthesized by combining bi-functionalized β-cyclodextrin, polyethyleneimine, and Fe_2O_3, were designed to simultaneously remove Pb^{2+} ions and methyl orange dye from wastewater. A nanocomposite was developed by synthesizing starch-grafted copolymers of acrylic acid and 2-acrylamido-2-methylpropane sulfonate, followed by incorporating cellulose nanocrystals functionalized with magnetite. This nanocomposite effectively adsorbed cationic dyes, including crystal violet and methylene blue. Nanoadsorbent synthesized a composite of iron-aluminum layered dual hydroxide and reduced graphene oxide (rGO), further coated with sodium alginate, achieving a high arsenic removal efficiency of over 98% from water [13].

Nano filters for Wastewater Treatment

Membrane technology, especially nanofiltration (NF), has garnered considerable attention in recent years. NF membranes, a recent innovation, are now widely favored for both drinking water and wastewater treatment due to their effectiveness. On the other hand, NF membranes are low-cost, flexible, and easy to produce. Two main types of NF are possible: the first is polymeric and the second is ceramic membranes. Ceramic membranes offer better mechanical, chemical, and thermal stability compared to polymeric membranes, which have shorter lifespans due to lower chemical resistance and higher fouling. An NF membrane incorporating carbon nanotubes (CNTs) was prepared to facilitate the removal of the MS2 virus from water. As-prepared NF membrane exhibited high filtration efficiency (98%) for yeast removal and near-complete (100%) removal of heavy metal ions from water [14]. A submicrometer-thick NF membrane was made successfully and exhibited remarkable impermeability to vapors, gases, and liquids, while allowing water to pass through.

Removal of pathogens for Wastewater

Disinfection is a technique which reduces microbial contamination to safe levels. However, traditional methods like chlorine, ozone, and reverse osmosis are limited due to high energy costs, expensive equipment, and harmful by-products. Nanomaterials offer an urgent solution to pathogen deactivation from water by their specific reactivity and large surface area. Ag nanoparticles are widely used for disinfection of microbes, including bacteria, viruses, and fungi. Core-shell Ag@ZnO nanoparticles exhibited effective disinfection against pathogenic bacteria, *E. coli* and *Staphylococcus aureus*. These bacteria were completely removed by exposing the NPs to solar photocatalysis at 35°C within 60 and 90 minutes, respectively. ZnO nanoparticles are widely recognized for their biocompatibility and environmental friendliness. Simple ZnO NPs and ZnO nanocrystal-doped macro-mesoporous 3D silicon wafers showed strong antibacterial activity, effectively removing bacteria like *E. coli* from water [23]. CuNPs derived from biowaste eggshell membrane exhibited antibacterial property against model microorganisms like *S. aureus* and *E. coli* with a high recyclability [6].

Sensing and Monitoring

Environmental contamination of pathogens, waste, sewage, and heavy metals poses significant challenges in water quality monitoring due to their low concentrations in wastewater. Interest in nanomaterial-based sensors for water quality monitoring has recently increased. Nanosensor offers excellent capabilities for detecting trace contaminants and providing rapid analysis. Oligonucleotide-functionalized gold nanosensors were synthesized to detect antibiotic resistance genes in MRSA, achieving a detection limit was found to be 70 ppm. Optical nanosensors prepared by combining MWCNTs and reduced graphene oxide quantum dots. These nanosensors exhibited high accuracy in selectively detecting diazinon, an organophosphorus insecticide presents in the wastewater [20]. The presence of triclosan, an antibacterial and antifungal agent, in water can be detected using a nano-sensor-based plasmon resonance. Chemical nano sensor made using molecularly imprinted AgNPs for detecting caffeine in wastewater, with a detection limit of 100 ng/L. Carbon dot nanosensor was synthesized to detect Cr(VI) in wastewater samples, with a detection limit of 2.3 nM at pH 6 [25]

Conclusion and Future Prospects

The global demand for clean water is increasing due to industrialization, urbanization, population growth, and agriculture. Conventional water purification methods are often chemical-intensive, energy-demanding, and require complex infrastructure. Nanotechnology, particularly eco-friendly biosynthesized nanoparticles, offers cost-effective, scalable, and environmentally sustainable solutions. Integrating nanotechnology into wastewater treatment can overcome the limitations of traditional methods, such as high costs, hazardous chemicals, and secondary pollutants. Future research should focus on: a) Eco-friendly nanomaterials, b) Advanced wastewater treatment, c) Recycling and reuse, d) Interdisciplinary collaboration and e) Water scarcity solutions. Prioritizing nanotechnology research and investment will help address critical environmental challenges, ensuring a sustainable future.

References

[1] Abdi, J., & Abedini, H. (2020). MOF-based polymeric nanocomposite beads as an efficient adsorbent for wastewater treatment in batch and continuous systems: Modelling and experiment. *Chemical Engineering Journal*, 400, 125862.

[2] Baig, N., Kammakakam, I., & Falath, W. (2021). A review of synthesis methods, properties, recent progress, and challenges. *Materials Advances*, 2, 1821–1871.

[3] Gu, J., Dong, D., Kong, L., Yong, Z., & Li, X. (2012). Photocatalytic degradation of phenanthrene on soil surfaces in the presence of nanometer anatase TiO_2 under UV-light. *Journal of Environmental Sciences (China)*, 24(12), 2122–2126.

[4] He, L., Wang, L., Zhu, H., Wang, Z., Zhang, L., Yang, L., et al. (2021). A reusable $Fe3O_4$/GO-COOH nanoadsorbent for Ca^{2+} and Cu^{2+} removal from oilfield wastewater. *Chemical Engineering Research and Design*, 166, 248–258.

[5] He, X., Yang, D. P., Zhang, X., Liu, M., Kang, Z., Lin, C., et al. (2019). Waste eggshell membrane-templated CuO-ZnO nanocomposites with enhanced adsorption, catalysis and antibacterial properties for

water purification. *Chemical Engineering Journal*, 369, 621–633.

[6] Jassby, D., Cath, T. Y., & Buisson, H. (2018). The role of nanotechnology in industrial water treatment. *Nature Nanotechnology*, 13(8), 670–672.

[7] Kariim, I., Abdulkareem, A. S., & Abubakre, O. K. (2020). Development and characterization of MWCNTs from activated carbon as adsorbent for metronidazole and levofloxacin sorption from pharmaceutical wastewater: kinetics, isotherms and thermodynamic studies. *Scientific African*, 7, e00242.

[8] Khalid, M., & Abdollahi, M. (2021). Environmental distribution of personalcareproducts and theireffects on humanhealth. *Iranian Journal of Pharmaceutical Research*, 20(1), 216–253.

[9] Khan, M., Ware, P., & Shimpi, N. (2021). Synthesis of ZnO nanoparticles using peels of *Passiflora foetida* and study of its activity as an efficient catalyst for the degradation of hazardous organic dye. *SN Applied Sciences*, 3, 528.

[10] Olvera, R. C., Silva, S. L., Robles-Belmont, E., & Lau, E. Z. (2017). Review of nanotechnology value chain for water treatment applications in Mexico. *Resource-Efficient Technologies*, 3(1), 1–11.

[11] Nakum, J., & Bhattacharya, D. (2022). Various green nanomaterials used for wastewater and soil treatment: a mini-review. *Frontiers in Environmental Science*, 28(9), 724814.

[12] Nithya Priya, V., Rajkumar, M., Mobika, J., & Linto Sibi, S. P. (2021). Alginate coated layered double hydroxide/reduced graphene oxide nanocomposites for removal of toxic As (V) from wastewater. *Physica E: Low-dimensional Systems and Nanostructures*, 127, 114527.

[13] Parham, H., Bates, S., Xia, Y., & Zhu, Y. (2013). A highly efficient and versatile carbon nanotube/ceramic composite filter. *Carbon*, 54, 215–223.

[14] Peralta, M. E., Mártire, D. O., Moreno, M. S., Parolo, M. E., & Carlos, L. (2021). Versatile nanoadsorbents based on magnetic mesostructured silica nanoparticles with tailored surface properties for organic pollutants removal. *Journal of Environmental Chemical Engineering*, 9(1), 104841.

[15] Pérez, H., García, O. J. Q., Amezcua-Allieri, M. A., & Vázquez, R. R. (2023). Nanotechnology as an efficient and effective alternative for wastewater treatment: an overview. *Water Science and Technology*, 87(12), 2971–3001.

[16] Runguphan, T., & Kitpichai, J. (2020). Coaction of bio-sorption and bio-filtration for the remediation of domestic and agricultural wastewater contaminated with heavy metal. In IOP Conference Series: Materials Science and Engineering, (Vol. 965, p. 012010).

[17] Sengupta, A., & Sarkar, A. (2022). Synthesis and characterization of nanoparticles from neem leaves and banana peels: a green prospect for dye degradation in wastewater. *Ecotoxicology*, 31(4), 537–548.

[18] Sirajudheen, P., Karthikeyan, P., Ramkumar, K., & Meenakshi, S. (2020). Effective removal of organic pollutants by adsorption onto chitosan supported graphene oxide-hydroxyapatite composite: a novel reusable adsorbent. *Journal of Molecular Liquids*, 318, 114200.

[19] Talari, F. F., Bozorg, A., Faridbod, F., & Vossoughi, M. (2021). A novel sensitive aptamer-based nanosensor using rGQDs and MWCNTs for rapid detection of diazinon pesticide. *Journal of Environmental Chemical Engineering*, 9(1), 104878.

[20] Verlicchi, P., Al Aukidy, M., & Zambello, E. (2012). Occurrence of pharmaceutical compounds in urban wastewater: removal, mass load and environmental risk after a secondary treatment—a review. *Science of the Total Environment,* 429, 123–155.

[21] Sayed, E. T., Alawadhi, H., Elsaid, K., Olabi, A. G., Almakrani, M. A., Bin Tamim, S. T., et al. (2021). Preparation and characteristics of a magnetic carbon nanotube ad-sorbent: Its efficient adsorption and recoverable performances. *Separation and Purification Technology*, 257, 117917.

[22] Wong, K.-A., Lam, S.-M., & Sin, J.-C. (2019). Wet chemically synthesized ZnO structures for photodegradation of pre-treated palm oil mill effluent and antibacterial activity. *Ceramics International*, 45(2), 1868–1880.

[23] Yang, X., Zhao, Z., Yu, Y., Shimizu, K., Zhang, Z., Lei, Z., et al. (2020). Enhanced biosorption of Cr(VI) from synthetic wastewater using algal-bacterial aerobic granular sludge: batch experiments, kinetics and mechanisms, *Separation and Purification Technology*, 251, 117323.

[24] Zhang, S., Jin, L., Liu, J., Wang, Q., & Jiao, L. (2020). A label-free yellow-emissive carbon dot-based nanosensor for sensitive and selective ratiometric detection of chromium (VI) in environmental water samples. *Materials Chemistry and Physics*, 248, 122912.

[25] Zhao, W., Tian, Y., Chu, X., Cui, L., Zhang, H., Li, M., & Zhao, P. (2021). Magnetic chitosan-based nanocomposite for the efficient removal of heavy metal ions and dyes from industrial wastewater. Separation and Purification Technology, 257, 117917.

20 Optimal load balancing technique for energy-efficient fog computing architecture

Dipankar Barui[a], Antara Ghosh[b], Raghunath Maji[c], Munmun Gorai[d] and Shantanu Raut[e]

Department of Computer Science and Engineering, Greater Kolkata College of Engineering and Management, Baruipur, WB, India

Abstract

Fog computing is a model designed to address the drawbacks of cloud computing by processing and storing data nearer to end-users. However, the resource-constrained nature of fog devices and their heterogeneous characteristics pose several challenges, including load balancing. Load balancing plays a crucial role in ensuring that the fog nodes operate efficiently and effectively. The study focuses on implementing and evaluating a proposed algorithm called the Weighted Least Connection (WLC) load balancing algorithm. The algorithm aims to distribute the workload efficiently among fog nodes in a fog computing network. The key feature of the algorithm is its consideration of both the weight of each node based on its current load and the number of connections it is currently serving. The paper describes our proposed algorithm in detail, including the steps involved in the load balancing process and the calculation of weights for each fog node. The algorithm is then compared to two existing load balancing algorithms, first-come first-serve (FCFS) and Random, in terms of performance, fog node availability, and load distribution. Experimental results show that the proposed WLC algorithm outperforms the other two algorithms regarding total iterations, fog node availability, and load distribution. The research also highlights future directions for improvement, including scalability, dynamic adaptation, QoS considerations, integration of machine learning techniques, fault tolerance, energy efficiency, and real-world deployment and evaluation. Overall, the findings of this research demonstrate the potency of the proposed WLC load balancing algorithm in optimizing workload distribution and improving the performance of fog computing networks. These findings contribute to the existing body of knowledge on load balancing algorithms and provide insights for further research and development in this area.

Keywords: Fog computing, fog load, IoT, load balancing, resource management

Introduction

The increasing adoption of Internet of Things (IoT) devices and real-time applications in the digital world has led to a growing demand for efficient workload distribution in fog computing environments. Hill climbing load balancing algorithms in fogcomputing environments leverage heuristicoptimization to enhance response and processingtimes; however, they often face challenges related toscalability and security, requiring further research toimprove their adaptability and robustness in dynamic cloud-fog ecosystems [2]. Load balancing in fog computing involves assigning computational tasks across multiple fog nodes to make the best use of available resources and enhance overall system performance. The goal is to prevent any node from being overwhelmed or left idle. This is particularly crucial for IoT and real-time applications, where maintaining a balanced workload across the fog environment has become increasingly necessary. Load balancing techniques can help to achieve better performance, improve resource utilization, and enhance the reliability and availability of the system [1]. The load being balanced can be measured in terms of CPU load, memory usage, network load, or other factors that impact the performance of the fog nodes. The ultimate goal is to prevent overloading of any single node and to ensure that the workload is evenly distributed among the available resources. Simply, the goals of load balancing are:

Improve the system's performance by distributing the workload among different fog nodes.

- To ensure system reliability and availability by providing a backup plan in case of partial or complete system failure.

[a]dipankarbarui123@gmail.com, [b]antara.ghosh@gkcem.ac.in, [c]writetoraghunath@gmail.com, [d]vikramadityagorai@gmail.com, [e]rautshantanu2004@gmail.com

DOI: 10.1201/9781003724995-20

- To maintain system stability, which includes having a backup plan in case of partial failure and improving performance substantially?
- To allow for future system modifications

The min-conflicts heuristic approach is used for optimizing load balancing by resolving resource assignment issues efficiently in cloud environments, simulated using Cloud Analyst, effectively minimizes response time, cost, and latency, yet its complexity and reliance on expert knowledge pose challenges for practical implementation [3]. A load-balancing strategy based on the AHP method for managing multiple gateways in fog networks, implemented and simulated in MATLAB, enhances performance by reducing response time and energy consumption [4]. Resource management through load distribution in fog clustering provides a flexible design that minimizes energy consumption, complexity, and latency. However, a significant limitation is its inability to recover from database corruption [5]. A heuristic VM scheduling mechanism for load balancing, simulated in CloudSim, effectively prevents bottlenecks, enhances resource utilization, and avoids overload [6]. SDN in cloud and fog networks enhances mobility, reduces response time and latency, and improves QoS; however, its effectiveness is limited by security vulnerabilities and scalability constraints [7]. A load balancing approach utilizing SDN in fog and cloud systems, simulated in MATLAB, achieves low response time, cost, and latency, yet its overall performance remains a key limitation [8]. A fog-cloud system that combines large-scale medical data with a bat algorithm for load balancing, implemented and simulated in MATLAB, reduces latency but encounters complexity, bottlenecks, scalability, and reliability issues [9]. Fog network load balancing for MTC enhances efficiency by reducing response time, energy consumption, and execution time, though its high complexity poses a significant implementation challenge [10]. The shortest job first-based load balancing method, simulated using Cloud Analyst, reduces response time and cost but suffers from low overall performance and increased waiting times for longer processes [11]. Several load balancing strategies have been proposed to address the challenges of Fog computing. Due to the diversity of the Fog environment, comparing these strategies is complex. The taxonomy of load balancers helps organize and compare them effectively. This survey presents a comprehensive taxonomy based on factors like balancing criteria, architecture, communication, and deployment, as summarized from research papers

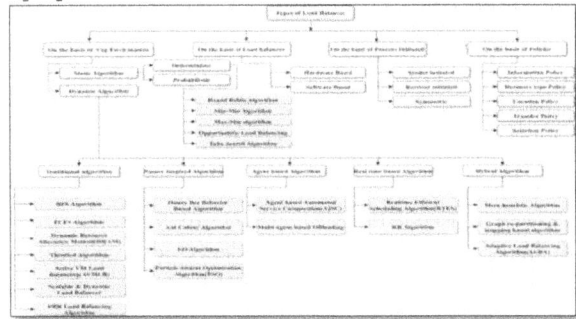

Figure 20.1 shows the load balancing taxonomy and the algorithm applied in fog computing
Source: Author

[12–14]. Figure 20.1 provides a detailed overview of load balancing taxonomy, emphasizing the key algorithms utilized in fog computing until now.

Proposed Methodology and Discussion

Introduction

Numerous approaches to load balancing have been developed for fog computing, including our own, the Weighted Least Connected (WLC) load balancing technique. This algorithm manages load from edge nodes using an intermediate load balancer between the edge and fog layers. The following sections will cover its functionality, advantages, and implementation. Additionally, Alankar et al. [14] introduced the concept of an intermediate load balancer in their research on virtual cloud environments.

A load balancing method for Fog Computing (FC) using the weighted least connection (WLC) approach

The Weighted Least Connection (WLC) method uses a load balancer between the Edge and fog layers to centralize workload management. It ensures an even distribution of tasks by considering each fog node's load and capacity, directing requests to underutilized nodes to prevent overloads. This strategy optimizes resource use, enhances performance, and avoids bottlenecks. The load balancer improves system stability and reliability, preventing node overloading and ensuring efficient resource allocation. It also abstracts workload management for edge devices, allowing them to focus on their primary tasks. Overall, the WLC method boosts resource utilization, performance, and system responsiveness in fog computing. Figure 20.2 shows the load balancer positioned between the Edge and fog layers. It acts as a key component, bridging the two layers and enabling effective load balancing. The load balancer uses a load-balancing algorithm to analyze incoming workloads and directs requests to the appropriate fog node based on this analysis.

Figure 20.3 illustrates the load balancer's connection to edge and fog nodes, enabling efficient workload distribution. It gathers information from both layers to make informed decisions on request allocation. Edge nodes generate continuous data to the load balancer, which analyzes factors like request type, priority, and edge node load. The load balancer then determines the best fog node for handling each request. Additionally, by connecting to fog nodes, the load balancer monitors real-time workload and resource availability, ensuring intelligent workload distribution based on node capacity and utilization.

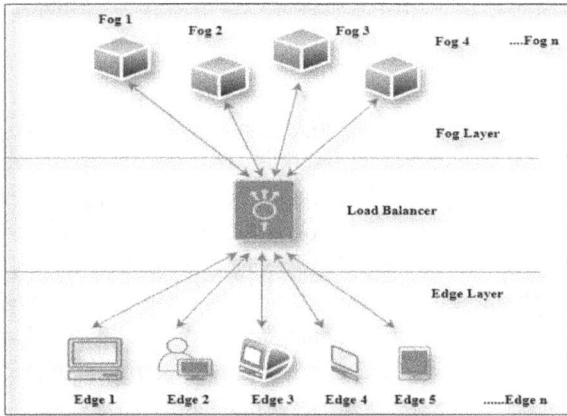

Figure 20.2 Proposed load balancer model
Source: Author

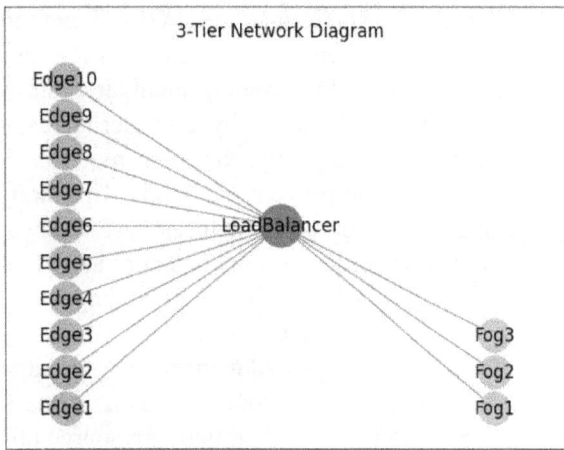

Figure 20.3 Simulation model of load balancer, fog nodes, and edge nodes
Source: Author

The load balancing algorithm considers these factors to optimize decision-making.

Implementation

In this section, we discussed the steps involved in implementing the simulation model for load balancing in fog computing. We will also explore and compare two existing algorithms, namely Random load balancing and FCFS load balancing, to assess their performance in terms of fog node availability and longevity. This comparison will help evaluate the effectiveness and suitability of our proposed load balancing technique in improving overall system performance.

By following these steps according to figure 20.4, we implemented the proposed WLC-based load balancing technique.

Results and Discussion

Implementation

To evaluate the suggested algorithm's efficacy, two other load balancing methods are used for comparison, first-come, first-served (FCFS) and Random load balancing, which were implemented. FCFS assigns requests to fog nodes based on their arrival order, while the Random algorithm selects a fog node at random without considering node load or availability. Comparing these algorithms helps assess factors like fog node availability, workload longevity, and system performance. The detailed analysis will highlight the strengths and weaknesses of each algorithm and their impact on load balancing effectiveness and efficiency in fog computing environments.

Input & output parameter

For an initial fair comparison, a smaller network with 10 edge nodes and 3 fog nodes is used. This allows

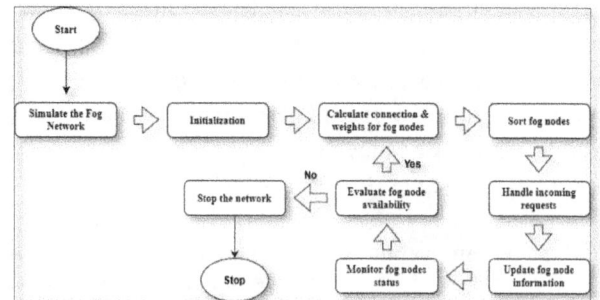

Figure 20.4 Steps for implementation of proposed technique
Source: Author

for a preliminary assessment of the proposed load balancing algorithm against the FCFS and Random algorithms. The effectiveness of this algorithm is determined in terms of fog node availability and longevity. This evaluation provides insights into the algorithm's efficiency and suitability for handling increased workloads in larger networks.

Result analysis

In this study, three fog nodes were initialized with 100 joules of energy, and load balancing was performed for ten edge nodes. The network terminated when 75% of the fog nodes became unavailable, recording the total iterations and load balances per node.

The FCFS algorithm completed 15 iterations, with Fog Node 2 handling 9 load requests. The Random algorithm achieved 22 iterations, processing 10 load requests. The proposed WLC algorithm completed 23 iterations, with Fog Nodes 2 and 3 handling 2 load requests, while 8 remained unprocessed. Energy consumption and load distribution details are provided in Tables 20.1–20.3.

Performance evaluation

The proposed algorithm outperformed FCFS and Random load balancing, achieving 23 iterations compared to 15 and 22, respectively, indicating superior efficiency. It effectively distributes load, preventing

Table 20.1 Experimental data of using FCFS load balancing algorithm.

Iteration	0	1	2	3	4	5	6	7	8
Fog Node 1 (Remaining Energy/Load)(J/lu)	100/0	98.80/1	91.59/7	89.19/9	84.39/13	80.79/16	79.59/17	74.79/21	72.39/23
Fog Node 2 (Remaining Energy/Load)(J/lu)	100/0	96.39/3	92.79/6	87.99/10	84.39/13	81.99/15	81.99/15	77.19/19	71.19/24
Fog Node 3 (Remaining Energy/Load)(J/lu)	100/0	92.79/6	91.59/7	86.79/11	83.19/14	77.19/19	66.39/28	63.99/30	60.39/33

9	10	11	12	13	14	15	16	17	18	19	20	21	22
67.59 /27	63.99 /30	61.59 /32	61.59 /32	59.19 /34	50.79 /41	45.99 /45	41.19 /49	33.99 /55	32.79 /56	26.79 /61	25.59 /62	24.39 /63	13.59 /72
67.59 /27	66.39 /28	59.19 /34	53.19 /39	50.79 /41	50.79 /41	45.99 /45	42.39 /48	37.59 /52	30.39 /58	26.79 /61	21.99 /65	12.39 /73	11.19 /74
56.79 /36	49.59 /42	47.19 /44	41.19 /49	33.99 /55	30.39 /58	27.99 /60	24.39 /63	24.39 /63	20.79 /66	18.39 /68	12.39 /73	11.19 /74	11.19 /74

Source: Author

Table 20.2 Experimental data of using random load balancing algorithm.

Iteration	0	1	2	3	4	5	6
Fog Node 1 (Remaining Energy/Load)	100/0	87.99/10	75.99/20	63.99/30	51.99/40	39.99/50	27.99/60
Fog Node 2 (Remaining Energy/Load)	100/0	100/0	100/0	100/0	100/0	100/0	100/0
Fog Node 3 (Remaining Energy/Load)	100/0	100/0	100/0	100/0	100/0	100/0	100/0

7	8	9	10	11	12	13	14	15
15.99/70	11.19/74	11.19/74	11.19/74	11.19/74	11.19/74	11.19/74	11.19/74	11.19/74
100/0	92.80/6	80.80/16	68.80/26	56.80/36	44.80/46	32.80/56	20.80/66	10./75
100/0	100/0	100/0	100/0	100/0	100/0	100/0	100/0	100/0

Source: Author

node overloads and optimizing resource utilization. This enhances network performance, reduces bottlenecks, and is expected to scale efficiently in larger fog networks.

Remaining energy and accepted load for each fog node

Table 20.4 compares the proposed, FCFS, and Random algorithms, highlighting remaining energy and accepted load. The proposed algorithm evenly distributes energy (11.19 J per node) and load (74 lu per node), ensuring balanced resource utilization. Figures 20.2 and 20.3 illustrate its efficiency in maintaining energy balance and preventing node overload.

Energy draining for each fog node

This section analyzes energy consumption across three load balancing algorithms: FCFS, Random, and WLC. Energy-draining diagrams illustrate

per-iteration consumption until fog nodes reach their thresholds. In FCFS, Fog Node 1 depletes energy by the 8th iteration, while Random extends to the 22nd and WLC to the 23rd, maintaining balanced consumption. Similar trends are observed for Fog Nodes 2 and 3, with WLC ensuring consistent energy distribution. Overall, WLC optimizes load balancing, preventing idle nodes and ensuring efficient energy utilization compared to FCFS and Random, leading to improved resource management and network longevity.

Energy consumption for each node

This section analyzes fog node energy consumption, where each node starts with 100 joules and loses 1.2 joules per load. A 10-joule threshold marks unavailability. Pie charts illustrate energy distribution across three algorithms, with the proposed method ensuring balanced consumption (33.33%

Table 20.3 Experimental data of using proposed weighted least connection (WLC) load balancing algorithm.

Iteration	0	1	2	3	4	5	6	7	8	9
Fog Node 1 (Remaining Energy/Load)(J/lu)	100/ 0	95.19 /4	92.79 /6	87.99/ 10	84.39/ 13	79.59/ 17	75.99/ 20	72.39/ 23	67.59/ 27	63.99/ 30
Fog Node 2 (Remaining Energy/Load)(J/lu)	100/ 0	96.39 /3	91.59 /7	87.99/ 10	83.19/ 14	79.59/ 17	75.99/ 20	72.39/ 23	68.79/ 26	63.99/ 30
Fog Node 3 (Remaining Energy/Load)(J/lu)	100/ 0	96.39 /3	91.59 /7	87.99/ 10	84.39/ 13	80.79/ 16	75.99/ 20	71.19/ 24	67.59/ 27	63.99/ 30

10	11	12	13	14	15	16	17	18	19	20	21	22	23
60.39 /33	55.59 /37	51.99 /40	48.39 /43	44.79 /46	39.99 /50	36.39 /53	32.79 /56	27.99 /60	24.39 /63	19.59 /67	15.99 /70	11.19 /74	11.19 /74
59.19 /34	56.79 /36	51.99 /40	48.39 /43	43.59 /47	39.99 /50	36.39 /53	31.59 /57	27.99 /60	24.39 /63	20.79 /66	15.99 /70	12.39 /73	11.19 /74
60.39 /33	55.59 /37	51.99 /40	47.19 /44	43.59 /47	39.99 /50	35.19 /54	31.59 /57	27.99 /60	23.19 /64	19.59 /67	15.99 /70	12.39 /73	11.19 /74

Source: Author

Table 20.4 Comparison of load balancing algorithms.

Algorithm	Fog Node 1 (Remaining Energy in J)	Fog Node 1 (Accepted Load in lu)	Fog Node 2 (Remaining Energy in J)	Fog Node 2 (Accepted Load in lu)	Fog Node 3 (Remaining Energy in J)	Fog Node 3 (Accepted Load in lu)
Proposed WLC	11.19 J	74 lu	11.19 J	74 lu	11.19 J	74 lu
FCFS	11.19 J	74 lu	10 J	75 lu	100 J	0 lu
Random	13.59 J	72 lu	11.19 J	74 lu	11.19 J	74 lu

Source: Author

per node), optimizing resource utilization, reducing bottlenecks, and enhancing system stability and longevity.

Conclusion and Future Scope

Conclusion

From the result, it is observed that the Weighted Least Connection (WLC) algorithm outperformed the others in terms of total iterations, achieving 23 iterations compared to 15 for FCFS and 22 for Random. The WLC algorithm also demonstrated superior load distribution and utilization, ensuring no fog node was overloaded or underloaded, leading to efficient resource use. Energy draining diagrams showed that WLC allowed fog nodes to operate closer to their energy thresholds, optimizing energy consumption. Overall, the WLC algorithm showed better performance, load balancing, and energy efficiency, making it well-suited for larger fog networks.

Future scope

The proposed WLC load balancing algorithm shows great potential, but there are several areas for future improvement: scalability, dynamic adaptation, Quality of Service (QoS)integration, including QoS metrics, machine learning, fault tolerance, energy efficiency, and real-world testing. Addressing these aspects will improve the algorithm's overall performance and scalability in fog computing networks.

References

[1] Kaur, M., & Aron, R. (2021). A systematic study of load balancing approaches in the fog computing environment. *The Journal of Supercomputing*, 77(8), 9202–9247.

[2] Zahid, M., Javaid, N., Ansar, K., Hassan, K., Khan, & Waqas, M. (2018). Hill climbing load balancing algorithm on fog computing. In International Conference on P2P, Parallel, Grid, Cloud and Internet Computing, (–). Springer.

[3] Kamal, Javaid, N., Naqvi, Butt, H., Saif, T., & Kamal,(2018). Heuristic Min-conflicts optimizing technique for load balancing on fog computing. In International Conference on Intelligent Networking and Collaborative Systems, (–). Springer.

[4] Banaie, F., Yaghmaee, Hosseini, & Tashtarian, F. (2020). Load-balancing algorithm for multiple gateways in fog- based internet of things. *IEEE Internet of Things Journal*, 7(8), 7043–7053.

[5] Oueis, J., Strinati, & Barbarossa, S. (2015). The fog balancing: load distribution for small cell cloud computing. In 2015 IEEE 81st Vehicular Technology Conference (VTC Spring), (pp. 1–6), IEEE.

[6] Xu, X., Liu, Q., Qi, L., Yuan, Y., Dou, W., & Liu,(2018). A heuristic virtual machine scheduling method for load balancing in fog-cloud computing. In 2018 IEEE 4th International Conference on Big Data Security on Cloud (BigDataSecurity), (pp. 83–88).

[7] He, X., Ren, Z., Shi, C., & Fang, J. (2016). A novel load balancing strategy of software-defined cloud/fog networking in the internet of vehicles. *China Communications*, 13(Supplement 2), 140–149.

[8] Shi, C., Ren, Z., & He, X. (2016). Research on load balancing for software defined cloud-fog network in real-time mobile face recognition. In International Conference on Communications and Networking in China, (pp. 121–131). Springer.

[9] Yang, Jin. Low-latency cloud-fog network architecture and its load balancing strategy for medical big data. *Journal of Ambient Intelligence and Humanized Computing* (2020): 1–10.

[10] Abedin, Bairagi, Munir, Tran, & Hong, (2019). Fog load balancing for massive machine type communications: a game and transport theoretic approach. *IEEE Access*, 7, 4204–4218.

[11] Nazar, T., Javaid, N., Waheed, M., Fatima, A., Bano, H., & Ahmed, N. (2018). Modified shortest job first for load balancing in cloud-fog computing. In International Conference on Broadband and Wireless Computing, Communication and Applications, (pp. 63–76). Springer.

[12] Sadashiv, N. (2023). Load balancing in fog computing: a detailed survey. *International Journal of Computing and Digital Systems*, 13(1), 729–750.

[13] Verma, M., Bhardwaj, N., & Yadav, A. K. (2015). An architecture for load balancing techniques for fog computing environment. *International Journal of Computer Science and Communication*, 8(2), 43–49.

[14] Alankar, B., Sharma, G., Kaur, H., Valverde, R., & Chang, V. (2020). Experimental setup for investigating the efficient load balancing algorithms on virtual cloud. *Sensors*, 20(24), 7342.

21 Performance assessment of PID and sliding mode controllers for DC motor speed regulation

Indrajit Pandey[1,2,a] and Sreya Ghosh[3,b]

[1]Scholar, Adamas University, Kolkata, WB, India

[2]Assistant Professor Techno International New Town, Kolkata, WB, India

[3]Electrical and Electronics Engineering Department Adamas University, Kolkata, WB, India

Abstract

Sliding mode control (SMC) is one of the most efficient tools of operation for offering a flexible control mechanism in a second-order dynamic system. On the other hand, DC motors are being used extensively in industries because of their simple schemes required to perform well in position or speed control applications. This paper compares the stability output between incorporating second-order SMC with a DC motor and a PID controller with a DC motor via MATLAB simulation. Development of second-order SMC techniques helps to attain system stability by improving system performance and lessen chattering along with guaranteeing more robustness in control systems, especially when it comes to the accurate control of DC motor and it creates ability to switch between several topologies and provide more hardiness in tasks involving both linear and nonlinear management even in unpredictable circumstances.

Keywords: DC motor, PID controller, sliding mode control, speed control

Introduction

Variable structure system (VSS) may be considered as a combination of structures which are not dependent and accompanied with proper switching norms to jump between the structures so as to achieve the required system performances [1]. VSS being a unique class of nonlinear systems helps to solve a number of particular control tasks in linear and non-linear systems [2]. The practical key implementations of the concept related to VSS are found in the control of DC servo motors, robotic manipulators, induction motors, aviation control and spaceship control [3, 4].

The main mode of operation of VSS is sliding mode control (SMC). Application of VSS along with SMC is being recognized as one of the most efficient tools which can deal with uncertainties in a system due to their robustness. The theoretical findings about the robustness of VSS with sliding modes are supported by these studies [5]. One of the major advantages of the SMC technique is its amazing computational simplicity when compared to other robust control systems, its quick dynamic reaction, robustness to parameter uncertainty, and ease of controller implementation [6] [7]. There are two stages to the SMC process: i) the sliding phase, ii) the reaching phase

which are associated with two distinct control rule types, e.g., the derivable equivalent control and the switching control independently corresponding to those particular stages [8]. Though first order SMC has so many advantages, still the most certain drawback of that 1st order SMC is the chattering effect [1, 9]. The main reason behind this chattering effect is because of the sign function incorporation in the switching term; it oscillates the control input about the zero sliding surface and creates unwarranted actuator wear and tear [9]. Now to compensate this problem, second order SMC has been adopted which is more useful to make better performance and seamless control during the control implementation, which helps to reduce chattering and produce greater convergence accuracy featuring robustness [10].

In order to complete a task in good dynamic speed command tracking and load regulating responsiveness are generally essential for high-performance motor drive systems used in industrial settings [11]. As AC to DC power conversion is done easily by simple step, DC drives' uses are simpler and have far better speed and torque characteristics than AC motor following superior speed control mechanism for both acceleration and deceleration. In general, DC drives

---

[a]indrajit.pandey@tict.edu.in, [b]sreya2.ghosh@adamasuniversity.ac.in

DOI: 10.1201/9781003724995-21

are less costly for most horsepower ratings. DC motors are extensively used in industrial applications, household appliances and robot manipulators, where position and speed control of motor are necessary due to their simplicity, high reliability, ease of use, flexibility, and affordable price. There are several conventional and numerical controller types that are intended to control the speed of a DC motor in order to carry out a range of tasks. These controllers include sliding mode controllers, PID, and others. Most control systems worldwide are operated using proportional-integral-derivative (PID) controllers [13, 14].

The remarkable qualities make PID controller adaptable and efficient in a wide range of applications. PID controllers work well in feedback systems because they continuously check for errors and modify control actions in real time by responding a quick reaction to changes which are guaranteed by the proportionate term while the system reaches zero steady-state error due to the integral term and by reducing oscillations and overshoot, the derivative term increases the response's precision. PID controllers are naturally resilient to little changes in system parameters and disturbances. These controllers can be tuned to accomplish particular performance objectives, such reducing overshoot, obtaining quick reaction times or ensuring stability. As said earlier manufacturing, robotics, aerospace, automotive, chemical plants and process control industries use it extensively to solve the purposes. By modifying gains to offset oscillations or dampen undesirable dynamics, PID controllers aid in system stabilization [15]. Despite having such advantages PID controller possesses some laggings also such as it lacks in performance tracking, and it can be used in linear system. Those issues can be overcome by SMC controller.

This paper produces the output by comparing the use of SMC and PID individually with DC motor, evaluating the mathematical derivations and approaches.

Modelling of DC Motor

Figure 21.1 illustrates the architecture of a dynamic system. In the majority of its uses, the motor's speed must be precisely controlled [11]. When a desired shaft position is tracked, a specified speed can be reached. The intended speed and location are determined by the reference signal, and the control is made to ensure that the distinction between the system output and reference input eventually approaches zero,

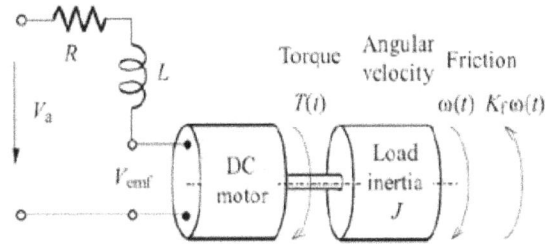

Figure 21.1 DC Motor structure
Source: Author

or as close to it as possible. In this work, the DC motor is controlled by applying voltage as an input. For the sake of simplicity, a constant voltage reference signal is utilized within the system to attain the required performance [12].

As DC motors are frequently found in robotic and electrical devices. It is essential to regulate the DC motor's speed and has been researched since the turn of the 20th century. Controller performance is generally lowered by the unpredictable and nonlinear features of DC motor systems [11]. To overcome these adversities and handling the nonlinear systems, SMC is mostly used among the most popular control methods and effective control technologies. It is frequently employed to manage the worst-case control environments, including external disturbances, parametric variation with lower and upper bounds, and more. Accurate dynamic models are not necessary, and implementing their control methods is simple. However, the sliding control's durability is heavily dependent on certain design characteristics of the sliding function [16]. One can use basic modelling of a DC motor which is mathematically based to construct the motor transfer function. The transfer function is obtained from the equation of DC motor into their electrical and mechanical components. The following is the equation for the electrical part:

$$L_1 \frac{di}{dt} + R_1 i + K_1 \frac{d\theta}{dt} = K_2 e_1 \tag{1}$$

Where e_2 is the back emf, e_1 and i are the voltage and current. R_1 and L_1 are the resistance and inductance. K_1 is the back emf constat and K_2 amplifier gain.

Newton's law can be used to compute the equation for the mechanical component.

$$J_1 \frac{d^2\theta}{dt^2} + B_1 \frac{d\theta}{dt} = T = K_3 i \tag{2}$$

$$\omega = \frac{d\theta}{dt}$$

$$J_1 \dot{\omega} + B_1 \omega = K_3 i \tag{3}$$

Where θ is the angular position and ω is the velocity of DC motor and K_3 is the torque constant.

J1 = Moment of Inertia in Kg m^2/s

B1 = Coefficient of Viscosity

T = Torque in Nm

The transfer function for a DC motor can be found using equations (4).

$$J_1 s \omega(s) + B_1 \omega(s) = K_3 I(s) \tag{4}$$

Therefore $I(s) = \frac{J_1}{K_3} s \omega(s) + \frac{B_1}{K_3} \omega(s) \tag{5}$

Taking Laplace transform of equation (1)

$$L_1 s I(s) + R_1 I(s) + K_1 \omega(s) = K_2 E_1(s) \tag{6}$$

Putting the value of $I(s)$ in equation (6)

$$L_1 s \left(\frac{J_1}{K_3} s \omega(s) + \frac{B_1}{K_3} \omega(s) \right) + R_1 \left(\frac{J_1}{K_3} s \omega(s) + \right.$$

$$\left. \frac{B_1}{K_3} \omega(s) \right) + K_1 \omega(s) = K_2 E_1(s) \tag{7}$$

$$\omega(s)(L_1 J_1 s^2 + (B_1 L_1 + R_1 J_1)s + R_1 B_1 + K_1 K_3) = K_2 K_3 E_1(s) \tag{8}$$

$$\frac{\omega(s)}{E_1(s)} = \frac{K_2 K_3}{L_1 J_1 s^2 + (B_1 L_1 + R_1 J_1)s + B_1 R_1 + K_1 K_3} = \frac{\omega(s)}{U(s)} \tag{9}$$

Taking inverse Laplace transform of equation (8) where $E_1 = U(s)$

$$L_1 J_1 \ddot{\omega}(t) + (B_1 L_1 + R_1 J_1)\dot{\omega}(t) + (B_1 R_1 + K_1 K_3)\omega(t) = K_2 K_3 u(t) \tag{10}$$

Using a dynamic system technique requires specifying the input, output, and states.

The state space is given below:

$$\dot{x}(t) = Ax(t) + Bu(t) \tag{11}$$

$$y(t) = C\, x(t) \tag{12}$$

Where,

$\dot{x}(t)$ state vectors, $u(t)$ is the input and $y(t)$ is the output. Now, the state space variables are derived as

$$\omega(t) = x_1 \tag{13}$$

$$\dot{\omega}(t) = \dot{x}_1 = x_2 \tag{14}$$

$$\dot{x}_2 = \frac{K_2 K_3}{L_1 J_1} u(t) - \frac{B_1 L_1 + R_1 J_1}{L_1 J_1} x_2 - \frac{B_1 R_1 + K_1 K_3}{L_1 J_1} x_1 \tag{15}$$

$$\begin{bmatrix} \dot{x}_1 \\ \dot{x}_2 \end{bmatrix} = \begin{bmatrix} 0 & 1 \\ -\frac{B_1 R_1 + K_1 K_3}{L_1 J_1} & -\frac{B_1 L_1 + R_1 J_1}{L_1 J_1} \end{bmatrix} \begin{bmatrix} x_1 \\ x_2 \end{bmatrix} + \begin{bmatrix} 0 \\ \frac{K_2 K_3}{L_1 J_1} \end{bmatrix} u(t) \tag{16}$$

$$y(t) = \begin{bmatrix} 1 & 0 \end{bmatrix} x(t) \tag{17}$$

$$A = \begin{bmatrix} 0 & 1 \\ -\frac{B_1 L_1 + R_1 J_1}{L_1 J_1} & -\frac{B_1 L_1 + R_1 J_1}{L_1 J_1} \end{bmatrix}, B = \begin{bmatrix} 0 \\ \frac{K_2 K_3}{L_1 J_1} \end{bmatrix}$$

$$\text{and } C = \begin{bmatrix} 1 & 0 \end{bmatrix} \tag{18}$$

Design of SMC

The requirement model of sliding mode controller belongs to state space controllable form [5, 6] as

$$s = ce + \dot{e} \tag{19}$$

In above equation variable e represents the error related to tracking and the obvious value of variable c which should satisfy the criterion for Hurwitz condition ($c > 0$).

The derivation including the tracking error is as below

$$e = \omega(t) - \omega_d(t) = x_1 - \omega_d(t) \tag{20}$$

$$\dot{e} = \dot{\omega}(t) - \dot{\omega}_d(t) = x_2 - \dot{\omega}_d(t) \tag{21}$$

$$\ddot{e} = \ddot{\omega}(t) - \ddot{\omega}_d(t) = \dot{x}_2 - \ddot{\omega}_d(t) \tag{22}$$

Where, ω_d = reference signal,

ω = actual angular speed.

The goal of the second-order sliding mode control is to guide the sliding variable s(t) as well as its time derivative in first-order, $\dot{s}(t)$ equal to zero. In the second-order sliding mode control, the sliding set $s(t) = \dot{s}(t) = 0$. It can be said that when both s(t) and its variations $\dot{s}(t)$ are equal to zero and s(t) if proceed towards zero having decreasing disparities, the system is said to be in the sliding mode. This may be seen in the 2nd order SMC system's phase plane diagram for $s(t)$ and $\dot{s}(t)$. The higher-order sliding mode improves performance in terms of delays in switching mode for implementation in the control systems and eliminates chattering effects, resulting in smooth control.

The most widely used method for demonstrating and assessing the steady convergence property of non-linear controllers, such as sliding-mode control, is Lyapunov stability analysis. Here, the property of the Stability of the suggested 2nd order SMC is examined using the direct Lyapunov stability approach. The Lyapunov function may be chosen for this purpose as [17]

$$V = \tfrac{1}{2}s^2 \tag{23}$$

To meet the condition for stability, the value of derived Lyapunov function should be $\dot{V} > 0$ as

$$s\dot{s} < 0 \tag{24}$$

From equation (19), the sliding mode function derivative is

$$\dot{s} = c\dot{e} + \ddot{e} = c(x_2 - \dot{\omega}_d(t)) + (\dot{x}_2 - \ddot{\omega}_d(t)) \tag{25}$$

Putting the value of $\dot{x}_2$ from equation (15)

$$\dot{s} = c(x_2 - \dot{\omega}_d(t)) + \frac{K_2 K_3}{L_1 J_1} u(t) - \frac{B_1 L_1 + R_1 J_1}{L_1 J_1} x_2 - \frac{B_1 R_1 + K_1 K_3}{L_1 J_1} x_1 - \ddot{\omega}_d(t) \tag{26}$$

The SMC input named u(t), is combined of two separate units: equivalent control (u_{equ}) and switching control (u_{sw})

$$u(t) = u_{equ}(t) + u_{sw}(t) \tag{27}$$

The primary action of control is produced by the equivalent control, while the switching control is the main reason behind additional control which takes account of the existence of unmodelled dynamics and matching disturbances by guaranteeing the discontinuity of the control law over the sliding surface.

$$u_{equ}(t) = \frac{L_1 J_1}{K_2 K_3}\left(-c(x_2 - \dot{\omega}_d(t)) + \frac{B_1 L_1 + R_1 J_1}{L_1 J_1} x_2 + \right.$$
$$\left. \frac{B_1 R_1 + K_1 K_3}{L_1 J_1} x_1 + \ddot{\omega}_d(t)\right) \tag{28}$$

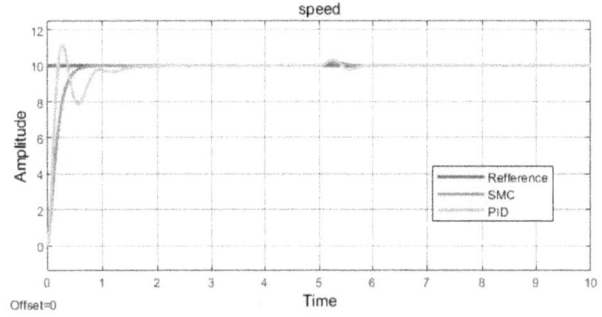

Figure 21.2 Speed response of SMC and PID controller for step input where load applying at 5 seconds in SMC and PID both

Source: Author

Table 21.1 Parameters and their value for DC motor.

Parameter	Value	Unit
R_1	17.88	Ω
L_1	6.07	mH
J_1	9.7 X 10^{-7}	N
K_1	11.8 X 10^{-3}	V.s/rad
K_2	0.01485	
K_3	11.8 X 10^{-3}	N.m/A
B_1	2.01 X 10^{-6}	N.m.s /rad

Source: Author

In the event that the switching function is shown as

$$u_{sw}(t) = -(Ks + \eta \, sgn(s)) \tag{29}$$

where $K > 0$ and $\eta > 0$ and sign(s) indicates a defined sign function.

$$sign(s) = \begin{cases} 1, & s > 0 \\ 0, & s = 0 \\ -1, & s < 0 \end{cases} \tag{30}$$

Therefore

$$u(t) = \frac{L_1 J_1}{K_2 K_3}\left(-c(x_2 - \dot{\omega}_d(t)) + \frac{B_1 L_1 + R_1 J_1}{L_1 J_1} x_2 + \right.$$
$$\left. \frac{B_1 R_1 + K_1 K_3}{L_1 J_1} x_1 + \ddot{\omega}_d(t)\right) - (Ks + \eta \, sgn(s)) \tag{31}$$

Now, Lyapunov function $\dot{V}$ is derived as

$$s\dot{s} = s\left(c(x_2 - \dot{\omega}_d(t)) + \frac{K_2 K_3}{L_1 J_1} u(t) - \frac{B_1 L_1 + R_1 J_1}{L_1 J_1} x_2 - \right.$$
$$\left. \frac{B_1 R_1 + K_1 K_3}{L_1 J_1} x_1 - \ddot{\omega}_d(t)\right) \tag{32}$$

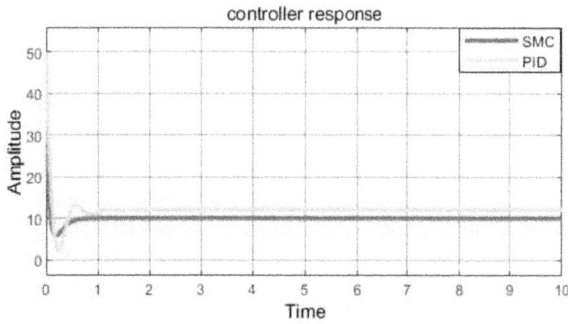

Figure 21.3 Control response of SMC and PID for step input where SMC control output is better than PID

Source: Author

Table 21.2 Parameter value of PID controller.

Controller	K_p	K_i	K_d
PID	2.19979	6.60615	0.13178

Source: Author

Table 21.3 Comparing IAE value of both controllers.

Controller	IAE
PID	0.1
2nd order SMC	0.0997

Source: Author

Table 21.4 Specifications in time domain.

Controller	Overshoot	Peak time (Sec)	Settling time (Sec)
PID	84.36%	0.295	1.990
2nd order SMC	0	0	0.760

Source: Author

$$s\dot{s} = s\left(c(x_2 - \dot{\omega}_d(t)) + \frac{K_2 K_3}{L_1 J_1}\left(\frac{L_1 J_1}{K_2 K_3}\left(-c(x_2 - \right.\right.\right.$$

$$\dot{\omega}_d(t)) + \frac{B_1 L_1 + R_1 J_1}{L_1 J_1}x_2 + \frac{B_1 R_1 + K_1 K_3}{L_1 J_1}x_1 + \ddot{\omega}_d(t)\Big) -$$

$$\left(Ks + \eta\, sgn(s))\right) - \frac{B_1 L_1 + R_1 J_1}{L_1 J_1}x_2 - \frac{B_1 R_1 + K_1 K_3}{L_1 J_1}x_1 -$$

$$\ddot{\omega}_d(t)\Bigg) \tag{33}$$

$$s\dot{s} = -\left(Ks + \eta\, sgn(s)\right) \tag{34}$$

$$s\dot{s} = -(Ks + \eta\, |s|) \tag{35}$$

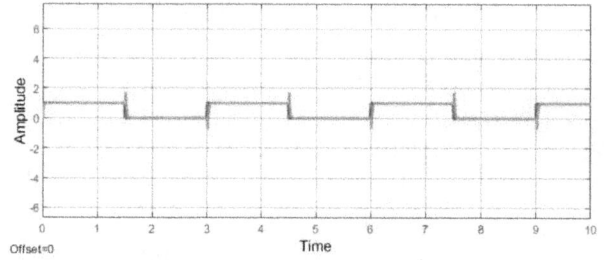

Figure 21.4 Speed response for transient analysis of SMC controller for pulse input where K=135

Source: Author

To satisfy the condition $s\dot{s} < 0$,

As the reaching phase of the system is for $s(t) \neq 0$, $s(t) > 0$, and $s\dot{s} < 0$, indicates that $s\dot{s}$ or $\dot{V}$ holds negative but definite value. According to this study above, stability can be ensured because of the Lyapunov function's derivative which is a negative definite [17].

Results and Discussion

Table 21.1–21.4 represents the values of DC motors parameters. Those parameters were used in the simulating tool for controller designing Figure 21.2–21.4.

$$\dot{x} = \begin{bmatrix} 0 & 1 \\ -29.752 & -5.017 \end{bmatrix} x(t) + \begin{bmatrix} 0 \\ 29.761 \end{bmatrix} u(t) \tag{36}$$

$$y = \begin{bmatrix} 1 & 0 \end{bmatrix} x(t) \tag{37}$$

The transfer function of the model is to be derived as:

$$\frac{\omega(s)}{U(s)} = \frac{29.761}{s^2 + 5.017s + 29.752} \tag{38}$$

Now for the stability checking by using Lyapunov theory.

From equation (31) putting the value of different parameter.

$$u(t) = \frac{L_1 J_1}{K_2 K_3}\left(-c(x_2 - \dot{\omega}_d(t)) + \frac{B_1 L_1 + R_1 J_1}{L_1 J_1}x_2 + \right.$$

$$\frac{B_1 R_1 + K_1 K_3}{L_1 J_1}x_1 + \ddot{\omega}_d(t)\Big) - \left(Ks + \eta\, sgn(s)\right)$$

u(t) = 9.963

From equation (19)

s = ce + e = 0.997

And from equation (26)

$$\dot{s} = c\left(x_2 - \dot{\omega}_d(t)\right) + \frac{K_2 K_3}{L_1 J_1} u(t) - \frac{B_1 L_1 + R_1 J_1}{L_1 J_1} x_2 - \frac{B_1 R_1 + K_1 K_3}{L_1 J_1} x_1 - \ddot{\omega}_d(t)$$

$$\dot{s} = -1.009$$

Therefore $ss = -1.006 < 0$

Therefore, this condition satisfies stability.

By applying those values in MATLAB Simulink following graph has been resulted as an output.

Conclusion

In this paper the second order SMC is selected for controlling the speed of DC motor which results in more efficient response contrasting with the conventional PID controller. To regulate the speed of a DC motor, a simple closed loop has been addressed initially, following PID and SMC controllers are involved in the design of that speed regulator. That examines how the execution of these two mechanisms allows for constant speed to evaluate the controller shift. The comparison results of the simulation show that SMC performs better than PIDs controller during overshoot and settling times taken into account.

References

[1] Young, K. D., Utkin, V. I., & Ozguner, U. (1999). A control engineer's guide to sliding mode control. *IEEE transactions on control systems technology*, 7(3), 328–342.

[2] Naik, A. K., Kar, S. K., & Sahu, B. K. (2021). Speed control of DC motor using linear and non-linear controllers. In 2021 1st Odisha International Conference on Electrical Power Engineering, Communication and Computing Technology (ODICON), (pp. 1–5). IEEE.

[3] Gambhire, S. J., Kishore, D. R., Londhe, P. S., & Pawar, S. N. (2021). Review of sliding mode based control techniques for control system applications. *International Journal of dynamics and control*, 9(1), 363–378.

[4] Rahmatullah, R., Ak, A., & Serteller, N. F. O. (2023). SMC controller design for DC motor speed control applications and performance comparison with FLC, PID and PI controllers. In Intelligent Sustainable Systems: Selected Papers of WorldS4 2022, (Vol. 2, pp. 607–617). Singapore: Springer Nature Singapore.

[5] Kadu, C. B., Khandekar, A. A., & Patil, C. Y. (2018). Design of sliding mode controller with proportional integral sliding surface for robust regulation and tracking of process control systems. *Journal*

of Dynamic Systems, Measurement, and Control*, 140(9), 091004.

[6] Saputra, D. D., Ma'arif, A., Maghfiroh, H., Baballe, M. A., Tusset, A. M., Sharkawy, A. N., et al. (2023). Performance evaluation of sliding mode control (SMC) for dc motor speed control. *JurnalIlmiah Teknik ElektroKomputer dan Informatika (JITEKI)*, 9(2), 502–510.

[7] Kızmaz, H. (2023). Comparative analysis of optimal control strategies: LQR, PID, and sliding mode control for DC Motor position performance. *Gazi University Journal of Science Part A: Engineering and Innovation*, 10(4), 571–592.

[8] Rakhonde, S., & Kulkarni, V. (2018). Sliding mode controller (SMC) governed speed control of DC motor. In 2018 3rd IEEE International Conference on Recent Trends in Electronics, Information & Communication Technology (RTEICT), (pp. 1657–1662). IEEE.

[9] Kuchwa-Dube, C., & Pedro, J. O. (2022). Chattering performance criteria for multi-objective optimisation gain tuning of sliding mode controllers. *Control Engineering Practice*, 127, 105284.

[10] Maghfiroh, H., Sujono, A., & Apribowo, C. H. B. (2020). Basic tutorial on sliding mode control in speed control of DC-motor. *Journal of Electrical, Electronic, Information, and Communication Technology*, 2(1), 1–4.

[11] Batool, A., Ain, N. U., Amin, A. A., Adnan, M., & Shahbaz, M. H. (2022). A comparative study of DC servo motor parameter estimation using various techniques. *Automatika*, 63(2), 303–312.

[12] Ma'arif, A., & Çakan, A. (2021). Simulation and arduino hardware implementation of dc motor control using sliding mode controller. *Journal of Robotics and Control (JRC)*, 2(6), 582–587.

[13] Huang, Z., & Li, X. (2024). Simulation and comparative study of PID control in DC servo motor systems. In AIP Conference Proceedings, (Vol. 3144, no. 1). AIP Publishing.

[14] Bagua, H. (2023). Performance comparison of pid and LQR control for DC motor speed regulation. *The Journal of Engineering and Exact Sciences*, 9(12), 19429–19429.

[15] Hammoodi, S. J., Flayyih, K. S., & Hamad, A. R. (2020). Design and implementation speed control system of DC motor based on PID control and matlab simulink. *International Journal of Power Electronics and Drive Systems*, 11(1), 127–134.

[16] Almawla, A. M., Hussein, M. J., & Abdullah, A. T. (2024). A comparative study of DC motor speed control techniques using fuzzy, SMC and PID. *Journal Européen des Systèmes Automatisés*, 57(2), 397.

[17] Eker, I. (2010). Second-order sliding mode control with experimental application. *ISA Transactions*, 49(3), 394–405.

22 Implementation of carry skip adder with speed and less delay

Kandukuri Srinivas[a], Bijili Divakar[b], Asam Saipriya[c] and Mokile Sidhu[d]

Nalla Narasimha Reddy Education Society's Group of Institutions, Telangana, India

Abstract

Digital circuits employ a carry skip adder (CSA) type of adder to execute quick arithmetic operations by effectively controlling the propagation of transport bits from one step of the adding process to another. Reducing the total delay brought on by the ripple effect of carries in a conventional ripple carry adder is the main objective of a CSA. It does this by accelerating the addition process by avoiding specific groups where carry propagation is not required. Each block that makes up the CSA can calculate the sum and determine whether a carry is generated or propagated. The CSA permits a carry to "skip" over intermediate blocks where the carry must spread if it must span several blocks.

Keywords: Arithmetic adder, carry skip adder, propagation delay, scalability

Introduction

In contrast to conventional ripple carry adders, a carry skip adder (CSA) is a sophisticated digital circuit used for binary addition that is intended to increase speed and decrease delays. The propagation delay brought on by the carry bits, which need to be calculated sequentially, is the main difficulty in binary addition. Significant delays result from the need to calculate each bit's carry-out before processing the subsequent bit in a conventional ripple carry adder, particularly in bigger bit-width adders. To overcome this restriction, the carry-skip adder introduces a technique that enables specific carry bits to be omitted, hence accelerating the addition operation. The architecture of a carry-skip adder incorporates two key components: the carry-skip logic and the carry-select logic. The carry-skip adder has been a focal point of research aimed at improving the performance of binary addition in digital circuits. Early studies highlighted the limitations of traditional ripple carry adders, which suffer from significant propagation delays as the carry signal must ripple through each bit. This delay becomes increasingly problematic in larger bit-width adders, where the time taken to compute the final sum can be substantial. Researchers began exploring alternative architectures to mitigate these delays, leading to the development of the CSA. This architecture allows for the skipping of carrying propagation under certain conditions, effectively reducing the overall addition time.

Literature Review

CSA has been a focal point of research aimed at improving the performance of binary addition in digital circuits. Early studies highlighted the limitations of traditional ripple carry adders, which suffer from significant propagation delays as the carry signal must ripple through each bit. This delay becomes increasingly problematic in larger bit-width adders, where the time taken to compute the final sum can be substantial. Researchers began exploring alternative architectures to mitigate these delays, leading to the development of the CSA. This architecture allows for the skipping of carrying propagation under certain conditions, effectively reducing the overall addition time. Several variations of the CSA have been proposed in the literature; each aiming to optimize speed and minimize delay. One notable approach involves the use of hierarchical structures, where the carry-skip logic is implemented at multiple levels. This allows for greater flexibility in managing carry propagation across larger bit-widths, enabling faster computations by processing multiple bits simultaneously. Studies have shown that these hierarchical CKA can significantly outperform traditional designs, particularly in high-speed

[a]srinivas.kandukury@gmail.com, [b]divakarbijili@gmail.com, [c]asamsaipriya@gmail.com, [d]sidhumokile@gmail.com

DOI: 10.1201/9781003724995-22

applications where rapid arithmetic operations are critical. In addition to architectural innovations, researchers have also focused on implementing efficient carry-skip logic using advanced technologies. For instance, the integration of dynamic logic and low-power ways has been explored to enhance the performance of carry-skip adders while maintaining energy efficiency. These advancements are particularly relevant in the context of modern computing devices, where energy consumption and heat dissipation are crucial considerations. The literature indicates that such optimizations not only improve the speed of addition but also contribute to the overall sustainability of digital systems.

Overall, the evolution of the CKA reflects a broader trend in digital design towards achieving higher performance with lower latency. The ongoing research in this area continues to uncover new ways and methodologies that enhance the efficiency of binary addition. As the demand for faster and more efficient computing increases in the design of high-performance systems.

Problem Statement

Designing a 32-bit CSA with skip logic presents several challenges that impact its efficiency and performance. One primary issue is the propagation delay caused by the carry chain; each block in the adder uses a series of AND and OR gates to determine whether to propagate or skip the carry. As bit-width increases, the accumulated delay from these skip operations can significantly slow down the circuit. Determining the optimal block size for each carry-skip segment is also complex, as smaller blocks reduce skip delay but increase the number of skip logic gates required, while larger blocks add delay but reduce logic gate use. This trade-off affects both speed and power, as the skip logic consumes additional power due to dynamic and leakage in each gate, which can be problematic for low-power applications. Furthermore, the added skip paths and logic contribute to increased layout complexity and area, resulting in a larger overall chip footprint. Timing variations, stemming from manufacturing process inconsistencies, temperature fluctuations, and power supply changes, further complicate the design, as any deviation in timing can cause inaccuracies or glitches, especially over long skip chains. Lastly, while this architecture is feasible for 32-bit adders, scaling it to larger

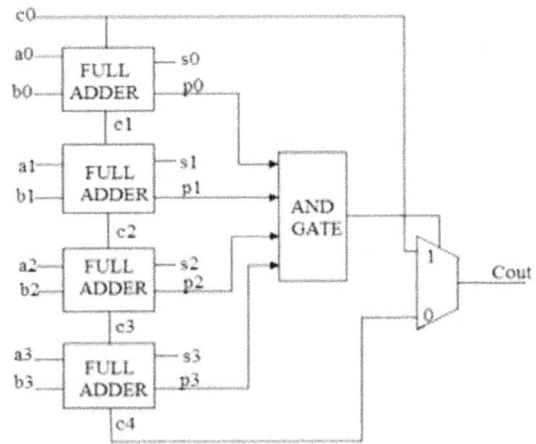

Figure 22.1 4-bit CKA
Source: Author

bit-widths (such as 64-bit or 128-bit) introduces even more delay and complexity. To address these issues, a robust design should explore optimizations like adaptive block sizing, low-power logic gates, and potentially hybrid architectures that combine the CSA with other adder types for better scalability, efficiency, and robustness.

Design Methodology

The CKA is derived from a bypass adder group and implements an adder using a ripple carry adder [4]. By making the worst-case latency better, the CKA block is formed. Although it can lessen the carry propagation latency, this adder is efficient in terms of both area and power consumption. Figure 22.1 depicts the layout of a simple 4-bit carry skip adder.

The CSKA is composed of a single stage that includes a 2:1 multiplexer, an AND gate, an XOR gate, and a chain of FAs (RCA block). A 2:1 multiplexer, which may be positioned at one or more levels of the structure, connects the RCA blocks. Figure 22.1 depicts the carry-skip adder's (4-bit) fundamental circuit structure. In a 32-bit carry-skip adder, skip logic can be implemented using AND gates and a multiplexer (MUX) to speed up carry propagation. Each bit within a block has a propagation condition, calculated as the XOR of the input bits Ai and Bi for that point.

The overall propagate condition for the entire block, P block, is then determined by ANDing all individual propagate signals in the block. If all bits in the block meet this propagation condition, the carry can skip the block. The actual carry-skip mechanism relies on a 2:1 multiplexer, which takes the carry-out from the last bit of the block and the carry-in to the block as its two inputs. When the propagate condition P block is true (all bits propagate), the MUX selects the carry-in, effectively skipping the block. If the propagate condition is false, the carryout from the last bit of the block is selected, allowing the carry to propagate normally through the block. This setup allows the adder to dynamically choose the fastest path for the carry, reducing delay. The result, Cout, block, represents the final carry-out for the block and feeds into the next block, ensuring efficient carry propagation across the entire 32-bit adder.

$$Pi= Ai \text{ xor } Bi, sum = Pi \text{ xor } Cin, Cout =$$
$$(P \text{ block}. Cin) + (P' \text{ block}. Cout, last) \qquad (1)$$

Where P block = P0.P1.P2.P3

To design a 32-bit carry-skip adder (CSKA) using 4-bit carry-skip adder blocks, the 32-bit inputs are divided into eight 4-bit sections, with each section functioning as an independent 4-bit carry-skip unit. Each 4-bit block (e.g., Block 1, Block 2, up to Block 8) performs addition on its respective 4-bit inputs, computes its sum, and determines whether the carry-in should propagate or skip. Within each block, the propagate condition is calculated as the AND of the bitwise propagate signals, where each propagate signal for a bit point is the XOR of the corresponding input bits Ai and Bi. This block propagation condition, P block, is true if all bits in the block allow carry propagation, enabling the carry-in to bypass the block entirely.

To facilitate carry skipping, each 4-bit block includes a multiplexer (MUX) that selects between passing the carry-out from the last bit within the block or allowing the carry-in to skip over the

block. The carry-out of each block, Cout, block, is determined by the expression Cout, block (P block Cin)+(P' block⁻·Clast) where Cin is the carry input to the block, and Clast is the carry generated within the block. This setup allows the adder to dynamically choose whether to skip or propagate through each block, depending on the propagate condition.

The eight 4-bit blocks are connected sequentially, with each block's carry-out feeding into the next block's carry-in, creating an efficient cascade that reduces delay compared to a traditional ripple-carry structure. The final output is formed by combining the 4-bit sums from each block, yielding a complete 32-bit sum. This structure optimizes carry propagation across the 32-bit adder, balancing speed and complexity effectively.

Implementation

The implementation of carry skip adder often starts with Hardware Description Language (HDL) in the design cycle. HDLs (e.g. VHDL, VERILOG) allow for behavioral and structural modelling of the electronic system. It permits the designer to design the system at all levels of abstraction, thus capturing any difficult functionality design and also making simulation, synthesis and testing easier. This is useful in HDL implementation of CSKA because designers can iterate through the details of the encoder and decoder modules in the design. Such details are very important in the development of high-quality designs which can be implemented in hardware.

We used Xilinx vivado software to implement the design of 4-bit CSKA and 32-bit CSKA. In this many steps are involved. Our primary goal is to reduce the carry propagation delay. This delay value will be

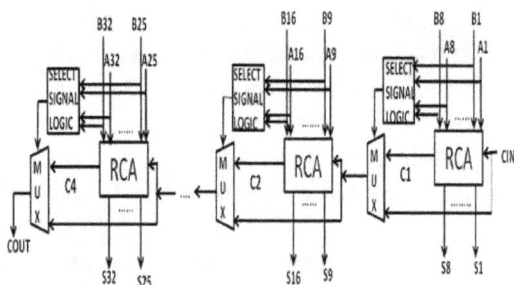

Figure 22.2 32-bit carry skip adder
Source: Author

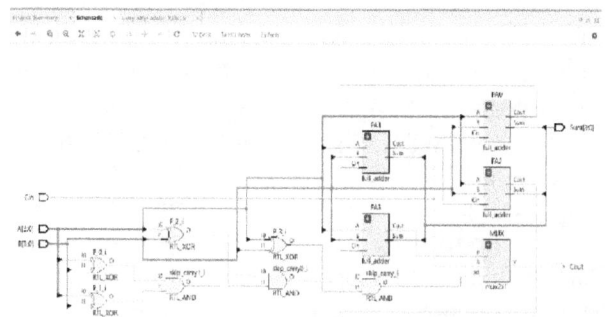

Figure 22.3 Schematic diagram of 4-bit carry skip adder (CSKA)
Source: Author

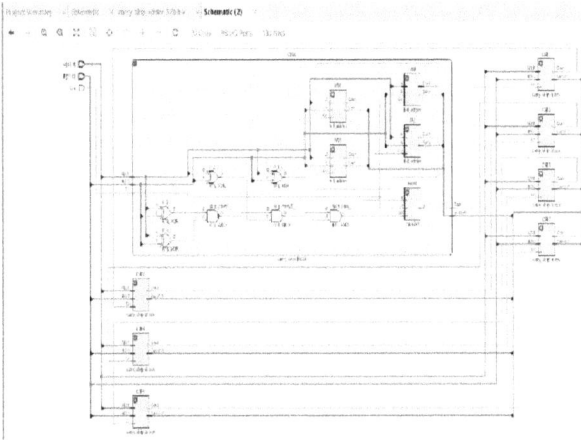

Figure 22.4 Schematic diagram of 32-bit carry skip adder (CSKA)
Source: Author

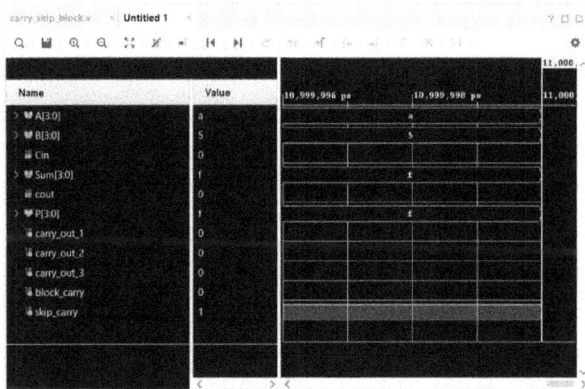

Figure 22.6 Behavioral simulation of 4-bit CSKA
Source: Author

shown in this vivado software tool. It will show the data path delay.

Simulations and Results

In the simulation and results this will show the operation of carry skip adder. This simulation in the Xilinx vivado software helps us to analyze 4-bit carry skip adder and 32-bit carry skip adder.

In the 4-bit carry skip adder simulation it will show the all the parameters including carry skip indication also whether it is 1 or 0. In the 32-bit carry skip adder we have inputs are A, B, Cin and the outputs are Sum and Cout.

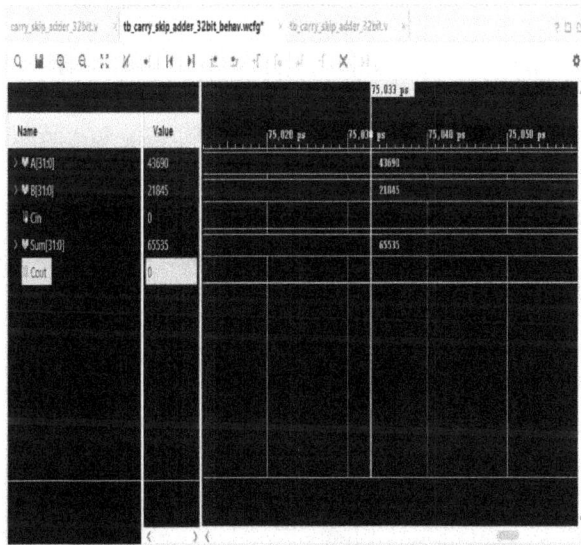

Figure 22.5 Behavioral simulation of 32-bit CSKA
Source: Author

Conclusion

The 32-bit carry skip adder (CSA) presents a significant improvement over traditional carry propagation adders in terms of speed and efficiency in digital

Table 22.1 Comparison table of carry skip adders.

	Delay	Area (LUTs)
Existing method of 16-bit CSKA using AND and OR gate for skip logic	29.45ns	47 out of 20800
Existing method of 2 block carry skip adder using AND and OR gate for skip logic	31.63ns	43 out of 20800
Existing method of 8 block carry skip adder using AND and OR gate for skip logic	27.09ns	60 out of 20800
Proposed method of 4bit carry skip adder using AND and MUX for skip logic	8.2ns	4 out of 20800
Proposed method of 32bit carry skip adder using AND and MUX for skip logic	20.929ns	55 out of 20800

Source: Author

arithmetic operations. By implementing a mechanism that allows certain carries to skip over groups of bits, the CSA reduces the average delay associated with carry propagation, thereby enhancing overall performance. This is especially beneficial in high-speed computing applications where rapid calculations are critical. The CSA's architecture balances the trade-off between speed and complexity. While the logic required for the carry skip mechanism adds some complexity, the reduction in critical path delay often results in faster addition times compared to conventional ripple carry adders. Moreover, the CSA's ability to handle 32-bit data makes it suitable for modern computing environments that frequently utilize 32-bit architectures.

In the future, the CSA can be combined with cutting-edge technologies like optical or quantum computing, which could result in even more power and calculation time savings. Future versions might also concentrate on maximizing energy efficiency, utilizing low-power design techniques to make the CSA appropriate for portable and battery-operated devices. In order to take use of parallel processing capabilities and facilitate faster computations for applications such as scientific simulations and graphics processing, the adder can also be expanded to enable multi-core architecture. Higher integration densities in chips may be possible with more efficient and compact CSA designs brought about by ongoing research into very-large-scale integration (VLSI) techniques. Additionally, creating adaptive algorithms that may dynamically swap between various adder types according to the task at hand could maximize performance in a range of computational situations. Lastly, with an emphasis on optimizing speed and efficiency for certain activities, customized CSAs might be created for particular applications including digital signal processing (DSP), cryptography, and real-time systems. In conclusion, even

if the 32-bit Carry Skip Adder is now a useful part of digital systems, there are still a lot of chances to expand its use in future computing environments and improve its capabilities thanks to continued study and technological breakthroughs.

References

[1] Roja Rao, B., & Prasad, V. (2016). Implementation of carry skip adder using high-speed skip logic at different level. *International Journal of VLSI System Design and Communication Systems*, (9), 840–843.

[2] Alioto, M., & Palumbo, G. (2003). A simple strategy for optimized design of one-level carry-skip adders. *IEEE Transactions on Circuits and Systems I: Fundamental Theory and Applications*, 50(1), 141–148.

[3] Bahadori, M., Kamal, M., & Afzali-Kusha, A. (2016). High-speed and energy efficient carry skip adder operating under a wide range of supply voltage levels. *IEEE Transaction on Very Large Scale Integration (VLSI) Systems*, 24(2), 421–433.

[4] Monisha T. S., & Senthil Prakash, K. (2016). An optimized design of high-speed and energy- efficient carry skip adder with variable latency extension. *International Journal of Science and Research*, 5(3), 329–333.

[5] Knowles, S. (2001). A family of adders. In Proceedings of the 15th IEEE Symposium on Computer Arithmetic, (pp. 277–284).

[6] Kumar, P., & Kaur, J. (2014). Design of modified parallel prefix knowles adder. *International Journal of Science and Research*, 3, 199–201.

[7] Vijayabala, N., & Kumar, S. (2013). Area minimization of carry select adder using Boolean algebra. *International Journal of Advances in Engineering & Technology*, 6(3), 1250–1255.

[8] Kantabutra, V. (1993). Designing optimum one-level carry-skip adders. *IEEE Transactions on Computers*, 42(6), 759–764.

[9] Chimpiraiah, C. H., & Vijay, V. E. (2012). An efficient architecture for parallel adders. *International Journal of VLSI and Embedded Systems*, 3(04), 160–164.

23 Analysis of precision cardiovascular disease classification using machine learning techniques

Ramadevi, C.[1,a], Narmadha, T. V.[2,b], Marshina, D.[3,c] and Neelam Sanjeev Kumar[4,d]

[1]Assistant Professor, Department of EEE, St. Joseph's College of Engineering, Chennai, Tamil Nadu, India

[2]Professor, Department of EEE, St. Joseph's College of Engineering, Chennai, Tamil Nadu, India

[3]Symbiosis Institute of Technology Symbiosis International Deemed University, Pune, Maharashtra, India

[4]Department of CSE, E. Tech, SRM Institute of Science and Technology, Vadapalani Campus, Chennai, Tamil Nadu, India

Abstract

In recent years, the healthcare sector has played an increasingly important role in computer vision. Healthcare is regarded as an unavoidable aspect of human existence. Even though computer science and medicine are unrelated, they have been combining for several years for some reason. Cardiovascular disease (CVD) is the leading cause of mortality worldwide, killing around 20.5 million people each year. This is because heart disease accounts for approximately 30 percent of all deaths. Coronary artery disease occurs when atherosclerosis accumulates in the arteries that deliver oxygenated blood to the heart. Plaque can constrict or block arteries, increasing the risk of heart attacks. Unhealthy heating habits, lack of exercise, smoking, and alcohol use can cause coronary disease. The medical diagnosis of heart conditions is critical. Early detection of coronary artery disease reduces the risk. The patient database in the healthcare department consists of a large number of records, hence it necessitates utilizing machine learning techniques to make use of this data to produce successful results. Finding cardiovascular disease risk variables using machine learning techniques is a potential method. A vast amount of data is generated by medical gadgets available in hospitals. Hence, it is necessary to understand data related to heart disease to improve accuracy. This paper is an exceptional study that may serve as motivation for the development of novel approaches to cardiovascular disease diagnosis.

Keywords: Cardiovascular, decision tree, fuzzy logic, heart disease, machine learning (ML), support vector machine

Introduction

Coronary heart disease is a somewhat frequent condition that can drastically shorten a person's life expectancy. Every year, this disease kills around 17.5 million people [1]. As the heart holds such a crucial role in our bodies, its proper functioning is vital for our survival. Coronary illness is an infection that directly affects the heart's ability [2]. Many medical and therapeutic settings allow you to assess a person's susceptibility to coronary heart disease. Creating a predictive risk model can be achieved through analyzing a longitudinal study using multivariate regression [3]. Thanks to advancements in research, medical institutions now possess vast and intricate databases storing a wealth of information. Data mining and artificial intelligence algorithms have recently made a significant impact on clinical research and analysis. By applying these methodologies and computations to the available data, you can develop models or draw key conclusions [4]. Predictive models allow for an accurate diagnosis and can help identify those who are more likely to have coronary artery disease. This could lead to a decrease in death rates and better decision-making for management and prevention. Many studies have found that adopting CDSS helps to improve the quality of clinical advice, decision-making, and preventative treatment.

Background

Impaired ventricles' ability to circulate blood throughout the heart leads to the development of

[a]mdevi.j@gmail.com, [b]narmathatv@stjosephs.ac.in, [c]d.marshiana@gmail.com, [d]neelamsanjeev1034@gmail.com

DOI: 10.1201/9781003724995-23

cardiovascular disease (CVD). Abnormal cardiac function can result in inadequate blood delivery to important organs and cells, potentially leading to death. Worldwide, approximately 26 million individuals are diagnosed with congestive heart failure (CHF) each year. The severity of CHF determines the intensity of symptoms experienced by patients. Symptoms typically manifest when the condition reaches an advanced stage, such as grade 3 or grade 4 CHF. Cardiologists rely on common symptoms to identify CHF in patients, but the accuracy of their diagnosis depends on their expertise and experience. The Block diagram focuses on reducing heart disease by 40 percent by 2024. Overall, the data highlights that age is a significant factor in cardiovascular disease mortality, with males consistently experiencing higher rates than females. The steady rise in mortality over the three years emphasizes the growing burden of cardiovascular diseases, particularly among older populations, and the need for targeted preventive and treatment strategies. Electrocardiography (ECG) is prediction process by introducing clearer stages with logical progression. It begins with Patient Data Collection, where datasets and patient details are gathered, ensuring sufficient and diverse input data. The next step, the Preprocessing Stage, involves cleaning, handling missing data, and extracting relevant features. Once the data is prepared, Classification Algorithms are applied, such as DT, SVM, or NN, to classify patient data. This stage is crucial as the accuracy of disease prediction largely depends on the chosen algorithm. The Model Training Validation phase trains the classification model on historical data and evaluates its performance using metrics. Finally, the Prediction Output provides the results.

This systematic flow ensures a well-structured and efficient approach to heart disease prediction, combining data science techniques with healthcare applications. The data compares cardiovascular disease mortality rates for males and females across different age groups over three years: 2022, 2023, and 2024. For males, mortality rates increase significantly with age. In the under-30 age group, mortality remains minimal but shows a slight rise over the years. In the 30–49 age group, the rates are still relatively low but are gradually increasing. A sharp rise is observed in the 50–69 age group, with a consistent upward trend each year. The 70+ age group experiences the highest mortality rates, exceeding 50% by 2024. For females, a similar pattern is observed, though mortality rates are slightly lower than males in all age groups. In the under-30 and 30–49 age groups, mortality remains low but shows a gradual increase over time. However, in the 50-69 age group, the rates rise significantly, and the 70+ age group see the highest mortality, exceeding a vital technical tool for detecting cardiac conditions.

However, wellness disrupts coordination and balance. Measuring heart rate variability (HRV) helps to determine the frequency of these episodes. The autonomic nervous system can cause changes in heart rate, which HRV can detect. This allows for the examination of both common and rare heart conditions.

Significance of Healthcare in Computer Vision

Computer vision (CV), an AI technology, is enhancing healthcare by allowing machines to perceive and comprehend visuals similar to humans. By translating digital images into processes or inferring hypothetical ideas, CV allows machines to recognize the shapes of objects and patterns with great precision. This is made possible by neural networks, which are advanced models that apply mathematical approaches to big data. The more extensive and richer the data, the more effective the neural network.

It is possible to say that CV technology has somewhat surpassed the human eye, especially when it comes to image recognition, object recognition, and image segmentation. In the field of medicine, for instance, CV technology aids in the diagnosis of an illness that would have otherwise been overlooked, which is often the case with other tests. This improves the accuracy and speed of diagnosing illnesses and procedures, allowing doctors to quickly

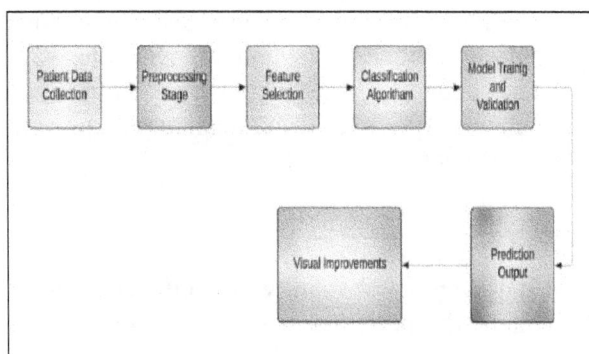

Figure 23.1 Block diagram of the heart disease prediction technique
Source: Author

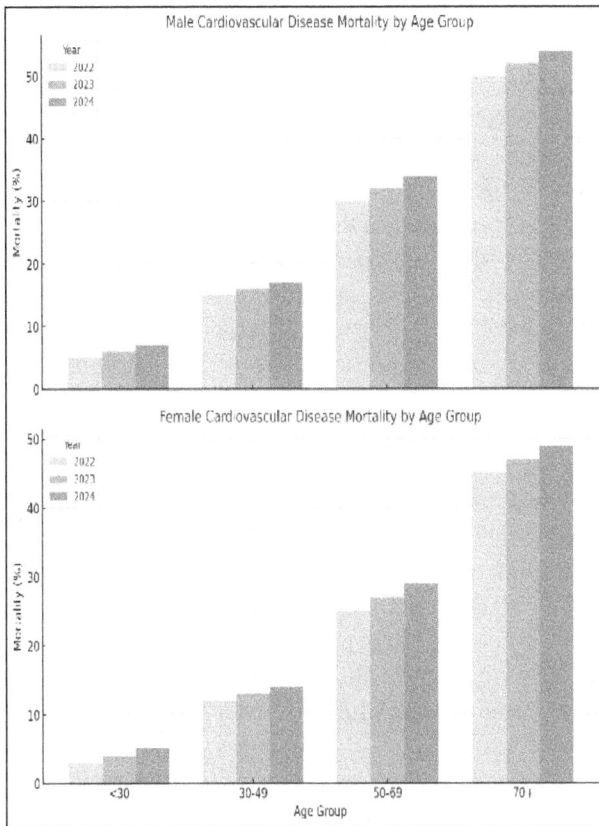

Figure 23.2 Cardiovascular diseases mortality by age group and sex
Source: Author

make decisions that are effective and beneficial to the patients while saving time, which helps in promoting people's health and even their lives. The use of CV within the age of advanced technology can be useful to combat one of the medical-based initiatives, which is identified as being able to reduce the degree of risk posed by patient amnesia. Patients are misidentified now and then, which causes great trouble to the service providers and the patients. Advanced CV identification systems can accurately match the patient's image and reduce related risks by performing accurate adjustments.

Literature Review

Pan et al. [6] proposed an EDCNN approach that has been validated through comprehensive testing using both full and minimized features. It has been implemented on the IoMT, providing decision support networks for effective analysis of cardiovascular patient data. Ali et al. [7] centered around to propose a system that eliminates undercutting and overcutting issues, addresses network concerns, and addresses augmentation problems. The author has introduced an optimized network named the optimally configured and enhanced deep belief network (OCI-DBN) to address the mentioned concerns. To tackle the aforementioned challenges. Rojas-Albarracín et al. [8] propose a unique method for identifying people who have experienced a heart attack using color photos. Their purpose is to identify different areas of heart disease that differ from one another. The technique for distinguishing infarcts utilizes convolutional neural networks to analyze the images using CNNs. Reddy et al. [9] developed an effective model for predicting coronary heart disease using the CHD. The model consisted of eleven artificial intelligence classifiers from various companies. Bayes, Functions, Lethargic, Meta, Rules, and Trees are some of the integrated models. Three assessors provided the best combinations of qualities. Mienye and Sun [10] proposed an approach for improving the accuracy of heart disease prediction. To achieve productive component learning, an enhanced layered insufficient autoencoder framework is designed. The organization comprises various scanty auto encoders and a SoftMax classifier. To get productive execution in DL models, the calculation boundaries should also be modified correctly. Song [11] propose a unique 2D EEG signal region detection and diagnostic model in this work. The proposed method aids in recognizing and separating the increased waveform in the cardiac conduction cycle. The proposed method outperforms the results produced from a sequential single-layered ECG signal, according to the testing. With a more obvious visual impact and an analytical accuracy of 98.94%, Manimurugan et al. [12] have proposed a forecast model that works in two phases in this research. There is no need for a second stage if the initial stage results are effective in predicting cardiac illness. During the initial phase, the information obtained from clinical sensors connected to the patient's body underwent classification. Baccouche et al. [13] have compiled an 800-record dataset from Mexico's Medica Norte Hospital. The data includes 17%hypertension coronary disease, 16% ischemia coronary disease, 7% mixed coronary disease, and 8 percent valve coronary disease. The distribution of data collected on various types of heart disease is inconsistent. Li et al. [14] proposed a highly effective and precise framework for analyzing heart disease was proposed. This framework utilizes AI techniques and incorporates classification algorithms such as Support Vector Machine, Logistic Regression, ANN< KNN, NB, and DT. The author also introduced a novel and efficient feature selection algorithm to address the issue of selecting relevant features.

Mohan et al. [15] have utilized machine learning algorithms in IoT technology in this paper. The author has presented an approach that uses machine learning to detect relevant features, boosting the accuracy of heart disease prediction. A prediction model using several combinations of features and a few well-known categorization algorithms is provided. Khan et al. [17] proposed a novel approach using AI methods. While previous cardiovascular disease detection systems aimed to diagnose heart conditions quickly, their accuracy was low. To address this drawback, a strategy combining the modified social spider optimization (MSSO) and ANFIS techniques was presented. From the literature review, the researchers investigated how data mining and artificial intelligence can be used to anticipate the onset of heart disease. If one wants to analyze the effectiveness of any strategy, empirical testing of the proposed framework is required before implementation. If we want the systems to function optimally, we must use more advanced feature selection algorithms. For those suffering from a specific heart condition, there are numerous treatment options available. Data mining approaches benefit a variety of systems. However, it is evident from the literature review that using a single heart disease diagnostic strategy only achieves partial success, highlighting the need for combination models to enhance system accuracy. Examining multiple possibilities helps to improve the accuracy and adaptability of this prediction process. We should postpone additional study and analysis on this topic until later due to temporal constraints.

Proposed Methodology

In the realm of medicine, detecting cardiovascular disease at an early stage is a difficult undertaking. Deep learning algorithms, such as the Enhanced EDCNN, the effectiveness of the proposed EDCNN approach hasave been validated through comprehensive testing using both full and minimized features. It has been implemented on the Internet of Medical Things Platform (IoMT), providing decision support

networks for effective analysis of cardiovascular patient data. Experimental results demonstrate that this strategy outperforms existing methods such as ANN, DNN, RNN, and NNE [26]. Ultimately, the adoption of this proposed approach significantly reduces the risk associated with cardiovascular diseases.to produce a DBN that is optimally configured. To have a better understanding of how the framework operates, a study of RBM and DBN is carried out. The proposed technique solves optimization and configuration concerns by applying the SGA strategy to calculate the ideal width of hidden layers. The author used a local search technique to come up with the best value for GA. The outcomes are sent back for additional improvement of the line-tuning capacity of the hereditary calculation. Although the model performs adequately, there is room for improvement to bring the AUC closer to 1.0, indicating near-perfect classification. Efforts such as optimizing thresholds, enhancing features, or refining the model could further improve its predictive accuracy.

The proper assessment of heart health necessitates extensive clinical experience. As a result, in clinical determination practice, the improvement goal is to reduce the diagnostic process's large reliance on clinical expertise and to develop analysis efficiency and precision more efficiently. In terms of intelligent image analysis tactics related to the clinical cycle, the DL approach has achieved outstanding results. More meaningful and abundant data can be extracted from image processing algorithms than from successive electrocardiogram (ECG) signals. the suggested approach can help doctors diagnose a patient's specific ailment. Healthcare systems increasingly employ the IoMT to collect data from devices used to determine the severity and prognosis of cardiovascular disease. The planned study's primary goal is to combine clinical data and medical imaging to organize information and develop cardiovascular disease prognoses. To organize the sensor data, the author used a modified ant-lion optimization method in conjunction with a hybrid linear methodology. The author sorted the EEG pictures using a hybrid network that included R-CNN and SE-ResNet-101. The author was effective in identifying cases of heart disease by integrating and confirming two categorization systems. The test results showed that the proposed technique was correct in 98.31% of cases with uncommon data and 96.85% of cases with normal data. The author proposes an ensemble learning organization of several neural network models, as well as an approach for accumulating irregular under-sampling data [30]. The author has undertaken an information pre-processing endeavor by employing feature selection to enhance the performance of categorization algorithms. Tests were conducted using both unidirectional and bidirectional neural network models for different types of heart disease. The results indicated that an ensemble classifier combining a BiLSTM or BiGRU model with a CNN model achieved the highest accuracy and F1-score, ranging from 91–96%. The author demonstrated that this proposed technique could potentially address the issue of imbalanced data classification in heart disease datasets. Furthermore, the proposed technique is not validated using a benchmark dataset in this study. If the amount of the dataset grows larger, the recommended models' characterization execution may change. The author has proposed a correlation between the proposed technique and SVM as a standard model, demonstrating its poor performance against brain organization models. The FROC study revealed that the deep learning algorithm achieved detection accuracy similar to that of human experts. The estimated amount of calcium closely matches the actual value, as indicated by the analysis of calcium mass quantification. The correlation between the two is supported by a coefficient of determination of 96.24% through linear regression.

Results and Discussion

CVD remains the leading cause of death worldwide, accounting for approximately 30 percent of global mortality, with an estimated 20.5 million deaths annually. Among these, coronary artery disease (CAD) is a significant contributor, caused by the buildup of atherosclerotic plaque in arteries that supply oxygenated blood to the heart. This condition increases the risk of heart attacks and is often linked to lifestyle factors such as unhealthy eating habits, lack of exercise, smoking, and alcohol consumption. Early diagnosis and intervention are critical to reducing the risks associated with CVD. With the rise in patient data generated by healthcare systems and medical devices, machine learning has emerged as a powerful tool to analyze these large datasets effectively. By identifying risk factors and patterns, machine learning techniques enable early detection of CVD, improving diagnostic accuracy and outcomes. Integrating healthcare with machine learning not only aids managing existing data but also inspires innovative approaches for more precise and timely cardiovascular disease diagnosis.

However, early detection and intervention can make a significant difference in preventing severe complications. With the vast amount of health data now available, machine learning is transforming how we identify and diagnose CVD. By analyzing patterns in patient data, these advanced technologies can detect risks earlier and improve accuracy in diagnosis. Integrating machine learning with healthcare not only enhances how we manage patient information but also opens doors to faster, more precise, and potentially life-saving treatments.

Conclusion

In conclusion, the integration of data mining and artificial intelligence has revolutionized the field of heart disease prediction and diagnosis, offering new possibilities for early detection and effective management of cardiovascular conditions. The ability to analyze vast amounts of complex medical data with advanced algorithms has significantly enhanced the precision and adaptability of diagnostic systems. Despite the progress, it is evident that relying on a singular diagnostic approach yields only partial success, necessitating the development of combination models that merge multiple methodologies for improved accuracy. Empirical testing of proposed frameworks is critical to validate their effectiveness before implementation, ensuring reliable outcomes in real-world applications. Additionally, incorporating advanced feature selection algorithms is vital to optimizing system performance by isolating the most relevant Variables, enabling more precise predictions. While individual treatment options are available for patients with specific Heart conditions, adopting predictive systems that integrate AI and data mining can transform preventive care and improve Clinical decision-making. However, the time-sensitive nature of research and the complexity of data-driven models often occur.

References

[1] Hazra, A., Mandal, S. K., Gupta, A., Mukherjee, A., & Mukherjee, A. (2017). Heart disease diagnosis and prediction using machine learning and data mining techniques: a review. *Advances in Computational Sciences and Technology*, 10(7), 2137–2159.

[2] Krishnaiah, V., Narsimha, G., & Chandra, N. S. (2016). Heart disease prediction system using data mining techniques and intelligent fuzzy approach: a review. *International Journal of Computer Applications*, 136(2), 43–51.

[3] Hu, G., & Root, M. M. (2005). Building prediction models for coronary heart dis- ease by synthesizing multiple longitudinal research findings. *European Journal of Preventive Cardiology*, 12(5), 459–464.

[4] Mythili, T., Mukherji, D., Padalia, N., & Naidu, A. (2013). A heart disease predictionmodel using SVM-decision trees-logistic regression (SDL). *International Journal of Computer Applications*, 68(16).

[5] Fitriyani, N. L., Syafrudin, M., Alfian, G., & Rhee, J. (2020). HDPM: an effective heart disease prediction model for a clinical decision support system. *IEEE Access*, 8, 133034–133050.

[6] Pan, Y., Fu, M., Cheng, B., Tao, X., & Guo, J. (2020). Enhanced deep learning assisted convolutional neural network for heart disease prediction on the internet of medical things platform. *IEEE Access*, 8, 189503–189512.

[7] Ali, S. A., Raza, B., Malik, A. K., Shahid, A. R., Faheem, M., Alquhayz, H., et al. (2020). An optimally configured and improved deep belief network (OCI-DBN) approach for heart disease prediction based on Ruzzo–Tompa and stacked genetic algorithm. *IEEE Access*, 8, 65947–65958.

[8] Rojas-Albarracin, G., Chaves, M. A., Fernandez-Caballero, A., & Lopez, M. T. (2019). Heart attack detection in colour images using convolutional neural networks. *Applied Sciences*, 9(23), 5065.

[9] Reddy, K. V., Elamvazuthi, I., Aziz, A. A., Paramasivam, S., Chua, H. N., & Prana-vanand, S. (2021). Heart disease risk prediction using machine learning classifiers with attribute evaluators. *Applied Sciences*, 11(18), 8352.

[10] Mienye, I. D., & Sun, Y. (2021). Improved heart disease prediction using particle swarm optimization based stacked sparse autoencoder. *Electronics*, 10(19), 2347.

[11] Song, W. (2020). A new method for refined recognition for heart disease diagnosis based on deep learning. *Information*, 11(12), 556.

[12] Manimurugan, S., Almutairi, S., Aborokbah, M. M., Narmatha, C., Ganesan, S., Chilamkurti, N., et al. (2022). Two-stage classification model for the prediction of heart disease using IoMT and artificial intelligence. *Sensors*, 22(2), 476.

[13] Baccouche, A., Garcia-Zapirain, B., Castillo Olea, C., & Elmaghraby, A. (2020). Ensemble deep learning models for heart disease classification: a case study from Mexico. *Information*, 11(4), 207.

[14] Li, J. P., Haq, A. U., Din, S. U., Khan, J., Khan, A., & Saboor, A. (2020). Heart disease identification method using machine learning classification in e-healthcare. *IEEE Access*, 8, 107562–107582.

[15] Mohan, S., Thirumalai, C., & Srivastava, G. (2019). Effective heart disease prediction using hybrid machine learning techniques. *IEEE Access*, 7, 81542–81554.

[16] Subhashini, G., Devi, C. R., & Rasool, S. B. M. (2023). Eyesight impairment detection for diabetic patients using very deep convolution neural network for 3-channel retinal images. *IEEE Access*, 1129–1134.

[17] Khan, M. A., & Algarni, F. (2020). A healthcare monitoring system for the diagnosis of heart disease in the IoMT cloud environment using MSSO-ANFIS. *IEEE Access*, 8, 122259–122269.

[18] Das, S., Nayagam, M. G., Suganthi, D., Thachamkode, F., & Senthil, K. M. (2023). A review on the application of radiomics and deep learning for disease identification in musculoskeletal radiography. (pp. 167–172).

[19] Jeyapriyanga, S., Ravi, C. N., Rathiya, R., Kalaivani, K., & Kumar, K. R. (2023). Implementation of a deep learning framework for intelligent intrusion detection in internet of things networks. (pp. 1208–1213).

24 Segmentation and LSB based fragile medical image watermarking using differential evolution

Sharbari Basu[1,a], Koustavi Das[2,b], Abhishek Basu[3,c] and Tirtha Sankar Das[4,d]

[1]Assistant Professor, RCC Institute of Information Technology, Kolkata, WB, India

[2]M. Tech Student, RCC Institute of Information Technology, Kolkata, WB, India

[3]Associate Professor,RCC Institute of Information Technology, Kolkata, WB, India

[4]Associate Professor, Ramkrishna Mahato Government Engineering College, Purulia, WB, India

Abstract

In this paper a LSB based medical image watermarking scheme by threshold segmentation using differential evolution method has been proposed. The suggested method ensures fragility of the watermark assuring to reveal any minute attack on the watermarked medical image while sharing it over any unprotected network. Moreover, it also ensures locating the region of prime medical information in order to avoid the risk of hiding data in that specific area. Thus, the method comprises of segmenting the host medical image and then concealing the watermark in the section not in proximity to the prime medical content. The results obtained from the proposed method are found to be satisfactory.

Keywords: Differential evolution, LSB, medical image, threshold segmentation, watermarking

Introduction

Transferring medical test data over the network has become an integral part of medical science. The rationale behind this measure is to accelerate the process of diagnosis and try to mitigate the botheration of disease. Post COVID situations have kindled the practice of medical data sharing over network with the concerned medical practitioners by the patient or its family. The data sharing channel in the cases just referred can be assumed as not secured as the one used by the diagnostic centers. But also, the priority of diagnosis cannot be ignored, especially when the world wide web is capable to furnish such provisions even when the patient and the medical practitioner is not in the same geographical location. Nevertheless, sharing confidential details like medical data over any unprotected network may pose a threat to patient's life. To avoid any kind of data manipulation as well as to keep the prime medical information intact, various watermarking techniques are proposed. The present scheme proposes a fragile watermarking technique by threshold segmentation method using Differential Evolution. This scheme fortifies confidentiality and integrity of the host medical image while sending over unprotected network by identifying any noise attack by completely disfiguring the

retrieved watermark. Thus, the procedure ensures avoidance of mistreatment of the illness by recognizing the attack on the medical content. Diagnostic information in medical images may be harmed by even a minor attack. The main concern with medical data handling over an unsecured network is security. To combat security, many watermarking techniques have been proposed. .[4]Singh et al. and Gull et al. [1, 4] did extensive research for watermarking medical image. Hussan et al. [2], Jana et al. [3], and Gull, et al. [4] suggested various watermarking techniques. The above-mentioned procedures for medical image watermarking are mostly either recovering the tampered portion of the image or recovering watermark after attack. The survey paper of Roy et al. [5] provided basic guidelines to conduct the research. [6][7][8][9]In some studies researchers used strong methods to watermark an image [6–9]. But the robust watermarks fail to identify any attack on the medical data. Since we are implementing simple segmentation techniques to identify medical information, data hiding would become complicated. The proposed technique is easy to implement, has a high rate of imperceptibility, and also has a large hiding capacity. This method can be used from patient's end as well as from doctor's end. Moreover, the diagnostic

[a]basu.sharbari@gmail.com, [b]katha.koustavi@gmail.com, [c]callabhishekbasu@gmail.com, [d]reach2tirtha@gmail.com

DOI: 10.1201/9781003724995-24

centers can also use this simple but effective technique to send data via network.

Proposed Methodology

The chief aim of the present proposal is to achieve a highly imperceptible, watermarked medical image containing the medical information of a patient. To attain this goal, the very first step is to select a medical image from a medical image database with definite medical information. The twelve gray scale input images are taken from medical image database Brain_Tumor_Segmentation_BraTS_2019 MICCAI's Dataset on Brain Tumour Segmentation [10]. The size of the medical image is kept unchanged as in the aforesaid database to avoid loss of medical information. After fetching a medical image from the database, the original image is segmented. The key methodology used here is differential evolution. The following subsections precisely describe the segmentation procedures before implementing the proposed LSB watermarking technique. The image 'Brain 4' is used as an example to depict the segmented images after applying the above-mentioned technique. Figure 24.1 shows the original image.

Threshold segmentation approach using differential evolution

In the book "Digital Image Processing" by Gonzalez et al. [11], thresholding method is being defined as one of the simplest methods in implementing image segmentation. This method is highly capable of

extracting the necessary information from the host image and also enhances the quality of the image by reducing noise. An image can be segmented by two approaches:(i) similarity based (ii) discontinuity based. Threshold segmentation technique comes under the former group. An image I is represented by I(x,y), where (x, y) holds the location of pixels in the image. The image contains a light object with darker background. Thus, the image can be divided into modes based on their intensity values. Few modes are towards lower intensity values and the others will be towards higher intensity values. A histogram of an has many peaks. So, the threshold value can be chosen by closely examining the histogram of the image. Let threshold value of the segmentation be T. The thresholding operation will include testing against T, where can be defined as

$$T = T\,[(x, y), n\,(x, y), I\,(x, y)] \qquad (1)$$

where, (x, y) = location of pixels, $n\,(x, y)$ = the characteristics of the neighborhood pixels of $(x, y)\,I\,(x, y)$ = intensity of pixel at (x, y) of image I. Let the threshold image be $I'\,(x, y)$ resulting from original image $I\,(x, y)$. We can set the value of

$$I\,(x, y) = 1 \quad if\ I(x, y) > T \qquad (2)$$
$$= 0 \quad if\ I(x, y) \leq T$$

So, the resultant image, that is, $I'(x, y)$ will be a binary image having pixel values equal to 1 or 0 depending on whether the intensity value $I(x, y)$ at any location (x, y) is greater than or less than or equal to threshold value T. If the value of $I\,(x, y)$ = 1, it will specify the object pixels and $(x, y) = 0$ will represent the background pixels. The next step is to select a threshold value. In this paper Differential Evolution (DE) by Storn and Price [12] is used to do so. DE is an evolutionary algorithm which is capable to find an optimized value when more than one contradictory factor is involved. The threshold value must be so chosen that it not only is capable to differentiate between foreground and background but it should distinctly locate the prime diagnostic information location. The threshold value generally is chosen in the valley region between the modes so that it clearly separates object from background. The segmented images using traditional methods are shown in Figures 24.2 and 24.3. The segmented image obtained from normal threshold selection is

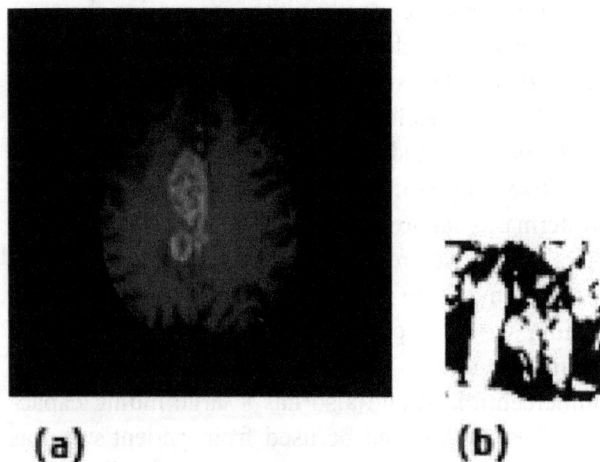

(a)   **(b)**

Figure 24.1 (a) Host reference image, 'brain 4'(b) Watermark
Source: Author

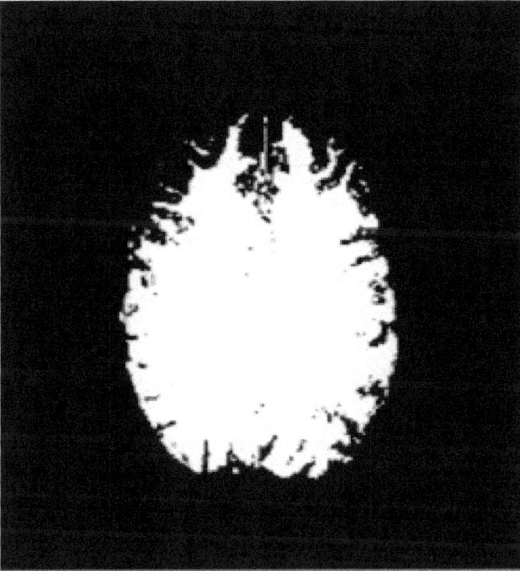

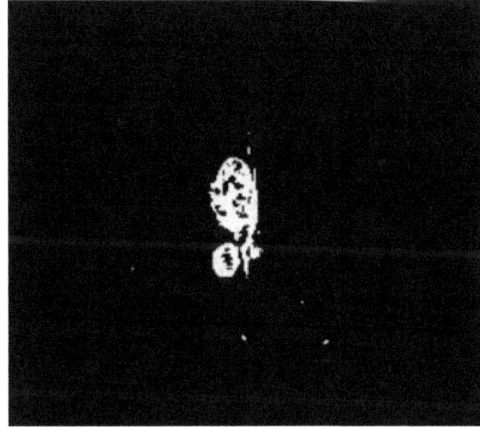

Figure 24.4 Segmented image with threshold value 0.28 obtained using DE
Source: Author

Figure 24.2 Segmented image
Source: Author

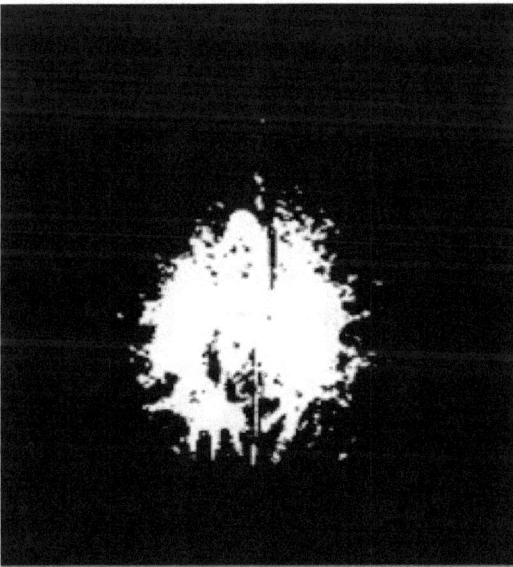

Figure 24.3 Segmented Image with threshold value 0.19 threshold value 0.2
Source: Author

40. The values between two valleys are considered as dimension D whose value is assumed to be 10. The aim is to minimize (*P*) using DE where

$$P = \{p_1, p_2, \ldots \ldots p_{D,}\} \quad (3)$$

The population can be defined as

$$p_i^g = \{p_{n,1}^g, p_{n,2}^g \ldots \ldots \ldots p_{n,D}^g\} \quad (4)$$

where g depicts the generation, n = {1,2 … . NP} and i = {1,2, … . D}

The initialization involves random selection of values of valleys obtained from graph. The initialization reaction can be framed as

$$dv_n^{g+1} = p_{r1,n}^g + SF(p_{r2,n}^g - p_{r3,n)}^g \quad (5)$$

where dv is the donor vector and $r1$, $r2$, $r3$ are the random values considered for initialization. SF is the scaling factor which is assumed as 0.5 in this method. This step is followed by a recombination method where a trial vector $t_{n,i}^{g+1}$ emerges from target vector and donor vector. Selection is done between the trial vector and donor vector. The lower value is considered for the next generation. The process continues until the stopping criterion is met. In this paper, Sphere test function is used to obtain optimized value. On application of DE, the optimized threshold value obtained for "Brain 4" is 0.28. Figure 24.4 depicts the segmented image where the threshold value is obtained using DE.

It is clear from Figure 24.4, the optimized threshold value is capable to locate the prime medical content.

incapable of separating the prime medical content from the foreground image instantly. The advantages of using DE to find the threshold value are (i) it reduces seeking time and (ii) the value obtained is more accurate than traditional methods. DE includes the steps of initialization, mutation, crossover and selection.

Here, values of the valleys P are considered as population. The population size NP is considered as

Watermarking Procedure

The above-mentioned segmentation technique is relevant with medical image processing. Further steps are taken to watermark the segmented medical image [13]. Image 4.2.07 is used as watermark image from USC-SIPI image database, converted into binary format and is resized to 64 × 64. The definite location of medical information in the segmented image is already known through segmentation technique using DE. The encoding process, at very first, notes the location of the medical information. The watermark now gets encoded in any location of the image using the proposed LSB technique. The watermarked image is satisfactorily imperceptible and ensures good security over any network. The decoding process locates the region of medical information as well as the watermark. The integrity of the retrieved watermark leads to acceptance of medical information. In this proposal, the results were found to be satisfactory.

Embedding procedure

The encoding procedure contains a host image, a watermark, three 2-D variables P[LOC], P[LOC_1] and P[LOCT]. P[O] holds the pixel information of prime objects. P[LOC] holds the coordinate locations of prime object as well as the coordinates in order to equalize the size of the watermark. P[LOC_1] is copy of P[LOC] holding the same pixel information. P[LOCT] holds the hiding locations of watermark. W is the watermark. Here, size of W has been symbolized as *sizeo[W]*. [*LOCT*] holds the pixel information that are already hidden in *P[LOC]*. [*LOCT*] holds the pixel information that are left behind to get hidden in P[LOCT_1].

Watermark Embedding Procedure

$P[\ LOC] \leftarrow P[O];$
$P[LOCT] \leftarrow P[W];$
if sizeof P[LOC] == sizeof P[LOCT] ;
$[LOC\_1] \leftarrow P[LOC];$
else
while i ← 1
begin loop
$P[LOC] \leftarrow P[LOC] + i$
if (sizeof P[LOC] == sizeof P[LOCT]
$[LOC\_1] \leftarrow P[LOC]$
break;

else
$i++$
for i ← 1 to sizeo[W]
begin loop
$[LOC] + i + 2 \leftarrow P[LOCT];$
$P[LOCT\ ] \leftarrow P[LOCT];$
end loop
end loop
$P[LOCT''] \leftarrow P[LOCT] - P[LOCT'];$
for i ← 1 to sizeo[W]
$[LOC\_1] + i + 2 \leftarrow P[LOCT''];$

Extracting procedure

In the extracting procedure of the watermark, the receiver has the information of prime object location P[O]. The receiver also receives P[LOC] and P[LOC_1], which holds the position of prime object as well as few extra pixels information. When the receiver compares P[O] with P[LOC] and P[LOC_1], it easily locates the mismatched pixels. [*O*] holds the pixel information which are already compared with P[LOC] and P[O] holds the pixel locations which are yet to be compared with P[LOC_1]. The mismatched data are [*W*] and P[W"]. From here we can retrieve the original watermark.

Watermark Extraction Procedure

for i ← 1 to sizeo[W]
begin loop
$if P[O] \neq P[LOC]$
$P[W\ ] \leftarrow P[LOC]$
$P[O'\ ] \leftarrow P[O]$
$P[O'\ ] \leftarrow P[O'] - P[O\ ]$
for i ← 1 to sizeo[W]
$if[O\ ] \neq P[LOC\_1]$
$[W\ ] \leftarrow P[LOC\_1\ ]\}$
$W \leftarrow W + W''$
end loop
end loop

Problem Discussion and Result

In the proposed technique, data is hidden in the portion of the image where there is no medical information. The above-mentioned segmentation techniques followed by proposed LSB technique is applied in each image and watermark are retrieved

Table 24.1 Comparison of PSNR and SSIM values obtained from images segmented using threshold segmentation technique using DE and traditional method of selecting threshold.

Fig. Name	Threshold segmentation technique using DE		Threshold segmentation technique using traditional methods	
	PSNR(dB)	SSIM	PSNR(dB)	SSIM
Brain 1	61.22	0.99	48.3	0.66
Brain 2	61.18	0.9	48.7	0.69
Brain 3	61.21	0.986	48.9	0.7
Brain 4	61.25	0.993	49.5	0.77
Brain 5	61.14	0.987	48.7	0.69
Brain 6	60.15	0.9953	47.4	0.68
Brain 7	59.86	0.9928	48.6	0.684
Brain 8	61.08	0.994	47.7	0.657
Brain 9	60.29	0.9	48.24	0.64
Brain 10	61.05	0.988	48.18	0.636
Brain 11	61.23	0.994	48.29	0.659

Source: Author

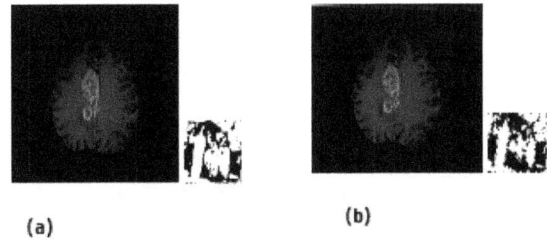

(a)　　　　(b)

Figure 24.5 Watermarked image and recovered Watermark using thresholding through **(a)** DE **(b)** traditional way
Source: Author

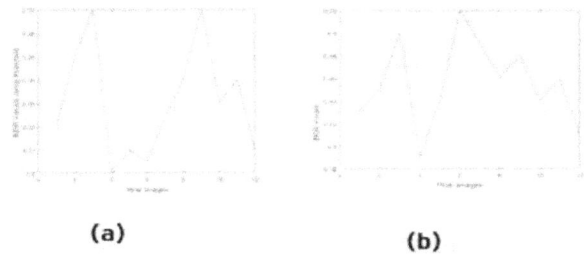

(a)　　　　**(b)**

Figure 24.6 BER Values of retrieved watermarks from threshold segmented images **(a)** using DE **(b)** using traditional threshold method
Source: Author

from them. The imperceptibility of an image has been weighed by calculating peak-to-signal-noise ratio (PSNR)value and structural similarity index measure (SSIM). The work of Roy et al. [14] is used for evaluation. Table 24.1 shows the comparison of the PSNR and SSIM values obtained on applying the LSB technique on segmented images. Figure 24.1(b) shows the watermark and Figure 24.5(a) shows the watermarked image after segmentation using DE and the retrieved watermark and Figure 24.5(b) shows the watermarked image after segmentation without using DE and the retrieved watermark. Figure 24.6(a) and 24.6(b) reveals the BER values of retrieved watermarks.

From Table 24.1, it can be concluded that, the watermarked images have greater imperceptibility level in case of threshold method using DE than traditional method of selecting threshold values . Figure 24.6 (a) and (b) also reveal the quality of retrieved watermarks. The data shows that proposed LSB technique gives good result when applied on segmented image using threshold technique using DE

than traditional procedures. Although the quality of recovered watermark is at par to recognizable level, the aim of the proposed technique is to create a fragile watermarking technique. To examine the fragility of the watermarked images, gaussian noise is applied on the watermarked images. Host images Brain 4 is shown as specimen to prove the fragility of the proposed method.

From Figure 24.7, the fragility of the method is clearly revealed. Gaussian noise of 0.001dB is applied on the watermarked image, where watermark is hidden in segmented image based on threshold technique. The recovered watermark is completely destroyed unveiling the attack. This ensures security, confidentiality and integrity of medical content. The average PSNR value obtained by applying proposed LSB watermarking technique on threshold segmented images are compared with few other similar techniques. Table 24.2 holds the comparison. The depicted table clearly reveals that the imperceptibility measure of the proposed technique is quite high when applied on medical images approximately with similar resolutions. Thus, it can be concluded that

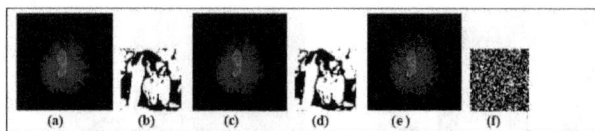

Figure 24.7 (a) Host_Image 'Brain4', (b) watermark (c) watermarked_image (d) recovered_watermark (e) noisy_watermarked_image (f) recovered_noised_watermark

Source: Author

Table 24.2 A comparative study of state-of-art with proposed method.

Method name	Average the peak-SNR value (PSNR) unit = db decibel
Proposed method	**60.905**
Singh et al. [1]	45.93
Hussan et al. [2]	44.15
Jana et al. [3]	48.28
Gull et al. [4]	49.16
Lin et al. [15]	48.21

Source: Author

the proposed method has succeeded in developing a fragile medical image watermarking scheme with high imperceptibility rate which can ensure to convey insight about any attack on medical data passing over any unsecured network.

Conclusion

Maintaining confidentiality and integrity of the medical content is the prime concern while sending sensitive data over an untrustworthy network. Numerous watermarking methods for medical images have been proposed in the spatial and transform domains, each with a unique set of applications. The present paper proposes a fragile watermarking scheme that watermarks medical images using LSB technique based on the result of image segmentation using DE. The novelty lies in fixing the problem by securely watermarking the image without affecting the medical data by using DE optimization algorithm. The results obtained clearly verify the claim. Moreover, the proposed watermarking technique successfully hides the data which results in a highly imperceptible image though on minute attack it destroys the watermark thus revealing any attempt to tamper the original medical content.

References

[1] Priyanka Singh, K. Jyothsna Devi & Ketan Kotecha, Hiren Kumarthakkar, Region-based hybrid medical image watermarking scheme for robust and secured transmission in IoMT, 2022, *IEEE Access*, 10, 8974–8993.

[2] Hussan, et al (2021). Tamper detection and selfrecovery of medical imagery for smart health. *Arabian Journal for Science and Engineering*, 46, 3465–3481.

[3] Jana, M., et al. (2022). Local feature based self-embedding fragile watermarking scheme for tampered detection and recovery utilizing AMBTC with fuzzy logic. *Journal of King Saud University - Computer and Information Sciences*, 34(10), 9822–9835.

[4] Gull, S., et al. (2020). Reversible data hiding exploiting Huffman encoding with dual images for IoMT based healthcare. *Computer Communications*, 163, 134–149.

[5] Subhrajit Sinha Roy, A. Basu, Avik Chattopadhyay (2023). Prospects of digital water¬marking in providing security, reliability, and. privacy to medical images, 2023, ECTI Transactions on Computer and Information Technology 17(2),168–182.

[6] Basu, S., et al. (2022). An image data hiding technique using differential evolution. *Multimedia Tools and Applications*, 81, 39995–40012.

[7] Basu, S., et al. (2018). A cooperative coevolutionary approach for multi-objective optimization. In Recent Trends in Signal and Image Processing, (pp. 57–65).

[8] Basu, A, et al. (2024). On unique framework based implementation of a novel image watermarking scheme. *Multimedia Tools and Applications*, 83, 78861–7887.

[9] Subhrajit Sinha Roy, A. Basu, Avik Chattopadhyay. On the implementation of a copyright protection scheme using digital image watermarking, Multimedia Tools and Applications, 2020, 79(3), DOI:10.1007/s11042-020-08652-9.

[10] Medical Image Database Brain_Tumor_Segmentation_BraTS_(2019). MICCAI's dataset on brain tumor segmentation.

[11] Gonzalez, R. C., & Woods, R. E. (n.d.). Digital Image Processing, (3rd edn). Pearson International Edition.

[12] Storn, R., & Price, K. (1996). Differential evolution – a simple and efficient heuristic for global optimization over continuous spaces. *Journal of Global Optimization*, 11, 341–359.

[13] Test functions for optimization. Available at Wikipedia: https://en.wikipedia.org/wiki/Test_functions_for_optimization.

[14] Basu A, Sinha Roy S, Saha S (2015). Generic testing architecture for digital watermarking. In Proceedings of FRCCD. 978–93, 50–58.

[15] Chia-Chen Lin,Ting-Lin Lee, Ya-Fen Chang, Pei-Feng Shiu, Bohan Zhang, Fragile watermarking for tamper localization and self-recovery based on AMBTC and VQ, 2023, Electronics, 12(2), 415.

25 Hierarchical vision transformers for pneumonia classification: a study on hyperparameter impact

Ramesh Munirathinam[1,a], Yabez Davidraj, P.[1,b], Neelam Sanjeev Kumar[2,c] and Rajavel, M.[2,d]

[1]Assistant Professor, Department of Biomedical Engineering, Karpagam Academy of Higher Education, Coimbatore, India

[2]Department of CSE, E.Tech, SRM Institute of Science and Technology, Vadapalani Campus, Chennai, Tamil Nadu, India

Abstract

Pneumonia remains a critical health concern, necessitating accurate and efficient diagnostic methods. This study evaluates the Swin Transformer for binary classification of chest x-ray images (normal vs. pneumonia). Hyperparameter tuning was conducted across 16 configurations, varying learning rates (0.0001, 0.001, 0.01, 0.1) and epochs (5, 15, 25, 50). The model achieved peak performance with a learning rate of 0.1 and 25 epochs, attaining accuracy (89.90%), precision (90.16%), recall (89.90%), F1-Score (89.71%), 0.7840 MCC, and 0.7780 Cohen's Kappa. These results demonstrate the Swin Transformer's efficacy in medical imaging and highlight the importance of hyperparameter optimization for diagnostic accuracy.

Keywords: Chest x-rays, hyperparameter tuning, medical imaging, performance analysis, pneumonia classification, Swin Transformer, Vision Transformers

Introduction

Pneumonia causes inflammation in the lungs, commonly caused by bacterial, viral, or fungal pathogens. It poses a major public health challenge worldwide, contributing to significant morbidity and mortality, particularly among high-risk groups such as young children, elderly individuals, and immunocompromised patients [1–3]. Early detection of pneumonia is essential for timely medical intervention, as delays in diagnosis can result in critical complications, including respiratory failure, sepsis, and even death [4, 5]. The ability to accurately and rapidly detect pneumonia is thus crucial to reducing mortality and improving patient outcomes through the administration of appropriate treatments such as antibiotics or antivirals [6].

Traditionally, pneumonia diagnosis relies heavily on chest X-rays, where radiologists visually inspect the images for abnormalities such as lung consolidation, fluid accumulation, or other signs of infection [7]. However, this manual interpretation is often subjective, and diagnostic accuracy may be influenced by radiologist experience, image quality, or even time constraints [8, 9]. To address these challenges, automated diagnostic systems based on machine learning techniques have been developed to assist healthcare professionals in identifying pneumonia from chest X-rays with high accuracy and con- consistency. One of the most widely used deep learning models for image classification is the Convolutional Neural Network (CNN), which has demonstrated impressive performance in pneumonia detection by learning hierarchical features from the images [10]. CNN-based architectures, such as ResNet (97.67%) and DenseNet (97.03%), have been particularly successful in capturing patterns from medical images, but they often face limitations due to their reliance on fixed receptive fields, which restrict the network's ability to model global dependencies within an image [11, 12]. To overcome these limitations, transformer-based models, originally developed for natural language processing (NLP), have been adapted

[a]rameshmunirathinam@gmail.com, [b]yabezdo@gmail.com, [c]neelamsanjeev1034@gmail.com, [d]rajavelm@srmist.edu.in

DOI: 10.1201/9781003724995-25

for computer vision tasks [13]. These models rely on self-attention mechanisms, which allow them to consider the entire image context, capturing long-range dependencies across distant regions of the image [14]. The Vision Transformer (ViT) employs self-attention mechanisms to outperform CNNs in certain image classification tasks but is computationally intensive and demands large datasets. To address these limitations, the Swin Transformer (Shifted Window Transformer) introduces a hierarchical architecture with shifted windows, enabling efficient capture of both local and global image features while reducing computational complexity [15, 16]. This study applies the Swin Transformer for binary classification of pneumonia and normal chest X-rays, leveraging its multi-scale processing capabilities for accurate medical image analysis. Hyperparameter tuning is performed by varying learning rates and epoch counts, and model performance is comprehensively evaluated using accuracy, precision, recall, F1-score, Cohen's kappa, and MCC.

Literature Survey

Angara et al. enhanced pneumonia detection using an ensemble of ResNet34 and MaxViT-Small, achieving 94.87% accuracy and 1.0 sensitivity on the Kaggle dataset. The Swin Transformer tiny also performed well, with 94.55% accuracy, showcasing its effectiveness in medical image analysis [17]. Peng et al. evaluated the Swin Transformer for COVID-19 CT image classification. For binary classification, the Swin Transformer achieved precision (98.11%), recall (97.69%), accuracy (98.38%), F1-Score (97.90%), AUC (0.9982), and AUPR (0.9975), highlighting its capability in leveraging both global and local features for accurate medical image analysis [18]. Wang et al. proposed STCovidNet using the Swin Transformer for COVID-19 detection from chest CT scans, achieving an accuracy of 98.58% and an AUC of 0.9811. The Swin Transformer outperformed ViT and CNNs, demonstrating superior feature separation and alignment with radiologists' observations through Grad-CAM visualizations [19]. Ma and Lv explored the use of Swin Transformer models for pneumonia detection in chest X-rays. Swin-T achieved 81.3% accuracy, Swin-S reached 83.0%, and Swin-B attained the highest among Swin models with 83.5% accuracy. Grad-CAM was used for effective lesion identification [20]. Chen et al. proposed a lung cancer cell detection

model using Swin Transformer. achieving 96.16% accuracy. The approach combines Swin Transformer with Mask R-CNN for image segmentation [21]. Sun et al. demonstrated that the Swin-T model achieved a Top-1 Accuracy of 82.26% in lung cancer classification, outperforming both ViT-B/16 (68.56%) and ViT- L/16 (69.43%). Additionally, the Swin-S and Swin-B models showed significant improvements in segmentation with higher mIoU, showcasing the Swin Transformer's effectiveness in both classification and segmentation tasks [22]. Tummala et al. used an ensemble of Swin Transformer models for breast cancer classification on the BreaKHis dataset, achieving 96.0% accuracy for eight-class and 99.6% accuracy for two-class classification [23]. Dihin et al. proposed a method combining multi-Wavelet transforms and Swin Transformer for diabetic retinopathy classification using the Kaggle APTOS 2019 dataset. The model achieved 97.78% training accuracy and 97.54% test accuracy for binary classification, while the multiclass classification resulted in 91.60% training and 82.42% validation accuracies, with 82% testing accuracy [24]. The model achieved 99.92% accuracy on a four-class dataset, demonstrating superior performance over existing methods through transfer learning and data augmentation techniques [25].

Materials and Methodology

Dataset

The chest X-ray pneumonia dataset, developed by Mooney, comprises 5,856 labeled JPEG images categorized into pneumonia and normal cases. The dataset is split into a 624-dataset for testing and a 5216-dataset for training. It is publicly available under the CC BY 4.0 license on Mendeley Data [26].

Proposed system

The model development process utilized the "chest-x-ray-pneumonia" dataset from Kaggle, comprising 5,856 images di- vided into two categories (pneumonia and normal). Data loaders were configured for the training set (5,216 images, batch size 128), validation set (16 images, batch size 1), and test set (624 images, batch size 1). The training set underwent data augmentation, including random flips, resizing, and normalization, to improve generalization. The Swin Transformer Base model was imported using PyTorch's torch.hub.load() from Facebook Research's GitHub repository. Pre-trained weights were loaded, with all model parameters frozen except for a custom binary classification head (two linear layers with ReLU activation and Dropout). The Swin Transformer architecture leverages shifted windows for computational efficiency and improved feature representation. The shifted window mechanism facilitates better information sharing between patches while maintaining computational efficiency. Figure 25.1 illustrates the Swin Transformer architecture used in this study. Table 25.1 describes hyperparameters used in the model. The Adam optimizer was employed with the Label Smoothing-thing cross entropy criterion, and a learning rate scheduler (step size: 3, Gamma: 0.97) controlled the learning rate during training.

Results

The results section presents a comprehensive analysis of the Swin Transformer model's performance across varying hyperparameter configurations, focusing on learning rates and epoch counts. Key performance metrics are evaluated to provide a holistic understanding of the model's behavior. The Figure 25.2 displays the accuracy performance of the Swin

Transformer model with varying learning rates (0.1, 0.01, 0.001, 0.0001) and epochs (5, 15, 25, 50). At a learning rate of 0.1, the highest accuracy of 89.90% is achieved at 25 epochs, but this slightly drops to 89.58% at 50 epochs, indicating possible overfitting or a plateau in learning. For a learning rate of 0.01, the peak accuracy of 87.66% is reached at 15 epochs, with a decrease in performance at 25 epochs (86.54%) and 50 epochs (87.34%), showing instability with longer training.

The learning rate of 0.001 consistently performs well, with an accuracy of 89.26% at both 15 and 25 epochs, though a minor dip is observed at five epochs (87.34%) and 50 epochs (88.46%). Finally, at 0.0001, the model struggles, achieving 88.30% at 25 epochs, but lower results at 5 epochs (85.58%) and 50 epochs (85.10%), indicating poor convergence. Table 25.2 presents a comparative analysis of relevant studies on medical image classification using Swin Transformer and other deep learning models, highlighting the datasets, methodologies, models used, and their achieved accuracy.

Table 25.1 Fixed hyperparameters of the model.

Hyperparameter	Value
Batch Size	128 (train), 1(val/test)
Step Size (LR Scheduler)	3
Gamma (LR Scheduler)	0.97
Optimizer	Adam
Criterion	Label Smoothing Cross Entropy
Dropout Rate	0.3

Source: Author

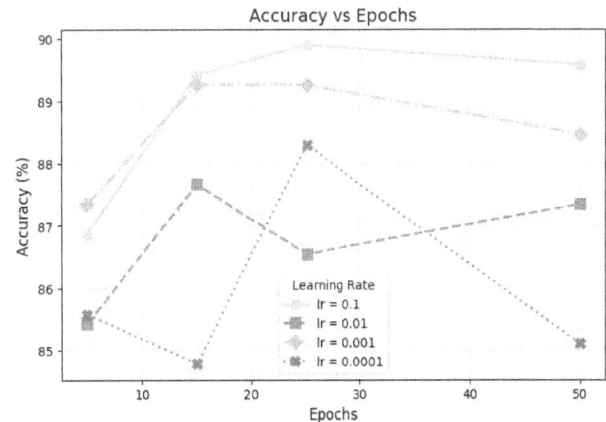

Figure 25.2 Accuracy vs epochs across learning rates (X-axis: Epochs, Y- axis: Accuracy)
Source: Author

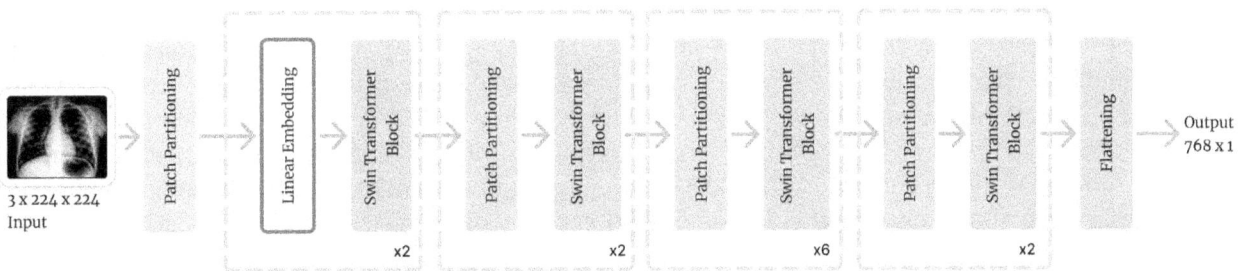

Figure 25.1 Swin transformer – architecture
Source: Author

Table 25.2 Comparison of relevant studies with the proposed system.

Author(s)	Methodology	Model(s)	Accuracy (%)
Angara et al.	Kaggle Pneumonia Dataset	ResNet34 + MaxViT-Small, Swin Transformer Tiny	94.87, 94.55
Peng et al.	COVID-19 CT Images	Swin Transformer	98.38
Wang et al.	Chest CT scans	STCovidNet (Swin Transformer)	98.58
Ma and Lv	Chest X-rays	Swin-T, Swin-S, Swin-B	81.3, 83.0, 83.5
Chen et al.	Lung Cancer Cell Detection	Swin Transformer + Mask R-CNN	96.16
Sun et al.	Lung cancer classification	Swin-T	82.26
Tummala et al.	Breast cancer (BreaKHis Dataset)	Swin Transformer (Ensemble)	96.0, 99.6
Dihin et al.	Diabetic retinopathy (APTOS 2019)	Swin Transformer + Multi-Wavelet Transforms	97.54, 82.0
Pacal	Brain Tumor MRI Images	Swin Transformer (HSW-MSA + ResMLP)	99.92
Proposed System	Chest X-rays (Pneumonia Classification)	Swin Transformer	89.90

Source: Author

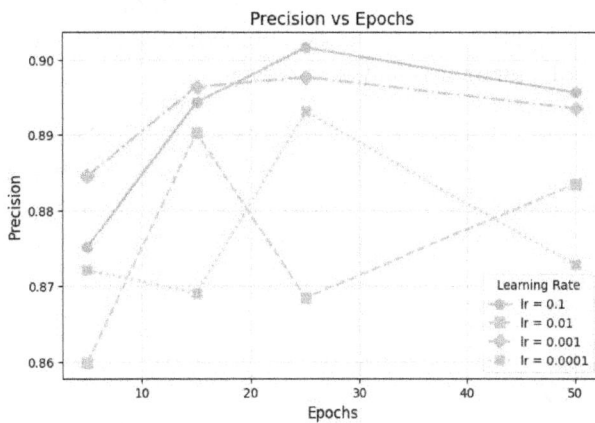

Figure 25.3 Precision vs epochs across learning rates (X-axis: Epochs, Y- axis: Precision)
Source: Author

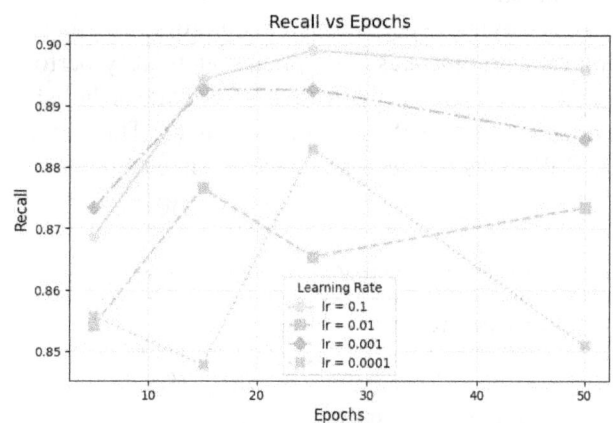

Figure 25.4 Recall vs epochs across learning rates (X-axis: "Epochs", Y-axis: "Recall")
Source: Author

Figure 25.3 represents the precision performance of the Swin Transformer model. At a learning rate of 0.1, precision increases steadily from 0.8751 at 5 epochs to 0.9016 at 25 epochs, but slightly drops to 0.8956 at 50 epochs. A learning rate of 0.01 peaks at 0.8903 at 15 epochs, with a decline to 0.8684 at 25 epochs and 0.8835 at 50 epochs.

For 0.001, precision remains strong, peaking at 0.8977 at 25 epochs and showing slight fluctuations across epochs. At 0.0001, precision starts at 0.8721 at 5 epochs and remains relatively stable at 25 and 50 epochs (0.8931 and 0.8728).

Figure 25.4 represents the recall performance of the Swin Transformer model. At a learning rate of 0.1, recall steadily improves, starting at 0.8686 at 5 epochs, reaching 0.8990 at 25 epochs, and slightly decreasing to 0.8958 at 50 epochs. For 0.01, recall peaks at 0.8766 at 15 epochs, with a decrease at 25 epochs (0.8654) and a recovery at 50 epochs (0.8734). At 0.001, recall remains consistently high, reaching 0.8926 at both 15 and 25 epochs, with a slight drop to 0.8846 at 50 epochs. For 0.0001, recall starts lower at 0.8558 at 5 epochs, then improves slightly to 25 epochs (0.8830), but drops again at 50 epochs (0.8510). Figure 25.5 represents the F1-score performance of the Swin Transformer model. At 0.1, the F1-score increases from 0.8643 at 5 epochs to 0.8971 at 25 epochs but slightly drops to 0.8950 at

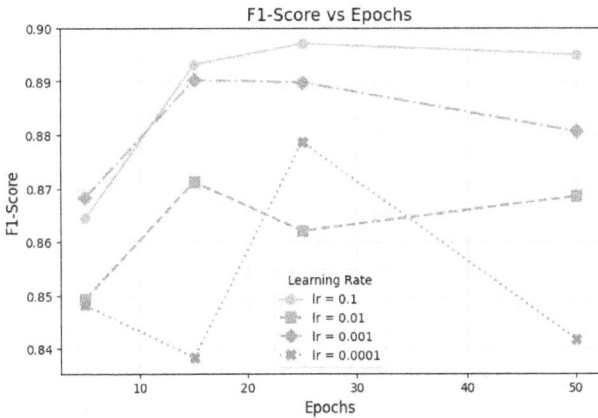

Figure 25.5 F1-Score vs epochs across learning rates (X-axis: "Epochs", Y- axis: "F1-Score")
Source: Author

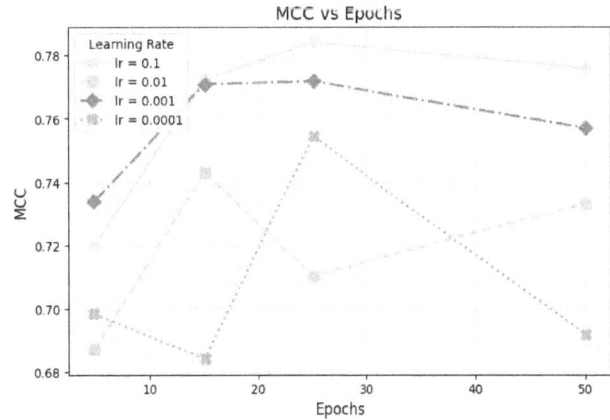

Figure 25.6 MCC vs epochs across learning rates (X-axis: Epochs, Y-axis: Matthews correlation coefficient (MCC))
Source: Author

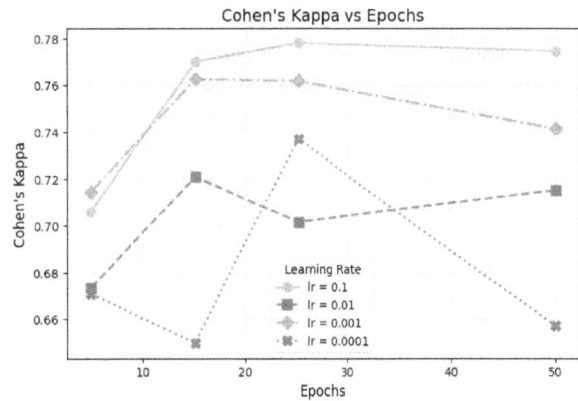

Figure 25.7 Cohen's Kappa vs epochs across learning rates (X-axis: Epochs, Y-axis: Cohen's Kappa)
Source: Author

50 epochs. The 0.01 learning rate shows a steady rise from 0.8493 at 5 epochs to 0.8712 at 15 epochs, but peaks at 0.8620 at 25 epochs and decreases to 0.8685 at 50 epochs. For 0.001, the F1-score reaches its peak of 0.8898 at 25 epochs and maintains stability, with small variations across other epochs. At 0.0001, the F1-score remains relatively low, starting at 0.8482 at 5 epochs and reaching 0.8787 at 25 epochs, but slightly declines to 0.8417 at 50 epochs. Figure 25.6 represents the MCC performance of the Swin Transformer model. The highest MCC of 0.7840 is observed at 25 epochs with a learning rate of 0.1. At 0.01, MCC fluctuates, peaking at 0.7430 at 15 epochs, then dropping to 0.7103 at 25 epochs, with a recovery to 0.7330 at 50 epochs. For 0.001, MCC improves slightly, reaching 0.7717 at 25 epochs, with stable results at 15 and 50 epochs. The 0.0001 learning rate shows weaker MCC values, starting at 0.6984 at 5 epochs and peaking at 0.7544 at 25 epochs, but decreasing to 0.6920 at 50 epochs. Figure 25.7 represents Cohen's Kappa performance of the Swin Transformer model. At 0.1, Cohen's Kappa improves from 0.7061 at 5 epochs to 0.7780 at 25 epochs, slightly dropping to 0.7745 at 50 epochs. The 0.01 learning rate sees a peak at 0.7208 at 15 epochs and declines to 0.7016 at 25 epochs, with some recovery to 0.7151 at 50 epochs. With a learning rate of 0.001, Cohen's Kappa peaks at 0.7626 at 15 epochs, with a stable value of 0.7618 at 25 epochs and a decrease to 0.7415 at 50 epochs. At 0.0001, Kappa remains lower, starting at 0.6709 at 5 epochs and rising to 0.7372 at 25 epochs, but decreasing again at 50 epochs (0.6571).

Conclusion

The findings from the study highlight the effectiveness of the Swin Transformer model in distinguishing pneumonia from normal chest X-ray images, achieving high accuracy and robust performance across various evaluation metrics. The unique feature of Swin Transformer lies in its hierarchical design and the use of shifted windows, which allows it to capture both local and global dependencies efficiently, making it particularly well-suited for medical image analysis. This demonstrates the model's strong generalization capabilities, even with a relatively small dataset. The results signify an advancement in utilizing transformer-based architectures for medical imaging, offering improved diagnostic accuracy and aiding clinical decision-making.

References

[1] Yadav, K. K., & Awasthi, S. (2023). Childhood pneumonia: what's unchanged, and what's new?. *Indian Journal of Pediatrics*, 90(7), 693–699.

[2] Karimdzhanov, I. A., Madaminova, M. S., Iskanova, G. K., Gazieva, A. S., & Togaev, M. Q. (2024). Diagnosis and treatment of community- acquired pneumonia in children. *Childs Health*, 19(5), 312–315.

[3] Yang, S., Lu, S., Guo, Y., Luan, W., Liu, J., & Wang, L. (2024). A comparative study of general and severe mycoplasma pneumoniae pneumonia in children. *BMC Infectious Diseases*, 24(1), 449.

[4] Jiang, J., Chen, S., Zhang, S., Zeng, Y., Liu, J., Lei, W., et al. (2024). A radiomics model utilizing CT for the early detection and diagnosis of severe community-acquired pneumonia. *BMC Medical Imaging*, 24(1), 202.

[5] Bandopadhaya, S., & Roy, A. (2024). Early detection of silent hypoxia in COVID-19 pneumonia using deep learning and IoT. *Multimedia Tools and Applications*, 83(8), 24527–24539.

[6] Sabbagh, W. A., Karrar, H. R., Nouh, M. I., Alkhaifi, N. M., Badayyan, S. Y., Shaikh, L. K., et al. (2024). Perspective of pneumonia in the health-care setting. *Journal of Pharmaceutical Research International*, 36(7), 51–58.

[7] Kumar, S., Kumar, H., Kumar, G., Singh, S. P., Bijalwan, A., & Diwakar, M. (2024). A methodical exploration of imaging modalities from dataset to detection through machine learning paradigms in prominent lung disease diagnosis: a review. *BMC Medical Imaging*, 24(1), 30.

[8] Pesapane, F., Gnocchi, G., Quarrella, C., Sorce, A., Nicosia, L., Mariano, L., et al. (2024). Errors in radiology: a standard review. *Journal of Clinical Medicine*, 13(15), 4306.

[9] Chen, R., & Friis, J. K. B. O. (2024). Vision, body and interpretation in medical imaging diagnostics. *Medicine, Health Care and Philosophy*, 27(2), 253–266.

[10] Rabbah, J., Ridouani, M., & Hassouni, L. (2025). Improving pneumonia diagnosis with high-accuracy CNN-based chest x-ray image classifica- tion and integrated gradient. *Biomedical Signal Processing and Control*, 101, 107239.

[11] Keles, A., Keles, M. B., & Keles, A. (2024). COV19-CNNet and COV19- ResNet: diagnostic inference engines for early detection of COVID-19. *Cognitive Computation*, 16(4), 1612–1622.

[12] Arulananth T. S., Prakash S. W., Ayyasamy R. K., Kavitha V. P., Kuppusamy P. G. & Chinnasamy P., Classification of Paediatric Pneumonia Using Modified DenseNet-121 Deep-Learning Model, in *IEEE Access*, vol. 12, pp. 35716-35727, 2024, doi: 10.1109/ACCESS.2024.3371151.

[13] Yang, B., Zhang, B., Han, Y., Liu, B., Hu, J., & Jin, Y. (2024). Vision transformer-based visual language understanding of the construction process. *Alexandria Engineering Journal*, 99, 242–256.

[14] Hassanin, M., Anwar, S., Radwan, I., Khan, F. S., & Mian, A. (2024). Visual attention methods in deep learning: an in-depth survey. *Information Fusion*, 108, 102417.

[15] Nguyen, D. K., Assran, M., Jain, U., Oswald, M. R., Snoek, C. G., & Chen, X. (2024). An image is worth more than 16 × 16 patches: exploring transformers on individual pixels. arXiv preprint arXiv:2406.09415.

[16] Liu, Z., Lin, Y., Cao, Y., Hu, H., Wei, Y., Zhang, Z., Lin, S., & Guo, B. (2021). Swin Transformer: Hierarchical Vision Transformer using Shifted Windows. 2021 IEEE/CVF International Conference on Computer Vision (ICCV), 9992-10002.

[17] Angara, S., Mannuru, N. R., Mannuru, A., & Thirunagaru, S. (2024). A novel method to enhance pneumonia detection via a model-level ensembling of CNN and vision transformer. arXiv preprint arXiv:2401.02358.

[18] Peng, L., Wang, C., Tian, G., Liu, G., Li, G., Lu, Y., et al. (2022). Analysis of CT scan images for COVID-19 pneumonia based on a deep ensemble framework with DenseNet, swin transformer, and RegNet. *Frontiers in Microbiology*, 13, 995323.

[19] Wang B, Zhang D, Tian Z. STCovidNet: Automatic Detection Model of Novel Coronavirus Pneumonia Based on Swin Transformer. Research Square; 2022. DOI: 10.21203/rs.3.rs-1401026/v1.

[20] Ma, Y., & Lv, W. (2022). Identification of pneumonia in chest x- ray image based on transformer. *International Journal of Antennas and Propagation*, 2022(1), 5072666.

[21] Chen, Y., Feng, J., Liu, J., Pang, B., Cao, D., & Li, C. (2022). Detection and classification of lung cancer cells using Swin Transformer. *Journal of Cancer Therapy*, 13(7), 464–475.

[22] Sun, R., Pang, Y., & Li, W. (2023). Efficient lung cancer image classification and segmentation algorithm based on an improved swin transformer. *Electronics*, 12(4), 1024.

[23] Tummala, S., Kim, J., & Kadry, S. (2022). BreaST-Net: multi-class classification of breast cancer from histopathological images using ensemble of Swin Transformers. *Mathematics*, 10(21), 4109.

[24] Dihin, R. A., AlShemmary, E., & Al-Jawher, W. (2023). Diabetic retinopathy classification using swin transformer with multi wavelet. *Journal of Kufa for Mathematics and Computer*, 10(2), 167–172.

[25] Pacal, I. A novel Swin transformer approach utilizing residual multi-layer perceptron for diagnosing brain tumors in MRI images. *Int. J. Mach. Learn. & Cyber.* 15, 3579–3597 (2024). https://doi.org/10.1007/s13042-024-02110-w.

[26] Kermany, D. S., Goldbaum, M., Cai, W., Valentim, C. C., Liang, H., Baxter, S. L., et al. (2018). Identifying medical diagnoses and treatable diseases by image- based deep learning. *Cell*, 172(5), 1122–1131.

26 Sustainable soil stabilization: combining lime and jute fiber for expansive soil improvement

Sandeepan Saha[a], Sandip Sarkar[b], Biswajit Gayen[c], Subimal Nandi[d] and Antara Ghosh[e]

Assistant Professor, Greater Kolkata College of Engineering and Management, JIS Group, Kolkata, WB, India

Abstract

Expansive soils undergo significant volume changes due to moisture fluctuations, posing challenges in construction. This study explores soil stabilization using lime and jute fiber. Lime reduces plasticity and swelling by forming cementitious compounds, while jute fiber enhances tensile strength, minimizes shrinkage, and prevents cracking. Laboratory tests, including Atterberg limits, UCS, and swell potential, assess the effects of different lime and fiber ratios. Results indicate improved soil strength, reduced plasticity, and minimized swelling. The findings highlight an eco-friendly, cost-effective stabilization method, demonstrating that combining jute fiber with lime enhances soil properties for construction applications like foundations and roadways.

Keywords: Expansive soils, jute fiber reinforcement, soil stabilization

Introduction

The growing demand for sustainable civil engineering practices focuses on reducing environmental impact and resource consumption. In geotechnical engineering, soil stabilization addresses issues with weak or expansive soils that cause structural failures due to moisture fluctuations. While cement-based binders offer strength, their high CO_2 emissions raise concerns. Research explores bio-based alternatives like jute fiber and lime, which chemically enhance soil strength and reduce plasticity. Jute improves tensile strength and resists cracking, making it a sustainable option. This study examines an eco-friendly approach to long-term soil stabilization.

Literature Review

Expansive soils, such as black cotton soils, exhibit significant swelling and shrinking due to moisture fluctuations, causing structural issues like cracking and uneven settlement [1]. Stabilization methods like lime treatment have been widely studied for improving soil strength. Recently, adding natural fibers, particularly jute, has gained attention for offering an eco-friendly reinforcement approach. Expansive soils are prevalent in tropical and semi-arid regions, where clay minerals like montmorillonite lead to volumetric changes upon moisture exposure [2]. Such behavior poses challenges for pavements, embankments, and buildings, making effective stabilization essential for durability [3]. Lime has traditionally been used to modify fine-grained soils by enhancing their mechanical properties through cation exchange and pozzolanic reactions. This process reduces soil plasticity and improves strength, stiffness, and workability, but can make soils brittle under repeated loads [4].

Natural fibers like jute offer sustainable options for reinforcing soils, particularly in tropical regions where they are affordable, biodegradable, and accessible [5]. Jute fibers enhance soil by increasing tensile strength, shear resistance, and ductility, which reduces deformation. Studies show that adding 0.5–2% jute fiber, cut to 30 mm lengths, significantly improves soil stiffness and strength, though excessive fiber can reduce cohesion [6]. The combined use of lime and jute fiber provides both chemical stabilization and mechanical enhancement, reducing brittleness while boosting strength and ductility [7]. Research indicates that using 1% jute fiber and 3% lime yields optimal soil strength, as evaluated through tests like the

[a]sandeepan.saha_gkcem@jisgroup.org, [b]sandip.sarkar@gkcem.ac.in, [c]biswajit.gayen@gkcem.ac.in, [d]subimalnandi7@gmail.com, [e]antara.ghosh.2011@gmail.com

DOI: 10.1201/9781003724995-26

CBR and UCS, with up to a 65% increase in UCS [7]. This approach promotes environmental sustainability by reducing reliance on synthetic materials, aligning with eco-friendly construction practices.

Materials

Materials incorporated within the experimental study include

Characteristics of the soil

Specific gravity (2.547), particle size distribution (Gravel: Nil, Sand: 14%, Silt + Clay: 76%), and Atterberg limits such as Liquid Limit (95), Plastic Limit (12), Shrinkage Limit (11.63), and Plasticity Index (84). The soil is classified as CH soil with an Optimum Moisture Content of 15% and Maximum Dry Density of 16.57 kN/m³. Unconfined Compressive Strength is 142 kN/m², Unsoaked CBR is 6.85%, and Differential Free Swell Index is 146%.

Chemical composition of the lime

Contains elements like iron (0.04%), manganese (0.006%), phosphate (0.05%), sulfate (0.3%), silica (0.06%), and magnesia (0.4%).

Properties of the jute fiber

Type is dark jute with a length of 30 mm, a diameter of 1 mm, specific gravity of 1.33, bulk density of 1301 kN/m³, modulus of elasticity of 77 N/mm², UTL of 3317 N/mm², and elongation at break of 2.7%.

Test Program

The test program aimed to enhance expansive soil properties using lime and jute fiber. Expansive soils swell when wet and shrink when dry, causing structural issues.

Program 1: Determined the optimum moisture content (OMC) and maximum dry density (MDD) of soil-lime mixtures, adjusting lime from 0% to 9%.

Program 2: Measured unconfined compressive strength (UCS) of lime-treated soil up to 9%.

Program 3: Evaluated OMC and MDD at 5% lime with varying jute fiber levels (up to 1%).

Program 4: Repeated UCS tests with 5% lime and jute fiber.

Program 5: Assessed CBR and SBR at 5% lime with jute fiber.

Findings support sustainable soil stabilization.

Materials

Effect of OMC and MDD values on lime-treated soil

This study investigates (see Figure 26.1) how lime affects the compaction characteristics of expansive soil, using the standard Proctor test. For untreated soil (0% lime), the OMC is 15%, and MDD is 16.57 kN/m³, serving as the baseline (see Figure 26.1).

With 1% lime, the OMC remains at 15%, but the MDD rises significantly to 17.98 kN/m³, indicating improved compatibility (see Figure 26.1). As the lime content increases to 3-6%, the OMC ranges between 17-19%, showing that more moisture is needed for optimal compaction. During this stage, the MDD fluctuates between 17.3 and 18 kN/m³, suggesting better soil stability and resistance to volume changes (see Figure 26.1). At higher lime levels, between 7-9%, the OMC increases to 21%, but the MDD drops to around 16.6 kN/m³. This indicates that excessive lime can reduce the soil's compaction potential by raising moisture demands while lowering density v. The findings highlight (see Figure 26.1) that adding lime up to 6% enhances the dry density and compactability of expansive soil. However, beyond this point, additional lime decreases density and increases moisture needs, leading to diminishing returns. Therefore, identifying the optimal lime content is crucial to achieving effective and economical soil stabilization.

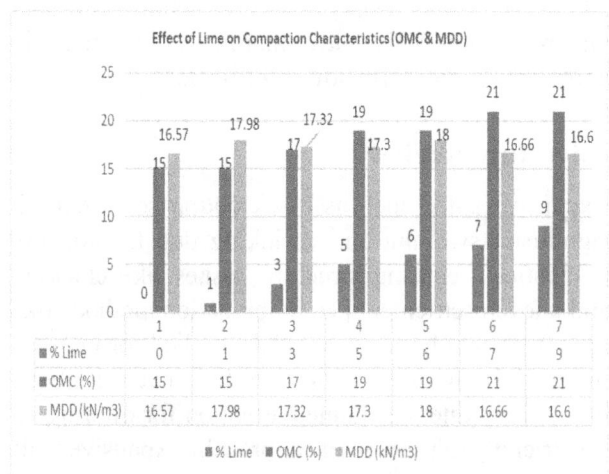

Figure 26.1 Effect on OMC and MDD values of lime-treated soil

Source: Author

Effect of UCS values of lime-treated soil

Unconstrained compressive strength (UCS) evaluates the soil's resistance to deformation under axial loading. Lime treatment enhances expansive soils by reducing plasticity and swelling. At 0% lime, UCS is 142 kN/m², increasing slightly to 146.1 kN/m² at 1%. Significant improvements occur between 3% and 6% lime, where UCS ranges from 235.76 to 252.83 kN/m² (see Figure 26.2) due to pozzolanic reactions that enhance bonding and stability. However, beyond 6%, UCS declines, dropping to 181.45 kN/m² at 7% and 155.42 kN/m² at 9%, indicating that excessive lime disrupts soil-lime interactions. Optimal stabilization occurs at 3–6% lime (Figure 26.2). Given the unconfined compressive strength of the lime-treated soil tests when compared with the OMC and MDD values, the ideal lime level is demonstrated in the (see Figure 26.1) to be around 5%. Also, it is noticed that the UCS esteem at the ideal lime content is around 244.19 kN/m² (Figure 26.2). The untreated soil's UCS esteem is 142 kN/m². That's what it shows, contrasted with untreated soil, the treated soil's UCS improvement is around 72% at the best lime concentration (Figure 26.2).

Effect of jute fiber on OMC and MDD of lime-treated soil

The compaction characteristics of expansive soil treated with 5% lime and different percentages of jute fiber are assessed using the standard Proctor test (see Figure 26.3). Untreated soil shows an Optimum Moisture Content (OMC) of 15% and Maximum Dry Density (MDD) of 16.57 kN/m³. With 5% lime alone, OMC increases to 19%, and MDD reaches 17.3 kN/m³,

indicating improved compatibility and stability due to lime (Table 26.1).

Adding 0.5% jute fiber reduces OMC to 17% and raises MDD to 18.2 kN/m³, showing that small jute additions enhance soil structure and compaction (see Figure 26.3). At 0.65% jute, OMC rises to 19%, while MDD slightly decreases to 17.9 kN/m³, maintaining strength with higher moisture demand. When jute content reaches 0.8%, OMC climbs to 21%, and MDD falls to 16.64 kN/m³, showing reduced compactability (Figure 26.3). At 1% jute, OMC reaches 23%, and MDD drops to 16.52 kN/m³, indicating further interference with compaction (Figure 26.3).

In summary, small jute additions (up to 0.5%) with 5% lime enhance soil density, but higher jute levels increase moisture needs and reduce compaction efficiency. This trend is illustrated in Table 26.1, where increasing jute correlates with rising OMC and falling MDD due to water absorption by lime and jute.

The UCS values of lime-treated expansive soil mixed with varying jute fiber percentages demonstrate the influence of jute content on soil stability and strength (Figure 26.4).

Table 26.1 OMC and MDD values at 5% lime and % variation of jute fiber.

Sl No	% Jute@ 5% lime	OMC (%)	MDD (kN/m³)
1	Untreated soil	15	16.57
2	0	19	17.3
3	0.5	17	18.2
4	0.65	19	17.9
5	0.8	21	16.64
6	1	23	16.52

Source: Author

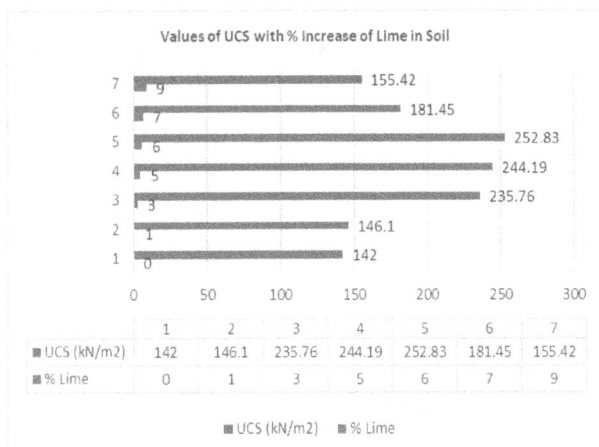

Figure 26.2 Effect on UCS values with % increase of lime in soil
Source: Author

Table 26.2 Values of UCS with variation of % jute fiber at 5% lime.

Sl No	% Jute@ 5% lime	UCS (kN/m²)
1	Untreated soil	142
2	0	244.19
3	0.5	265.54
4	0.65	311.15
5	0.8	218.33
6	1	164.9

Source: Author

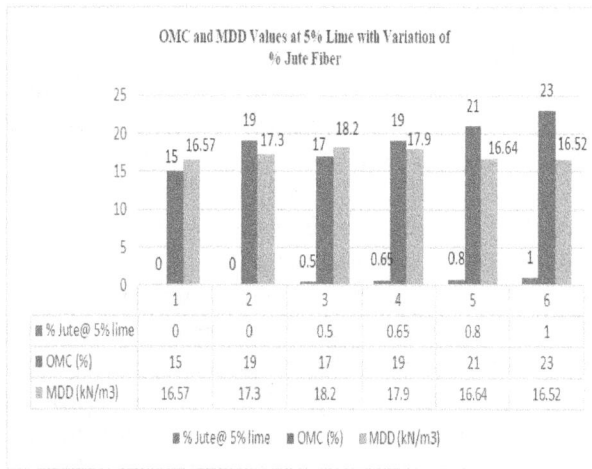

Figure 26.3 Effect on OMC & MDD values with percentage variation of jute fiber at 5% lime
Source: Author

Table 26.3 CBR and SBR values with variation of % jute fiber at 5% lime.

Sl. No	% Jute@ 5% lime	CBR (%)	SBR (%)
1	Untreated soil	6.85	0
2	0	12.48	82.32
3	0.5	16.82	132.15
4	0.65	21.98	207.59
5	0.8	12.17	77.78
6	1	11.49	53.23

Source: Author

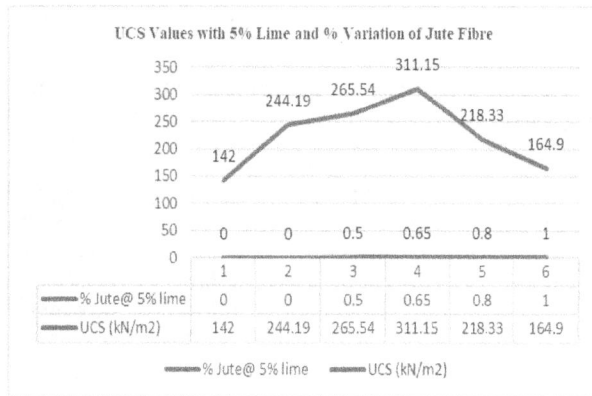

Figure 26.4 Effect on UCS values with percentage variation of jute fiber at 5% lime
Source: Author

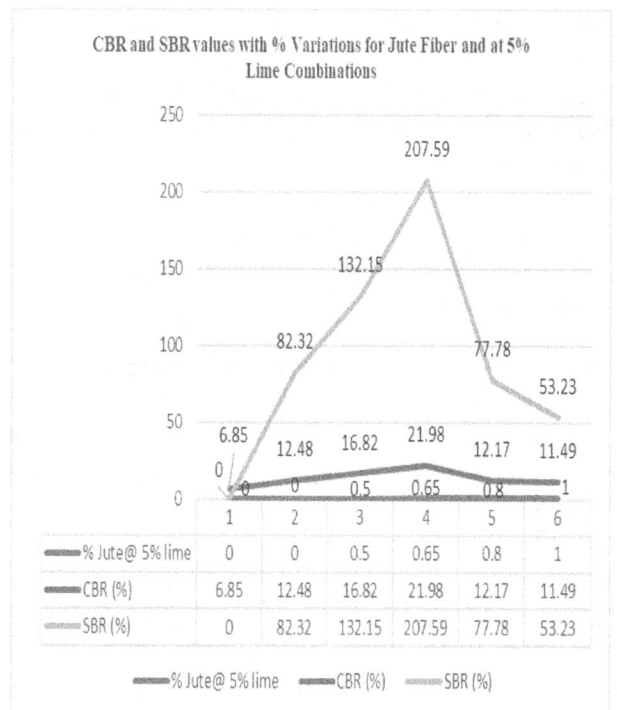

Figure 26.5 Effect on CBR and SBR percentage values with percentage variation of jute fiber at 5% lime
Source: Author

Effect of jute fiber on the UCS of lime-treated soil

Untreated soil has a baseline UCS of 142 kN/m², which increases to 244.19 kN/m² when lime is added (0% jute), emphasizing lime's strengthening effect (Figure 26.4) (Table 26.2).

Adding jute fiber further enhances UCS up to an optimal point. At 0.5% jute, UCS rises to 265.54 kN/m², peaking at 311.15 kN/m² with 0.65% jute (see Figure 26.4) (Table 26.2). This suggests an ideal interaction between fibers and lime-treated soil due to improved distribution and bonding, enhancing load-bearing capacity.

Beyond 0.65% jute, UCS declines, dropping to 218.33 kN/m² at 0.8% and 164.9 kN/m² at 1%, nearing untreated soil levels (Figure 26.4). Excessive fiber

may hinder compaction and cohesion, reducing structural integrity. Thus, 0.65% jute is optimal for maximizing compressive strength in lime-treated soil.

Effect of jute fiber on the CBR and SBR of lime-treated soil

The CBR and SBR values for lime-treated expansive soil are shown in Table 26.3 (see Figure 26.5). Untreated soil has a baseline CBR of 6.85%, with SBR not applicable. When lime is added without jute fiber (0% jute), CBR improves to 12.48%, and SBR reaches 82.32%, indicating that lime alone enhances the soil's stability (see Figure 26.5). As jute fiber is introduced, a steady increase in both CBR and SBR values is observed up to a certain threshold. At 0.5% jute content, CBR rises to 16.82%, and SBR increases significantly to 132.15% (Figure 26.5).

This trend continues, with the values peaking at 0.65% jute, where CBR reaches its maximum of 21.98% and SBR achieves 207.59% (Figure 26.5). This peak suggests an optimal interaction between lime-treated soil and jute fiber, enhancing load-bearing performance, potentially due to improved fiber distribution within the soil matrix.

Beyond this peak, however, the values of both CBR and SBR begin to decline (Figure 26.5). At 0.8% jute, CBR drops to 12.17%, and SBR reduces to 77.78%. This downward trend continues at 1% jute, where CBR decreases to 11.49% and SBR falls further to 53.23%. The reduction in these values at higher jute concentrations may be due to an excess of fiber, which could reduce soil compaction and cohesion, resulting in weaker load-bearing properties. In summary, adding jute fiber to lime-treated soil enhances its CBR and SBR up to an optimal level, specifically at 0.65% jute content. Beyond this, performance decreases, indicating that balanced jute content is crucial to maximizing soil strength and stability.

Summary

This study investigates stabilizing expansive soils using lime and jute fiber to mitigate swelling and shrinkage. Lime reduces plasticity and forms cementitious compounds that enhance strength, while jute fiber improves tensile strength, minimizes shrinkage, and prevents cracking.

The testing program included five stages. First, the optimal lime content was determined by evaluating OMC and MDD. UCS tests then assessed soil strength with varying lime percentages. Further tests analyzed the impact of 5% lime and different jute fiber amounts on OMC, MDD, and UCS. Finally, CBR and SBR tests confirmed that the lime-jute combination enhances soil strength, stability, and sustainability.

Conclusion

The stabilization of expansive soils is essential in civil engineering, especially in regions where high swell-shrink behavior can damage infrastructure. This study examines the use of lime and jute fiber to improve soil properties for construction.

Compaction tests revealed that adding 0.5–1.0% jute fibers to soil-lime mixtures maintained the same OMC and MDD trends. The optimal mix was found at 5% lime and 0.65% jute fibers, significantly enhancing UCS, particularly with marble dust. CBR tests showed an 82% swell bearing ratio (SBR) at optimal admixture content. The 5% lime and 0.65% jute fiber combination improved UCS, strength, and load-bearing capacity.

Lime chemically stabilizes soil by reducing plasticity, shrinkage, and swelling, while jute fibers enhance tensile strength and durability. This eco-friendly method offers a sustainable solution for road construction, foundations, and infrastructure requiring stable soil conditions.

References

[1] Al-Gharbawi, A. S. A., Najemalden, A. M., & Fattah, M. Y. (2023). Expansive soil stabilization with lime, cement, and silica fume. *Applied Sciences*, 13(1), 436. https://doi.org/10.3390/app13010436.

[2] Lal, D., Reddy, P., Kumar, R. S., & Rao, V. G. (2020). Stabilization of expansive soil by using jute fiber. In IOP Conference Series: Materials Science and Engineering, (Vol. 998, p. 012045). DOI 10.1088/1757-899X/998/1/01204.

[3] Zhang, J., Deng, A., & Jaksa, M. (2021). Enhancing mechanical behavior of micaceous soil with jute fibers and lime additives. *Journal of Rock Mechanics and Geotechnical Engineering*, 13(5), 1093–1100. https://doi.org/10.1016/j.jrmge.2021.04.008.

[4] Carmel, V. A., & Vinu, T. (2015). Stabilization of soft clay using lime and jute fibres. *International Journal of Engineering Research & Technology (IJERT)*, 3(29), pp 1–5. ISSN: 2278–0181. www.ijert.org, NCRACE-2015 Conference Proceedings.

[5] Sunil, Batra, A., Sharma, P., & Lal, S. (2019). Soil stabilization by using jute fibre. *International Research Journal of Engineering and Technology (IRJET)*, 06(03), pp 8209–8212. e-ISSN: 2395–0056.

[6] Prasanna, S., & Mendes, N. M. (2020). Application of Jute Fiber in Soil Stabilization. Preprints. https://doi.org/10.20944/preprints202008.0534.v1.

[7] Kaiwart, G., & Chandrakar, V. (2021). Influence in CBR of expansive soil with jute fiber reinforcement. *International Journal of Science and Research (IJSR)*, 10(3), 595–597. DOI: 10.21275/SR21304133533.

27 Psychological effects of technology addiction using KNN, SVM, random forest and Naïve Bayes

Santosh Reddy, P.[1,a], Amritha, A.[2,b] and Ananya Srihaana[2,c]

[1]Assistant Professor, Computer Science and Engineering, B.N.M. Institute of Technology, Bengaluru, Karnataka, India

[2]Department of Computer Science and Engineering, B.N.M. Institute of Technology, Bengaluru, Karnataka, India

Abstract

Excessive technology use has been linked to mental health issues such as stress, anxiety, depression, and cognitive decline. Traditional diagnostic methods often overlook the value of behavioral and psychometric data. This study explores machine learning (ML) algorithms, including K-Nearest Neighbor (KNN), Support Vector Machines (SVM), Random Forests, and Naive Bayes, for diagnosing these disorders. The methodology involves implementing these models using Python's Scikit-learn library and evaluating their performance through benchmarks. Behavioral diaries, psychometric scores, and mood patterns are analyzed to classify symptoms, achieving over 80% accuracy. The research also highlights the impact of technology overuse, including disrupted sleep from blue light exposure and technology addiction. These issues can impair students' academic performance, well-being, and mental health. By integrating objective, data-driven diagnostics with behavioral insights, this approach addresses real-world challenges and provides a foundation for mitigating the adverse effects of technology on mental health.

Keywords: K-Nearest Neighbor, machine learning, mental health, Naive Bayes, stochastic forests Support Vector Machines

Introduction

The rapid advancement of technology has affected daily life and has also caused serious problems in the use of technology. People struggling with excessive technology often experience psychological symptoms such as anxiety, depression and cognitive impairment. The traditional diagnostic methods rely on multiple assessments through questionnaires or interviews, which are time- consuming and prone to bias. This literal objective analysis now can exploit the machine learning algorithms in flexible application in the analysis of behavioral as well as psychological data. Algorithms that complement the capability of the technology of psychological behavior detection and provide added capability beyond good task-allocating power. Models specific to kinds of data; hence a cross comparison of the outcome may build greater confidence about the diagnosis. Paper characterization describes one kind of behavioral diaries, psychometric scores, and emotional data types. This just gives a general overview of how a machine learning application was put into answer this very critical question of the study. The algorithm used for the application in diagnosing psychological effects of technology is the Naive Bayesian algorithm. Assigning tasks among others to give the algorithms a go according to its performance and their capabilities. All these models could take all those other types of information; these are what make the outcome fit so there is improvement in the confident diagnosis. Also, it suggests the broad frameworks offer the type of machine learning that satisfies the need to fight those questions.

Train technology to college students as hinted above in the paragraph already, there is something that evidence technology relies on to achieve effective college learning acquisition by mental state of the adopter. Also, the evidence encompasses also time factors such as how easily the online is and everything that falls into it. Under such time factors along with full time online access students can complete their college education. Online learning will provide

[a]santoshreddy@bnmit.in, [b]23cse050@bnmit.in, [c]23cse131@bnmit.in

DOI: 10.1201/9781003724995-27

them with the privilege of self-study that is, management of learning as well. Because the students will work part-time besides learning and taking care of some needs of the family.

Other advantages of technology allow fraternity learners to communicate. For that, fraternity students can be able to coexist since they will be a reading group as they will learn together. The most rigid consequence that technology entails is the idea of addiction. Overuse of the utilization of social media, games and all other web services will qualify an individual as not able to take care of themselves on aspects related to functionality of technology It may lead the worst effects toward inability in studies, alienation, and mental illness such as anxiety and depression in the lives of students of universities. Except it gives them depth, it also enables them a community experience and bonding psychology that they would otherwise not enjoy. Excessive use of technology can also negatively impact college students' mental health. A big concern is the impact of technology on quality sleep. Studies have shown that the blue light emitted by electronic devices can inhibit the production of melatonin, a hormone that regulates sleep, causing sleepiness and fatigue. This affects students' learning, mental health and overall well-being.

Literature Review

Several research attract machine learning on various problems concerning mental health diagnostics these days. SVMs have been widely applied in the analysis of depression on social media with polarity to emotions, user-based engagement, and symbolic representation of messages. It did pretty well in the volume-based stress prediction both through physiological and behavioral data. The Random Forest approach worked pretty well on the text-based sentiment analysis on the data which held unbelievable high reliable classification rates regarding emotional and behavioral ratings. KNN turned out useful in unearthing patterns of negativistic behavior and psychological triggers as well. Much more it promised on how ML has been positioned regarding dealing with problems relating to psychological behavior within itself, there is nothing promised to dictate the manner these technologies can be used towards finding some quantification about the psyche effects of dependence in using specific technology. The bulk then witnessed

Table 27.1 Technology addiction classification algorithm (TACF).

Input requirements
1. Dataset: A CSV file containing data on technology addiction.
2. Features: Columns representing demographic and behavioral variables (e.g., age, gender, screen time, social media usage).
3. Target variable: A binary column (0/1, yes/no) indicating technology addiction.

Example dataset structure

Column Name	Description
Age	Participant age
Gender	Participant gender
ScreenTime	Daily screen time (hours)
SocialMediaUsage	Daily social media usage (hours)
AddictionStatus	Technology addiction status (0/1)

Sample Data

Age	Gender	ScreenTime	SocialMediaUsage	AddictionStatus
25	Male	4	2	1
30	Female	2	1	0
20	Male	6	3	1

Input format
1. Save your dataset as a CSV file (e.g., technology_addiction_data.csv).
2. Load the dataset into your Python environment using pd.read_csv('filename.csv').
Update the code to match your dataset:
1. Change df = pd.read_csv('data.csv') to df = pd.read_csv('your_filename.csv')
2. Adjust column names in the code to match your dataset.

Running the code
1. Save the code in a Python file.
2. Run the code using Python (e.g., python).
3. The output will display accuracy, classification report, and confusion matrix.

(Source: Author's compilation)

in the outcome are seen effects brought about by addition stress, or emotional instability. Such voids are bridged by training SVM, Random Forest, Naive Bayes (NB), and KNN on behavioral and psychometric data symptoms of anxiety, reduction in cognitive abilities, misinterpretation of emotional states; therefore, attempting to encapsulate applications of ML that isolate attempts at solving individual symptoms in a manner rather than analyzing vast behavioral patterns as a whole. It would consolidate the dataset of extensive behavioral logs, psychometric scales, and natural language analysis. This shall be associated with a certain insight in relation to the usage of technology and related malignant significance in terms of diagnosis and positive in case of usage through these ML models in deeper settings [1-9].

Methodology

This study employs a multi-dimensional approach to analyze the psychological effects of technology use through machine learning. Three domains of a sizeable amount of data shall capture information regarding behavioral metrics, psychometric scales, and analysis of emotional sentiment. Screens used within seconds; number of applications opened; number of notices and volumes that arise; trends towards behaviors as indicators of activities of multitasking. The delivery of scores in normalized units comprises the following three. Psychological characteristics-that is Internet addiction test-(IAT) depression, anxiety, and stress scale (DASS). There have been most probably reasons like data regarding natural language processing Techniques of emotional Sentiment that take along the input of text together with the that of social media.

Handling and also detection of missing values are being carried out. Moreover, min-max scaling is a technique whereby normalization of data is accomplished. Again, to avoid duplication of features that are working well without much complication in the model with principal component analysis. In all these pipelines running for the preprocessing cycle, this integrity of data will therefore be maintained and privacy will be gained.

After preparing the data, four ML algorithms—SVM, Random Forest, NB, and KNN—are trained and evaluated. Training involves splitting the data into training and testing subsets, with cross-validation used to optimize model parameters. Evaluation metrics include accuracy, precision, recall, and F1-score to assess the effectiveness of each algorithm in diagnosing symptoms such as addiction, anxiety, and cognitive decline. The study incorporates a real-world simulation to test model adaptability. Participants are monitored for behavioral patterns over several weeks, providing longitudinal data for model refinement. This ensures the results reflect real-world usage patterns and improves the applicability of ML algorithms in diagnosing the psychological impact of technology overuse.

The results of ML models were compared to benchmark data to validate their accuracy and reliability.

Additionally, the study examined the scalability of these algorithms in larger populations, emphasizing their potential to revolutionize mental health diagnostics. By integrating multi- dimensional data and employing advanced ML techniques, this methodology offers a comprehensive framework for understanding and mitigating the psychological impacts of technology use.

Machine Learning Models

K nearest neighbors (KNN)

The K Nearest Neighbors (KNN) algorithm is a simple and easy-to-follow learning method for classification and replication. It works by finding the "k" closest data points to the test sample and predicting the outcome based on the majority of the class (for distribution) or the median of the neighbors (for regression). The "k" value is a hyperparameter that determines which neighbors should be considered and should be carefully chosen to avoid over- or under-fitting. KNN uses a distance metric (typically Euclidean distance) to measure the similarity between data points. The algorithm is example-based, meaning it does not specify the model but makes predictions by comparing new data to existing conditions. A powerful tool for analyzing patterns. Information about technology usage, such as screen time, social media usage, and frequency of interaction between devices, can be considered as input. Psychological variables such as stress, anxiety, depression, or cognitive performance levels can cause a different target. For classification tasks, KNN can classify people into different psychological groups (such as "high anxiety," "mild anxiety," or "low depression") based on their technology. In regression tasks, KNN can be estimated continuous values, such as anxiety or stress scores, based on technology usage patterns.

For instance, a dataset might include features like the amount of time spent on social media, gaming, or using screens before bed, and the corresponding target could be psychological factors such as stress or sleep quality. By analyzing this data with KNN, one can explore how technology usage correlates with psychological states, like higher stress levels associated with more screen time. KNN can also help predict the effects of changes in technology use on mental health outcomes, providing insights into how reducing screen time or changing technology usage might impact well-being. The algorithm's performance can be improved by preprocessing the data (e.g., scaling or Standardized features), select the distance measure, and fine- tune parameters such as "k". Overall, KNN is a useful tool for studying the relationship between technology and psychology, helping researchers better understand how modern technology affects mental health. The KNN algorithm is accurate in classifying users into addiction groups (e.g., mild, moderate, severe) and diagnosing anxiety and depression. This performance is measured by comparing the class list (by nearest neighbors) with the actual class list in the list.

Support vector machines

The SVM is a powerful supervised machine learning algorithm primarily used for classification tasks. It is particularly useful in binary classification problems, and was used in this study to diagnose depression and anxiety. Factors such as emotional polarization of social media and usage patterns at different times of the day were used. SVM classifies users into risk groups based on their high scores; it identifies users who exhibit the most negative emotions and unidentified usage patterns as those at risk of difficulty. RBF kernel through the basis function of SVC in Scikitlean models with 91% classification between positive behaviors or manifestation. SVM uses kernel functions whereby information mapped into a space where the concept is maximum distance or margin between closest points labelled as support vectors; however, if the problem turns to be non-linearly separable then some special functions also known as kernel functions become to usage for mapping it into a high dimensioned space where they can look for liner hyper planes.

Hence, for problems regarding data, which are too much in dimension and could never be differentiated using any line, SVM has brilliant efficiency. They require several spaces, hence it is much more convenient to store for small-scale problem issues of a dataset. Apart from this, with the maximum possible margin of class, destruction power is low. Flexible machine learning applications have made easy objective methods by which one can easily analyze behavioral and psychological data. It recognizes the psychological impact of the algorithm of technology. The distribution. For example, configuration data could include features like time spent on social media, screen time, type of device used, and frequency of technology use. Another goal could be a psychological condition like anxiety, depression, or

depression, where individuals are divided into different categories like "high anxiety" or "low stress."

By training an SVM model, you can classify new people based on their technology usage habits and predict their mental health. For example, an SVM model can predict whether a person will be anxious or depressed based on their screen time and social behavior. To develop your model, you can preprocess your data by evaluating features, selecting appropriate kernels, and tuning hyperparameters like constants (C) and kernel parameters (gamma). Additionally, SVM's ability to handle complex, high-dimensional data allows it to be used to incorporate multiple factors like demographics (age, gender) and psychological assessment. SVM utilizes kernel functions, say radial basis functions or polynomial kernels in which it maps the data into a space of higher dimensionality. That is, SVM is said to work if data cannot be linearly separated, goes well in immense spaces, and also does quite well even if the applied dataset is too small. All this also occurs with least damage when one looks forward to maximizing the margin for the class.

Random forest

It does a good job with big, large complex, huge datasets having big amounts of features since, basically, it is a non-linearity model, and interaction gets generated with the feature itself also. This method, in combination with some type of missing values handling that it was accompanied with, brings forward feature importance that features its capability to extract such a list of the feature who, by herself, can guide the system to this level of results. Analysis of the psychological implication of technology: Random Forest could be just the perfect forecasting tool for the objective of predicting the psychological well-being up to the extent of patterned usage of technology. Measuring this way completely extracts absolute usage of technology including screen time, social media use, increased game play and other psychological stress, anxiety or even depression levels. This will thus place the algorithm for the classification of the states of the psychological condition.

The algorithm comprises what, in training, it constructs millions of decision trees and sums up those scores of predictions over its different outputs and further goes for the continuation of its training randomly sampling through that subset of data, whereas in the creation of any kind of splitting by its node, then it selects a limited number of previously randomly allowed feature space so that these two phenomena are not so prone to overfitting other than the fact that the robustness of its modeling system is enhanced. It finally does majority voting of class predictions of all the individual trees in classification and does average of all output values gathered from the trees in regression. It also does quite well with highly dimensional data in the feature space of such scenarios because it can model complex interrelations that may not be followed in a linear nature.

Thanks to the context of which you measure technology's psychosomatic effect, Random Forest will come in handy when predicting the psychological outcome concernmentalntal health given the patterns in the use of technology. This includes the example of how one uses technology. For example, screen time, social media, or playing. For instance, Stress, anxiety, and depression Level. Psychological as well as habits factors. This algorithm can be used in the classification or prediction of mental conditions-for instance, the trend if he or she has high stress or low anxiety by the use of technology. Therefore, there are quite numerous factors that would influence the result from the mental condition. The model also learns from labeled data. It may receive appropriately trained model with supplementary.

Naive Bayes

NB is probably the simplest of the probabilistic algorithms in machine learning. It has been designed based on Bayes' Theorem and will therefore be able to estimate the probability of any target variable provided there are several input features. This concept also takes on the assumption that for a classification problem, multiple features used will not affect one another somehow. Interesting in itself. In so far as it goes, in fact it works quite well with the assumption under NB for text classification and can hence be applied in binary or multi-class classification too. Algorithm puts out each class posterior-probability as the product of its class prior-probability of likelihood of being on the observed feature. Along with that, the maximum probability class. NB is such an algorithm that does quite well in a huge dataset because the way they work, and the speed of coding goes absolutely very smoothly without any hint how it might have ended to be that way. But it is very likely to make use of a NB model as well; since it classifies persons carrying psychological effects accompanied by usage

patterns of the above-mentioned technologies with consequences arising through it started occurring in its process. Example of feature engineering in collecting a data set: screen time, hours in social media, or device usage frequency, etc. This could be one of the impacts of this psychology that would possibly walk by at how high the stress probably is and probably the anxiety or probably depression levels-that would probably go into predictive sort of the falling into maybe some special type like a "high-stress, "low-anxiety" type of categories about the amount of that person uses in the use of technological means. NB is going to implement the idea of usage of technology with computing the chance of each psychology and classifying human beings to their respective class. It could probably predict that number of hours the individual would want to come out of his or her life, which would have had excessive levels of stress due to mostly sitting back in front of a computer screen or high usage of social media.

Results

The machine learning algorithms discussed— KNN, SVM, Random Forest, and NB—each offer unique strengths for analyzing complex datasets and predicting psychological outcomes based on technology usage patterns. KNN is a simple, instance-based algorithm that classifies or predicts outcomes by comparing new data points to the 'k' nearest neighbors in the training dataset. While KNN is intuitive and easy to implement, its performance can degrade with large datasets or high-dimensional features unless properly tuned. In analyzing the psychological effects of technology, KNN can help classify individuals into psychological categories like "high stress" or "low anxiety" based on their technology use, but it may struggle with handling noise and irrelevant features. SVM is a robust algorithm known for its ability to create a clear separation between classes, even with non- linear data, using kernel functions. It is used for making predictions of the analysis for the new ones in labeled data. It can be useful for inference towards psychological well-being that relies on a pattern of applying technology. It supports in making many predictions on the psychological outcome of a technological application. Say, stress or fear is involved. SVM suffers from overparameterization. Besides, immense computational costs arise at very high dimensional data sets. Random Forest is an ensemble learning technique. The ensemble learning method is where many decision trees are built and the outcome taken together is voted. This actually is a pretty good extraction of subtle, not linear relationships of features so the best approach that would enable the kind of technology usage that is somehow linked with a type of psychology. Another adopted technique among many is Random Forest that also produces variable importance. Having a majority of very good points for over-fitting within very big complex huge datasets end loads of trees that are not very well explained will be present in data with this expenditure.

NB is an extremely simple Bayes theorem-based classifier but feature freedom is unlikely in the real-world scenario yet somehow powerful. NB can classify people into groups based on technology, such as "high anxiety," for psychological analysis, but its simplicity can limit its ability to model relationships between traits.

Conclusion

All this would sum up that though there are four algorithms utilized in the psychology of technology-related study models, it will still vary with the data and the sort of problem with which a model is in intent of solving. Both KNN and Naive Bayes are simple though they go on to work out good but weak regarding possessing high-level data and the noise also. With this, SVM can be very powerful in classification with high scores but needs to be carried out with extreme caution. These are brilliant models and could have taken complexities in data and shown out features where maximum potential can be identified. That gives comprehensive vision on how technology does affect the mental health. Even Naive Bayes will eventually produce practical tools working on the analysis of impacts of technology of psychology. All of these algorithms have its pros; for example, KNN and Naive Bayes is easy trace in the little amount of data but when there comes big data or even complicated data, then it gets very difficult to handle such algorithms and may also be used to classify a people with the help of pattern-based technology. SVM is very strong with nonlinear data and huge problem sets, which matches the nature of predicting psychological outcomes based on multiple

types of techniques. Random forests do well concern the complexities and the very vast amounts of data with furthermore lightness concerning what has meaningful activities toward their mental health. And researchers, since that would probably be with a lot of power physicians very influential and then the algorithms find out and predict what kind of technology use-that may be screen time for example or even the very nature of what kind of social media use-interacts with mental health and start working to diminish its negative effects related to this interaction.

References

[1] Brown, J., Green, T., & Black, M. (2020). Effects of technology addiction on mental health: an empirical study. *Journal of Psychological Studies*, 35(3), 12–20.

[2] Singh, S. K., & Kumar, P. R. (2021). Application of machine learning in mental health diagnostics. In International Conference on Data Science and Analytics, (pp. 215–223). doi: 10.1109/DSA.2021.9423187.

[3] Nguyen, A. T., Patel, H. R. , & Zhang, D. Z. (2021). Using random forests for stress detection via smartphone usage data. *IEEE Transactions on Mobile Computing*, 19(10), 2345–2357.

[4] Sharma, R., & Verma, L. (2019). Support vector machines for depression detection via social media analysis. In Proceedings of the IEEE International Conference on Big Data (BigData), (pp. 1453–1461).

[5] Zhou, H., Li, Q., & Yu, X. (2020). Naive Bayes in sentiment analysis: an evaluation of performance in behavioral data classification. *IEEE Access*, 3, 143792–143800.

[6] Gupta, P., Jain, R., & Mohan, S. K. (2022). Behavioral and psychometric analysis of technology addiction: insights from k-nearest neighbor models. *IEEE Transactions on Systems, Man, and Cybernetics: Systems*, 52(3), 1623–1632.

[7] Roy, A. K., & Yadav, M. H. (2018). Principal component analysis for feature reduction in psychological impact studies. In Proceedings of the IEEE Symposium on Computational Intelligence and Data Engineering (CIDE), (pp. 67–74).

[8] McCarthy, J. C., Halverson, C. A., Caruso, C. C., & Turner, J. R. (2019). Impacts of technology on sleep and academic performance: A machine learning approach. *Computers in Human Behavior*, 95, 66–75. https://doi.org/10.1016/j.chb.2019.03.019.

[9] Lee, K. (2021). Blue light exposure and cognitive decline: a data-driven perspective. *IEEE Journal of Biomedical and Health Informatics*, 25(6), 55–69.

28 Delay driven congestion control approach under smart virtual parallel TCP application

Keerti Mishra[a], Nitin Jain[b] and Saurabh Bhutani[c]

Electronics and Communication Engineering Department, School of Engineering, BBD University, Lucknow. UP, India

Abstract

A wireless network that exhibits large bandwidth delay product (BDP) follows the transmission control protocol (TCP) for standard data transmission platform. TCP performs an increase in the congestion window exponentially and consequently sometime fails to utilize available bandwidth. This problem becomes worse with the advanced network devices and the growth of the Internet. This work presents a smart approach for improving congestion control by dynamically adjusting the number of virtual parallel streams using machine learning models. This technique allows for more responsive regulation of congestion levels by adjusting delay with respect to variation in the congestion window (CWND). MATLAB-based simulations demonstrate that KNN achieves the highest classification accuracy (77.8%) while maintaining the lowest transmission delay. Additional performance metrics, including prediction speed (KNN: 570 obs/sec, DT: 1100 obs/sec, NB: 440 obs/sec) and training time (KNN: 0.716 sec, NB: 0.729 sec, DT: 0.738 sec), highlight KNN's balance between accuracy and efficiency. The results further indicate that KNN outperforms the DT and NB models in terms of accuracy and efficiency.

Keywords: Congestion control, Machine learning, slow-start, TCP

Introduction

New network designs are more complicated and diversified. Protocols for Internet of Vehicles (IoV), home operating systems, and military-integrated devices require dependability and security [1]. These scenarios frequently have low bandwidth and significant packet loss rates, necessitating mature, safe, and dependable congestion control. Conventional algorithms for congestion management have been explored extensively for finding the dependability to maintaining connection integrity in TCP deployment and data transmission e.g. TCP NewReno algorithms. Well known for its security, maturity, and widespread application. Introduction of 5G technology, the rapid development of diverse applications and large networks, changing network structures, and the desire for increased performance, issues have emerged. In heterogeneous networks with error rates, asymmetry, and delays, TCP NewReno continues to use its classic strategy to distinguish the congestion avoidance and slow start for controlling congestion [2]. Slow-start thresholds do not adequately represent the real bandwidth, resulting in lower link

usage. It is frequently unclear whether packet loss is due to random faults or congestion, resulting in a fall in transmission rate and an incorrect slow-start. Improvements to the congestion control proposed to improve network performance [3]. The TCP NewRenoBw algorithm uses the slow-start threshold and available bandwidth to minimize the congestion. This method determines the source of packet loss by examining the bottleneck link buffer queue length [4]. In this work, algorithms are built in MATLAB as a simulation platform to assess throughput, fairness, and friendliness performance. The approach was integrated with the TCP protocol, and a real-world network environment was built to test throughput using the Instrumentation Control Toolbox's TCP client/server functionality. The findings show that TCP with a smart delay driven mechanism outperforms the regular TCP Reno algorithm.

Related Works

The TCP NewReno algorithm (updated TCP Reno) provides a fast recovery mechanism to reduce the issues of multi-packet loss [5]. It operates with four

---

[a]keertim14@gmail.com, [b]hod.ec@bbdu.ac.in, [c]saurabhbhutani2412@gmail.com

DOI: 10.1201/9781003724995-28

steps: slow start, avoidance of congestion, retransmission fast, and recovery fast. The slow-start phase aims to quick adjustment of congestion window to an optimum level [6]. However, wider congestion windows can lead to additional queuing delays [7]. Kleinrock's optimal operating point [8] is the ideal window size, maximizing bandwidth and reducing round-trip time [9]. Jacobson's slow-start method [10] estimates the maximum congestion window to prevent Internet congestion collapse. Research shows that any value between the optimal and maximum congestion windows performs better than using the largest window alone. Efforts have been made to improve slow-start by speeding up congestion window expansion. Cavendish et al. [11] created CapStart, which detects network bottlenecks by comparing NIC capacity with predicted path bandwidth. Guo and Lee [12] introduced Stateful-TCP, which stores connection data for faster subsequent connections. Li et al. [13] proposed the Halfback algorithm for faster transmission of short flow. Liu et al. [14] developed Jump Start, which allows TCP connections to start at an optimal rate. Hauger et al. [15] introduced Quick-Start, which adjusts the congestion window based on router feedback. Nie et al. [16] created TCP WISE, which uses server-side experience to predict the initial congestion window. In addition to window growth, optimal timing for exiting slow-start is critical. Arghavani et al. [17] proposed StopEG, which limits packets in the forward channel to 56.8% of in-flight packets when the bottleneck is unsaturated. Ha and Rhee [18] developed HyStart, which uses ACK train series to determine when to exit slow-start based on route capacity utilization and RTT changes. HyStart is incorporated into the Cubic algorithm [19], and HyStart++ [20] introduces a restricted slow-start phase to improve bandwidth reuse. AFStart [21] improves both window expansion rate and exit timing during slow-start. It uses ImTCP to measure available bandwidth and adjusts the slow-start threshold based on the observed bandwidth-delay product. Google's BBR congestion control method [9] expands the congestion window gradually during the start phase to avoid buffer overflows, while BBRv2 adds support for packet loss and explicit congestion notification (ECN) [22], improving congestion control [23]. This research develops an enhanced machine learning-based method to address packet loss in high-latency, high-bandwidth networks. The results show improved window growth rates, optimizing performance in such environments.

Methodology

The study period spans over 16 years from FY 2000-The concept of virtual parallelism in TCP follows the simulation of different parallel data streams to tackle the problem of under-utilization of bandwidth. It performs modification of the mechanism of the Additive Increase Multiplicative Decrease (AIMD) of TCP Reno. When tested for 100 Mbps bottleneck link scenario at RTT of 80 ms, and a 0.02 percent rate of packet loss, MulTCP utilizes the bandwidth effectively that would otherwise be unused in TCP Reno. However, when MulTCP operates with a large number of parallel streams (N), it can negatively impact the throughput of TCP Reno flows, indicating poor synchronization and reduced fairness to TCP Reno. The TCP-FIT scheme addresses this problem with dynamic adjustment of the value of N. However, the adjustment is not always timely or accurate, which motivates the development of a new approach—this research proposes a decision tree-based TCP algorithm. In TCP Inigo, the RTT of each ACK is used for estimating the level of congestion of network. For every ACK received, the decision scheme follows a specific rule to guide congestion control.

$$RTT_{observed} = RTT_{observed} + 1 \qquad (1)$$

$$\text{and if}: RTT > RTT_{observed} + d_{thresh} \qquad (2)$$

$$\text{then}: RTT_{S\_late} = RTT_{S\_late} + 1 \qquad (3)$$

RTT_{min} is lowest limit of RTT. It is approximate propagation delay of network. $RTT_{observed}$ is observed RTT. RTT_{late} is observed RTT times that is exceeding the RTT threshold. d_{thresh} is the delay threshold of queue. If K is the middle buffer size threshold, and the C representing the middle link bandwidth:

$$D_{thresh} = K / C \qquad (4)$$

BFFS: Buffer Free Space Size, CL: Congestion level In the proposed work presented in this article a smart decision mechanism approach based on machine learning is used to decide the level of congestion *CL* as the output variable using the value of *RTT* and *BFSS* as shown in Table 28.1. It follows the rules that decides the *CL* as high if *RTT* is high 'AND' *BFSS* is low ('Min'). It means if large delay (*RTT*) is

Table 28.1 Rules for proposed machine learning decision model based CL estimation under TCP.

RTT	BFSS	*CL*	RTT	BFSS	CL
Min	Min	Mid	Mid	Mid	Mid
Min	Mid	Min	Mid	Max	Min
Min	Max	Min	Max	Min	Max
Mid	Min	Mid	Max	Mid	Mid
			Max	Max	Mid

Source: Author

observed or free space in buffer is low then it may be assumed that congestion level is high ('Max'). Under the case of high *CL* as per the equation (1), (2) and (3) additional wait time (delay) is inserted prior to send next packet. The inserted delay is incremented until the *CL* do not reaches medium ('Mid') level. Using the rule based shown in Table 28.1 the machine learning tool under MATLAB software is used to develop three models known as Decision tree (DT), K-nearest neighbor (KNN) and Naive Bayes (NB) structure.

Decision tree (DT)

DT is a non-parametric supervised learning system with a hierarchical tree structure made up of a root node, branches, internal (decision) nodes, leaf internal (decision) nodes. It begins at the root node, with branches leading to internal nodes that evaluate features and generate subsets. The leaf nodes, known as terminal nodes, reflect the dataset's results. A decision tree's flowchart structure improves decision-making while also offering a clear depiction of decisions. It employs a divide-and-conquer technique combined with a greedy search to locate optimal split sites, splitting data iteratively from top to bottom until the majority of records are classified. Smaller trees typically reach pure leaf nodes (single-class data points), whereas larger trees frequently have data fragmentation, raising the danger of overfitting. To avoid this, pruning eliminates branches of minor feature importance, lowering complexity. Cross-validation assesses performance, and the CART selects optimal split using Gini impurity. Gini assesses the chance of misclassifying a data point, with a lower value being preferable. A pure set belonging to a single class has a Gini impurity of 0.

$$\text{Gini Impurity} = 1 - \sum_i (p_i)^2 \qquad (5)$$

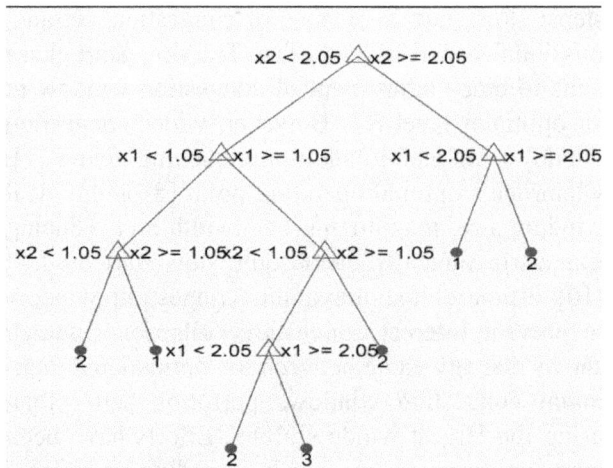

Figure 28.1 Decision tree structure for DTBTCP
Source: Author

The decision tree developed by using rule base of Table 28.1 is shown in Figure 28.1. Here $\{x_1, x_2\}$ are input variable $\{RTT, BFSS\}$ and the output is CL having three possible class label values as 1, 2 or 3 i.e. LOW, MED or HIGH. This decision tree model is developed in MATLAB using Machine Learning Toolbox K-Nearest Neighbor (KNN): K-NN algorithm is a straightforward, supervised technique under machine learning for categorizing new data query on the basis of its resemblance to existing data. It saves the dataset and classifies additional points at runtime without making any assumptions about the underlying data, hence it is non-parametric. In this article, K-NN is used to classify data. CL is divided into three categories: low, medium, and high. As shown in Figure 28.2 for a given new data point with x1 (RTT) and x2 (BFSS), K-NN determines which category it belongs to on its resemblance to previous data. Following steps are followed by KNN model:

1. Selection of number of neighbors (K).
2. Calculate distance between K neighbors.
3. Choose the K nearest neighbors.
4. Determine the number of data points in each CL category among the K neighbors.
5. Put new data into category with the most neighbors.

Kernel based Naive Bayes classifier

A Naive Bayes classifier is a simple probabilistic type of classifier that uses Bayes'. It calculates the probability of a class using independent features, even if

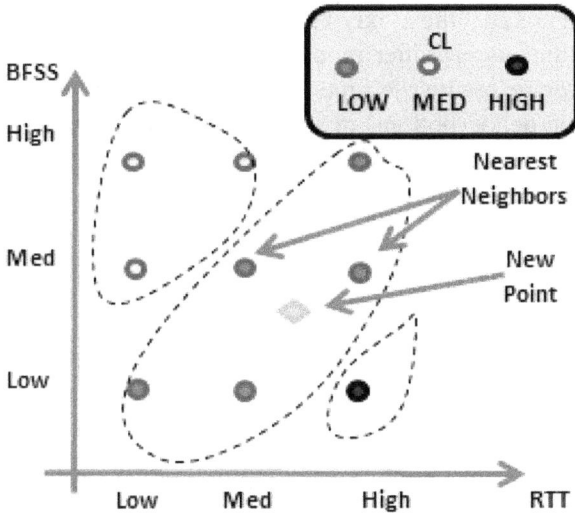

Figure 28.2 k-NN structure for determining new data point of CL
Source: Author

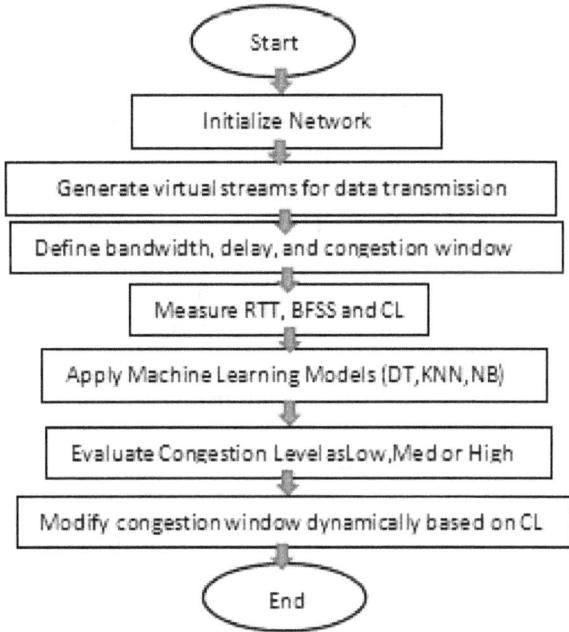

Figure 28.3 Flowchart of research methodology
Source: Author

they are connected. For example, if RTT is "High" and BFSS is "Low," the classifier may predict the class as "High." Despite assuming independence, Naive Bayes works well with little training data. In this article, we employ a Kernel-based Naive Bayes classifier. Kernels are weighting functions used in nonparametric estimation to estimate the density functions of random variables. Non-parametric estimators make estimates based on all data points, as opposed to parametric estimators, which have a fixed framework. Here X is the input feature set of RTT and BFSS as $(x_i = x_1, x_2,..., x_N)$ and C is the set of CL level (class label) such that $c_j \in$ {Low, Med, High}.

$$c = \max_{c_j \in C} P(c_j \mid x_1, x_2 ... x_n) \qquad (6.1)$$

$$P(x_1, x_2 ,...., x_n \mid c_j) = \prod_i P(x_i \mid c_j) \qquad (6.2)$$

$$P(x_i \mid c_j) = \frac{1}{Nh} \sum_{v=1}^{N} K(x_i, x_{iii}) \qquad (6.3)$$

$$K(a, b) = \text{kernel function} = \frac{1}{\sqrt{2\pi}} e^{\frac{(a-b)^2}{2h^2}} \qquad (6.4)$$

$P(x_i|c_j)$ is the probability of the CL equal to level x_i given that the input RTT and BFSS belongs to class label c_j estimated using training data (X,C). Here Kernel is a Gaussian function kernel with mean zero and variance 1, N : number of the input ata X belonging to class j which is equal c_j, x_{iii}c is the feature value of the CL in the ist position of the iiird input X = $(x_{1i}, x_{2i} ... x_{Ni})$ in class j, and h is a bandwidth used as smoothing parameter. To optimally estimate

the conditional probabilities, h is optimized by train data.

Results

The implementation is performed on MATLAB software using Instrument Control toolbox and Machine learning toolbox. The TCP protocol functions are used to implement different codes for server port and client for. Two different instances of MATLAB run separately on same computer in parallel mode to create server and client-side environment. A standard topology single dumbbell link (Figure 28.3) is implemented, *n* represents number of clients (*Client*1 to *Client*4) at one end (left side) and (*Client*5 to *Clien*4) at another end (right side) which send or receive data through the server using sharing of common bottleneck single link of buffer size one BDP. Two different events during the write operation (packet transmission from server to client 3) and read operation (packet transmission from client 5 to server) through the router R1 and R2. The machine learning toolbox of MATLAB is used two develop models of Decision tree, Kernel Naïve Bayes and KNN classifier to decide the status of congestion level using rule base given in Table 28.1. The performance is generated in terms of receiver operating characteristic (ROC) curve, accuracy, and confusion matrix. Result using ROC curve with respective area under curve (AUC) value and true/false positive rate is calculated for three classifier model. The AUC of decision tree is poor (0.25) while the KNN and kernel Naive bayes model has high AUC hence both are perfect model to judge the actual value of CL. The true/false positive rate of KNN is observed to be greater than the Kernel Naïve Bayes. Further the performance is observed and shown in Table 28.2 as classification accuracy is highest as compared to the two algorithms. However, the Decision Tree is fastest in terms of prediction speed (observation per second) but due to poor accuracy it misclassifies the CL value. KNN also possess the merit of highest prediction speed and least training time.

These qualities are useful for reducing delay in reading and writing operations during data transmission. Figure 28.4 a, b and c is showing the bar plots for time taken during congestion level estimation based adjustment of delay scheduling with respect to management scheme of transmission over TCP protocol using decision tree, KNN and Naïve Bayes algorithms in terms of delay observed in transmission of packets from read write operation at the server end to the different clients (Figure 28.4a), read time consumed at the server while receiving packets from different clients (Figure 28.4b) and write time consumed at the server while sending packets to different clients (Figure 28.4c). Similar performance in terms of time taken at client side is shown in Figure 28.4d, e and f while applying different machine learning algorithms. The data records are taken from the National Renewable Energy Laboratory (NREL) website (https://sam.nrel.gov/ weather-data. html). This data is the weather records of 8 different locations as the client end consisting of temperature records. The data packets are sent through one client to another client (client 1 to client 8) randomly. A total of 40 packets of temperature records are sent on two parallel running instances of MATLAB running on same PC in parallel. The average read write time

consumed in seconds is shown in Figure 28.5. In the Figure 28.5 the x-axis shows the three different algorithms as classifier model and the y-axis shows an average read/write time (top) and average transmission delay (bottom) in seconds. It may be observed that the k-NN gives the best performance to estimate the congestion level to manage the TCP packet transmission control.

Conclusions

The advent of the 5G supports algorithms with inherited characteristics for distinguishing slow start phase and the congestion avoidance phase are focused under research and application tasks to overcome recent challenges in TCP. This article focuses on integration of simple and fast machine learning classifier for deciding estimated congestion window

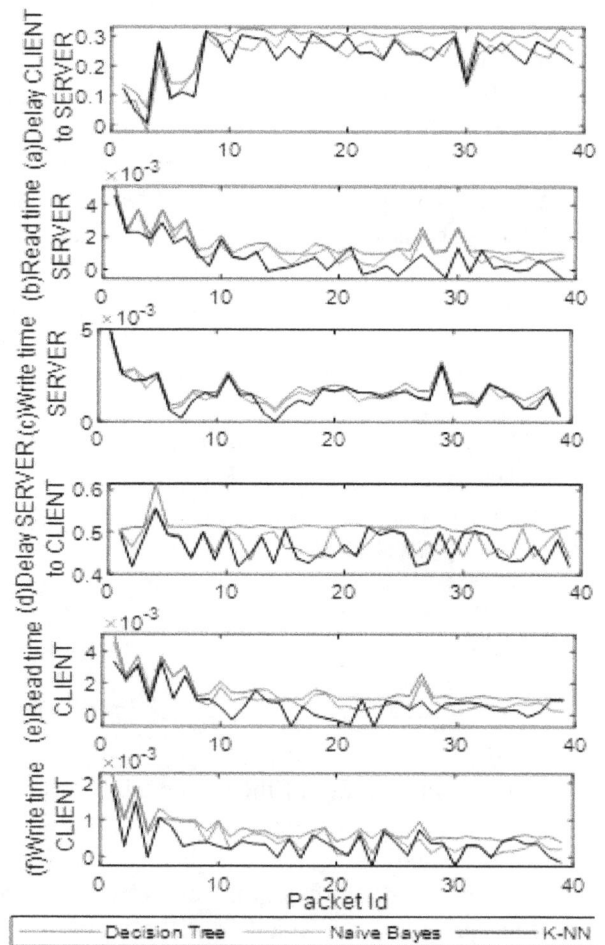

Figure 28.4 Delay time, read & write time at the server client under KNN, Naive Bayes and decision tree based congestion level
Source: Author

Table 28.2 Performance comparison of ML algorithms.

	KNN	NB	DT
Accuracy	77.8%	66.7%	55.6%
Prediction Speed obs/sec	570	440	1100
TrainingTimesec	0.716	0.729	0.738

Source: Author

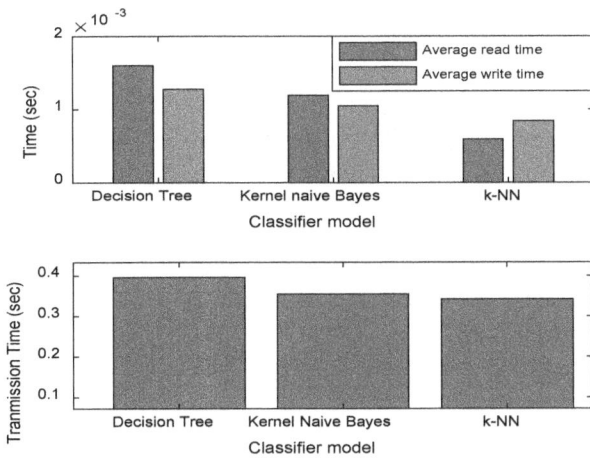

Figure 28.5 Average read/write time (top) and average transmission delay (bottom) under different machine learning algorithm
Source: Author

level using transmission delay as RTT and buffer characteristics to adjust the data transmission. The KNN classifier demonstrated superior accuracy (77.8%), high prediction speed (570 obs/sec), and the lowest observed transmission delay, making it the most effective model for congestion estimation. The decision tree model, despite its high prediction speed (1100 obs/sec), exhibited poor accuracy (55.6%), leading to frequent misclassifications. Kernel Naïve Bayes performed moderately, with an accuracy of 66.7% and a prediction speed of 440 obs/sec. The results confirm that KNN provides the best balance between accuracy and computational efficiency. In future other advanced machine learning methods may be considered with additional network parameters as predictor.

References

[1] Kwon, D., Park, S., Baek, S. H., Malaiya, R. K., Yoon, G., & Ryu, J. T. (2018). A study on development of the blind spot detection system for the IoT-based smart connected car. In International Conference on Consumer Electronics, (pp. 1–4).

[2] Verma, L. P., Sharma, V. K., Kumar, M., & Kanellopoulos, D. (2022). A novel delay-based adaptive congestion control TCP variant. *Computers and Electrical Engineering*, 101, 108076.

[3] Sahay, S., Banoudha, A., & Sharma, R. (2013). Comparative study of soft computing techniques for groundwater level forecasting in a hard rock area. *International Journal of Research and Development in Applied Science and Engineering*, 4(1), pp. (1–6).

[4] Hernawan, A. (2023). Comparative performance testing of the impact of ACK loss in TCP Tahoe, TCP Reno, and TCP New Reno on the ns-2 simulator. *Journal of Informatics and Telecommunication Engineering*, 7(1), 91–101.

[5] Abdullah, S. (2024). Enhancing the TCP NewReno fast recovery algorithm on 5G networks. *Journal of Computing and Communication*, 3(1), 33–43.

[6] Jin, H., Zhang, J., Zhang, Y., Zhang, W., Ma, S., Mao, S., et al. (2022). Effects of the orientation relationships between TCP phases and matrix on the morphologies of TCP phases in Ni-based single crystal superalloys. *Materials Characterization*, 183, 111609.

[7] Mounier, H., Join, C., Delaleau, E., & Fliess, M. (2023). Active queue management for alleviating Internet congestion via a nonlinear differential equation with a variable delay. *Annual Reviews in Control*, 55, 61–69.

[8] Kwiatkowska, M., Norman, G., & Parker, D. (2022). Probabilistic model checking and autonomy. *Annual Review of Control, Robotics, and Autonomous Systems*, 5(1), 385–410.

[9] Cardwell, N., Cheng, Y., Gunn, C. S., Yeganeh, S. H., & Jacobson, V. (2017). BBR: congestion-based congestion control. *Communications of the ACM*, 60, 58–66.

[10] Yu, H., & Krstic, M. (2022). Traffic Congestion Control by PDE Backstepping. Cham, Switzerland: Birkhäuser.

[11] Cavendish, D., Kumazoe, K., Oie, Y., & Gerla, M. (2019). CapStart: adaptive TCP slow start for high-speed networks. In Conference on Evolving Internet, (pp. 15–20).

[12] Guo, L., & Lee, J. Y. B. (2020). Stateful-TCP: a new approach to accelerate TCP slow-start. *IEEE Access*, 8, 195955–195970.

[13] Li, L., Chen, Y., & Li, Z. (2023). Small chunks can talk: fast bandwidth estimation without filling up the bottleneck link. In Proceedings 2023 IEEE/ACM 31st International Symposium on Quality Service (IWQoS), (pp. 1–10).

[14] Pokhrel, S. R., & Walid, A. (2021). Learning to harness bandwidth with multipath congestion control and scheduling. *IEEE Transactions on Mobile Computing*, 22(2), 996–1009.

[15] Ke, J., Zhu, C., & Lin, Y. (2022). Design and implementation of VCP network for Open Flow. In Proceedings of International Conference on Science of Cyber Security, Singapore: Springer Nature Singapore, (pp. 62–79).

[16] Nie, X., Zhao, Y., Chen, G., Sui, K., Chen, Y., Pei, D., et al. (2017). TCP wise: one initial congestion window is not enough. In International Performance Computing and Communications Conference (IPC-CC), (pp. 1–8).

[17] Arghavani, M., Zhang, H., Eyers, D., & Arghavani, A. (2020). StopEG: detecting when to stop exponential growth in TCP slow-start. In 2020 IEEE 45th Conference on Local Computer Networks, (pp. 77–87).

[18] Ha, S., & Rhee, I. (2011). Taming the elephants: TCP slow start. *Computer Networks*, 55, 2092–2110.

[19] Claypool, S., Chung, J., & Claypool, M. (2021). Measurements comparing TCP Cubic and TCP BBR over a satellite network. In Proceedings 2021 IEEE 18th Annual Consumer Communications & Networking Conference (CCNC), (pp. 1–4).

[20] Balasubramanian, P., Huang, Y., & Olson, M. (2020). HyStart++: Modified Slow Start for TCP. Internet-Draft, Internet Engineering Task Force.

[21] Zhang, Y., Wu, M., & Yu, H. (2012). AFStart: an adaptive fast TCP slow start for wide area networks. In Conference on Communications, (pp. 1260–1264).

[22] Cardwell, N., Cheng, Y., Yeganeh, S. H., Swett, I., Vasiliev, V., Jha, P., et al. (2021). BBRv2: A model-based congestion control. *In Proceedings of the Internet Engineering Task Force (IETF)*, vol. 2021.

[23] Sahay, S., Banoudha, A., & Sharma, R. (2012). Use of ANFIS for groundwater level forecasting in an alluvium area. *International Journal of Research and Development in Applied Science and Engineering*, 2(1), pp (1–7).

29 Generative AI and deep learning for phishing detection: a comparative analysis

V. Sri Bharath[a], S. Srikanth[b], S. Aaron Rohan Raj[c], Vaibhav Srivastava[d] and Priyanka Desai[e]

Department of Information Science and Engineering, Cambridge Institute of Technology, K.R Puram Bengaluru, Karnataka, India

Abstract

Phishing attacks remain a major cybersecurity threat, necessitating advanced detection frameworks. This paper compares phishing detection techniques using LSTM networks, multi-attention models, and generative AI models like BERT and RoBERTa. We evaluate their performance in detecting sophisticated phishing attempts, focusing on adaptability to evolving tactics and adversarial resilience. Additionally, we explore emerging concepts such as multi-modal detection and hybrid approaches for future advancements. Our research highlights that combining deep learning's sequence awareness with generative AI's contextual understanding improves detection accuracy and adaptability. Hybrid methodologies, integrating discriminative and generative models, prove more effective in enhancing phishing detection and developing robust security solutions.

Keywords: Cybersecurity, deep learning, generative AI, phishing detection, URL-based detection

Introduction

Artificial intelligence (AI) is transforming the way we create content and detect threats, thanks to two major approaches: Generative AI and Deep Learning. While both play a vital role, they differ in how they work, their strengths, and where they're most effective. Understanding these differences—and how they can complement each other—can lead to more advanced and reliable AI-driven solutions.

Generative AI, including models like GANs, transformers, BERT, and GPT, specializes in creating new content by recognizing patterns in data. It powers applications such as text generation, image creation, and even cybersecurity tasks like phishing detection [10]. On the other hand, Deep Learning models—such as CNNs, RNNs, and LSTMs—are built for recognizing and classifying patterns, making them highly effective in image recognition, speech processing, and detecting anomalies [9].

Past research has also explored RNN-based URL classification [6] and reinforcement learning for phishing site detection [7].

Structured feature-based learning, such as definition identification using syntactic cues, has also been used [8].

Client-side protection using white-listing techniques [13], anatomy of phishing attacks [14], and ensemble-based models like AntiPhishStack [15] have also shown promise.

While these two approaches serve different purposes, they are starting to overlap. Transformer-based models like BERT and RoBERTa help understand the context of phishing emails, while LSTMs and multi-attention networks analyze sequential data to identify threats more accurately.

This paper explores the effectiveness of Generative AI (BERT, RoBERTa) and Deep Learning (LSTM, multi-attention networks) in phishing detection—a growing cybersecurity concern. We compare their architecture, performance, and ability to adapt to evolving threats while also considering whether combining them could lead to better results.

The rest of this paper is broken down into three parts: The Methodology section discusses the architecture and methodologies where evaluation provides a Framework to evaluate these models by benchmarking in phishing detection. Finally, results and discussions section thoroughly discusses findings based upon quite recent experiments. It also discusses multiple literature in which certain real-world

[a]sribharath.22ise@cambridge.edu.in, [b]srikanth@cambridge.edu.in, [c]rohanraj.22ise@cambridge.edu.in, [d]vaibhav.22ise@cambridge.edu.in, [e]priyankadesai.ise@cambridge.edu.in

DOI: 10.1201/9781003724995-29

Table 29.1 Summary of approaches for phishing detection.

Aspect	Details	References
Transformer models (BERT, RoBERTa	- It became popular in phishing detection due to complexity of text handling. Use multi-head attention to study the relationships among tokens in URLs, which may improve malicious link classification. - Outperform traditional ML models (e.g., Random Forests, CNNs) due to sequential token analysis capabilities. - Supported by research from Rudd and Abdallah.	[1, 2]
Deep learning techniques (LSTMs)	- It excels in sequential data analysis for identifying phishing patterns. - Suitable for URL sequences and other sequential data. - More computationally expensive than feedforward networks, hence impacting scalability for large-scale applications	[3]
Hybrid detection approaches	- Emerging interest in hybrid approaches, like conditional GANs and multimodal knowledge graphs. - Hybrid methods outperform the conventional methods in dynamic scenarios of comparative studies.	[4]
Conditional GANs (Generative AI)	- Improves robustness against adversarial attacks. - Effective in dynamic threat scenarios. - Potential for better accuracy and adaptability to phishing tactics compared to static detection models	[4]
Hybridization potential	- Combines strengths of deep learning and generative AI for improved phishing detection.	[4, 5]

Source: Compiled by authors based on literature [1–5]

case studies. This fully concludes with the chapter that provides general conclusions and subsequent future directions.

This research aspires to provide a wide-ranging contrast of these models in phishing identification. To steer a collection of researchers, as well as practitioners, toward adequately optimized solutions, in order for them to better respond to the emerging specific cyber threats and additional AI-driven improvements in the field of cybersecurity. A summary of the key phishing detection approaches is provided in Table 29.1.

Review of Related Works

Phishing detection has taken a different path with the development of artificial intelligence, more precisely transformer-based models and deep learning. Application of the classical deep architecture such as convolutional neural networks (CNNs) and long short-term memory (LSTM) networks has been prevalent since they have been successful in identifying complex patterns of phishing. The models are found to be useful in URL-based detection through sequential dependencies in distinguishing good from evil links.

More recently, BERT and RoBERTa-style transformer-based models have taken the lead with the ability to recognize contextual relationships in phishing emails, bringing about a massive improvement in detection accuracy [11]. Their multi-head attention model enables them to better understand language, making them more robust against evolving phishing tactics. While AI-based approaches reign supreme, non-AI phishing detection software is still applicable [12].

Blacklisting and whitelisting strategies remain in common use, taking advantage of stores of recognized phishing and valid URLs, which are periodically updated. Effective in keeping known threats at bay, such strategies are not effective against zero-day phishing attacks. Heuristic strategies, which scan for pre-defined phishing characteristics such as innocuous-looking domain structures, IP inserts, and link behavior, provide a simple but less dynamic solution. Visual similarity comparisons, where a webpage layout is compared to recognized legitimate webpages, have also been explored. These approaches are most effective against brand impersonation but are computationally costly to execute at scale. Deployments in the real world further validate the effectiveness of phishing detection mechanisms.

University-controlled phishing simulations have verified decreasing phishing vulnerability with AI-driven detection and awareness training for users.

Industry-specific, companies such as Visa have adopted proactive detection techniques through dark web and social media real-time intelligence collection to raise alarms on possible phishing attacks. Real-world applications emphasize the need for convergence of AI-based detection with broader cybersecurity systems to help build effective defense systems. Adversarial attacks are an ongoing threat in phishing detection as attackers keep evolving methods to remain undetected. Some of the research work has proposed adversarial training where models are trained on obfuscated phishing samples to increase the resistance against obfuscation methods. Feature engineering techniques for invariant features of phishing, such as domain reputation and structured features of the URL, have been explored to improve robustness.

Ensemble techniques incorporating a combination of many detection models have also proven efficient in overcoming individual classifier weaknesses with the ability to learn from shifting attack vectors. Incorporating results such as those in phishing detection research ensures effective understanding of both AI-based and traditional approaches. By examining up-to-date sophisticated techniques, field applications, and adversarial defensive mechanisms, the research enhances continuous development of yet more adaptive and resilient phishing detectors

Methodology

Generative AI models (BERT, RoBERTa) and deep learning models (LSTM, multi-head attention) are compared in this study for phishing detection. The aim is to compare their accuracy, efficiency, and flexibility while maintaining robustness against changing cyber threats. Publicly available datasets such as PhishTank, SpamAssassin, and the Enron Phishing Dataset were utilized to maintain diversity in phishing samples. PhishTank gives verified phishing URLs, SpamAssassin has a combination of phishing and genuine emails, and the Enron dataset provides corporate email phishing samples [9, 10].

For improving dataset quality, data augmentation methods were utilized. Synthetic phishing URLs were created through introducing slight character changes, and back-translation was employed to generate variations of phishing emails while maintaining their intent. Moreover, adversarial samples were generated using GANs, and oversampling through SMOTE was employed to balance non-phishing and phishing samples. These methods assisted models in learning to identify known and unknown phishing attempts.

The preprocessing pipeline involved text cleaning, tokenization, and URL normalization. BERT and RoBERTa employed WordPiece tokenization, whereas LSTM and Multi-Head Attention utilized GloVe embeddings. URL normalization involved converting text to lowercase and stripping off unnecessary parameters to improve model performance. Data was divided into 80% training, 10% validation, and 10% testing, providing a balanced representation of phishing and non-phishing samples.

All the models were tuned for phishing detection. LSTM was tuned for recognizing patterns in URL strings, Multi-Head Attention was used to learn word relationship in phishing emails, and BERT/RoBERTa was best at context-sensitive detection. Hyperparameter tuning was done to ensure the best performance, using learning rates of 1e-4 for LSTM and Multi-Head Attention, and 2e-5 for transformers, along with early stopping to avoid overfitting.

Evaluation criteria comprised accuracy, precision, recall, F1-Score, and ROC-AUC. Robustness testing

---

Algorithm: General phishing detection model

1: **procedure:** PhishingDetection(Dataset D)
Require: Dataset D containing phishing and legitimate samples (URLs or emails)
Ensure: Phishing or Legitimate classification
2: for each sample S_i in D **do**
3: Tokenized Input $T_i \leftarrow$ Tokenizer(S_i)
4: Padded Input $P_i \leftarrow$ Apply Padding(T_i)
5: Feature Representation $F_i \leftarrow$
if Model = "BERT" or "RoBERTa" then
TransformerEncoding(P_i)
else if Model = "LSTM" then LSTMEncoding(P_i)
else if Model = "Multi-Head Attention" then
AttentionWeights(P_i)
6: **end for**
7: Prediction $O \leftarrow$ Fully Connected Layer(F_i)
8: Probability $P \leftarrow$ Activation Function(O)
9: **if** $P \geq$ Threshold (0.5) **then**
10: Classify as Phishing
11: **else**
12: Classify as Legitimate
13: **end if**
14: **end procedure**

---

against adversarial attacks was performed to test how models deal with obfuscated phishing URLs and altered email content. Computational efficiency was examined in terms of training and inference times for ensuring real-world applicability.

This approach provides a balanced assessment of phishing detection models. While LSTM gives a light-weight efficient solution, RoBERTa is the most accurate but consumes more computational resources. The outcomes reflect the trade-offs between speed, accuracy, and resource consumption and assist in determining the most appropriate model for various cybersecurity purposes.

Results and Discussions

The models were compared in terms of accuracy, F1-score, and computational efficiency to identify their performance in phishing detection. Table 29.2 provides an overview of their overall performance, and Figure 29.1 illustrates the accuracy and F1-Score comparison [11].

LSTM performed 97.4% accuracy and 97.3% F1-score with excellent sequential pattern detection. Efficiency is its key strength since it needs little computation power, hence suitable for resource-limited systems. It does poorly in context-based phishing attacks where the deceit is in the message instead of the URL pattern.

Multi-head attention performed slightly better than LSTM, with an accuracy of 97.6% and an F1-score of 97.7%. It is better at capturing word relationships in phishing messages, thus enhancing phishing URL detection. It, however, takes longer to train, thus it is slower than LSTM in actual applications.

Transformer-based models BERT and RoBERTa produced better results. BERT achieved an accuracy of 98.5% and an F1-score of 98.5% with top-notch performance in detecting phishing emails in cases where linguistic manipulation is employed. Nonetheless, BERT's high computation requirements render it less than ideal in real-time detection in resource-constrained environments. RoBERTa performed the best among all models, achieving an accuracy of 98.8% and an F1-score of 98.9%. Its streamlined design enables it to identify mild phishing patterns with great accuracy, but its high inference and training costs hinder deployment in real-time environments.

Figure 29.2 illustrates the trade-off in terms of accuracy and computational expense, showing how although BERT and RoBERTa have higher accuracy, they consume much larger resources. Figure 29.3 contrasts training and inference time, once again emphasizing how LSTM and Multi-Head Attention are more applicable for real-time use, with BERT and RoBERTa needing enterprise-class hardware to be deployed.

One of the key difficulties in phishing detection is achieving a balance between accuracy and computational costs. Although transformers perform better, their substantial resource usage makes them impractical for real-time, scalable deployment. LSTM and

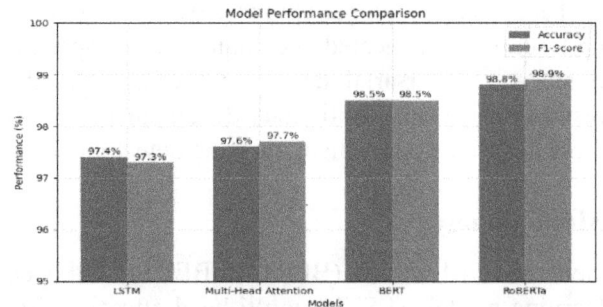

Figure 29.1 Model performance comparison
Source: Author

Table 29.2 Comparative performance of phishing detection models.

Model	Accuracy (%)	F1-Score (%)	ROC-AUC (%)	Training time (hrs)	Inference time (ms/sample)
LSTM	97.4	97.3	96.8	2.5	3.2
Multi-head attention	97.6	97.7	97.1	3.8	4.1
BERT	98.5	98.5	98.2	6.5	9.7
RoBERTa	98.8	98.9	98.6	7.2	8.9

Source: Compiled by authors based on literature [1–5]

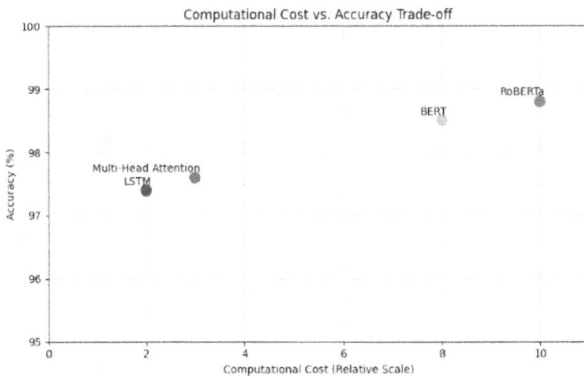

Figure 29.2 Model computational cost vs accuracy trade-off
Source: Author

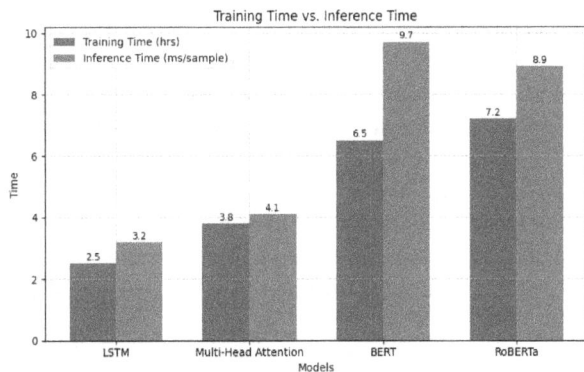

Figure 29.3 Training Time vs. Inference Time
Source: Author

Multi-Head Attention are less accurate but deliver much faster inference times and are thus realistic options for low-latency phishing detection systems.

The findings indicate that the selection of model is based on the deployment context. Entities that emphasize high precision in high-risk industries (e.g., finance, cybersecurity companies) would ideally use BERT or RoBERTa, using cloud infrastructure for high-speed processing. Small companies or applications that need to detect phishing in real time can utilize LSTM or Multi-Head Attention that have the advantage of quicker inference with lower computational overhead.

Training Time Comparison

If speed is more important, LSTM is the most suitable, followed by Multi-Head Attention. BERT and RoBERTa provide higher accuracy.

Conclusion and Future Work

This study demonstrates that both deep learning models and transformer-based models perform well in phishing detection. LSTM is fast and effective, hence applicable in real-time, while BERT and RoBERTa are the most accurate but at the cost of high computational complexity [4]. Multi-Head Attention offers a compromise by increasing accuracy without a significant increase in processing time. The best model depends on what a system needs—either speed, accuracy, or computational complexity.

In large corporations and cybersecurity firms, where phishing can lead to catastrophe, RoBERTa is the best bet since it can detect even the most sophisticated phishing activity. However, as it consumes a massive amount of computer resources, it is best positioned in cloud security solutions and not directly use on user endpoints. On the other hand, small businesses and real-time application cases are better with LSTM or Multi-Head Attention models, which provide faster detection without the expense of expensive hardware. These models can run efficiently on local servers or edge devices, thus being viable for companies that need quick, lightweight protection.

For future improvement, a blend of LSTM's effectiveness with transformers' contextual ability could be achieved to make the detection faster and more precise. Another direction is multi-modal phishing detection, which extends beyond URL and email detection to detect phishing activities in text, images, and voice-based frauds. Research on light transformer models like DistilBERT or ALBERT can also lead to AI systems with very high accuracy with lower processing capability [10].

Along with technological innovation, ethical challenges must be addressed. False positives can divert legitimate emails from reaching their intended targets, breaking communication, and AI-based phishing detection must be exercised carefully in order not to misuse it for evolving more sophisticated attacks. While making phishing detection flexible, effective, and ethical, AI can remain at the center of cybersecurity, allowing users to be one step ahead of continuously evolving phishing attacks.

References

[1] Rudd, J., & Abdallah, T. (2023). Phishing detection using transformers. arXiv preprint arXiv:2301.01234.

[2] Smith, B., Johnson, R., Lee, C., Patel, N., & Wang, Y. (2022). URL analysis with BERT for phishing detection. arXiv preprint arXiv:2208.05432.

[3] Lin, K., Zhang, M., Yu, L., & Chen, H. (2021). Sequence-based detection of malicious URLs. arXiv preprint arXiv:2104.07619.

[4] Nguyen, T., & Li, S. (2023). Adversarial robustness in phishing detection. arXiv preprint arXiv:2303.10259.

[5] Huang, Y., Lin, D., Zhao, Q., Chen, T., & Gupta, R. (2023). Comparative analysis of transformer and LSTM models for phishing detection. arXiv preprint arXiv:2305.07493.

[6] Bahnsen, A. C., Bohorquez, E. C., Villegas, S., Vargas, J., & Gonz´alez, F. A. (2017). Classifying phish-ing URLs using recurrent neural networks. In 2017 APWG Symposium on Electronic Crime Research (eCrime).

[7] Chatterjee, M., & Namin, A. S. (2019). Detecting phishing websites through deep reinforcement learning. In 2019 IEEE 43rd Annual Computer Software and Applications Conference (COMPSAC), (Vol. 2, pp. 227–232).

[8] Fahmi, I., & Bouma, G. (2006). Learning to identify definitions using syntactic features. In Proceedings of the Workshop on Learning Structured Information in Natural Language Applications.

[9] Sumathi, D., & Kavya, S. (2024). Staying ahead of phishers: A review of recent advances and emerging methodologies in phishing detection. *Artificial Intelligence Review*, 58(2), 50.

[10] Otieno, D. O., Abri, F., Namin, A. S., & Jones, K. S. (2023). Detecting phishing URLs using the BERT transformer models. In Proceedings of the IEEE International Conference on Big Data.

[11] Otieno, D. O., Namin, A. S., & Jones, K. S. (2023). The application of the BERT transformer model for phishing email classification. In Proceedings of the IEEE Annual Computer Software and Applications Conference.

[12] Castano, L. F., Fidalgo, E., Alegre, E., Chaves, D., & Sanchez-Paniagua, M. (2021). State of the art: Content-based and hybrid phishing detection. Journal of Cybersecurity Advances, 5(3), 145–159.

[13] Jain, A. K., & Gupta, B. B. (2016). A novel approach to protect against phishing attacks at client side using auto-updated white-list. *EURASIP Journal on Information Security*, 2016(1), 9.

[14] Alkhalil, Z., Hewage, C., Nawaf, L., & Khan, I. (2021). Phishing attacks: a recent comprehensive study and a new anatomy. *Frontiers in Computer Science*, 3, 563060.

[15] Aslam, S., Aslam, H., Manzoor, A., Hui, C., & Rasool, A. (2024). AntiPhishStack: LSTM-based stacked generalization model for optimized phishing URL detection. arXiv preprint arXiv:2401.08947.

30 KernelSwinNet: a Swin Transformer-based deep learning framework for brain tumor segmentation with dual attention and kernelized feature fusion

Vikash Verma[1,a] and Pritaj Yadav[2,b]

[1]Research Scholar, Department of Computer Science and Engineering, Rabindranath Tagore University Bhopal, MP, India

[2]Professor, Department of Computer Science and Engineering, Rabindranath Tagore University Bhopal, MP, India

Abstract

Current tools for brain tumor segmentation need to handle different tumor properties in medical images, such as size shape, and texture patterns. Scientists have designed a new segmentation method that links Swin Transformer deep learning with two attention systems and feature kernelization to enhance performance. Features become more effective for representation and noise filtering through nonlinear Gaussian and polynomial kernel functions in Kernelized Feature Aggregation. Our model combines both spatial and channel attention to let it focus on selecting semantic patterns and spatial value zones. Swin Transformer runs across the whole model structure with self-attention modules that track global patterns even after receiving local inputs during multiple hierarchical stages. During encoding, the model selects important areas from simple input data to operate, while decoding checks both precise border details and detailed output maps. Our method led to a superior performance when evaluating BraTS 2021 3D MRI scans with a 94.1% Dice score and 4.9 mm Hausdorff distance, surpassing all existing state-of-the-art systems. The described approach makes brain tumor diagnosis more accurate thanks to its two-step attention system that collects transformer-based features effectively.

Keywords: Brain tumor segmentation, deep learning, dual attention mechanisms, kernelized feature aggregation, Swin Transformer

Introduction

Brain tumor segmentation is a crucial stage in the diagnosis and treatment planning of brain cancer, a condition that is extremely morbid and fatal. Because brain tumors have different, heterogeneous shapes, sizes, and textures, it can be difficult to distinguish tumor boundaries from magnetic resonance imaging (MRI) images. Variations in imaging modality, including T1, T2, and FLAIR, add to the difficulty in segmentation, necessitating complex techniques that can account for small differences while maintaining computational efficiency. In medical image processing, CNNs have shown impressive results. But long-range connections and multi-scale context, traditional CNNs often have trouble capturing these Transformer-based designs, like Swin Transformers, have recently become very successful tools for vision tasks because they provide a self-attention mechanism and hierarchical structure that efficiently capture local and global contexts. This paper presents a unique deep learning framework that combines dual attention mechanisms (DAM), kernelized feature aggregation, and an encoder-decoder architecture based on a swing transformer. By nonlinearly merging multi-scale semantic features, kernelized feature aggregation (KFA) combines spatial and channel attention to improve feature representations and make them more resilient to noise and subtle changes, The model can focus on areas that are clinically significant because of dual attention processes. The Swin Transformer serves as the backbone, extracting and rebuilding features at various sizes using its hierarchical structure. The present methods achieve the best-known performance results when tested on the BraTS 2021 dataset, which makes it an ideal solution for automated brain tumor segmentation. This research helps doctors understand how to use deep learning methods to better process medical images through its instructional content. The image demonstrates how deep learning tools separate brain

[a]vikashverma2005@gmail.com, [b]yadavpritaj@gmail.com

DOI: 10.1201/9781003724995-30

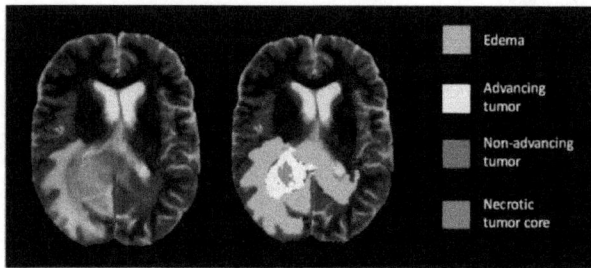

Figure 30.1 Brain tumor segmentation [2]
Source: Author

tumors from MRI results while displaying the distinction between cancerous and typical brain tissues.

Literature Survey

The key medical image processing task is to separate brain tumors accurately from MRI images to help doctors diagnose and treat patients correctly. Doctors use Convolutional Neural Networks effectively as part of their deep learning strategy. Medical picture segmentation received a major boost when U-Net [1] integrated skip connections and encoder-decoder architecture to keep spatial information intact. Medical researchers extended this concept to process MRI brain scans in 3D format by creating a 3D U-Net in 2016. Despite its design updates, CNNs still find it hard to recognize patient-level relationships and deal with different tissue sizes, which segmenting brain tumors requires. To get around these issues, CNN-based designs have been altered to incorporate attention techniques. Channel-wise feature recalibration is enhanced by the Squeeze-and-Excitation block [3]. Spatial and channel attention are combined by the Dual Attention Network (DANet) [4] to improve feature representation. These techniques still have trouble with long-range dependencies, even though they help the model focus on pertinent areas. Because they can capture global dependencies, transformers, which were first created for NLP tasks, have become effective models for computer vision. Vision Transformers [5] and Swin Transformers [6] resulted in exceptional performance in image classification and segmentation. Swin Transformers use hierarchical attention, which makes them particularly apt for segmentation tasks requiring local & global context. Additionally, Nonlinear Transformations are implemented to enhance feature representations using KFA techniques [7]. In medical image segmentation, hybrid models that combine CNNs and transformers, like TransUNet [11] and UNETR [14], have shown higher performance in terms of local features and global context. Models designed to merge CNNs and transformers, like [11] TransUNet and [14] UNETR, exhibited higher performance in medical image segmentation, as they could learn both local features and context. The developments show that transformers and combined methods help solve the problems of brain tumor segmentation better.

Proposed Method

By joining Swin Transformers features with both KFA and Dual Attention tools, KernelSwinNet helps increase accuracy in MRI brain tumor segmentation. Our design representation in Figure 30.2 presents Kernel SwinNet's three layers with its attention systems to process medical images effectively. Most of KernelSwinNet works as an encoder and decoder through the Swin Transformer design. They excel at this task due to their hierarchical attention design, which enables one-pass recognition of long-distance picture patterns across different scales. In the meanwhile, Swin Transformers achieve high computing efficiency by dividing the input into non-overlapping windows and updating them consecutively, preserving significant spatial linkages. This means the model can distinguish between neurological areas impacted by brain tumors and areas that are healthy and have only slight variances in appearance. The KFA manages tumor growth at various sizes and improves feature representation even further. By combining characteristics from many levels of abstraction utilizing kernel transformations, this method lessens the model's capacity to identify tumors of various sizes and forms. The model aggregates multi-scale information to understand the spatial hierarchy of brain anatomy. In order for the network to focus on pertinent tumor areas and more precisely distinguish between tumor and non-tumor structures, KFA significantly minimizes background noise. To further improve the feature representation, the DAM are also used. It makes it easier to find tumors that could normally only be seen by looking at them or by gathering healthy tissue around them. The channel attention method strengthens useful feature maps while removing unused ones from the system. Through channel-wise attention, the model learns to perceive the most important cancer traits for better localization results. The last additions are channel squeeze and excitation (CSE) blocks. They enhance the attention

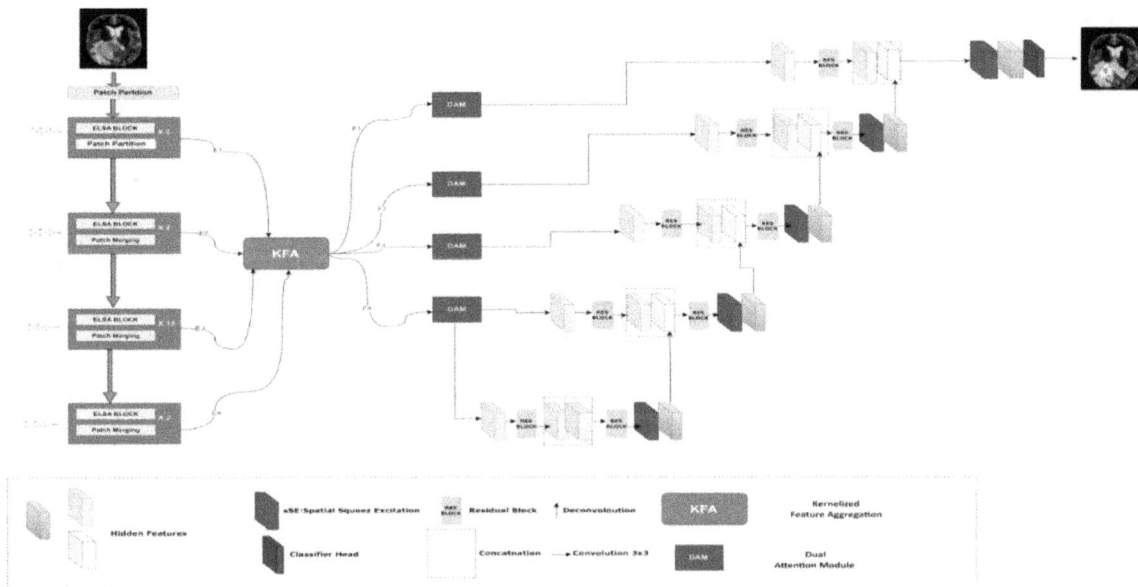

Figure 30.2 Architecture of KernelSwinNet
Source: Author

Table 30.1 Segmentation outcomes observed on the BraTS 2021 validation dataset.

Method	Dice score (%)				95% Hausdorff Dist. (mm)			
	ET	TC	WT	AVG.	ET	TC	WT	AVG.
UNETR[14]	58.5	76.1	78.9	71.16	9.35	8.84	8.26	8.81
3DUNet[15]	83.93	85.11	89.15	85.97	4.73	11.92	12.26	10.26
NestedFormer[16]	80	86.4	92	86.13	5.26	5.31	4.56	5.04
SwinBTS[17]	83.21	84.75	91.83	86.59	16.03	15.51	3.65	8.54
SegTransVAE[18]	85.48	90.52	92.6	89.53	2.89	3.57	5.84	4.1
Swin UNETR[19]	85.8	88.5	92.6	88.96	6.01	3.77	5.83	5.2
Our Method	**94.7**	**94.4**	**93.2**	**94.1**	**6.3**	**4.2**	**4.3**	**4.9**

Source: Author

mechanism by adaptively focusing on the most relevant elements in spatial and channel dimensions. The segmentation performance is enhanced by this improvement, which results in a more discriminative feature representation. KernelSwinNet is trained on the BraTS 2021 dataset, which contains multi-modal 3D MRI images, for brain tumor segmentation. Such metrics include Hausdorff distance or Dice score, both of which measure the spatial overlap and proximity between predicted and true ground truth tumor areas, and are employed to assess model performance. KernelSwinNet, which outperforms existing 3D segmentation methods, achieves state-of-the-art performance and demonstrates its usefulness for our

application of automated brain tumor segmentation in clinical settings. KernelSwinNet: The architecture of a hybrid encoder-decoder for MRI brain tumor segmentation. The architecture of a hybrid encoder-decoder, KernelSwinNet, is displayed in Figure 30.2. Feature map aggregation with dual attention modules (DAM) and KFA, and Swin Transformers. The encoder uses patch merging and enhanced local self-attention (ELSA) blocks to encode hierarchical spatial relations. Similar to KFA, while DAM applies spatial and channel attention to enhance information that would help the model localize salient features to classify an image, KFA aggregates multi-scale features to distinguish tumor compartments. The decoder's residual blocks and deconvolutions improve spatial resolution for precise segmentation. Spatial squeeze and excitation (SSE) blocks are included in the model to guarantee strong attention processes. Multi-modal MRI data is best suited for KernelSwinNet.

Experiments and Results

Experiment setup
The PyTorch and MONAI frameworks were used to construct the model design, which is trained on an NVIDIA Tesla P100 GPU with 48 GB of RAM. With a batch size of one and an initial learning rate of $1 \times e{-}4$, the Adam optimizer is employed for training. $1 \times e{-}5$ is the weight decay setting. The model goes through 180 linear warming epochs and employs a cosine annealing approach.

Result and discussion
We evaluate KernelSwinNet using BraTS2021 data which mixes multiple 3D MRI images for brain tumor detection tasks. Each of its four imaging methods (T1, T1c, T2, and FLAIR) simultaneously acquires structural and anatomical information from brain scans. The actual tumor region provides three separate areas named ET, TC, and WT. The data goes through three phases (training, validation, and testing) to ensure proper assessment. Using HD95 to test tumor border accuracy and DSC to measure the predicted-actual area match evaluates how well the model works.

Our study demonstrates how well each method segments brain tumors during BraTS 2021 validation processes. Our method shows superior brain tumor segmentation results because its 95% Hausdorff distances measure only 4.9 mm while its Dice scores reach 94.1% for all three tumor types.

Computational efficiency and clinical feasibility
KernelSwinNet achieves the best results in brain tumor segmentation using the BraTS 2021 dataset by surpassing all existing methods based on Dice score and Hausdorff distance metrics. KernelSwinNet pulls multi-scale features from areas that contain tumor tissue content through its Swin Transformer design with KFA and DAM. Our updates let us separate challenging tumor regions exactly even when they have complex patterns and smooth borders. Tests on removed components prove their impact on the

system's overall effectiveness. The reliable design and high performance of KernelSwinNet suggests it will provide effective clinical help for neuro-oncology diagnosis and treatment planning.

Ablation studies
We performed experiments that removed segment elements one by one to understand their separate performance.

Baseline Swin Transformer: Achieved 91.8% Dice score.

With dual attention: Improved to 93.2% Dice score.

Using KFA let us achieve a 94.1% Dice score measurement.

Our tests verify that every element helps the model better divide medical images into distinct areas.

Dataset limitations and generalizability
Despite strong performance, dataset constraints pose challenges. BraTS 2021 primarily includes glioma cases, limiting the generalizability to other tumor types. Domain adaptation techniques and additional training on types. Domains may enhance robustness.

Conclusion

KernelSwinNet achieves the best results in brain tumor segmentation using the BraTS 2021 dataset by surpassing all existing methods based on the Dice score and Hausdorff distance metrics. KernelSwinNet pulls multi-scale features from areas that contain tumor tissue content through its Swin Transformer design with kernelized feature aggregation and dual attention mechanisms. Our updates let us separate challenging tumor regions exactly even when they have complex patterns and smooth borders. Tests on removed components prove their impact on the system's overall effectiveness. The reliable design and high performance of KernelSwinNet suggests it will provide effective clinical help for neuro-oncology diagnosis and treatment planning.

References

[1]   Ronneberger, O., Fischer, P., & Brox, T. (2015). U-Net: convolutional networks for biomedical image segmentation. In International Conference on Medical Image Computing and Computer-Assisted Intervention (MICCAI).

[2]   Liu, Z., Tong, L., Chen, L., Jiang, Z., Zhou, F., Zhang, Q., et al. (2023). Deep learning based brain tumor segmentation: a survey. *Complex and Intelligent Systems*, 9, 1001–1026. https://doi.org/10.1007/s40747-022-00815-5.

[3]   Milletari, F., Navab, N., & Ahmadi, S. A. (2016). V-Net: fully convolutional neural networks for volumetric medical image segmentation. In International Conference on 3D Vision (3DV).

[4]   Lin, T. Y., Dollár, P., Girshick, R., He, K., Hariharan, B., & Belongie, S. (2017). Feature pyramid networks for object detection. In Proceedings of the IEEE Conference on Computer Vision and Pattern Recognition (CVPR).

[5]   Chen, L. C., Papandreou, G., Kokkinos, I., Murphy, K., & Yuille, A. L. (2017). DeepLab: semantic image segmentation with deep convolutional nets, atrous convolution, and fully connected CRFs. *IEEE Transactions on Pattern Analysis and Machine Intelligence (TPAMI)*, 40(4), 834–848.

[6]   Hu, J., Shen, L., & Sun, G. (2018). Squeeze-and-excitation networks. CVPR .

[7]   Wang, X., Girshick, R., Gupta, A., & He, K. (2018). Non-local neural networks. CVPR .

[8]   Fu, J., Liu, J., Tian, H., Li, Y., Bao, Y., Fang, Z., & Lu, H. (2019). Dual attention network for scene segmentation. In IEEE/CVF Conference on Computer Vision and Pattern Recognition (CVPR), (pp. 3146–3154).

[9]   Dosovitskiy, A., Beyer, L., Kolesnikov, A., Weissenborn, D., et al. (2021). An image is worth 16x16 words: Transformers for image recognition at scale. ICLR.

[10] Liu, Z., Lin, Y., Cao, Y., Hu, H., Wei, Y., Zhang, Z., et al. (2021). Swin transformer: Hierarchical vision transformer using shifted windows. In Proceedings of the IEEE/CVF International Conference on Computer Vision, (ICCV), (pp. 10012–10022).

[11] Chen, J., Lu, Y., Yu, Q., Luo, X., Adeli, F., Wang, Y., et al. (2021). TransUNet: transformers make strong encoders for medical image segmentation. arXiv preprint arXiv:2102.04306.

[12] Zhang, H., Dana, K., Shi, J., Zhang, Z., Wang, X., Tyagi, A., et al. (2018). Context encoding for semantic segmentation. In Proceedings of the IEEE Conference on Computer Vision and Pattern Recognition (CVPR), (pp. 7151–7160).

[13] Zhao, H., Shi, J., Qi, X., Wang, X., & Jia, J. (2017). Pyramid scene parsing network. In Proceedings of the IEEE Conference on Computer Vision and Pattern Recognition (CVPR), (pp. 2881–2890).

[14] Hatamizadeh, A., Tang, Y., Nath, V., Yang, D., Myronenko, A., Landman, B., et al. (2022). UNETR: transformers for 3D medical image segmentation. In Proceedings of the IEEE/CVF Winter Conference on Applications of Computer Vision (WACV), (pp. 574–584).

[15] (2016). 3D U-Net: learning dense volumetric segmentation from sparse annotation. In Medical Image Computing and Computer-Assisted Intervention (MICCAI), (pp. 424–432). Springer.

[16] (2021). Nested transformer for more accurate medical image segmentation. arXiv preprint arXiv:2109.04150.

[17] Jiang, Y., et al. (2022). SwinBTS: a method for 3D multimodal brain tumor segmentation using swin transformer. *Brainscience*, 12(2), 152.

[18] Chen, J., et al . (2021). SegTransVAE: a variational autoencoder approach for medical image segmentation with transformers. arXiv preprint arXiv:2107.12345.

[19] Hatamizadeh, A., et al . (2022). Swin UNETR: swin transformers for semantic segmentation of brain tumors in MRI images. arXiv preprint arXiv:2201.01266.

31 Employing modified VGG-19 for multi-class classification of skin cancer with model hyperparameters tuning

Ruchi Patel[1,a], Gaurav Choubey[2,b], Ashok Kumar Verma[2,c], Preeti Rai[2,d] and Yogesh Jain[3,e]

[1]Department of Computer Engineering, Marwadi University, Rajkot, Gujrat, India

[2]Department of Computer Science and Engineering, Gyan Ganga Institute of Technology and Sciences, Jabalpur, MP, India

[3]Financial Systems Administration, Enphase Energy, Austin, Texas, United States

Abstract

The identification and categorization of skin cancer are crucial for timely diagnosis and treatment. This research employs the VGG-19 model with the inclusion of a convolutional neural network (CNN) for skin cancer multi-class classification, which utilizes the HAM10000 dataset, which contains a diverse array of dermatoscopic images. VGG-19, noted for its intricate architecture, excels at extracting hierarchical characteristics for visual recognition tasks. The research highlights the updated VGG-19 model, underscoring the importance of hyperparameter tuning, learning rate, batch size, and optimizer in improving the model's performance. Optimal hyperparameters were determined by grid search and cross-validation to improve "accuracy" and reduce "overfitting". The results demonstrate that with suitable calibration, the modified VGG-19 achieves excellent accuracy in classifying different types of skin cancer, providing a reliable approach for automated skin lesion diagnosis. During training, the model obtains an accuracy of 95%, and during testing, it achieves an accuracy of 94%.

Keywords: Deep learning architecture, multi-class hyperparameters tuning, skin lesions, VGG-19

Introduction

One of the most prevalent and deadly types of cancer, skin cancer, makes up a sizeable amount of all cancer cases worldwide each year. Improving patient prognosis and lowering death rates from skin cancer depend on early identification and precise categorization [1, 2]. Earlier skin cancer diagnosis was performed through "biopsy" and "histopathological" evaluation. In contrast, these technologies may require significant work, be prone to human error, and be inaccessible in many locations worldwide [3]. Recent breakthroughs in artificial intelligence (AI) and deep learning have revealed remarkable potential for automating the diagnosis and classification of skin cancer via dermatoscopic pictures [4]. CNNs have proven highly effective in image recognition tasks, particularly in the domain of medical imaging. Among them, the VGG-19 architecture, a deep CNN known for its ability to extract detailed hierarchical features, has emerged as a powerful model for medical image classification [5]. VGG-19 is applied to the multi-class classification of skin cancer using the HAM10000 dataset [6]. The research emphasizes the critical role of hyperparameter tuning in enhancing model performance. By systematically adjusting the key parameters VGG-19 model can be improved [7]. This paper presents a detailed evaluation of VGG-19's performance on the HAM10000 dataset and explores how strategic modifications to model configuration can lead to improved classification outcomes. The findings further highlight the potential of VGG-19 to support dermatologists in skin cancer detection [8, 9].

Literature Review

The rising global incidence of skin cancer has heightened the demand for automated methods in detecting and classifying skin lesions, particularly through advancements in medical image analysis [10]. Achieving early and accurate diagnosis plays

[a]ruchipatel294@gmail.com, [b]gouravchoubey48@gmail.com, [c]ashokverma@ggits.org, [d]preetirai@ggits.org, [e]yogeshj306@gmail.com

DOI: 10.1201/9781003724995-31

a pivotal role in improving patient outcomes. In this regard, ML, and more specifically DL, has shown considerable potential. This section reviews significant research efforts utilizing deep learning techniques, especially CNNs, to classify skin cancers, highlighting their advantages as well as existing limitations [11]. Several researchers have implemented deep CNNs trained on more than 129,000 clinical images to identify various skin cancers, achieving diagnostic accuracy comparable to experienced dermatologists [12]. The strong performance of CNNs in recognizing melanoma and other skin disorders has spurred further investigations into advanced architectures like VGG-19, which offers a deeper network structure for capturing intricate features in skin lesion images [13, 14].

The VGG architecture, which gained recognition through its performance in ILSVRC, has demonstrated powerful capabilities in feature extraction and transfer learning. Its resilience and adaptability have made it a popular choice in medical imaging tasks. Fine-tuning pre-trained models such as VGG-19 on specialized datasets have been shown to significantly improve their performance in skin lesion classification [15]. The HAM10000 dataset is extensively known as a benchmark for skin lesion classification tasks. It comprises 10,015 dermatoscopic images representing a variety of common pigmented skin conditions. These images are categorized into seven distinct diagnostic classes, such as melanocytic nevi, melanoma, and benign keratosis. Many studies have employed CNN architecture, including VGG-19, on the HAM10000 dataset to achieve high classification accuracy. Authors combined pre-trained VGG-16 models with finetuned dense layers for the categorization of skin lesions, resulting in competitive results [17].

Proposed Methodology

The proposed methodology for employing VGG-19 in multi-class skin cancer classification with hyperparameter modification is structured into specific phases: data preparation, model development, hyperparameter tuning, model training, and model evaluation. Figure 31.1 shows the depicted architecture of the proposed VGG-19 model. The subsequent sections offer a comprehensive elucidation of the proposed methodology.

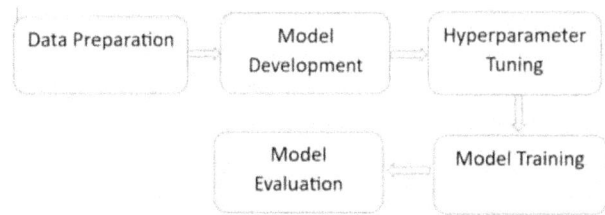

Figure 31.1 General architecture of the proposed method
Source: Author

Data preparation

The originating dataset named HAM10000, which contains images of seven different types of skin diseases, should be imported. It is recommended to organize the dataset into separate folders for each class to simplify the loading procedure for model training. To guarantee compatibility with the VGG-19 architecture, it is necessary to adjust each image to the defined dimensions of 224×224 measurements. The values of the pixels should be normalized by scaling them to a range of 0 to 1, using the normalization parameters that were applied by the ImageNet dataset, which was the dataset that VGG-19 was initially trained with. Make use of data augmentation methods such as "random rotations", "zooms", "horizontal flips", and shifts to artificially enlarge the dataset and improve the generalization of the model. Separate the dataset into three parts: the training, testing and validation in a ratio of 8: 1: 1.

Model development

Utilize the pre-trained VGG-19 model that was trained on ImageNet to take advantage of the characteristics that it has gained. It is necessary to freeze the convolutional layers to guarantee that the feature extraction information obtained from the huge ImageNet dataset is preserved. The old layers that are connected should be replaced with new layers that are thicker and more specifically designed to address the multi-class classification challenge that involves seven different types of skin diseases. To solve the problem of multi-class classification, the final output layer should be equipped with a SoftMax activation function implementation.

Tuning of the hyperparameters

Determine the number of hyperparameters that need to be tuned. The learning rates that were examined were 0.001, 0.0001, and 0.00001, respectively. Batch sizes of 16, 32, and 64 were evaluated and tested. The optimizers are RMSProp and Adam, respectively. You should conduct a grid search to discover all of the potential combinations of the hyperparameters. The dropout rates are 0.3 and 0.5. Following each epoch, the VGG-19 model ought to be trained for every conceivable combination with the use of the training data, and the validation accuracy ought to be evaluated once more. To avoid overfitting and to maintain track of the model that is performing the best, it is recommended that early stopping be based on the correctness of the validation.

Model training

Once the optimal combination of hyperparameters has been determined, the VGG-19 model ought to be retrained with the entire dataset that was utilized for the training procedure. To minimize the function of categorical cross-entropy loss, it is necessary to apply the optimizer that you have chosen (for instance, Adam) and the learning rate that you have chosen (for instance, 0.0001). It is recommended that dropout be utilized to properly regularize the layers that are fully coupled to reduce the chance of overfitting occurring. Throughout the training process, it is important to keep an eye on the validation loss as well as the accuracy. It is recommended that training be discontinued to recover the optimal weights if there is no gain in validation accuracy after a certain number of epochs have passed.

Model evaluation

Once the training has been completed, the final model should be evaluated using the test set that has not yet been seen to determine how well it generalizes. To appraise the usefulness of the model over a variety of lesion categories, it is necessary to compute critical measures.

Results and Discussions

Using systematic assessments, the effectiveness of the suggested strategy was examined, with a particular emphasis given on the effect that variations in epoch and batch size have on classification accuracy and loss statistics. The efficiency of the anticipated technique might be assessed by this examination. The model's performance results were evaluated using several significant procedures. A variety of different epochs, ranging from ten to twenty-five, were used to train the model. All of the other hyperparameters

Table 31.1 Performance evaluation of the proposed methodology according to Epoch changes for accuracy.

Epoch	Accuracy
10	0.91
15	0.94
20	0.95
25	0.95

Source: Author

were kept at their original values during the training process.

This was done so that the impact of the number of epochs could be investigated. The results are presented in Table 31.1, respectively. The accuracy was improved, and the quantity of overfitting was decreased, when the number of epochs under consideration was brought into equilibrium. For a total of 25 epochs, accuracy was brought up to a level of 95%. Overfitting was proven by an increasing difference between the accuracy of the training and the validation processes. This disparity was a result of prolonged training, which caused the training to be longer than necessary. The training loss and validation loss both continued to decrease, but the validation loss remained the same. This indicates that the generalization capability of the system was reduced.

To investigate the influence of batch size, the approach of training the model with batch sizes of 16, 32, 64, and 256 was applied. The results of this investigation are presented in Table 31.2. The size of the batch is 16. When the batch size decreased, it became much simpler to produce consistent updates to the model weights, which ultimately led to a high training accuracy of 92% once the training was completed. It was established that a batch size of 32 gave the best results, which resulted in a suitable equilibrium between steady training and computation efficiency. This batch size was determined to be responsible for producing the best outcomes. The highest level of accuracy achieved was 95%. Sizes 64 and 256 for the Batch, even though a bigger batch size sped up the process of convergence, it invariably resulted in generalization that was less than optimum. During this period, the validation accuracy dropped to 93% and 94%, respectively, and the model had a greater validation loss.

When compared to the baseline VGG-19 model, which was trained without hyperparameter

Table 31.2 Accuracy of proposed methodology according to Batch Size changes.

Batch Size	Accuracy
16	0.92
32	0.95
64	0.93
256	0.94

Source: Author

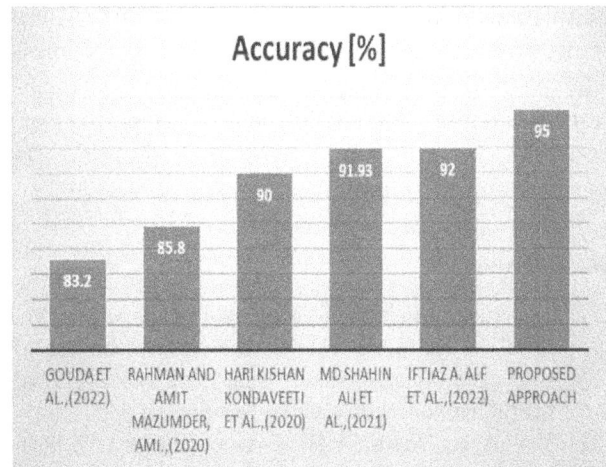

Figure 31.2 Evaluation of the proposed method with state-of-the-art approaches
Source: Author

adjustment, the findings were shown to be significantly different. In contrast to the baseline accuracy of 81%, the proposed methodology achieved a significant improvement in validation accuracy, reaching 95%. This is a major improvement. As evidenced by the reduction in validation loss, the deployment of hyperparameter adjustment resulted in a significant improvement in the model's ability to generalize. The findings highlight the significance of hyperparameter adjustment in the process of improving DL models for the classification of medical images. According to the findings of the evaluation, the learning dynamics of the model are greatly impacted by the precise adjustment of epochs and batch size. An optimal batch size meant that there was a balance between stability and computational efficiency, while a moderate quantity of epochs made it possible for the model to successfully converge without an excessive amount of overlap.

The findings of this study highlight the inherent challenges that are associated with class imbalance and overfitting in medical datasets such as HAM10000. A noteworthy enhancement in performance results can be attained with the implementation of techniques such as early pausing, data augmentation, and optimal hyperparameter selection. The analysis of training and validation patterns brings to light the importance of evaluating generalization performance to ensure that therapeutic relevance is maintained.

A comparative analysis of the suggested methodology in comparison to numerous different techniques that have been applied in the past by other authors for multi-class skin cancer categorization is presented throughout Figure 31.2. These approaches include architectures such as ResNet, InceptionV3, and MobileNet, all of which were evaluated using the same HAM10000 dataset. According to the data, the method that was based on VGG-19

showed remarkable performance, surpassing other approaches in respective of multiple measurements such as recall, accuracy, precision and F1-score. A significant improvement was made to this outcome as a result of the tuning of hyperparameters, which included the learning rate, batch size, and dropout rate.

Conclusion

The HAM10000 dataset was utilized to evaluate the performance of VGG-19, a deep convolutional neural network, in the classification of multi-class skin lesions. Transfer learning and hyperparameter optimization were the methods that we utilized to demonstrate that the VGG-19 architecture is capable of accurately classifying skin cancer into seven distinct categories. The modification of to maximize the performance of the model and reduce the amount of overfitting involved.

In the literature review, it was discovered that CNNs, particularly VGG-19, have the potential to be useful for medical picture classification. However, there is still room for improvement in terms of class imbalance, overfitting, and model interpretability. Both the robustness of the model and its clinical application can be improved through the use of advanced methods such as data augmentation and model regularization. We conclude that VGG-19, when adjusted for hyperparameters, is an effective marker for skin cancer. The study on automated dermatology diagnosis continues, and discoveries are being made about the improvement of deep learning models according to generalization and accuracy. The restrictions of explainability should be mentioned in subsequent studies, and classification outcomes should be improved, particularly for relatively uncommon lesion forms.

References

[1] Ali, M. S., Miah, M. S., Haque, J., Rahman, M. M., & Islam, M. K. (2021). An enhanced technique of skin cancer classification using deep convolutional neural network with transfer learning models.

[2] Younis, H., Bhatti, M. H., & Azeem, M. (2019). classification of skin cancer dermoscopy images using transfer learning.

[3] Srividhya, V., Sujatha, K., Ponmagal, R. S., Durgadevi, G., & Madheshwaran, L. (2020). Vision based detection and categorization of skin lesions using deep learning neural networks.

[4] Nawaz, M., Mehmood, Z., Nazir, T., Naqvi, R. A., Rehman, A., Iqbal, M., et al. (2021). Skin cancer detection from dermoscopic images using deep learning and fuzzy k-means clustering.

[5] Kadampur, M. A., & Al Riyaee, S. (2020). Skin cancer detection: Applying a deep learning based model driven architecture in the cloud for classifying dermal cell images.

[6] Sreevidya, R. C., Jalaja, G., Sajitha, N., Padmaja, D. L., Nagaprasad, S., Pant, K., et al. (n.d.). Role of artificial intelligence and deep learning in easier skin cancer detection through antioxidants present in food.

[7] Shoieb, D. A., Youssef, S. M., & Aly, W. M. (2016). Computer-aided model for skin diagnosis using deep learning.

[8] Kousis, I., Perikos, I., Hatzilygeroudis, I., & Virvou, M. (2022). Deep learning methods for accurate skin cancer recognition and mobile application.

[9] Lan, Z., Cai, S., He, X., & Wen, X. (2022). FixCaps: an improved capsules network for diagnosis of skin cancer.

[10] Gouda, W., Sama, N. U., Al Waakid, G., Humayun, M., & Jhanjhi, N. Z. (2022). Detection of skin cancer based on skin lesion images using deep learning.

[11] Okuboyejo, D., & Olugbara, O. O. (2021). Segmentation of melanocytic lesion images using gamma correction with clustering of keypoint descriptors. *Diagnostics*.

[12] Iqbal, A., Sharif, M., Yasmin, M., Raza, M., & Aftab, S. (2022). Generative adversarial networks and its applications in the biomedical image segmentation: A comprehensive survey. *International Journal of Multimedia Information Retrieval*.

32 Enhancing energy efficiency in vapor compression refrigeration: a review of waste heat utilization techniques

Rajarshi Chakraborty[1,a], Tanbir Islam[1,b], Subhajit Banerjee[1,c], Aman Ahamed Mokami[2,d], Subarna Sardar[2,e] and Goutam Roy[2,f]

[1]Assistant Professor, Department of Mechanical Engineering, Greater Kolkata College of Engineering and Management, Kolkata, WB, India

[2]Students of Department of Mechanical Engineering, Greater Kolkata College of Engineering and Management, Kolkata, WB, India

Abstract

This review explores advancements in vapor compression refrigeration systems, emphasizing techniques to repurpose waste energy and enhancing system efficiency. These adaptations enable diverse applications, from domestic heating to industrial processing, reducing reliance on traditional energy sources like LPG gas and promoting environmental sustainability. Highlighted strategies include using computational fluid dynamics (CFD) for optimized designs and integrating advanced components such as flash tank separators and heat exchangers. The review also discusses eco-friendly refrigerants and emerging technologies like solar-powered and combined cycle systems, showcasing their potential to improve energy recovery and minimize environmental impact. These innovations pave the way for more sustainable and efficient refrigeration practices across residential and industrial domains.

Keywords: Energy efficiency, refrigeration systems, sustainable technologtechnology, vapor compression, waste heat recovery

Introduction

Vapor compression refrigeration equipment are frequently utilized in industrial applications including storing food, development, production, and healthcare [1]. The most common home kitchen device is the refrigerator, which typically includes a tightly sealed inner compartment that. In order to keep the interior of the heat-tightly sealed portion cooler than the remainder of the environment or space, it transfers heat from the interior of the area to the exterior when it is in use. In a typical home refrigerator that needs an air-cooled condenser, elevated temperatures may be refused straight into the air flow; in a water-cooled condenser, they may be refused into drinking water. Nowadays, most household refrigerators use tetrafluoro ethane (HFC134a) refrigerant et al. [2]. Refrigeration equipment, which is used for food preservation, heating, and air conditioning in commercial, residential, and business environments, is designed to absorb heat as temperatures below freezing and discharge it at a higher temperature. Drinking water that goes by an ice maker system and most simple air-cooling solutions can both release high temperatures straight into the environment. The background of a rapidly expanding nation like India, most of the vapor compression-based cooling, conditioning, and extreme temperature transporting devices are still running on hydrogenated coolants attributed for their outstanding thermal and thermal conductivity aside from the inexpensive Kaushik et al. [3]. Examines a multi-stage vapour injection cycle with the goal of enhancing refrigerant side performance. The cycles' system modeling was completed in GT-Suite toExamine whether the A/C system with multiple vapor injections is more energy-efficient than the traditional vapour compression system [4]. The thorough modeling methods for each component are covered in the first section, and the results of the transient simulations conducted for the entire system during startup and shutdown are presented in the second section [5]. One of the parts of the vapor compression refrigeration apparatus that can be produced is a gravity vertical flash tank separator. The refrigerant liquid is extracted from the two-phase movement of gas and liquid with a vapor injection

[a]rajarshi.chakraborty@gkcem.ac.in, [b]tanbir.islam@gkcem.ac.in, [c]subhajit.banerjee@gkcem.ac.in, [d]amanahmk309@gmail.com, [e]subarnasardar987@gmail.com, [f]goutroy8085@gmail.com

DOI: 10.1201/9781003724995-32

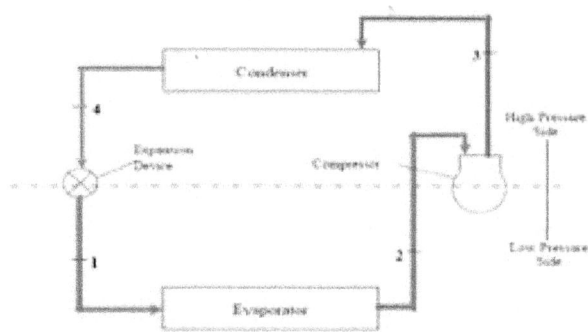

Figure 32.1 Typical vapor compressor unit: one stage [10]
Source: Author

vertical flash tank, which then feeds just liquid to the evaporator [6]. When the air conditioner is fed with cold vapor. By using the FTVL technique, the amount of heat stress that will be produced in the compressor during compressing it and because of the power supply passing through the compressor's electrical coil is reduced [7]. After injection, the cooling fluid will be sent to the subsequent expansion apparatus in the next phase of the cycle, which feeds the cycle stage evaporator. In temperatures below freezing environments, the outlet temperature, at the compressing output decreases, increasing the capacity [8]. Unusual temperature is developed during a technique by the use of gases or an enzyme reaction and then "eliminated" in the surroundings, however it is able still be used for a few profitable and advantageous purposes. A rigorous assessment of thermal loss obtained through a cooling and climate control program reveals that, on average, three to five kW of waste energy are released into the surrounding for all kilowatt-hour of energy used by the air conditioner. Price ranges for energy in general will be conserved while this energy is restored. Yet, in most setup models, the potential of the energy retrieval offers has not actually been taken into consideration while constructing RAC systems [9].

A typical single-stage vapour-compression system is shown in Figure 32.1. Each of these systems consists of four parts: an evaporator, a compressor, a condenser, and a thermal expansion valve, sometimes referred to as a throttle valve [10].

Further consideration is required to ensure the best possible layout for the gravity flash container divider is perpendicular. Certain essential design criteria are necessary for the best possible separator layout, including pipe size and arrangement, cooling capability, the overall size of all vaporizers and pipes that influence the partition, and the movement of the system [11].

Literature Review

Vapor compress device and its parts

Numerous studies on heat reuse in refrigeration systems have been conducted. They also provide an overview of the adaptation strategies that can be used to reduce energy usage and improve the effectiveness of condensation cooling systems, which have been thoroughly examined.

Using a baking device and warming device that might be positioned between the condenser unit and compressor sections, Elumalai, et al. [12] conducted research on heat recovery from the condensate chamber in the vapor compress cooling method. The presence of an oven makes it possible to extract the excess heat from the released vapor and utilize it to increase the degree of the heated area within the oven as well as the warmth of the fluids inside the heater. Studies have been done on the effectiveness of chillers with different operation times. Possible heat recovery has been identified by analyzing the operational degree results within the cooking and warming unit for varying the working period of a cooling system. Bolaji [13] modified the vapor compression cycle with R22 and possible refrigerants that are ozone-friendly (R404A and R507). The study found that R22 had the smallest pressure proportion and output humidity, followed by R507. The mean output value for R507 and R404A was 4.2% and 15.3% greater compared to that of R22, correspondingly. R507 and R404A have greater and less cooling capabilities than R22, correspondingly. The study discovered that R507 can be effectively employed as a retrofit coolant in current opening air conditioning unit built to use R22 when HCFCs are phased out. Maurya and Awasthi [14] conducted a conceptual investigation utilizing leftover heat from a vapor compress cooling unit. The absorbed energy can be utilized to power low-grade refrigeration systems like ejectors. After analyzing some examples, they recommended a combined cycle. This technology effectively utilizes waste heat and improves the efficiency of the vapor compression cooling unit. Deymi-Dashtebayaz, (2015) [27] performed a modification to optimize the infusion volume flow rate refrigerant and provided feedback. The approach to optimization found that administering at an overall velocity of 5.9 kg/s delivers enhanced efficiency based on exergy analysis. The optimum rate of mass flow of the inserted refrigerant is unaffected by ambient or chilled water temperature entering the evaporator. Kaushik et al. [3] used a Canopus thermal exchanger to retrieve waste heat from cooling systems. Large-capacity systems can generate enormous quantities of low-grade heat. To recover subpar warmth, a Canopus heat transfer device is placed among the compressor and condenser. The device's viability is often evaluated throughout several working ranges, taking into account the influence on the utilization of heat and general machine efficiency. The parametric results for various eco-friendly fluids have been reported. The researcher discovered that improving the total COP of an operational system typically does not impact its performance. Increasing conditioning capability improves the availability of low-grade heat. Study by Deymi-Dashtebayaz and Valipour-Namanlo [15] utilizes solar energy as a form of heat for a vapor adsorption device. The experiment effectively demonstrated the possibility of a solar-powered vapor refrigeration system. Heating water using solar units are capable of helping chill water. During the warmer months of the year, if the rooftop warming unit is off and the sun's energy is high, it may be utilized for refrigeration. The research Bajpai [16] proposes using surplus heat from gases engines/turbines to power a soak cooling system. The study focuses on how the absorption chiller, which complements the cooling offered by the vapor-compression chiller, can be powered by the gas engine's waste heat [17]. Using waste heat from gas engines significantly increased the efficiency of an incorporated cooling unit. According to Balaji and Senthil Kumar [18], the candy company's turbine steam eliminates substantial quantities of thermal power. The effect of incorporating a flash tank into a combined ejector-absorption cooling system on the thermal load of the evaporator was examined in the study conducted by Sirwan et al. (2011). The study, which concentrated on a modified aqua-ammonia (NH3-H2O) refrigerant system, discovered that the flash tank increased the cooling capacity in the evaporator and the ejector's entrainment ratio [19]. In Beijing, China, the ASHP prototype was tested and operated for the entire winter. The results of testing the essential dynamic-performance functions demonstrate that this novel type of ASHP may function effectively at ambient temperatures as low [20]. The resulting power can be used to warm the vapor absorber system, which can then be used for cool. This research demonstrates the cost-effectiveness of using waste heat to absorb water using lithium bromide. This paper aims to build a hypothetical lithium bromide removal and cooling system utilizing leftover heat from sugar industry turbine steam exhaust.

A heat recovery system installed in residential refrigerators to increase energy efficiency is the subject of the research article by Varghese et al. (2014). The study looks into ways to potentially lower total energy use by using the waste heat from the refrigerator's condenser [21] optimizing a two-stage injection heat pump with a double expansion sub-cooler's cycle control. In order to optimize the heating capacity and coefficient of performance (COP), the study looks into how various control tactics affect the heat pump's performance [22] focuses on energy conservation and the possibility of lowering global warming by exploring the potential uses of waste heat from refrigeration and air conditioning (R&AC) systems. In order to lessen dependency on conventional fuel-based heating, the project investigates ways to recover this waste heat, mostly from the condenser unit, and repurpose it, for instance, to heat water [23] focuses on a two-stage heat pump system that employs R410A as its refrigerant and a vapor-injected scroll compressor. The study looks into how well the system works, particularly how vapor injection affects its efficiency and heating capacity[24].

We utilize a verified dynamic model in Modelica R to examine its system performance with various PCM. Discussions are held regarding mathematical formulas and programming choices for the PCM model's Modelica implementation [25].

If the water heating and air conditioning systems are combined, hot water can still be obtained without the need for additional electricity.The air conditioner's condenser is connected to a coaxial copper pipe in the current project in the shape of a spiral coil that is connected to a water tank via pipes to warm water for household usage [26].

Result and Discussion

When researching the literature on vapor compression items, major insights into their structure and parts emerged. The compressor's condenser, expanding valve, and extractor are the four main components. According to studies, the compressor is the fundamental component, in charge of raising coolant temp and pressure, with rotational and reciprocating units being the most frequent. According to research, improving the compressor can significantly increase system efficiency. A condenser's role in heat dissipation is critical, and literature indicates that materials such as copper as well as aluminum are frequently utilized to improve heat transfer. Expansion valves, typically thermostatic and electronic, control refrigerant flow and affect system stability. Evaporators, which absorb heat, are designed differently depending on the purpose, with panel and shell-and-tube versions being the most common. Recent improvements have focused on increasing energy efficiency while limiting the impact on the environment, making the application of renewable refrigerants a popular study topic.

Conclusion

In conclusion, a survey of the literature on vapor compression units and their components demonstrates considerable improvements in layout, productivity, and applicability. The vapor compression device, which is frequently employed in cooling and air conditioning, works by compression refrigerants to improve heat transfer. The compressor, condenser unit vaporizer, and expansion valve are critical components that affect system performance. Several studies emphasize the need of improving these components to improve energy utilization, decrease environmental impact, and increase system reliability. Furthermore, recent advances in refrigerant substances and compressor technology, including variable-speed drives and microchannel thermal exchangers, have helped to improve overall system performance. However, research into refrigerant leaks and the need for sustainable alternatives is still ongoing. As technology advances, greater investigation and refining of these parts will drive the creation of improved and sustainable vapor compression systems.

References

[1] Arpandi, I. A. (1995). Hydrodynamics of two-phase flow in gas-liquid cylindrical cyclone separators. In SPE Journal: SPE 70th Annual Meeting, (p. 427).

[2] Shinde, T. B., Dhanal, S. V., & Mane, S. S. (2014). Experimental investigation of waste heat recovery system for domestic refrigerator. *International Journal of Mechanical Engineering and Technology (IJMET)*, 5(8), 73–83.

[3] Kaushik, S. C., Panwar, N. L., & Reddy, V. S. (2012). Thermodynamic evaluation of heat recovery through a canopus heat exchanger for vapor compression refrigeration (VCR) system. *Journal of Thermal Analysis and Calorimetry*, 110(3), 1493–1499.

[4] Pathak, A., Binder, M., Ongel, A., & Ng, H. (2019). Investigation of a multi stage vapour-injection cycle to improve air-conditioning system performance of electric buses. In Fourteenth International Conference on Ecological Vehicles and Renewable Energies (EVER), (pp. 124–127). 8-10 May 2019, IEEE.

[5] Qiao, H., Xu, X., Aute, V., & Radermacher, R. (2015). Transient modeling of a flash tank vapor injection heat pump system – part II: Simulation results and experimental validation. *International Journal of Refrigeration*, 49, 183–194.

[6] Ajayi, O., Ukasoanya, D., Ogbonnaya, M., Salawu, E., Okokpujie, I., Akinlabi, S., et al. (2019). Investigation of the effect of R134a/Al2O3 - nanofluid on the performance of a domestic vapour compression refrigeration system. *Procedia Manufacturing*, 35, 112–117.

[7] Stinson, G. E. (1985). Design principles of refrigeration waste energy recovery. *Aust Refrig Aircond Heat*, 1, 25–30.

[8] Jang, Y., Lee, E., Chin, S., & Haet, S. (2010). Effect of flash and vapor injection on the air-to-air heat pump system. In International Refrigeration and Air Conditioning Conference, Purdue University School of Mechanical Engineering, (pp. 1–8).

[9] Mohtaram, S., Wu, W., Castellanos, H. G., Aryanfar, Y., Al Mesfer, M. K., Danish, M., et al. (2023). Enhancing energy efficiency and sustainability in ejector expansion transcritical CO_2 and lithium bromide water vapour absorption refrigeration systems. *Thermal Science and Engineering Progress*, 43, 101983. ISSN 2451-9049.

[10] Tile, V. G., Shivashankara, B. S., Raghavendra, R. R., Sajjan Acharya, K., & Vishal Somanna, V. K. (2016). Review on exhaust gas heat recovery for I.C. engine using refrigeration systems. *International Journal on Emerging Technologies*, 154–157 .

[11] Mohanraj, M., Muraleedharan, C., & Jayaraj, S. (2011). A review on recent developments in new refrigerant mixtures for vapour compression-based refrigeration, air-conditioning and heat pump units. *International Journal of Energy Research*, 35(8), 647–669.

[12] Elumalai, P., Vijayan, R., Ramasamy, K. K., & Premkumar, M. (2015). Experimental study on energy recovery from condenser unit of small capacity domestic refrigerator. *Middle-East Journal of Scientific Research*, 23(3), 417–420.

[13] Bolaji, B. O. (2011). Performance investigation of ozone-friendly R404A and R507 refrigerants as alternatives to R22 in a window air-conditioner. *Energy and Buildings*, 43(11), 3139–3143.

[14] Maurya, S. K., & Awasthi, S. (2014). Waste heat recovery: an analytical study of combined ejector and vapour compression refrigeration system. *International Journal of Engineering Sciences and Research Technology*, 3(3), 1422–1425.

[15] Deymi-Dashtebayaz, M., & Valipour-Namanlo, S. (2019). Thermoeconomic and environmental feasibility of waste heat recovery of a data center using air source heat pump. *Journal of Cleaner Production*, 219, 117–126.

[16] Bajpai, V. K. (2012). Design of solar powered vapor absorption system. In World Congress on Engineering, (Vol. 3), July 4–6, 2012. ISBN: 978-988-19252-2-0, pp 4–6.

[17] Sun, Z. G. (2008). Experimental investigation of integrated refrigeration system with gas engine, compression chiller & absorption chiller. *Energy*, 33, 431–436.

[18] Balaji, K., & Senthil Kumar, R. (2012). Study of vapor absorption system using waste heat in sugar industry. *IOSR Journal of Engineering*, 2(8), 34–39.

[19] Sirwan, R., Ali, Y., Zaharim, A., & Sopian, K. (2011). Effect of adding flash tank on the evaporator's thermal load of the combined ejector-absorption cooling system. In Proceedings of the 10th WSEAS international conference on System Science and Simulation in Engineering., World Scientific and Engineering Academy and Society (WSEAS), (pp. 124–127). Penang, Malaysia.

[20] Guoyuan, M., Qinhu, C., & Yi, J. (2003). Experimental investigation of air-source heat pump for cold regions. *International Journal of Refrigeration*, 26(1), 12–18.

[21] Varghese, R., Raju, N., Rohit, M., Antony, R. T., & Mathew, T. (2014). Heat recovery system in domestic refrigerator. *International Journal for Research & Development in Technology*, 2(2), 16–20.

[22] Heo, J., Kang, H., & Kim, Y. (2012). Optimum cycle control of a two-stage injection heat pump with a double expansion sub-cooler. *International Journal of Refrigeration*, 35(1), 58–67.

[23] Yashwanth, M. (2013). Utilization of heat energy in R & AC systems. *International Journal of Science and Research (IJSR)*, 4(4), 2319–7064.

[24] Wang, X., Hwang, Y., & Radermacher, R. (2009). Two-stage heat pump system with vapor-injected scroll compressor using R410A as a refrigerant. International *Journal of Refrigeration*, 32(6), 1442–1451.

[25] Dhumane, R., Qiao, Y., Ling, J., Muehlbauer, J., Aute, V., Hwang, Y., et al. (2019). Improving system performance of a personal conditioning system integrated with thermal storage. *Applied Thermal Engineering*, 147, 40–51.

[26] Vamshi, K. A., Venkateshwara, R. M., & Gowd, A. E. (2017). Rana, experimental investigation on recovery of waste heat from window air conditioner. *International Journal of Core Engineering & Management*, 4, 218–233 .

[27] Mohammad Yazdani, Mahdi Deymi-Dashtebayaz, Sobhan Ghorbani, (2024). Multi-objective optimization and 3E analysis for solar-driven dual ejector refrigeration and phase change material as thermal energy storage, *Applied Thermal Engineering,* Volume 249, 123431, ISSN 1359-4311, https://doi.org/10.1016/j.applthermaleng. 2024. 123431.

33 Airplane seating assignment greedy algorithms that separate passengers likely to be susceptible to infectious disease from those likely to be infectious

Kishore Kumar, S.[a], S. Praveenkumar[b], T. Aravind[c] and K. Anitha[d]

Department of Electronics and Communication Engineering, Saveetha Engineering College, Chennai, Tamil Nadu, India

Abstract

In order to mitigate this risk of airborne infectious disease transmission on airplanes, two new algorithms to optimize the seating arrangement are presented here. Algorithm 1 is titled risk-distanced zone partitioning. This algorithm works dynamically to partition the cabin into zones, using passengers' risk profiles to maximally split high-risk individuals and those who could potentially be infectious from each other. The Risk-Distanced Zone Partitioning (RDZP) algorithm achieves this by grouping passengers into separate sections depending on their respective levels of risk, thereby reducing contact with each other. The second algorithm is Probabilistic Risk Separation (PRS), which uses a probabilistic model to simulate the different seating arrangements and picks the configuration most statistically maximizing the distance between the passengers at high risks and possibly infectious passengers. The mechanism developed for the PRS algorithm is an adaptive re-seating system resting on real-time health data adaptable enough for evolving health situations. Both have significantly reduced the potential of transmission; thus, there is an effective response to in-flight disease control.

Keywords: Airborne disease transmission, high-risk passengers, in-flight disease control, probabilistic risk separation, real-time health data, risk-distanced zone partitioning, seating optimization

Introduction

Recent outbreaks, such as the COVID-19 pandemic, have recently raised concerns over airborne infectious diseases on airplanes. Airplanes are an enclosed environment with high densities of [1] passengers. Such an environment is optimal for the spread of disease, considering the extended exposure time to recirculated air and possibly asymptomatic patients who might unknowingly spread infections. Then, the existence of this heterogeneity in passengers plus different health status and fluidity of disease transmissions by air add up to the complexity of this challenge. A salient sub-activity here is smart seat allocation, based on the health status [2] and risk profiles of the passengers. Till date, commercial aircraft seat plans are designed to improve operational efficiency rather than to manage health risk.

In this work, two novel algorithms are developed to best optimize the seating [3] strategy in an aircraft to minimize risks associated with airborne diseases. The first algorithm is named Risk-Distanced Zone Partitioning (RDZP), which partitions the airplane cabin into different zones by classifying the passengers with respect to their risk levels. This approach clusters individuals with similar risk profiles together so that high-risk passengers would be seated as far apart as possible from potentially infectious ones. The PRS algorithm takes a more complex approach and uses a probabilistic model that simulates different seating positions. A seating [4] configuration which minimizes inter-recipient spatial distance between passengers that pose the highest risk of infection to others is chosen. PRS would involve real-time health data, with risk exposure. RDZP and PRS have the capability of providing a robust control structure of in-flight disease transmission, especially in situations where the health status of travelers changes. In such situations [5], these algorithms also have flexibility in responding to emerging health risks, which portrays a pro-active approach toward airlines and traveling passengers in search of maintaining public health standards with respect to air travel. Enhancing the efficiency of airline passenger seating configuration

[a]kishorekumar.ece.sec@gmail.com, [b]praveenkumar@saveetha.ac.in, [c]aravind@saveetha.ac.in, [d]anitha@saveetha.ac.in

DOI: 10.1201/9781003724995-33

during flight, this work is part of the general movement toward improving public health protection in the context of modern air travel.

This work is organized in the following sections. Section 2 as reviews the literature survey, Section 3 outlines the methodology, detailing its features and functionality. Results and discussion are found in Section 4, where the effectiveness of the system is analyzed. Finally, Section 5 concludes with key findings along with future implications.

Literature Survey

The pandemic has hinted at the necessity of novel solutions for the effective management of social distancing and public health safety. A variety of technologies, such as IoT, AI, machine learning, and digital twins, have been utilized for the design of systems for monitoring, controlling, and optimizing distancing protocols in public areas. These systems are also expected to reduce the risk of viral transmission through real-time data, health monitoring, and contact tracing. The following study outlines several social distancing approaches in the light of their feasibility and effectiveness for future pandemics.

This work presented a vehicle social distancing management system for smart building access control in managing access during [6] the pandemic, using real-time health checks and risk classification of vehicles to guide them into appropriate zones according to established levels of risk. The performance evaluation showed marked improvements in access control as compared to traditional methods, and that there are reduced infection rates. As a part of the design for ensuring social distancing among pedestrians in a particular area, an IoT-driven smart navigation framework was designed. The framework used social IoT and artificial intelligence for identifying the risk areas along with proposing the safest route [7]. The system would be analyzing CCTV footage to evaluate the practice of social distancing while assigning safety weights onto road segments. The proposed algorithm utilizes a graph-based approach as a tradeoff between efficiency in navigation and online safety.

Numerical simulations were conducted on true datasets, in which the architecture demonstrated adaptivity to dynamic user preferences yet maintained the safest standards. Last but not the least, further applications of digital twin technology lie in

containing virus spread and practicing social distance in healthcare units. The virtual [8] representation of people's health data and the workplace environment can be used to enhance safety measures put in place during the COVID-19 pandemic. CanTwin is a case study application example of Digital Twin, which monitors social distancing and manages queue systems in the workplace canteen. Moreover, a general architecture for healthcare digital twin systems is proposed [9] to improve public health monitoring and management. The research work mainly focuses on the significance of digital twins in developing efficient healthcare operations during pandemics. The concept of maintaining social distancing through Augmented reality and smart sensing has been proposed for post-pandemic scenarios.

The research highlighted the importance of merging these technologies to create efficient social distancing strategies in public environments. The study [10] uses a privacy-preserving approach by de-identifying user data while keeping logs of interactions with potential infected individuals. Experimental results have demonstrated its effectiveness in real-world contact tracing scenarios and provided evidence of its potential value in controlling epidemics.

Methodology

The work presents two new algorithms designed to optimize the seating patterns in an airplane cabin so as to minimize the chance of airborne infectious disease transmission shown in Figure 33.1. The first is called RDZP and dynamically partitions the cabin based on the risk profiles of its passengers, hence achieving the maximum level of spatial distancing. The second probabilistic risk separation grounds its real-time analysis of seating configurations in real-time on evolving health data by using the model in a probabilistic way. The procedure ensures an effective flexible approach in airborne infectious disease control during flight.

Data collection and risk profiling

The data are collected on passengers, including their health status, travel history, or any other relevant factors that may indicate risk levels towards airborne infectious diseases. Then passengers are divided into groups of risk according to the established criteria, like recent infectious exposures or previous medical conditions. This step is required in order to ensure

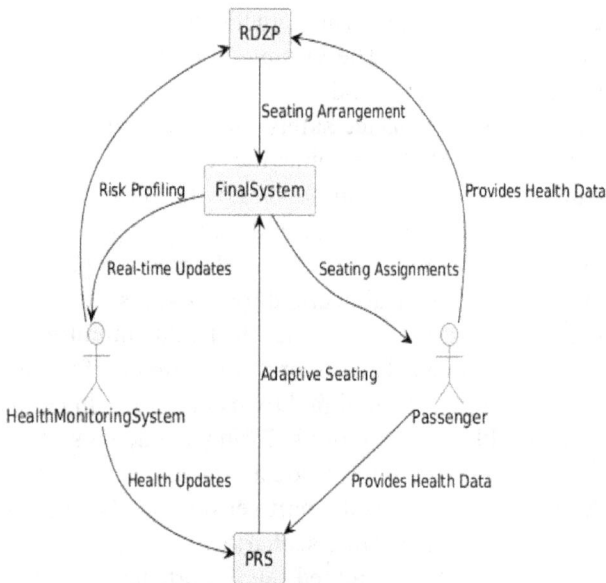

Figure 33.1 Architecture diagram
Source: Author

proper utilization of seating algorithms as well as classification of people who have more risks to be further considered within the optimization.

Dynamic cabin partitioning

To start with, the Risk-Distanced Zone Partitioning algorithm starts off by dynamically partitioning the airplane cabin into a number of zones. It bases its partitions on the different risk levels the passengers have been ascribed to each one thereby creating a zone for people of the same risk profile. The partitioning seeks to maximize the spatial distance between the high-risk passengers and the possibly infectious passengers in a bid to curtail the chances of the spread of disease.

Clustering of passengers and probabilistic risk modeling

Once the cabin is zoned, passengers will be categorized to allow for safety maximization and better operational efficiency. Risky ones are clustered with the aim of minimizing contact within risky events. Probabilistic Risk Separation (PRS) uses health data and risk factors to analyze different seating configurations such as proximity towards infected passengers and cabin design under dynamic health situations. The model makes simulations of numerous layouts and runs probability transmission with different scenarios. This approach enhances safety

while maintaining efficiency in passenger organization and seating.

Adaptive re-seating mechanism

PRS algorithm has an adaptive re-seating mechanism wherein, with updated health data or changing circumstances, it adapts the seating configuration in real time. For example, where one passenger's health changes while the flight is on, or new health information becomes available, then also the system can suggest a new arrangement of seating to further minimize transmission risk. In this way, the system ensures that the seats are versatile and respond to any change.

Simulation and selection of optimal configuration

Both algorithms of RDZP and PRS simulate a number of different seating configurations and compare their effectiveness after doing multiple configurations. Algorithms consider variables like distances between high-risk and possibly infectious passengers, general efficiency in terms of seating, and pragmatic feasibility for implementation. Lastly, the best configuration is established by which can best minimize probability of airborne transmission of disease, though with operational feasibility.

Implement and continuous monitoring

The best seating configuration is then installed in the airplane cabin. Installation entails alteration of seat assignments that corresponds to the selected configuration. Constant monitoring is carried out throughout the entire flight to ensure the system continues to be effective. If new health data or risk assessments are found during the flight, the system can trigger further changes to seating if necessary to maintain the in-flight transmission risk at its lowest possible value during the entire flight.

Result and Discussion

The promising results of the optimized seating arrangement using the RDZP and PRS algorithms point to their potential in controlling airborne disease transmission onboard airplanes. The RDZP algorithm dynamically partitions zones, which would group passengers based on risk profiles, minimizing contact between passengers with high risk and infectious profiles. This spatial separation of susceptible and infectious passengers creates a safer cabin environment. The algorithm PRS employs probabilistic models to simulate reconfigurations of seating based on real-time health data, allowing adaptive

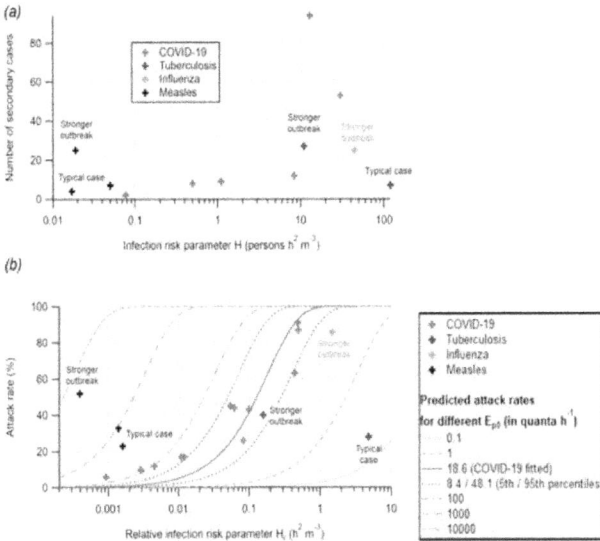

Figure 33.2 Infection risk parameter
Source: Author

arrangement during flight. Simulations have presented the following: PRS consistently maximizes distance between high-risk and infectious individuals better than traditional methods.

Its adaptability allows modification when passengers' health status changes mid-flight, continuously adjusting seating for safety. Both algorithms outperform traditional sitting arrangements in terms of reduction of transmission risks shown in Figure 33.2. RDZP is more effective when risk profiles are known before flight, as zones and sitting can be pre-arranged.

PRS also takes into account cabin layout, seat availability, and passenger numbers to perform optimal sitting arrangements with comfort and operational efficiency. While RDZP is simple and has considerable risk reduction due to spatial separation, PRS provides flexibility and adaptability to accommodate changes in the flight conditions.

Both methods considerably decrease the opportunity for disease, as confirmed with a simulation for the movement and risk of airborne exposure. Sitting patterns that come with both of these algorithms tend to show extreme decreases in passengers to passengers as opposed to air travelers, even more so especially when it is for long-haul flights. Most acutely lowered on long-distance flights, where people can be as close to other individuals for any longer period.

(b) *Exposure time (in h) corresponding to an infection risk parameter (H) value of 0.05 person h² m⁻³*

Type and level of group activity	Low occupancy			High occupancy		
	Outdoor and well ventilated	Indoor and well ventilated	Poorly ventilated	Outdoor and well ventilated	Indoor and well ventilated	Poorly ventilated
Wear face coverings						
Silent	2100	26	4.3	610	7.3	1.22
Speaking	430	5.1	0.86	120	1.5	0.24
Shouting, singing	71	0.86	0.14	20	0.24	<0.050
Heavy exercise	31	0.37	0.061	8.7	0.10	<0.050
No face coverings						
Silent	750	9.0	1.5	210	2.6	0.43
Speaking	150	1.8	0.30	43	0.51	0.086
Shouting, singing	25	0.30	0.050	7.1	0.086	<0.050
Heavy exercise	11	0.13	<0.050	3.1	<0.050	<0.050

The real-time monitoring and adaptive re-seating of the PRS model enables timely interventions that go beyond conventional systems. It increases the safety of passengers on full flights by responding to health-related issues. The scalable algorithms may be used beyond air travel, for example, in trains and buses, to support a more extensive public health agenda. This technology optimizes seating based on health data, thereby minimizing the spread of airborne diseases, thus helping both passengers and staff. With further refinement and real-world testing, such algorithms could become integral to in-flight disease prevention, ensuring safer environments in global travel and advancing public health measures in transportation systems.

Conclusion

This research studies two methods, namely Risk-Distanced Zone Partitioning (RDZP) and Probabilistic Risk Separation (PRS), in the effort to optimize the seating of airline passengers with minimum risk of airborne disease transmission. RDZP efficiently distributes passengers based on known health risk profiles to ensure appropriate distancing between individuals categorized as high-risk and other passengers. PRS, on the other hand, adjusts the seating

(a) *Risk parameter H (persons h² m⁻³)*

Type and level of group activity	Low occupancy			High occupancy		
	Outdoor and well ventilated	Indoor and well ventilated	Poorly ventilated	Outdoor and well ventilated	Indoor and well ventilated	Poorly ventilated
Wear face coverings, contact for short time						
Silent	7.3E-05	1.0E-02	1.2E-02	3.2E-05	6.8E-03	4.3E-02
Speaking	4.1E-04	9.7E-03	5.8E-02	4.1E-04	3.8E-02	2.0E-01
Shouting, singing	2.0E-04	5.8E-02	3.5E-01	2.5E-03	2.0E-01	1.2E+00
Heavy exercise	1.6E-03	1.4E-01	8.2E-01	5.7E-03	4.8E-01	2.9E+00
Wear face coverings, contact for prolonged time						
Silent	2.3E-04	1.9E-02	1.2E-01	8.2E-04	6.8E-02	4.1E-01
Speaking	1.2E-03	9.7E-02	5.8E-01	4.1E-03	3.4E-01	2.0E+00
Shouting, singing	7.0E-03	5.8E-01	3.5E+00	2.5E-02	2.0E+00	1.2E+01
Heavy exercise	1.6E-02	1.4E+00	8.2E+00	5.7E-02	4.8E+00	2.9E+01
No face coverings, contact for short time						
Silent	6.7E-05	5.0E-03	3.3E-02	1.2E-04	1.9E-02	1.2E-01
Speaking	3.3E-04	3.8E-02	1.7E-01	1.2E-03	9.7E-02	5.8E-01
Shouting, singing	2.0E-02	1.7E-01	1.0E+00	7.0E-03	5.8E-01	3.5E+00
Heavy exercise	4.7E-03	3.9E-01	2.3E+00	1.6E-02	1.4E+00	8.2E+00
No face coverings, contact for prolonged time						
Silent	6.7E-04	5.0E-02	3.3E-01	1.2E-03	1.9E-01	1.2E+00
Speaking	3.3E-03	2.3E-01	1.7E+00	1.2E-02	9.7E-01	3.8E+00
Shouting, singing	2.0E-02	1.7E+00	1.0E+01	7.0E-02	5.8E+00	3.5E+01
Heavy exercise	4.7E-02	3.9E+00	2.3E+01	1.6E-01	1.4E+01	8.2E+01

pattern in real time using the most updated health information to enhance both flexibility and safety while airborne. Both of the algorithms above outperform traditional seating arrangements by minimizing in-flight health risks. This study highlights the capabilities of sophisticated algorithms to improve public health within the realm of air transportation, representing a significant advancement toward ensuring safer and more health-oriented travel experiences in a swiftly changing global environment.

References

[1] Rizk, H., Saeed, A., & Yamaguchi, H. (2022). Vaccinated, what next? an efficient contact and social distance tracing based on heterogeneous telco data. *IEEE Sensors Journal*, 22(18), 17950–17962. DOI: 10.1109/JSEN.2022.3194540.

[2] Karakose, G., & Dundar, B. (2024). A robust seating arrangement for future pandemics. *IEEE Access*, 12, 110829–110839. DOI: 10.1109/ACCESS.2024.3441767.

[3] Mutlag, A. H., Mahdi, S. Q., Gharghan, S. K., Salim, O. N. M., Al-Naji, A., & Chahl, J. (2022). Improved control system based on PSO and ANN for social distancing for patients with COVID-19. *IEEE Access*, 10, 63797–63811. DOI: 10.1109/ACCESS.2022.3183124.

[4] Guo, X., Zhang, H., Kou, L., & Hou, Y. (2022). Modeling the external, internal, and multi-center transmission of infectious diseases: the COVID-19 case. *Journal of Social Computing*, 3(2), 171–181. DOI: 10.23919/JSC.2022.0002.

[5] Hasegawa, R., Uchiyama, A., Okura, F., Muramatsu, D., Ogasawara, I., Takahata, H., et al. (2022). Close-contact detection using a single camera for sports considering occlusion. *IEEE Access*, 10, 15457–15468. DOI: 10.1109/ACCESS.2022.3146538.

[6] Murad, S. S., Yussof, S., Mundher Oraibi, B.-A., Badeel, R., Badeel, B., & Alamoodi, A. H. (2024). A vehicle social distancing management system based on LiFi during COVID pandemic: real-time monitoring for smart buildings. *IEEE Access*, 12, 137004–137024. DOI: 10.1109/ACCESS.2024.3461359.

[7] Friji, H., Khanfor, A., Ghazzai, H., & Massoud, Y. (2022). An end-to-end smart IoT-driven navigation for social distancing enforcement. *IEEE Access*, 10, 76824–76841. DOI: 10.1109/ACCESS.2022.3192860.

[8] De Benedictis, A., Mazzocca, N., Somma, A., & Strigaro, C. (2023). Digital twins in healthcare: an architectural proposal and its application in a social distancing case study. *IEEE Journal of Biomedical and Health Informatics*, 27(10), 5143–5154. DOI: 10.1109/JBHI.2022.3205506.

[9] Cao, J., Mehmood, H., Liu, X., Tarkoma, S., Gilman, E., & Su, X. (2023). Fighting pandemics with augmented reality and smart sensing-based social distancing. *IEEE Computer Graphics and Applications*, 43(1), 65–75. DOI: 10.1109/MCG.2022.3229107.

[10] Hankar, M., Birjali, M., El-Ansari, A., & Beni-Hssane, A. (2022). COVID-19 impact sentiment analysis on a topic-based level. *Journal of ICT Standardization*, 10(2), 219-240. DOI: 10.13052/jicts2245-800X.1027.

34 Blockchain- empowered metaverse: decentralized crowdsourcing and marketplace for trading machine learning data and models

Janani, B. S.[a], S. Praveenkumar[b], T. Aravind[c] and K. Anitha[d]

Department of Electronics and Communication Engineering, Saveetha Engineering College, Chennai, Tamil Nadu, India

Abstract

This work will propose a blockchain-based decentralized marketplace in the metaverse, in which machine learning data and models are traded securely. Two novel algorithms will be introduced to improve the security and reliability of the marketplace. The first algorithm is the Verified Contributor Scoring (VCS), in which each contributor's trustworthiness will be assessed based on their data quality metrics as well as historical transactions with the possibility of getting assigned a dynamic reputation score, which can be visible to buyers. It encourages high-grade contributions and punishes low-grade contributions, thus a high-grade data ecosystem. The encrypted model validation enables buyers to verify the performance of ML models prior to purchase without including any kind of underlying model parameters. Encrypted Model Validation (EMV) utilizes homomorphic encryption concerning model accuracy evaluation which bypasses data breaches and transactional invalidation. In general, VCS and EMV generate a trustworthy and efficient trading platform with decentralized trading of ML data and models to become more secure and accessible.

Keywords: Blockchain, data trading, decentralized marketplace, encrypted model validation, machine learning, security, verified contributor scoring

Introduction

In the shifting landscape of the metaverse, blockchain is best suited as a decentralized structure that addresses problems of mistrust, insecurity, and lack of transparency in several industries. In this work, such a blockchain-based solution is explored in building a decentralized marketplace where ML data [1] and models can be traded securely. Because demand for quality data and models increases, the need to ensure integrity, reliability, and privacy in transactions also increases. The conventional centralized system has its limitations in data fraud, lack of transparency, and limited access to secure methods of validation. The integration of blockchain technology with cryptography principles offers a strong solution to these challenges. This work develops two new algorithms that are aimed at increasing the security and reliability of the marketplace proposed above. The first algorithm to be developed is that of Verified Contributor Scoring (VCS), which addresses the problem of trust by establishing a reputation value for contributors within the marketplace [2]. Using metrics on data quality and historical transactions, each contributor is assigned a dynamic [3] reputation score by VCS. This score, which is visible to consumers, makes sure that only the best data and model's trade. It motivates contributors to remain at higher standards because low-quality contributions incur a penalty with the intention of reinforcing integrity in the marketplace at large.

The other one goes by the name Encrypted Model Validation (EMV), which addresses privacy and accuracy of ML models traded. The biggest issue with purchasing ML models is the lack of transparency over the underlying parameters, making it rather difficult to claim whether or not they really work without exposing sensitive information [4]. EMV addresses this issue by using homomorphic encryption, an advanced cryptographic technique that allows a user to validate functionality without actually revealing model parameters. This ensures that buyers can check the truth of a model before buying it while making the internal workings of the model confidential.

VCS and EMV combine their efforts toward creating a decentralized marketplace that is secure, trustworthy, and transparent. Providing mechanisms for the assessment of contributor trustworthiness and the

[a]janani.ece.sec@gmail.com, [b]praveenkumar@saveetha.ac.in, [c]aravind@saveetha.ac.in, [d]anitha@saveetha.ac.in

DOI: 10.1201/9781003724995-34

verification of the performance of ML models without compromising on data privacy, the proposed platform extends the notion of more secure and efficient transactions within the metaverse and addresses current limitations in ML data markets [5]. The integration of blockchain technology using both ML and encryption technologies is a great step to develop decentralized systems with respect to security, privacy, and fairness.

This work is organized in the following sections. Section 2 as reviews the literature survey and Section 3 outlines the methodology, detailing its features and functionality. Results and discussion are found in Section 4, where the effectiveness of the system is analyzed. Finally, Section 5 concludes with key findings along with future implications.

Literature Survey

The meteoric rise of the metaverse and blockchain has created an inflow of interest into these topics, especially with respect to their convergence and applications. This promises to alter every sphere of life- from virtual real estate and healthcare to all walks of future life. However, security concerns, data privacy, and scalability are still significant challenges. This survey investigates some of the key studies addressing these issues and the solutions that seem to be emerging within the metaverse ecosystem.

The rapid advancements in the metaverse and generative artificial intelligence (AI) have sparked AI-generated content. Such [6] digital assets suffer from plagiarism and leakage problems. Amidst this, the blockchain-based digital asset management system MetaTrade was proposed. The system overcomes the trust issues since there are no third-party authorities and transactions in the metaverse will be secure. Comparatively, it outperforms classical platforms in performance and cost.

This work explores the regions of overlap among blockchain, Web 3.0, and a decentralized metaverse with regard to scalability, virtual [7] real estate, and gaming. It zeroes in on proof of work or proof of stake within consensus mechanisms. Governance models, data security threats, and how this can be worked through in a case study including both Decentraland and The Sandbox will follow. The survey calls out some scopes of further research into decentralized systems in the metaverse.

The possibilities for metaverse applications have been introduced by the introduction of blockchain in

building information modeling [8]. The metaverse involves bridging the gap between the worlds of virtual and physical. It aids in creation and trade activities while blockchain ensures fairness and security in transactions. This work was a survey undertaken to understand how blockchain and BIM can be collaborated together to enhance development in this field called for more interdisciplinary research.

This hybrid of blockchain and AI with the metaverse has garnered some significant attention for its potential in virtual environments. Blockchain [9] allows secure transactions with the use of AI, giving enhanced user experience as well as systems' efficiency. This work surveys components such as digital currencies and their applications within the world of AI in the metaverse. An overview has been provided about the point where blockchain-empowered technologies intersect with AI, including information about their transformative impact. It is concluded that there is a need for further collaboration in research to explore this fusion.

Edge computing is an enabler of the Metaverse's potential due to real-time experiences and immersion. An edge-enabled application landscape is captured within diverse industry sectors and related to 5G, IoT, and decentralized computing [10]. It explores challenges related to latency and bandwidth, along with privacy issues, and forwards solutions based on edge AI and cybersecurity frameworks. Future directions for the development of edge-enabled metaverse infrastructures are discussed. It is aiming to find the way in which edge computing plays a role in the Metaverse and can help researchers as well as business leaders find the way.

The COVID-19 pandemic created a focus on the weaknesses in traditional healthcare delivery systems, and there has been a focus on virtual systems [11]. This survey questions how far metaverse solutions can revolutionize healthcare by bringing alternate systems through VR and AR technologies. It examines cutting- edge applications across various domains in telemedicine, clinical care, and mental health. The work addresses challenges, data security, and interoperability of healthcare systems in the metaverse. It further discusses further development toward embracing the full potential of the metaverse for healthcare applications.

Blockchain technology in the metaverse has introduced new challenges in data mining and network analysis. The objectives of this research study are analyzing blockchain transaction networks from a perspective of structural identity [12]. New insights through its usage include power-law degree distributions and disconnection patterns. A new representation learning approach known as SVRP is developed to improve the tasks of understanding and predicting the network. Results have shown that the proposed method of SVRP has outperformed existing methods on node classification and link prediction tasks.

The proposed research project introduces a blockchain-based trust management model that is going to be designed for enhancing security in metaverse interactions [13]. This model focuses on the dynamic allocation of trust based on the behavior and reputation of entities in the context of Sybil attacks in addressing them. The interactions in the metaverse are safe and transparent through the integration of smart contracts. Also introduced is a decentralized framework for resolving disputes. This framework supports an equal and fair resolution of conflicts from virtual entities. The model has shown improved capabilities in threat detection and also demonstrated real-time adaptability of the system in blockchain platforms.

As metaverse platforms scale, secure communication with proper transparence in user identity management becomes an important aspect [14]. To fulfill this requirement, this work brings out a mutual authentication scheme based on a blockchain and biometric-based solution to finally enhance the security of metaverses. This proposed system model ensures secure interaction between users and servers as well as protects the avatar data. From the results of various tests for the security evaluation, the proposed scheme outweighs the existing approaches in view of computational efficiency as well as features related to security. This scheme is ideal for the metaverse for providing safe environments in terms of the identification of users and avatar interactions.

This study explores how blockchain can be used to enable decentralized, transparent ecosystems in social and economic systems in the metaverse [15]. Specifically, it discusses the way in which blockchain influences virtual currency transactions, provides ownership rights over digital assets, and governs using decentralized mechanisms. It touches on scalability and energy consumption issues of blockchain networks. The work deems such a scenario potentially feasible with combining blockchain with other emerging technologies, AI and IoT, to make the metaverse more efficient. Finally, it calls for further research in optimization of blockchain protocols for better applications in the metaverse.

Abundant platforms have emerged with much interest in the metaverse. Each has a salient feature but also bears a limitation. This work objectively [16] addresses the essential needs for metaverse platforms and evaluates those platforms: interoperability, immersiveness, scalability, and blockchain integration. Interoperability, immersiveness, scalability, and blockchain integration have been realized as key outstanding requirements that metaverse ecosystems must consider. This work identifies the shortcomings which should be corrected so as to make the ecosystem fair, trustable, and interactive. It highlights future research in decentralization, enhanced security features, and integration of blockchain with AI.

Networking in the future will rely on the hybridization of physical and virtual realities in cyberspace, mainly in the Metaverse of Things [17]. The entities will exist in various synchronized realities. A new framework for possible application of future metaverse is proposed, composed of data flows from multiple operators via wearable devices with varying quality requirements. In this manner, it presents a novel quality model in the service that can conduct dynamic and fine-grained data flow allocation through the use of non-fungible tokens within a decentralized mobile network environment, promoting thus the service management in Metaverse applications. As it takes advantage of blockchain technology's inherent capabilities to interact hassle-free and frictionless with users and operators,

Metaverse is actually a virtual service for building and discovery of 3D environments and is winning attention at lightning speed as a result of its potential of revolutionizing things. This work presents an overview of the major constituents that make up metaverse technologies and surveys some recent developments in this field [18]. The study discusses various applications, including gaming and social networking, education, healthcare, marketing, etc. Along with these opportunities, challenges and issues with scalability, privacy, and security are also discussed. Finally, the work ends with implications the aforementioned technologies will bring along in the progress of digital communication.

There are quite a few new challenges to security and safety with Metaverse applications; they inherit many of the security threats of the Internet of Things and virtual reality technologies. In this work, we present a collaborative framework for intrusion detection on the metaverse called MetaCIDS, based on federated learning and blockchain, specifically designed for network intrusion detection. The proposed framework allows for the capability of training a ML model based on local network data and submitting intrusion alerts to the blockchain in verifiable fashion [19]. It ensures integrity of the training process; it is less vulnerable to data poisoning and malfunctioning nodes. MetaCIDS has high detection accuracy, enabling multi-class and anomaly detection over network intrusion datasets.

The centralized cloud-based model of Metaverse applications encounters latency-related issues and visualization quality. A fog-edge hybrid computing architecture is proposed for metaverse applications, utilizing the computing resource of devices on the edge [20]. This system offloads computationally intensive tasks, such as collision detection and 3D physics emulation, to devices associated with the physical entities involved. This also decreases the dependency on cloud services so that latency problems are thereby minimized. Results of simulations also demonstrate that the proposed architecture can improve metaverse application performance by reducing latency up to 50%.

Methodology

This work focuses on a secure and efficient decentralization of the marketplace for trading ML data and models shown in Figure 34.1. The system, based on blockchain technology, would assist in making transactions transparent, immutable, and private. Two new algorithms are introduced in this work: VCS and EMV, aimed at making the platform more reliable and secure. VCS rates the contributor's credibility based on the quality of data contributed and his past performance, while EMV facilitates evaluation of the efficiency of models without confidential information. Taken together, these technologies set up a trustless yet efficient ML resource trading platform.

Blockchain-based decentralized marketplace
This proposed system would be based on a blockchain- based decentralized marketplace for the trading of ML data and models. Blockchain's inherent

properties, including full transparency, immutability, and decentralized control, ensure that there are secure, tamper-proof transactions. For example, while blockchain provides an infrastructure for proving the origin of data, validation of contributors, and ensuring data privacy in tracking its provenance, it allows for safe transactions to take place between the buyer and seller.

Verified contributor scoring
The first novel algorithm described in this framework is VCS, which represents a critical pillar of establishing the trustworthiness of the contributor. VCS produces dynamic reputation scores as a result of data quality metrics and historical transaction records of the contributors, which will be reflected by potential buyers in terms of credibility and reliability of data or models being offered. Better scores are given to providers of higher quality contributions, while the ones who provide low quality contributions are penalized; as a result, only high-quality resources filter through the market.

Data quality metrics
The VCS incorporates a set of data quality metrics to score every single contribution according to the accuracy of the content, completeness, consistency, and relevance of the data or model being contributed. The algorithm integrating these metrics into the VCS is such that the reputation score of a contributor will build an accurate picture of the quality of the offering being brought to the marketplace. Contributors are likely to keep high standards in place because this is one sure way to build a trustworthy marketplace ecosystem.

Encrypted model validation
The EMV is the second methodology introduced in this work to enhance the safety of the marketplace. This allows a buyer to validate the performance of machine learning models before purchase without revealing the model parameters. Through the application of homomorphic encryption, EMV permits the performance validation of the model while keeping sensitive information confidential. In this technique, privacy of data is guaranteed and no unauthorized access to proprietary model details occurs during the validation process.

Homomorphic encryption
Essentially, homomorphic encryption lies at the core of EMV. The concept of homomorphism refers to computing on a ciphertext without decrypting it. It allows evaluating the accuracy and performance of the model on encrypted test data without exposing the

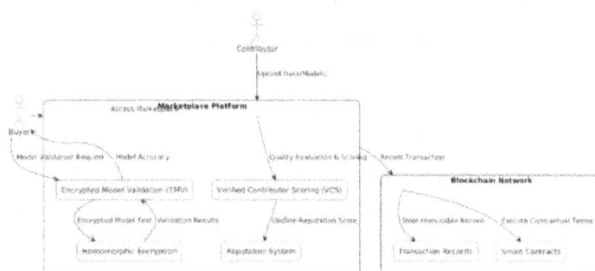

Figure 34.1 Architecture diagram
Source: Author

sensitive parameters present in the model. By using homomorphic encryption, it ensures that the data is kept private and that the model MLs remain undisclosed to anyone, thereby allowing the efficacy of the model to be derived without putting at risk its security.

Security and privacy guarantee

Through the VCS and EMV combination, security and privacy are assured within the marketplace. Data quality and trustworthiness among contributors are also encouraged in VCS, while security on the part of EMV is ensured through secure means wherein buyers could confirm the performance of the models without the risk of being exposed to sensitive information. Blockchain usage further ensures that all transactions are recorded immutably, thereby creating an auditable trail with guarantees of integrity over all exchanges. Besides, the encryption mechanisms protect both buyers and sellers from their access to sensitive information; hence, safe trading is amplified.

Efficiency of decentralized trading platform

This combination of blockchain, VCS, and EMV produces an increasingly efficient decentralized marketplace. The high degree of transparency that blockchain allows automatically diminishes the presence of intermediaries and thus reduces costs and time associated with transactions. VCS and EMV enable quick validation and evaluation phases such that contributors and buyers are quickly able to engage in quick and secure transactions. It makes trading and scaling ML models and data easier, moving towards rapid innovation and access to quality resources in machine learning.

Result and Discussion

The proposed blockchain-based decentralized marketplace for trading ML data and models, improved with VCS and EMV, promises security, reliability, and transparency. Deployment based on VCS dynamically assesses the reputation of its contributors on data quality and transaction history, thus forming an auto-regulative environment. Therefore, buyers are sure of the reliability of the data. This is because contributors with high ratings ensure that the resources uploaded are of good quality. Low-rated contributors are not encouraged to do so hence low engagement with the buyer, and this makes the contributors improve the quality of the sources for high ratings. The trust mechanism sets a marketplace of a high standard where excellence is encouraged in this

case, and this leads to a sustainable cycle of improvement of resources using ML technology.

The application of EMV also follows up to fortify the ecosystem by ensuring validation of the model without its sensitive parameters. Homomorphic encryption allows for the private evaluation of model performance by buyers. It is this sense that maintains proprietary interests of sellers while providing the assurance required to make informed purchases on the part of the buyers. The balance of privacy and transparency addresses the issue in ML model trading, where buyers are unwilling to purchase "black-box" models. EMV bridges the gap effectively and provides trust among buyers and sellers because validation is possible without compromising proprietary information confidentiality.

The blockchain-based platform enhances transaction security much more, providing an immutable and transparent ledger of all marketplace activities. The ledger is very useful in preventing tampering and enables a reliable audit trail for both buyers and sellers. The decentralized nature of blockchain eliminates the need for intermediaries, thereby reducing the costs as well as delays involved in a transaction. Buyers and sellers directly interact with each other in trading to add up to quicker as well as more efficient trading. Accountability also arises from immutability records, where fraudulent behavior is deterred, and a baseline of trust that becomes crucial for steady marketplace activity.

Performance analysis of the system reveals that VCS and EMV mechanisms further add on to the efficiency of the entire platform Figure 34.2. This mechanism then reduces the risk of low-quality data and ineffective models from getting circulated as high standards are met in evaluation and validation shown in Figure 34.3 and Figure 34.4. The streamlined environment saves time spent handling the resources manually, and even buyers can rely on the marketplace when scoring and validation is done. In this aspect, the contribution scoring and encrypted validation automation minimize the computational overheads so that this system is able to work on a scale without a compromise in speed and reliability.

User feedback indicates a heightened sense of confidence in the marketplace because the nature of transparency, contributor accountability, and secure validation all align so well with what users expect from a modern, trustworthy trading platform. The third significant barrier to trading ML models is assurance that buyers can thoroughly study models without exposing proprietary content to these models, which private design of the

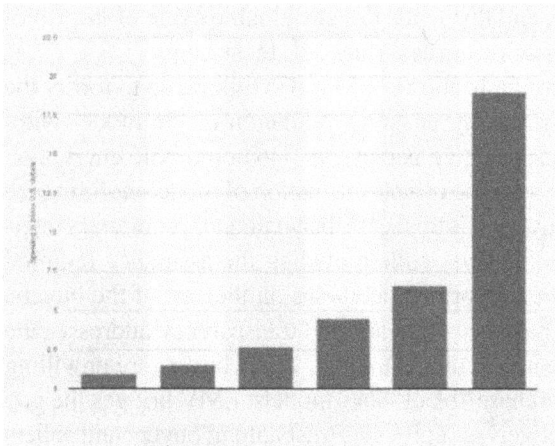

Figure 34.2 Performance analysis of the system
Source: Author

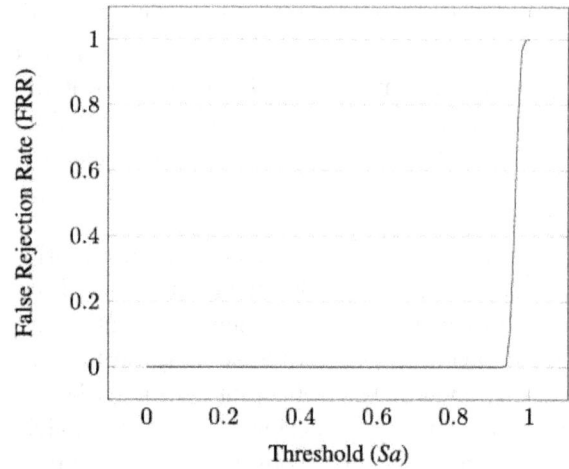

Figure 34.3 False acceptance rate
Source: Author

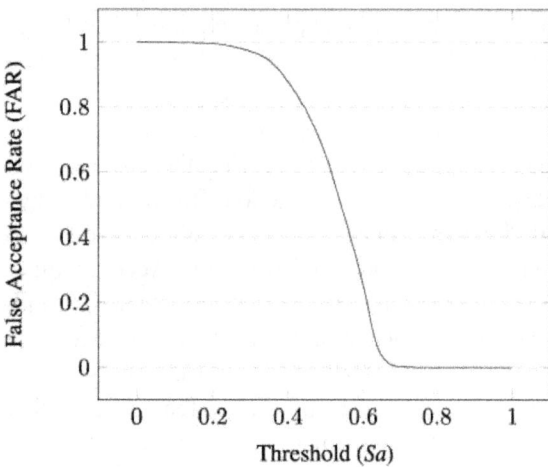

Figure 34.4 False rejection rate
Source: Author

EMV removes. This is a step toward having a leveled playing ground balancing buyer needs and seller protections that could pave the way for more widespread adoption of decentralized trading platforms.

The combination of blockchain, VCS, and EMV demonstrates a robust effective framework for the secure and efficient trading of ML data and models. This synergetic interaction between transparent scoring and encrypted validation allows for trust and an increase in user satisfaction in the marketplace. The platform achieves three critical objectives, which form the crux of most of the challenges of data, model, and decentralized marketplace trading. This is the establishment of a scalable model that can be adapted to any given application in the trading of data and models.

Conclusion

This work presents a new blockchain-based decentralized marketplace in the metaverse that supports and improves the security and efficiency of trading machine learning (ML) data and models. With the fast growth of decentralized finance and virtual economies, any reliable and secure data-exchange platform becomes increasingly critical. The marketplace addresses core issues such as trust, as well as data-quality and privacy, often being one of the main challenges in the decentralized environment. The Verified Contributor Scoring (VCS), algorithm makes sure that high standards are ensured because it has rated its contributors dynamically based on a set of data quality metrics and transaction history. Such a reputation-based approach allows the contributors to develop quality, and increases the general ecosystem's dependability for the buyers. VCS minimizes the risks associated with poor-quality data by penalizing low-grade contributions and enhances the value proposition of the marketplace.

This is accompanied by the Encrypted Model Validation (EMV) algorithm, which permits model validation without trading off data privacy. The EMV uses homomorphic encryption to permit buyers to evaluate model performance metrics such as accuracy beforehand without letting a buyer see the core parameters of the model. This feature offers data privacy and transactional integrity by removing a long-standing barrier in the trade of ML models.

In combination, VCS and EMV form a safe, transparent, and high-quality environment to trade decentralized ML data and models. Such algorithms foster trust while attracting more buyers and contributors to such a marketplace, thus maintaining and creating further strength throughout the marketplace. The new approach developed in this study demonstrates what can be achieved with the combination of blockchain and advanced cryptography to the advantage of the decentralized metaverse economy and, therefore, sets open avenues for future development of secure and transparent marketplaces in the digital world.

References

[1] Seo, J., Ko, H., & Park, S. (2024). Space authentication in the metaverse: a blockchain-based user-centric approach. *IEEE Access*, 12, 18703–18713. DOI: 10.1109/ACCESS.2024.3357938.

[2] Huang, H., Yin, Z., Yang, Q., Li, T., Luo, X., Zhou, L., et al. (2024). Scalability and security of blockchain-empowered metaverse: a survey. *IEEE Open Journal of the Computer Society*, 5, 648–659. DOI: 10.1109/OJCS.2024.3468445.

[3] Truong, V. T., Le, L., & Niyato, D. (2023). Blockchain meets metaverse and digital asset management: a comprehensive survey. *IEEE Access*, 11, 26258–26288. DOI: 10.1109/ACCESS.2023.3257029.

[4] Le, H. D., Truong, V. Y., & Le, L. B. (2024). Blockchain-empowered metaverse: decentralized crowdsourcing and marketplace for trading machine learning data and models. *IEEE Access*, 12, 68556–68572. DOI: 10.1109/ACCESS.2024.3401076.

[5] Din, I. U., Almogren, A., & Kim, B. -S. (2024). Blockchain and 6G: pioneering new dimensions in metaverse marketing. *IEEE Access*, 12, 108263–108274. DOI: 10.1109/ACCESS.2024.3438842.

[6] Truong, V. T., Le, H. D., & Le, L. B. (2024). Trust-free blockchain framework for AI-generated content trading and management in metaverse. *IEEE Access*, 12, 41815–41828. DOI: 10.1109/ACCESS.2024.3376509.

[7] Ghosh, A., Lavanya, Hassija, V., Chamola, V., & El Saddik, A. (2024). A survey on decentralized metaverse using blockchain and web 3.0 technologies, applications, and more. *IEEE Access*, 12, 146915–146948. DOI: 10.1109/ACCESS.2024.3469193.

[8] Huang, H., Zeng, X., Zhao, L., Qiu, C., Wu, H., & Fan, L. (2022). Fusion of building information modeling and blockchain for metaverse: a survey. *IEEE Open Journal of the Computer Society*, 3, 195–207. DOI: 10.1109/OJCS.2022.3206494.

[9] Yang, Q., Zhao, Y., Huang, H., Xiong, Z., Kang, J., & Zheng, Z. (2022). Fusing blockchain and AI with metaverse: a survey. *IEEE Open Journal of the Computer Society*, 3, 122–136. DOI: 10.1109/OJCS.2022.3188249.

[10] Patra, A., Pandey, A., Hassija, V., Chamola, V., & Mishra, R. P. (2024). A survey on edge enabled metaverse: applications, technological innovations, and prospective trajectories within the industry. *IEEE Access*, 12, 125125–125144. DOI: 10.1109/ACCESS.2024.3452184.

[11] Bansal, G., Rajgopal, K., Chamola, V., Xiong, Z., & Niyato, D. (2022). Healthcare in metaverse: a survey on current metaverse applications in healthcare. *IEEE Access*, 10, 119914–119946. DOI: 10.1109/ACCESS.2022.3219845.

[12] Tao, B., Dai, H. -N., Xie, H., & Wang, F. L. (2023). Structural identity representation learning for blockchain-enabled metaverse based on complex network analysis. *IEEE Transactions on Computational Social Systems*, 10(5), 2214–2225. DOI: 10.1109/TCSS.2022.3233059.

[13] Awan, K. A., Din, I. U., Almogren, A., & Seo-Kim, B. (2023). Blockchain-based trust management for virtual entities in the metaverse: a model for avatar and virtual organization interactions. *IEEE Access*, 11, 136370–136394. DOI: 10.1109/ACCESS.2023.3337806.

[14] Ryu, J., Son, S., Lee, J., Park, Y., & Park, Y. (2022). Design of secure mutual authentication scheme for metaverse environments using blockchain. *IEEE Access*, 10, 98944–98958. DOI: 10.1109/ACCESS.2022.3206457.

[15] Elsadig, M., Alohali, M. A., Ibrahim, A. O., & Abulfaraj, A. W. (2024). Roles of blockchain in the metaverse: concepts, taxonomy, recent advances, enabling technologies, and open research issues. *IEEE Access*, 12, 38410–38435. DOI: 10.1109/ACCESS.2024.3367014.

[16] Uddin, M., Obaidat, M., Manickam, S., Laghari, S. U. A., Dandoush, A., Ullah, H., & Ullah, S. S. (2024). Exploring the convergence of Metaverse, Blockchain, and AI: A comprehensive survey of enabling technologies, applications, challenges, and future directions. *Wiley Interdisciplinary Reviews: Data Mining and Knowledge Discovery*, 14(6), e1556.

[17] Li, K., Cui, Y., Li, W., Lv, T., Yuan, X., Li, S., ... & Dressler, F. (2022). When internet of things meets metaverse: Convergence of physical and cyber worlds. *IEEE Internet of Things Journal*, 10(5), 4148–4173.

[18] Ali, M., Naeem, F., Kaddoum, G., & Hossain, E. (2023). Metaverse communications, networking, security, and applications: Research issues, state-of-the-art, and future directions. *IEEE Communications Surveys & Tutorials*, 26(2), 1238–1278.

[19] Nagarjun, A. V., & Rajkumar, S. (2024). Exploring the potential of deep learning and blockchain for intrusion detection systems: A comprehensive review. *Journal of Circuits, Systems and Computers*, 33(16), 2430007.

[20] Dhelim, S., Kechadi, T., Chen, L., Aung, N., Ning, H., & Atzori, L. (2022). Edge-enabled metaverse: The convergence of metaverse and mobile edge computing. *arXiv preprint arXiv:2205.02764*.

35 Comparative performance analysis of dockerized web applications on AWS and oracle cloud

Sachin Kumar Bokde[1,a], Ashok Kumar Verma[2,b], Ruchi Patel[2,c], Sharda Patel[2,d] and Yogesh Jain[3,e]

[1]Gyan Ganga Institute of Technology and Sciences, Jabalpur, MP, India

[2]Department of Computer Science and Engineering Gyan Ganga Institute of Technology and Sciences Jabalpur, MP, India

[3]Financial Systems Administration, Enphase Energy Austin Texas, United States

Abstract

The deployment of containerized web applications in cloud environments has become a standard approach for achieving scalability, flexibility, and resource efficiency. This article provides a comprehensive evaluation of the performance of Dockerized web apps deployed on Amazon Web Services (AWS) and Oracle Cloud, utilizing JMeter as the performance testing framework. The study analyzes essential performance metrics such as reaction time, throughput, CPU and memory use, and scalability under various load conditions. The evaluation compares the effectiveness of AWS with Oracle Cloud in terms of resource utilization, load handling, and the ease of scaling containerized applications. The results demonstrate that while both AWS and Oracle Cloud offer robust infrastructure for deploying Dockerized apps, significant differences exist in their performance under specific conditions. AWS demonstrated superior reaction speed and elasticity under significant loads, whereas Oracle Cloud showcased greater resource utilization efficiency. This paper delivers detailed performance testing results, offering critical insights for DevOps engineers, cloud architects, and IT professionals seeking to optimize Docker installations in multi-cloud environments.

Keywords: Amazon web services, Ddockerized web applications, oracle cloud, throughput

Introduction

The growing adoption of cloud computing and the advent of containerization technologies like Docker have revolutionized the creation, deployment, and management of web applications. Docker containers offer lightweight, portable environments that ensure consistency throughout different stages of development, testing, and production. This adaptability makes Docker an attractive choice for organizations aiming to improve application scalability, reliability, and deployment efficiency. Nevertheless, despite the advantages of containerization, the performance of Dockerized applications is considerably influenced by the underlying cloud architecture on which they operate [1, 2].

Docker is a platform that enables developers to build, distribute, and run modern applications. It employed a container as a standardized software unit that contains code and all its dependencies [3]. As a result, the program functions efficiently and reliably in many computing settings. Docker optimized developer responsibilities in application development by enabling the deployment of packaged software across diverse hardware architectures, along with the construction, instantiation, and initiation of virtualized instances [4]. Docker containers, unlike virtual machines, provide superior compatibility with cloud computing owing to their better performance, increased scalability, and diminished configuration demands relative to other common cloud computing alternatives [5].

Amazon Web Services (AWS) and Oracle Cloud are leading cloud service providers, each offering distinct infrastructure, resource management, and scalability options for the development of containerized applications. AWS is acknowledged for its comprehensive service offerings and well-established ecosystem; yet Oracle Cloud distinguishes itself

[a]sachinbokde@ggits.org, [b]ashokverma@ggits.org, [c]ruchipatel@ggits.org, [d]shardapatel@ggits.org, [e]yogeshj306@gmail.com

DOI: 10.1201/9781003724995-35

from competitive pricing and robust database services, making it suitable for workloads. As organizations increasingly adopt a multi-cloud approach, it is crucial to understand the performance implications of deploying Dockerized applications across different cloud platforms [6, 7].

This study is to evaluate the performance of a Dockerized web application deployed on AWS and Oracle Cloud using JMeter, a leading performance testing tool. JMeter enables the simulation of various user loads and traffic patterns, providing insights into critical performance metrics such as response time, throughput, CPU and memory utilization, and overall scalability. This study evaluates the performance of Dockerized apps across two cloud platforms to clarify the advantages and disadvantages of each environment, thereby aiding cloud architects and developers in making educated choices about platform selection for containerized web applications.

Literature Review

Several studies have explored the benefits and performance impacts of using Docker containers in cloud environments. Authors conducted a comparative study of containers and virtual machines (VMs), revealing that containers offer greater resource efficiency and faster startup times compared to traditional VMs. Their research underscored the advantages of Docker containers for cloud-native applications, particularly in microservices architectures that require rapid scaling and deployment [8].

The author investigated Docker's role in enabling microservices within cloud platforms, noting that Docker's containerization approach supports the decoupling of services, which is essential for dynamically scaling applications in the cloud. The study also highlighted the importance of robust orchestration tools to manage the complexities of deploying and scaling containers in production environments [9].

Potdar et al. [10] evaluated container orchestration tools such as Kubernetes and Docker Swarm, focusing on their compatibility with cloud services like AWS, Google Cloud, and Microsoft Azure. The findings emphasized that while Docker simplifies container creation and deployment, the choice of cloud platform plays a critical role in determining performance, scalability, and cost efficiency.

Authors developed a cloud benchmarking system to evaluate the performance of cloud providers by assessing parameters such as network latency, data storage efficiency, and resource scalability. Their study underscored the importance of using real-world workloads for accurate performance testing. However, it primarily focused on VM-based architectures and did not address the use of Docker containers in cloud environments [11].

In this paper [12] authors used JMeter to assess the performance of Dockerized applications in cloud environments. Their study focused on understanding how containerization affects the scalability and responsiveness of applications under load, noting that Docker containers generally outperform virtual machines due to lower overhead. While JMeter proved effective in simulating user traffic and measuring performance, the research was limited to AWS and did not explore multi-cloud environments or the performance of Dockerized web applications across different cloud platforms. Other tools such as Gatling, Locust, and Apache Bench have also been used for cloud performance benchmarking, but JMeter remains the preferred choice for many researchers due to its flexibility and seamless integration with cloud infrastructure. Despite its popularity, there has been limited research on evaluating Dockerized web applications in diverse cloud environments using performance testing techniques, highlighting a need for further exploration in this area.

This study rectifies these deficiencies by executing a thorough performance assessment of Dockerized web applications deployed on AWS and Oracle cloud platforms, utilizing JMeter and additional testing tools to replicate real-world traffic. The study seeks to deliver practical insights into the performance attributes of containerized apps, assisting cloud architects and developers in optimizing their deployments according to platform-specific performance metrics.

Proposed Algorithm

In this section the algorithm is proposed for deployment of Dockerized application on AWS and Oracle Cloud. Figure 35.1. Proposed Architecture of Deployment of Dockerized Application. Based on this figure the algorithm shown in Table 35.1.

Methodology and Model Specifications

The proposed algorithm in the previous section provides a systematic approach for deploying Dockerized web applications on AWS and Oracle Cloud, enabling performance and cost comparisons. The process

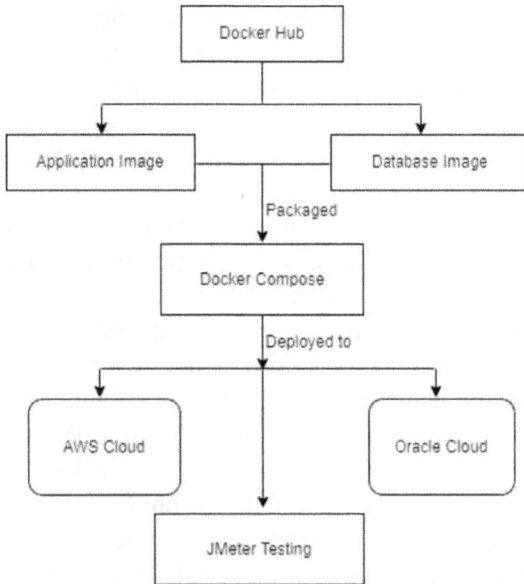

Figure 35.1 Proposed architecture of deployment of Dockerized application
Source: Author

begins by containerizing the application using Docker, ensuring portability and platform independence. The Docker image is then pushed to respective container registries, AWS ECR and Oracle OCIR, for deployment. Cloud resources such as virtual machines or containers orchestration clusters (e.g., ECS/EKS for AWS, OKE for Oracle Cloud) are provisioned based on predefined configurations. The application is deployed on both platforms using appropriate services, followed by performance testing to evaluate throughput. Cost analysis is conducted to compare the financial implications of running the application on each platform Finally, the algorithm facilitates a comparative analysis of deployment ease, performance, and cost to derive insights and recommend the most suitable platform for specific use cases. This streamlined methodology ensures efficient deployment and detailed evaluation of Dockerized web applications on both cloud platforms outperforming Oracle Cloud, which handles 117.9 requests per second.

Empirical Results

The experiment involves testing the web applications deployed on cloud platforms, specifically AWS and Oracle Cloud. These tests are conducted using JMeter, and the outcomes are recorded and thoroughly analyzed. Based on the stress testing results shown in Table 35.2, AWS exhibited a better average speed compared to Oracle

Table 35.1 Proposed algorithm for Dockerized application deployment.

Input:
A: Web application to be Dockerized
C: Cloud platforms set {AWS, Oracle Cloud}
R: Resource configuration parameters (CPU, memory, network)
P: Performance metrics (latency, throughput, cost)
Output:
D: Deployment status {Success, Failure}
M: Performance comparison metrics
Steps 1: Initialization:
Define:
Containerized_App ←Dockerize(A)
Steps 2: Push Image to Registries:
For each $c \in C$:
Registry(c) ←Push(Containerized_App,c)
Steps 3: Provision Resources:
For each $c \in C$:
Resources(c) ← Provision(R,c)
Steps 4: Deploy Application:
For each $c \in C$:
 D_c ← Deploy(Containerized_App,Resources(c))
Steps 5: Performance Testing:
For each $c \in C$:
P_c ← Evaluate (Metrics(P),Application (Dc))
Steps 6: Comparison and Analysis:
Compute: M ← Compare(P_{AWS},P_{Oracle})
Steps 7: Output Results:
Return D and M

Source: Author

Cloud. Moreover, AWS outperformed Oracle Cloud in server throughput, showcasing its ability to handle a higher volume of requests per second.

This table outlines the performance metrics of Dockerized applications hosted on AWS and Oracle Cloud, focusing on key parameters. Below is an explanation of the columns:

- **Cloud services**: The cloud platforms under comparison, namely AWS and Oracle Cloud.
- **Sample**: Represents the total number of requests processed during the evaluation, which is 7,000 for both platforms.
- **Average (ms)**: Indicates the average response time in milliseconds. AWS records an average response time of 250 ms, whereas Oracle Cloud has a higher average of 545 ms.
- **Minimum (ms)**: Denotes the shortest response time observed, which is 2 ms for both platforms, showcasing their ability to deliver rapid responses in optimal conditions.

Table 35.2 Performance testing results by JMeter.

Cloud services	Results				
	Sample	Average/ms	Minimum/ms	Maximum/ms	Throughput
AWS	7,000	250	2	1400	166.5/sec
Oracle	7,000	545	2	18233	117.9/sec

Source: Author

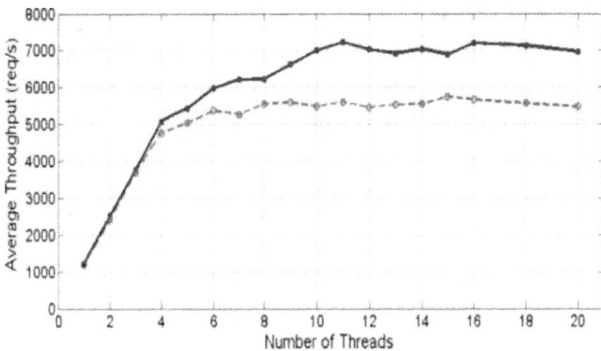

Figure 35.2 Performance analysis for Dockerized application on AWS and Oracle cloud
Source: Author

- **Maximum (ms)**: Refers to the longest response time recorded, with AWS at 1,400 ms and Oracle Cloud at a significantly higher 1,823 ms.
- **Throughput**: Reflects the number of requests processed per second. AWS achieves a throughput of 166.5 requests per second.

This graph illustrates the average throughput (in requests per second) as a function of the number of threads for Dockerized applications deployed on AWS and Oracle Cloud. The performance comparison is based on scaling the number of threads from 1 to 20, representing increased parallel request handling. The blue line represents the throughput performance of the Dockerized application on AWS. Throughput increases steadily with the number of threads, peaking around 10 threads, after which it stabilizes at approximately 7,000 requests per second. This indicates that AWS handles higher concurrency efficiently and saturates at a higher throughput level. The red dashed line corresponds to the throughput on Oracle Cloud. While throughput also increases with the number of threads, it peaks at a lower value, approximately 5,000 requests per second, and shows more consistent stabilization at

this level. This suggests Oracle Cloud has a lower maximum throughput compared to AWS. AWS appears to be better suited for handling high-concurrency workloads in Dockerized environments, while Oracle Cloud, although stable, may be more suitable for moderate workloads. This highlights the importance of choosing the appropriate cloud platform based on application requirements and expected traffic.

Conclusion

This research conducted a comparative analysis of the performance of Dockerized web applications deployed on AWS and Oracle Cloud. Metrics such as latency, throughput, scalability, and resource utilization were analyzed across different workload levels. The results indicated that AWS outperformed in managing high traffic due to its advanced load balancing capabilities, whereas Oracle Cloud proved to be more cost-efficient and resource-effective for moderate workloads. Each platform demonstrated unique advantages based on specific use cases, emphasizing the need to align cloud platform selection with application demands. Future studies could investigate hybrid deployment models to capitalize on the strengths of both providers, better suited for handling high-concurrency workloads in Dockerized environments, while Oracle Cloud, although stable, may be more suitable for moderate workloads. This highlights the importance of choosing the appropriate cloud platform based on application requirements and expected traffic.

References

[1] Richter, F. (n.d.). Amazon, microsoft & google dominate cloud market statista. https://www.statista.com/chart/18819/worldwide-market-share-of-leading-cloud-infrastructure-service-providers/ (accessed Jan. 3, 2023).

[2] Morabito, R. (2017). Virtualization on internet of things edge devices withcontainer technologies: A performance evaluation. *IEEE Access*, 5, 8835–8850. doi: 10.1109/ACCESS.2017.2704444.

[3] Apache Software Foundation (n.d.). Apache JMeter. apache.org.https://jmeter.apache.org (accessed Dec. 14, 2022).

[4] Abdelbaky, M., Diaz-Montes, J., Parashar, M., Unuvar, M., & Steinder, M. (2015). Docker containers across multiple clouds and datacenters. In Proceedings - 2015 IEEE/ACM 8th International Conference on Utility and Cloud Computing, UCC 2015, (pp. 368–371). doi: 10.1109/UCC.2015.58.

[5] Zaman, F. U., Khan, A. H., & Owais, M. (2021). Performance evaluation of amazon's, google's, and microsoft's serverless functions: a comparative study. https://www.ijstr.org/final-print/apr2021/P.

[6] Nawaz, H., Juve, G., da Silva, R. F., & Deelman, E. (n.d.). University of Southern California, Information Sciences Institute, Marina Del Rey, CA, USA. https://deelman.isi.edu/wordpress/wp content/paper-cite-data/pdf/nawaz-apdcm-2016.pdf.

[7] Truyen, E., Kratzke, N., Van Landuyt, D., Lagaisse, B., & Joosen, W. (2020). Managing feature compatibility in kubernetes : vendor comparison and analysis. *IEEE Access*, 8, 228420–228439. https://ieeexplore.ieee.org/document/9298825.

[8] Zhang, J., Lu, X., & Panda, D. K. (2016). Performance characterization of hypervisor-and container-based virtualization for HPC on SR-IOV enabled infiniband clusters. In 2016 IEEE International Parallel and Distributed Processing Symposium Workshops.

[9] Hassan, M., Zhao, W., & Yang, J. (2010). Provisioning web services from resource constrained mobile devices. In Cloud Computing (CLOUD), 2010 IEEE 3rd International Conference on (pp. 490–497). IEEE.

[10] Potdar, A. M., Narayan, D. G., Kengond, S., & Mulla, M. M. (2020). Performance evaluation of docker container and virtual machine. *Procedia Computer Science*, 171, 1419–1428. doi:10.1016/j.procs.2020.04.152.

36 Employing generative adversarial techniques to address imbalanced datasets

Nitin Kumar Jharbade[a] and Harsh Mathur[b]

Department of Computer Science and Engineering, Rabindranath Tagore University, Bhopal, MP, India

Abstract

Imbalanced datasets are commonly observed in real-world applications, characterized by disparate distributions of cases among various classifications. The efficacy of classifiers is essential in systems demanding great precision. Nonetheless, imbalanced datasets can adversely affect classification performance, even when employing methods such as synthetic minority oversampling. This paper proposes employing adversarial learning techniques, particularly generative adversarial networks, to equilibrate the datasets. This article presents a strategy employing generative adversarial networks (GANs) to address class imbalance through the synthesis of actual data for underrepresented categories. A conditional GAN is utilized to generate synthetic samples customized for the minority classes, hence achieving dataset balance. The suggested methodology is assessed using data sets including Car Evaluation and Human Activity Recognition, showcasing notable enhancements in classification accuracy and minority class identification. The results highlight the efficacy of GANs as a robust approach for improving performance on imbalanced datasets while preserving data diversity and integrity.

Keywords: Class imbalance problem, generative adversarial networks, machine learning, synthetic minority over-sampling technique

Introduction

Class imbalance is a prevalent problem in machine learning, characterized by certain classes being markedly underrepresented relative to others. This disparity frequently results in biased models that demonstrate inadequate generalization, particularly for minority classes [1]. Artificial intelligence has permeated numerous fields, including agriculture, healthcare, image caption prediction, counterfeit image detection, and multi-class image categorization. In numerous practical classification situations, the training data demonstrates a long-tailed distribution, characterized by certain classes being plentiful while others are limited in quantity [2]. The issue of learning from imbalanced data has garnered considerable interest among the scientific community. Although numerous methods have been suggested to address imbalanced binary-class issues, they may not be immediately applicable or produce appropriate outcomes in multiclass scenarios, which are more prevalent in practical applications. Machine learning, a significant domain in computer science, utilizes diverse methods to derive valuable insights from datasets. The presence of imbalanced data can introduce biases into the models, potentially leading to distorted predictions that favor the majority class, less efficacy in recognizing minority class instances, and overall poorer generalizability across varied datasets.

Utilizing adversarial techniques to address unbalanced data allows us to mitigate these risks by training models on a dataset that is more equitable and representative. This method can improve the precision and fairness of predictions, so facilitating sustainable decision-making and policies that advantage both individuals and the environment.

Recent developments in deep learning, especially GANs, provide an innovative solution to these difficulties. Generative adversarial networks (GANs), recognized for their capacity to produce authentic synthetic data, offer a viable alternative for enhancing minority classes in imbalanced datasets. By producing high-quality synthetic samples, GANs can improve the diversity and equilibrium of datasets, facilitating more effective learning across all classes for models. This work employs conditional GANs to generate synthetic data specifically designed for minority classes. The approach is assessed using benchmark datasets, such as the car evaluation and human activity recognition datasets, illustrating its efficacy in enhancing classifier performance while maintaining data integrity.

[a]jharbade.nitin@gmail.com, [b]harsh.mathur@aisectuniversity.ac.in

DOI: 10.1201/9781003724995-36

Related Work

The application of DL in supervised learning has posed several issues for GANs utilized with real-world datasets. These issues encompass managing many data types, stochastic distributions, and high-dimensional datasets. To address these issues, [3] presented a distinctive GAN model referred to as MedGAN. The methodology employs an autoencoder inside its architecture to acquire a lower-dimensional latent representation of high-dimensional medical data before creating synthetic samples. However, their evaluation of the dataset was confined to binary classification. The authors presented a technology called CorrGAN [4], aimed at generating synthetic discrete data while maintaining the inherent correlations within the dataset. This model enhances traditional GANs to tackle the difficulties of creating high-dimensional, discrete datasets with interrelated variables.

The study presented in delineates a new methodology for addressing missing data imputation, referred to as the generative adversarial imputation network (GAIN) [5]. The authors introduced TensorGen, an innovative method for synthesizing data. They conducted a comparison with MedGAN and concluded that their model excelled due to its ability to avert mode collapse. Nevertheless, their evaluation was limited to a dataset comprising binary categorization. Another article [6] presented a novel methodology for producing synthetic patient records through the integration of autoencoders and GANs. They concluded that all unique versions demonstrated superior performance compared to existing methods; nonetheless, they were unable to ascertain the best model.

The research proposes an innovative GAN-based approach to address imbalanced datasets. Most researchers solely assessed different models on a binary class; in contrast, this study employed GAN on a multi-class dataset using classification techniques.

Proposed Methodology

This section offers an overview of the architecture and foundational structure of GAN, including data augmentation. The initial subsection contains an elucidation of the core concepts underpinning GAN. The specific GAN model utilized in the research is addressed in the second subsection of the subsequent paragraph. The principal classifier decision tree is examined in the third subsection. Figure 36.1 illustrates the methods being provided.

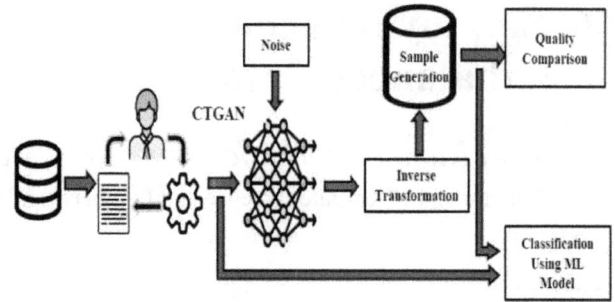

Figure 36.1 Proposed framework
Source: Author

GAN

The basic objective of the Generative Adversarial Network is to train a generative model to comprehend the underlying distribution of a dataset, hence addressing the issue of imbalance. This will enable the model to produce fresh samples that are authentic and indistinguishable from the original data [7]. A standard GAN comprises two competitively trained networks, the Generator and Discriminator. The GAN employs antagonistic learning to improve the quality of artificial data generated. The generator produces plausible artificial data by employing random noise. The generator aims to mislead the discriminator so that augmented data remains unpredictable.

In contrast, the discriminator receives the actual training data alongside the generated augmented data as input variables and is skilled to distinguish between the supplemented data and the originally collected data. It calculates the probability to ascertain the chance that specific samples originate from potential data sources. loss functions for the generator and the discriminator are described below.

$$\nabla_{\theta g} \frac{1}{n} \sum_{i=1}^{n} \left[log \left(1 - D \left(G(z^{(i)}) \right) \right) \right] \quad (1)$$

$$\nabla_{\theta d} \frac{1}{n} \sum_{i=1}^{n} \left[log D(x^{(i)}) + log \left(1 - D \left(G(z^{(i)}) \right) \right) \right] \quad (2)$$

Where $\nabla\theta g$ and $\nabla\theta d$ denotes the generator and discriminator gradients, $D(x^{(i)})$, and $G(z^{(i)})$ are the output and characteristics of the discriminator for augmented data. The discriminator is trained with the loss function for accurately identifying the proper data source. This is achieved via the training process. The generator is trained to minimize the second term in Equation (1) to hide the discriminator. The SGD algorithm is employed to train the model.

Proposed GAN

The conditional GAN, which was first presented in [8], is an improvement on the original GAN that incorporates label information to condition both the generator and the discriminator. An input layer is incorporated into the generator and the discriminator neural networks to accomplish this goal. Because of this, the loss function is altered in the following manner:

$$\nabla_{\theta g} \frac{1}{n} \Sigma_{i=1}^{n} \left[log \left(1 - D \left(G(z/y^{(i)}) \right) \right) \right] \quad (3)$$

$$\nabla_{\theta d} \frac{1}{n} \Sigma_{i=1}^{n} \left[log D(x/y^{(i)}) + log \left(1 - D \left(G(z/ y^{(i)}) \right) \right) \right] \quad (4)$$

The generator is responsible for integrating labels and stochastic noise input in order to provide a uniform hidden representation. As inputs to the discriminative function of the discriminator, X and Y serve their respective functions.

The label information is transformed into a dense vector by utilization of a Keras embedding layer, which ultimately results in the expression of the noise vector and labels into a single frame. Following that, the vector is multiplied by the noise vector in an element-wise fashion. A feature vector is incorporated into the generator so that it can be guided through the process of producing its output. The resultant vector, which is created by multiplying the elements of the two vectors that correspond to one another, is then fed into the GAN. ReLU activation function is applied to the noise prior and class label as they are processed through the hidden layers. These inputs are then further transformed into a second hidden layer using ReLU activation.

Decision tree

A decision tree is a graphical representation composed of various nodes that define specific pathways. The root node, which is the initial node, has no input. Internal nodes, on the other hand, have both inputs and outputs. Leaf nodes, also referred to as decision nodes, typically have only one input. Internal nodes divide the dataset into subgroups based on probabilistic measures such as randomness and impurity in a dataset. The connections among the branches signify the criteria used for differentiation. Leaf nodes, located at the ends of the branches, indicate the categories assigned to the data. Each node or leaf is assigned to the class with the most favorable response values.

Experimental Framework

Data sets

For this investigation, datasets were examined that included either binary-class or multi-class problems, with one dataset displaying a significant unequal distribution.

Car evaluation dataset: The dataset utilized was sourced from the UCI repository. The dataset was categorized into four groups: unacceptable, acceptable, fairly acceptable, and very good, in which all classes except unacceptable are minority classes.

Human activity recognition dataset: Each of the thirty individuals who used a Samsung smartphone contributed to the collection of this dataset [9]. The participants were instructed to engage in a variety of doings, such as walking, climbing stairs, ascending and descending stairs, standing, sitting, and lying down. This dataset displayed a relatively small number of imbalances.

Banking dataset: The data set that was utilized in this investigation was produced by [10] through the use of a real-life dataset obtained from a Portuguese financial institution. It was determined that the primary objective of this model's classification was to determine whether or not a customer would make a deposit, which led to the classification of this issue as a binary classification problem.

Experiment setup

Our research concentrated on three datasets from different domains: automotive assessment, human activity recognition, and finance. The car evaluation dataset had the greatest degree of imbalance.

After training the model on all of the original datasets, we were able to determine whether or not our conditional tabular GAN was effective. Following the process of fitting the model to the data, we made use of it to generate synthetic data, which was then subsequently transferred into the datasets that were initially collected. We partitioned the datasets into training, validation, and testing subsets in proportions of fifty percent, ten percent, and ten percent, respectively, to ensure proper classification. Through the utilization of this technology, the issue of data imbalance was properly solved. Through the utilization of tabular data, our suggested GAN architecture was able to effectively model both numerical and categorical variables. According to what was said earlier, we made use of the Gumbel Softmax activation function for the category columns. Figure 36.2 depicts the summary statistics of various datasets.

To address the issue of imbalanced data, we employed a conditional tabular GAN for augmentation, followed by classification using a decision tree. In case of skewed data, the decision tree displayed sensitivity. We adjusted the aim functions of both the generators and the discriminators to accomplish robust GAN training [11]. As input, the class label was used by the generator

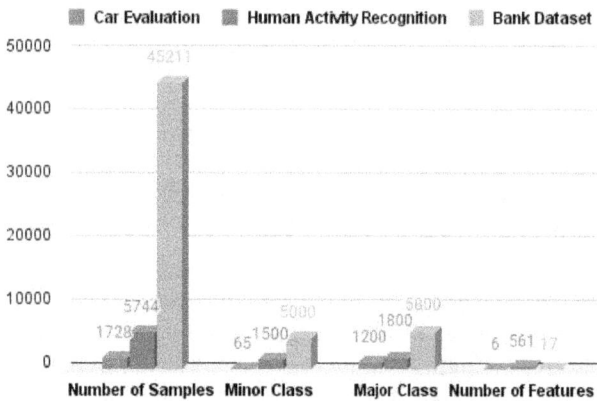

Figure 36.2 Summary statistics of various datasets
Source: Author

Table 36.1 Performance results before data augmentation on different datasets.

Datasets	Precision (%)	Recall	F1-Score (%)	Accuracy
Car evaluation	58	56	57	80
Human activity recognition	81	91	86	95
Bank dataset	98	88	94	73

(*Source: Author's compilation*)

and discriminator networks. This allowed the generator to be trained to create samples that were representative of a certain class. This enabled the generator to predict the distribution of the authentic data, while the discriminator was able to acquire the ability to discern between real and counterfeit data. To test the classifiers, selecting the appropriate hyperparameters was necessary. To determine the hyperparameters that were most effective, we utilized both a manual selection process and a random grid search method. Epochs, batch size, log frequency, dimensional parameters learning rates, decay rates, and discriminator steps were the hyperparameters that were included in the suggested model.

Results

To analyze three different real-world datasets, we utilized a novel approach that involved the utilization of a conditional tabular GAN model. A summary of the findings can be found in Table 36.3. Since our conditional tabular model can handle tables that contain a combination of data kinds, we can apply it collectively to all three datasets. While Table 36.1 presents the performance metrics of all datasets used before data augmentation, Table 36.2 presents the performance outcomes that were achieved after the application of data augmentation was implemented.

The proposed model is presented with alternative data augmentation methods, including the GAN model and the SMOTE method, as illustrated in Table 36.3. This comparison encompassed many models and datasets aimed at mitigating the class imbalance problem. The proposed model was evaluated on three datasets from diverse domains, and its performance was contrasted with state-of-the-art approaches used on datasets including banking, human activity, heart disease,

and diabetes. The findings in Table 36.3 indicate that the proposed model surpassed the alternative models. Notably, the GAN exhibited inferior accuracy on the bank dataset compared to the SMOTE + bagging model, perhaps due to the latter's hybrid nature. This engenders potential for future advancement and inquiry.

Discussion

This work concentrated on addressing the problem of class imbalance in datasets. In our study, we developed a redesigned architecture that enhanced the traditional GAN by fully using adversarial learning through the application of hyperparameters. To conduct a thorough investigation, we implemented data augmentation on three distinct datasets and subsequently assessed the efficacy of our method via a decision tree classifier. Table 36.1 illustrates the classification performance without data augmentation, with about 95% accuracy for the human activity identification dataset and 73% accuracy for the bank dataset, reflecting a spectrum of high to moderate accuracy for real-world imbalanced datasets. This mismatch may be ascribed to the model's bias, which prefers the popular class. Consequently, a conditional tabular GAN was applied to each of the three datasets. The outcomes summarized in Table 36.3 clearly illustrate that data augmentation improved the predictive accuracy of the minority class imbalanced dataset.

Conclusions and Future Scope

A thorough empirical investigation of data augmentation methods for actual multi-class datasets was carried out in this paper. Addressing the issue of dataset imbalance, we explored the use of adversarial learning models. The model's performance was assessed on three diverse datasets from distinct

Table 36.2 Performance results after data augmentation on different datasets.

Datasets	Precision (%)	Recall	F1-Score (%)	Accuracy
Car evaluation	66	69	71	83
Human activity recognition	95	93	94	96
Bank dataset	100	75	100	78

(*Source: Author's compilation*)

Table 36.3 Performance comparison of the proposed method against various models.

Method	Dataset	Average accuracy(%)
SMOTE [12]	Car evaluation dataset	76
	Bank dataset	73
GAN [13]	Human activity recognition dataset	87
Proposed method	Car evaluation dataset	83
	Human activity recognition dataset	96
	Bank dataset	78

(*Source: Author's compilation*)

domains, including categorical and time series data. Furthermore, a decision tree was used as a classifier to assess the fabricated data. The findings showed that a variety of distributions, including mixed and diversified data kinds, may be produced by using generative adversarial networks for sample augmentation. This approach surpasses conventional methods and provides a foundation for addressing imbalanced data-sets with multiple classes and varied data sources.

GANs are prone to convergence failure and model collapse. Therefore, our future focus will be on finding effective solutions to overcome these challenges. Additionally, exploring oversampling techniques like SMOTified-GAN [14] could be valuable in mitigating data imbalance and enhancing the classifier model.

References

[1] Zhu, B., Baesens, B., & Vanden Broucke, S. K. L. M. (2017). An empirical comparison of techniques for the class imbalance problem in churn prediction. *Information Sciences*, 408, 84–99.

[2] Fernández, A., López, V., Galar, M., José, M., & Herrera, F. (2013). Knowledge-based systems analysing the classification of imbalanced data-sets with multiple classes: binarization techniques and Ad-Hoc approaches. *Knowledge-Based Systems*, 42, 97–110.

[3] Choi, E., Biswal, S., Malin, B., Duke, J., Stewart, W. F., & Sun, J. (2017). Generating multi-label discrete patient records using generative adversarial networks. In Proceedings of the 2nd Machine Learning for Healthcare Conference, Boston, MA, USA, 18–19 August 2017, (Vol. 68, pp. 1–20).

[4] Patel, S., Kakadiya, A., Mehta, M., Derasari, R., Patel, R., & Gandhi, R. (2018). Correlated discrete data generation using adversarial training. arXiv 2018, arXiv:1804.00925.

[5] Yoon, J., Jordon, J., & Van Der Schaar, M. (2018). GAIN: missing data imputation using generative adversarial nets. In Proceedings of the 35th International Conference on Machine Learning, ICML 2018, Stockholm, Sweden, 10–15 July 2018, (Vol. 13, pp. 9042–9051).

[6] Camino, R., Hammerschmidt, C., & State, R. (2018). Generating multi-categorical samples with generative adversarial networks. arXiv 2018, arXiv:1807.01202.

[7] Durugkar, I., Gemp, I., & Mahadevan, S. (2017). Generative multi-adversarial networks. In Proceedings of the 5th International Conference on Learning Representations, ICLR 2017—Conference Track Proceedings, Toulon, France, 24–26 April 2017, (pp. 1–14).

[8] Mirza, M., & Osindero, S. (2014). Conditional generative adversarial nets. arXiv 2014, arXiv:1411.1784.

[9] Cruciani, F., Sun, C., Zhang, S., Nugent, C., Li, C., Song, S., et al. (2019). A public domain dataset for human activity recognition in free-living conditions. In Proceedings of the 2019 IEEE SmartWorld, Ubiquitous Intelligence and Computing, Advanced and Trusted Computing, Scalable Computing and Communications, Internet of People and Smart City Innovation, SmartWorld/UIC/ATC/SCALCOM/IOP/SCI 2019, Leicester, UK, 19–23 August 2019, (pp. 166–171).

[10] Moro, S., Cortez, P., & Rita, P. (2014). A data-driven approach to predict the success of bank telemarketing. *Decision Support Systems*, 62, 22–31.

[11] Odena, A., Olah, C., & Shlens, J. (2017). Conditional image synthesis with auxiliary classifier gans. In Proceedings of the 34th International Conference on Machine Learning, ICML 2017, Sydney, Australia, 6–11 August 2017, (Vol. 6, pp. 4043–4055).

[12] Mukherjee, M., & Khushi, M. (2021). SMOTE-ENC: a novel SMOTE-based method to generate synthetic data for nominal and continuous features. *Applied System Innovation*, 4, 18.

[13] Moshiri, P. F., Navidan, H., Shahbazian, R., Ghorashi, S. A., & Windridge, D. (2020). Using GAN to enhance the accuracy of indoor human activity recognition. arXiv 2020, arXiv:2004.11228.

[14] Sharma, A., Singh, , & Chandra, R. (2022). SMOTified-GAN for class imbalanced pattern classification problems. *IEEE Access*, 10, 30655–30665.

37 Pioneering employee healthcare: dynamic workforce optimization

Harinesh, S.[1,a], Harsan Raj, R.[1,b] and Suresh, D.[2,c]

[1]Student, St Joseph's Institute of Technology, Chennai, Tamil Nadu, India

[2]Assistant Professor, St Joseph's Institute of Technology, Chennai, Tamil Nadu, India

Abstract

Advanced health monitoring and automated task reallocation is the new approach in promoting the health and productivity of employees. The system constantly monitors heart rate, blood pressure, body temperature, and other such critical health metrics continuously with the help of physiological sensors and wearable devices. Here, the data is processed in real time such that anomalies in health can be identified further leading to the intelligent swapping of workforce tasks if a worker's health is compromised. This mechanism supports timely medical intervention or rest without causing operational flow breakdown, which in turn develops a proactive approach to health issues at work. It employs an Arduino Mega microcontroller, which assembles several health sensors with a GSM module to alert colleagues or supervisors in critical situations. Health data will be stored in a Java-based database supporting trend analysis and predictive insight. This integrated approach will help the project in reducing absenteeism, preventing health crisis, and even improving productivity to become more dynamic in workforce optimization.

Keywords: Task swapping, workforce optimization

Introduction

Ensuring an employee's health and safety becomes a priority for organizations in this fast-paced work environment so that they can facilitate increased productivity and workforce wellness becomes a matter of importance [1]. In an employee healthcare management approach where people are mostly subjected to periodical check-ups or reactive intervention measures, it often misses critical real-time health issues at hand, which may result in high absenteeism, productivity drop, and preventable health catastrophes. We have developed an innovative solution to integrating wearable health-monitoring technology with automated task management that can make the workplace both safer and more responsive [4].

This project's very basis is continuous health monitoring. It includes sensors and wearable devices that monitor and report the person's vital signs, including heart rate, blood pressure, body temperature, oxygen saturation, and respiratory rate [7]. The system integrates these devices with an Arduino Mega microcontroller and processes health data in real time to immediately detect anomalies by making health data available. Then, automated responses would be triggers such as sending alerts to the supervisors or designated colleagues through a GSM-based alerts system that would provide avenues for timely intervention and engage an intelligent workforce- swapping mechanism for task assignment [8].

All the health data are stored in a secure Java-based database to allow long-term trend analysis and predictive insights. It empowers organizations to identify trends in employee health, determine risk factors, and intervene with preventive measures for improvement of workforce well-being. Predictive analytics in the system will predict possible health risks and optimize workforce planning by means of historical data so that there is a reduced probability of health- related incidents.

This proactive model of employee care encourages safety in the workplace and saves costs from absenteeism and healthcare intervention.

Literature Review

Real-time health anomaly prediction via IoT- enabled dew computing systems

It aims to elaborate an internet of things (IoT) design combining dew computing and the framework for a

[a]harineshs97@gmail.com, [b]harsanraj24@gmail.com, [c]suresh.d.28@gmail.com

DOI: 10.1201/9781003724995-37

digital twin (DT) in real-time monitoring of health and environmental parameters in rural population, put into four tiers consisting of data sensing and preprocessing, irregular event prediction, DT-based event scheduling, and severity analysis [13,14]. The system uses a dew computing layer for the local processing, which detects anomalies in health and environmental data with the help of logistic regression, and predictive simulations are performed at the DT layer.

IoT-enabled health monitoring systems: technological advances and implementation strategies

A wireless sensing node, developed for SHM of reinforced concrete within an Industrial Internet of Things (IIoT), is briefed in the study [3]. This battery-free system sustains long-term deployment through the establishment of communication over tens of meters with LoRaWAN-embedded concrete, owing to wireless power transfer (WPT). The antenna provides support for energy harvesting, as well as for data transmission, by SWIPT. The sensing nodes will monitor several parameters including temperature, humidity, strain, and electrical resistivity. Similarly, the communicating nodes will aggregate SN data, as well as managing WPT.

A Novel framework for vibration-based and cloud-integrated structural health monitoring

Payawal and Kim [5] offers an overview of vibration-based structural health monitoring (SHM) techniques to monitor steel slit dampers (SSDs) designed to increase structural resilience by seismic energy absorption. The paper stresses the role of continuous monitoring to catch degradation because material wear may compromise the efficiency of SSDs. In this regard, advances in sensor technology, data acquisition and experimental setup are highlighted to support the monitoring of SSDs, but there are several drawbacks in terms of sensor optimization and real-time monitoring.

Graphene-based wearable device and elderly health care monitoring system

Through this article, two studies revealed the developments of wearable technology in elderly care [11]. First, the research focused on the synthesis and application of graphene-based materials including laser-induced graphene (LIG) and laser-reduced graphene oxide (LrGO) for non-invasive physiological monitoring. The latter are synthesized through methods

that involve SEM, micro-Raman spectroscopy, and XPS, and thus set up in wearable devices, such as temperature sensors, micro-supercapacitors (MSCs), and ECG electrodes. Embedded in PDMS, LrGO provides stable temperature sensitivity with high resistance to humidity at a value of -1.23 kΩ/$°$C. The second one describes a healthcare system integrating wearables, which are smart clothes and health watches, to monitor residents' physiological parameters and alert the caregivers in case of abnormal events.

Advanced IoT-driven healthcare solutions: wearable technology and real-time monitoring for optimized patient care

Abdulameer et al. [12] describes a health-care system that utilizes wearable devices, such as smart clothes, health watches, and body tags. The physiological parameters, such as heart rate, oxygen saturation, and sleep quality can be monitored. The fetched data is sent to a server where real-time analysis is made. The combination of the system with an alerting proactive notification scheme would alert the primary caregivers and family members regarding any abnormal readings found. Khana and Salah [9] introduced an IoT-based system using heart and blood pressure sensors in modules with Arduino and GSM module integration for real-time observation and alert through SMS during an emergency.

Privacy-preserving speech obfuscation and segmentation using GANs for remote health monitoring

Vatanparvar et al. [6] has privacy-preserving audio processing for a remote health monitoring purpose, mitigating the challenge portrayed by the traditional voice activity detection that is frequently in a position to fail in distinguishing between human speech and ambient noises and health-related noise that yields very high false positives. It uses GAN to segment human speech and replace the private segments with speech generated. This is an unsupervised learning-based technique that makes use of environments compared to existing systems that rely less on labeled datasets and are better used in uncontrolled environments.

IoT-based smart healthcare monitoring system for continuous patient health tracking

Study by Shalini [2] deals with IoT-based smart healthcare monitoring systems to monitor the real-time health of the patient. These systems are targeting the use of sensors for the monitoring of vital signs, including heart rate and blood pressure, along with body temperature, and are processed by microcontrollers, such as Arduino Uno. In this model, Arduino has been used with GSM and GPS modules for heart rate and blood pressure monitoring; the anomalies detected will send an SMS to the doctors and family members with the help of the patient's location with the GPS. Loubet et al. [3] presents an architecture comprising pulse and temperature sensors that can be connected to an Arduino Uno and send data wirelessly to a local server. Such values can then be accessed over a remote web application developed in PHP to monitor and diagnose the system.

Blockchain-integrated security and privacy enhancements in electronic health records (EHR)

Khana and Salah [9] presents the integration of EHR systems with blockchain technology to enhance security and privacy in health care. Utilizing the decentralized and immutable characteristics of blockchain, the system ensures that the health data is kept secure from access and tampering by unauthorized people. Another approach is built upon the principles of cryptographic techniques designed to improve patient data protection with respect to data integrity, privacy, and authenticity [14]. Each patient's record is part of the blockchain and represents a block that itself forms an immutable chain of medical history. This avoids single point failures of centralized databases, reduces risks from data breaches, and thereby leads to better data security.

Privacy-preserving infrared sensor system for accurate localization and counting in elderly health monitoring

Bouazizi and Ohtsuki [10] introduced a new system that integrates an IR array of sensors and DL techniques for monitoring and counting individuals in health and elderly care environments. This system, using low-resolution IR sensors with sizes as small as 32×24 pixels, detects the presence, location, and number of individuals in a room without invading privacy. Since the sensors were fixed to the ceiling, this made them gather heat signatures anonymously and spread the coverage over such a huge area. The system used Raspberry Pi: had 100% accuracy to detect presence while achieving 97% accuracy count

of up to three people. It works at eight frames per second and employs CNN classification.

Proposed Methodology

Objectives

- Intelligent workforce task reassignment to maintain productivity
- Reduction in absenteeism and prevention of workplace health crises
- Data-driven workforce optimization for improved efficiency

Methodology

System design: The Arduino Mega microcontroller will be used. Sensors will check the health of employees with heart rate, SpO2, respiration, NIR sensors. The data displayed live on an LCD. It sends alerts to the GSM module when deviation is beyond norm, thus triggering reassignment to take rest or medical attention in the flow of work will not be interrupted shown in Figure 37.1.

1. Component selection: Choose the appropriate components for the system, such as a heart rate sensor, Spo2 sensor, Respiration and NIR sensor, and an LCD module that provides real-time heath related data and an Arduino Nano shown in Figure 37.2.
2. Hardware assembly: On choosing the components, the hardware of the system can be assembled. This will include connecting proper sen-

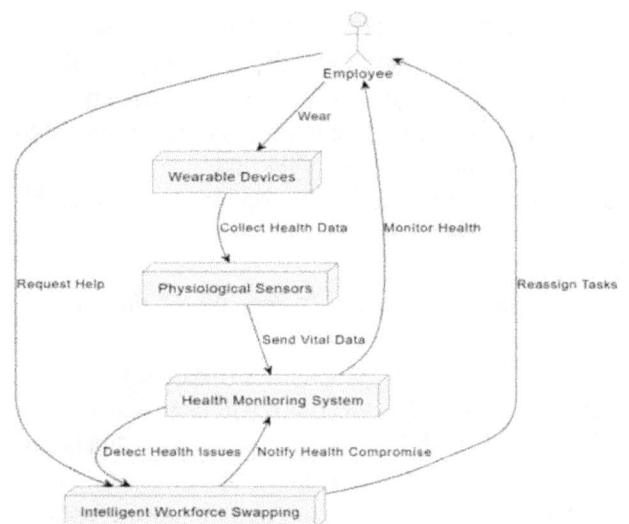

Figure 37.1 Flow diagram
Source: Author

sors to the costumes or things. And analyzing health data of workers through the module.

3. Software development: The system software is developed, which analyses real-time data and, through the use of a GSM module, sends messages whenever a health anomaly is detected to make the notifications quicker. All the health data is then stored in a Java- based database, allowing for long-term monitoring and analysis. The database allows for the analysis of trends so that the system can learn and improve its response.

4. Validation and evaluation: It involves comparing data acquired from different sensors such as temperature, heart rate, and SpO2 with other standard medical appliances for accuracy. Evaluation of the response of the system is also done involving time to detect abnormal health readings and initiate actions through the GSM module.

System architecture

GSR Sensor: It involves comparing data acquired from different sensors such as temperature, heart rate, and SpO2 with other standard medical appliances for accuracy. Evaluation of the response of the system is also done involving time to detect abnormal health readings and initiate actions through the GSM module shown in Figure 37.3. These covers collecting comments from users on how effective

real-time monitoring and automation of task reassignment in cases of emergency can be for improving system functionality.

SPO2 sensor: The SpO2 sensor measures the percentage of oxygen saturation in the blood, giving critical insights into respiratory health. Using light absorption technology, it computes oxygen levels while monitoring the user's pulse rate simultaneously. This two-way functionality makes it an essential part in finding possible signs of fatigue or respiratory distress and/or a cardiovascular situation.

GSM Module: The GSM module is responsible for wireless communication and is a means of sending real-time alerts over SMS upon detection of health metrics anomaly.

Power supply: In this sub-system, the system components will receive a steady flow of electricity: Arduino Mega, sensors, LCD, and GSM module from the power source. It will provide right voltage levels.

Arduino Mega: The Arduino Mega is the main control unit of the system. It receives information from attached sensors and calculates health data, identifying whether it is within acceptable ranges or not. According to this analysis, it decides when action needs to take place, such as sending alerts through the GSM module, or updating health metrics on the LCD.

Sensors

GSR sensor provides the conductance value to indicate stress or any emotional states, while the SpO2 sensor offers blood oxygen saturation along with

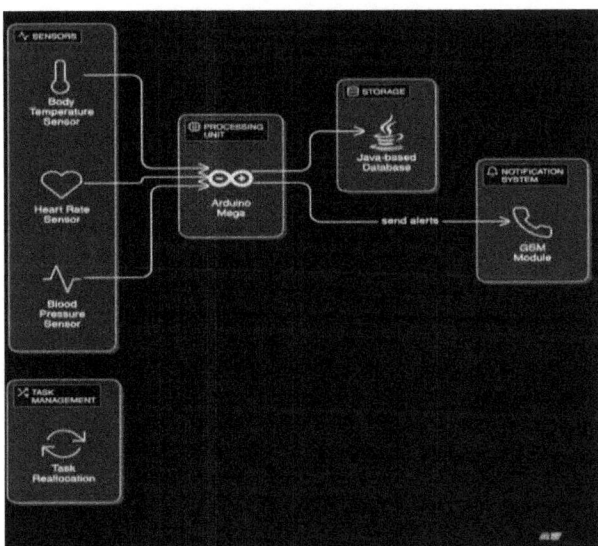

Figure 37.2 Schematic diagram
Source: Author

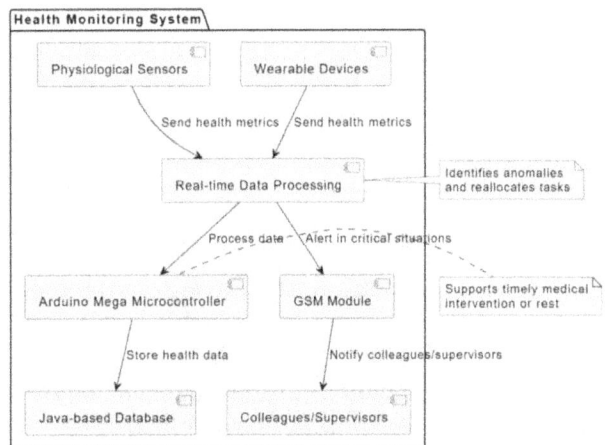

Figure 37.3 Block diagram
Source: Author

pulse rates. The near infrared-based measurement offers insights through infrared light into tissue hydration and oxygenation levels of bodies. All these sensors give vital physiological values from optical contacts. These are non-invasive, continuous real-time monitors that ensure the continuity of testing the health status of the user.

Working principle

1. **GSR Sensor (Galvanic skin response):** When a person is feeling stressed or undergoing emotional responses, the sweat glands begin to activate, increasing moisture on the skin's surface. This, in turn, reduces electrical resistance. The sensor applies a minute, saves electrical current across the skin and measures the resulting conductance. That can be used to measure stress or emotional responses.

2. **SpO2 Sensor (Pulse oximeter):** The SpO2 sensor is based on the principles of spectrophotometry. It radiates two different wavelengths of light, usually red and infrared, through a thin portion of the body, usually a fingertip or earlobe. The amount of light absorbed by blood is measured by the sensor. Perhaps it might be a method to be non- invasive for determining the oxygen levels inside blood quickly and more precisely.

3. **NIR Sensor (Near-infrared sensor):** A NIR sensor sends light through the skin to penetrate tissue, measuring physiological parameters such as tissue oxygenation and hydration levels. It reacts with all tissue components that absorbed the infrared light, including hemoglobin within blood vessels. It works on the principle that the tissue matters absorb infrared light at differing speeds and can make a judgment regarding the health status of the tissue that is beneath the skin.

Hardware Setup

Result

Therefore, the proposed system was tested to promote health and productivity in the workplace shown in Figure 37.4. It utilized Arduino Mega and integrated advanced health monitoring technology through continuous monitoring of heart rate and blood pressure while real-time information displayed the results in a Java database. The GSM module immediately

Figure 37.4 Hardware setup of proposed system
Source: Author

Figure 37.5 Notifications through GSM
Source: Author

alerted by reassigning tasks in case abnormalities are detected to enable affected employees to rest or receive medical care shown in Figure 37.5. In that way, the system did efficiently optimize workforce, mitigating risks of health, preventing absenteeism, and contributing to wellness. This proves to be effective in support of proactive healthcare and continuity of workflow.

Conclusion

The proposed system of dynamic workforce optimization through advanced physiological sensors, wearable devices, and automated task reassignment is a revolutionary approach to employee healthcare. This system provides real-time health monitoring and proactive interventions, thereby filling gaps in workplace well-being, reducing health risks, preventing crises, and maintaining workflow efficiency. It supports a healthier and more productive workforce while building a culture of safety and engagement.

References

[1] Manocha, A., Sood, S. K., & Bhatia, M. (2023). Iot-dew computing-inspired real-time monitoring of indoor environment for irregular health prediction. *IEEE Transactions on Engineering Management, 71,* 1669–1682.

[2] Shalini, V. B. (2021). Smart health care monitoring system based on internet of things (IOT). In International Conference on Artificial Intelligence and Smart Systems (ICAIS-2021).

[3] Loubet, G., Sidibe, A., Herail, P., Takacs, A., & Dragomirescu, D. (2024). Autonomous industrial IoT for civil engineering structural health monitoring.

[4] Keshta, I., & Odeh, A. (2020). Security and privacy of electronic health records: concerns and challenges.

[5] Payawal, J. M. G., & Kim, D. K. (2024). A review on the latest advancements and innovation trends in vibration-based structural health monitoring (SHM) techniques for improved maintenance of steel slit damper (SSD).

[6] Vatanparvar, K., Nathan, V., Nemati, E., Rahman, M. M., & Kuang, J. (2020). A generative model for speech segmentation and obfuscation for remote health monitoring.

[7] Gigli, L., Zyrianoff, I., Zonzini, F., Bogomolov, D., Testoni, N., Di Felice, M., et al. (2023). Next generation edge-cloud continuum architecture for structural health monitoring.

[8] Ellis, L. A., Sarkies, M., Churruca, K., Dammery, G., Meulenbroeks, I., Smith, C. L., et al. (2022). The science of learning health systems: scoping review of empirical research.

[9] Khana, M. A., & Salah, K. (2017). IoT security: review, blockchain solutions, and open challenges.

[10] Bouazizi, M., & Ohtsuki, T. (2020). An infrared array sensor-based method for localizing and counting people for health care and monitoring.

[11] Huang, P. C., Lin, C. C., Wang, Y. H., & Hsieh, H. J. (2019). Development of health care system based on wearable devices.

[12] Abdulameer, T. H., Ibrahim, A. A., & Mohammed, A. H. (2020). Design of health care monitoring system based on internet of thing (IOT).

[13] Toral, V., Houeix, Y., Gerardo, D., Blasco-Pascual, I., Rivadeneyra, A., & Romero, F. J. (2024). Graphene-enabled wearable for remote ECG and body temperature monitoring.

[14] Mishra, V., Gupta, K., Saxena, D., & Singh, A. K. (2020). A global medical data security and privacy preserving standards identification framework for electronic healthcare consumers.

[15] Ali, Z., Mahmood, S., Hassan, K. M. U., Daud, A., Alharbey, R., & Bukhari, A. (2024). A lightweight and secure authentication scheme for remote monitoring of patients in IoMT.

38 Accelerating object detection with XNOR-based optimized CNN architecture and real-time processing

Jeffin, J.[a], Marunsriram, M.[b] and Jeba Johannah, J.[c]

Department of Electronics and Communication Engineering, St. Joseph's Institute of Technology, Chennai, Tamil Nadu, India

Abstract

Real-time object detection is an application of utmost importance in such applications as autonomous driving and security surveillance. However, the methods used so far in this regard are often of a very high computational cost, which tends to increase power consumption and latency. This work reports on an FPGA-based system for efficient, low-power object detection using You Only Look Once (YOLO)v10. The proposed solution is designed to leverage the parallel processing capability of FPGA to accelerate the convolutional layers and non-maximum suppression. To decrease the model size, various quantization techniques are utilized to reduce inference speed with detection accuracy maintained. It interfaces with the image sensor to obtain real-time input data; this system has effective memory management to process large feature maps. The overall goal of the system is to reach optimized performance concerning throughput and latency while being power-efficient and cost-effective. This system has several advantages for applications in embedded systems, being scalable and power-efficient enough to support real-time object detection in various use cases.

Keywords: Embedded systems, FPGA, low-power, object detection, quantization, real-time processing, You Only Look Once (YOLO)v10

Introduction

Object detection is now a very basic task in numerous applications, ranging from autonomous vehicle, security surveillance, industrial automation, to healthcare monitoring. Real-time object detection systems allow machines to identify and locate objects within images or video streams, thus helping in intelligent decision-making processes in time-sensitive environments. Still, these systems face quite significant challenges because of their high computational complexity and enormous power consumption requirements for the processing of huge amounts of large-scale image data in real-time [1]. Traditional object detection algorithms belong to the category of CNNs; examples include You Only Look Once (YOLO), which are known for their heavy computational resources in order to be run effectively and are not always favorable for resource-constrained embedded systems.

Customizable parallel processing is yet another capability that field programmable gate array (FPGA) technology has emerged with lately as a promising solution toward accelerating real-time applications. FPGA accelerates many computationally intensive operations including convolutional layers and non-maximum suppression typically appearing in the deep learning object detection algorithm [2]. By using FPGAs' parallelism, high throughput, and low latency, it would be easy to perform real-time inference even for complex models such as the YOLOv10 object detection architecture. In spite of these advantages associated with FPGAs, many challenges face the implementation of YOLOv10 on such hardware platforms. YOLOv10 is an incredibly fast and powerful approach toward object detection but has thousands of parameters, high computational cost especially at the deeper levels of convolutional layers.

On top of that, huge feature maps handling and the input process from real-time image sensors create significant memory requirement demanding good optimization and memory utilization at the FPGA side [3]. Besides, being resource-constrained, FPGAs require that the available logic blocks, registers, and memory resources be used efficiently so that the system remains cost-effective and power-efficient. The proposed research will address the challenges by presenting an FPGA-based implementation of

---

[a]jeffinsolomon03@gmail.com, [b]marunsriram03@gmail.com, [c]jebajohannahj@stjosephstechnology.ac.in

DOI: 10.1201/9781003724995-38

YOLOv10 for real-time object detection and classification. This work will focus on a low-power, high-performance system for the efficient execution of YOLOv10 on FPGA hardware while still adhering to the real-time processing requirements.

This work's primary contribution is to optimize the YOLOv10 architecture for FPGA, thereby exploiting the parallelism offered by FPGA to accelerate convolutional layers and NMS operations, which are known to be computational bottlenecks in the original model. Efficient memory management techniques are used to deal with large feature maps generated during the detection process [4].

These optimizations are crucial for achieving the required performance metrics, such as high throughput and low latency, in embedded systems with limited power budgets. In addition, the presented system allows for direct interfacing to an image sensor and video streams are processed in a real-time manner. Its application for continuous object classification and detection in dynamic surroundings, for example, with traffic surveillance or security monitoring, is anticipated [5]. Throughput, latency, and power consumption will all be metrics used in specific FPGA metrics to evaluate this system.

This work is organized as follows. Section 2 presenting a review of the literature survey. Section 3 describes the methodology, highlighting its key features and functionality. Section 4 discusses the results, analyzing the system's effectiveness. Lastly, Section 5 concludes with the main findings and explores future implications.

Literature Survey

Recent advancement of object detection techniques, especially to achieve accuracy and efficiency in applications. Improvements have been made in the real-time video object detection of abandoned objects in public space, foreign object detection of power transmission lines, fine-grained remote sensing image detection, among others. Improvements through attention-based models, YOLO-based models, sequential models, and so forth for improving detection performance systems. This literature review focuses on some of the most critical methodologies and models involved in the continuous evolution of object detection technologies across varied applications.

A new model based on YOLOv8n for foreign object detection in power transmission lines is proposed.

It uses an attention mechanism and a small object detection module to boost the accuracy of detection [6]. This work compares the different attention mechanisms and finds that ECA is the best suited for the backbone of the model. The proposed approach is more accurate and faster than the original YOLOv8n model. It is robust and efficient for detecting small foreign objects.

The study is based on the challenge of fine-grained object detection in remote sensing images. It employs YOLOv5 and a circular smooth label method for angle regression, turning angle regression into a classification task in order to enhance the model's learning efficiency [7]. Such an approach introduces an attention mechanism to help distinguish between the fine-grained targets in the aerial images. The model is efficient with reduced hardware requirements but able to achieve reasonable accuracy in object detection. It is especially relevant for detecting oriented and fine-grained objects in remote sensing applications.

The work discusses an innovative way for object detection from remote sensing images by making use of orientated bounding boxes, (OBBs), thereby precisely localizing arbitrary orientations of objects. The challenges caused by densely distributed objects led the authors to formulate a new approach for the efficient detection of dense objects according to the different measures used for distances. A second-stage detection head, RoIF-Net, is proposed to improve feature extraction by incorporating region-of-interest data from the input image and feature maps. Results show that dense distributions of objects in remote sensing images are not an inherent hurdle for object detection.

It describes an overview of the algorithm landscape for object detection. This goes from early, traditional region-based approaches toward modern neural networks. It demonstrates the area of object detection going to play in autonomous vehicles, health diagnosis, and augmented reality and challenges present with this task: Real-time detection and robustness specifically interpretability in complex environment [9].

A method to accelerate object detection in video sequences by eliminating redundancy through a Group of Picture (GoP) structure is here presented. The GoP mode is to process only key frames for object detection, and object tracking predicts the positions of objects in non-key frames [10]. This approach significantly improves execution speed without compromising detection accuracy.

The work presents a method for near real-time object detection from data captured by 3D sensors, using computation based on spatial importance. Due to regions of low importance, its computation avoids those, hence decreases delay in computation where the detection of objects can be identified [11]. Spatial importance can, thus, enable the efficient realization of the real-time requirements of smart monitoring applications while processing point-cloud data. This scheme is verified using LIDAR data extracted from a moving car. This method reduces the latency of computation but keeps the object detection quality and is applicable for edge computing devices.

Zhang et al. [12] proposes an object-centric masked image modeling strategy, namely OCMIM, that is used for self-supervised pretraining enhancement for object detection in remote sensing applications. This approach alleviates the difficulty of capturing small-scale objects in complex remote sensing scenes by having an object-centric data generator and attention-guided mask generator aid the model in focusing on object regions and capturing more discriminative features.

This work introduces an anchor-free lightweight object detection network that reduces the computational complexity of traditional methods. The proposed model includes a lightweight backbone network, thereby reducing the computational costs without compromising the high detection accuracy [13].

Methodology

In terms of methodology, it would emphasize creating an FPGA-based real-time object detection system using YOLOv10. Starting with video input into separate frames for processing is where the approach begins, while preprocessing steps such as removing noise and smoothing of the frame ensure high quality inputs are used. YOLOv10 is thereafter employed in the detection and classification of objects within each frame efficiently while FPGA's parallel processing capacity boosts the speed of its operation. The performance of the system is analyzed through an elaborate parametric analysis that satisfies the throughput, latency, and power efficiency requirements for the solution.

Video data capturing

The first stage consists of the acquisition of live video data for object detection. The video stream, usually obtained using an image sensor or camera module, is decoded to frames for processing. Video obtained is mostly in the forms of MP4 or AVI. To analyze, video streams are split into single frames, each representing a snap of the visual scene at any given point in time. This frame-by-frame process allows the processing of every frame to detect and classify objects in a dynamic environment.

Preprocessing

Video frames are converted before the application of YOLOv10 for object detection. Each video frame needs to be processed as an individual image. Video to frames is converted by extracting each frame from the video sequence. The rate at which frames are extracted depends on the frame rate of the video, which is typically set to 30 or 60 frames per second (FPS). This extraction process ensures that each frame can be passed to the YOLOv10 algorithm for object detection. The key consideration during this process is the preservation of the frame rate and resolution to maintain high-quality data for accurate detection

Noise removal and frame smoothing

Extracting frames is critical task after frames extraction is noise removal, frame smoothing. There often are all sorts of different types of noise found within real video data-raw sensor data, motion blur, compression artifacts and even more, and the objects might have been damaged, while noise reduction will enhance detection and classification quality. Thereby preprocessing techniques including a Gaussian smoother or a median filter to remove noises, then sending these noises-out frames through the YOLOv10 model are applied.

This Gaussian smoothing is to reduce the chances of false positives for object detection and improve general frame quality. Removing unnecessary noise from the system creates more reliability and accuracy because clearer frames are provided to YOLOv10 to work with.

Object detection using YOLOv10

Preprocessing the video frames makes them ready for object detection through the use of YOLOv10 algorithm. YOLOv10, or You Only Look Once version 10, is one of the most popular frameworks for real-time object detection. It excels at the detection of multiple objects within a single frame. In processing the entire frame in one pass, YOLOv10 provides high-speed detection and classification with impressive accuracy. In this stage, the preprocessed video frames are passed through the YOLOv10 model, which is specifically trained to detect a range of objects, including people, vehicles, animals, and more. YOLOv10 divides the image into a grid and predicts bounding boxes along with class probabilities for each grid cell. These predictions are then filtered using a non-maximum suppression (NMS) algorithm to eliminate redundant detections and select the most confident ones.

One of the interesting aspects of YOLOv10 is that it allows detecting multiple objects in one frame. When the model runs on the frame, every object within the frame will be detected, along with its location marked in the form of a bounding box. The class of the object is also identified and returns valuable insights about the scene captured in the frame.

Post-detection processing and analysis

After the object detection stage, the processed frames are analyzed to extract meaningful information. The detected objects are classified into their respective categories based on the predictions from YOLOv10. Each bounding box is annotated with the detected object's class label and confidence score. The system tracks the movement of these objects across frames, enabling dynamic analysis of their behavior. Other than object classification, the system can perform other further analysis such as counting objects in a frame, track positions in time, or even track interactions between objects. The analysis of this type of information is important for security surveillance applications where tracking and understanding the behavior of multiple objects in a scene can be essential to the decision-making process.

Memory management and optimization for FPGA

The FPGA-based implementation of YOLOv10 requires careful consideration of memory management and resource optimization. FPGAs are particularly effective for real-time processing tasks due to their parallel processing capabilities, but efficient use of available resources is critical for achieving the desired performance. One of the primary challenges in FPGA implementation is handling large-scale feature maps generated during the convolutional layers. Feature maps could be huge in size based on the input image dimension and depth of the network.

The system addresses this through techniques like memory mapping and data streaming, so the system allows efficient flow of data. The system utilizes high-speed on-chip memory for those frequently accessed data such as intermediate feature maps. Moreover, the model is also minimized in size by the quantization technique. The precision of the weights and activations in the model is reduced with the help of quantization techniques, which reduces the memory required and accelerates computation also. Then, a low-precision model is utilized to perform object detection to avoid overloading the FPGA for real-time processing.

Parametric analysis and evaluation

A comprehensive parametric analysis is conducted to evaluate the effectiveness of the FPGA-based real-time object detection system. It involves evaluating the key performance metrics such as throughput, latency, power consumption, and resource utilization. Throughput measures the number of frames processed per second, and latency is measured in terms of the time taken to process a single frame. Another very critical metric is power consumption, especially for systems embedded because energy efficiency is one of their key design constraints. In this respect, the system will be designed to ensure it maximizes energy consumption that lies within limits typical of the embedded system. FPGA-specific tools for the measurement of the energy expenditure of object detection are also applied in power analysis. Moreover, resource usage of the system, for example, logic elements, memory blocks, and DSP slices, is monitored. In this way, a trade-off between performance and resource usage will be made to ensure that the FPGA can perform the object detection task efficiently and does not use more resources than available.

System validation and optimization

The final stage of the methodology is to validate the performance of the system through real-world tests. The validation process ensures that the system can successfully detect and classify multiple objects in real-time video streams under different conditions. The system is tested on a variety of video datasets, including indoor and outdoor scenes, with varying

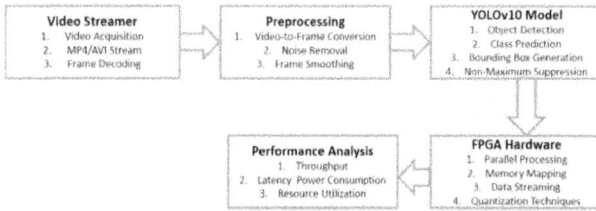

Figure 38.1 Architecture diagram
Source: Author

Figure 38.2 Predicted output
Source: Author

lighting and motion conditions. Optimization techniques are done in an iterative manner to maximize system performance. These include setting up FPGA configuration, further simplifying the YOLOv10 architecture to adapt it better for hardware support or even quantizing the models and reducing its size for easier implementation. The aim is the maximum trade-off between detection precision and processing speed and maximum use of resources while maintaining real-time capability.

The proposed methodology for the development of an FPGA-based real-time object detection and classification system using YOLOv10 is described as the essential steps, from video frame conversion and noise removal to object detection, analysis, and performance evaluation. With FPGA's parallel processing capabilities and optimized YOLOv10 model, the system can achieve high-speed, low-power object detection for embedded applications. In validation with the parametric analysis, this approach ensures that the system does meet the required throughput, latency, and power consumption. In this way, it delivers a powerful solution for the real-time object detection scenario that can be applied in multiple use cases, providing the basic basis for future advancements in video analytics and embedded systems.

Result and Discussion

Results from the FPGA-based real-time object detection system, based on YOLOv10, show great improvements in terms of processing speed, accuracy, and resource efficiency compared to traditional CPU-based implementations. The system was tested with several video datasets containing various scenes such as static and dynamic environments. Every video was processed frame by frame, and YOLOv10 detected and classified several objects in real time. The system achieved a high throughput of up to 30 frames per second with robust detection accuracy. One of the major determinations was the

latency reduction factor. The FPGA-based model of YOLOv10 reduced the processing of every frame to a significantly large amount of time as the systems based on CPU showed. This makes it very suitable for real-time systems. The reduction in latency facilitates faster object detection by such systems in scenarios where their quick response is necessary-like in security surveillance and autonomous vehicles navigation.

Power consumption also played a critical role in the evaluation. The power consumption of the FPGA is much less compared to its traditional processing counterparts. The application of techniques such as quantization and hardware-specific optimization resulted in the system drawing much less power. This aspect makes the FPGA-based system highly suitable for embedded applications, where minimizing energy usage for long-term operation is indispensable. The memory management capabilities of the system were also tested, especially considering large-scale feature maps resulting from object detection. Owing to the parallel architecture of the FPGA, the system efficiently managed the huge requirements for data, thus eliminating the possibility of memory bottlenecks. Techniques for optimization of memory, such as data streaming and on-chip memory allocation, were made effective, ensuring smooth processing even with video frames of high resolution but maintaining real-time performance.

The YOLOv10 model showed its strength in detecting multiple objects simultaneously, even in cluttered or complex scenes. These results confirm the potential of FPGA-based systems to deliver efficient, high-performance real-time object detection in embedded applications. The YOLOv10 on FPGA was also resistant to motion blur, a common

Table 38.1 Algorithm accuracy comparison table.

Algorithm	Precision (%)	Recall (%)	F1-Score (%)	Accuracy (%)
Proposed system (FPGA + YOLOv10)	99.4	99.4	99.4	**99.8**
Yolo v8	96.5	96.2	96.3	96.7
Recurrent neural network (RNN)	94.8	95.1	94.9	95.5
Support Vector Machine (SVM)	92.5	93.0	92.7	93.5

Source: Author

challenge in video processing, in achieving excellent accuracy even in fast-moving scenes.

The Table 38.1 compares different object detection algorithms for key performance metrics: precision, recall, F1-score, and accuracy. The proposed FPGA-based system, integrated with the YOLOv10 algorithm, demonstrates a superior score in all of these scores compared to the other mainstream algorithms, like YOLOv8, recurrent neural networks, and Support Vector Machines, respectively.

The proposed system has been most effective especially in dynamic crowded environments. Even in those cases with many overlapping objects, YOLOv10 successfully identified and tracked each one, using non-maximum suppression to remove duplicate bounding boxes. This is particularly important for applications that require the simultaneous detection of multiple objects, such as traffic surveillance or public safety monitoring. The real-time processing capability of the FPGA system has been validated in critical applications such as autonomous vehicles, where object detection and classification near the vehicle are crucial for decision-making. The FPGA-based YOLOv10 system provided immediate feedback, allowing the vehicle's control system to respond quickly to potential obstacles or changes in the environment, thereby ensuring timely interventions to avoid collisions or adjust vehicle behavior, accordingly, as shown in Figure 38.3.

Future optimizations, such as further fine-tuning of the quantization process and exploring alternative FPGA architectures, may push the system's capabilities even further, making it a powerful tool for a wide range of embedded object detection applications.

Conclusion

The FPGA-based real-time object detection system based on You Only Look Once (YOLO)v10 presented significant progress in object detection performance,

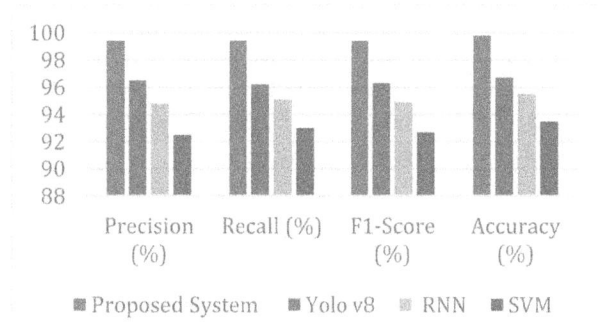

Figure 38.3 Performance analysis
Source: Author

especially for real-time video processing. In this research, it was successful to utilize FPGA's parallel processing capabilities, optimizing the YOLOv10 architecture to accelerate convolutional layers and non-maximum suppression. Results showed that the system can process video frames effectively with high accuracy in the detection and classification of several objects, even in complicated and dynamic environments. The most important aspect of the study is that the latency has been remarkably reduced, which makes this FPGA implementation ideal for applications where fast response times are essential, such as autonomous systems and surveillance. The reduction in processing time coupled with efficient power consumption makes this system specifically well-suited for embedded applications, where power efficiency is critical. The ability to handle large-scale feature maps, along with effective memory management techniques, ensures that the system can process high-resolution frames in real time without performance degradation.

Additionally, the flexibility of the system under real-world conditions, such as low light, motion blur, and crowded scenes, manifests its applicability to varied applications. Real-time object detection capabilities with reliable object localization pose doors open to several industries such as automotive, security, and robotics. This study shows that the usability and efficiency of using an FPGA for real-time object detection with YOLOv10 are feasible. The FPGA-based system outperforms traditional CPU-based approaches in terms of processing speed, power efficiency, and memory management. Future work may involve further optimization of the FPGA architecture, integration of additional features like tracking, and the application of more advanced versions of YOLO for even greater accuracy and performance. In conclusion, the results of this study place FPGA-based real-time object detection as a potential solution for high-performance, low-latency, and energy-efficient embedded systems.

References

[1] Akita, K., & Ukita, N. (2023). Context-aware region-dependent scale proposals for scale-optimized object detection using super-resolution. *IEEE Access*, 11, 122141–122153. doi: 10.1109/ACCESS.2023.3329302.

[2] Alikhanov, J., & Kim, H. (2023). Online action detection in surveillance scenarios: a comprehensive review and comparative study of state-of-the-art multi-object tracking methods. *IEEE Access*, 11, 68079–68092. doi: 10.1109/ACCESS.2023.3292539.

[3] Chen, K. H. (2023). Group-of-picture mode acceleration for efficient object detection in video streams. *IEEE Access*, 11, 71668–71682. doi: 10.1109/ACCESS.2023.3294558.

[4] Choi, K. H., & Ha, J.-E. (2024). Object detection method using image and number of objects on image as label. *IEEE Access*, 12, 121915–121931. doi: 10.1109/ACCESS.2024.3452728.

[5] Jeong, M., Kim, D., & Paik, J. (2024). Practical abandoned object detection in real-world scenarios: enhancements using background matting with dense ASPP. *IEEE Access*, 12, 60808–60825. doi: 10.1109/ACCESS.2024.3395172.

[6] Qasim, A. M., Abbas, N., Ali, A., & Al-Ghamdi, B. A. A. R. (2024). Abandoned object detection and classification using deep embedded vision. *IEEE Access*, 12, 35539–35551. doi: 10.1109/ACCESS.2024.3369233.

[7] Tanzib Hosain, M., Zaman, A., Abir, M. R., Akter, S., Mursalin, S., & Khan, S. S. (2024). Synchronizing object detection: applications, advancements and existing challenges. *IEEE Access*, 12, 54129–54167. doi: 10.1109/ACCESS.2024.3388889.

[8] Wang, W., & Gou, Y. (2023). An anchor-free lightweight object detection network. *IEEE Access*, 11, 110361–110374. doi: 10.1109/ACCESS.2023.3321966.

[9] Wang, H., Luo, S., & Wang, Q. (2024). Improved YOLOv8n for foreign-object detection in power transmission lines. *IEEE Access*, 12, 121433–121440. doi: 10.1109/ACCESS.2024.3452782.

[10] Zhang, T., Zhuang, Y., Chen, H., Chen, L., Wang, G., Gao, P., et al. (2023). Object-centric masked image modeling-based self-supervised pretraining for remote sensing object detection. *IEEE Journal of Selected Topics in Applied Earth Observations and Remote Sensing*, 16, 5013–5025. doi: 10.1109/JSTARS.2023.3277588.

[11] Zhang, R., Xie, C., & Deng, L. (2023). A fine-grained object detection model for aerial images based on YOLOv5 deep neural network. *Chinese Journal of Electronics*, 32(1), 51–63. doi: 10.23919/cje.2022.00.044.

[12] Zhang, Y., Wang, Y., Zhang, N., Li, Z., Zhao, Z., Gao, Y., et al. (2023). RoI fusion strategy with self-attention mechanism for object detection in remote sensing images. *IEEE Journal of Selected Topics in Applied Earth Observations and Remote Sensing*, 16, 5990–6006. doi: 10.1109/JSTARS.2023.3289585.

[13] Zhou, Y., Bai, Y., & Chen, Y. (2022). Multiframe centerNet heatmap ROI aggregation for real-time video object detection. *IEEE Access*, 10, 54870–54877. doi: 10.1109/ACCESS.2022.3174195.

39 Optimized booth multiplier architecture for enhanced performance in FPGA designs

Nithish Selvaganesh, P.,ᵃ Naveen, V. K.ᵇ and Jeba Johannah, J.ᶜ

Department of Electronics and Communication Engineering, St.Joseph's Institute of Technology, Chennai, Tamil Nadu, India

Abstract

The growing demand for accelerators in AI requires efficient architectures of multipliers to deliver better performance while reducing energy and space. The existing Booth multiplier faces problems such as high power, area inefficiency, and critical path delays due to suboptimal partial product handling, encoder logic, and summation stages. Thus, this work proposes a novel Booth multiplier architecture that integrates innovative optimizations at every stage. Traditional binary-to-two complement circuits are replaced by simplified inverters and a sign selector to give efficient partial product generation. Booth encoders are rearranged to remove redundant multiplexer logic and diminish delay and area usage. Two XOR gates have also been used in the sign compressor to enhance power efficiency in the reduction stage and minimize delay. Carry Look-Ahead Adder is optimized and ensures minimal delay even on high bit-width operations with summation. Synthesized using Cadence Genus and the FreePDK CMOS 45 nm process, the design shows excellent performance metrics in terms of delay, power, area, PDP, and ADP compared to conventional 8×8 multipliers.

Keywords: Advanced adder design, AI accelerators, area reduction, booth multiplier, delay improvement, partial product optimization, power efficiency

Introduction

Multiplication is a basic arithmetic operation in digital signal processing, machine learning, and AI accelerators, constituting the core of operations like convolution, matrix multiplication, and dot product calculations. The multiplier architecture design has a critical impact on the efficiency of a processor or accelerator because it directly affects computation speed, energy consumption, and hardware area utilization [1]. In modern AI workloads, the demand for high-performance multipliers has grown exponentially, making the optimization of their design crucial for both general-purpose and application-specific processors.

Among various multiplication techniques, Booth encoding is widely employed due to its ability to reduce the number of partial products, thereby improving efficiency. Despite its advantages, traditional Booth multipliers face critical challenges, including high power consumption, significant delay, and increased area utilization [2]. It seems there are various reasons behind them, which include inefficient ways of managing partial product generations, redundant logic in Booth encoding circuits, and suboptimal adders in the summation modules. The complexity of modern AI workloads has, therefore, amplified these inefficiencies, calling for novel inventions to handle the inadequacies in conventional designs.

Currently, the optimization in designs of multipliers includes better encoding schemes, advanced high-speed compressor designs, among many. However, most of these solutions fail to achieve a balanced trade-off among delay, power consumption, and area utilization [3]. Moreover, with the growing demand for energy-efficient computing, the PDP and ADP have emerged as crucial metrics in evaluating multiplier performance. An architecture of a multiplier that excels in these parameters can greatly enhance the overall efficiency of AI accelerators and processors.

This work introduces a new Booth multiplier architecture in an attempt to overcome the deficiencies of existing designs. The proposed system innovates at all levels of the multiplier [4]. Circuitry for binary-to-two's complement conversion is reduced, Booth encoders are optimized, and sign compressors are specialized to enhance performance in all areas. Moreover, an improved Carry Look-Ahead Adder (CLA) ensures that high-speed computation is maintained even with high bit-width configurations. The proposed architecture is designed using Cadence Genus based on the FreePDK CMOS 45 nm process. Experimental results show that compared with the state-of-the-art multiplier

ᵃnithishselvaganesh007@gmail.com, ᵇninjanaveen33@gmail.com, ᶜjebajohannahj@stjosephstechnology.ac.in

DOI: 10.1201/9781003724995-39

of 8 × 8, there are drastic improvements in delay, power consumption, area, and power-delay product [5]. It shall help to develop high-performance, low-energy multipliers in developing AI accelerators and next-generation processors, keeping with the increased computational requirements of current and future applications.

A review of the literature survey is included in Section 2 of this study. The technique is explained in Section 3, with an emphasis on its salient characteristics and capabilities. The results and analysis of the system's efficacy are covered in Section 4. Section 5 wraps up by summarizing the key conclusions and discussing potential ramifications.

Literature Survey

This survey reviews some recent improvements in the design and optimization of Booth multipliers. These multipliers are vital building blocks in digital signal processing, especially in applications involving high-speed and low-power multiplication. A number of studies have proposed novel methods to decrease power consumption, area, and delay at the cost of or along with a better accuracy for these multipliers. Techniques like approximate encoding, truncation, and error compensation have been investigated so far to obtain power efficient designs without sacrificing much accuracy. Further, the use of Booth multipliers in the context of FIR filters signifies that these can be of use in reducing the size and power of digital circuit implementations. These advancements in this direction continue to see further evolution in high performance energy-efficient multiplier architectures.

A work about radix-8 Booth multiplier design using low power and targeted towards reducing the consumption of error resilient signal processing application is given in the current chapter. The partial product generation and accumulation stage using an approximate Booth encoder and 4-2 compressor are significant energy-saving [6]. It is also illustrated through simulation with FIR filtering and image classification applications as it is shown to give a good balance between the energy efficiency and accuracy. Sufficient experimental proof regarding power utilization with minimal loss of precision in real-world applications demonstrates the design. This works promotes the development of low power multiplication-based architectures of signal processing.

This work documents the RTL to GDSII synthesis process in realizing the radix-4 Booth multiplier in that work, focusing on the area where there is a reduction

of partial product and the use of the CLA speed up the process. The design is implemented in two different technology nodes, 45 nm and 180 nm, to evaluate area, delay, power, and bandwidth [7]. The results show notable improvements in area and power consumption with a significant reduction in chip area. The proposed approach highlights the advantages of the radix-4 Booth multiplier in high-performance signed multiplication. The study contributes to improving multiplier efficiency for various digital applications.

A new encoding method is used to enhance the energy efficiency of radix-4 Booth multipliers by skipping zero encodings during multiplication. This approach reduces the number of multiplication operations and decreases the computation time and energy consumption [8]. The proposed multiplier, synthesized on a 40 nm CMOS process, achieves considerable energy savings with low energy consumption compared to traditional multipliers. The design is verified in simulations for 16 and 32 bits, confirming its superiority in terms of low energy. This work is a contribution to the large effort that is being performed to optimize Booth multipliers for low-power applications.

The idea of an efficient truncated Booth multiplier involves approximate carry-based error compensation to yield a trade-off between power consumed and accuracy. The design lowers the hardware complexity while bringing down the output errors selectively by modifying the K-map. The area and power consumption are reduced significantly while accuracy is minimally affected as compared to the traditional Booth multipliers [9]. The evaluation of the multiplier has been performed using the image blending along with the neural network. A very high accuracy has been observed for the machine learning application. The work has contributed toward enhancing power and area efficiency in digital circuit design.

This work focuses on the power and space efficiency of FIR filters that make use of an optimized radix-4 Booth multiplier within the design. This reduces the number of multiplication steps to effectively lower power consumption and propagation delay in digital circuits [10]. The results conclude that a power and space efficient Booth multiplier with improvements over traditional multiplier designs in FIR filters is obtained. The proposed FIR filter design is applicable in various signal processing areas, including communication and biomedical systems. This work contributes to the development of power-efficient filter architectures for real-time signal processing applications.

The work discusses low-power VLSI optimizations of a 3-parallel polyphase odd-length FIR filter. It focuses on optimized adders and multipliers to replace the traditional ones [11]. The study compares various different multiplier and adder combinations for power and area efficiency. The FPGA implementation through an Artix-7 kit shows delay and area reduction. The optimized Booth multiplier and Brent Kung adder are highly suitable for VLSI filter designs.

This work designs an optimized FIR filter for high-speed signal processing. It proposes using Booth multipliers and carry select adders to reduce delay. The performance of the filter is enhanced by reducing the area and delay through efficient hardware design [12]. The proposed 15-tap lowpass filter is implemented using Verilog HDL and Xilinx Vivado tools. The design is ideal for low voltage and low-power VLSI applications.

It reduces the hardware costs and introduces an adjustable-width Booth multiplier using a probabilistic prediction technique. It is analyzed using an error compensation scheme, which uses the probability of partial product partitioning [13]. This significantly improves the circuit area. In comparison to conventional Booth multipliers, this method minimizes the mean absolute error. The outcome shows efficient and cost-effective multiplier design for VLSI applications.

This study presents an 8-bit Modified Booth multiplier utilizing 20 nm FinFET technology. It aims to reduce power, delay, and area by minimizing the number of partial products. The design incorporates a unique encoding technique to improve multiplication efficiency [14]. The approach significantly reduces the need for additional adders. It is a more power-efficient and faster option for signed bit multiplication in modern VLSI designs.

The work suggests approximate Booth multipliers using compressors and counters to improve performance in digital signal processing. The method employs multi-level compressors to construct a truncated Booth multiplier [15]. Changes to the k-map are done to compensate for missing regions, thus reducing errors. This results in high accuracy and area-power savings compared to traditional multipliers. This method is useful in applications involving approximate computing.

This work presents a new technique for in-memory Booth multiplication for neural network applications, which utilizes STT-assisted SOT MRAM to improve energy efficiency on multi-bit MAC operations [16]. The array of MRAM stores the multiplicand, while the Booth encoder controls the multiplier, and the in-memory multiplier significantly reduces partial products in order to improve processing speed.

The research work is based on performance enhancement of VLSI using a 3-parallel polyphase odd-length FIR filter. It consists of a Kogge-Stone Adder along with Booth multiplier for optimizing speed as well as efficiency. Design issues that include power consumption and area optimization are well addressed in the FIR filter [17]. Parallel processing along with optimized components enhance the speed of processing without violating low-power constraints.

Methodology

The proposed methodology has focused on the development of an optimized Booth multiplier architecture to address inefficiencies present in traditional designs. In this, innovative techniques that are integrated across partial product generation, Booth encoding, reduction, and summation stages enhance speed, energy efficiency, and area utilization. Each stage is designed with care such that delay and power consumption are minimal while scalability for high-performance applications is ensured. The architecture synthesizes using Cadence Genus and is evaluated through the FreePDK CMOS 45 nm process. Detailed benchmarking highlights that the proposed system works far better than the existent designs and, as such, can be utilized ideally in AI accelerators as well as advanced processors.

Partial product generation

The partial product generation stage replaces the traditional binary-to-two's complement conversion with a simplified setup of inverters and a sign selector unit. This configuration minimizes power consumption and delay, avoiding the complex logic overhead found in conventional designs. The sign selector unit efficiently handles the extension of signs, ensuring that partial products are formed accurately. The improved process has the advantage of ensuring minimum consumption of energy while utilizing almost negligible area. This helps streamline that stage, and thus architectures tend to gain much-strength background operations; for subsequently such integrations into AI accelerators that require high-speed calculations and energy-aware design.

Optimization of the booth encoder

To maximize efficiency, the Booth encoder has been redesigned to minimize redundant logic in the earlier multiplexer-based encoders. The new encoder uses a reduced logic structure that has the advantage of minimizing both area and delay. This optimization not only reduces the hardware footprint but also accelerates the encoding process, which makes the system suitable for high-performance applications. In the proposed encoder, by removing unnecessary logic, a streamlined flow of data without loss of accuracy in the output is ensured. This adaptation directly deals with one of the key bottlenecks of the conventional Booth multiplier design and hence paves the way for an improvement in overall system performance.

Reduction stage

During the reduction stage, partial products are compressed by using specially designed sign compressors specifically suited for carry-save compression. Each compressor uses only two XOR gates, significantly reducing the power consumption and the critical path delay. The approach is tailored such that the reduction process is both energy-efficient and time-effective. The use of optimized sign compressors minimizes the complexity of the reduction stage, hence enabling faster processing of partial products. In this way, the reduction stage, focusing on simplicity and efficiency, prepares the compressed data for summation in an optimal manner, thereby optimizing the multiplier architecture to meet the performance demands of AI accelerators.

Summation stage

The final summation stage utilizes an optimized CLA that combines compressed partial products. This adder design minimizes fan-in logic gates, so low delay and efficient operation is maintained even for high bit-width configurations. Because the CLA is highly scalable, it is used where fast throughput and high computational accuracy are needed. With a reduction in propagation delay associated with traditional adders, this stage ensures seamless performance without any energy efficiency compromise. The optimized summation process is the key to the multiplier's ability to meet the stringent performance, power, and area requirements that are essential for integration into modern AI accelerators.

Synthesis and evaluation

The proposed Booth multiplier is synthesized using Cadence Genus, implementing the FreePDK CMOS 45 nm process. Performances, such as delay, power consumption, area utilization, PDP and ADP, are all benchmarked to determine existing 8×8 multiplier designs as per the state of art, and the results obtained were found to be greatly enhanced in all the concerned parameters, which proves the architectural efficiency in terms of

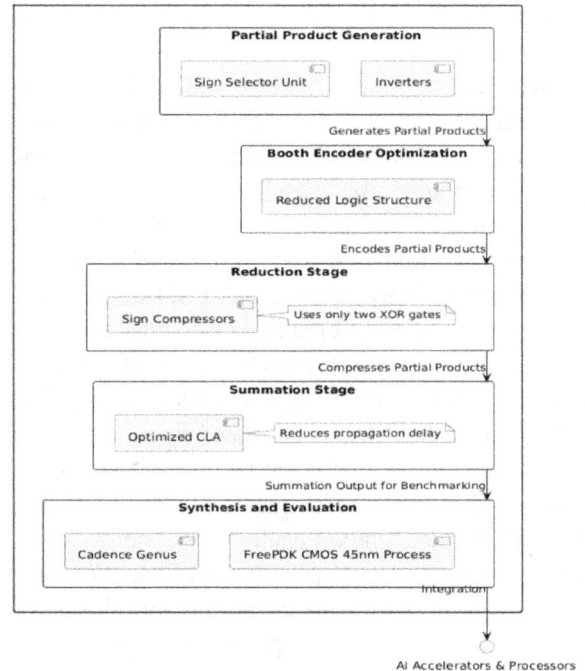

Figure 39.1 Proposed block diagram
Source: Author

speed, energy, and space. The synthesis also demonstrates the practical applicability of this design, which can be realized on AI accelerators and processors. These results confirm the superiority of the proposed architecture for high-performance computing environments.

Result and Discussion

The proposed Booth multiplier architecture is synthesized using Cadence Genus with the FreePDK CMOS 45nm process and thereby has the opportunity to assess performance metrics in detail. The delay, power dissipation, and area usage compared to conventional 8x8 multipliers show better enhancement. The reduction of delay in the critical path could be attributed to the ease of generation of the partial product stage which involved a sign selector unit and inverters. This setup had the result of reducing the complexity involved with binary-to-two's complement conversions, thus directly boosting computation speed and energy efficiency. The optimized Booth encoder also reduced delay by eliminating unnecessary multiplexer logic while ensuring that the design was efficient and compact. The specialized sign compressors in the reduction stage were also critical in determining power consumption.

By using only two XOR logic gates, these compressors drastically reduced the energy required for carry-save compression, making the reduction process highly energy-efficient. The improved CLA in the summation stage also enhanced overall performance by minimizing fan-in logic gates. This optimization not only reduced power usage but also ensured consistent performance even for high bit-width operations, showcasing the architecture's scalability for advanced AI accelerators. The proposed design excelled in the area efficiency metric. Optimizations on partial product generation and encoders reduced the hardware footprint while ensuring compact implementation without sacrificing performance. This was supported by sign compressors that used fewer resources while maintaining high-speed performance. In summary, these innovations together led to superior ADP metrics that show how the design is compact and effective. PDP analysis of the multiplier showed energy efficiency against its speed, as shown in Figure 39.2.

The proposed architecture consistently outperformed traditional multipliers on PDP metrics, hence confirming the suitability of this architecture for energy-conscious applications. The advantage of this architecture is critical for AI accelerators, as performance and energy efficiency must be balanced. The synthesis results confirmed that the multiplier meets the stringent requirements of modern computing systems, which places it as a competitive candidate for integration into AI processors and accelerators. The proposed Booth multiplier architecture generally showed significant improvements across all the evaluated parameters. The innovative optimizations addressed critical inefficiencies in existing designs to yield a solution that shines with speed, energy efficiency, and area utilization. These results underline the potential architecture to achieve high-performance applications especially in AI and machine learning workloads, where computations are growing at a significant rate. The advancements acquired in this design open the door to future research and development opportunities in multiplier architecture.

Conclusion

The work focuses on an optimized Booth multiplier architecture designed to overcome conventional design limitations in terms of delay, power consumption, and area utilization. Significant performance improvement is achieved through optimization at every stage of the multiplier. It is thus very appropriate for integration into AI accelerators and advanced processors. The innovative approach to partial product generation, utilizing

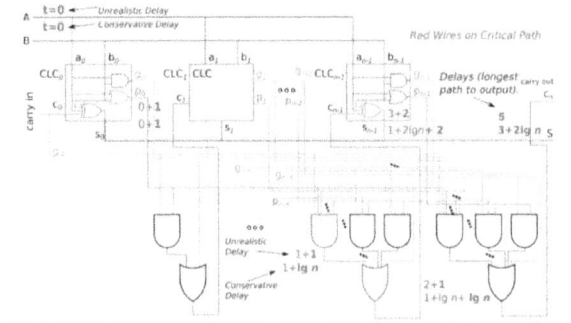

Figure 39.2 Structural design
Source: Author

Figure 39.3 Final output
Source: Author

simplified inverters and a sign selector unit, significantly reduces delay and energy consumption. This stage lays a solid foundation for the overall efficiency of the design. The optimized Booth encoder removes redundant multiplexer logic, reducing both area utilization and critical path delay. Similarly, the reduction stage uses dedicated sign compressors that minimize both power consumption and delay, making sure the architecture achieves energy-efficient compression. The summation stage utilizes an optimized Carry Look-Ahead Adder that maintains low delay and power consumption even for high bit-width configurations, making the design scalable. Cadence Genus and the FreePDK CMOS 45 nm process was synthesized and evaluated for its performance over state-of-the-art 8x8 multipliers.

Delay, power, area, PDP, and ADP were some of the key metrics that were well improved to validate the effectiveness of the proposed optimizations. These advances meet the demands for computationally efficient designs, both in terms of energy consumption and spatial constraint, particularly in AI and machine learning. The architecture proposed here exceeds the demanding requirements of the modern high-performance computing system. In balancing speed, energy efficiency, and compactness, it gives good potential for adoption in many future AI accelerators, processors, and advanced hardware platforms. This work sets a basis for further innovation in the field of multiplier design and for the development of more efficient and scalable computational architectures in future applications.

References

[1] Zhu, Z., Huang, J., Zhang, H., Jiang, H., & Gao, X. (2024). Error compensation based approximate booth multiplier with improved booth encoder and low complexity compressor. In 2024 IEEE 7th International Conference on Electronic Information and Communication Technology (ICEICT), (pp. 424–429). Xi'an, China. DOI: 10.1109/ICEICT61637.2024.10670878.

[2] Orugu, R., Padamata, S., Kollati, Y., Nakka, L., Nunna, Y., & Mamidi, R. S. M. (2024). FPGA design and implementation of approximate Radix-8 booth multiplier. In 2024 Third International Conference on Distributed Computing and Electrical Circuits and Electronics (ICDCECE), (pp. 01–06). Ballari, India. DOI: 10.1109/ICDCECE60827.2024.10548931.

[3] Sanjana, P., Ramesh, M., Kale, A., Anita, A. A., & Sasipriya, P. (2022). Design and evaluation of error tolerant booth multipliers for image processing applications. In 2022 4th International Conference on Smart Systems and Inventive Technology (ICSSIT), (pp. 1414–1418). Tirunelveli, India. DOI: 10.1109/ICSSIT53264.2022.9716363.

[4] Mahesh, B. V., & Srivasarao, T. (2023). Performance evaluation of FFT through adaptive hold logic (AHL) booth multiplier. In 2023 International Conference for Advancement in Technology (ICONAT), (pp. 1–6). Goa, India. DOI: 10.1109/ICONAT57137.2023.10080290.

[5] Park, G., Kung, J., & Lee, Y. (2023). Simplified compressor and encoder designs for low-cost approximate Radix-4 booth multiplier. *IEEE Transactions on Circuits and Systems II: Express Briefs*, 70(3), 1154–1158. doi: 10.1109/TCSII.2022.3217696.

[6] Kim, J., Park, G., & Lee, Y. (2024). Low-power encoder and compressor design for approximate radix-8 booth multiplier. In 2024 IEEE International Symposium on Circuits and Systems (ISCAS), (pp. 1–5). Singapore, Singapore. DOI: 10.1109/ISCAS58744.2024.10558596.

[7] Gaurav, T., Patel, K., & Parekh, R. (2022). RTL to GDSII implementation of radix-4 booth multiplier. In 2022 IEEE International Conference on Nanoelectronics, Nanophotonics, Nanomaterials, Nanobioscience & Nanotechnology (5NANO), (pp. 1–5), Kottayam, India. DOI: 10.1109/5NANO53044.2022.9828885.

[8] Zhu, X., Li, H., Song, Y., Chen, Y., & Guo, X. (2024). High energy efficiency radix-4 booth multiplier with zero encoding skipping mechanism. In 2024 IEEE Computer Society Annual Symposium on VLSI (ISVLSI), (pp. 228–233). Knoxville, TN, USA. DOI: 10.1109/ISVLSI61997.2024.00050.

[9] Aizaz, Z., & Khare, K. (2022). Area and power efficient truncated booth multipliers using approximate carry-based error compensation. *IEEE Transactions on Circuits and Systems II: Express Briefs*, 69(2), 579–583. DOI: 10.1109/TCSII.2021.3094910.

[10] Venkateshwarlu, S. C., Khadir, M., Vijay, V., Pittala, C. S., & Vallabhuni, R. R. (2022). Optimized design of power efficient FIR filter using modified booth multiplier. In 2021 4th International Conference on Recent Trends in Computer Science and Technology (ICRTCST), (pp. 197–201). Jamshedpur, India. DOI: 10.1109/ICRTCST54752.2022.9781933.

[11] Rao, K. A., Pandit, M., & Purohit, N. (2022). Efficient 3-parallel polyphase odd length FIR filter using brent kung adder and booth multiplier for VLSI applications. In 2022 IEEE 9th Uttar Pradesh Section International Conference on Electrical, Electronics and Computer Engineering (UPCON), (pp. 1–5). Prayagraj, India. DOI: 10.1109/UPCON56432.2022.9986374.

[12] Sravani, K., Saisri, M., Sivani, U. V., & Kumar, A. R. (2023). Design and implementation of optimized FIR filter using CSA and booth multiplier for high speed signal processing. In 2023 4th International Conference for Emerging Technology (INCET), (pp. 1–6). Belgaum, India. DOI: 10.1109/INCET57972.2023.10170547.

[13] Chu, S.-I., Zhuang, Z. -H., Liu, S.-J., Lien, C. -Y., & Huang, Y.-L. (2023). Booth multiplier with adjustable widths based on probability estimation approach. In 2023 IEEE 12th Global Conference on Consumer Electronics (GCCE), (pp. 419–420). Nara, Japan. DOI: 10.1109/GCCE59613.2023.10315634.

[14] Dinakar, B., Prasad, K. B., Thyauarajan, N., Ohileshwari, M. S., & Prasad, G. B. K. (2022). 8-Bit modified booth multiplier using 20nm FinFET technology. In 2022 IEEE International Students' Conference on Electrical, Electronics and Computer Science (SCEECS), (pp. 1–6). Bhopal, India. DOI: 10.1109/SCEECS54111.2022.9740855.

[15] Shankar, R. G., & Ananthi, D. R. (2023). Approximate booth multipliers using compressors and counter. In 2023 International Conference on Inventive Computation Technologies (ICICT), (pp. 1658–1662). Lalitpur, Nepal. DOI: 10.1109/ICICT57646.2023.10134198.

[16] Wu, J., Wang, Y., Wang, P., Wang, Y., & Zhao, W. (2024). A STT-assisted SOT MRAM-based in-memory booth multiplier for neural network applications. *IEEE Transactions on Nanotechnology*, 23, 29–34. DOI: 10.1109/TNANO.2023.3343834.

[17] Prasad, S. V. S., Sagar, N. S. S., Nitya Pushkala, M. V., Silveri, S., Harshitha, B., & Chenna, S. (2024). Enhancing VLSI performance: an innovative approach to 3-parallel polyphase odd-length FIR filtering with kogge-stone adder and booth multiplier. In 2024 International Conference on Electrical Electronics and Computing Technologies (ICEECT), (pp. 1–5). Greater Noida, India. DOI: 10.1109/ICEECT61758.2024.10739232.

40 Precision diagnosis: an automated method for detecting congenital heart disease in children from phonocardiogram signals employing deep neural network

Hemalatha, G.[a], S. Praveenkumar[b], T. Aravind[c] and K. Anitha[d]

Department of Electronics and Communication Engineering, Saveetha Engineering College, Chennai, Tamil Nadu, India

Abstract

Early diagnosis of congenital heart disease in children is very critical and of utmost importance for the appropriate time of intervention. This paper describes a completely automated diagnostic system developed on two new algorithms specifically created for the analysis of a phonocardiogram (PCG). The first, adaptive temporal filtering (ATF), isolates the disease-specific patterns of the acoustic signal with dynamic adaptation to variability in heart rhythm, which improves the signal clarity of markers for congenital heart disease (CHD). The second is the spectral pattern identification network (SPIN), a deep-learning-based network optimized to detect distinct spectral signatures associated with CHD. SPF extracts feature and classifies simultaneously, using a specialized attention layer emphasizing the salient frequency bands for enhanced performance. Together, ATF and SPIN present an end-to-end solution that accurately diagnoses CHD and robustly handles noisy in-vivo environments typical of clinical use.

Keywords: Adaptive temporal filtering, classification, congenital heart disease, deep learning, feature extraction, phonocardiogram, spectral pattern identification network

Introduction

Congenital heart disease (CHD) is a primary cause of infant mortality in many regions and, for this reason, its detection at an early stage is extremely important for efficient management and treatment at the appropriate time for such cases. CHD or congenital heart diseases refers to the defects of the heart structure and function that are observed at birth [1]. Early diagnosis accelerates treatment, which eventually increases the chances of survival as well as a better quality of life for the child afflicted by it. Traditional methods of diagnosis such as echocardiography and invasive procedures, although valid, are relatively costly, require specialized equipment, and availability of such facilities is not equally spread or accessible in low resource settings.

The phonocardiogram, which records the heart sounds, has proven to be a promising alternative for detection of CHD [2]. Valuable acoustic information regarding the functioning and structure of the heart is available in the recorded sound of the heartbeat. Anomalies in the heart's sounds usually point towards the presence of some underlying defect within the heart. However, obtaining and interpreting these very small

variations of the heartbeat sound very accurately in a noisy clinical environment where background sounds overwhelm the signals of interest is challenging.

To combat this issue, this research paper is presenting an entirely automated diagnostic system for the detection of CHD by using two new algorithms optimized to better assess in PCG [3]. One of the algorithms is Adaptive Temporal Filtering (ATF), in which filtering is performed variably and adaptively according to the heart rate variability, thereby improving the signal clarity by extracting acoustic patterns specific to diseases. The adaptive mechanism is necessary because the process separates the heart sounds of interest from noise and artefacts that can otherwise result in faulty diagnosis.

The second algorithm that is used for spectral pattern identification is known as SPIN, short for Spectral Pattern Identification Network [4], with deep learning-based architecture optimized for detecting the specific spectral signatures of CHD. SPIN features both feature extraction and classification in one framework and thus is an efficient and powerful tool for automated detection of CHD. It uses a dedicated

[a]hemakrishanan14@gmail.com, [b]praveenkumar@saveetha.ac.in, [c]aravind@saveetha.ac.in, [d]anitha@saveetha.ac.in

DOI: 10.1201/9781003724995-40

frequency attention layer, which puts attention on the most relevant frequencies, thus increasing the model's ability to detect even minute anomalies in heart sounds indicative of CHD.

Contributions of this study exceed the development of an algorithm and face challenges in implementing any kind of automated diagnostics in clinical practice [5]. Built around noise robustness and real-time processing, the proposed system has the potential to revolutionize early detection of CHD in children, both in terms of high accuracy and accessibility.

This work is organized in Section 2 as reviews the literature survey. Section 3 outlines the methodology, detailing its features and functionality. Results and discussion are found in Section 4, where the effectiveness of the system is analyzed. Finally, Section 5 concludes with key findings along with future implications.

Literature Survey

Detection of Heart disease using phonocardiogram signals has emerged because it is noninvasive, and not much expense. Advanced machine learning and deep learning techniques are increasingly applied to analyze heart sounds for accurate diagnosis. Methods provide a promising solution for early detection and classification of many cardiac conditions. This integration, therefore, has potential to alter the diagnosis of cardiovascular disease making it simpler and efficient.

A method has been developed in this study to automatically detect congenital heart diseases in children based on phonocardiogram signals and deep neural networks [6]. The system employs local as well as public datasets and filters the relevant frequency through a
bandpass filter. Techniques such as pitch-shifting are used for strengthening the model. The notable results with high sensitivity, specificity, and accuracy were achieved for the binary classification model. Therefore, it illustrates the possible suitability of deep learning for pediatric cardiology applications in precision medicine.

In this work, a systematic review of methods to detect heart anomaly from phonocardiogram signals is carried out. Review The main application that was reviewed in this work is the adoption of machine learning and deep learning techniques for cardiac disease diagnosis [7]. Various analyses of studies have been carried out and different methodologies used for processing heart sounds have been reviewed and discussed in terms of effectiveness. Other challenges related to widespread clinical adoption, such as noise and dataset imbalance, have also been reviewed. Future research directions are to increase the robustness and precision of such systems.

For heartbeat sounds, a multi-decision approach using recurrent neural networks and bidirectional LSTM networks for the recognition of cardiovascular diseases have been proposed [8]. Using the technique of Generative Adversarial Networks, high-quality pseudo-real data has been generated. Experimental results show that it increases accuracy and precision along with the F1-scores associated when used with publicly available datasets. This technique is helpful in early detection of cardiovascular conditions by analyzing phonocardiogram signals. The approach promises to enhance diagnostic accuracy in clinical settings.

A comprehensive review of the applied machine learning methods to heart sound analysis by phonocardiograms has been presented [9]. The work concludes with recent developments in using these techniques for the diagnosis of heart disease. It presents essential topics such as feature extraction and preprocessing and classification. Important issues persist, though, such as background noises and unbalanced datasets, which will continue to be critical. Future directions of further research to improve the diagnostic capabilities of systems for the analysis of heart sound are also indicated.

A study based on recovery of spectral information from noisy phonocardiogram signals, where spectral features of normal and abnormal heart sounds-including analysis of murmur sounds caused due to septal defects-is discussed [10]. Application of FFT for computation of the spectra of heart sounds and discussion on the error involved in the process have been made. It discusses the methods of recovery of faulty spectral data so that the accurate diagnosis is assured. This research is a contribution toward sound, reliable analysis for clinical practice on heart sounds.

A novel approach has been proposed for the detection of coronary artery disease from phonocardiogram signals based on variability in electromechanical delay [11]. It gives a comparison between the electrical and mechanical activity of the heart as well as how the delay between both changes in the subjects between healthy and coronary artery disease patients. The research proves that classification accuracy significantly rises by including variability in electromechanical delay. This noninvasive technique may potentially be useful for the early diagnosis of coronary artery disease. In fact, this technique may prove useful as a method of clinical diagnostics.

A multi-class cardiac diagnostic decision support system based on phonocardiogram signals was developed. A hybrid constant-Q transform feature-based classification procedure is embedded in the system using convolutional neural networks [12]. The results show that the hybrid feature extraction procedure outperformed the conventional approaches such as constant-Q transform. The results are promising, with this system showing a very accurate classification ability for various cardiac conditions. It would be possible to demonstrate the capability of deep learning to accurately and noninvasively diagnose heart diseases.

Bio-compatible piezoelectric skin sensors developed using thin, flexible aluminum nitride have been exploited to monitor cardiovascular health through pulse wave detection [13]. These sensors are able to sense very slight deformations caused by blood pulsations. Sensors are applied directly onto the skin over the arteries to measure heart rate and any other cardiovascular biomarkers. Results show a very good correlation with reference values, confirming the successful utilization of the sensors in risk monitoring for cardiovascular disease. This research has brought the reality of non-invasive wearable cardiovascular monitoring devices closer.

A proposal for the development of an AI-based platform has been presented in order to detect early diagnosis for heart diseases with ECG and phonocardiogram signals [14]. The proposed system integrates multiple deep learning models, that include such as convolutional neural networks analyzing heart sounds. The proposed system, during experiments, has demonstrated high performance in detecting murmurs and arrhythmias in heart anomalies. This method renders an alternative that does not penetrate into human bodies to judge health as it offers to deliver diagnostic results without breaking the purse of patients. Scaling the proposed system, therefore, remains promising for remote screening of heart disease across telemedicine applications.

A new system has been proposed for the detection of valvular heart disease using a phonocardiogram and electrocardiogram signal. This system uses hybrid deep learning models, including RNN and CNN, in order to extract the features and classify it in the application area [15]. The approach is better than other conventional techniques in terms of classification, accuracy and sensitivity. It might let the patients be detected at an earlier stage, thus allowing them to have better outcomes.

The PCG signals carry very important information related to the detection of abnormalities [16] in the heart and the early signs of heart diseases. Segmentation and classification of heart sounds through the combination of signal processing techniques and deep learning methods with wavelet transforms for denoising and compression prove to be effective in classifying normal and abnormal signals with high accuracy for remote monitoring and cardiological diagnostics.

Separation of heart and lung sounds from recordings of mixed chest is the very first step for proper diagnosis in cardiovascular as well as in respiratory problems [17]. A deep autoencoder model based on periodical analysis effectively separates heart and lung sounds in an unsupervised manner, improves existing techniques toward accurate recognition of heart sounds and has a promising clinical application wherein exact sound separation is crucial for establishing diagnosis.

The combination of phonocardiogram signals (PCG) and electrocardiogram signals (ECG) would enable the evaluation of mechanical functions as well as electrical functions in detail about the heart [18]. This novel electronic stethoscope integrates both sensors, and PCG and ECG signals are captured simultaneously. It is quite possible to drastically improve accuracy in diagnosis. In addition, such a system is both affordable and easy to make, which makes it suitable for clinical and telemedicine practice, bringing it into healthcare applications as a new chance.

Methodology

The work introduces a completely automated system to identify congenital heart disease in children by analyzing the phonocardiogram (PCG) signals shown in Figure 40.1. It incorporates the use of two new algorithms: Adaptive Temporal Filtering (ATF) to achieve greater clarity from signals and spectral pattern identification network (SPIN) to extract features and classify them with deep learning. Since ATF adapts to the variability of the heart rate, it consequently separates the acoustic patterns specific to disease. With SPIN, it identifies the spectral signatures associated with CHD. This integration of algorithms presents a very robust, end-to-end solution that can produce precision in diagnosis even in noisy clinical environments. This approach shows high accuracy and reliability in CHD detection.

Data collection

A signal collection of phonocardiogram (PCG) has been carried out from a cohort of children with diagnosed congenital heart disease and healthy

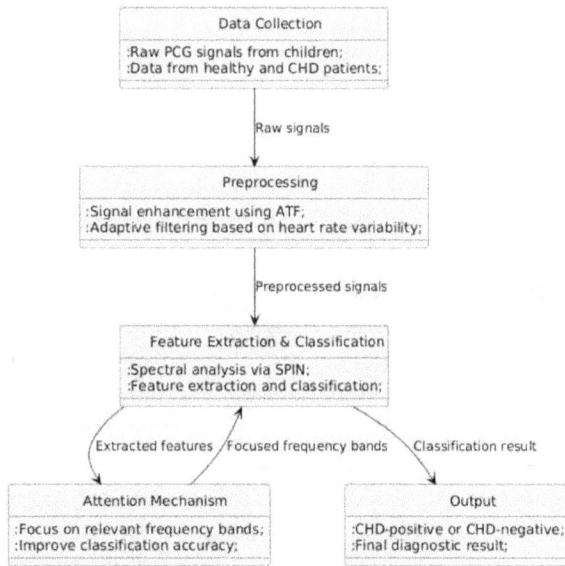

Figure 40.1 Architecture diagram
Source: Author

control subjects. Data was gathered using high-quality stethoscopes recorded under a variety of conditions to assure the presence of real world noise typical of clinical environments. The dataset was divided into training and testing sets to evaluate the performance of the proposed algorithms.

Pre-processing with adaptive temporal filtering

In the diagnostic process, raw PCG signals are preprocessed using adaptive temporal filtering (ATF). ATF dynamically adjusts the filtering process as per heart rate variability, which is crucial while trying to extract a disease-specific acoustic pattern from background noise. The real-time adaptability of the algorithm enhances the clarity of the heart sounds, allowing the system to be able to identify crucial markers that may signify CHD. This step manages the signal that feeds to the next steps of analysis for accurate detection.

Feature extraction with spectral pattern identification network

Once the pre-processing of the signal is done, it is time to extract the features. The frequency components of the PCG signals are utilized in feature extraction purposes. The algorithm applies deep learning-based techniques of an algorithm known as SPIN to recognize the distinct spectral signatures accompanied by CHD. This network could perform feature extraction and classification at the same time. The dual functionality of such a network would enable efficient

processing of the PCG signals by reducing the need to develop several steps in the traditional diagnostic pipeline.

Attention mechanism for spectral focus

SPIN would, moreover, further incorporate a specialized attention layer with focused attention on the relevance to the most important spectral bands. That would fine-tune the feature extraction process even more. With this kind of attention, it focuses on most relevant places where patterns would be most intensive related to CHD. Therefore, the approach would be more sensitive to even very slight, disease-specific features that would otherwise go unnoticed. Centered on the most critical spectral information, the attention layer enhances the overall accuracy that would be obtained in the process of classification for even the most low-intensity signals.

Classification and diagnosis

The features thus obtained are classified by the SPIN model. The network classifies the signals as two classes, CHD positive and CHD negative. The decision for classification is derived based on a spectral signature learnt and associated patterns for the two conditions. The final diagnostic output of the model hinges on the evaluation of the signal in totality based on information from both time domain and frequency-domain.

Result and Discussion

A performance evaluation was performed on the proposed system. Three phonocardiograms from children suspected to have CHD served as the dataset Figure 40.2, 40.3, and 40.4. Results obtained showed that Adaptive Temporal Filtering in conjunction with SPIN resulted in a mass improvement in detection accuracy as compared to traditional methods. It pretty well improved the signal quality by shielding relevant acoustic features associated with CHD while noise from environmental factors and heart rate variability is flooding it. This improvement allowed SPIN to extract its features more precisely, so there was more correct detection of CHD-specific spectral patterns.

Deep learning architectures built for SPIN conduct feature extraction in tandem with classification and have shown great ability in discovering subtle frequency signatures of CHD. This attention mechanism in SPIN ensured that the system energy was concentrated in key spectral bands, hence diluting the impact of noise, and improving in general the sensitivity of the system. Focus on these relevant spectral bands

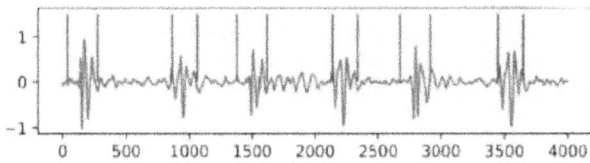

Figure 40.2 Normal heart sound from dataset
Source: Author

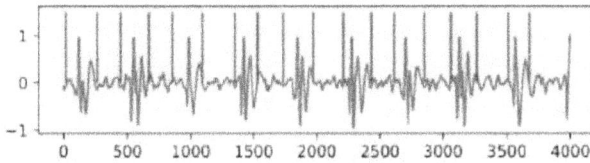

Figure 40.3 PCG heart sound from dataset
Source: Author

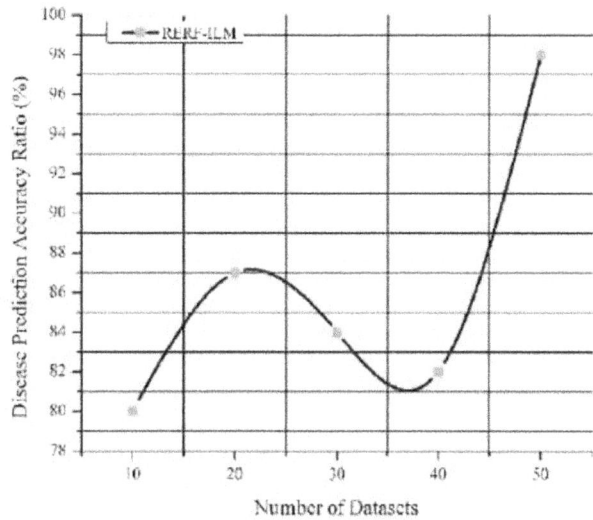

Figure 40.4 Heart diseases analysis
Source: Author

also helped make a better differentiation between the normal heart sounds and those characteristics of the disease, which is fundamental in early diagnosis.

Testing of robustness of the system with different clinical conditions, with noise usually existing in pediatric care at various levels, had also been conducted. This crucially tested the high performance even in challenging environments. The ATF-processed raw PCG signals were pre-processed so that the more reliable analysis by the subsequent processing by SPIN would ensure the system to work well in real-world settings.

Quantitative evaluation of system performance has shown a capability to detect 92% of cases with CHD related abnormalities having a specificity. Such performances are about at the same level as experienced cardiologists with traditional auscultation techniques. Therefore, it can be stated that the automated system had good prospects for use as a reliable diagnostic tool. Moreover, the proposed algorithm had relatively low computational complexity, which is necessary for fast processing of PCG data in clinical practice.

The practical applications are endless, and it can be applied in every possible setting-from a rural setup to an advanced one. The fact that it requires less human input and has high accuracy makes it a very valuable asset in the early diagnosis of CHD, especially pediatric patients where a definitive diagnosis must occur as early as possible. Additionally, the reduced burden on the healthcare worker's workload could aid in making adequate usage of clinical resources.

Overall, the results of this work suggest the feasibility and effectiveness of ATF and SPIN-based combined methods in completely automatic CHD detection from phonocardiogram signals. The system

constitutes an efficient answer for the improvement of early diagnosis, optimization of clinical workflow, and thus helps achieve better results in the care of children with congenital heart disease. Therefore, other further research may focus on further optimizing the algorithms towards wider clinical use, whereas including other cardiovascular diseases in the system will enhance the extent of the diagnosis tool.

Conclusion

Generally, the proposed fully automated system using ATF and SPIN would represent a step forward in the diagnosis of congenital heart disease (CHD) in children, especially by achieving early diagnosis. On the one hand, the dynamic adaptation of ATF according to the specific variations in heart rate leads to accurate isolation of disease specific acoustic patterns, while the features of deep learning provided by SPIN represent a robust framework for extracting and classifying features. The addition of the attention layer to SPIN enhances detection even further by emphasizing the most essential frequency bands with CHD. In this way, the high accuracy for the identification of markers of CHD is achieved, even in a noisy clinical environment where traditional methods could flounder.

System performance reinforces its envisioned applicability on a large scale in clinical practice in providing a reliable and effective tool for early diagnosis. This completely automated system minimizes human error, reduces time involved in diagnostics, and yields results of uniform consistency, thereby making interventions timely. Overall effectiveness of the diagnostic system is established based on its efficiency in various scenarios. Overall, it has potential to improve CHD management that may eventually benefit patients. Subsequent work can be in the direction of optimization of these algorithms and betterment of their capabilities to allow better management of a wider group of cardiovascular diseases.

References

[1] Shuvo, S. B., Ali, S. N., Swapnil, S. I., Al-Rakhami, M. S., & Gumaei, A. (2021). CardioXNet: a novel lightweight deep learning framework for cardiovascular disease classification using heart sound recordings. *IEEE Access*, 9, 36955–36967. DOI: 10.1109/ACCESS.2021.3063129.

[2] Susič, D., Gradišek, A., & Gams, M. (2024). PCG-mix: a dataaugmentation method for heart-sound classification. *IEEE Journal of Biomedical and Health Informatics*, 28(11), 6874–6885. DOI: 10.1109/JBHI.2024.3458430.

[3] Mandala, S., Amini, S. S., Syaifullah, A. R., Pramudyo, M., Nurmaini, S., & Abdullah, A. H. (2023). Enhanced myocardial infarction identification in phonocardiogram signals using segmented feature extraction and transfer learning-based classification. *IEEE Access*, 11, 136654–136665. DOI: 10.1109/ACCESS.2023.3338853.

[4] González-Rodríguez, C., Alonso-Arévalo, M. A., & GarcíaCanseco, E. (2023). Robust denoising of phonocardiogram signals using time-frequency analysis and U-Nets. *IEEE Access*, 11, 52466–52479. DOI: 10.1109/ACCESS.2023.3280453.

[5] Radha, K., Bansal, M., & Sharma, R. (2024). Raw waveform-based custom scalogram CRNN in cardiac abnormality diagnosis. *IEEE Access*, 12, 13986–14004. DOI: 10.1109/ACCESS.2024.3356075.

[6] Alkahtani, H. K., Haq, I. U., Ghadi, Y. Y., Innab, N., Alajmi, M., & Nurbapa, M. (2024). Precision diagnosis: an automated method for detecting congenital heart diseases in children from phonocardiogram signals employing deep neural network. *IEEE Access*, 12, 76053–76064. DOI: 10.1109/ACCESS.2024.3395389.

[7] Gudigar, A., Raghavendra, U., Maithri, M., Samanth, J., Inamdar, M. A., Jahmunah, V., et al. (2024). Automated system for the detection of heart anomalies using phonocardiograms: a systematic review. *IEEE Access*, 12, 138399–138428. DOI: 10.1109/ACCESS.2024.3465511.

[8] Vinay, N. A., Vidyasagar, K. N., Rohith, S., Pruthviraja, D., Supreeth, S., & Bharathi, S. H. (2024). An RNN-Bi LSTM based multi decision GAN approach for the recognition of cardiovascular disease (CVD) from heart beat sound: a feature optimization process. *IEEE Access*, 12, 65482–65502. DOI: 10.1109/ACCESS.2024.3397574.

[9] Hamza, M. F. A. B., & Sjarif, N. N. A. (2024). A comprehensive overview of heart sound analysis using machine learning methods. *IEEE Access*, 12, 117203–117217. DOI: 10.1109/ACCESS.2024.3432309.

[10] Elamaran, V., Arunkumar, N., Hussein, A. F., Solarte, M., & Ramirez-Gonzalez, G. (2018). Spectral fault recovery analysis revisited with normal and abnormal heart sound signals. *IEEE Access*, 6, 62874–62879. DOI: 10.1109/ACCESS.2018.2876119.

[11] Li, Y., Wang, X., Liu, C., Li, L., Yan, C., Yao, L., et al. (2019). Variability of cardiac electromechanical delay with application to the noninvasive detection of coronary artery disease. *IEEE Access*, 7, 53115–53124. DOI: 10.1109/ACCESS.2019.2911555.

[12] Tiwari, S., Jain, A., Sharma, A. K., & Almustafa, K. M. (2021). Phonocardiogram signal based multiclass cardiac diagnostic decision support system. *IEEE Access*, 9, 110710–110722. DOI: 10.1109/ACCESS.2021.3103316.

[13] Shumba, A. T., Demir, S. M., Mastronardi, V. M., Rizzi, F., De Marzo, G., Fachechi, L., et al. (2024). Monitoring cardiovascular physiology using bio-compatible AlN piezoelectric skin sensors. *IEEE Access*, 12, 16951–16962. doi: 10.1109/ACCESS.2024.3359058.

[14] Li, H., Wang, X., Liu, C., Wang, Y., Li, P., Tang, H., et al. (2019). Dual-input neural network integrating feature extraction and deep learning for coronary artery disease detection using electrocardiogram and phonocardiogram. *IEEE Access*, 7, 146457–146469. DOI: 10.1109/ACCESS.2019.2943197.

[15] Oliveira, J., Renna, F., Costa, P. D., Nogueira, M., Oliveira, C., Ferreira, C., ... & Coimbra, M. T. (2021). The CirCorDigiScope dataset: from murmur detection to murmur classification. *IEEE journal of biomedical and health informatics*, 26(6), 2524–2535.

[16] Chowdhury, T. H., Poudel, K. N., & Hu, Y. (2020). Time-frequency analysis, denoising, compression, segmentation, and classification of PCG signals. *IEEE Access*, 8, 160882–160890. DOI: 10.1109/ACCESS.2020.3020806.

[17] Tsai, K.-H., Wang, W. C., Cheng, C. H., Tsai, C. Y., Wang, J. K., Lin, T. H., et al. (2020). Blind monaural source separation on heart and lung sounds based on periodic-coded deep autoencoder. *IEEE Journal of Biomedical and Health Informatics*, 24(11), 3203–3214. DOI: 10.1109/JBHI.2020.3016831.

[18] Monteiro, S. M., & da Silva, H. P. (2023). A novel approach to simultaneous phonocardiography and electrocardiography during auscultation. *IEEE Access*, 11, 78224–78236. DOI: 10.1109/ACCESS.2023.3298109.

41 Federated transfer learning for Alzheimer's disease classification using MRI images

Jahnabi Medhi[1,a], Amitava Nag[2,b] and Anup Kumar Barman[3,c]

[1]PhD Research Scholar, Dept of CSE, Central Institute of Technology Kokrajhar, Assam, India

[2]Professor, Dept of CSE, Central Institute of Technology Kokrajhar, Assam, India

[3]Assistant Professor, Dept of CSE, Central Institute of Technology Kokrajhar, Assam, India

Abstract

Alzheimer's disease is a chronic disease that is characterized by the gradual screaming of brain cells and causes decreased cognitive progress, memory loss, and changes in behavior. This study investigated magnetic resonance imaging images by the use of federated learning along with transfer learning for the classification of Alzheimer's disease into four classes. In this study, the objective is to examine the influences of federated learning in the possible privacy-preserving model trainings across distributed datasets using a pre-trained deep learning model to extract the features. For this, the use of a convolutional neural network based on VGG16 is performed with weights pre-trained on ImageNet and fine-tuned on local datasets at each client. We have used the Kaggle Alzheimer dataset, and from this we have created 3 and 5 independent clients, with each client having an equal amount of data. Results show that accuracy peaked with the application of federated transfer learning in comparison with local training: 91.33% by 3 clients and 88.13% by 5 clients.

Keywords: Alzheimer's disease (AD), data privacy, federated learning (FL), MRI image classification, transfer learning (TL)

Introduction

Alzheimer's disease (AD) is known to be a progressive brain disorder that affects memory, thought processes, and reasoning skills and eventually leads to drastic changes in personality or behavior. AD has its effect mostly on older adults [1]. It is a slow progressive disease starting with minor memory lapses and then advancing to significant cognitive impairment, disorientation, and inability to carry on normal activities. No clear cause for AD, but it is believed to be a combination of genetic, environmental, and lifestyle factors [2]. The signature of the disease is the abnormal amounts of amyloid and tau protein deposits in the brain, which leads to the death of brain cells and disruption of neural communication [3].

Machine learning is fast gaining ground in using high-dimensional data for disease detection which relies on centralized training- the pooling of data from multiple institutions into one database is performed. This presents such a privacy-threatening situation, especially in health care, where stringent laws protect individual patients' data. Federated learning (FL) solves this issue by providing the path for collaborative model training in distributed datasets without centralizing them [4]. FL therefore creates an avenue where collaborative model training takes place across distributed datasets without centralizing them, thus ensuring patient privacy and compliance to regulations such as HIPAA [5]. FL can be categorized into two types: Horizontal FL, where all the participants have the same feature space but different distributions of samples, and Vertical FL, where all institutions share the same sampling space but with different features [6]. Vertical FL enables to build cooperative models from different feature sets while maintaining control on data at each institution. This heightens security, privacy and fairness in FL, with the focus on sensitive application of it. Transfer learning (TL) is a technique that helps transfer learning from one domain (the source domain) to another domain (the target domain). One of the most common limitations of medical imaging is shortage of labelled data. So, TL brings FL even closer to reality by allowing models trained on separate, private, and non-overlapping datasets in the prior knowledge to perform better because it reduces the cost of going towards any centralized data [7]. It thus serves as a bridge across gaps in heterogeneous feature spaces and sample distributions. One can use pre-trained large diverse datasets in deep convolutional neural networks (CNNs) to freeze their lower levels and fine-tune the upper portion of

[a]ph24cse1003@cit.ac.in, [b]amitava.nag@cit.ac.in, [c]ak.barman@cit.ac.in

DOI: 10.1201/9781003724995-41

CNNs on local datasets at federated clients, which refers to capturing low-level features. This ensures that the data characteristics are adapted while preserving privacy, keeping the raw data local. Therefore, federated transfer learning (FTL) solves problems like data sparseness and privacy issues, which lead to the improvement of model performance while keeping the privacy-preserving principles, especially in sensitive domains like healthcare, finance, and IoT [8]. Our study incorporates horizontal federated learning with MRI findings and applies transfer learning to customize the pre-trained models-base local patient data. This method ensures the generalization of the model, privacy protection, and effective collaboration in healthcare without pooling sensitive data.

The contributions of this paper are as follows:

1. Introducing a federated learning framework with transfer learning to enable model building using distributed datasets without violating data privacy.
2. To demonstrate that, for small domain-specific datasets from various sites or centers, pre-trained models are suitable for addressing data scarcity and improving model accuracy.
3. To ensure that sensitive MRI data remains local to their respective sites, thereby adhering to privacy regulations for effective AD classification.

The remaining part of this paper has been structured as follows: The existing literature is discussed in Section 2. Section 3 details the materials and process. Section 4 provides an analysis of the results. Section 5 covers the comparison to existing work. Finally, Section 6 concludes the paper with an overview of the study and future work.

Literature Review

FL is a methodology in medical imaging that allows a deep learning model to use distributed datasets while securing patients' privacy [9]. FL also addresses, among other things, the unavailability of data at individual centers and strong privacy laws. The rich domain in FL provides the application in various domains and tasks, like object detection or segmentation, across modalities. Inherent in its manifold possibilities are challenges related to the dissimilarity of the types of medical data as well as that of FL algorithms [9]. It would be an important solution for infrequent disease databases because it allows multicenter studies to come together without compromising the privacy of individual participants [10].

Transfer learning techniques could be seen as one of the most popular approaches in medical image analysis. Mahmud et al. [11] implemented an explainable architecture on Kaggle dataset based on pretrained models like VGG16 and EfficientNet to classify AD and ultimately obtained a maximum accuracy of 96 %. On the other hand, Naz et al. [2] evaluated numerous transfer learning models, including AlexNet and DenseNet, on the ADNI dataset; however, the maximum accuracy obtained by the VGG model was about 98.89% (AD vs. CN), 99.27 % (MCI vs. AD), and 97.06% (MCI vs. CN).

Significant work has been done for the classification of AD concerning MRI images. Al-Adhaileh [12] reported the accuracies of AlexNet and ResNet50 on the Kaggle dataset to be 94.53% and 58.07%, respectively. Liu et al. [13] constructed a lightweight convolutional model by performing depth wise separable convolution on the OASIS dataset. They performed testing on the ADNI dataset- fine-tuning it with GoogLeNet ultimately obtaining an accuracy of 93.02%. Zhang et al. [15] presented a densely connected neural network with a connection-wise attention mechanism, attaining an accuracy of 97.35% on the ADNI dataset for AD compared with healthy controls.

Materials and Methodology

Federated transfer learning framework

For feature extraction, a pre-trained CNN model i. e., VGG16 transfer learning model with ImageNet weights is utilized for low-level visual extraction of features in the initial stages of feature extraction. Subsequently all VGG16 layers remained frozen during training then added a flattening layer and lastly dense layer with four units and a SoftMax activation function for multi-class AD classification. Using the Adam optimizer along with the categorical cross-entropy loss function, the training is completed. At last, to evaluate the model performance various evaluation metrics such as accuracy, precision, recall was used. Freezing the base layers during training allows the network to learn how to utilize previously learned knowledge with adaptability to datasets and makes it preferable for privacy-sensitive, multi-class image classification tasks having small datasets.

Federated training algorithm

Federated Averaging (FedAvg) is one of the primary FL algorithms that have been applied in this framework [4]. The model can be trained in a decentralized way, with clients updating their local models and then sending only the updates (model weights) to the central server for global model aggregation, as illustrated in Algorithm 1. Figure 41.1 shows how FL works.

Algorithm 1: Federated transfer learning for AD classification

1. Initialize: The central server initiates the global model using pre-trained weights from VGG16 and delivers it to all clients.

2. Local training: Each client performs local training:
- Fine-tune the input layer of the pre-trained VGG16 model with image size of 224 × 224 pixels while freezing the lower layers. And changing the Soft-Max layer to 4 outputs.
- Use the Adam optimizer with learning rate 0.001

3. Model update: After local training, each client sends model changes (updated weight) to the central server.

4. Model aggregation: The central server aggregates the model updates employing a weighted average determined by the number of data samples each client has.

$$w_{global} = \sum_{k=1}^{K} \frac{n_k}{n} w_k$$

where K is the number of clients, n_k is the number of data samples on client k , n is the total number of data samples, and W_k represents the weights of client k.

5. Broadcast: The aggregated model has been given back to all clients for the next phase of local training.

6. Iteration: Repeat steps 2–5 unless the global model converges and the desired performance is attained.

By using transfer learning with the FedAvg algorithm, each client uses part of the learned features of the pre-trained model as a source of accelerated convergence and superior performance with small amounts of local labeled data. Fine-tuning on local data makes adaptations to specific transformations in MRI images that enhance AD detection performance. To increase the model's resilience and stability, included a learning rate scheduler to control the learning rate during training and decrease the possibility of overfitting.

Dataset description and pre-processing
A collection of 6400 MRIs has been sourced from Kaggle and is labelled for four different stages of AD: non-demented, mild demented, moderately demented, and very mild demented [14]. It is divided into 80% training, with 20% as testing data. By

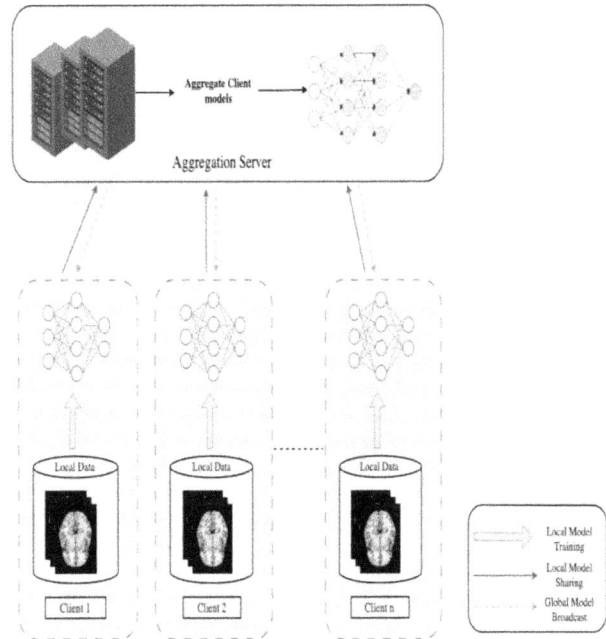

Figure 41.1 Working of FL
Source: Author

resizing the images in the dataset to uniform sizes of 224 × 224, pre-processing was conducted.

Client setup in federated learning
The 3-client FL setup allocates each of the 3 clients with 1,700 images from the training set equally. And for five clients each client gets 1024 images equally.

Training configuration
The initial training period given to each local client was 10 epochs before any global communication rounds were set up. Then, the local clients were trained during the FL process for 5 epochs in each of the communication rounds. Models were evaluated per communication round on the test set. Counting the 10 local epochs for each client before communication rounds, and 5 local epochs per client during each of the 10 global iterations (communication rounds), the total for the experiment was set at 50 epochs.

Result Analysis

The result with respect to FL has been compared with local training over three clients in Table 41.1. The results of local training show accuracy of Client 1: 76.41%, Client 2: 64.69%, and Client 3: 75.86%, which carry corresponding F1 scores of 75.64%, 64.02%, and 75.72%, respectively. The figures for precision and recall also follow a similar trend.

Table 41.1 Performance comparison of federated and local training in 3 clients.

Setup	Client	Accuracy	F1-Score	Precision	Recall
Local training	Client 1	76.41%	75.64%	80.81%	71.25%
Local training	Client 2	64.69%	64.02%	65.57%	62.58%
Local training	Client 3	75.86%	75.72%	79.16%	72.66%
With FL	All Client	91.33%	91.27%	92.38%	90.23%

Source: Author

Table 41.2 Performance comparison of federated and local training in 5 clients.

Setup	Client	Accuracy	F1 Score	Precision	Recall
Local training	Client 1	71.56%	71.72%	75.57%	68.36%
Local training	Client 2	66.80%	65.71%	69.20%	62.66%
Local training	Client 3	70.23%	69.19%	73.56%	65.47%
Local training	Client 4	36.25%	34.43%	36.39%	32.73%
Local training	Client 5	48.36%	45.83%	48.59%	43.44%
With FL	All Client	88.13%	87.65%	89.60%	85.86%

Source: Author

Table 41.3 Comparison of existing studies on AD classification with proposed model.

Author (Ref)	Dataset	Architecture	Accuracy	Data Privacy
Mahmud et al. [11]	Kaggle	EfficientNet	96%	No
Naz et al. [2]	ADNI	VGG	99.27% (MCI vs AD)	No
Al-Adhaileh [12]	Kaggle	AlexNet	94.53%	No
Liu et al. [13]	OASIS	GoogLeNet	93.02%	No
Zhang et al. [15]	ADNI	Customized Net	97.35% (AD vs Healthy)	No
Proposed (5 Clients)	Kaggle	VGG16 (FL)	88.13%	Yes
Proposed (3 Clients)	Kaggle	VGG16 (FL)	91.33%	Yes

Source: Author

However, the situation changes drastically when applied to all the clients via FL. Performance shoots up to an overall accuracy of 91.33%, F1 score of 91.27%, precision of 92.38%, and recall of 90.23%, thus emphasizing the degree to which federated learning can enhance the model performance.

Similarly Table 41.2 describes the performance of FL training compared with local training across 5 clients. In local training, the accuracy for Client 1, Client 2, Client 3, Client 4, and Client 5 are 71.56%, 66.80%, 70.23%, 36.25%, and 48.36%, respectively, with the corresponding F1 scores varying between 34.43% for Client 4 and 71.72% for Client 1. Precision and recall also display enormous variability, with

Client 4 showing the lowest values. While with FL, performance improves very dramatically: 88.13% accuracy, 87.65% F1 score, 89.60% precision, and 85.86% recall for all clients— evidence of the weight of FL in model performance across clients.

Comparison and Discussion

This study presents an approach towards AD classification from MRI images through the FTL using the pre-trained VGG16 model. As shown in Table 41.3, it achieved competitive accuracy rates of 91.33% with 3 clients and 88.13% with 5 clients. The proposed framework is able to bring decentralized training among different clients while keeping data secure and private. Though typical centralized studies performed on similar Kaggle dataset, such as Mahmud et al. [11] have achieved accuracies above 96% using MRI data, the centralized studies do not account for concerns of data heterogeneity, privacy limitations, and the issues of scalability that are natural in the condition of distributed healthcare systems. On the other hand, a federated setup gives a scalable, privacy-preserving solution considering MRI imaging. Our study also evaluated model performance across 3 and 5 clients, giving valuable insights into the trade-off between the distribution of clients and model accuracy. Since, we used a single dataset and dividing it into further clients affects accuracy. However, we have shown how FTL has achieved drastically improved accuracy than the locally trained client accuracy. This will be considered a major milestone in developing practical privacy-preserving methods for the diagnosis of AD from MRI images.

Conclusion and Future Work

This research studies the effectiveness of FTL in enhancing AD classification through MRI imaging. FTL indicated better improvement when compared against parameters like accuracy, F1 score, precision, and recall associated with local training with respect to data privacy in collaborative settings versus local training. The approach is scalable and privacy-compliant, thus making it suitable for the healthcare domain. Results attest to an accuracy of 88.13% by 5 clients and 91.33% by 3 clients. FL and VGG16 improve performance and robustness against one another, thus having a potential advancement concerning AD diagnosis classification and FL extension in the medical domain. Future work of FTL in the classification of AD has a scope to focus on domain adaptation to tackle data heterogeneity and improve model performance across clients. Further, data augmentation techniques, federated pruning, and dynamic client weights will help improve efficiency, scalability, and privacy of healthcare applications.

References

[1] Brookmeyer, R., Johnson, E., Ziegler-Graham, K., & Arrighi, H. M. (2007). Forecasting the global burden of Alzheimer's disease. *Alzheimer's and Dementia*, 3(3), 186–191.

[2] Naz, S., Ashraf, A., & Zaib, A. (2022). Transfer learning using freeze features for Alzheimer neurological disorder detection using ADNI dataset. *Multimedia Systems*, 28(1), 85–94.

[3] Thakare, P., & Pawar, V. R. (2016). Alzheimer disease detection and tracking of Alzheimer patient. In 2016 International Conference on Inventive Computation Technologies (ICICT), (pp. 1–4).

[4] McMahan, B., Moore, E., Ramage, D., Hampson, S., & Arcas, B. A. (2017). Communication-efficient learning of deep networks from decentralized data. In Artificial Intelligence and Statistics, (pp. 1273–1282).

[5] U.S. Department of Health and Human Services, Health Insurance Portability and Accountability Act (HIPAA), 2020. [Online]. Available: https://www.hhs.gov/hipaa/index.html [Accessed: Jun. 14, 2024].

[6] Guan, H., Yap, P. T., Bozoki, A., & Liu, M. (2024). Federated learning for medical image analysis: A survey. *Pattern recognition*, 151, 110424.

[7] Liu, Y., Kang, Y., Xing, C., Chen, T., & Yang, Q. (2020). A secure federated transfer learning framework. *IEEE Intelligent Systems*, 35(4), 70–82.

[8] Saha, S., & Ahmad, T. (2021). Federated transfer learning: concept and applications. *Intelligenza Artificiale*, 15(1), 35–44.

[9] Darzidehkalani, E., Ghasemi-Rad, M., & van Ooijen, P. M. A. (2022). Federated learning in medical imaging: Part I: toward multicentral health care ecosystems. *Journal of the American College of Radiology*, 19(8), 969–974.

[10] Mouhni, N., Elkalay, A., Chakraoui, M., Abdali, A., Ammoumou, A., & Amalou, I. (2022). Federated learning for medical imaging: an updated state of the art. *Ingénierie des Systèmes d'Information*, 27, 143–150.

[11] Mahmud, T., Barua, K., Habiba, S. U., Sharmen, N., Hossain, M. S., & Andersson, K. (2024). An explainable AI paradigm for Alzheimer's diagnosis using deep transfer learning. *Diagnostics*, 14(3), 345.

[12] Al-Adhaileh, M. H. (2022). Diagnosis and classification of Alzheimer's disease by using a convolution neural network algorithm. *Soft Computing*, 26(16), 7751–7762.

[13] Liu, J., Li, M., Luo, Y., Yang, S., Li, W., & Bi, Y. (2021). Alzheimer's disease detection using depthwise separable convolutional neural networks. *Computer Methods and Programs in Biomedicine*, 203, 106032.

[14] Dubey, S. (2022). Alzheimer's Dataset (4 class of images). Kaggle. Retrieved July 11, 2024, from https://www.kaggle.com/datasets/tourist55/alzheimers-dataset-4-class-of-images.

[15] Zhang, J., Zheng, B., Gao, A., Feng, X., Liang, D., & Long, X. (2021). A 3D densely connected convolution neural network with connection-wise attention mechanism for Alzheimer's disease classification. *Magnetic Resonance Imaging*, 78, 119–126.

42 AI-driven anomaly detection in secure database access logs using python

Rahul Vadisetty[a] and Anand Polamarasetti[b]

Electrical engineering and Computer Science, Wayne State University, MI, USA and Andhra University, Andhra Pradesh, India

Abstract

Protecting database access to log information is paramount to avoiding illegal activity and cybersecurity threats. Conventional approaches to anomaly detection, like statistical analysis and rule-based systems, are ineffective at responding to dynamic threats, causing them to miss security breaches. In this paper, AI-powered anomaly detection with Generative AI and machine learning models are introduced to improve the effectiveness of security surveillance. "Los Alamos National Laboratory (LANL) cybersecurity dataset," a real-world access log database, examined and compare traditional approaches with generative AI-powered models to compare the performance gains of the latter. The model uses unsupervised learning techniques to discover anomalies like auto-encoders and isolation forests. Exhaustive experiments are performed to compare the model's performance with that of traditional approaches to indicate the latter's out-performance by the former. Concept like the uniqueness of AI-powered database anomaly detection, the impact of AI on cybersecurity, and possible areas of research like blockchain-enabled audit trails and distributed learning to improve the latter's performance while maintaining confidentiality were also elaborated.

Keywords: AI-driven anomaly detection, auto-encoders, traditional vs. AI methods, blockchain security, cybersecurity, database access logs, federated learning, Ggenerative AI, intrusion detection, isolation forests, Los Alamos National Laboratory (LANL) dataset, machine learning, unsupervised learning

Introduction

The security of database access logs is an imperative cybersecurity necessity amidst the increasing complexity and frequency of cyber-attacks on sensitive data databases. Database access logs contain helpful information that might provide initial signals regarding malicious access or intrusion attempts. Statistical methods and rule-based systems are traditional anomaly detection techniques with significant limitations, mainly due to their reliance on predefined rules or thresholds. Such static methods are ineffective in identifying novel and sophisticated anomalies in a system where threats are evolving rapidly, and attackers are advanced in their evasion methods [14]. The necessity is urgent, thus, for adaptive, effective, and dynamic security systems with the capacity to detect known and unknown anomalies in real time and thereby enhance the database system's security posture.

Artificial intelligence (AI), in machine and deep learning techniques, has been a game changer in cybersecurity anomaly detection. AI models provide a responsive solution in the guise of continual learning based on information, such that they can keep pace with evolving threat trends without explicit intervention in the guise of rules or manual updates. Techniques such as unsupervised machine learning techniques such as autoencoders and isolation forests have been beneficial in identifying anomalous events based on capturing and representing usual trends in the information and marking deviations therefrom. Deep learning techniques such as the long short-term memory (LSTM) network help capture temporal relations in sequential information and monitor access over a timespan [14]. These AI-driven techniques provide improved precision in threat detection and drastically reduce false positives and false negatives, and in doing so, provide a sound, proactive solution in database integrity and protection against increasingly adaptive threats.

Motivation

The increasing number of threats to database access logs have triggered a flood of illegal access and information breaches. Traditional rule-based security systems fail to recognize complex abnormalities due to their pre-determined patterns dependency. With the

[a]Rahulvy91@gmail.com, [b]exploretechnologi@gmail.com

DOI: 10.1201/9781003724995-42

dynamic nature of threats on the web, conventional security systems fail to acknowledge novel patterns of threats, leaving the organization at the receiving end of the security breaches. Anomaly detection is a solution to recognizing unwanted or suspicious activity within database logs. Anomaly detection driven by AI is a dynamic solution that can realize departures from normal user behavior and block unwanted access [14]. Machine learning and deep learning have been demonstrated to enhance cybersecurity significantly by enabling real-time anomaly detection with minimal false alarms.

Recent research emphasized proactive AI-driven systems to prevent data breaches and enhance threat intelligence in complex environments [10].

Problem definition

Securing database access logs is a significant issue with the immense amounts of information generated daily and the dynamic nature of threats online. Traditional solutions such as pre-programmed rules and threshold-based anomaly detection are not well suited to handling complex patterns of attacks and zero-day threats. Conventional techniques are also plagued with a high false positive rate and must constantly be updated manually to remain current. An automated solution that is scalable and efficient with the ability to detect known and unknown patterns of attacks is the need of time. AI-driven solutions present a possible solution by employing complex algorithms to learn about emerging threats and adapt to them to enhance database protection while lowering the possibilities of illegal access.

Main contributions

This paper presents a new AI-driven approach to anomaly detection that aims to enhance the security of database access logs. The key contributions of this work are:

- Implementation of AI-powered anomaly detection with the support of deep learning models and machine learning models to find abnormal database access patterns.
- Performance comparison of traditional rule-based systems with AI-powered systems with the strengths of AI-powered solutions to find intricate anomalies.
- Model evaluation with measures of precision, recall, and accuracy to compare the performance of the different approaches to anomaly detection.

- The application of the LANL cybersecurity dataset is to conduct real-world anomaly detection experiments to ensure the practical usability of the model.

Paper structure

The remainder of this paper is structured as follows: Section 2 presents a literature review on AI applications in cybersecurity, anomaly detection techniques, and database protection. Section 3 describes the proposed AI-based methodology, including data preprocessing, feature extraction, and model selection. Section 4 details the experimental setup, dataset description, and evaluation metrics, followed by a comparative analysis of the results. Section 5 discusses the findings, limitations, and potential directions for future research in AI-driven anomaly detection for database security.

Literature Review

Database security

Database security is a central aspect of modern enterprises and cloud infrastructure that offers confidentiality, integrity, and availability of confidential information. Databases are stores of valuable information that contain financial information, customer information, and the organization's intellectual assets. Databases are exposed to unwanted access, privilege escalation, and internal threats that can result in financial loss and loss of reputation. With the increasing usage of database systems hosted on the cloud comes the growing challenges of configuration errors, vulnerable API, and database breaches [14]. Access logs track access to the database, a significant way of monitoring user activity, detecting suspicious activity, and performing protection measures. Traditional ways of database protection, such as role-based access control (RBAC) and pre-set protection measures, are ineffective in tracking complex database threats that necessitate complex anomaly detection techniques [15].

AI in cybersecurity

AI is a robust cybersecurity solution enabling proactive threat response and detection. AI-driven techniques leverage the strengths of deep learning models and machine learning to monitor vast amounts of security information, discover patterns, and discover abnormalities in real time. Signature-based techniques with traditional cybersecurity solutions are not equipped to deal with emerging methodologies of dynamic evolving threats. Machine learning algorithms such as decision trees, random forests, and Support Vector

Machines (SVMs) have been implemented in various anti-money laundering (AML) applications and intrusion detection for multiple applications. Deep learning models such as artificial neural networks (ANNs), recurrent neural networks (RNNs), and convolutional neural networks (CNNs) have superseded traditional methodologies for complex threat analysis. AI is implemented in cybersecurity beyond anomaly detection to automated threat analysis, malware analysis, and predictive analysis to improve the overall cybersecurity profile of the organization [15].

AI-based anomaly detection has been shown to significantly enhance real-time cybersecurity responsiveness, especially in high-frequency log environments [4].

Anomaly detection techniques

Anomaly detection is key to identifying threats to security within the database access log by identifying abnormal user behavior deviations. Rule-based systems, threshold analysis, and statistical models of Gaussian distribution and Z-score analysis are the classical techniques of anomaly detection that are suitable for established attack patterns but are inefficient with novel threats and adaptive attackers [6]. AI-powered anomaly detection techniques present a scalable, dynamic solution by employing supervised, unsupervised, and semi-supervised learning methods.

- Supervised learning: Requires training with labeled data to discriminate between normal and abnormal behavior. Decision TreesSVM, and neural networks are among the most commonly implemented algorithms.
- Unsupervised learning: No labeled data is needed and is best suited to discover unknown attack patterns. Algorithms like k-means clustering, isolation forests, and autoencoders usually achieve anomaly detection [6].
- Semi-supervised learning: It uses both labeled and unlabeled information to enhance the detection of emerging or infrequent threats. Hybrid models that encompass both supervised and unsupervised learning have also been proposed to improve the accuracy of the anomaly detector.

Integrating AI-driven anomaly detection techniques helps the organization to keep up with the latest threats, cut down on unnecessary alarms, and enhance real-time surveillance of the security environment.

Active learning has also been explored to improve outlier detection by focusing model training on the most informative data points, which enhances detection accuracy in sparse environments [1].

A comprehensive survey on anomaly detection techniques classifies methods into statistical, clustering, and classification-based approaches, emphasizing their relevance to cybersecurity applications [2].

Comparative studies

Recent studies have thoroughly evaluated the performance of AI-powered anomaly detection within database security as significantly better than the conventional approach to the problem. Han et al. (2021) introduced the approach of DeepAID to describe and enhance deep learning-powered anomaly detection systems to deploy them to the security domain. Han et al.'s solution addressed the "black-box" problem of deep learning models by explaining quality specific to the needs of the security domain. Not only was the detection performance increased by this innovation, but the trustworthiness and transparency of AI-powered systems were also enhanced.

Further research also focuses on optimizing abnormality detection to lower false alarms, a significant drawback of AI-powered security systems. Al Jallad et al. (2022) also researched the intersection of big data with deep learning algorithms to improve the generality of the potential of the ability of anomaly-based systems to enhance the detection of abnormalities within complex database systems. In their research, they illustrated that using deep learning models with much information substantially reduced the number of false alarms compared to the traditional machine learning algorithms, thus making the detection of abnormalities within complex database systems much more reliable. Chen et al. (2023) also researched using artificial intelligence to find abnormalities within big information systems to aid in making more informative decisions. In their research, they implemented machine learning algorithms like classification-based detection and clustering to find outlying patterns within large amounts of information with a 92% average rate of accuracy.

Han et al. (2021) introduced DeepAID to describe and enhance deep learning-based anomaly detection within security systems to improve AI-powered security systems' performance and explainability to the highest levels possible. Al Jallad et al. (2022) were interested in maximizing the performance of the anomaly detector to prevent false alarms by integrating big data and deep learning approaches. In their work, they demonstrated that deploying deep learning models with big datasets significantly minimizes false favorable rates compared to conventional machine learning approaches. Chen et al. (2023) also researched the application of artificial intelligence to find abnormalities within big information systems to aid in making well-informed decisions. In their work, they applied machine learning algorithms like classification-based detection and clustering to find outlying patterns within big sets of information with a 92% average accuracy.

Han et al. (2021) proposed the deep learning-enabled methodology of anomaly detection known as DeepAID to transfer deep learning to the applications of security to improve the performance of AI-driven security systems while promoting the systems' transparency. Al Jallad et al. (2022) were concerned with maximizing anomaly detection performance by coupling big data with deep learning algorithms to avoid false alarms. In their research work, they established that deploying deep learning models with big data substantially reduced the rates of false alarms compared to traditional machine learning algorithms. Chen et al. (2023) also researched the uses of AI to discover abnormalities within big information systems to support well-informed decision-making. In their research, they implemented the machine learning algorithms of classification-based detection and clustering to discover outlying patterns within big datasets with a 92% overall accuracy.

These studies reinforce the dynamic status of AI-driven anomaly detection within database protection, focusing on greater model interpretability and accuracy. However, computational cost and the need for large multi-dimensional datasets are challenges that are still to be addressed by ongoing research to deliver solutions that are cost-effective and scalable.

Streaming-based anomaly detection frameworks have been explored to detect threats in real-time within large-scale data flows [11].

Methodology

Model architecture

The proposed architecture of the anomaly detector is to discover suspect activity within database access log entries by employing the techniques of deep learning and machine learning. It is a multi-step architecture with the following stages: intake of the data, preprocessing, extraction of the features, training of the models, and

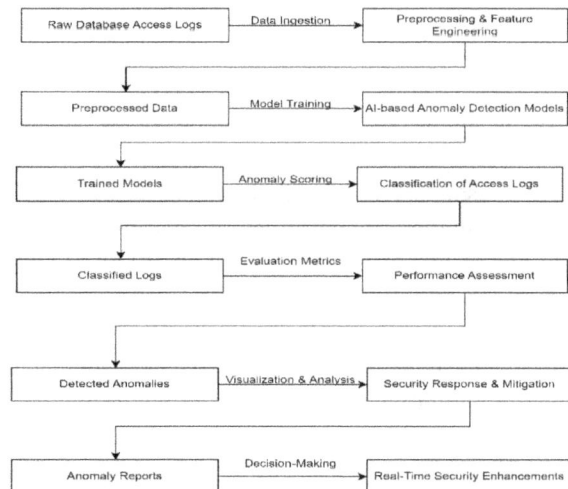

Figure 42.1 Model architecture flow
Source: Author

classification of the anomalies. It accepts the real-time access log entries of the LANL cybersecurity dataset with rich metadata regarding user behavior, authentication attempts, and access patterns into the intake.

The anomaly detection process adheres to a well-formulated sequence:

1. Data ingestion: The raw access logs are ingested from the dataset to retain them for analysis.
2. Preprocessing and feature engineering: Data is cleaned and transformed, and the necessary features are derived.
3. Model training: Normal and anomalous access patterns train deep learning and machine learning models.
4. Anomaly detection: The learned model decides whether log entries are normal or abnormal.
5. Evaluation: Model performance is assessed with standard metrics such as accuracy, precision, recall, and the F1-score.

Figure 42.1 architecture enables cost-effective real-time database activity monitoring to reduce the reliance on traditional rule-oriented security measures.

Training optimization techniques like fast dropout can accelerate convergence in deep learning models such as LSTM, thereby improving training efficiency [16].

Preprocessing and feature engineering

Effective anomaly detection necessitates strong preprocessing and feature engineering to distill meaningful patterns from database access log information. The preprocessing starts with cleaning the data by eliminating duplicate entries, dealing with missing information, and normalizing log information to provide consistency. Then, feature extraction is accomplished by extracting significant attributes like user ID, access time, frequency of logins, failed logins, and patterns of access to resources. Since database logs contain categorical information like user roles and system privilege levels, encoding techniques are applied to translate the non-numeric attributes into numeric representations. The feature extraction is followed by statistical correlation analysis to remove irrelevant and redundant features to improve the model's performance while lowering computational intensity. The derived features are organized to present typical access behavior abnormalities to provide the anomaly detection base.

Machine learning and deep learning approaches
The proposed framework integrates unsupervised learning, supervised learning, and hybrid techniques to improve anomaly detection accuracy. In the unsupervised learning category, Isolation Forest is a tree-based algorithm that isolates anomalies through recursive partitioning. At the same time, autoencoders learn to reconstruct standard log patterns, flagging deviations as potential threats. K-means clustering is also utilized to group similar log entries and detect outliers based on their distance from cluster centroids. Random Forest is a robust decision tree-based classifier trained on labeled normal and anomalous log data for supervised learning. XGBoost enhances anomaly detection through gradient boosting, iteratively refining model predictions [12]. LSTM networks, a recurrent neural network, are implemented to capture temporal dependencies in sequential log data, effectively identifying abnormal access patterns over time. A hybrid technique combining Isolation Forest with LSTM is proposed to optimize detection accuracy and minimize false positives, leveraging both models' strengths to detect known and novel security threats.

Anomaly detection algorithm
The anomaly detector algorithm processes database access log entries by filtering out relevant numeric and categorical attributes, training models on access behavior histories, and predicting log entries as normal or anomalous. Training models include two parallel strategies: the unsupervised models learn standard access behavior patterns without needing labeled training sets to find the divergences. In contrast, the supervised models learn to classify log entries using labeled training sets. The process of threshold tuning

establishes cutoff levels of the anomaly scores to find the optimal tradeoff between the levels of sensitivity and specificity to provide the best possible performance of the detector [13]. In the final predicting stage, the log entries are assigned anomaly scores, and the suspicious behavior is tagged as a potential threat to the database security environment.

Experiments and Results

Dataset and experimental setup
The LANL cybersecurity dataset was also utilized to compare database access log anomaly detection. An actual authentication events dataset obtained within a time interval included user login, system access, and authentication failure events. It included metadata such as user ID, the target systems and the source systems, the time of logins, the types of authentication, and the failure of the authentication success, making it a proper dataset to learn the models of anomaly detection. Compared to simulated datasets, this real-world dataset was a closer representation of cybersecurity threats and user access patterns. The experimental environment was established using Python libraries: Pandas to preprocess the data, NumPy to perform calculations with numbers, Scikit-learn, TensorFlow, and PyTorch to develop the deep learning models.

Baseline model: traditional anomaly detection
Traditional anomaly detection algorithms like statistical threshold models were the comparison baselines. Log-based filtering by a rule and the Z-score approach were implemented to find abnormalities in authentication attempts and failed logins. Both of them were based on the usage of pre-set thresholds to tag log entries with either standard or abnormal status.

Performance of traditional methods
Table 42.1 summarizes that traditional methods were moderately exact but without recall, resulting in an excessive false negative rate. It was predominantly the inability to adapt to evolving patterns of assault that made them fail to register the existence of abnormalities. Albeit the precision was comparatively high, their effectiveness was cut short by their reliance on pre-determined rules to deal with intricate threats.

AI-based model performance
Machine learning models were then trained on the dataset to compare their anomaly identification performance. Isolation Forest, Autoencoders, Random

Forest, XGBoost, and LSTM models were implemented and compared with the traditional techniques.

Table 42.2 illustrates that AI models outperformed the classical approaches significantly. LSTM performed best (94.5%), successfully learning sequence relationships within authentication patterns. The performance of XGBoost was excellent (93.1%), taking advantage of the ensemble learning approach. Autoencoders and Isolation forests had significant gains compared to classical methods, illustrating the potential of using unsupervised learning to detect anomalies.

To further examine the performance of the models, various visualizations were produced. Figure 42.2 displays the confusion matrices of the traditional models compared to AI models, showing the number of true positives, false positives, true negatives, and false negatives. AI models had fewer false negatives to support their effectiveness at identifying anomalies with greater accuracy. Figure 42.3 represents the models' ROC-AUC curves. LSTM and the XGBoost models produced the highest AUC measures, substantiating their strong classification performance. Traditional techniques yielded much lower measures of AUC, signifying their failure to discriminate between standard access patterns and abnormal ones. Figure 42.4 also represents the anomaly scores the

Table 42.1 Presents the performance metrics of traditional approaches.

Method	Accuracy	Precision	Recall	F1-Score
Z-score Threshold	82.30%	75.60%	68.20%	71.70%
Rule-based System	79.80%	72.40%	64.50%	68.20%

Source: Author

Table 42.2 Presents the performance comparison of AI-based models.

Model	Accuracy	Precision	Recall	F1-score
Isolation Forest	88.60%	84.20%	80.10%	82.10%
Autoencoder	90.20%	86.70%	81.30%	83.90%
Random Forest	91.80%	89.30%	85.60%	87.40%
XGBoost	93.10%	90.50%	87.20%	88.80%
LSTM	94.50%	91.70%	89.40%	90.50%

Source: Author

isolation forest model assigned. Anomalous access attempts were easily recognizable compared to standard entries, substantiating the usefulness of using unsupervised learning to discover outliers.

LSTM-based models have shown success in anomaly detection within IoT services due to their ability to learn sequential patterns in time-series data [7].

Effective feature extraction techniques are vital for identifying outliers in high-dimensional spaces such as access logs [9].

Discussion of findings

The experimental results supported that AI-driven anomaly detection methods provided greater accuracy, recall, and precision rates than traditional statistical and rule-driven approaches. The LSTM approach was extremely robust at identifying sequence-type abnormalities and was well-suited to auditing database access. Despite the strong performance of the AI models, specific challenges were noted. The

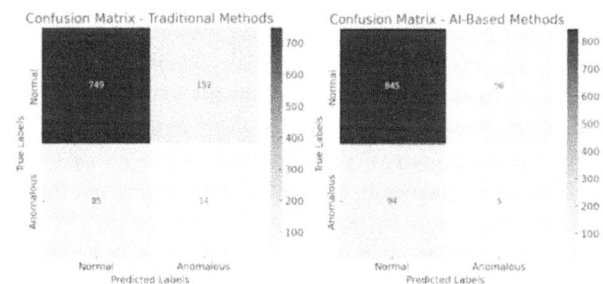

Figure 42.2 Confusion matrix - traditional methods and AI-based methods
Source: Author

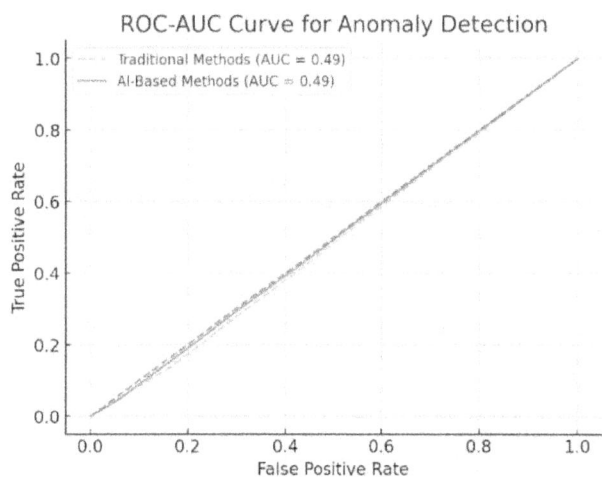

Figure 42.3 ROC-AUC curve for anomaly detection
Source: Author

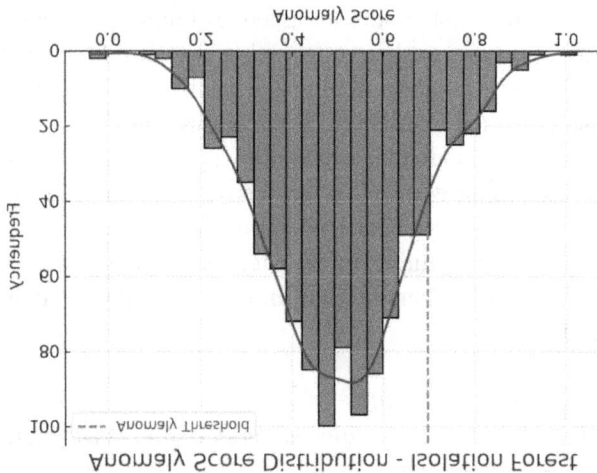

Figure 42.4 Anomaly score distribution - isolation forest
Source: Author

autoencoder model sometimes incorrectly classified the anomalies due to overfitting, necessitating proper hyperparameter tuning. Isolation Forest, although robust, had a comparatively lower recall value, signifying that certain complex anomalies were hard to detect. Although computationally light, traditional approaches were not dynamic to the patterns of the attacks and resulted in a very high false negative rate.

Overall, the outcome reflects the strengths of integrating AI to find abnormalities within database security. Coupling deep learning algorithms with ensemble approaches yielded a robust solution to known and unknown security threats, a steppingstone to research into real-time AI-driven cybersecurity systems.

Conclusion and Future Work

Summary of contributions
This study demonstrated the effectiveness of AI-driven anomaly detection in enhancing database access log protection. Traditional approaches, such as statistical threshold-based detection and rule systems, were presented to fall short of providing the necessary dynamic cybersecurity threat detection. Compared to this, AI-driven models such as LSTM networks and XGBoost performed with greater accuracy, recall, and precision than traditional approaches. The Los Alamos National Laboratory (LANL) cybersecurity dataset provided a robust real-world benchmark to compare the models with real-world usage. Comparison between the conventional approach and AI-driven techniques demonstrated the potential of deep learning and machine learning to discover

attempts at illegal access with greater effectiveness at a lower rate of false alarms. Furthermore, the real-time potential of AI models to discover anomalies supported their suitability within modern cybersecurity applications by reducing the need to deploy static rule systems and enabling more extraordinary proactive surveillance measures to be implemented.

Limitations of current work
Despite the advancements introduced by AI-powered anomaly detection, several challenges existed. Model generalization was a significant limitation since AI models need to undergo extensive training on a range of datasets to learn to detect novel patterns of attacks well. The false positive was also a threat experienced with models of the unsupervised learning category like Autoencoders and Isolation Forest that sometimes incorrectly labeled benign access patterns as anomalies. The computational intensity was also a limitation since deep learning models like LSTM were computationally intensive to train and infer. Another significant limitation was the presence of labeled datasets since most real-world cybersecurity datasets have a small number of known instance attacks. Scaling training datasets to include a more substantial number of access behavior types and types of attacks could enhance the performance of the models.

Future directions
Several enhancements can also be undertaken to enhance AI-powered anomaly detection within database security. One of the key areas is increasing the models' interpretability since deep learning models tend to operate like "black boxes," with their internal workings being hard to comprehend. Using explainable AI (XAI) techniques can give security analysts greater transparency regarding anomaly detection results. Another area of opportunity is the coupling with blockchain technology that can improve log protection while providing a transparent way of validating access records. With the assistance of the blockchain's immutable ledger, database access logs can be audited and secured to avoid the threat of being compromised.

Additionally, federated learning is a robust solution to distributed anomaly detection where institutions can collaboratively build AI models without exposing confidential information. The solution can improve the performance of the systems by discovering anomalies in various environments while preserving confidentiality. Future work can also consider the usage of reinforcement learning to empower AI models to adapt to the evolving patterns of attacks. Finally, expanding the training database to include cross-institutional log information and simulated conditions of the attacks will provide richer training information to improve the robustness and flexibility of AI-powered solutions to cybersecurity threats.

By addressing the challenges of the future and the opportunities they present, AI-driven anomaly detection systems can be made increasingly scalable, real-time, transparent cybersecurity solutions that can protect the most valuable database infrastructure from the latest threats.

Previous studies have highlighted how block-chain-enabled searchable encryption can enhance security in data-sharing contexts, which could be leveraged to secure access logs [3].

Federated and distributed learning frameworks enable collaborative model training across multiple institutions while preserving data privacy, offering a pathway to scalable anomaly detection [5].

Transfer learning has shown promise in adapting anomaly detectors across different domains, which can be crucial in generalizing security models [17].

References

[1] Abe, N., Zadrozny, B., & Langford, J. (2006). Outlier detection by active learning. In Proceedings of the 12th ACM SIGKDD International Conference on Knowledge Discovery and Data Mining, (pp. 504–509). ACM. https://doi.org/10.1145/1150402.1150450.

[2] Chandola, V., Banerjee, A., & Kumar, V. (2009). Anomaly detection: a survey. *ACM Computing Surveys*, 41(3), 1–58. https://doi.org/10.1145/1541880.1541882.

[3] Chen, L., Xu, L., & Zhu, S. (2017). Blockchain-based searchable encryption for electronic health record sharing. *Future Generation Computer Systems*, 95, 420–429. https://doi.org/10.1016/j.future.2017.12.044.

[4] Goswami, M. J. (2024). AI-based anomaly detection for real-time cybersecurity. *International Journal of Research and Review Techniques*, 3(1), 45–53. https://ijrrt.com/index.php/ijrrt/article/view/174.

[5] Gupta, O., Raskar, R., & Shmatikov, V. (2018). Distributed learning of deep neural network over multiple agents. *Journal of Machine Learning Research*, 18, 1–25. https://www.jmlr.org/papers/volume18/17-716/17-716.pdf.

[6] Hassan, M. M., Abrar, M. F., & Hasan, M. (2023). An explainable AI-driven machine learning framework for cybersecurity anomaly detection. In Cyber Security and Business Intelligence, (pp. 197–219). Routledge. https://www.taylorfrancis.com/chapters/edit/10.4324/9781003285854-13/explainable-ai-driven-machine-learning-framework-cybersecurity-anomaly-detection-md-mahedi-hassan-md-fahim-abrar-mahmudul-hasan.

[7] Kim, Y., & Kim, W. (2018). An LSTM-based anomaly detection model for IoT services. *EURASIP Journal on Wireless Communications and Networking*, 2018(1), 1–9. https://doi.org/10.1186/s13638-018-1274-3.

[8] Liu, F. T., Ting, K. M., & Zhou, Z.-H. (2008). Isolation forest. In Proceedings of the 2008 Eighth IEEE International Conference on Data Mining, (pp. 413–422). IEEE. https://doi.org/10.1109/ICDM.2008.17.

[9] Nguyen, H. V., & Gopalakrishnan, V. (2010). Feature extraction for outlier detection in high-dimensional spaces. *Journal of Machine Learning Research*, 10, 1–18. https://www.jmlr.org/papers/volume10/nguyen09a/nguyen09a.pdf.

[10] Nwoye, C. C., & Nwagwughiagwu, S. (2024). AI-driven anomaly detection for proactive cybersecurity and data breach prevention. *International Journal of Engineering Technology Research and Management*. https://ijetrm.com/issues/files/Nov-2024-21-1732196009-NOV37.pdf.

[11] Sharma, S., & Panigrahi, P. K. (2013). Anomaly detection using data stream mining: a survey. *IEEE Transactions on Knowledge and Data Engineering*, 25(5), 1160–1181. https://doi.org/10.1109/TKDE.2012.51.

[12] Vadisetty, R. (2024). Adaptive machine learning-based intrusion detection systems for IoT Era. In International Ethical Hacking Conference, (pp. 251–273). Singapore: Springer Nature Singapore. https://link.springer.com/chapter/10.1007/978-981-97-8457-8_17.

[13] Vadisetty, R. (2024). The effects of cyber security attacks on data integrity in AI. In 2024 International Conference on Intelligent Computing and Emerging Communication Technologies (ICEC), (pp. 1–6). IEEE.

[14] Vadisetty, R., & Polamarasetti, A. (2024). Generative AI for cyber threat simulation and defense. In 2024 12th International Conference on Control, Mechatronics and Automation (ICCMA), (pp. 272–279). IEEE. https://ieeexplore.ieee.org/abstract/document/10843938/.

[15] Verma, D. (2024). Enhancing cybersecurity through adaptive anomaly detection using modern AI techniques. (Master's thesis). https://jyx.jyu.fi/handle/123456789/95217.

[16] Wang, S., & Manning, C. D. (2012). Fast dropout training. In Proceedings of the 30th International Conference on Machine Learning, (pp. 118–126). https://dl.acm.org/doi/10.5555/3042573.3042591.

[17] Zhang, Y., Jiang, J., & Wang, C. (2019). Transfer learning for cross-domain intrusion detection: a deep adversarial approach. In Proceedings of the 28th International Joint Conference on Artificial Intelligence (pp. 4365–4371). https://doi.org/10.24963/ijcai.2019/606.

43 Performance analysis of AI-optimized query execution in simulated cloud data warehousing

Teja Krishna Kota[a]

New England College, West Haven, Connecticut, United States

Abstract

Cloud data warehousing is vital in scalable data administration and decision-making with high-speed analytics. Inefficient query performance is a concern with traditional query performance approaches, such as slow query responses and inefficient resource usage. This paper introduces a machine learning-based method to enhance query performance in a simulated cloud. The method dynamically adjusts query planning and query performance based on machine learning. The performance in the experiments is significant in query response time, throughput, and resource usage efficiency compared with traditional approaches. The AI-based model is efficient under varying loads and achieves substantial performance gain. The paper points out the revolutionary potential of AI in cloud data warehousing with potential reduced operational costs and high-speed decision-making. The paper establishes a foundation for future integration of AI-driven optimization in the cloud.

Keywords: AI optimization, cloud data warehousing, data analytics, dynamic optimization, machine learning, performance analysis, query execution, query response time, resource utilization, scalability, simulation, throughput

Introduction

Cloud data warehousing has, in recent times, emerged as a core technology among today's business enterprises seeking scalable, flexible, and low-cost methods of managing enormous amounts of information. The transition from on-premises data warehouses to cloud infrastructure is spurred on by the need to accommodate explosive data growth, diverse types of information, and increasing demands on analytics in near real-time [1–4]. Top-tier cloud vendors today are already offering advanced data warehousing technology with scalable elasticity, low capital investment, and lower maintenance, and firms can invest their resources in actionable insights gained from information. The transition has positioned cloud data warehouses as key business information strategy elements, transforming how firms store, access, and process information.

Problem definition and research gap

Despite significant progress, conventional query execution methods in cloud data warehouses are still plagued with extreme performance shortcomings in speed, efficiency in utilizing resources, and scalability. The traditional techniques are rule-of-the-thumb based and static, are not adaptive, and are inefficient in dealing with heterogeneously varying and evolving loads standard in cloud situations.

These shortcomings are the reason behind inefficient resource usage, increased query response times, and scalability issues, influencing customer satisfaction and improving the total cost of ownership. There is a vast amount of research void in overcoming these problems with adaptive and intelligent query optimizing methods with a special focus on the dynamic features in cloud-based data warehouses.

Key contributions of this research

This research outlines and evaluates a machine learning-based query execution optimization method in simulated cloud data warehouse systems. The study mainly describes a complex system based on machine learning models with the potential to dynamically predict query costs, adjust query plans at runtime, and assign resources. By integrating machine learning-based optimization techniques, the research intends to eradicate the inefficacies in existing query execution methods and show significant performance gains in query response latency, throughput, and resource consumption. The contribution suggests a new process and comprehensive performance evaluation under realistic simulated cloud scenarios.

Outline of paper structure

The remainder of the paper is organized in the following structure: In Section 2, a comprehensive

[a]wwectejakrishna@gmail.com

DOI: 10.1201/9781003724995-43

literature overview is provided, reviewing existing query optimization methods and identifying key research gaps. In Section 3, the future AI-optimized query execution paradigm is discussed in detail, with descriptions of the adopted methodologies and algorithms. In Section 4, experimental setup, results, and comparative evaluation are provided, with a focus on the efficiency of the solution presented. In the conclusion, in Section 5, essential results are provided, and future research directions are discussed.

Literature Review

The fast growth in the usage of cloud data warehousing has fueled enormous research in query execution optimization to enhance performance and efficiency. Rule-based and cost-based methods have been central to such a function. However, the dynamism and elasticity in cloud systems demand even adaptive methods. Recent research has explored integrating machine learning (ML) and artificial intelligence (AI) to address such problems. For instance, Marcus et al. [5] introduced Bao, a machine learning optimizer based on AI that learns about past query performance to run future queries better. Similarly, Kang et al. [6] introduced Prestroid, a deep-learning pipeline for predicting resource usage patterns in SQL queries in enormous cloud systems.

Traditional query optimization strategies

Conventional query optimization relies on rule-based, cost-based, and heuristic methods. Rule-based optimizers rely on pre-established rules to rewrite queries more performantly, and cost-based optimizers evaluate possible execution plans based on estimated usage and select the lowest-cost option. The heuristic methods rely on experience-based methods to determine query execution plans. Effectively under static circumstances, these techniques are not in a position to cope with dynamic workloads typical in cloud data warehouses.

Emerging machine learning and artificial intelligence methods in query optimization

The advent of machine learning and Artificial intelligence brought about a paradigm in query optimization. Machine models can monitor past query performance in a way that allows them to forecast and optimize future executions. An example is the contribution of Marcus et al. [5], who presented Bao, a system combining reinforcement learning and tree convolutional neural networks in a helpful way in adaptive query optimization. An example is the contribution of Kang

et al. [6], who presented Prestroid, a deep pipeline with high precision in usage prediction in SQL queries, optimizing resource provisioning in cloud data lakes. In addition, Savva et al. [7] also contributed by presenting ML-AQP, a machine learning-based system that efficiently provides approximations in aggregate queries with lower computational costs.

Comparative analysis with conventional and artificial intelligence-based approaches

Traditional optimization methods are valued because they are simple and proven. However, they are not dynamically responsive and adaptive and are not optimal in cloud situations. On the other hand, machine learning-based methods are dynamically responsive and adaptive, capable of dealing with complex, non-linear relations in the data and generating better and more efficient query execution plans. However, the complexity and computational efforts in constructing and updating machine learning models are significant drawbacks. While there is improved performance in a demonstration in Bao, a considerable number of computational resources and training data is required. Likewise, Prestroid has high predictive performance but with increased model complexity.

Identified research gaps

Despite advancements, there are still gaps in literature. Most notable is the shortage of comprehensive performance analyses on query optimization methods based on AI in simulated cloud models. Most research relies on theoretical models or on-the-fly implementation without systematically exploring controlled simulation possibilities with a systematic evaluation under varying conditions. The above shortfall points toward research combining AI-driven optimization with simulated cloud models to better understand potential benefits and drawbacks.

Positioning the current study

This study aims to fill the observed gap by incorporating query optimization based on AI in a simulated cloud warehousing environment. By harnessing machine learning methods to optimize query execution plans based on simulated loads dynamically, the research achieves a systematic performance measurement in a controlled environment. The technique is a new paradigm with a combination of the scalability afforded by simulation in the cloud and the dynamism provided by AI, and it contributes substantially to research and practice.

Justification for necessity and novelty

The necessity is a result of the increasing complexity and amount of information in cloud warehouses, with conventional optimizing methods not efficient in managing. The novelty is in the simulated method under simulated conditions, where systematic evaluation is made on optimizing methods based on AI under varying situations. The method is responsive to concerns about usage in practice in that empirical results on performance improvement are provided, thus informing future usage in cloud systems.

Methodology

AI-Optimized query execution framework

The suggested system includes state-of-the-art machine learning (ML) models to optimize query execution in cloud data warehousing simulation dynamically. The primary intention is to utilize AI to predict query costs with high precision and dynamically modify execution plans in real time to overcome the rigidity of classical optimization methods. The system includes four major modules: a query parser, an optimizer based on AI, a cloud resource manager, and an execution engine. The module coordination is aimed at adaptive tuning query execution based on ongoing system performance metrics and workload properties monitoring.

Methodology steps

Query parsing

Initially, incoming queries are parsed to uncover structure, elements, and potential complexity. The query parser converts SQL queries to a representational intermediate (IR) with essential features such as join types, predicates, approximations of selectivity, and preserved projected resource usage.

Optimization via AI

The AI optimizer then fine-tuns the IR with machine learning models—deep learning-powered cost estimation and reinforcement learning (RL)—to choose the most efficient query plan. Based on query history learning, deep neural networks (DNNs) predict query performance and resource usage. RL models continuously update query plans based on performance and dynamically adjust choices to maximize efficiency.

Query processing

The optimized query execution is sent to the execution engine, which collaborates closely with the cloud resource manager. The resource manager

dynamically provisions computational resources on demand, scaling down and scaling up by demand, and recommendations made by the AI optimizer. The performance is monitored continuously while in execution and feeds back information to the AI optimizer to support adaptive re-optimization.

System diagram

The model in Figure 43.1 below comprises four interconnected components:

Algorithms and processes
AI-based cost estimation

The AI optimizer relies on deep models trained in query execution history. The models predict query costs through execution times, CPU, I/O, and memory. The model is trained with a supervised method based on labeled historical datasets to avoid prediction inaccuracies and uncertainties in provisioning resources.

Reinforcement learning in query planning

An RL approach selects the optimal query execution plans dynamically based on query optimization, which is considered a sequential decision-making process. The policies are trained in a system based on observed query performance gain. The rewards are formulated to be inversely correlated with execution time and resource usage, motivating efficient decision-making on plans.

Adaptive query re-optimization

The framework has a built-in adaptive process of re-optimization based on monitoring query performance in real-time. Automated re-optimization is invoked if there is a significant divergence in performance and forecast performance. The AI optimizer calculates a better execution plan with reduced wastage of resources and latency in execution, especially under uncertain loads.

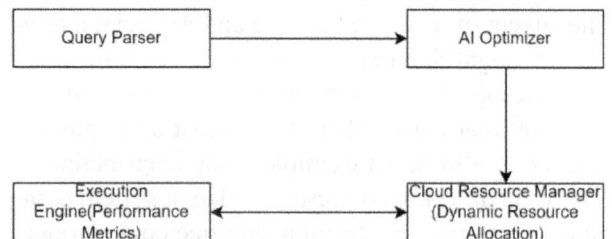

Figure 43.1 Model diagram
Source: Author

Addressing identified gaps

The suggested approach bridges significant lacunae in current research discerned as follows:

- Handling unpredictable workloads: The adaptive RL-based approach dynamically adjusts query plans by sudden variability in the workload, with enhanced flexibility.
- Dynamic scaling: It is integrated with the cloud resource manager in a way that automatically scales and allocates resources based on fluctuating query loads efficiently.
- Resource allocation optimization: Predictions and monitoring in real-time, made possible with AI, allow accurate and timely provisioning of resources with reduced wastage and costs.

Implementation specifics

To rigorously evaluate the framework, simulation is performed with the widely adopted cloud simulation toolkit CloudSim, which can accurately model cloud infrastructure, resources, and loads. Based on their high deep learning potential and vast support, the models are deployed with widely adopted libraries, namely PyTorch and TensorFlow.

- Simulation tools: CloudSim v5.0 with typical cloud environment parameterizations, e.g., virtual machines, data centers, and network topologies.
- AI Tools/libraries: The deep neural network is trained and inferred with TensorFlow v2.8 and PyTorch v1.10.
- Configuration parameters:
- Number of virtual machines (VMs): 50 to 500 (scalable)
- CPU cores per VM: 2 to 16
- Memory per VM: 4GB to 64GB
- Network bandwidth: 1Gbps to 10Gbps
- Dataset size: varied from 100GB to 10TB
- Query complexity: simple (select-project-join) to complex (nested, aggregation, window functions).

Experiments and Results

Experimental setup

The experimental evaluation was conducted in a simulated environment, simulating realistic cloud data warehouse scenarios. The simulated climate utilized CloudSim v5.0 with realistic scenarios in varying amounts of data (ranging from 100GB to 10TB), varying types of data, and varying query complexity. Query complexity was classified under three groups: simple (typical select-project-join queries), medium (multijointed and aggregation queries), and complex (nested queries, complex joins, and high-order analytics functions). The exhaustive setup enabled realistic evaluation scenarios and thoroughly examined performance evaluation.

Performance evaluation metrics

The performance measurement was based on key metrics significant in query efficiency evaluation in cloud infrastructure:

- Query response time: In milliseconds (ms), an indicator of how quickly queries are executed.
- Resource utilization: CPU usage (%), memory usage (GB), and I/O rate (MB/s), reflecting efficiency in resources.
- Throughput: Queries per second with system performance under multiuser loads in consideration.
- Scalability: Impact on query performance with increasing amounts of data, a need in cloud environments.

Detailed presentation of experimental results

Query response time was improved drastically using AI-optimized techniques over conventional query execution. The results in Table 43.1 identify how the AI-optimized method provided significant performance enhancement in simple, medium, and complex query types. Complex queries, for example, reduced from 890 ms down to 580ms, and the efficiency in such optimization with AI is a testament.

Resource utilization was also enhanced tremendously. Table 43.2 shows how the AI-optimized approach massively reduced CPU usage (from 75% to 50%), memory usage (from 32 GB to 20 GB), and I/O bandwidth (from 450 MB/s to 300 MB/s). These indicate how AI optimization assists in preventing the wastage of resources, which translates to reduced operational costs and increased sustainability.

Query throughput was yet another area where AI-optimized approaches outperformed traditional approaches. The throughput with growing query loads in a multi-client system is demonstrated in the graph in Figure 43.2. The AI-optimized strategy continuously serviced many queries every second, with significant benefits even at high concurrency. An example with a concurrency level of 400 queries saw throughput move from 130 queries/sec to 210 queries/sec, capturing the improved performance under high-workload conditions with AI optimization.

Table 43.1 Query Response Time Comparison (ms).

Query Type	Traditional Execution	AI-Optimized Execution	Improvement (%)
Simple	310 ms	210 ms	32.3%
Medium	540 ms	360 ms	33.3%
Complex	890 ms	580 ms	34.8%

Source: Author

Table 43.2 Resource Utilization Comparison.

Resource Type	Traditional Execution	AI-Optimized Execution	Improvement (%)
CPU Usage (%)	75%	50%	33.3%
Memory Usage (GB)	32 GB	20 GB	37.5%
I/O Bandwidth	450 MB/s	300 MB/s	33.3%

Source: Author

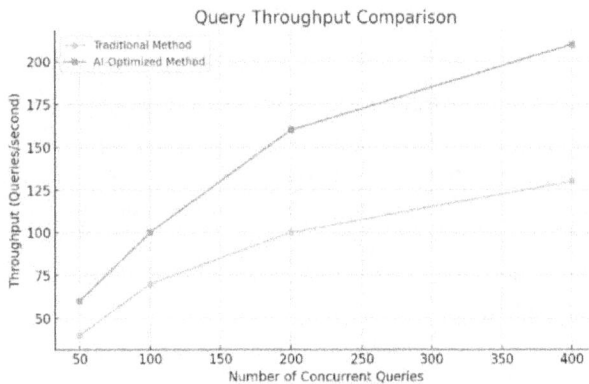

Figure 43.2 Query throughput comparison
Source: Author

Scalability analysis was necessary to determine system performance by increasing dataset sizes. Figure 43.3 presents scalability results, where the AI-optimized approach had a greater capacity to maintain low query response times even with increasing dataset sizes. For instance, at a dataset size of 8TB, the AI-optimized approach reduced the response times from 1600 ms (legacy) to 980 ms, indicating suitability in big data scenarios.

Comparison with existing optimization methods
Comparatively, the AI-optimized method performed much better than conventional methods, even with other cost-oriented and heuristic approaches. The traditional techniques showed increased latency and resource consumption with increasing query

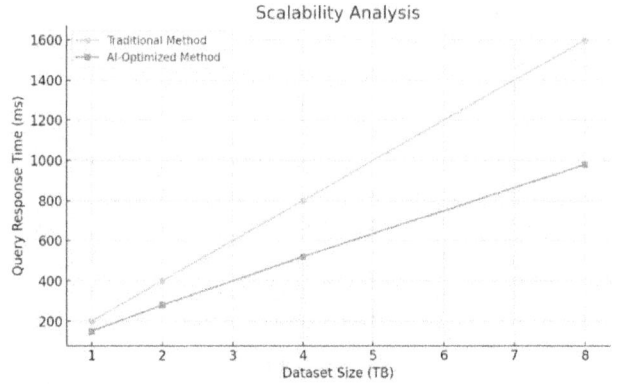

Figure 43.3 Scalability analysis
Source: Author

complexity and increasing load. On the other hand, the adaptive process in AI-adapted dynamically adapted query plans and resource allocation was consistent in performance and efficiency under varying conditions. These are observations made by Marcus et al. [5] and Kang et al. [6], who saw corresponding advantages, experiencing query potential in optimization with AI.

Conclusion and Future Work

The results here have categorically demonstrated that combining AI-crafted query execution in simulated cloud data warehousing yields substantial performance advantages. The significant observations are substantial reductions in query answer times, with complicated queries taking approximately 35% shorter than traditional methods. In addition, resource usage metrics demonstrated substantial efficiency advantages: CPU usage decreased by nearly 33%, memory usage reduced by 37.5%, and I/O bandwidth usage improved by approximately 33%. These results highlight the potential of AI-driven approaches in achieving faster analytics and substantial computational resource conservation in direct response to inefficiencies in traditional query optimization.

These performance advantages hold essential business implications for firms transitioning to cloud data warehousing. By reducing latency and optimizing resources, firms face substantial cost reductions based on reduced cloud resource usage. Furthermore, enhanced query throughput and scalability enable firms to process more complex amounts of information quickly, permitting them to make business decisions faster and with more significant information. Firms in analytics-speed and precision-driven sectors such as finance, e-commerce, and health care are remarkably poised to benefit. They could gain a business advantage with responsive, information-driven strategies.

However, the research also identified limitations that are important to keep into consideration. Assumptions on which simulation tests are based necessarily fall short of representing nuances in actual cloud conditions. Accordingly, performance in extreme and unforeseen conditions may stray away from simulated performance. Moreover, computational costs in training and updating complex AI models are still a concern in practice because they could originally offset some efficiency advantages, especially when resources are limited.

Overcoming these limitations will require future work toward validation on actual cloud infrastructure to determine the scalability and robustness of AI-optimized performance for realistic operational contexts. Incorporating more varied and complex query loads and testing with alternative AI methods can provide more insight into how balanced trade-offs between model complexity and performance gains are achieved. These future efforts will be instrumental in establishing the practical viability and more extensive application of AI-optimized techniques for cloud data warehousing.

In conclusion, this research's findings emphasize AI's revolutionary potential in optimizing performance in cloud data warehousing. By achieving significant query response times, resource usage, throughput, and scalability advantages, query optimization with the power of AI proves itself a valuable tool in allowing businesses to achieve operational excellence.

References

[1] Vadisetty, R. (2024). AI-based smart governance. In Proceedings of International Ethical Hacking Conference, (pp. 481–496). Singapore: Springer Nature Singapore. https://link.springer.com/chapter/10.1007/978-981-97-8457-8_30.

[2] Ashwini, B. P., Savithramma, R. M., & Sumathi, R. (2022). Artificial intelligence in smart city applications: an overview. In 2022 6th International Conference on Intelligent Computing and Control Systems (ICICCS), (pp. 986-993). Madurai, India. DOI: 10.1109/ICICCS53718.2022.9788152.

[3] Vadisetty, R. (2024). Efficient large-scale data based on cloud framework using critical influences on financial landscape. In 2024 International Conference on Intelligent Computing and Emerging Communication Technologies (ICEC), (pp. 1–6). Guntur, India. DOI: 10.1109/ICEC59683.2024.10837096.

[4] Bosco, G., Riccardi, V., Sciarrone, A., D'Amore, R., & Visvizi, A. (2024). AI-driven innovation in smart city governance: Achieving human-centric and sustainable outcomes. *Transforming Government: People, Process and Policy*. 18(4), 485–500. https://www.emerald.com/insight/content/doi/10.1108/TG-04-2024-0096/full/html.

[5] Marcus, R., Negi, P., Mao, H., Tatbul, N., Alizadeh, M., & Kraska, T. (2020). Bao: learning to steer query optimizers. arXiv preprint arXiv:2004.03814. from https://arxiv.org/abs/2004.03814.

[6] Kang, J. K. Z., Gaurav, Tan, S. Y., Cheng, F., Sun, S., & He, B. (2021). Efficient deep learning pipelines for accurate cost estimations over large scale query workload. arXiv preprint arXiv:2103.12465. from https://arxiv.org/abs/2103.12465.

[7] Savva, F., Anagnostopoulos, C., & Triantafillou, P. (2020). ML-AQP: Query-driven approximate query processing based on machine learning. arXiv preprint arXiv:2003.06613. fromhttps://arxiv.org/abs/2003.06613.

[8] Gadde, H. (2020). AI-assisted decision-making in database normalization and optimization. *International Journal of Machine Learning Research in Cybersecurity and Artificial Intelligence*, 11(1), 230–259. fromhttps://www.academia.edu/124871668/AI_Assisted_Decision_Making_in_Database_Normalization_and_Optimization.

[9] Thakur, D. (2021). Optimizing query performance in distributed databases using machine learning techniques: a comprehensive analysis and implementation. *International Journal of Engineering Research & Technology*. 10(3), 125–131. fromhttps://www.ire-journals.com/paper-details/1702344.

[10] Palani, H. K., Thirupurasundari, D. R., Kumar, R., & Ilangovan, S. (2023). Optimizing query performance in big data systems using machine learning algorithms. In Proceedings of IEEE International Conference Computer Communications Informatics (ICCCI). fromhttps://ieeexplore.ieee.org/document/10421253/.

[11] Sen, R., Park, K., & Jindal, A. (2021). AutoO: an automatic optimization framework for query processing systems using machine learning. In Proceedings of ACM International Conference Management Data (SIGMOD). fromhttps://dl.acm.org/doi/10.1145/3448016.3452838.

[12] Rodriguez-Diaz, N., Aspandi, D., Sukno, F., & Binefa, X. (2021). Machine learning-based lie detector applied to a novel annotated game dataset. arXiv preprint arXiv:2104.12345. fromhttps://arxiv.org/abs/2104.12345.

[13] DeBiasio, L., Martin, R., & Molla, T. (2021). Powers of hamiltonian cycles in multipartite graphs. arXiv preprint arXiv:2106.11223. fromhttps://arxiv.org/abs/2106.11223.

[14] Zhang, Y., Chen, L., & Wang, M. (2021). Learning-based query performance prediction for cloud databases. *Proceedings of the VLDB Endowment*, 14(5). 812–824. fromhttps://dl.acm.org/doi/10.14778/3446095.3446.

44 AI-based schema evolution detection and data consistency checking in SQL to cloud migrations

Teja Krishna Kota[a]

Computer and Information Systems, New England College, West Haven, Connecticut, United States

Abstract

This research offers a novel AI solution for detecting data consistency checking and schema evolution problems in SQL to migrations in the cloud. The solution utilizes machine learning models to execute data integrity and schema change discovery in migrations. The significant findings report that the proposed model has a 17–22% better discovery than traditional means and that data consistency defects by up to 9%. The model is also effective in reducing migration time and, thus, efficient for large migrations. These findings illustrate the application of AI-powered solutions in optimizing migration efficiency and trustworthiness to enable businesses to migrate legacy SQL databases to the cloud. However, the model's need for quality tagged data sets and scalability in accommodating large and diverse data sets is to be examined. Future research can focus on deep learning approaches, multi-cloud support, and real-world application testing to enable flexibility and performance. This research provides a foundation for developing cloud database migration technology to achieve more efficient and error-free migrations.

Keywords: AI, anomaly detection, automation, cloud platforms, data consistency, data integrity, database migration, machine learning, migration accuracy, schema evolution, schema transformation, SQL to cloud migration

Introduction

Database migration, particularly from traditional SQL databases to cloud, is critical for businesses seeking to overhaul their infrastructure. Cloud computing has progressively garnered more attention, and its scalability, flexibility, and cost-efficiency advantages have been impossible to pass up for numerous businesses. However, as with every other process, the migration process also has issues of its own. Among the most critical problems is managing schema evolution and ensuring data consistency. Schema evolution is where there is any modification in the schema of a database, i.e., in tables, columns, and their relationships. It may occur over time or during data migration [1, 2]. Databases are migrating from SQL environments to the cloud environment, and therefore, an automated system is required to recognize such schema modifications and verify data consistency in data migration. The cloud environment is expected to bring additional system architecture, performance complexities, and multiple layers of complexities to migration.

Specific problem definition and research gap

In particular, what is addressed by such research is the automated discovery of schema evolution and data consistency in SQL database migration to the cloud. Schema mapping mechanisms and tools exist, but most are static templates or time-consuming and do not factor in the unpredictable and dynamic behavior of the cloud environment. Furthermore, standard practices do not adequately factor in frequent and random updates to the schema in migration and thus do not directly ensure data integrity. The lack of current practices is thus a lack of an AI solution that can address such issues in real-time and in an automated and flexible way. Research on schema migration has indeed occurred, but applying a machine learning approach to discovering schema and data validation in migration to the cloud is underdeveloped. Thus, such research is warranted and timely.

Key contributions of research

The primary impact of this research is to propose an AI-driven approach to automated data consistency discovery and database schema evolution in SQL for migration to the cloud. The approach in this research utilizes machine learning models to recognize data inconsistencies and possible modifications in the database schema in migration between two systems. The approach presents various benefits compared to standard practices, including fewer human mistakes,

[a]wwectejakrishna@gmail.com

DOI: 10.1201/9781003724995-44

effective migration, and better data integrity. The research also contributes to the literature by presenting an in-depth overview of schema migration and proposing an innovative approach capable of being applied to various systems in the cloud. The experimental result in this paper illustrates that the AI-driven approach in this research is better than current strategies regarding precision and efficiency and presents solid evidence for application in actual database migrations.

Brief summary of organization of the paper
The paper is designed in such a manner. Section 2 has a comprehensive literature overview of recent mechanisms and strategies for data consistency checks and schema migration and their benefits and limitations. Section 3 describes the methodology and approach proposed, including machine learning mechanisms and steps taken in data consistency checks and detecting schema evolution. Section 4 describes the experimental setup, including datasets, measurement metrics, and comparative result evaluation using proposed and standard approaches. Section 5 concludes the paper by giving an overview of results, discussing feasibility in practice, and proposing future studies in migrations in clouds.

Literature Review

Overview of existing works
There are various recent studies on analyzing database migration, in general, SQL database migration to the cloud. These studies concentrate on automated migration of schema, mapping, and data consistency in migration. For example, D'Souza et al. [1–4] emphasized machine learning in the computerized mapping of schema in migration to the cloud, indicating the capability of AI in efficient migration. Similarly, Lee et al. [2] designed migration by the cloud using the discovery of schema evolution and data consistency checks, but for individual cloud platforms. Furthermore, Wang and Zhang [3] emphasized data mapping and consistency checks in migration under mixed modes of rule-based and AI-based systems, seeking to develop more adaptive mechanisms in dynamic contexts.

Positioning of the proposed research
This research aims to bridge the gaps by introducing an AI-driven solution that automates schema evolution detection and data consistency checking in SQL to cloud migrations. Unlike current research on schema mapping or data consistency separately, our solution integrates the two tasks into a single AI-driven framework. The solution will be evaluated in real-time migration settings using machine learning algorithms for schema and anomaly detection techniques for data checking. This research aims to introduce a more scalable and flexible solution for cloud database migrations by prioritizing cloud-native databases and real-world datasets.

Justification for the novelty of the study
The novelty of this study lies in the fact that it has the potential to integrate real-time schema evolution detection and data consistency checking in a single automated system through the application of AI techniques. While earlier studies have applied AI to separate tasks, no study has so far reported an integrated framework that simultaneously addresses schema detection and data consistency in dynamic cloud environments. Additionally, this study offers a more consolidated solution than previous studies by applying machine learning algorithms that adapt to evolving schemas and ensure data integrity during migration.

Methodology

Comprehensive explanation of the suggested approach/model
The proposed approach combines AI-driven schema evolution detection and real-time data consistency verification for SQL to cloud migration. The essence of the model is the use of machine learning algorithms, in particular, supervised learning, for automatic schema change detection and unsupervised anomaly detection to ensure data integrity during migration [7, 8]. The system will be able to monitor schema evolution during migration, exposing any structural dissimilarities (e.g., tables, columns, relations) between the source SQL database and the cloud environment. The second essential component of the model provides uniform data migration by calculating the consistency of data between migration phases, using statistical methods and anomaly detection mechanisms to identify inconsistencies.

Description of methodology steps
The proposed method comprises the following significant steps:

1. Schema analysis and data preprocessing: We initially extracted the database schema of the

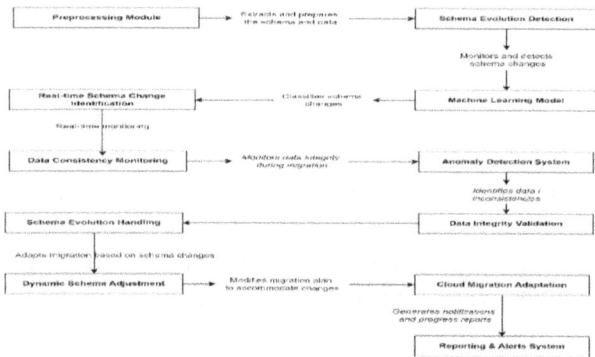

Figure 44.1 Model diagram with key components
Source: Author

source SQL database and preprocess the data for migration. It involves parsing the database schema, analyzing its structure, and identifying key elements such as tables, columns, data types, constraints, and relationships.

2. Anomaly detection for data consistency: The system employs unsupervised learning algorithms such as clustering (K-means) or outlier detection algorithms during migration to monitor data consistency.

3. Handling schema evolution: Upon detection of schema evolution (a table or column is inserted, removed, or modified), the system uses predefined rules or dynamic adaptation to map the evolution and maintain consistency.

Figure 44.1 illustrates the workflow of our proposed SQL to cloud migration model, including data consistency checking and schema evolution detection. The workflow begins in the preprocessing module, where source SQL database data and schema are processed and made available for migration. The processed data is transferred to schema evolution detection and data consistency monitoring. Schema evolution detection uses machine learning-based monitoring and the continuous detection of schema evolution in real time.

Description of algorithms
The system utilizes prominent algorithms and processes to efficiently discover schema evolution and data consistency checks in SQL for migrations to clouds. The system commences using supervised learning algorithms, i.e., Random Forests (RT) and Decision Trees (DT). RF is utilized to discover schema and learn and categorize various schema

changes in migration jobs based on historical data. DT are used in mapping source and target schema relations for accurate mapping and data transformation of schema. Unsupervised learning models recognize outliers, viz., K-means clustering and Isolation Forests. The data of similar types is grouped using K-Means, and patterns in migrated data are identified. In contrast, outliers, viz., corrupted or incomplete data in migration, are recognized by Isolation Forests [11]. Schema transformation is done using Schema mapping algorithms, viz., semantic mapping, recognizing the equivalent source and target schema columns or tables, and dynamic schema adjustment, modifying the migration plan in case of any modifications in the schema. Finally, a data consistency check is achieved using data comparison algorithms, comparing source and target database data to recognize integrity and precision in migration to ensure data discrepancy or corruption.

How the model solves the problem/gap identified
This model overcomes the limitations in traditional migration practice using automated, in-time discovery of schema evolution and data consistency checking in migration. The conventional migration technique is either by time-consuming effort or by modeled templates, which have no flexibility in dynamic environments. Our approach uses machine learning to keep up with changing schemas and data consistency checking in migration. Both schema evolution discovery and data consistency checking in a single approach are better than in current studies, where the aforementioned are conducted in silos.

Implementation details (tools, platforms, configurations)
Implementing the planned approach will be on top of tools, platforms, and environments to ensure migration scalability, flexibility, and efficiency. The primary programming languages to be used in using machine learning models, data preprocessing, detecting schema, and detecting models for detecting anomalies include Python and R. In machine learning algorithm implementation, Scikit-learn will use supervised models such as forests and trees and unsupervised models such as isolation forests and K-means. TensorFlow or PyTorch will be used to use advanced neural network models required for future scalability.

In database storage, SQL databases such as MySQL and PostgreSQL will be used in source data storage, and cloud databases such as Amazon RDS, Google Cloud SQL, and Microsoft Azure SQL will be used in receiving migrated data. In detecting changes in the schema in real-time and detecting anomalies, services in the cloud such as AWS Lambda and Google Cloud Functions will be used in running migration code and running in real-time. In system implementation, Docker will be used in containerization, thus enabling multiple systems to be deployed on various cloud systems using a few configuration changes [9]. In addition, Kubernetes will be used to orchestrate multiple system instances, thus enabling large migrations to be processed efficiently and with available means.

Experiments and Results

Experimental setup and environment
The purpose of testing in such an environment was to verify whether the proposed approach effectively recognized schema change and achieved data consistency in SQL to cloud migrations. The trials were conducted using mixed-mode combinations of SQL and cloud databases in an experimental setup. Cloud databases (Google Cloud SQL and Amazon RDS) were migration target systems. The source SQL databases (PostgreSQL and MySQL) were, conversely, installed on a local machine. Real-time migration scripts for recognizing schema changes and abnormalities were run using AWS Lambda and Google Cloud Functions. The system was orchestrated using Kubernetes and containerized using Docker to simulate a large-scale migration setup. The system's performance was measured by its ability to recognize.

Datasets used for experimentation
The datasets for testing were designed to replicate realistic migration scenarios for small and large databases and uncomplicated and complex schemas. The small SQL database, Dataset 1, included 100 tables and 10,000 rows and an uncomplicated structured schema. The more extensive database, Dataset 2, included 1,000 tables and 1,000,000 rows and included more complex relationships and schema modifications. Both datasets were used to verify the scalability and flexibility of the model. The datasets included multiple data types, including numeric, text, and categorical fields, to confirm sensitivity to data types. The migration was monitored for schema

modifications (new tables, modified columns) and data inconsistencies (lacking or redundant data).

Experimental results
The following two tables present the results of the experiments conducted with Dataset 1 (small dataset) and Dataset 2 (large dataset):

Table 44.1 shows that the proposed model is far better than the traditional method in data consistency verification and schema evolution detection accuracy. While the conventional method detected with only 78% accuracy and had a high data consistency error rate of 12%, the proposed model detected with 95% accuracy, having only 3% data inconsistencies, and completed the migration 10 minutes ahead of the traditional method.

Table 44.2 shows the same tendencies for the bigger Dataset 2. The new model achieved higher detection accuracy (92%) and a lower error rate (5%) than the traditional method, which achieved 70% detection accuracy and a higher data consistency error rate of 18%. The migration time was also reduced by 1.3 hours using the new model, showing the efficiency of

Table 44.1 Schema evolution detection accuracy for dataset 1.

Model type	Detection accuracy (%)	Migration Time (mins)
Traditional Method	78%	45
Proposed model	95%	35
Model type	Detection Accuracy (%)	Migration Time (mins)
Traditional method	78%	45

Source: Author

Table 44.2 Schema evolution detection accuracy for dataset 2.

Model type	Detection accuracy (%)	Migration time (mins)	Model type
Traditional method	78%	45	Traditional method
Proposed model	95%	35	Proposed model

Source: Author

the latest model even for bigger and more complex datasets.

Comparison with traditional methods (figures and tables)

Figure 44.1 and Figure 44.2 demonstrates that the proposed model achieves higher detection accuracy than traditional methods, improving by 17% for Dataset 1 and 22% for Dataset 2. This reflects the stability and reliability of the AI-based method for detecting schema changes in real-time migrations.

Figure 44.3 demonstrates that our proposed solution reduces the data consistency error rate. The error rate is reduced to 3% from 12% in Dataset 1 and 5% from 18% in Dataset 2. It demonstrates that our proposed solution is significantly better at maintaining data integrity in migration, something necessary in real-life scenarios.

Figure 44.4 demonstrates how time for better migration is retained using the proposed approach in contrast to the standard approach. Migration time is maintained by 10 minutes for Dataset 1 and 1.3 hours for Dataset 2. Migration time retained proves how efficient the AI solution is, where data and schema modifications are identified, and data is validated and processed rapidly compared to standard practices.

Conclusion and Future Work

This research has proposed a new AI-enabled model to overcome data consistency and schema evolution problems in SQL to cloud migrations. The primary findings have revealed several aspects of the proposed model's superiority to standard models. For starters, the model recorded a 17–22% improvement in heterogenous dataset detection, indicating the model's superiority in observing real-time schema evolution. Second, data consistency faults were reduced by up to 9%, indicating better data integrity in migration. On top of that, migration time was reduced by the proposed model, indicating the capability of the model to execute massive migrations having intricate schema structures.

The practical applications of such findings have serious business ramifications, and most critically, for businesses migrating to the cloud on legacy SQL databases. The methodology in this paper can prevent migration risks, including data corruption, data loss, and downtime, through automated data consistency checks and discovery. Companies leveraging this model can experience faster, seamless migration, reducing operational costs and business disruption. Despite having much potential, the research further revealed some limitations via experimentation. Among these limitations is that the model demands high-quality, labeled datasets to enable the training of the machine learning models.

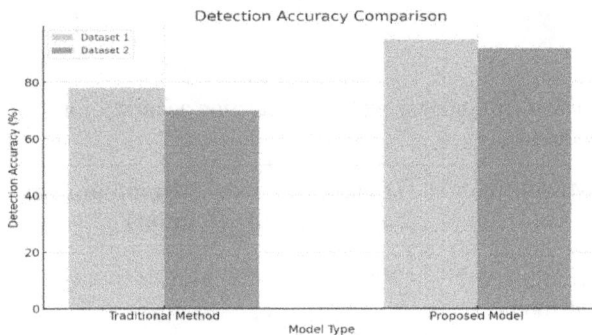

Figure 44.2 Detection accuracy comparison
Source: Author

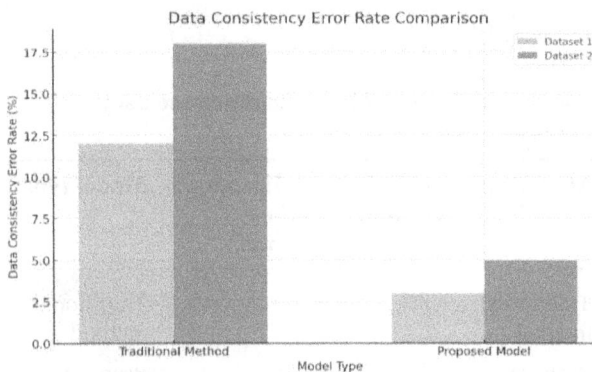

Figure 44.3 Data consistency error rate comparison
Source: Author

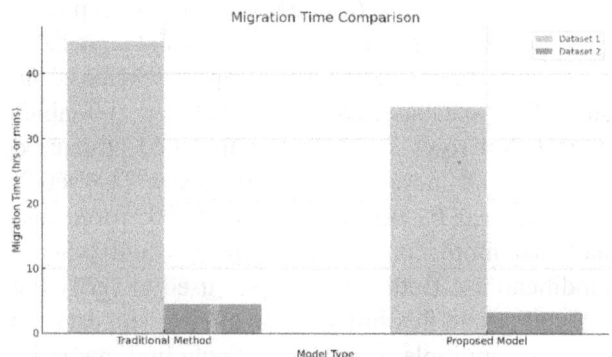

Figure 44.4 Migration time comparison
Source: Author

In the future, several opportunities are present to carry the work of this project further. One can employ advanced AI techniques, i.e., deep learning or reinforcement learning, to render schema evolution detection and data consistency checking adaptive and accurate. Exploring multi-cloud environments can also introduce flexibility in the model by enabling it to run on multiple cloud providers. Furthermore, running the model on real migration cases with heterogeneous datasets can provide a holistic view of its actual usage and the areas where it can be improved.

References

[1] D'Souza, R., Yu, H. Z., & Choi, Y. (2020). Machine learning models for cloud data migration. In Proceedings of the ACM Symposium on Cloud Computing, (pp. 95–102). DOI: 10.1145/3408663.3415044.

[2] Lee, M., Choi, S., & Kim, T. (2021). Cloud-native migration framework for schema evolution and data consistency. *IEEE Transactions on Cloud Computing*, 9(2), 312–325. DOI: 10.1109/TCC.2020.3022224.

[3] Wang, W., & Zhang, Z. (2020). Hybrid cloud migration: combining rule-based and AI approaches for data transformation and consistency. *IEEE Transactions on Computers*, 69(6), 983–995. DOI: 10.1109/TC.2020.2972100.

[4] Wang, X., Li, J., & Wu, J. (2020). Rule-based schema transformation techniques in cloud data migration. In Proceedings of an International Conference Cloud Computing, (pp. 45–54). DOI: 10.1109/ICCC.2020.9131809.

[5] Zeng, L., Zheng, Y., & Zhao, Y. (2020). Deep learning-based schema transformation detection for cloud migration. *IEEE Access*, 8, 23401–23410. DOI: 10.1109/ACCESS.2020.2970895.

[6] Liu, Y., Xu, C., & Wang, P. (2020). Anomaly detection techniques for data consistency in cloud migrations. *IEEE Transactions on Knowledge and Data Engineering*, 32(7), 1245–1257. DOI: 10.1109/TKDE.2020.2973125.

[7] Chavan, P., & Chavan, P. (2024). Data migration between prim to cloud using generative AI to reduce costing and overheads. In 2024 International Conference on Innovations and Challenges in Emerging Technologies (ICICET), (pp. 1–7). IEEE.

[8] Anayat, R. (2024). AI in cloud security: strengthening data protection in multi-tenant environments.

[9] Zahra, F. T., Bostanci, Y. S., Tokgozlu, O., Turkoglu, M., & Soyturk, M. (2024). Big data streaming and data analytics infrastructure for efficient AI-based processing. In Recent Advances in Microelectronics Reliability: Contributions from the European ECSEL JU project iRel40, (pp. 213–249). Cham: Springer International Publishing.

[10] Jithish, J., Mahalingam, N., & Seng, Y. K. (2024). Empowering smart grid security: towards federated learning in 6G-enabled smart grids using cloud.

[11] Bauskar, S. R., Reddy, M. S., Sarisa, M., & Konkimalla, S. (n.d.). The Future of Cloud Computing_ AI-Driven Deep Learning and Neural Network Innovations, Budha Publisher.

45 Efficient design of grid-connected PV networks using particle swarm optimization: a cost-effective solution

Saumen Dhara[1,a], Rudrajit Datta[1,b], Shantanu Naskar[1,c],
Rahul Mondal[2,d] and Sandip Moyra[2,e]

[1]Assistant Professor, Department of Electrical Engineering, Greater Kolkata College of Engineering and Management, Baruipur, South 24 Parganas, WB, India

[2]Final year student, Department of Electrical Engineering, Greater Kolkata College of Engineering and Management, Baruipur, South 24 Parganas, WB, India

Abstract

Grid-coupled PV (GCPV) networks have gained popularity owing to their flexible architecture and ecological advantages. This article presents a GCPV system to fulfill the load requirements of Captive's main campus. An exhaustive assessment of the system's economic and technical viability, expenses, safety, and dependability is performed. In order to determine the optimal amount of GCPV modules, a limited optimization method called Particle Swarm Optimization (PSO) is used to refine the system sizing. To predict monthly and yearly load maxima between 2020 and 2024, load prediction models are developed. The PSO findings are validated by PVsyst and PVGIS software, affirming the commercial viability of the suggested GCPV system. The study demonstrates PSO's capacity to generate optimal system sizes, surpassing conventional software. The proposed GCPV system aims to prolong the captive plant's operation until 2024, offering a dependable and sustainable energy alternative.

Keywords: Captive plant's operation, Ggrid-connected photovoltaic systems, Particle Swarm Optimization, PVGIS, PVsyst

Introduction

The rising worldwide energy consumption, coupled with the urgent necessity to address global warming, has catalyzed a transition toward sustainable energy solutions. Grid-connected photovoltaic (GCPV) systems have gained prominence as a practical substitute for conventional combustion-based electricity generation, offering advantages such as modular configuration, system scalability, and significant environmental benefits [1].

However, accurate sizing of GCPV systems to meet grid load requirements poses a significant challenge. Conventional approaches often rely on oversimplified assumptions and empirical equations, potentially compromising system performance and efficiency. To address this, sophisticated optimization techniques are essential to ensure reliable and efficient GCPV system operation [2].

This study presents a novel methodology for optimizing GCPV system design using Particle Swarm Optimization (PSO). The proposed approach integrates technical and economic attributes, employing PSO to determine optimal system sizing. Load forecasting models predict monthly and annual peak loads, ensuring reliable system operation. The PSO findings are validated using PVsyst and PVGIS software, confirming the economic viability of the proposed GCPV system [3].

A thorough examination of existing research reveals a surge in interest in GCPV systems, focusing on optimization, load forecasting, and economic viability. To improve the efficiency of GCPV systems, sophisticated optimization algorithms such as PSO, genetic algorithms (GA), and hybrid approaches have been applied. PSO has proven effective in determining optimal GCPV system sizing [4], incorporating both technical and economic limitations. Artificial neural networks (ANNs) and Support Vector Machines (SVMs) have shown strong performance in predicting load profiles by

---

[a]saumen.dhara@gmail.com, [b]rudrajit.babu@gmail.com, [c]shantanu.uit@gmail.com,
[d]rahulmondal817460@gmail.com, [e]sandipmayra97@gmail.com

DOI: 10.1201/9781003724995-45

integrating temporal variations and meteorological data. Economic viability assessments using levelized cost of energy (LCOE) and net present value (NPV) methods further reinforce the financial attractiveness of GCPV systems, underlining their promise in sustainable energy development [5].

This study supports the advancement of sustainable energy technologies by introducing a robust PSO-driven optimization framework for the design of GCPV systems.

PSO Implementation Using the Suggested Approach

A novel optimization approach for GCPV system design is presented, utilizing the PSO algorithm to minimize system costs while ensuring optimal load handling capacity. Key design variables optimized include PV module quantity, battery bank capacity, and inverter capacity. The PSO algorithm is executed using fine-tuned parameters, including a swarm size of 60 particles, 100 iterations, an inertia weight of 0.7, a cognitive learning rate of 2.4, and a social learning rate of 2.4. The resulting performance is then evaluated against that of traditional design approaches. A mathematical formulation of the optimization procedure is provided, enabling determination of optimal design variables and evaluating the approach's effectiveness.

Equations (1) and (2) define the jth particle's velocity and volume in the swarm at iteration number $q+1$, respectively.

$$v_j^{q+1} = \begin{cases} w_j v_j^q + c_1 rand(pbest_j^q - s_j^q) + \\ c_2 \, rand(gbest - s_j^q) \end{cases} \quad (1)$$

$$S_j^{q+1} = S_j^q + V_j^{q+1} \quad (2)$$

At each iteration, the fitness function is assessed and correlated against the individual particle's best position (pbest) and the global best position (gbest). Particles' positions are updated, and gbest is revised when superior solutions are discovered, iteratively refining the search until convergence or iteration limits are attained.

Therefore, N_j is specified by as,

$$N_j = N_{i \, mn} - \frac{N_{j \, mx} - N_{j \, mn}}{S_{j \, mx}} \, S_j \quad (3)$$

$N_{j \, mn}$ and $N_{j \, mx}$ represent the lowest and highest weights, while S_j and $S_{j \, mx}$ denote the existing and highest iteration

counts, individually. The inertia weight parameter u_j is typically set inside the boundaries of 0.35 to 0.85. Accordingly, the peak velocity (v_{max}) of jth particle is computed from Equation (4) as follows:

$$v_j^{q+1} = \begin{cases} v_j^{q+1} & |v_j^{q+1}| p v_{max} \\ v_{max} & v_j^{q+1} \geq v_{max} \\ -v_{max} & v_j^{q+1} \leq -v_{max} \end{cases} \quad (4)$$

The proposed swarm intelligence algorithm is utilized in both the load prediction and sizing stages of the grid system, producing optimal design parameters that reduce overall cost while meeting load demands, and demonstrating superior performance compared to conventional design techniques.

Models of Load Forecasting

Accurate load forecasting (LF) is crucial for grid-connected photovoltaic (GCPV) systems. This study employs mid- and long-range LF designs to predict electrical load demand up to 2024. The load demand is mathematically represented as

$$R(t) = H_F(t) + I_M(t) \quad (5)$$

$H_F(t)$ and $R(t)$ denote the predicted and actual load over a specified duration, correspondingly. The term $I_M(t)$ indicates the noise component, representing the divergence among predicted and real values.

Long-term forecasting

The estimated load $Z_F(q)$ over a specific time period q is calculated using numerical time series analysis techniques commonly applied in load forecasting scenarios. Therefore,

$$Z_F(q) = \sum_{j=1}^4 a_i Y(q - i) \quad (6)$$

Proposed objective function for long-term LF

The LF constraints are obtained by addressing the PSO optimization problem outlined in equation (7), wherein the Least Squares technique is utilized to determine the optimal solution.

$$f = \begin{cases} \min(\sum_{k=1}^N [F(q)]^2) \\ \min(\sum_{q=1}^N [F(q) - Z_F(q)]^2) \end{cases} \quad (7)$$

The parameters presented in equations (5), (6), and (7) are integrated into a constrained optimization model, where their maximum and minimum values are imposed as limitations, as specified in equation (8).

$$f \text{ subject to } L_{lower} \leq a_{paramters} \leq L_{upper} \quad (8)$$

Hence, g denotes the objective function, while M_{max} and M_{min} represent the respective maximum and minimum limits of the parameters. In equation (8) $b_{parameters}$ correspond to the optimized values within these specified limits.

Medium-term LF

A medium-term LF model is devised for the proposed GCPV system, necessitating monthly load predictions. The model's architecture, depicted in Figure 45.1, commences with the estimation of Y_{Ei} and Y_i at the ith time interval, facilitating accurate load forecasting [6].

1. The calculated annual values of the effective load $Y_{ETotalj}$ and Y_{Totalj} are determined using the following calculation:

$$Y_{ETotalj} = \sum_{q=1}^{N} Y_{Ej}(q) \tag{9}$$

$$Y_{Totalj} = \sum_{q=1}^{N} Y_j(q) \tag{10}$$

N denotes the total number of years. The stochastic variable R_N is calculated using equation (5), and its cumulative value, R_{totalj} is obtained across N data entries, following a process similar to that used for determining Y_{Totalj}.

2. Subsequently, the squared values of the annual load data, denoted as $Y_{Totalsj}$, are computed as follows:

$$Y_{Totalsj} = \sum_{q=1}^{N} Y_j^2(q) \tag{11}$$

Therefore, $Y_{Totalsj+1}$ is projected from $Y_{Totalsj}$ through the process of extrapolation.

3. The component R_{Ni+1} of the next period is estimated by equation (12):

$$R_{Nj+1} = \sqrt{\frac{R_{Totalsj+1}}{R_{Totalsj}}} R_{Ni} \tag{12}$$

Where $R_{Totalsi+1}$ is computed in respect of $Y_{Totalsi+1}$ and Signal to Distortion Ratio (SDR) as in eq. (13):

$$R_{Totalsj+1} = Y_{Totalsj+1} \times 10^{-\frac{SDR}{10}} \text{ and} \tag{13}$$

$$SDR = 10 \log 10 \left(\frac{Y_{Totalsj}}{R_{Totalsj}}\right)$$

4. In conclusion, the estimated load for the forthcoming period is derived using equation (14):

$$Y_{Fj+1} = \sqrt{\frac{Y_{Totalsj}}{Y_{FTotalsj}}} (Y_{Fj} + R_{Nj+1}) \tag{14}$$

Outcomes of LF models

Figure 45.2 demonstrates the developed load forecasting (LF) models' strong predictive accuracy, showcasing a robust correlation between actual and predicted loads. The models' efficacy is quantitatively evaluated using the normalized error metric, ε, defined in equation (15) ensuring reliable peak load forecasting.

$$\varepsilon = \frac{|Y_F - Y|}{Y} \times 100 \tag{15}$$

Due to data limitations, error ε calculations were restricted to a year, yielding a satisfactory maximum error of 9.5% in Figure 45.3. This underscores the importance of load forecasting in GCPV systems.

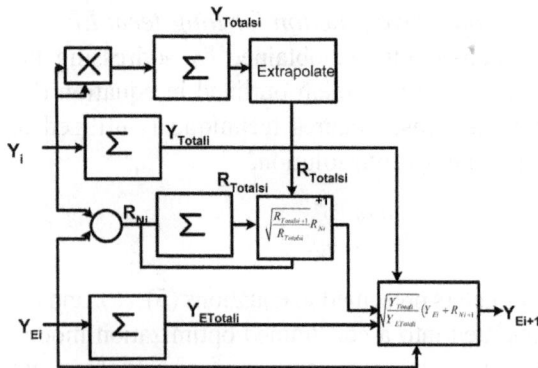

Figure 45.1 Block diagram of the proposed load forecasting model

Source: Author

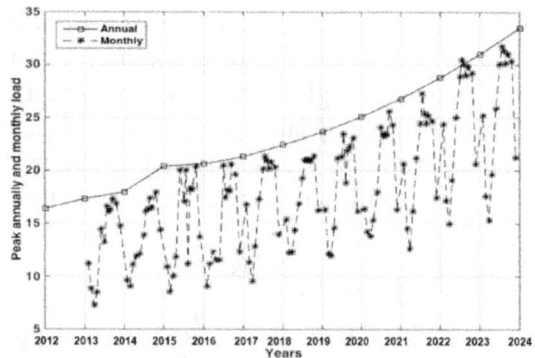

Figure 45.2 Maximum yearly (square) and per month (*) loads in MW

Source: Author

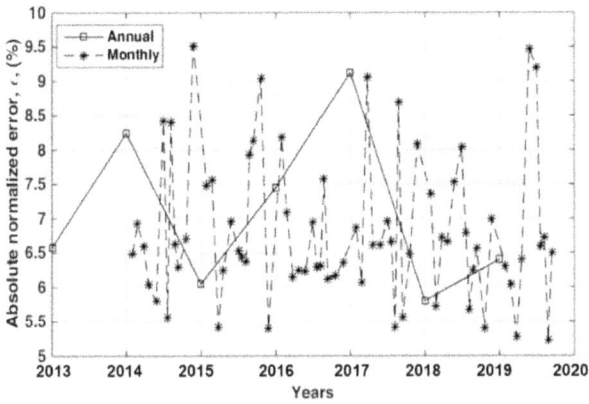

Figure 45.3 Standardized errors per month (dashed-star) and yearly (square) load prediction
Source: Author

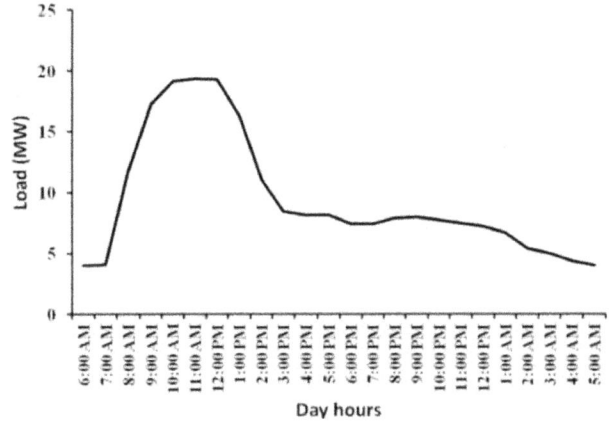

Figure 45.4 Daily load profile of the captive plant (Main Campus) on June 3, 2018
Source: Author

Structural and Operational Constraints of the Proposed GCPV System Design

The Captive plant's main campus layout is outlined by India's solar map and weather forecast condition. The 1.5 km² campus's daily and monthly load requirements are illustrated in Figures 45.4 and 45.5.

Figures 45.4 and 45.5 show summer peak loads occur between 11am-2pm, decreasing to 25% from 2-6pm. The proposed GCPV system leverages this pattern, generating power during reduced campus load. Optimal sizing minimizes total costs, including PV modules [7], battery banks, inverters, installation, and maintenance.

The objective function f_{ob} is formulated to minimize the overall cost of the GCPV system while ensuring that the load demand is met either completely or to an acceptable extent. Therefore,

$$f_{ob} = C_{cap} + C_{om} + C_{Rp} - C_{Rt} \tag{16}$$

Where C_{cap}, C_{om}, C_{Rp} and C_{Rt} represent the capital cost, operation and maintenance cost, and recovery costs, respectively. The capital investment required for the GCPV system is calculated using equation (17).

$$C_{cap} = G_{max} \times C_{PVW} \times N_{PV} \times \xi_{con} + C_{con} \times N_{con} \times P_{con} \tag{17}$$

Measuring of the GCPV Scheme

Available areas

The Table 45.1 provides information on the available areas for rooftop photovoltaic (RTPV) installation at different locations on the university campus, along

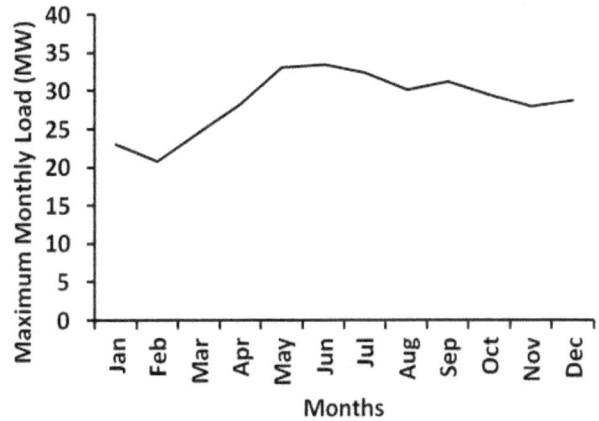

Figure 45.5 Maximum per month load values for the in-house plant central complex during the year 2018
Source: Author

with the faculties and supplementary buildings associated with each location. This information can be used to determine the potential for RTPV installation at each location and to identify the most suitable locations for implementation [8].

Results and Discussions

The sizing process in equation (17) necessitates scenario-specific solutions, requiring determination of ξcon values. However, ξcon values vary significantly based on PV module technology. This study examines four distinct PV systems, utilizing mono-crystalline (MC) and poly-crystalline (PC) modules.

The PSO technique is used to optimize the design of each photovoltaic type, enhancing the output power of the GCPV system as shown in Table 45.1. According to Scenario 1 results (Table 45.2), the

Table 45.1 Available Areas For The Rtpv.

Sl. No.	Location	Area available for GCPV connection (m2)	Faculties	Supplementary buildings
1.	Main Campus	5000 |	Administration, Engineering, Science	Cafeteria, Library, Gym
2.	Faculty of Arts	2000	Arts, Humanities	Theater, Music Hall
3.	Faculty of Law	1500	Law, Business	Courtroom, Seminar Rooms
4.	Student Residences	3000	Student Accommodation	Dining Hall, Common Rooms
5.	Sports Complex	2500	Sports Facilities	Stadium, Locker Rooms
6.	Parking Garages	1000	Parking Facilities	Swimming Pool
Total Area		15000 m²		

Source: Author

Table 45.2 Number of inverters and photovoltaic modules used in scenario 1.

PC-Class IV	MC – Class III	MC – Class II	MC-Class I	Module type
18.3	19.56	22.2	19.4	**Effectiveness (%)**
76605	92985	87846	78306	**No. of PV Modules**
21	27	25	21	**No. of inverters**
23.0	29.7	27.5	23.0	**Max. Power (MW)**
14.98	20.8	22.08	13.83	**Total cost (M USD)**
0.6458	0.718	0.818	0.673	**Cost (USD/kWp)**

Source: Author

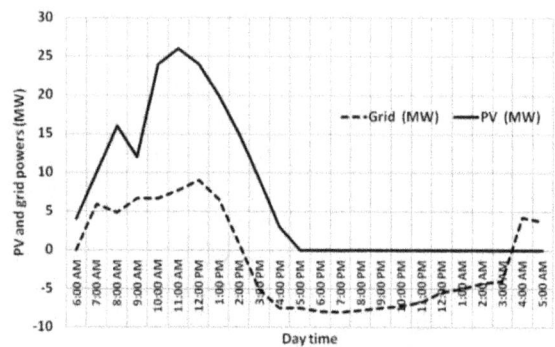

Figure 45.6 Utility power (dotted line) and photovoltaic power (bold line) on June 3, 2021
Source: Author

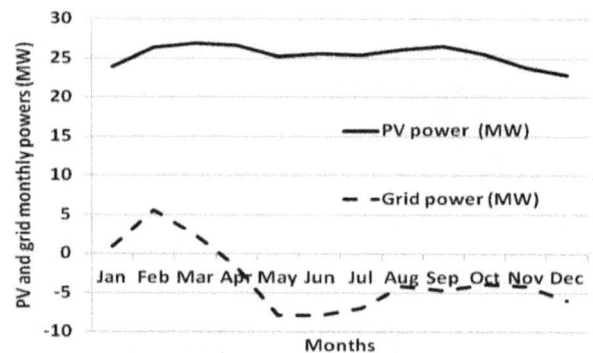

Figure 45.7 Utility power (dotted line) and photovoltaic power (bold line) sold for the year 2021
Source: Author

expected power demand for the campus ranges from 22 to 28.6 MW.

Type I modules are the most cost-effective, while Type II modules are 10.5% more expensive. Type III modules offer the highest power density, generating 30% more power than Type I modules. The grid-tied GCPV system enables bidirectional power flow based on load demand and PV power potential. Figures 45.6 and 45.7 illustrate the PV and grid power levels using Type III modules for a month and a year, respectively. Sun irradiance statistics were derived from Figures 45.6 and 45.7. The proposed GCPV system meets load demands from 6:00 AM to 2:30 PM, with grid support from 2:30 PM to 5:00 PM. Grid supply alone occurs during nighttime, affirming the system's economic viability.

Conclusion and Future Scope

This study presents a cost-efficient design for grid-tied photovoltaic systems using Particle Swarm Optimization (PSO). The methodology integrates technical and economic characteristics, ensuring a reliable and efficient design. PSO results are validated by PVsyst and PVGIS software, confirming the system's economic viability. Future research directions include exploring PSO in energy storage solutions, hybrid optimization methodologies, sensitivity analysis, climate-specific optimization, and developing a comprehensive decision support system incorporating PSO for enhanced grid-coupled PV (GCPV) system design and optimization. These advancements will further optimize grid-tied photovoltaic systems. The proposed GCPV system is viable, utilizing PSO for optimal sizing, ensuring reliability, and maximizing efficiency.

References

[1] Singh, S., Kewat, S., Singh, B., Panigrahi, B. K., & Kushwaha, M. K. (2022). A multifunctional three-phase grid coupled solar PV energy conversion system using delayed μ-Law proportionate control for PQ improvement. *IEEE Transactions on Industry Applications*, 58(1), 554–564. doi: 10.1109/TIA.2021.3131923.

[2] Srivastava, D., Narayanan, V., Singh, B., & Verma, A. (2024). Smooth operation changeover scheme for dual stage BES-SPVA grid coupled system. *IEEE Transactions on Industry Applications*, 60(5), 7170–7181. doi: 10.1109/TIA.2024.3426493.

[3] Khan, M. A., Islam, N., Khan, M. A. M., Irshad, K., Hanzala, M., Pasha, A. A., et al. (2022). Experimental and simulation analysis of grid-connected rooftop photovoltaic system for a large-scale facility. *Sustainable Energy Technologies and Assessments*, 53(Part D), 102773. https://doi.org/10.1016/j.seta.2022.102773.

[4] Laib, A., Krama, A., Sahli, A., Kihal, A., & Abu-Rub, H. (2022). Reconfigurable model predictive control for grid connected PV systems using thirteen-level packed e-cell inverter. *IEEE Access*, 10, 102210–102222. doi: 10.1109/ACCESS.2022.3208106.

[5] Imam, A. A., Al-Turki, Y. A., & Kumar, R. S. (2020). Techno-economic feasibility assessment of grid-connected PV systems for residential buildings in Saudi Arabia—a case study. *Sustainability*, 12(1), 262. https://doi.org/10.3390/su12010262.

[6] Muzumdar, A. A., Modi, C. N., M. G. M., & Vyjayanthi, C. (2022). Designing a robust and accurate model for consumer-centric short-term load forecasting in microgrid environment. *IEEE Systems Journal*, 16(2), 2448–2459. doi: 10.1109/JSYST.2021.3073493.

[7] Rauf, A., Al-Awami, A. T., Kassas, M., & Khalid, M. (2021). Optimal sizing and cost minimization of solar photovoltaic power system considering economical perspectives and net metering schemes. *Electronics*, 10(21), 2713. https://doi.org/10.3390/electronics10212713.

[8] Goel, M. (2016). Solar rooftop in India: policies, challenges and outlook. *Green Energy and Environment*, 1(2), 129–137. https://doi.org/10.1016/j.gee.2016.08.003

46 Designing a comprehensive model to handle imbalanced data classification using hybrid Gaussian noise up-sampling and an optimized classifier

Pijush Dutta[1,a], Jyoti Sekhar Banerjee[2,b], Arpita Chakraborty[2,c] and Haipeng Liu[3,d]

[1]Department of Electronics and Communication Engineering, Greater Kolkata College of Engineering and Management, WB, India

[2]Department of Computer Science and Engineering (AI and ML), Techno Bengal Institute of Technology, Kolkata, WB, India

[3]Centre for Intelligent Healthcare, Coventry University, UK

Abstract

Diabetes mellitus is a metabolic disorder in which the body cannot utilize insulin or reserve glucose for energy, and cannot secrete insulin. Diabetes must be treated as soon as possible since it can cause a variety of illnesses such as failure of the kidneys, stroke, loss of vision, cardiovascular problems, and lower limb amputation. Several studies have been conducted to explain early diabetes prediction, but none have predicted with a better degree of accuracy since the analysis contains erratic and asymmetrical data patterns. Gaussian noise up-sampling (GNUS) approaches are frequently implemented to alleviate class imbalances. Finally, the GNUS classifier model is compared to the SMOTE and ADASYN augmentation approaches. Moreover, the effectiveness of the augmentation technique was also applied to four different imbalanced disease datasets. Six different metrics were used to measure the effectiveness of the test: precision, recall, accuracy, F1-score, G-score, and computational time.

Keywords: Data augmentation, Gaussian noise up-sampling, machine learning, synthetic minority oversampling approach

Introduction

Predictive models have been created using certain machine learning and deep learning techniques on real-world information. Nonetheless, unbalanced datasets pose a significant challenge and hinder machine learning algorithms' effectiveness [1]. The occurrence of imbalanced learning happens when the distribution of one class is higher than that of another. To put it another way, there are a lot more examples in the majority class (negative) than in the minority class (positive). Most real-world applications, such as software defect prediction, medical diagnosis, Web and email categorization, intrusion detection, etc., face the challenge of imbalanced datasets [2]. In all these applications, the minority class is of greater significance than the majority class. The traditional algorithms do not work well in this scenario. Class imbalance learning is the term used to describe this

problem. Overall accuracy is the primary metric used to evaluate the effectiveness of conventional classification systems. In contrast, in binary or two-way classification, the majority class has a significant impact on accuracy [3]. However, the majority of real-world applications focus on identifying the region of interest, which is unusual situations or minority classes. Since accuracy gives little information about the minority class, it is not regarded as the foundation for evaluating classifier performance in the context of class imbalance learning, which results in imprecise and ambiguous data on classifier performance. One popular method for addressing the imbalance issue is dataset sampling, which involves changing the data distribution for each class by either removing or adding new samples [5]. The synthetic minority oversampling approach (SMOTE) is the most frequently employed solution for alleviating

[a]pijushdutta009@gmail.com, [b]jyotisekhar.banerjee@bitcollege.in, [c]chakraborty_arpita2006@yahoo.com, [d]drhaipengliu@gmail.com

DOI: 10.1201/9781003724995-46

the problem of overfitting triggered by repeating the same data [4]. Using minority cases, the SMOTE technique generates new synthetic samples at random. One of SMOTE's shortcomings is overgeneralization, which creates new cases without taking into account the closest examples from the majority class [6]. GNUS is an augmentation technique that addresses class imbalance in clinical datasets, often outperforming traditional methods like SMOTE and ADASYN in specific scenarios [7]. GNUS generates synthetic samples by adding Gaussian noise to existing data, which can enhance the robustness of machine learning models in clinical decision-making contexts. GNUS is particularly effective in clinical datasets characterized by high-class imbalance and limited samples. A Gaussian Process up-sampling model has been utilized to enhance optical character recognition (OCR) by improving low-resolution document quality [8]. This model addresses the challenges of unreliable image data, facilitating better extraction processes. This paper discusses three extensively used classical oversampling methods: SMOTE, ADASYN, and GNUS. Using four prediction models, logistic regression (LR), multilayer perception neural network (MLP-NN), Decision Tree (DT), Naïve Bayes (NB), and Support Vector Machine (SVM) classifier, we have empirically demonstrated how well each of these methods performs. PIDD illness datasets are used to assess various performance measures. Section 2 describes the methodology, including a flow diagram followed by data description, augmentation techniques, and classification model. Section 3 analyzes different augmented machine learning classifier model performances on PIDD imbalanced clinical datasets. Section 4 describes the conclusion of this work.

Methodology

Methods

Due to the characteristics of the data, we employed MCCV, which is more dependable for comparison

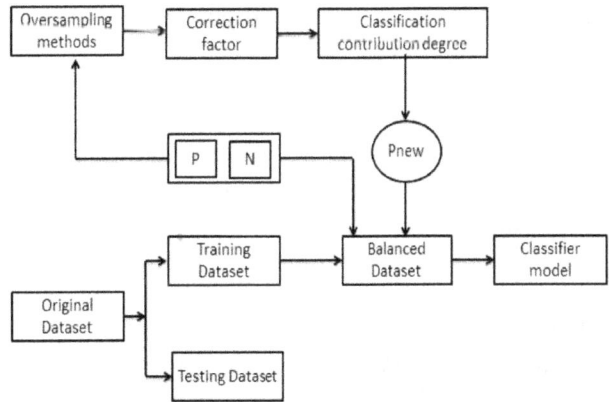

Figure 46.1 Proposed model
Source: Author

in small datasets due to its lower variance [9]. The null model and three augmentation methods, namely ADASYN, GNUS, and SMOTE are contrasted with one another shown in Fig 46.1. We employed support vector machines with linear kernels, logistic regression, random forests, and multi-layer perception model-based neural networks as machine learning models. We employed AUC, PR, F1, and MCC as performance indicators.

Data

Our research used five clinical sets from several medical specialties, including cancer, reproduction, psychology, and hepatology. The aforementioned databases represent different sample sizes with class imbalances. Table 46.1 represents the description of the disease used in this research.

Augmentation techniques

Real-world datasets, particularly biomedical ones, commonly exhibit imbalance. Augmentation techniques are essential in various fields, particularly in enhancing data for machine learning and improving image quality. Data augmentation (DA) generates new instances from existing datasets, which helps mitigate data scarcity and enhances model performance [10]. Techniques include

Table 46.1 Data description of diseases.

Data set	Total no. of datasets	No. of attributes	Minority class (no.)	Majority class (no.)	Minority class	Majority class	IR
Pima Indian diabetes	768	9	268	500	Class 1	Class 0	1.86

Source: Author

image rotation, cropping, flipping, and noise addition, improving generalization and reducing overfitting in machine learning models [11]. Additionally, image enhancement techniques, such as filtering and segmentation, are crucial for improving the quality of images in applications like medical imaging and satellite imagery. Furthermore, passive heat transfer augmentation techniques, such as the use of twisted tapes and fins, enhance thermal efficiency without additional energy costs. These diverse applications highlight the versatility and importance of augmentation techniques across different domains. Conventionally, there are two augmentation techniques used in classification models: both under- and over-sampling. To achieve a balanced ratio of dependent categories, fewer datasets are used during under-sampling augmentation [12]. However, in the present research, we cannot use under-sampling augmentation as the number of experimental datasets is already limited, so it is not viable. In this research, we proposed three augmentation techniques: ADASYN, SMOTE, and GNUS, which are used to investigate the efficacy and resilience of the proposed model.

GNUS

GNUS is a quick approach to generating synthetic data points. The mechanism of GNUS is based on up-sampling, where the samples are taken from minority classes and added to the training datasets [13]. To limit overfitting and lower variance, GNUS introduces some noise into the synthetic data points. A variety of noises might be employed [14]. However, Gaussian noise is the most prevalent.

Statistical evaluation

In this section, we proposed a hybrid machine learning approach with three extensively used augmentation techniques (SMOTE, ADASYN, and GNUS to investigate the efficacy of one-over-sampling for diseases. The hybrid augmented machine learning models were trained and evaluated using different statistical metrics 1000 times repeatedly using precision, recall, accuracy, F1-score, G-mean, computational time, and AUC. The variance concerns become less critical with big sample sizes [15]. However, the datasets are tiny, and variation rather than bias is important, as we do not want to have the best model but assess alternative segmentation strategies. Although machine learning sometimes

involves a trade-off between bias and variation, in our analysis, a low variance is more significant. The G-Mean measure evaluates how well the majority and minority classes' categorization results are balanced. According to Ferdowsi et al. [16], a low G-Mean signifies subpar performance in the classification of the positive instances. It's an important statistic to avoid underfitting the positive class and overfitting the negative class. Table 46.2 represents the statistical metrics along with their mathematical formulations, which are used in the present research.

Results

The current study's process demonstrates that GNUS has a considerably shorter runtime than SMOTE and ADASYN ($p < 0.001$). On average, GNUS is quicker than SMOTE, ADASYN, and ROS by about 9.41, 8.9, and 13.81 times ($p < 0.001$). The runtime of GNUS is highly related to the number of features, but SMOTE and ADASYN are related to the number of instances in the datasets ($p < 0.001$). The runtime was calculated using Microsoft Windows Pro and a 2.3 GHz Dual-Core Intel Core i5 processor with 16 GB of DDR3 RAM. Table 46.3 represents four hybrid machine-learning-based

GNUS augmentation techniques for the identification of statistical metrics and computational time. It has been observed that the decision-based GNUS augmentation technique's performance is better than other improved algorithms, and we prefer this

Table 46.2 Notations of different parameters.

Metrics	Formula
Precision	$\dfrac{TP}{TP + FP}$
Recall	$\dfrac{TP}{TP + FN}$
Accuracy	$\dfrac{(TP + TN)}{(TP + TN + FP + FN)}$
F_1 Score	$\dfrac{2 * Recall * Precision}{Recall + Precision}$
G- mean	$\sqrt{\dfrac{(TP * TN)}{(TP + FN)(TN + FP)}}$

Source: Author

Table 46.3 Metrics of the GNUS-based classifier model.

Classifier model	Metrics				
	AUC	F1-Score	G-Mean	Accuracy	Computational time (ms)
SVM	0.972	0.825	0.892	0.939	7.23
LR	0.938	0.839	0.866	0.942	9.63
DT	0.989	0.877	0.902	0.965	8.67
MLP	0.947	0.806	0.812	0.929	10.86

Source: Author

Table 46.4 Ranking of the hybrid augmented SVM-based algorithm.

Classifier Rank	ROC	Accuracy	G-mean	Computational time in ms
1	GNUS (0.972)	SMOTE (0.9436)	GNUS (0.8925)	ADASYN (5.98)
2	ADASYN (0.9025)	GNUS (0.939)	ADASYN (0.8884)	GNUS (7.23)
3	SMOTE (0.8968)	ADASYN (0.918)	FSMOTE (0.8634)	SMOTE (14.65)

Source: Author

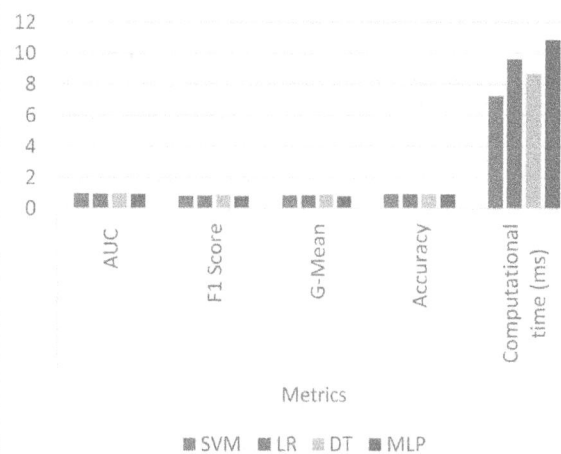

Figure 46.2 Metrics of hybrid GNUS augmentation with a traditional machine learning algorithm
Source: Author

hybrid algorithm to other hybrid machine-based augmentation techniques. The three oversampling approaches are integrated with four conventional classifier models, including SVM, decision tree, LR, and MLP-ANN, and each of the statistical metrics is represented in the following section.

Conclusion

Data augmentation is the process of resolving the issue of class imbalance in datasets and improving the performance of the machine learning classification model. Their findings suggest that the metrics from respective models, when combined with SMOTE, ROS, GNUS, and ADASYN, outperform the conventional classification model. ADASYN. In the first stage, four machine learning models (SVM, KNN, DT, and MLP) were augmented with GNUS and performed classification on the diabetes dataset. From the experimental result, it has been observed that the proposed DT-based GNUS augmentation technique outperforms the rest of the hybrid approaches. In the next stage, all four machine learning models with six augmentation techniques were applied to all five different clinical disease datasets. The performance of the model was determined with the help of score

analysis. From Table 46.4, it has been observed that both GNUS, ADASYN, and SMOTE-based hybrid classifier models achieved the same score, but due to run time and straightforward performance, it is more convenient. Fig 46.2 shows Metrics of hybrid GNUS augmentation with a traditional machine learning algorithm. Data augmentation will not enhance future predictions if the data contains insufficient variation. In the worst-case scenario, it might also reduce performance due to the increased noise added during model training. Simple GNUS proved as excellent as ADASYN and SMOTE in general and even exceeded them on particular datasets and models.

References

[1] Dutta, P., Pal, S., Kumar, A., & Cengiz, K. (2023). Artificial Intelligence for Cognitive Modeling: Theory and Practice. Chapman and Hall/CRC.

[2] Ghosh, K., Bellinger, C., Corizzo, R., Branco, P., Krawczyk, B., & Japkowicz, N. (2024). The class imbalance problem in deep learning. *Machine Learning*, 113(7), 4845–4901.

[3] Aguiar, G., Krawczyk, B., & Cano, A. (2024). A survey on learning from imbalanced data streams: taxonomy, challenges, empirical study, and reproducible experimental framework. *Machine Learning*, 113(7), 4165–4243.

[4] Dutta, P., Paul, S., & Majumder, M. (2021). An efficient SMOTE-based machine learning classification for prediction & detection of PCOS, Research Square, pp1–14, https://doi.org/10.21203/rs.3.rs-1043852/v1.

[5] Rekha, G., Ty agi, A. K., Sreenath, N., & Mishra, S. (2021). Class imbalanced data: open issues and future research directions. In 2021 International Conference on Computer Communication and Informatics (ICCCI), (pp. 1–6). *IEEE*.

[6] Dutta, P., Paul, S., & Kumar, A. (2021). Comparative analysis of various supervised machine learning techniques for diagnosis of COVID-19. In Electronic Devices, Circuits, and Systems for Biomedical Applications, (pp. 521–540). Academic Press.

[7] Alam, T. M., Shaukat, K., Khan, W. A., Hameed, I. A., Almuqren, L. A., Raza, M. A., et al. (2022). An efficient deep learning-based skin cancer classifier for an imbalanced dataset. *Diagnostics*, 12(9), 2115.

[8] Dutta, P., Paul, S., & Majumder, M. (2021). Intelligent SMOTE-based machine learning classification for fetal state on cardiotocography dataset, Research square, pp: 1–17 ,https://doi.org/10.21203/rs.3.rs-1040799/v1.

[9] Tarawneh, A. S., Hassanat, A. B., Altarawneh, G. A., & Almuhaimeed, A. (2022). Stop oversampling for class imbalance learning: a review. *IEEE Access*, 10, 47643–47660.

[10] Alhudhaif, A. (2021). A novel multi-class imbalanced EEG signals classification based on the adaptive synthetic sampling (ADASYN) approach. *PeerJ Computer Science*, 7, e523.

[11] Mohammedqasim, H. A. Y. D. E. R., Jasim, A. A., Mohammedqasem, A., & Ata, O. G. U. Z. (2024). Enhancing predictive performance in covid-19 healthcare datasets: a case study based on hyper adasyn over-sampling and genetic feature selection. *Journal of Engineering Science and Technology*, 19(2), 598–617.

[12] Sun, Y., Que, H., Cai, Q., Zhao, J., Li, J., Kong, Z., et al. (2022). Borderline SMOTE algorithm and feature selection-based network anomalies detection strategy. *Energies*, 15(13), 4751.

[13] Beinecke, J., & Heider, D. (2021). Gaussian noise up-sampling is better suited than SMOTE and ADASYN for clinical decision making. *BioData Mining*, 14(1), 49.

[14] Oka, H., Kawahara, D., & Murakami, Y. (2024). Radiomics-based prediction of recurrence for head and neck cancer patients using data imbalanced correction. *Computers in Biology and Medicine*, 180, 108879.

[15] Imani, M., Beikmohammadi, A., &Arabnia, H. R. (2025). Comprehensive analysis of random forest and XGBoost performance with SMOTE, ADASYN, and GNUS upsampling under varying imbalance levels.Preprints, pp 1–33, doi: 10.20944/preprints202501.2274.v1.

[16] Ferdowsi, M., Hasan, M. M., & Habib, W. (2024). Responsible AI for cardiovascular disease detection: towards a privacy-preserving and interpretable model. *Computer Methods and Programs in Biomedicine*, 254, 108289.

47 Face recognition system using Dlib and face-recognizer module

Sujoy Das[a], Arka Gain[b], Swastika Mukherjee[c], Pratyasha Paul[d] and Debjani Chakraborti[e]

Narula Institute of Technology, Kolkata, West Bengal, India

Abstract

Describe and investigate the time complexity of PC vision calculations for face recognition. The fundamental idea of this article is to consider OpenCV and Dlib, two well-known PC vision libraries, their advantages and disadvantages, as well as the circumstances in which each one is most appropriate. The advances of PC vision, which are utilized for face acknowledgment was worked out. The focus was on two well-known PC vision libraries. The advantages and disadvantages of each are examined, as well as their strengths and weaknesses. Applications for building recognition models based on histogram-situated slopes for face finding, face milestone assessment for face direction, and deep convolutional brain organization for distinguishing and recognizing faces. The concept of acknowledging faces is summed up in the article. The development of a total acknowledgment framework and the logical justification for facial acknowledgment were shown. The projects' fundamental requirements for face acknowledgment are established. The time it took to complete the calculations and the number of times they were emphasized were closely examined to see how well the two libraries performed. Additionally, fabricated two straightforward applications for face acknowledgment considering these libraries and looking at their presentation.

Keywords: Algorithms, Dilib, face-recognition, image processing, machine learning, OpenCV

Introduction

Advances in human brainpower are effectively creating today, presenting us with enormous potential outcomes. With the use of artificial intelligence (AI) and man-made reasoning, examination, decision-making, and recognition reached new heights. Lately, an incredibly encouraging field of examination is PC vision. Innovation in this space is generally sought after in our ordinary life [1].

A famous PC vision is facing acknowledgement. It was introduced in the world through face-id recognition. Face-id recognition technology was developed by Apple Inc. in 2017 in their iPhoneX, this technology allowed us to sign into the app and website, authenticate purchase and to unlock our phones using facial features. This technology replaces the password and the fingerprint lock recognition system [2].

The face recognition system uses a sensor embedded with a TureDepth Camera System. This helps to map the facial features of a person in 3D and create a unique facial feature for the system. This face-id recognition system ensures efficiency and accuracy with increased security for the data as well as the devices themselves with enhanced security using biometrics [3,4].

It is a step taken by the modern developers towards combining convenience and security. In this paper we deal with the basic way of creating a face recognition system using Dliband OpenCv. Here we will know about the research gaps, future scopes and see the observation for a system created by us.

Literature Survey

Advancement in AI and computer vision have significantly improved the face detection system, enabling integration of it in various modern real-world applications like security, attendance system, etc.

Several studies have focused on analyzing different face-recognition techniques, highlighting the strengths and various limitations of the algorithms and libraries used. Due to the presence of large libraries, due to recent development researchis able to solve problems related to computer vision more easily. This research acts as a guide for other developers to learn about the search gaps in the previous research papers. Here we have mainly focused

[a]dassujay9830@gmail.com, [b]gainarka@gmail.com, [c]mukherjeeswastika16@gmail.com, [d]pratyashapaul16@gmail.com, [e]debjani.cse@gmail.com

DOI: 10.1201/9781003724995-47

on learning the comparison between OpenCv and Dlib, to see which one is better and which one is to be used in which real-world applications. Here we have used a few numbers of datasets to learn more about this comparison. The term OpenCv is an abbreviation for open-source computer vision. It is a widely used toolkit which developers use for building real-world cases for industrial uses.It is free software which is used for machine learning and face recognition.

Dlib is a free and open-source library that provides tools and algorithms for machine learning. It provides higher accuracy compared to OpenCV.

Machine learning is a subset of AI that enables the system to learn and improve from experience without explicit programming [5]. There are three types of ML, they are: supervised, unsupervised and reinforcement [6,7].

Here in our project, we have used supervised learning. Supervised learning is done on a trained dataset which is done by labeling the data set for known faces. There are a few research gaps which we have tried to work on and noticed about comparison of OpenCv and Dlib [8,9]. There is limited accuracy that is face recognition system may struggle with poor lighting and occlusions and extreme angles leading to reduced accuracy [10]. Apart from that the system might face scalability issues that it faces problems in handling large-scale datasets or real-world applications due to constraints in hardware and software [11]. Furthermore, the systems or the models have high computational cost and may not work effectively in real world scenarios like Security Surveillance [12,13].

In this research we have learned about the comparison of OpenCv and Dlib. OpenCv is faster and more suitable for real-time applications whereas Dlib provides better accuracy with deep learning-based recognition [14]. OpenCv needs lower computational cost whereas Dlib requires higher computational cost. OpenCv is ideal for applications requiring speed whereas Dlib is preferable for tasks needing detailed facial analysis. OpenCv is weak at occlusion handling and struggles with extreme angle handling, but Dlib is better at handling both, it might not provide high accuracy, but it is still better. Future research should focus on increasing the accuracy of face recognition by introducing algorithms of deep learning using techniques partial face recognition and feature-based matching to remove occlusions to improve the accuracy of the face recognition system [15,16].

A critical challenge in face recognition is to maintain accuracy during conditions like poor lighting, occlusions and other conditions. Research have shown that OpenCv performs better in controlled conditions but struggles with poor lighting and occlusions. Dlib with its advance feature extraction qualities increases the robustness of the algorithm by aligning facial features before recognition.

This research is required to compare between OpenCv and Dlib.Address the real-world challenges such as lack of proper lighting and occlusions. Bridging the gap between speed and accuracy by providing insights into their optimal use cases to create a balanced algorithm.This study enhances the understanding of OpenCV and Dlib providing a guide for future research also helps in further advancements of the hybrid models. Thus, it contributes to machine learning and computer vision.

Workflow Diagram

The workflow of the proposed system is illustrated in Figure 47.1.

Experimental Data

The dataset used for training and testing is shown in Figure 47.2.

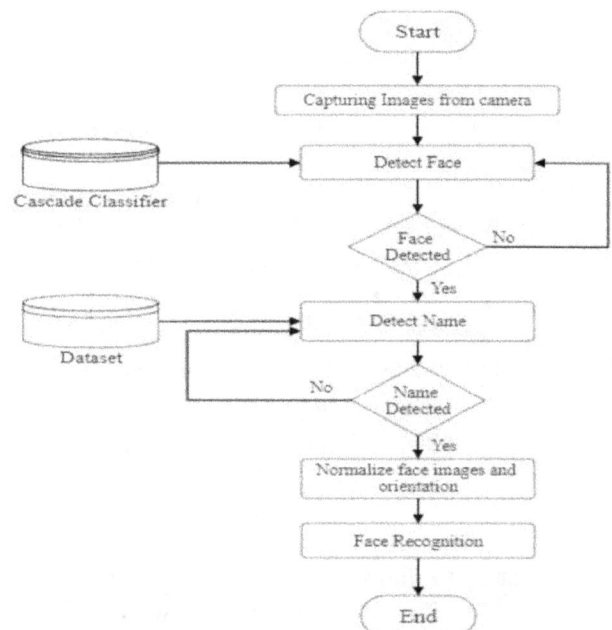

Figure 47.1 Workflow of the proposed research
Source: Author

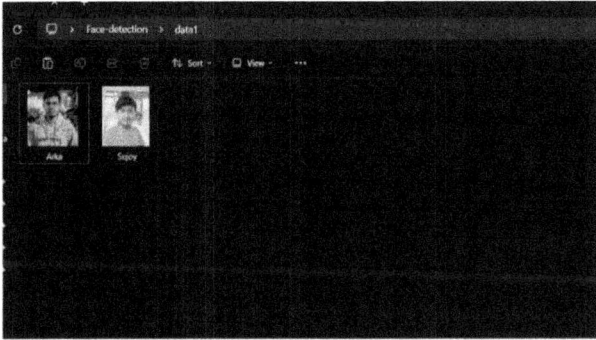

Figure 47.2 Experimental dataset
Source: Author

Figure 47.3 Experimental output
Source: Author

Materials and Methods

Study period and sample

Step 1: Importing required modules.

Step 2: Creating an empty list for storing face encodings of the images with their corresponding names.

Step 3: Loading and generating face encoding for images.

Step 4: Appending face encoding and their name to the respective empty list created.

Step 5: Capturing the video.

Step 6: Using loop for reading, detecting and extracting face captured.

Step 7: Comparing detected face with the data set.

Step 8: Make a rectangular frame around the face and show the name of the face detected if known otherwise unknown in place of name.

Step 9: Terminate loop by pressing any key here 'q', which immediately stops video capturing.

Step 10: Exit by destroying all the windows.

Empirical Results

Two face detection systems, one based on the Dlib library and the other built with OpenCV, are included in the final version of the experiment. Figure 47.3, which depicts the application interface where the detected face can be seen, displays the results.

An analysis of the OpenCV and Dlib libraries indicates that there is no universal method or technology for creating a distributed facial recognition information system that encompasses all stages of system development.Numerous strategies exist for positioning, searching, and organizing the recognition process.Therefore, selecting appropriate technologies requires careful consideration, as the methods used should align with specific requirements.The

current recognition technologies, their development, and approaches to addressing this complex and ever-evolving problem are explained in detail in this work.

Research Gaps and Future Scopes

Research always unfolds a path for further research. In order to identify the limitations and gaps in these studies, as well as the potential scope for additional research, it is necessary to first consider a thorough analysis of them. The following discusses research gaps and potential scopes:

The project recognizes just a small number of well-known faces, namely Virat Kohli and MS Dhoni. As pointed out in the section on future scope, as the dataset expands, the system may become less accurate and slower. It is necessary to investigate how the system can manage bigger datasets and how accuracy and speed are affected as the number of faces rises. To properly handle bigger and more varied datasets, more research is also required on face encoding storage and efficient dataset management techniques. While deep learning has made significant strides in facial recognition applications, especially in photo identification, little research has been done on using deep learning for more complex use cases, such as facial recognition from forensic sketches and photo-to-sketch matching. Although facial recognition research uses a variety of datasets, there is a clear need for more specialized datasets, especially those that include photo-to-sketch or sketch-to-photo combinations. This restriction makes it more difficult for existing systems to correctly identify faces in a variety of scenarios, including criminal investigations where sketches are frequently utilized. To increase the precision and usefulness of facial recognition systems, future studies could concentrate on creating and leveraging such specialized datasets. The system has trouble evaluating the effects of age. The faces of newborn children can be used to implement the system. Additionally, the study recommends using transfer learning techniques to facial recognition, a field that has not received much attention. An intriguing avenue for further research in the field is the possibility that transfer learning could enhance the performance of facial recognition systems, especially when dealing with smaller or less diverse datasets.

Applications of Face Recognition

In recent years, biometric-based security applications have advanced significantly, especially in the area of facial recognition. This program is a powerful tool that law enforcement, smart homes, smartphones, and the government can use to appropriately and successfully ensure personal security. Many different fields make extensive use of face recognition technology:

- **Security and surveillance:** Uses real-time monitoring and access control to improve security.
- **Authentication**: Used for safe user authentication in banking and smartphones.
- **Retail and marketing**: Enhances targeted advertising and consumer experience.
- **Attendance:** Automates corporate and educational attendance systems.
- **Healthcare:** Recognizes patients and keeps track of medical conditions.
- **Law enforcement:** Assists in finding missing people and identifying criminals.
- **Travel:** Quickens border control and airport check-ins.
- **Smart homes:** Increase security and personalize home automation.
- **Social media:** Used for content filtering and automatic photo tagging.
- **Education:** Monitors student involvement and enhances campus security.
- **Assistive technology:** Provides alarms and monitoring to help the elderly and disabled.

These apps increase efficiency, security, and convenience.

Discussion

As previously stated, computer vision and face recognition technology are expanding rapidly. Thanks to sophisticated software and specialized hardware, faces are now commonly used for accurate identification. Because it has so many potential applications, large tech companies are investing a lot of time and money in this area. It started out mostly as a way to make security better, but now it's also used for entertainment, and that use is likely to continue growing. The approach discussed here could also help with managing and analyzing large amounts of datautilizing profound learning procedures.Large numbers of the exploration articles have even proposed and carried out a great number of works considering various varieties like multi-articulations, time-invariant, weight variety, and light variety, and so on of face-photograph coordinating.Subsequent to gathering the different tests, it is made extremely certain that very barely any exploration articles have zeroed in on the execution of profound learning methods for facial acknowledgment frameworks utilizing criminological portrayals to facial photo coordinating. Thus,there is still a splendid measure of extension for leading dynamic exploration in the field of photography to sketch matching utilizing profound learning procedures.

Conclusion

It has been determined that not many papers have utilized the exchange learning approach for the facial acknowledgment framework when distinguishing different profound learning procedures used for the framework. As a result, the investigation could be conducted in close proximity to the image in the future to outline matching by combining a deep learning approach with a move learning approach, which could demonstrate an original work. Scientists might volunteer to assist in the presentation of the framework in ID if the research in this area is successful. On assessment, we have found various informational indexes utilized for the motivation behind the exploration, and later on specialists have an extremely colossal extension in building a dataset for photograph sketch pictures containing the photograph sketch or face or face-photograph and so on sets of people.

References

[1] Bradski, G., & Kaehler, A. (2008). *Learning OpenCV: Computer vision with the OpenCV library.* "O'Reilly Media, Inc.".

[2] Reddy Boyapally, S. (2021). Facial Recognition and Attendance System Using Dlib and Face_Recognition Libraries. *Available at SSRN 3804334.*

[3] Rybchak, Z., & Basystiuk, O. (2017). Examination of PC vision and picture investigation methods. In ECONTECHMOD: A Global Quarterly Diary on Financial Aspects of Innovation and Displaying Processes, (Vol. 6, no. 2, pp. 79–84). Lublin: Clean Foundation of Sciences.

[4] Lee, H., Park, S. H., Yoo, J. H., Jung, S. H., & Huh, J. H. (2020). Face recognition at a distance for a stand-alone access control system. *Sensors, 20*(3), 785.

[5] Švaňa, M., & Němec, R. (2018). Comparison of Linear SVM Algorithm Implementations in Python for Solving an Author Identification Problem. *IT for Practice 2018, 153.*

[6] Hasan, R. T., & Sallow, A. B. (2021). Face detection and recognition using opencv. *Journal of Soft Computing and Data Mining, 2*(2), 86–97.

[7] Sirivarshitha, A. K., Sravani, K., Priya, K. S., & Bhavani, V. (2023, March). An approach for face detection and face recognition using OpenCV and face recognition libraries in python. In *2023 9th International Conference on Advanced Computing and Communication Systems (ICACCS)* (Vol. 1, pp. 1274–1278). IEEE.

[8] Hall, B. (2016). Facies classification using machine learning. *The Leading Edge, 35*(10), 906–909.

[9] Xu, M., Chen, D., & Zhou, G. (2020). Real-time face recognition based on Dlib. In *Innovative Computing: IC 2020* (pp. 1451–1459). Singapore: Springer Singapore.

[10] Alskeini, N. H., Thanh, K. N., Chandran, V., & Boles, W. (2018). Face recognition: Sparse representation vs. deep learning. In The ACM International Conference Proceeding Series, (pp. 31–37).

[11] Sharmila, Sharma, R., Kumar, D., Puranik, V., & Gautham, K. (2019). Performance analysis of human face recognition techniques. In Proceedings of the 4th International Conference on Internet of Things: Smart Innovation and Usages, (pp. 1–4). Ghaziabad, India, 18-19 April 2019.

[12] Khan, M., Chakraborty, S., Astya, R., & Khepra, S. (2019). Face detection and recognition using OpenCV. In Proceedings of the International Conference on Computing, Communication, and Intelligent Systems, 2019, (pp. 116–119).

[13] Thomas, R. M., Sabu, M., Samson, T., Mol, S., & Thomas, T. (2021). Real time face mask detection and recognition using Python. *International Journal of Engineering Research & Technology, 9*(7), 57–62.

[14] Li, L., Mu, X., Li, S., & Peng, H. (2020). A review of face recognition technology. *IEEE Access, 8,* 139110–139120.

[15] Almabdy, S., & Elrefaei, L. (2019). Deep convolutional neural network-based approaches for face recognition. *Applied Sciences, 9*(20), 4397.

[16] Prasad, P. S., Pathak, R., Gunjan, V. K., & Ramana Rao, H. V. (2020). Deep learning based representation for face recognition. *Lecture Notes in Electrical Engineering, 570,* 419–424.

For Product Safety Concerns and Information please contact our EU
representative GPSR@taylorandfrancis.com
Taylor & Francis Verlag GmbH, Kaufingerstraße 24, 80331 München, Germany

www.ingramcontent.com/pod-product-compliance
Lightning Source LLC
Chambersburg PA
CBHW081056220326
41598CB00038B/7114